J. J. FLY

Highlights of the Bible Commentary

A Brief Review and Commentary on Selected Key Scriptures

First published by Self 2021

Copyright © 2021 by J. J. Fly

All rights reserved. No part of this publication may be reproduced, stored or transmitted in any form or by any means, electronic, mechanical, photocopying, recording, scanning, or otherwise without written permission from the publisher. It is illegal to copy this book, post it to a website, or distribute it by any other means without permission.

v 1.1

First edition

This book was professionally typeset on Reedsy. Find out more at reedsy.com

"If you abide in My word, you are My disciples indeed. And you shall know the truth, and the truth shall make you free."

John 8:31,32 (NKJV)

"But even to this day, when Moses is read, a veil lies on their heart. Nevertheless when one turns to the Lord, the veil is taken away."

2 Corinthians 3:15-16 (NKJV)

Contents

Preface   iv
Acknowledgement   v

1. Genesis - HIGHLIGHTS of the BIBLE - OLD TESTAMENT...   1
2. Exodus   16
3. Leviticus   25
4. Numbers   35
5. Deuteronomy   41
6. Joshua   55
7. Judges   60
8. Ruth   65
9. 1 Samuel   67
10. 2 Samuel   73
11. 1 Kings   78
12. 2 Kings   81
13. 1 Chronicles   84
14. 2 Chronicles   96
15. Ezra   113
16. Nehemiah   118
17. Esther   125
18. Job   127
19. Psalms   138
20. Proverbs   204
21. Ecclesiastes   240
22. Song of Solomon   246
23. Isaiah   248
24. Jeremiah   265

25	Lamentations	274
26	Ezekiel	277
27	Daniel	286
28	Hosea	292
29	Joel	296
30	Amos	298
31	Obadiah	301
32	Jonah	302
33	Micah	304
34	Nahum	307
35	Habakkuk	308
36	Zephaniah	309
37	Haggai	311
38	Zechariah	313
39	Malachi	318
40	Matthew - HIGHLIGHTS of the BIBLE - THE GOSPELS COMMENTARY -...	321
41	Mark	353
42	Luke	370
43	John	412
44	Acts - HIGHLIGHTS of the BIBLE - ACTS to REVELATION...	457
45	Romans	471
46	1 Corinthians	485
47	2 Corinthians	499
48	Galatians	510
49	Ephesians	521
50	Philippians	530
51	Colossians	538
52	1 Thessalonians	544
53	2 Thessalonians	549
54	1 Timothy	552
55	2 Timothy	559
56	Titus	563

57	Philemon	566
58	Hebrews	568
59	James	575
60	1 Peter	586
61	2 Peter	598
62	1 John	602
63	2 John	609
64	3 John	611
65	Jude	613
66	Revelation	616
67	Conclusion	642
About the Author		644

Preface

Some people say the Bible contains the most important words ever written and explains the mysteries of life. If so, important questions need answers. Could the mysteries revealed in the Bible fill you with a peace beyond understanding? Are beliefs presented in the Bible unique? Could these beliefs transform your life? I wrote this commentary to answer my existential questions. I hope it helps you answer yours.

Acknowledgement

Thanks to my wife, for encouraging me to retire from regular full-time employment, allowing time for completing this project. Also, thanks for providing valuable input on the commentary.

Thanks to my sister-in-law for providing corrections to scriptural references.

Thanks to J. Wolf, Ph.D., who provided suggestions for improvements to this project's writing.

Thanks to HomeGroup members who continue to be encouraging and inspirational in this journey.

Thanks to the pastors of the churches I've attended for their enlightened and balanced teaching.

1

Genesis - HIGHLIGHTS of the BIBLE - OLD TESTAMENT COMMENTARY - VOLUME I

[1]**GENESIS** - Genesis may be the most popular and unique book ever written. The book itself seems to support these opinions. Of course, popularity alone does not denote importance. The book does claim to provide a wealth of information on universal truths. Maybe, like me, you were curious or, perhaps you were interested because of its influence throughout the history of modern people. Let's get into the highlights of the book starting with the critically important first verse.

The structure of this commentary is as follows: each selected section of scripture is stated in **bold** print followed by the commentary in standard text.

---

[1] NSB quotations are from the Nelsons Study Bible, copyright (c) 1997 by Thomas Nelson, Inc., Nashville, TN; used by permission; scripture taken from the New King James Version, Copyright (c) 1979, 1980, 1982 used by permission. All rights reserved.

Genesis 1:1 In the beginning God created the heavens and the earth. This verse says God created all the physical world and the cosmos. The scripture does not appear to say how this was done other than to say God spoke it into existence (Psalm 33:9). Since "**God is spirit**" (John 4:24), this means that the spiritual created the physical that constitutes our observable world.

Among various theories, scientists have postulated a "Big Bang Theory," which some say is consistent with the laws of physics except for the universally observable fact that in the physical world, based on the laws of physics, something (like a big bang) does not come from nothing. Thus, if the big bang is how God created the universe, it would seem to confirm the existence of power (or spirit) outside the laws of physics.

As I understand it, one person considered to be a genius postulates that because there is a law such as "gravity," the universe will "create itself" from nothing. However, the belief that nothing created everything would seem to be a scientific impossibility. From where did that law of gravity come? Wouldn't that have to be a power outside the law of gravity?

Could the law of gravity create itself? A law describes what happens under certain conditions. To my knowledge, it does not create or produce anything. If I write a song, did I or the laws of music write the song? The obvious answer is that I wrote the song. In my opinion, the same reasoning applies whether a person wants to make (a) gravity, (b) spontaneous creation, (c) the laws of physics, (d) aliens, or (e) anything else out to be their god. What caused that gravity, spontaneous creation, law, or aliens to exist? From a purely rational perspective, it seems like there has to be something outside of the natural world that is uncreated, uncaused, and supernatural or there would not be a natural world.

Thus, an accurate explanation of the cosmos appears to require a supernatural creator. (**2 Corinthians 4:18... while we do not look**

at the things which are seen, but at the things which are not seen. For the things which are seen *are* temporary, but the things which *are* not seen are eternal.) If there is a supernatural creator, He allows us the free will to believe something different; whatever we want. A friend said, "What if one just accepts what is without a point of view." That position certainly is an option. On the other hand, if you accept what the Bible presents about the natural and supernatural (i.e., spiritual), the words need to be understood. This commentary seeks to offer one person's perspective on the interpretation. This first verse of Genesis is so important it demanded an expanded explanation. Comments on other verses will mostly be more succinct.

Genesis 1:3 Then God said: "Let there be light"; and there was light. God's command creates reality as we know it and the light, without which we would be eternally in the dark. On second thought, we would not be in the dark. Without light, we would not exist.

Genesis 1:26 Then God said, Let us make man in Our image, according to Our likeness;... God refers to Himself as "us" and later reveals the Trinity (Father, Son, and Holy Spirit) in the New Testament. Wow, what a revelation! Many people and belief systems cannot accept this concept.

Not only that, but the verse states that *we* are in His likeness (image). Since God is spirit, I assume this means we also have a spiritual aspect. Based on enlightenment from the New Testament, it appears there are three aspects (or persons) to the one and only God (Father, Son, and Holy Spirit). God, the Father is spirit, God the Son took on a physical body on earth and now has a glorified body, God the Holy Spirit is the Spirit of God here with us and in believers (1 Corinthians 6:19). This is understandable since natural beings infused with a spirit also seem to have three different components. These components are the mind (the intellect or soul), body (our physical person), and spirit. These are three aspects of a natural human being like the Father, Son, and Holy Spirit are the three different aspects of the supernatural God (John 4:24). Yes, these are complex concepts to comprehend or explain, and that's why this analogy is inadequate but may be somewhat helpful.

Genesis 2:18 And the LORD God said, "*It is* not good that man should be alone; I will make him a helper comparable to him." Interestingly, the first negative assessment in the Bible is against loneliness. It is good to have a helper.

Genesis 3:1 Now the serpent was more cunning than any beast of the field which the LORD God had made. And he said to the woman, "Has God indeed said, 'You shall not eat of every tree of the garden'?" Satan's point of attack began at the Word of God. Some choose a literal interpretation of this scripture. Others view it as allegorical, symbolic, or metaphorical. The "serpent" is later identified as being Satan (Revelation 12:9; 20:2) so to me, it makes sense to view the reference in this story as symbolic rather than literal.

Whether you view the story as literal, symbolic, or metaphorical, the same attack mode continues today. There are many examples of the trustworthiness of the Word of God being questioned by well-meaning, scholarly, and intelligent people. Often, the appeal to challenge the Word of God is an appeal to our pride. In the Bible, a statement by the serpent that appeals to the pride of man is **3:4 "you will not surely die."** Self-will (i.e., pride) against the instruction of God begins here. The serpent symbolizes something both repulsive but fascinating at the same time (opposites can attract). Throw in a desire for self-will, and you have rebellion against God's instruction. The defining issue seems to be one of obedience or disobedience to the Word of God. Whether one views this story as symbolic or literal, the point appears to be the same. Note that without disobedience, forgiveness would not be necessary. There is more on this tragic sense of life in subsequent parts of this commentary.

Genesis 3:17 Then to Adam He said, "Because you have heeded the voice of your wife, and have eaten from the tree of which I commanded you, saying, 'You shall not eat of it':
"Cursed *is* the ground for your sake;
In toil you shall eat *of* it
All the days of your life.
3:18 Both thorns and thistles it shall bring forth for you,
And you shall eat the herb of the field. It appears that before the fall (when Adam disobeyed God), the ground wasn't filled with unpleasant weeds, and the work of harvesting food was probably much more pleasant. It is clear that although his wife encouraged Adam to disobey the Lord, he was still responsible for his actions and would have to suffer the consequences along with all the rest of us who have followed in his footsteps. However you view this part of scripture, the underlying message that man has the free will and propensity to disobey our maker seems evident. Note that in verse 22 of this chapter, God says the man has now become "**like one of Us to know good and evil.**" Thus, in this respect, man now appears to reflect more of the image of God than he initially did. When I use the term "man" here, I mean man and woman. The woman suffered the consequences, as did the man.

Genesis 3:21 His brother's name *was* Jubal. He was the father of all those who play the harp and flute. Here in the first book of the Bible, we have mention of musical instruments. God gave humanity the gift of the ability to pursue music. As with the gift of life, it is evident that He gave us the free will to use the gift of music however we want.

Genesis 3:24 And Enoch walked with God; and he *was* not, for God took him. Enoch and Elijah (2 Kings 2:11) didn't die; it appears that they were just taken from the earth by God.

Genesis 4:8 Now Cain talked with Abel his brother; and it came to pass, when they were in the field, that Cain rose up against Abel

his brother and killed him. Here, in the first family story in the Bible, after Adam and Eve disobeyed God (the fall), we see what the fall did for family relationships. Cain turned against his brother Abel with such anger that he killed him.

Abel had done nothing wrong to deserve this anger. All Abel did was demonstrate his true faith through offering to God the best that he had to offer, not just a token gift. Cain became jealous to the point of murder because his brother obtained favor for good behavior. The propensity of humankind for this type of sentiment and jealousy has not changed over the ages. (Consider the Romans throwing Christians to the lions or banning the Bible in various countries now and over the centuries).

The scripture does not say whether Abel gloated or not, but it does indicate that Cain was angry apparently because he did not do as well as his brother in the sight of the Lord. Even today, we see the same kind of anger from grown offspring who have not done as well in the sight of God or their parents. They may lash out in anger and jealousy toward their parents or toward the siblings they think are in some way more favored.

It is important to note that sometimes, this anger and hatred is not based on anything that the parents or siblings have done wrong. It can be based on the jealousy of the offspring who has not done well in the sight of their parent, or their God. A lesson we can learn from this story is that whenever someone demonstrates what appears to be irrational or obsessive hatred or anger toward a family member, we need to consider that it might not have anything to do with what the family member did to them. It could be due to their jealousy about relationships, siblings, or parents have with God or others.

A little further along in this book, we have another family story of jealousy and hatred between siblings. Joseph's brothers conspire to kill him in this story, but he winds up sold into slavery instead. Again the target of the hatred and jealousy did not deserve all the cruel treatment he received. These stories let us know early on that obsessive jealousy and anger can be very destructive and those compulsive feelings can even lead to murder.

Proverbs 6:16 says: **"These six *things* the Lord hates, Yes, seven *are* an abomination to Him:.....one who sows discord among the brethren"** so, we don't want to be one of the people who sow discord. It can be hard to accept that the Lord hates some things, but that *is* what this scripture states.

Genesis 6:4 There were giants on the earth in those days, and also afterward when the sons of God came into the daughters of men and they bore *children* to them. Those *were* the mighty men who *were* of old, men of renown. I don't know much about what this means, and it appears that even scholars have different opinions. Thus, I will just say it is a very interesting statement that I hope to understand someday. Archaeology does indicate that there were giant animals on earth in prehistoric times.

Genesis 8:21 And the LORD smelled a soothing aroma. Then the LORD said in His heart, "I will never again curse the ground for man's sake, although the imagination of man's heart *is* evil from his youth; nor will I again destroy every living thing as I have done. This is a serious charge against humanity. Our hearts are evil from our youth, but the gift of salvation is available to all. Note that until Adam's disobedience (the fall), man's heart was not evil. Herein is a major difference between many different belief systems (other religions) and Christianity. Some systems state that man is good, whereas Christianity posits that man is born bad. If you are good without God, then you may not think you need God. If you are bad, you may think that you need God's forgiveness and redemption. Also, note that it appears Noah, who built the Ark, **walked with God** (vs. 6:9) by seeking to obey Him. We'll get into the concept of bad but innocent in succeeding commentary.

Genesis 9:6 For in the image of God He made man. Only humankind is said to possess God's image. I take this to mean that we have a spiritual aspect in addition to our natural/material status. God is spirit (John 4:24), so this verse must have to do with how we have some spiritual aspect to be in His image. We have a rational volitional (free will) component also and can reason. Perhaps some of these attributes are also in the image of God. When we create something original, we are also acting somewhat in the image of God since that is something that God does. It is interesting to note that, in His glorified body, apparently Christ had both spiritual and physical attributes. When believers receive their glorified resurrected bodies (1 Corinthians 15:35-50), I expect these glorified bodies will have both spiritual and physical-like qualities.

Initially, we were created in righteousness and innocence, which can be viewed as a reflection of God's holiness (Genesis 1:27). We are social and can enjoy fellowship with others. This seems to reflect an aspect of God. It was God who first declared that it was not good for man to be alone (Genesis 2:18). Though it does not appear that man was created "evil", man became so through Adam's free will choice to disobey God whereby sin entered the world. Thereafter for all men, the imagination of our hearts has been evil (8:21).

Today we still have some vestige of the moral nature that man was initially given, but we also have the damaged likeness or image that Adam passed on to all of his descendants (Romans 5:12). Thus, while we are on earth, our physical aspect continues to battle with the spiritual (Galatians 5:16-18). Interestingly, without a rule/law, there *is* sin, but sin is not imputed when there is no law (Romans 5:13). In other words, a person would not be responsible for their misdeeds/sins if there was no standard/rule by which to measure their actions. This approach seems fair and also partly explains why the Bible can engender such animosity. It sets rules of behavior that make it clear when we miss the mark/sin. Before I came to faith, I did not want to know these rules even though I did have an innate conscience that let me know when I was getting out of line. (Romans 2:14-15).

The good news is that when God redeems us, we begin to become set apart for His use through the process of sanctification that He starts in us (Ephesians 4:24). This process is only by God's grace through faith (Ephesians 2:8-9). Through faith, we become new creations in the likeness of God (2 Corinthians 5:17). Important Note: We don't become a god; we only reflect His righteousness. It is like the moon reflecting the light of the sun. The moon has no light of its own to give, but it reflects the sun's light, which is especially visible at night when it is dark.

Genesis 11:6 Come, let us go down and confuse their language so they will not understand each other." Here is another time in the Old Testament that reveals the Trinity. It appears that God confused their language to keep them from becoming too prideful and arrogant. This move may have delayed the development of our pride.

Genesis 12:3 I will bless those who bless you,
   And I will curse him who curses you;
   And in you all the families of the earth shall be blessed." This is part of what the Lord said to Abram. It conveys a concept about Abram and his descendants that I think we need to understand. God renamed Abram Abraham (Genesis 17;1-8), and his name is one of the most honored, respected, and famous names in human history. Christianity, Islam, and Judaism all honor his name.

Genesis 12:11 And it came to pass, when he was close to entering Egypt, that he said to Sarai his wife, "Indeed I know that you *are* a woman of beautiful countenance. This scripture presents one of the very few times in the Bible that mention a person's looks. In contrast, looks get way too much attention in our culture. Perhaps we should seek to change our focus. God puts much more emphasis on the heart and spirit than the physical appearance.

Genesis 14:22 But Abram said to the king of Sodom, "I have raised my hand to the LORD, God Most High, the Possessor of heaven and earth,... Here, we find out who owns everything on earth: the Lord. While we are on earth, we are just temporary stewards of a minuscule part of what the Lord owns. Think of this: a light-year is 182,000 miles times the number of seconds in a year (nearly 6 trillion miles). Then consider that we can identify a star that is about 1550 light-years away from the earth (that is 9,300,000,000,000,000 miles if my calculations are correct). It is a big God who can make a universe that big. Also, it is interesting to note that prominent scientists (Einstein, Hubble, et al.) have determined, based on their observations and measurements, that our universe is about 13.7 billion years old and that it started with what they refer to as a "big bang." According to *The Atlantic*, 99.9 percent of the National Academies of Sciences members agree with this big bang theory. However, since no sound can be transmitted in space (because there is no air in space and sound waves are contractions and refractions of air molecules), it would probably be more appropriate to call it the big expansion theory. As I understand it, the basic scientific measurements prove that the universe is expanding, and from this, they measure how many years it has been in existence.

Genesis 15:1 After these things the word of the LORD came to Abram in a vision, saying, "Do not be afraid, Abram. I *am* your shield, your exceedingly great reward." In addition to other ways God has used to communicate to humanity, He sometimes speaks in visions. This scripture indicates that our relationship with the Lord is an exceedingly great reward.

Genesis 15:6 And he believed in the LORD, and He accounted it to him for righteousness. Wow! This statement is straightforward and very important to know. One interpretation: we can believe in God and be saved. With this belief, faith in the only living God is what saves us from sin (John 12:11). We are not saved by our good deeds or anything else that we can do. In the Old and New Testament times, people are saved the same way, by the grace of God through faith. Note that there is a vast difference between Christianity and all the other religions on this point. There is absolutely nothing we can do to save ourselves, nor can we save anyone else. It is the complete work of God that cost Him a lot but is given to us as a free gift (Romans 6:23). Of course, as with any gift, we have to accept it and use it. If someone gives me a plane ticket, I have to accept it and board the flight for it to have any value to me.

Genesis 22:5 And Abraham said to his young men, "Stay here with the donkey; the lad and I will go yonder and worship, and we will come back to you." Abraham seemed deliberate and determined to worship. There are times when we need to have this kind of attitude because the cares of this world can hinder us in what we need to do. We do need some discipline.

Genesis 22:11 But the angel of the LORD called out to him from heaven, "Abraham! Abraham!" "Here I am," he replied. 12 "Do not lay a hand on the boy," he said. "Do not do anything to him. Now I know that you fear God, because you have not withheld from me your son, your only son." Abraham was completely obedient to God. He completely trusted God. God appears to be testing Abraham to allow him the opportunity to show his true character. God, of course. knew how this event would turn out.

Genesis 24:26 Then the man bowed down his head and worshiped the LORD. Here Abraham's servant follows his example of worship. This is the kind of example we need to be.

Genesis 24:63 And Isaac went out to meditate in the field in the evening; and he lifted his eyes and looked, and there, the camels *were* coming. Here we have one of the first mentions in the Bible of meditation. The modern technique of meditation is focusing the mind on a particular object, thought or activity to achieve a mentally clear and emotionally calm state. Scripture encourages us to meditate on (a) God (Psalm 63:6), (b) the work of God (Psalm 77:12),(c) the precepts of God (Psalm 119:15), (d) the statutes of God (Psalm 119:48), (e) the Word of God (Psalm 119:148), (f) the majesty of God (Psalms 145:5), (g) His name (Malachi 3:16), and (h) whatever is true, whatever things are noble, whatever things are just, whatever things are pure, whatever things are lovely, whatever things are of good report or virtuous (Philippians 4:8). Thus from a Biblical perspective, these are things we are directed to fill our minds with when we meditate. In one of my college classes, we were given the assignment to try to empty our minds in the process of meditating. That would appear to be the opposite of what the Bible says though it might be part of listening to God as we meditate on His word.

Genesis 28:22 ... And this stone which I have set as a pillar shall be God's house, and of all that You give me I will surely give a tenth to You." Everything belongs to God. Here Jacob commits to tithe a tenth of what the Lord lets him control back to the Lord. There is some disagreement regarding whether the tithe of a tenth still applies in New Testament times. It has been my experience that the more we have given, the more we have been blessed to earn. In other words, Malachi 3:10 has proven true for us. Though I do not think it is a good idea to give expecting to get, this verse in Malachi appears to say that the people could test the Lord in their tithing and see if He blessed them. The LORD has given us everything we have, even our very life when you think about it. When we give back some of what He has temporarily entrusted to us, I think it changes us for the better. Because He is a giving God, we become a little more in His image. It is also essential to take care of your family's needs. I did say "needs." Taking care of "wants" should probably be farther down the list of expenditures. A 2007 study by The Barna Group found that five percent of Americans give the ten percent tithe or more. They also found that among the most charitable groups were evangelicals, of whom 24% tithe. By comparison, 2% of Catholics tithed. I'm just reporting the findings of that one study here. Other investigations may have different outcomes.

Genesis 33:19 And he bought the parcel of land, where he had pitched his tent, from the children of Hamor, Shechem's father, for one hundred pieces of money. It is interesting that although God had promised the land to Abraham's family, they had to buy it one piece at a time. He didn't just give it to them, they were going to get it but not all at once, and they had to work for it. This principle seems to be the way with some of what God gives us. He knows that people often do not appreciate, value, or respect that for which they do not have to work. This is a principle that we could apply in our government systems. We often do not allow people the dignity of earning what they receive. For those who are capable of earning their keep, we could allow them to do so. We could probably solve many human service problems by designing systems to preserve the dignity of the people receiving assistance and letting them earn what they need.

Genesis 35:22 And it happened, when Israel dwelt in that land, that Reuben went and lay with Bilhah his father's concubine; and Israel heard *about it*. Sin can result in loss of blessing that, ironically, the sinner thought they would get through partaking of the sin (see 49:3-4). By this act, Reuben attempted to solidify his claim as the firstborn son, but instead was told, as a result of his action he would not excel.

Genesis 38:6 Then Judah took a wife for Er his firstborn, and her name *was* Tamar. But Er, Judah's firstborn, was wicked in the sight of the LORD, and the LORD killed him. Interestingly, Judah intermingled his family with the Canaanite wife for Er but the Lord did not judge the Canaanite woman Tamar but did judge Er. Tamar went on to become a heroine in the Bible (Ruth 4:12, Matt. 1:3).

Genesis 39:3 And his master saw that the LORD *was* with him and that the LORD made all he did to prosper in his hand. This scripture demonstrates how we can view the situation when we do things the right way, and it prospers; the LORD made what we did to prosper (39:23). When Joseph was in prison, the warden didn't even have to check on anything under Joseph's authority because everything he did, "The LORD made it prosper." Joseph had quite a good reputation even when he was a convict. When he was an ex-convict, he gained an even more widespread reputation as he became second in command over all of Egypt and saved Egypt and others from starving during a seven-year famine. If you have had things in your life prosper, perhaps you should also say: "The LORD made it prosper." In addition, don't ever think that the Lord cannot use an ex-convict to further His plans. He used Joseph mightily.

Genesis 40:8 And they said to him, "We each have had a dream, and *there is* no interpreter of it." So Joseph said to them, "Do not interpretations belong to God? Tell *them* to me, please." This scripture demonstrates how Joseph did things. He announced his faith and immediately proceeded to act upon it. He's a good role model in this respect.

Genesis 41:16 So Joseph answered Pharaoh, saying, "*It is* not in me; God will give Pharaoh an answer of peace." This approach is typical of Joseph; he didn't take credit for the ability to interpret dreams nor use his innocence to plead for his freedom. He accepted his fate as what God wanted and just went with it. In the end, he didn't even blame his brothers for what they had done to him. What a testimony of forgiveness! We probably need more of that kind of attitude in our lives (see 45:8).

Genesis 49:33 And when Jacob had finished commanding his sons,

he drew his feet up into the bed and breathed his last, and was gathered to his people. It is interesting that when Jacob died, the scripture says he was gathered to his people. I take this to mean that there is an afterlife, and our people are there. Along with 2 Samuel 12:23, this verse indicates that believers will go to be with our loved ones who are in heaven and that babies who die are there already. In other words, those who die on earth before they are accountable for their choices go to heaven and are with the Lord. They will not come back to us, but we can go to them. The question comes to mind: If David's baby was in heaven, we might ask what happens in the case of a stillbirth or a miscarriage, or other premature death? The scripture says that God knew the prophet even before he was formed in the womb (Jeremiah 1:5). Thus, it appears that life begins before physical birth so, in all of the cases where death occurs before birth or before the age of accountability, my opinion would be that these people are in heaven.

2

Exodus

[2]**EXODUS** - How the Israelites Left Slavery

Exodus 3:14 God said to Moses, "I AM WHO I AM. This is what you are to say to the Israelites: 'I AM has sent me to you.'" That is an amazing statement that we can't even comprehend. He is. He is eternal and does not have a cause. He always existed. We have a hard time understanding these concepts. Faith is the answer. All creatures owe their existence to Him. And, it does not appear that the dimensions of space and time bind Him as we are bound in the physical world. When you think about it, if He is the spirit that created the space and time dimensions that we live in, it makes sense that the rules controlling these dimensions would not apply to Him. By the way, though God is referred to using a masculine pronoun, gender must be very different from what it is in the physical world. In the spiritual realm, there is no marriage (Matthew 22:11) and no procreation, nor are these representations needed. However, the glorified bodies in heaven still carry some gender identity appearance (1 Corinthians 15:42-44). So, it appears that our

---

[2] NSB quotations are from the Nelsons Study Bible, copyright (c) 1997 by Thomas Nelson, Inc., Nashville, TN; used by permission; scripture taken from the New King James Version, Copyright (c) 1979, 1980, 1982 used by permission. All rights reserved.

gender is recognizable in the spiritual realm, but it will not have anything to do with procreation or marriage. These spiritual bodies will be eternal, powerful, and honorable. Thus, gender is a very different concept in the afterlife. Also, the Bible indicates that when it comes to salvation, gender doesn't matter (Galatians 3:28).

Exodus 4:21 The LORD said to Moses, "When you return to Egypt, see that you perform before Pharaoh all the wonders I have given you the power to do. But I will harden his heart so that he will not let the people go. Interestingly, the Lord hardened Pharaoh's heart. So the next time we run up against someone whose attitude we think we need to change, we may want to be patient and persistent as Moses was with Pharaoh. Note that Pharaoh did not begin to believe what Moses believed but did let the Israelites go.

Exodus 9:14 ...for at this time I will send all My plagues to your very heart, and on your servants and on your people, that you may know that *there is* none like Me in all the earth. 15 Now if I had stretched out My hand and struck you and your people with pestilence, then you would have been cut off from the earth. 16 But indeed for this *purpose* I have raised you up, that I may show My power *in* you, and that My name may be declared in all the earth. The Lord had a purpose for hardening Pharaoh's heart. Pharaoh had set himself up as a god. The Lord's judgment on him was appropriate and demonstrated His power. We don't always know what is going on and, we are often not the key player. We need to keep in mind that we are just observers of the bigger things going on in the universe in many situations. In these situations, we are like fans in the stands at a baseball game watching the action but not impacting the outcome. Just as the sun does not revolve around the earth as some early men thought it did, the earth does not revolve around us as we sometimes think it does. In this section of scripture, it appears that God decided to teach Pharaoh a lesson because Pharaoh refused to humble himself. We always need to remember that

God resists the proud but gives grace to the humble (Ps. 18:27; 147:6; Isa. 57:15-21; 1 Pet. 5:5). It would not be good for us if God hardened our hearts because we refused to humble ourselves.

Exodus 12:6 Now you shall keep it until the fourteenth day of the same month. Then the whole assembly of the congregation of Israel shall kill it at twilight. 7 And they shall take *some* **of the blood and put** *it* **on the two doorposts and on the lintel of the houses where they eat it.** In that day, this was the Lord's provision for avoiding physical death. The blood of Christ is the Lord's provision for us to avoid spiritual death which is separation from Him. Note that there are two types of death in the Bible. One is the death of our physical body (when the soul separates from the body). The other is the separation from God, which is spiritual death (when the spirit is separated from God). There is a spiritual and physical element to human life. We can be spiritually dead but physically alive (Eph. 2:1, 5). We could also be spiritually alive but physically dead (Matt. 22:32).

Exodus 12:27 …that you shall say, 'It *is* **the Passover sacrifice of the LORD, who passed over the houses of the children of Israel in Egypt when He struck the Egyptians and delivered our households.'" So the people bowed their heads and worshiped. 28 Then the children of Israel went away and did** *so;* **just as the LORD had commanded Moses and Aaron, so they did.** The Israelites worshiped, believed, and obeyed the Lord at this point. For this level of faith, God's laws should be with us at all times. We can use reminders, memorials, and symbols to help us in this respect. We can also read and study the Bible regularly.

Exodus 15:1 Then Moses and the children of Israel sang this song to the LORD, and spoke, saying:
  "**I will sing to the LORD,**
  For He has triumphed gloriously!
  The horse and its rider

He has thrown into the sea!
**2 The LORD *is* my strength and song,
And He has become my salvation;
He *is* my God, and I will praise Him;
My father's God, and I will exalt Him.** God is the reason for singing. He is the purpose. He is a strong song. God was the audience when they sang this song. They brought God beauty by praising Him, and this is appropriate because He created all beauty.

Exodus 15:20 Then Miriam the prophetess, the sister of Aaron, took the timbrel in her hand; and all the women went out after her with timbrels and with dances. It is interesting to note that the women-led worship in this passage **with timbrels and with dances**. It is good to look at this passage in light of the culture of the time. We can get an idea about the culture through books written by many sources around that time and by looking at modern-day cultures that carry on some of the same attitudes. It appears that Christianity was a major force in bringing more equality of treatment for women.

Exodus 15:26...and said, "If you diligently heed the voice of the LORD your God and do what is right in His sight, give ear to His commandments and keep all His statutes, I will put none of the diseases on you which I have brought on the Egyptians. For I *am* the LORD who heals you." God brought on the disease in this situation. This verse does not say He brings on all diseases, but the rest of the verse does imply that He is the one who heals us. Note that even though God does something or gives us something in other parts of scripture, this may not mean that no work is required. In the case of God's healing, he certainly can heal through having doctors work to accomplish His healing. When God promised land to Abraham's family, they still had to buy it or obtain it through other means. Acquiring the land required effort on their part. They were going to get it, but they had to work and pay for it. Healing can be like this. We may get it, but many in the healing professions may have to work on the problem before the healing is finally given.

Exodus 16:4 Then the LORD said to Moses, "Behold, I will rain bread from heaven for you. And the people shall go out and gather a certain quota every day, that I may test them, whether they will walk in My law or not. The Lord will sometimes test us to see if we will obey Him or not. There does not seem to be much question that He wants us to pass these tests of faith and obedience.

Exodus 17: 15 And Moses built an altar and called its name, The-LORD-Is-My-Banner; 16 for he said, "Because the LORD has sworn: the LORD *will have* war with Amalek from generation to generation." Israel continues to war with the descendants of Esau to this day.

Exodus 17:16 Then it came to pass on the third day, in the morning, that there were thunderings and lightnings, and a thick cloud on the mountain; and the sound of the trumpet was very loud, so that all the people who *were* in the camp trembled. It appears that a visitor from heaven brought their trumpet with them when they came down. It was a very loud trumpet that would be expected of a trumpet from heaven. Because of this, the people were afraid. Nice to know that there are musical instruments in heaven.

Exodus 20:3 "You shall have no other gods before Me. This one of the ten commandments clarifies that He is the only living God who is to be worshiped and obeyed. We refer to the 10 Commandments as law. The Hebrew word: law can mean instruction. Thus, here God is mercifully giving us instruction in following His ways for our benefit. He is pointing out the way we should go in our life.

Exodus 20:5 Thou shalt not bow down thyself unto them, nor serve

them, for I Jehovah thy God am a jealous God, visiting the iniquity of the fathers upon the children, upon the third and upon the fourth generation of them that hate me, Of course, as noted in the New Testament, faith in Christ conquers all sin and judgment for those who believe. However, the consequences of a father's sins can have impacts on his ancestors for multiple generations.

Exodus 22:1 "If a man steals an ox or a sheep, and slaughters it or sells it, he shall restore five oxen for an ox and four sheep for a sheep. It would probably be good for us to adopt more restitution principles in place of today's incarceration policy. Indeed, the victims would be better off with quintuple or quadruple repayment instead of what they might get from an insurance company. Also, when the offenders are incarcerated without mandatory restitution, the victim is victimized again through having to pay a tax rate high enough to feed, house, clothe and take care of all the medical, dental, and vision needs of offenders. As is abundantly evident with our punitive versus restitution system, the victim is victimized twice, once by the offender and once by our criminal justice system. Punishment sometimes helps, but rehabilitation, training, and education programs are also needed.

Exodus 22:14"And if a man borrows *anything* from his neighbor, and it becomes injured or dies, the owner of it not *being* with it, he shall surely make *it* good. This concept is what I was taught growing up. It's good to see that the teaching was in line with scripture.

Exodus 22:18 "Do not allow a sorceress to live..." God prescribed heavy-duty punishment for sorcery at that time. However, this punishment was not for any individual to impose, but rather only the highest authority. Now, we do not have this law against sorcery. However, the scripture gives us an idea of what God thought about sorcery and makes me think it is best to stay away from it. Sorcery or wizardry, for that matter, is a process of denying divine providence. We do need to view this law in the context of the older dispensation explicitly given to Israel instead of the dispensation of grace that we are now under (Luke 9:55). In other words, I do not view all of the laws given to Israel under the Old Testament as applying to Christians in the modern New Testament days. (See comments on Exodus 40:35) Still, reviewing these laws gives us a good idea of what pleases God and what does not. Sorcery does not.

Exodus 22:28 "You shall not revile God, nor curse a ruler of your people. Our culture is removed from the second part of this warning, even by many who call ourselves Christians. If we curse a ruler of our people, who God allowed to be there in His sovereignty, are we also disrespecting God's authority? Does it depend on why we are cursing the ruler? We will look at other examples of how Christians should respond to governing authorities in the book of Romans. Until we get there, there is scripture regarding authorities at the family level. Exodus 20:12 required the Israelites to honor their fathers and mothers. Also, in Deuteronomy 27:16, we have scripture that says: **"Cursed is the one who treats his father or mother with contempt."** Thus, the one who does not respect even this lower level of family authority structure has their contempt boomerang on them in the form of a curse. It would appear that these principles still apply even if the punishments meted out in those days by the governing authorities are different than what would happen today to violators.

Exodus 23:3 You shall not show partiality to a poor man in his dispute. In other words, justice is justice regardless of a person's riches or lack of riches. The poor or rich should be held to the same standards of conduct. Greedy or criminal behavior is not excused by economic status. Our culture often appears to have difficulty implementing this kind of equality/fairness. The Lord also encourages compassion on the poor and discourages favoritism toward the rich (James 2:2-9), a very fair approach.

Exodus 25:34 On the lampstand itself four bowls *shall be* made like almond *blossoms, each with* its *ornamental* knob and flower. Interesting that the Lord appears to like artistry here.

Exodus 28:3 So you shall speak to all *who are* gifted artisans, whom I have filled with the spirit of wisdom, that they may make Aaron's garments, to consecrate him, that he may minister to Me as priest. God gives skills to gifted artisans and fills them with the spirit of wisdom. These artisans were spiritually guided. We could use more artisans "**with the spirit of wisdom**" in our culture.

Exodus 32:14 So the LORD relented from the harm which He said He would do to His people. This is a remarkable statement that can be hard to understand. It appears that Moses pleaded to the Lord and the Lord relented. Though this is the sequence of events, a different translation may help with understanding this passage. The New International Version translates this passage as follows: **14 Then the LORD relented and did not bring on his people the disaster he had threatened.** This version makes sense because the Lord threatened His people to bring them into line with what He expected of them. After Moses prayed for the people to receive mercy, He granted that mercy in harmony with His intentions from the beginning. Rather than reminding the Lord what He had promised, Moses wound up reminding himself of what the Lord had promised to Israel and others.

Exodus 32:33 And the LORD said to Moses, "Whoever has sinned against Me, I will blot him out of My book. It's not a great fate to sin against the Lord, but to consider the whole counsel of the Lord, we need to also look at the following passages: "**the Son of Man has power on earth to forgive sins**" (2 Cor. 2:7). And "**If we confess our sins, He is faithful and just to forgive us our sins and to cleanse us from all unrighteousness**" (1 John 1:9). It is great that God has provided how a man can have his sins forgiven because every human being has fallen short of the standard and needs forgiveness no matter how or by whatever means we may try to deny this reality. When a person humbles themself and repents, it is a joyous occasion on earth and in heaven as even the angels in heaven rejoice (Luke 15:10).

Exodus 40:35 And Moses was not able to enter the tabernacle of meeting, because the cloud rested above it, and the glory of the LORD filled the tabernacle. Here we see that God lived among His people in Old Testament times. However, until New Testament times when Jesus came, no one could get near His Shekinah glory. Now we have the Holy Spirit indwelling us (Acts 2). It's a very different dispensation that we are now in even though God is still the same yesterday, today, and tomorrow (Hebrews 13:8, Psalm 102:25-27 et al.). He does not change. He has always been the great "I Am."

3

Leviticus

[3]**LEVITICUS** - God's holiness requires holiness and He provides a means for atonement.

Leviticus 1:3 If his offering be a burnt sacrifice of the herd, let him offer a male without blemish: he shall offer it of his own voluntary will at the door of the tabernacle of the congregation before the LORD. The burnt offering was entirely consumed. It was a complete offering with nothing held back. The message seems to be that our commitment to the Lord should be (1) freely given and (2) complete. We should joyfully give to the Lord. That's what we were made to do. These offerings required the active participation of the people. When Christ offered Himself for us, it was complete as our commitment to Him should be. This system was the Old Testament method of allowing people to approach God as **"without the shedding of blood there is no remission"** of sin (Hebrews 9:22). Note that the sacrificial system before Christ's death on the Cross was so the people could have fellowship with God without being destroyed because of their sin. The Israelites looked

---

[3] NSB quotations are from the Nelsons Study Bible, copyright (c) 1997 by Thomas Nelson, Inc., Nashville, TN; used by permission; scripture taken from the New King James Version, Copyright (c) 1979, 1980, 1982 used by permission. All rights reserved.

forward to Christ's atonement while we look back to it. Through His atonement, we can come into the presence of God.

Leviticus 4:1 Now the LORD spoke to Moses, saying, 2 "Speak to the children of Israel, saying: 'If a person sins unintentionally against any of the commandments of the LORD *in anything* which ought not to be done, and does any of them, 3 if the anointed priest sins, bringing guilt on the people, then let him offer to the LORD for his sin which he has sinned a young bull without blemish as a sin offering. This scripture makes it known that it is possible to sin unintentionally. Still, an offering needed to be made to the Holy God to atone for the sin. Sin is sin; whether we acknowledge it or know it, we are still guilty and bear responsibility. Again, the offering to be made was to be of the best they had to offer.

Leviticus 5:17 "If a person sins, and commits any of these things which are forbidden to be done by the commandments of the LORD, though he does not know *it*, yet he is guilty and shall bear his iniquity... This verse lays it out clearly. We need forgiveness for breaking the commandments of God even if we don't realize we are breaking them. In other words, ignorance does not make the sin any less destructive; it just makes it unintentional. Later we will see that intent does have a bearing on punishment and makes a difference in that respect.

Leviticus 7:29 "Speak to the children of Israel, saying: 'He who offers the sacrifice of his peace offering to the LORD shall bring his offering to the LORD from the sacrifice of his peace offering. 30 His own hands shall bring the offerings made by fire to the LORD. The fat with the breast he shall bring, that the breast may be waved *as* a wave offering before the LORD... We cannot delegate worship or have proxy worship for us. It needs to be done in person.

Leviticus 8:12 And he poured some of the anointing oil on Aaron's

head and anointed him, to consecrate him. Note what the Nelson Study Bible says about this scripture: "Jesus combines in His person the offices of High Priest, King, and Prophet, so He is the Anointed One, which is the meaning of the names Messiah and Christ." Also, concerning the priesthood, the Nelson Study Bible states: "Through His death on the Cross, the formal priesthood was abolished (Hebrews 10:11, 12)." In its stead, all believers become priests - not to offer sacrifices but to pray, worship God, and witness to others about Jesus (Hebrews 13:15, 16; 1 Peter 2:5, 9; Revelation 1:5, 6)." How about that? Most Christians probably don't think of themselves as priests.

Leviticus 10:3 And Moses said to Aaron, "This is what the LORD spoke, saying:
   'By those who come near Me
   I must be regarded as holy;
   And before all the people
   I must be glorified.'"
   So Aaron held his peace. Worship is fellowship with God and must glorify Him and regard Him as Holy. Here's a test for worship: If it does not glorify God, it does not pass the test and should not be part of Christian worship.

Leviticus 10:8 Then the LORD spoke to Aaron, saying: 9 "Do not drink wine or intoxicating drink, you, nor your sons with you, when you go into the tabernacle of meeting, lest you die. *It shall be* **a statute forever throughout your generations, 10 that you may distinguish between holy and unholy, and between unclean and clean, 11 and that you may teach the children of Israel all the statutes which the LORD has spoken to them by the hand of Moses."** I take this as a strong warning that those who teach in the sanctuary and probably those who lead worship should be clear-headed with no mood-altering chemicals/intoxicants in their systems. In Aaron's time, the penalty for violating this direction prevented any repeat violations. The message is: don't violate the holiness of God when it comes to teaching or leading His people. Thankfully, God has provided the ultimate solution for even this type of sin in the blood of Christ. Still, the message is clear through many scriptures that we should always approach the presence of God with reverence but also with joy (1 Timothy 1:17; Romans 15:6).

Leviticus 13:40 "As for the man whose hair has fallen from his head, he *is* bald, *but* he *is* clean. This is just a comforting scripture for some of us.

Leviticus 17:1 And the LORD spoke to Moses, saying, 2 "Speak to Aaron, to his sons, and to all the children of Israel, and say to them, 'This *is* the thing which the LORD has commanded, saying:... God directed Moses in this and many other scriptures to provide the information to **"all the children of Israel."** Thus, the priests could be held accountable by the people if they deviated from the instructions, and the priests could not have the ability to exploit or oppress the people with knowledge that only they possessed.

Leviticus 19:16 You shall not go about *as* a talebearer among your people; nor shall you take a stand against the life of your neighbor: I *am* the LORD. Interesting that this particular issue is dealt with in scripture shortly after a sin referred to as an abomination. A talebearer is probably someone who is actively spreading false or distorted stories to destroy someone's reputation. This is a very harmful thing that one person can do to another. It also can cause disharmony within the body of Christ. The fact is that this activity if it sows discord among the brethren, is also an abomination to the Lord (see Proverbs 6:19). And, we deceive ourselves when we think that it is just the behavior of other people that can be an *abomination* to the Lord. Unfortunately, too many Christians do participate in telling tales that sow discord.

Leviticus 19:26 'You shall not eat *anything* with the blood, nor shall

you practice divination or soothsaying. Divination and soothsaying seem to be techniques that demonstrate a lack of trust in God.

Leviticus 20:9 'For everyone who curses his father or his mother shall surely be put to death. He has cursed his father or his mother. His blood *shall be* **upon him.** In conjunction with Deuteronomy 27:16, which indicates that one who holds his mother or father in contempt is cursed, it is clear that the Lord has little tolerance for those who denigrate their father or mother. It has been my experience that people who denigrate their mother, father, or both cause much discord in (a) their families, (b) the families of other bystanders associated with the denigrated parents, and (c) among the brethren. With the advent of instant communication facilities, this type of abuse can be spread worldwide with the press of a button.

In his day, it probably took Absalom a lot more time to garner supporters for his cause to overthrow his father, King David. He had to sit at the city gates and spread his carefully worded criticisms to individuals and small groups. Even in those days, gossip and negative criticism probably spread as fast as wildfire. A modern-day Absalom can accomplish the same kind of destruction to their parent's reputation much easier and quicker to a large audience using the available communication technology.

Note that this scripture says *everyone* who curses one of their parents shall be put to death. Of course, the laws of our times are different. Now, with our freedom of speech laws, anyone can curse their father or mother ad infinitum with impunity. It is not uncommon for some people to denigrate their parents publicly for their sins. Sometimes this is done posthumously. Whether true or a matter of perception, it does similar damage to the parent's reputation, and like the feathers scattered by the wind, cannot be taken back. Thankfully, even this type of sin can be forgiven by God's grace through faith.

Leviticus 23:3 'Six days shall work be done, but the seventh day *is* a Sabbath of solemn rest, a holy convocation. You shall do no work *on it*; it *is* the Sabbath of the LORD in all your dwellings... The Lord worked six days, so we are in the image of the Lord when we work six days of the week. Maybe work is not so bad. Though it is good for us to have a day of rest each week, a legalistic approach to the Sabbath was discouraged by Christ (see Mark 2:27). There are also other laws for the Israelites in the Old Testament regarding circumcision, dietary restrictions, and other things that, based on the teachings of Christ, do not apply to believers in this dispensation.

Sometimes, you hear an older person advising a younger person to find what they love to do and make that their career. If the young person is fortunate enough to love doing something that pays a good wage, that might be okay advice. However, for most of us, we better figure out a way to love (or at least stand) what we wind up doing for pay, than wait to find something we love doing.

The reality is that work is work and may not be what we love doing. However, it still may put food on the table. Thus, since almost everyone loves to eat, the end result of our work will still be pleasurable even if we do not love every bit of the work we do to earn the food.

Another thing to realize about the Bible is that it does not encourage freeloading off the work of others. At one point, Paul advises the Thessalonian believer that those who do not work should not be allowed to eat (2 Thessalonians 3:10). Of course, we know from other parts of the Bible that applying this rule would be for non-disabled people who could work. The problem with feeding people who can work without having them work is that it creates a perverse dependency in which lack of effort is rewarded rather than reasonable effort. This creates what can be called learned helplessness. Once this attitude is learned, it can be debilitating and destructive to a person's mental attitude toward being self-sufficient and productive.

Learned helplessness can cause tremendous harm to a person. This kind of false charity rewards indolence rather than productive effort. Unfortunately, this is how much of our welfare system works. It appears to have fostered multiple generations of family members crippled by being paid for doing nothing rather than rewarded for work. Eventually, even though we are one of the wealthiest countries on the face of the earth, we will not be able to afford to create too many citizens who are rewarded for being unproductive.

Note: Part of Jesus' mission on earth was to proclaim liberty from the old letter of the law (Romans 7:6). Here is what the scripture says in Galatians: **23 Before the coming of this faith, we were held in custody under the law, locked up until the faith that was to come would be revealed. 24 So the law was our guardian until Christ came that we might be justified by faith. 25 Now that this faith has come, we are no longer under a guardian.** Thus, we are now under the law of faith instead of the letter of the old law. The law of faith only requires faith as opposed to perfect obedience. The ten commandments are not what can provide salvation. No person can keep them perfectly. They show us our need for grace. It appears that many do not understand this. Even some highly thought of theologians seem to have a different understanding of the purpose of the ten commandments. The reality that many want to refute is that "**all have sinned, and come short of the glory of God**" (Rom. 3:23). Unfortunately, the law requires death as the penalty for sin and, it still appears to be in effect. Thus if we were under the letter of the law, we all would deserve the sentence of death.

Thankfully, that penalty has been paid on our behalf, and now by the grace of God through faith, we can be spared from the just penalty for our lawbreaking and provided with eternal life. Remember that the law can point out sin, but it cannot save us from sin. But through faith, salvation is a gift. We cannot earn it. If we could, we would take pride in the fact that we earned it.

"Therefore by the deeds of the law there shall no flesh be justified in his sight: for by the law is the knowledge of sin" (Rom. 3:20). What the law (the Ten Commandments) does is demonstrate to us that we do sin and will sin and need forgiveness.

Christ paid the price for our sin and offers that forgiveness to those who, through faith, want to receive it. One other thought: even though the Ten Commandments cannot save us, it is to our benefit to follow them because breaking these commandments brings negative consequences. The law is like a mirror. We can see the dirt on our face with a mirror, but the mirror cannot make it disappear.

Also, note that people are saved in the same way in the New Testament and the Old Testament: by grace through faith. Noone was saved in the Old Testament through perfectly keeping the commandments and laws. Abraham was saved in the same way that we can be: by grace through faith (Rom. 4:3,4). He was not perfect, nor was David or Solomon. In Old Testament days, they looked forward to the atoning death of Christ, and we look backward. The same grace of God saves us as saved them. Unfortunately, no one can earn their way into heaven. It has always been a gift and, even the faith a believer has comes from God.

Leviticus 25:23 'The land shall not be sold permanently, for the land *is* Mine; for you *are* strangers and sojourners with Me. Again, we have the concept that we do not own the land, it belongs to the Lord. We are just temporary inhabitants. After that, believers will go to our permanent home with Christ in paradise/heaven.

Leviticus 25:35 'If one of your brethren becomes poor, and falls into poverty among you, then you shall help him, like a stranger

or a sojourner, that he may live with you. God is generous, and we should imitate Him in this area of His character. From other scripture, we know that this help is the help to become productive, not help to remain dependent and helpless.

Leviticus 26:14 'But if you do not obey Me, and do not observe all these commandments, 15 and if you despise My statutes, or if your soul abhors My judgments, so that you do not perform all My commandments, *but* break My covenant, 16 I also will do this to you: I will even appoint terror over you, wasting disease and fever which shall consume the eyes and cause sorrow of heart. And you shall sow your seed in vain, for your enemies shall eat it. 17 I will set My face against you, and you shall be defeated by your enemies. Those who hate you shall reign over you, and you shall flee when no one pursues you. There was a blessing for Israel's obedience, but not the same for disobedience. This scripture has proven true over and over throughout history. Later in this chapter, the Israelites would be scattered among the nations, which was also prophetic.

Leviticus 26:40 '*But* if they confess their iniquity and the iniquity of their fathers, with their unfaithfulness in which they were unfaithful to Me, and that they also have walked contrary to Me, 41 and *that* I also have walked contrary to them and have brought them into the land of their enemies; if their uncircumcised hearts are humbled, and they accept their guilt — 42 then I will remember My covenant with Jacob, and My covenant with Isaac and My covenant with Abraham I will remember; I will remember the land. Our glorious God is still gracious to forgive them (and us) when we humble ourselves and confess our sin. His character has always been grace, mercy, love, and redemption. We should seek to follow these characteristics.

Leviticus 27:34 These *are* the commandments which the LORD commanded Moses for the children of Israel on Mount Sinai. Per this scripture, these commandments were specifically for the children of Israel. Even so, it appears that there are many concepts here that apply just as well to our lives in the modern age. We have been redeemed by more precious blood than they had at the time, and our goal should still be to obey God and to live by his precepts and teaching. Why? Because God is holy holy holy, and our disobedience is worthy of death. Due to His holiness, we could not survive a direct encounter with God in our sinful state, but the appropriate price was paid on our behalf so that we can be in His presence. The price of our disobedience was paid, just like if someone paid your fine in a court of law, the judge can set you free without further punishment. Christ paid the just punishment for our crimes. That is good news.

4

Numbers

[4]**NUMBERS** - History of the Israelites

Numbers 2:2 "Take a census of the sons of Kohath from among the children of Levi, by their families, by their fathers' house, 3 from thirty years old and above, even to fifty years old, all who enter the service to do the work in the tabernacle of meeting. The work in the tabernacle was apparently done by 30 to 50-year-old people, perhaps because these people were physically able to do the work of bearing burdens in the tabernacle of meeting and mature enough to handle the responsibility (see 4:47).

Numbers 3:10 ...So you shall appoint Aaron and his sons, and they shall attend to their priesthood; but the outsider who comes near shall be put to death." In those days, only the high priest could go into the Most Holy Place where the presence of God was. Now, all believers receive the forgiveness of sins, not because of what we have done but because of what Christ has done for us. Thus, we can be in the presence

---

[4] NSB quotations are from the Nelsons Study Bible, copyright (c) 1997 by Thomas Nelson, Inc., Nashville, TN; used by permission; scripture taken from the New King James Version, Copyright (c) 1979, 1980, 1982 used by permission. All rights reserved.

of God. We are saints in his sight with our sins removed from us as far as the East is from the West (Psalm 103:12).

Numbers 4:2 "Take a census of the sons of Kohath from among the children of Levi, by their families, by their fathers' house, 3 from thirty years old and above, even to fifty years old, all who enter the service to do the work in the tabernacle of meeting. The work in the tabernacle was done by 30 to 50-year-old people, perhaps because these people were physically able to do **the work of bearing burdens in the tabernacle of meeting** (see 4:47).

Numbers 6:24 "The LORD bless you and keep you;
  25 The LORD make His face shine upon you,
  And be gracious to you;
  26 The LORD lift up His countenance upon you,
  And give you peace.
  27 "So they shall put My name on the children of Israel, and I will bless them." What a great blessing from the Lord, and what a great brand to have. This blessing is known as the Aaronic benediction and was how Aaron and his sons were to bless the children of Israel. God's grace and mercy come through clearly in this blessing. The last line appears to be a type of branding for the people similar to the "Christian" branding believers are known by today.

Numbers 8:24 "This *is* what *pertains* to the Levites: From twenty-five years old and above one may enter to perform service in the work of the tabernacle of meeting; 25 and at the age of fifty years they must cease performing this work, and shall work no more. 26 They may minister with their brethren in the tabernacle of meeting, to attend to needs, but they *themselves* shall do no work. Thus you shall do to the Levites regarding their duties." Here's one of the very few places in the Bible where there is anything relating to retiring from a type of work. In this case, when they were over 50 years of age, they retired from the heavy lifting. In this case, it appears that the word "work" is referring to the burdensome work, as noted in verse 4:47. The scripture states that it did not mean they were to cease all of what we might also refer to as work, such as ministering to others and attending to their needs. It seems that they were to cease the heavy physical type of work. To the disappointment of many, there does not seem to be the equivalent of what we call retirement mentioned in the Bible other than this section having to do with quitting the heavy lifting while continuing to be actively involved. Retirement, as we envision it, seems to be a modern-day concept.

Numbers 11.17 Then I will come down and talk with you there. I will take of the Spirit that *is* upon you and will put *the same* upon them; and they shall bear the burden of the people with you, that you may not bear *it* yourself alone. The Holy Spirit was upon these elders.

Numbers 12:3 (Now the man Moses *was* very humble, more than all men who *were* on the face of the earth.) Interesting that God chose the most humble man to be His leader. He was not proud or arrogant. Moses knew his proper place and had an accurate assessment of himself. He generally did not rebel against the precepts of God nor try to put himself above God even though he was given great authority among men.

Numbers 15:29 You shall have one law for him who sins unintentionally, *for* him who is native-born among the children of Israel, and for the stranger who dwells among them. God is fair in that there is one law for all.

Numbers 15:36 So, as the LORD commanded Moses, all the congregation brought him outside the camp and stoned him with stones, and he died. This man knew the rules about the Sabbath that God had established for these people, but he deliberately chose to violate these orders and disobey them. In this case, the Lord did not allow this blatant disobedience and did not delay the appropriate consequence. The direct rebellion against God received the inevitable result for all who chose to rebel against God. The man just accelerated the unavoidable result through his direct, blatant, and public disobedience. The Lord will not be mocked. One day every knee will bow, and every tongue will confess that Jesus Christ is Lord (Romans 14:11, Philippians 2:10). What a powerful statement!

Numbers 16:8 Then Moses said to Korah, "Hear now, you sons of Levi: 9 *Is it* **a small thing to you that the God of Israel has separated you from the congregation of Israel, to bring you near to Himself, to do the work of the tabernacle of the LORD, and to stand before the congregation to serve them; 10 and that He has brought you near** *to Himself,* **you and all your brethren, the sons of Levi, with you? And are you seeking the priesthood also?** They, as do we, need to be satisfied with the position the Lord places us in. These people were not satisfied with the ministry God had assigned them. Dissatisfaction is not a good thing and demonstrates arrogance, a trait the Lord is not fond of.

Interestingly, they accused Moses and Aaron of exalting themselves above others, the very thing of which they were guilty. This technique (projection) is not uncommon among the arrogant who are jealous of the people they report to and want to usurp their authority. In this situation, they rebelled against the Lord's chosen servants and reaped the appropriate consequence: death.

Yes, it sounds harsh, but why should the maker of man tolerate a rebel. Since He is God, He has every right to make some vessels for honor and some for dishonor out of the same lump of clay (Romans 9:21-23).

We tend to view God as if He were a human being. He did humble

Himself and come to earth in the form of a human for a brief period as Jesus Christ as part of His plan for our redemption. However, He is so far above being a human being that there is no comparison. He is omniscient, omnipresent and omnipotent. We can barely fathom what these words mean, let alone have any of these attributes. We are not even a speck of dust in comparison. Nevertheless, He cares for us as part of His creation and has provided a way for our redemption and relationship with Him.

Numbers 18:20 Then the LORD said to Aaron: "You shall have no inheritance in their land, nor shall you have any portion among them; I *am* your portion and your inheritance among the children of Israel. As with Aaron, our inheritance is in the future kingdom (Romans 8:17).

Numbers 20:8 "Take the rod; you and your brother Aaron gather the congregation together. Speak to the rock before their eyes, and it will yield its water; thus you shall bring water for them out of the rock, and give drink to the congregation and their animals." This verse is the specific direction from God that Moses did not follow or believe. As a result of his failure to follow this particular instruction to "Speak to the rock," Moses was prevented from bringing the people into the promised land (Numbers 20:12).

Numbers 23:5 Then the LORD put a word in Balaam's mouth, and said, "Return to Balak, and thus you shall speak." The Lord can use anyone to facilitate His purpose.

Numbers 27:18 And the LORD said to Moses: "Take Joshua the son of Nun with you, a man in whom *is* the Spirit, and lay your hand on him; In choosing a successor, Moses was guided to a man **in whom is the Spirit**. In the New Testament (Acts 6:3) are similar qualifications. Joshua began to take on some of the work before Moses died so there was a gradual transition of authority and responsibility (Joshua 1:1).

Numbers 30:1 Then Moses spoke to the heads of the tribes concerning the children of Israel, saying, "This *is* the thing which the LORD has commanded: 2 If a man makes a vow to the LORD, or swears an oath to bind himself by some agreement, he shall not break his word; he shall do according to all that proceeds out of his mouth. Honesty is the best policy.

Numbers 35:30 Whoever kills a person, the murderer shall be put to death on the testimony of witnesses; but one witness is not *sufficient* testimony against a person for the death *penalty*. There were different punishments for someone who intentionally killed another person (murder) and for someone who accidentally killed another person (accidental manslaughter). The congregation was to judge between the two. If someone accidentally killed another, they could flee to a city of refuge and stay there until the death of the high priest. Note that the death penalty was an option but required at least two witnesses.

5

Deuteronomy

[5]**DEUTERONOMY** - Blessings and Curses Depending on Belief and Behavior

Deuteronomy 1:16 "Then I commanded your judges at that time, saying, 'Hear *the cases* **between your brethren, and judge righteously between a man and his brother or the stranger who is with him. 17 You shall not show partiality in judgment; you shall hear the small as well as the great; you shall not be afraid in any man's presence, for the judgment** *is* **God's. The case that is too hard for you, bring to me, and I will hear it.'** The judges judge with wisdom (the ability to bring harmony) to deal fairly with all parties regardless of their position in society.

Deuteronomy 3:25 I pray, let me cross over and see the good land beyond the Jordan, those pleasant mountains, and Lebanon.' 26 "But the LORD was angry with me on your account, and would not listen to me. So the LORD said to me: 'Enough of that! Speak no

---

[5] NSB quotations are from the Nelsons Study Bible, copyright (c) 1997 by Thomas Nelson, Inc., Nashville, TN; used by permission; scripture taken from the New King James Version, Copyright (c) 1979, 1980, 1982 used by permission. All rights reserved.

more to Me of this matter. Here Moses finds out that sometimes the answer to a deeply desired prayer is: "no."

Deuteronomy 4:1 "Now, O Israel, listen to the statutes and the judgments which I teach you to observe, that you may live, and go in and possess the land which the LORD God of your fathers is giving you. 2 You shall not add to the word which I command you, nor take from it, that you may keep the commandments of the LORD your God which I command you. Here we have one of the warnings from the Lord not to add to or take from His Word.

Deuteronomy 4:9 Only take heed to yourself, and diligently keep yourself, lest you forget the things your eyes have seen, and lest they depart from your heart all the days of your life. And teach them to your children and your grandchildren, 10 *especially concerning* **the day you stood before the LORD your God in Horeb, when the LORD said to me, 'Gather the people to Me, and I will let them hear My words, that they may learn to fear Me all the days they live on the earth, and** *that* **they may teach their children.'** We are encouraged to teach God's commandments to our children and grandchildren for their benefit. It should be noted that Moses usually deferred to the Lord as the source of the good instruction he gave the people. He did disobey and misrepresent the Lord once and wound up paying the price for it. He was not allowed to enter the promised land (Numbers 20:12).

Deuteronomy 4:23 Take heed to yourselves, lest you forget the covenant of the LORD your God which He made with you, and make for yourselves a carved image in the form of anything which the LORD your God has forbidden you. 24 For the LORD your God *is* **a consuming fire, a jealous God.** In another verse, the Lord mentioned: **the likeness of male or female, any animal, any winged bird, anything that creeps on the ground, any fish, the sun, the moon, the stars and all the host of heaven.** This list is a fairly extensive list of idols humankind might be tempted to make and worship, especially the images of men and women. None of these things could serve as a representation of the creator. God did not ever allow them to see His form when He spoke to anyone, as He did not want them to act corruptly and try to make an image of Him in any of the forms mentioned.

You might notice that dictators often have images of themselves erected. It seems like they want the people to see and treat them as a god. Adherence to the Lord's direction regarding images would diminish this type of idolatry.

Note also that God refers to Himself as a jealous God, and it doesn't appear that He takes disobedience in this area lightly. It is one of the ten commandments. Apparently, even if some image were serving as an image of the one and only true God, it would still divert our attention from the living God.

What about the cross? Some do not believe we should even have those, but most believers under the dispensation of grace are not as legalistic about this issue and are open to some symbols like the cross that you see in most churches. We still might want to avoid making images as the pagans had in Old Testament times.

Deuteronomy 4:39 Therefore know this day, and consider *it* **in your heart, that the LORD Himself** *is* **God in heaven above and on the earth beneath;** *there is* **no other. 40 You shall therefore keep His statutes and His commandments which I command you today, that it may go well with you and with your children after you, and that you may prolong** *your* **days in the land which the LORD your God is giving you for all time."** Suppose everyone on earth accepted this one thing that **the LORD Himself is God;** what a different world this would be. Note that the promises of things going well for them in the land depended on their obedience. Could this concept be true for us today, such that we need to follow God's statutes and His commandments so that it will go well with us? That is certainly something about which to think.

Deuteronomy 5:21 'You shall not covet your neighbor's wife; and you shall not desire your neighbor's house, his field, his male servant, his female servant, his ox, his donkey, or anything that *is* your neighbor's.' This commandment is the only one of the ten commandments that seems to prohibit an attitude. This total lack of concern for the neighbor and wanting to take what belongs to him would be the precursor to adultery, stealing, murder, or other sin.

Here, and in other scripture, we see that even wanting to have what belongs to someone else that they don't have for sale is sinful. Almost everyone knows intuitively that thinking about some sin is often the first step to participating in it. In the New Testament, we find out that the greatest commandments are to love the Lord and our neighbors (Mark 12:28-31). Christ said: **"There is no other commandment greater than these."** If we love our neighbors, we are concerned for their welfare and would not take from them for ourselves. Especially when you consider greedy thoughts, it is evident that we all need forgiveness for our sins.

Deuteronomy 6:4 "Hear, O Israel: The LORD our God, the LORD *is* one! 5 You shall love the LORD your God with all your heart, with all your soul, and with all your strength. There is none other like the Lord. He has no beginning or end. He created everything we can see and that which we cannot see. This is a fundamental concept that we need to teach our children. The Lord is alone in His attributes. There is none other like Him. We need to keep His commands in mind.

Deuteronomy 7:25 You shall burn the carved images of their gods with fire; you shall not covet the silver or gold *that is* on them,

nor take *it* for yourselves, lest you be snared by it; for it *is* an abomination to the LORD your God. 26 Nor shall you bring an abomination into your house, lest you be doomed to destruction like it. You shall utterly detest it and utterly abhor it, for it *is* an accursed thing. Here is one of the few times in the Bible where something was pronounced an abomination. This one has to do with idols. In our culture, we have contests to see who has the most talent, and we call them idols and pay them lots of money to perform their talent. Movie stars and sports figures get this same kind of adoration. I wonder how the Lord feels about this part of our culture? In 1 Corinthians 3:4, some people said that they followed Paul, and others followed Apollos. Paul sets them straight and tells them that we need to follow God, not mere men. He implies that this is how people of the world act, but we should be faithful to and worship only God. That does not mean that we cannot enjoy watching the stars perform. It means that we do not want to make them into our idols and worship them as gods.

Deuteronomy 8:3 So He humbled you, allowed you to hunger, and fed you with manna which you did not know nor did your fathers know, that He might make you know that man shall not live by bread alone; but man lives by every *word* that proceeds from the mouth of the LORD. We have a lot of life based on what is communicated to us through the Word of the LORD. We have the life here on earth that he breathed into us, which is very short, and we have eternal life through the gift that we learn about in the Word of the LORD.

This scripture also lets us know that there is a spiritual component to life and that it is interconnected with obeying the Word of the LORD. Life for man is not just material. Spirit is kind of like the opposite of material and earthly. Spirit is what the flesh lusts against and vice versa (Galatians 5:17).

How do we know when we are operating under the control of the Holy

Spirit? We see the fruit which is: love, joy, peace, longsuffering, kindness, goodness and faithfulness, (Galatians 5:22). That's how we know. All of those sound good except longsuffering, but longsuffering is also a fruit of the Spirit. When we follow the Word, we will sometimes suffer just as almost all the spiritual leaders in the Bible did. It seems that there are two main types of suffering. One is the consequence that comes from disobedience and sin. The other comes from the world's opposition to the LORD and His followers (2 Corinthians 2:16).

Deuteronomy 8:18 "And you shall remember the LORD your God, for *it is* **He who gives you power to get wealth, that He may establish His covenant which He swore to your fathers, as** *it is* **this day.** This is very important. He gives us the power to do well. He gives, and He can take away. We don't want to forget that. We want to continue to give Him thanks, praise, and worship for any success or gifts He gives us.

Deuteronomy 9:18 And I fell down before the LORD, as at the first, forty days and forty nights; I neither ate bread nor drank water, because of all your sin which you committed in doing wickedly in the sight of the LORD, to provoke Him to anger. The number forty seems significant. Moses prayed for forty days and nights. Christ fasted and was tempted forty days and nights. Israel wandered for 40 years in the desert. Christ presented Himself alive after His suffering for forty days. In Deuteronomy, the number of stripes a person could receive as punishment was forty. The flood was forty days and forty nights. The front of the temple that Solomon built was forty cubits long. It appears that often the number has to do with trial or testing.

Deuteronomy 10:12 "And now, Israel, what does the LORD your God require of you, but to fear the LORD your God, to walk in all His ways and to love Him, to serve the LORD your God with all your heart and with all your soul, 13 *and* **to keep the commandments of the LORD and His statutes which I command you today for**

your good? 14 Indeed heaven and the highest heavens belong to the LORD your God, *also* the earth with all that *is* in it. The Lord's commandments and statutes are for our good. Again, we see that we are just temporary stewards of what the Lord owns. He makes all the elements in the physical world and owns it all.

Deuteronomy 10:19 Therefore love the stranger, for you were strangers in the land of Egypt. The message we see here is that as we are taken care of by the LORD, we should, in turn, show love and kindness to the disadvantaged strangers in our midst. This warning can apply to many different groups and needs to be considered in light of other scripture regarding how people should be treated.

In the Bible, there is almost always balance if you consider the whole counsel of God. As a general rule, we are instructed to treat the sojourner among us with hospitality as if they are one of us. The rules for them should be the same as for the native; no more, no less. We should leave some fruit on the vines and trees for the poor and the sojourner. Notice that they still have to do the work of picking the fruit themselves.

On the other hand, the sojourner is expected to follow our laws and practices as if they were citizens (Numbers 9:14; Exodus 12:48-49; Leviticus 24:16). If they do not follow the law, they shall suffer the consequences. In addition, we are expected to exercise common sense (Proverbs 3:21; 2:6; 1 Corinthians 15:33). Thus, would it make sense to let a person come into your home (or country) who has said he wants to kill you and annihilate your country? This is an issue that some countries may deal with daily. Does it make sense to welcome someone who has already said they will not respect your laws and only want to come in to infiltrate and destroy your system?

Another common sense question we can ask is: what is the appropriate order of priority when caring for people? Well, it seems that there is a priority in taking care of your own family (1 Timothy 5:8) and then the poor and sojourners. Everyone should follow the laws of the land (Romans 13:1-4), including the aliens. But what do you do if the laws are not enforced? It can get complicated when children are involved.

That brings up the issue of selective enforcement of the laws. That should not be happening, but it does. These issues are beyond the scope of this commentary, except to say that basic principles can be applied when figuring out solutions.

Deuteronomy 11:26 "Behold, I set before you today a blessing and a curse: 27 the blessing, if you obey the commandments of the LORD your God which I command you today; 28 and the curse, if you do not obey the commandments of the LORD your God, but turn aside from the way which I command you today, to go after other gods which you have not known. 29 Now it shall be, when the LORD your God has brought you into the land which you go to possess, that you shall put the blessing on Mount Gerizim and the curse on Mount Ebal. Here is a crucial concept for everyone to grasp. Obedience brings blessing and disobedience, the curse. The story of Job lets us know that the blessing or curse is not necessarily immediate. There are times when more significant issues are at play than our tiny world. Still, the result for us is in harmony with this scripture. A curse is the opposite of a blessing. When we are blessed, we are incurring the favor of God, which brings happiness. When we are cursed, we invoke evil, calamity, injury, or destruction, which brings unhappiness. A curse is like judgment, which causes people to become weak, sick, and die (1 Corinthians 11:30; James 1:15).

Deuteronomy 12:18 ...and you shall rejoice before the LORD your God in all to which you put your hands. This verse sounds like we are to rejoice in our work. Also, see Colossians 3:23, which specifically says: **"whatever you do, do it heartily, as to the Lord and not to men."**

Deuteronomy 13:1 If a prophet, or one who foretells by dreams, appears among you and announces to you a sign or wonder, 2 and if the sign or wonder spoken of takes place, and the prophet says, "Let us follow other gods" (gods you have not known) "and let us worship them," 3 you must not listen to the words of that prophet or dreamer. The LORD your God is testing you to find out whether you love him with all your heart and with all your soul. There also appear to be people like this who God allows to operate to test us in our day. If we love the Lord and therefore want Him to be pleased with us, we will not let these false teachers influence us. This warning is part of why we need to know the scriptures to discern these dreamers who can even come clothed as pastors of megachurches. They may teach a viral message that everyone is eventually saved or that there really isn't hell, or that the Bible is just a book put together by well-meaning men and is not the inspired Word of God.

Deuteronomy 14:28 At the end of every three years, bring all the tithes of that year's produce and store it in your towns, 29 so that the Levites (who have no allotment or inheritance of their own) and the foreigners, the fatherless and the widows who live in your towns may come and eat and be satisfied, and so that the LORD your God may bless you in all the work of your hands. We don't hear much about this use of tithes. It appears that fully one-third of the tithe in those days was to be used for the purposes noted in these verses and in verses 26:12-14. Also, they were to have a Sabbath (suspension) for debts every seven years (Leviticus 25:1-7), which gave the poor a break when also the land was given a break from sowing and cultivation.

Deuteronomy 15:11 There will always be poor people in the land. Therefore I command you to be open handed toward your fellow Israelites who are poor and needy in your land. This verse was a command. They were to be generous toward the poor and needy. The poor were allowed to glean from what was left in the fields. Note, there was still work to be done by the poor and needy to gather the gleanings, and scripture in the New Testament indicates that those who refused to work would not be allowed to eat of the produce. "**If anyone will not work, neither shall he eat**" (2 Thessalonians 3:10). Note that the way this is worded implies that the person is capable of working but still refuses. In this situation, they were not to be given food to eat if they refused to work for it.

Deuteronomy 18:10 Let no one be found among you who sacrifices their son or daughter in the fire, who practices divination or sorcery, interprets omens, engages in witchcraft, 11 or casts spells, or who is a medium or spiritist or who consults the dead. 12 Anyone who does these things is detestable to the LORD; because of these same detestable practices the LORD your God will drive out those nations before you. 13 You must be blameless before the LORD your God. Here's where we find out how God feels toward people trying to find out about the future through these prognosticators. It is detestable. Based on this and other warnings, we need to avoid people who seem to be communicating with the dead or maybe demons. All we need to be concerned about is the Lord's revelation.

Deuteronomy 19:18 The judges must make a thorough investigation, and if the witness proves to be a liar, giving false testimony against a fellow Israelite, 19 then do to the false witness as that witness intended to do to the other party. You must purge the evil from among you. This judgment is fair. When one person lies to hurt another, it's only fair that they suffer the consequences they were trying to inflict on another unfairly. However, even if we never see this happen in our brief time on earth, we need to remember that "**God is not mocked: for whatever a man sows, that he will also reap**" (Galatians 6:7).

Deuteronomy 21:18 If someone has a stubborn and rebellious son

who does not obey his father and mother and will not listen to them when they discipline him, 19 his father and mother shall take hold of him and bring him to the elders at the gate of his town. 20 They shall say to the elders, "This son of ours is stubborn and rebellious. He will not obey us. He is a glutton and a drunkard." 21 Then all the men of his town are to stone him to death. You must purge the evil from among you. All Israel will hear of it and be afraid. Here's the concept: respect and obey your parents or suffer severe consequences for your rebellion. This concept wouldn't get much traction today. Even with this concept in place in Old Testament times, it probably never happened because parents would not bring their children to be stoned to death no matter how bad they were.

Parents generally would be the first to make excuses for their children even if the child held the parent in extreme contempt and blamed them for every problem there is. Most parents would probably continue to support their offspring even if they turned out to be a pedophile or a murderer. Look how King David mourned for Absalom, who was trying to kill him. Even Absalom's murderous actions toward his father did not turn David totally against him. A parent's forgiveness of even extreme rebellion reminds us of the Lord's gift of salvation to us even while we were still sinners. According to the Nelson Study Bible commentary, "the community could not allow the rebellious youth to spread his immoral practices. They were God's holy people." It seems that this was a specific law for the Israelites at that time. However, today, some religious groups reject the teaching of grace in the New Testament and impose severe punishments for things they do not accept.

Deuteronomy 22:5 "A woman shall not wear anything that pertains to a man, nor shall a man put on a woman's garment, for all who do so *are* an abomination to the LORD your God. Cross-dressing was not an accepted practice in ancient Israel. Some of the rules for the Israelites appear to be specific to their time to help the chosen people remain holy as a group. These rules were under the dispensation of the law. We are now under the dispensation of grace. In our time, we are justified by the grace of God through faith, not by living up to the law. By the law, no man is justified (Galatians 3:11). Galatians 3:13-15 (NKJV) puts it as follows: **13 Christ has redeemed us from the curse of the law, having become a curse for us (for it is written, "Cursed *is* everyone who hangs on a tree"), 14 that the blessing of Abraham might come upon the Gentiles in Christ Jesus, that we might receive the promise of the Spirit through faith.** This is excellent news without which we are not in a good situation. From this, it is clear that man cannot save himself by doing all that the law requires. We need to humble ourselves to be saved by the grace of God through faith.

Deuteronomy 26:10 …and now, behold, I have brought the firstfruits of the land which you, O LORD, have given me.' "Then you shall set it before the LORD your God, and worship before the LORD your God. Note that worship involves both love for God and obedience.

Deuteronomy 27:16 'Cursed *is* the one who treats his father or his mother with contempt.'

"**And all the people shall say, 'Amen!'** To understand this curse, we need to know what contempt is in this context. It is the state of despising, dishonoring, disdaining, or scorning a parent. Contempt for a parent is also usually an infraction of the fifth commandment. Notice that there are no exceptions noted. What if the parent was a child abuser? What if the parent neglected their child? The judgment of these sins is not the responsibility of the offspring. This curse and others were part of the covenant renewal ceremony where the Levites were to speak the curses with a loud voice, and all the people agreed with them. The curses were so important that the last one was a curse for anyone who did not confirm them. All the people were to say, "Amen," indicating their agreement.

The Lord gives us instructions that will make our lives better. When we violate those rules, and things don't go well for us, we have ourselves to blame. However, those who treat their mother or father with contempt will justify their actions. Unfortunately for them, there doesn't seem to be any indication that the curse would not apply if they had a reason to treat their parent with contempt. Perhaps this has something to do with the disharmony from offspring treating their mother or father with contempt. More about those who sow discord, especially among the brethren (Proverbs 6:19), is in other scripture. It is also possible that the offspring have no justification for their contempt and are just angry and exercising their self-will. In this case, Proverbs 17:15 is instructive: **"He who justifies the wicked, and he who condemns the just, both of them are an abomination to the Lord."** Thankfully, Jesus Christ became a curse for those cursed under the law (Galatians 3:13), so there is still hope for those who have held their mother or father in contempt if they repent and believe.

Deuteronomy 29:29 "The secret *things belong* to the LORD our God, but those *things which are* revealed *belong* to us and to our children forever, that *we* may do all the words of this law. Some things are secret and not for us to know; others we are to know and obey. However, like many valuable things, it may still take some work to uncover and learn the things that are not secret.

Deuteronomy 30:1 "Now it shall come to pass, when all these things come upon you, the blessing and the curse which I have set before you, and you call *them* to mind among all the nations where the LORD your God drives you, 2 and you return to the LORD your God and obey His voice, according to all that I command you today, you and your children, with all your heart and with all your soul, 3 that the LORD your God will bring you back from captivity, and have compassion on you, and gather you again from all the nations where the LORD your God has scattered you. We don't know if they returned to the LORD, but it does appear that, since 1948, many have been gathered again from all the nations back to Israel in accord with this prophecy which was made thousands of years ago. It is incredible that after all the years of being dispersed, many Jewish people have gone back to Israel, according to this scripture. What other book written thousands of years ago accurately predicts current events?

Deuteronomy 32:43. " Rejoice, O Gentiles, *with* His people;
  For He will avenge the blood of His servants,
  And render vengeance to His adversaries;
  He will provide atonement for His land *and* His people." Note that Gentiles were invited to rejoice with Israel even in Moses' time.

Deuteronomy 34:8 And the children of Israel wept for Moses in the plains of Moab thirty days. So the days of weeping *and* mourning for Moses ended. It appears that the time of mourning in Old Testament times was 30 days for a man of Moses' stature. Note that there was a consequence to his sin even though he was called a servant of God. Moses was allowed to see the land while he was alive but not allowed to cross over there.

6

Joshua

⁶JOSHUA (the Lord saves) - In this book, we learn of the adventures of Joshua, who experienced what we would view as severe hardships but always seemed to keep a positive (God-focused) perspective.

Joshua 1:8 This Book of the Law shall not depart from your mouth, but you shall meditate in it day and night, that you may observe to do according to all that is written in it. For then you will make your way prosperous, and then you will have good success. This is a great encouragement for the reader of the scriptures that success depends on obedience. This concept is demonstrated over and over again through the story of the Israelites. Many can talk the talk, but not as many walk the walk. That is partly because after we learn that to please God with our actions, our actions have to be led by the Holy Spirit. However, our flesh continually rebels against letting the Spirit take control (Galatians 5:16-18). And, our flesh will not die until the Spirit of life leaves it. When our bodies are reconstituted, they will be glorified, and we won't have the problem of the flesh always trying to retake control (Daniel 12:13).

---

[6] NSB quotations are from the Nelsons Study Bible, copyright (c) 1997 by Thomas Nelson, Inc., Nashville, TN; used by permission; scripture taken from the New King James Version, Copyright (c) 1979, 1980, 1982 used by permission. All rights reserved.

Joshua 1:18 Whoever rebels against your command and does not heed your words, in all that you command him, shall be put to death. Only be strong and of good courage. The penalty for rebelling against God's chosen leader in Joshua's time was death. Nowadays, we have a hand in choosing our leaders, and they don't always follow the Lord. Scripture still tells us to submit to the government except in limited situations (Romans 13:1-7).

Joshua 1:6 For the children of Israel walked forty years in the wilderness, till all the people *who were* **men of war, who came out of Egypt, were consumed, because they did not obey the voice of the LORD—to whom the LORD swore that He would not show them the land which the LORD had sworn to their fathers that He would give us, "a land flowing with milk and honey."** Here and in other scriptures, we see that disobedience brought disqualification for the benefits of the covenant. This concept seems to be throughout scripture. How, then, can we obey? We have to have the help of the Holy Spirit, and we can't get that without faith in God and a belief that there is a Holy Spirit who can provide us counsel, comfort, and help to obey.

Joshua 5:14 So He said, "No, but *as* **Commander of the army of the LORD I have now come."**

And Joshua fell on his face to the earth and worshiped, and said to Him, "What does my Lord say to His servant?" 15 Then the Commander of the LORD's army said to Joshua, "Take your sandal off your foot, for the place where you stand *is* **holy." And Joshua did so.** This is another place in the Bible where a human is told to take off their sandal because the place they are standing is holy. Perhaps the Commander of the army of the LORD was a pre-incarnate appearance of Christ (see John 1:18). Joshua's immediate response to the presence of the Commander was to worship. That is probably a good idea for us to consider in situations where we are aware of the Lord's presence.

Joshua 6:20 So the people shouted when *the priests* blew the trumpets. And it happened when the people heard the sound of the trumpet, and the people shouted with a great shout, that the wall fell down flat. Then the people went up into the city, every man straight before him, and they took the city. When the Lord is involved on one side of a battle, the other side does not have a chance of winning. We see this over and over in the scriptures. If the Lord is with us, who can be against us (Romans 8:31)?

Joshua 8:7 Then you shall rise from the ambush and seize the city, for the LORD your God will deliver it into your hand. Joshua's plan to win the battle for this city used deception. It was a very successful plan.

Joshua 10:14 And there has been no day like that, before it or after it, that the LORD heeded the voice of a man; for the LORD fought for Israel. Here's an example of the Lord listening to the voice of Joshua and acting upon his request. This was a unique occurrence. Most of the time, our prayers are to align our goals with the Lord's and not the other way around.

Joshua 10:42 All these kings and their land Joshua took at one time, because the LORD God of Israel fought for Israel. Joshua utterly destroyed the Canaanites. Though it is hard to accept, their level of sin, including incest, child sacrifice, and bestiality, to name some, justified their destruction. Their society was apparently hostile to all God's ways (Deuteronomy 9:4-5). It appears that they brought this judgment upon themselves because of their wickedness.

Joshua 11:20 For it was of the LORD to harden their hearts, that they should come against Israel in battle, that He might utterly destroy them, *and* that they might receive no mercy, but that He might destroy them, as the LORD had commanded Moses. Here's another situation where the Lord hardened the hearts of people who were opposed to His people. In this case, it appears the Lord hardened their hearts so that they would do battle and be destroyed. He could have destroyed them in another way, but He chose to use Joshua and his army to destroy these people committed to evil.

Joshua 14:13 And Joshua blessed him, and gave Hebron to Caleb the son of Jephunneh as an inheritance. Some of the blessings from the Lord in life here on earth can include children, land, wealth, and a positive reputation (Genesis 1:28; 26:3; 28:12-14; 22:18).

Joshua 20:1-3 The Lord also spoke to Joshua, saying, 2 "Speak to the children of Israel, saying: 'Appoint for yourselves cities of refuge, of which I spoke to you through Moses, 3 that the slayer who kills a person accidentally *or* unintentionally may flee there; and they shall be your refuge from the avenger of blood. Here we see how the punishment is different depending on the intent. Our current laws continue this example, and the penalties differ depending on the degree of the crime a person is convicted of doing. For example, there are several other possible findings when one person kills another. It can be first-degree murder or second degree. Or, it could be voluntary or involuntary manslaughter. Each of these levels carries different penalties.

Joshua 21:45 Not a word failed of any good thing which the LORD had spoken to the house of Israel. All came to pass. The simple message here is that the Lord keeps His promises.

Joshua 22.20 Did not Achan the son of Zerah commit a trespass in the accursed thing, and wrath fell on all the congregation of Israel? And that man did not perish alone in his iniquity.'" The sin of one person can hurt many others.

Joshua 24:14 "Now therefore, fear the LORD, serve Him in sincerity

and in truth, and put away the gods which your fathers served on the other side of the River and in Egypt. Serve the LORD! Leaders need to be committed to the truth regardless of what others do.

Joshua 24.15...But as for me and my house, we will serve the LORD." This is a great scripture and commitment.

7

Judges

[7]**JUDGES** - History of Judges and the Israelites

Judges 2:13 They forsook the LORD and served Baal and the Ashtoreths. 14 And the anger of the LORD was hot against Israel. So He delivered them into the hands of plunderers who despoiled them; and He sold them into the hands of their enemies all around, so that they could no longer stand before their enemies. 15 Wherever they went out, the hand of the LORD was against them for calamity, as the LORD had said, and as the LORD had sworn to them. And they were greatly distressed. There are terrible consequences to turning against the Lord. Don't do it.

Judges 2:21 I also will no longer drive out before them any of the nations which Joshua left when he died, 22 so that through them I may test Israel, whether they will keep the ways of the LORD, to walk in them as their fathers kept *them*, or not." It appears that corrupt people were left to test Israel. Perhaps some corrupt people are

---

[7] NSB quotations are from the Nelsons Study Bible, copyright (c) 1997 by Thomas Nelson, Inc., Nashville, TN; used by permission; scripture taken from the New King James Version, Copyright (c) 1979, 1980, 1982 used by permission. All rights reserved.

still here to test us.

Judges 4:4 Now Deborah, a prophetess, the wife of Lapidoth, was judging Israel at that time. Deborah is one of five prophetesses mentioned in the Old Testament. She and a fellow named Barak sang a song of praise and triumph called the Song of Deborah and Barak.

Judges 6:15 So he said to Him, "O my Lord, how can I save Israel? Indeed my clan *is* the weakest in Manasseh, and I *am* the least in my father's house."
16 And the LORD said to him, "Surely I will be with you, and you shall defeat the Midianites as one man." This is a great promise from God; that He will be with Gideon. The Lord made similar promises to Moses and Joshua. Despite the weakness of these leaders and our own weaknesses, God can accomplish what He wants through us if we trust and obey even if our trust waivers a bit from time to time.

Judges 9:4 So they gave him seventy *shekels* of silver from the temple of Baal-Berith, with which Abimelech hired worthless and reckless men; and they followed him. 5 Then he went to his father's house at Ophrah and killed his brothers, the seventy sons of Jerubbaal, on one stone. But Jotham the youngest son of Jerubbaal was left, because he hid himself. Here is another case of a jealous, power-hungry sibling making sure that his brothers would not be able to challenge him in his quest to rule over the people. Based on this story and others in the Bible, it is evident that siblings can be ruthless with each other and hold their parents in contempt when they get jealous or power-hungry. Some things don't change.

Judges 9:22 After Abimelech had reigned over Israel three years, 23 God sent a spirit of ill will between Abimelech and the men of Shechem; and the men of Shechem dealt treacherously with Abimelech, Interesting that God will put a spirit of ill will between people at times to accomplish His purposes. It appears here that both sides deserved judgment for their sins and that's what they wound up getting as follows: **56 Thus God repaid the wickedness of Abimelech, which he had done to his father by killing his seventy brothers. 57 And all the evil of the men of Shechem God returned on their own heads, and on them came the curse of Jotham the son of Jerubbaal.**

Judges 10:16 So they put away the foreign gods from among them and served the LORD. And His soul could no longer endure the misery of Israel. Here's an interesting reference to God's soul. He is apparently hurt by the suffering of His children just as we would be if our children were suffering.

Judges 11:30 And Jephthah made a vow to the LORD, and said, "If You will indeed deliver the people of Ammon into my hands, 31 then it will be that whatever comes out of the doors of my house to meet me, when I return in peace from the people of Ammon, shall surely be the LORD's, and I will offer it up as a burnt offering." Here we see Jephthah trying to make a deal with the Lord to manipulate the outcome of the battle. He surely knew that human sacrifice was forbidden by the law of Moses, but he made this offer anyway. Jephthah was foolish and lacked faith, which was the basis of this reckless offer. He didn't have to make this offer as the Lord had apparently already determined how the battle would turn out.

Judges 13:3 And the Angel of the LORD appeared to the woman and said to her, "Indeed now, you are barren and have borne no children, but you shall conceive and bear a son. 4 Now therefore, please be careful not to drink wine or *similar* drink, and not to eat anything unclean. Here's an example of the Lord providing proper instruction for a woman before any controlled studies would demonstrate the potential for fetal alcohol syndrome. This is also another bit of advice that was good thousands of years ago and is still useful today. Of course, this is no surprise at all to those who believe the Lord knows about His own creation. This kind of intelligence does pose a problem for those who think the life of man came to be (a) through chance occurrences, (b) from aliens who have no beginning, (c) from a material world that had no beginning, (d) is un-caused or (e) just always existed.

To be fair though, which God always is, they could also reason that some smart person who figured out fetal alcohol syndrome thousands of years ago wrote this scripture and attributed these words to God to make it look like God is all-knowing. It appears that the Lord gives us a free choice to believe in Him or not and if we choose not to, He even allows there to be some kind of explanation other than that He created the world and all that is in it. Now that is ultimate fairness to the side that wants to convince people there is no God who created everything. Again, we are reminded that the world does not revolve around us. Though we are important to God, we are just a small part of a much larger universe where God is in charge.

Judges 13:24 So the woman bore a son and called his name Samson; and the child grew, and the LORD blessed him. 25 And the Spirit of the LORD began to move upon him at Mahaneh Dan between Zorah and Eshtaol. Here we have scripture noting that it was initially the Spirit of the Lord motivating Samson to carry out the Lord's work. In the Old Testament, the Spirit of the Lord is mentioned many times often in relation to providing power for great feats of strength beyond the normal human capability or for speaking God's Word. At some point in Samson's life, scripture says that **"he did not know that the Lord had departed from him"** (16:20). At a certain point in David's life, the Spirit stayed with him consistently and in Psalm 51:11 David had this to say about the Spirit's ongoing presence with him: **"Do not cast me away from Your presence, And do not take Your Holy Spirit from me."** The New Testament has a lot to say about living in the ongoing presence of the Holy Spirit.

Judges 17:6 In those days *there was* no king in Israel; everyone did *what was* right in his own eyes. This is a terrible thing in that the people were not even trying to live by what the Lord said was right but doing whatever they wanted. This attitude can generally lead to a lot of sin and oppression. It should be noted that some cultures that don't even know the Lord's commandments have at least some cultural mores that are in harmony with the Lord's laws and consequently, they avoid some of the sin, pain, and oppression that will come from anarchy.

8

Ruth

[8]**RUTH** (grace) - History and God's Grace

Ruth 2:2 So Ruth the Moabitess said to Naomi, "Please let me go to the field, and glean heads of grain after *him* in whose sight I may find favor." And she said to her, "Go, my daughter." Here we have the concept of gleanings left for the poor. They were not handed the gleanings; they had to get them and thus could maintain at least a portion of their dignity in that they worked for their food. This was part of the law of Moses (Leviticus 23:22).

Ruth 2:11 And Boaz answered and said to her, "It has been fully reported to me, all that you have done for your mother-in-law since the death of your husband, and *how* you have left your father and your mother and the land of your birth, and have come to a people whom you did not know before. 12 The LORD repay your work, and a full reward be given you by the LORD God of Israel, under whose wings you have come for refuge." Now there's a great thought:

---

[8] NSB quotations are from the Nelsons Study Bible, copyright (c) 1997 by Thomas Nelson, Inc., Nashville, TN; used by permission; scripture taken from the New King James Version, Copyright (c) 1979, 1980, 1982 used by permission. All rights reserved.

coming under the Lord's wings for refuge. Ruth has shown loyal love for her mother-in-law, which Boaz took notice of, and later, he took Ruth under his wing, and she became his wife. Boaz became for her like a redeemer as Christ has become for us.

9

1 Samuel

[9]**1 SAMUEL** - History of Ancient Israel

1 Samuel 1:12 And it happened, as she continued praying before the LORD, that Eli watched her mouth. 13 Now Hannah spoke in her heart; only her lips moved, but her voice was not heard. Therefore Eli thought she was drunk. 14 So Eli said to her, "How long will you be drunk? Put your wine away from you!" 15 But Hannah answered and said, "No, my lord, I *am* a woman of sorrowful spirit. I have drunk neither wine nor intoxicating drink, but have poured out my soul before the LORD. 16 Do not consider your maidservant a wicked woman, for out of the abundance of my complaint and grief I have spoken until now." Note that prayer does not have to be vocalized: **"she spoke in her heart."** She was not drunk. Eli had misinterpreted her actions as happened in other parts of scripture when people were under the influence of the Holy Spirit. We are directed to be filled with and controlled by the Holy Spirit (Ephesians. 5:18) as opposed to being filled with intoxicating drinks which in the end: **"bites like a**

---

[9] NSB quotations are from the Nelsons Study Bible, copyright (c) 1997 by Thomas Nelson, Inc., Nashville, TN; used by permission; scripture taken from the New King James Version, Copyright (c) 1979, 1980, 1982 used by permission. All rights reserved.

serpent, And stings like a viper" (Prov. 23:30).

1 Samuel 2:35 I will raise up for myself a faithful priest, who will do according to what is in my heart and mind. I will firmly establish his priestly house, and they will minister before my anointed one always. Here the Lord refers to His heart and mind.

1 Samuel 6:19 Then He struck the men of Beth Shemesh, because they had looked into the ark of the LORD. He struck fifty thousand and seventy men of the people, and the people lamented because the LORD had struck the people with a great slaughter. It appears here that the men of Beth Shemesh didn't have the reverence they should have had for the holy things of God as the law of Moses directed (Numbers 4:20-21).

1 Samuel 8:7 And the LORD said to Samuel, "Heed the voice of the people in all that they say to you; for they have not rejected you, but they have rejected Me, that I should not reign over them. Here God yields to the people who wanted a king over them. Then they had to pay the price. Having a King would create many problems for them. The king would draft their young men into the military to go to war. Their young women would have to work in his palace. He would tax them. He would take the best of their products and force other people into his service. Their personal freedoms would be taken away. All this is the result of the people rejecting God and favoring a King. Some of this behavior sounds familiar though we now have many government systems (federal, state, county, city) instead of a single King.

1 Samuel 9:15 Now the LORD had told Samuel in his ear the day before Saul came, saying, 16 "Tomorrow about this time I will send you a man from the land of Benjamin, and you shall anoint him commander over My people Israel, that he may save My people from the hand of the Philistines; for I have looked upon My people,

because their cry has come to Me." God hears the prayers of the people and takes action.

1 Samuel 10:27 But some rebels said, "How can this man save us?" So they despised him, and brought him no presents. But he held his peace. There always seems to be some rebels. Moses had them, King Saul had them, and every King/leader appears to have had them after that. Although the Israelites wanted a King, it seems that God's permissive will allowed them to have Saul as their king.

1 Samuel 11:6 Then the Spirit of God came upon Saul when he heard this news, and his anger was greatly aroused. 7 So he took a yoke of oxen and cut them in pieces, and sent *them* throughout all the territory of Israel by the hands of messengers, saying, "Whoever does not go out with Saul and Samuel to battle, so it shall be done to his oxen." And the fear of the LORD fell on the people, and they came out with one consent. Saul knew who God was (Proverbs 2:5) and responded to good and evil at this time in his life (Proverbs 16:6). In this case, it appears that the Spirit of God brought up anger in him and aroused him to do something about the problem.

1 Samuel 12:13 "Now therefore, here is the king whom you have chosen *and* whom you have desired. And take note, the LORD has set a king over you. 14 If you fear the LORD and serve Him and obey His voice, and do not rebel against the commandment of the LORD, then both you and the king who reigns over you will continue following the LORD your God. 15 However, if you do not obey the voice of the LORD, but rebel against the commandment of the LORD, then the hand of the LORD will be against you, as *it was* against your fathers. Note that this scripture says that if the people don't rebel, both the people and the king will continue following the Lord. It appears that there is a symbiotic relationship between what the people do and what the king does. The consequences of rebellion are noted in Deuteronomy 28:15-68. Here is the summary of these verses: **28**:**20 "The Lord will send on you cursing, confusion, and rebuke in all that you set your hand to do, until you are destroyed and until you perish quickly, because of the wickedness of your doings in which you have forsaken Me"** (see below for more on this issue).

1 Samuel 12:4 Only fear the LORD, and serve Him in truth with all your heart; for consider what great things He has done for you. 25 But if you still do wickedly, you shall be swept away, both you and your king." Both the king and the people can experience great things or be swept away in judgment.

1 Samuel 15:3 Now go and attack Amalek, and utterly destroy all that they have, and do not spare them. But kill both man and woman, infant and nursing child, ox and sheep, camel and donkey.'" This is hard justice that can come when a people's extreme unrepentant hard-headed sin demands it. Some people judge God for allowing this justice. However, human beings have no standing that would give them authority to judge God. For a person to think this way shows a lack of understanding of their status in the universe. Nevertheless, some people will still do so.

1 Samuel 15:10 Now the word of the LORD came to Samuel, saying, 11 "I greatly regret that I have set up Saul *as* king, for he has turned back from following Me, and has not performed My commandments." And it grieved Samuel, and he cried out to the LORD all night. Saul did not live up to the Lord's expectation of him. In this chapter, we find that obedience is more important than sacrifices, and rebellion is like witchcraft and stubbornness is like idolatry. Thus, the Lord regrets anointing Saul as king and rejects him from serving in this capacity. Saul's excuse that he feared the people, so he obeyed them was not an adequate justification for his sin. From this, we also learn that, at least in Old Testament times, the Spirit of the Lord's influence on a man could be temporary and withdrawn due to disobedience.

1 Samuel 16:7 But the LORD said to Samuel, "Do not look at his appearance or at his physical stature, because I have refused him. For *the LORD does* not *see* as man sees; for man looks at the outward appearance, but the LORD looks at the heart." Here we learn that the Lord is more concerned with the heart of a person than the looks. The state of a man's heart is far more critical to the Lord than his physical appearance or abilities.

1 Samuel 16:13 Then Samuel took the horn of oil and anointed him in the midst of his brothers; and the Spirit of the LORD came upon David from that day forward. So Samuel arose and went to Ramah. Upon anointing from Samuel, the Spirit of the Lord came upon David and stayed upon him.

1 Samuel 16:23 And so it was, whenever the spirit from God was upon Saul, that David would take a harp and play *it* with his hand. Then Saul would become refreshed and well, and the distressing spirit would depart from him. David's playing had the desired effect, at least temporarily, on the distressing spirit that the Lord allowed to afflict Saul. It appears that God allowed the distressing spirit to come upon Saul rather than put it upon him. This spirit may have had something to do with Saul's own bad self-centered attitude.

1 Samuel 17:36 Your servant has killed both lion and bear; and this uncircumcised Philistine will be like one of them, seeing he has defied the armies of the living God." 37 Moreover David said, "The LORD, who delivered me from the paw of the lion and from the paw of the bear, He will deliver me from the hand of this Philistine." Note David's confidence is based on the preparation and understanding that the Lord delivered him from beasts time after time in the wilderness. After these experiences and development, along with the Holy Spirit upon him, David had good reason for his confidence. David showed a great contempt of Goliath for coming against the **"armies of the living God"** and referred to him as the "uncircumcised Philistine." We know how this turned out. When they went out to face each other, Goliath cursed David. Note that in Genesis 12:3, God says: **"I will bless those who bless you, and I will curse those who curse you."** Thus, through cursing David, Goliath brought a curse from God on his head, and it didn't take long for David's stone to find its way into Goliath's head and David's hand to cut off Goliath's head with the very sword with which Goliath had planned to kill David. David made a point that: "the battle is the Lord's" regardless of the sword or spear of the enemy.

1 Samuel 18:12 Now Saul was afraid of David, because the LORD was with him, but had departed from Saul. Saul's disobedience appears to have caused the Lord to let his mind be troubled and fear David.

1 Samuel 23:2 Therefore David inquired of the LORD, saying, "Shall I go and attack these Philistines?" Note that just because there was a need, David did not pursue fulfilling the need until he inquired of the Lord whether it was a need he was to fulfill. This was his custom before making a big decision.

10

2 Samuel

[10]**2 SAMUEL** -King David's Anointing and Reign

2 Samuel 1:14 So David said to him, "How was it you were not afraid to put forth your hand to destroy the LORD's anointed?" 15 Then David called one of the young men and said, "Go near, *and* execute him!" And he struck him so that he died. David seemed to exhibit great respect for the authority of even his enemy. To demonstrate that respect, he had the person who killed Saul killed. Today, people often gossip about, disdain, criticize and show contempt for government leaders, church leaders, and parents. Based on this scripture and others, it seems that the Lord does not like this type of attitude toward higher authorities. These actions would appear to be the opposite of the respect with which David treated Saul even when Saul was trying to kill him.

2 Samuel 3:2 Sons were born to David in Hebron: His firstborn was Amnon by Ahinoam the Jezreelitess; 3 his second, Chileab, by Abigail the widow of Nabal the Carmelite; the third, Absalom

---

[10] NSB quotations are from the Nelsons Study Bible, copyright (c) 1997 by Thomas Nelson, Inc., Nashville, TN; used by permission; scripture taken from the New King James Version, Copyright (c) 1979, 1980, 1982 used by permission. All rights reserved.

the son of Maacah, the daughter of Talmai, king of Geshur; Note that David took multiple wives apparently to cement alliances between Israel and foreign nations. This was contrary to God's instruction against polygamy (Deuteronomy 7:3 and 17:17). There were significant problems with some of David's children from these wives.

2 Samuel 6:5 Then David and all the house of Israel played *music* before the LORD on all kinds of *instruments of* fir wood, on harps, on stringed instruments, on tambourines, on sistrums, and on cymbals. Here we have the use of many musical instruments used in celebration before the Lord

2 Samuel 6:21 So David said to Michal, "*It was* before the LORD, who chose me instead of your father and all his house, to appoint me ruler over the people of the LORD, over Israel. Therefore I will play *music* before the LORD. 22 And I will be even more undignified than this, and will be humble in my own sight. But as for the maidservants of whom you have spoken, by them I will be held in honor." Michal had criticized David for how he was dressed when he was dancing and celebrating about the Ark of the Lord being brought back into his city. Michal did not accept her lot in life and became bitter at her husband, David. The criticism noted in this episode probably had deeper roots of resentment. Nevertheless, scripture says she suffered the consequence of childlessness for what she said to David about how he looked to the maids in his celebration before the Lord. It appears that the Lord did not like her criticism of David's method of worship. Perhaps it is not good to criticize the worship style of other believers.

2 Samuel 7:25 "And now, LORD God, keep forever the promise you have made concerning your servant and his house. Do as you promised, 26 so that your name will be great forever. Then people will say, 'The LORD Almighty is God over Israel!' And the house of your servant David will be established in your sight. Nelson's Study

Bible has this to say about this prayer of David: "As David undoubtedly knew, God's will would be accomplished whether he prayed for it or not. But, like David, when we pray *in* God's will *for* God's will, we become a *part* of His will." To become a part of His will seems to be one of the most significant aspects of prayer and life. Even Christ modeled this attitude and behavior for us. When we can pray honestly for *His will to be done*, it seems that we are getting close to the approach we always need.

This is the way that Joab expressed this attitude: "**And may the Lord do what is good in His sight**" (2 Sam. 10:12). Note that this doesn't mean that we don't play a part in the process. Joab had done all he could to prepare for the battle he was about to enter before he expressed this prayer. So the message is: prepare and trust. It is not: do nothing and trust.

2 Samuel 12:13 Then David said to Nathan, "I have sinned against the LORD." Nathan replied, "The LORD has taken away your sin. You are not going to die. 14 But because by doing this you have shown utter contempt for the LORD, the son born to you will die."
   15 After Nathan had gone home, the LORD struck the child that Uriah's wife had borne to David, and he became ill. Here we see how humility and confession lead to grace. However, there are still consequences to sin. God forgives sin, but there are still consequences.

2 Samuel 12:21 His attendants asked him, "Why are you acting this way? While the child was alive, you fasted and wept, but now that the child is dead, you get up and eat!" David fasted and prayed until the very end. As long as the situation was not finished, he prayed and fasted. After his son died, there was no more reason to do so.

2 Samuel 15:6 In this manner Absalom acted toward all Israel who came to the king for judgment. So Absalom stole the hearts of the men of Israel. Absalom was a son who appeared jealous of his own father's position as king. He devised a method of garnering favor with the people, and eventually, he tried to unseat his father. David committed the situation to the Lord's hands in contrast to Absalom, who devised deceitful words to facilitate the overthrow of his father as king. In the end, Absalom's contempt for his father, which brings a curse, was his undoing. He was killed, and the people heaped a large pile of stones over his dead body. Even after all Absalom had done against King David, David still mourned for Absalom.

2 Samuel 21:1 Now there was a famine in the days of David for three years, year after year; and David inquired of the LORD. And the LORD answered, "*It is* because of Saul and *his* bloodthirsty house, because he killed the Gibeonites." Here is a clear indication that God sometimes uses the weather for His purposes.

2 Samuel 22:4 I will call upon the LORD, *who is worthy* to be praised; So shall I be saved from my enemies. There is a place for contemplative worship, and there is a place for joyful worship boasting of what God has done, is doing, and what He will do. We see examples of these types of songs in the Psalms and other parts of the Bible.

2 Samuel 22 33 God *is* my strength *and* power, And He makes my way perfect. This is a familiar concept for the believer. God provides the strength and capability for us to live righteously.

2 Samuel 22:50 Therefore I will give thanks to You, O LORD, among the Gentiles, And sing praises to Your name. The phrase "**give thanks**" means to provide public acknowledgment. Thanksgiving appears to be one of the most used words in the Psalms, having to do with praise.

2 Samuel 23:3 'He who rules over men *must be* just, Ruling in the fear of God. Now there's a good idea. If all the people in authority were just, it would be great.

2 Samuel 24:11 Now when David arose in the morning, the word of the LORD came to the prophet Gad, David's seer, saying, 12 "Go and tell David, 'Thus says the LORD: "I offer you three *things*; choose one of them for yourself, that I may do *it* to you."'" 13 So Gad came to David and told him; and he said to him, "Shall seven years of famine come to you in your land? Or shall you flee three months before your enemies, while they pursue you? Or shall there be three days' plague in your land? Now consider and see what answer I should take back to Him who sent me." This is interesting. The Lord let David choose the punishment for the people. It was like multiple choice punishment. He chose a plague that killed seventy thousand men. Here it appears that the people suffered the consequences of their leader's sin. *The Nelson Study Bible* says: "Moses had warned of all the punishments for breaking God's covenant" (Deuteronomy 28:15-68). David asked for it to be left to the hand of the Lord, and the LORD sent a plague.

2 Samuel 24:24 Then the king said to Araunah, "No, but I will surely buy *it* from you for a price; nor will I offer burnt offerings to the LORD my God with that which costs me nothing." So David bought the threshing floor and the oxen for fifty shekels of silver. Here's another concept of David's. He believed that his worship of the Lord should cost him something. It seems that his idea was that if there was a cost, there was a sacrifice, and he wanted to practice sacrificial giving to the Lord. If there is no cost, there is no real sacrifice. In the New Testament, the Corinthians exhibited this kind of giving. Even though they were poor and afflicted, they freely gave beyond their means with great joy (2 Cor. 8:2-5).

11

1 Kings

[11] **1 KINGS** - God's blessings are tied to obedience.

1 Kings 13:9 Therefore give to Your servant an understanding heart to judge Your people, that I may discern between good and evil. For who is able to judge this great people of Yours?" The next verse says that it pleased the Lord that Solomon had asked for understanding and discernment, so he gave Solomon a wise and understanding heart. There had not been anyone like him before him, and none would be after him. The people took note **that the wisdom of God was in him to administer justice.** According to Proverbs 2:6, discernment is from the Lord, so the people were correct in their assessment. In his time, **he spoke three thousand proverbs** and **one thousand five songs.**

1 Kings 6:22 The whole temple he overlaid with gold, until he had finished all the temple; also he overlaid with gold the entire altar that *was* by the inner sanctuary. They estimate that about 21 tons of gold went into building Solomon's Temple. That's a lot of valuable gold,

---

[11] NSB quotations are from the Nelsons Study Bible, copyright (c) 1997 by Thomas Nelson, Inc., Nashville, TN; used by permission; scripture taken from the New King James Version, Copyright (c) 1979, 1980, 1982 used by permission. All rights reserved.

but as The Nelson Study Bible makes clear, "Although gold was valued highly and continues to be, the Scripture asserts that certain qualities are to be valued more: wisdom (Job 28:17), loving favor (Proverbs 22:1), and the judgments, law, and commandments of the Lord (Psalms 19:9, 10: 119:72, 127)."

1 Kings 8:27 ...Behold, heaven and the heaven of heavens cannot contain You. How much less this temple which I have built! Here, Solomon realized that though the glory of the Lord filled the house of the Lord so that the priests could not continue ministering, God is beyond the heaven or heaven of heavens and cannot be contained. He is infinite.

1 Kings 11:14 Now the LORD raised up an adversary against Solomon,... Solomon is an example of a king who started well but went astray. He did evil and did not wholly follow what the Lord had directed him to do even though the Lord had directly appeared to him two times. He had loved many foreign women, and they turned his heart away from the Lord, compromising his faith through worshiping foreign gods. So one of the critical things about Solomon's life is how the Lord turned against him and used unbelievers against him after Solomon was corrupted and began to worship other gods. This is something to guard against as we experience success from following the living God.

1 Kings 14:15 For the LORD will strike Israel, as a reed is shaken in the water. He will uproot Israel from this good land which He gave to their fathers, and will scatter them beyond the River,... This is what happened to Israel. They were scattered throughout the earth but eventually came back per another prophecy in the Bible.

1 Kings 17:22 Then the LORD heard the voice of Elijah; and the soul of the child came back to him, and he revived. Here we see that it is the soul that gives life to the body. Most of what we have left without the soul is just water, organic molecules, oxygen, carbon, hydrogen, nitrogen, calcium, and phosphorus. Without the soul, these materials don't do much.

1 Kings 18:28 So they cried aloud, and cut themselves, as was their custom, with knives and lances, until the blood gushed out on them. Here's a case where pagan people who worshiped Baal had a tradition of cutting themselves as part of trying to get their god to take some action.

1 Kings 19:12 ...and after the fire a still small voice. The Lord sometimes speaks to men in **a still small voice** as he did in this passage to Elijah. There are instances in the Bible where Christ went into the wilderness to pray and commune with God. This is probably a good model for us. There are times when we need to get away from all the confusion and noise of modern-day life. We need to go into the beautiful wilderness that God created to be still and know that he is God and listen for His still small voice

1 Kings 21:29 "See how Ahab has humbled himself before Me? Because he has humbled himself before Me, I will not bring the calamity in his days. In the days of his son I will bring the calamity on his house." Here's a section on the value of humility before God in the Old Testament. Ahab's humility resulted in God delaying calamity that would have befallen the people sooner had not Ahab humbled himself before the Lord.

12

2 Kings

[12]**2 KINGS** - The Lord fulfills His promises.

2 Kings 2:11... and Elijah went up by a whirlwind into heaven. In a dramatic exit from the earth, Elijah was taken into heaven with horses of fire. What a spectacular way to go!

2 Kings 2:23 Then he went up from there to Bethel; and as he was going up the road, some youths came from the city and mocked him, and said to him, "Go up, you baldhead! Go up, you baldhead!" After this, Elisha pronounced a curse on them in the name of the Lord, and two female bears came out and mauled forty-two of these irreverent youths.

2 Kings 3:15 But now bring me a musician." Then it happened, when the musician played, that the hand of the LORD came upon him. It appears that in this case, the music and prophecy were intertwined. Perhaps the music helped him concentrate on the divine revelation. As

---

[12] NSB quotations are from the Nelsons Study Bible, copyright (c) 1997 by Thomas Nelson, Inc., Nashville, TN; used by permission; scripture taken from the New King James Version, Copyright (c) 1979, 1980, 1982 used by permission. All rights reserved.

in many instances, the prophecy directed the people to do something intertwined with God's action. Humankind was working with God. Often, it seems that man has to do his part for the Lord to work in his life and accomplish His purpose.

2 Kings 6:17 And Elisha prayed, and said, "LORD, I pray, open his eyes that he may see." Then the LORD opened the eyes of the young man, and he saw. And behold, the mountain *was* full of horses and chariots of fire all around Elisha. Elisha was a prophet of God who had the privilege of having his eyes opened by God to see some of his guardians. The young man who accompanied Elisha was also granted this privilege, and he was able to see the spiritual world that very few men have the ability to see. Many churches have angels associated with them in the New Testament (Rev. 2:1; 2:8; 2:12), and the Angels of the Lord are mentioned throughout the Bible. Sometimes they are seen by specific individuals, as in this verse.

2 Kings 8:1 ...for the LORD has called for a famine, and furthermore, it will come upon the land for seven years." Here's a situation where the Lord actually implemented a famine to reprimand the people and cause them to repent. There are other instances of this type of punishment. Note: this scripture does not say that the Lord calls all natural disasters. There are also times when the Lord allowed Israel's enemies to get the best of them as a judgment on His people (1 Kings 19:15-17). Note that the kingdom that God uses as an instrument of judgment can also themselves fall under judgment (2 Kings 10:31-36).

2 Kings 17:20 And the LORD rejected all the descendants of Israel, afflicted them, and delivered them into the hand of plunderers, until He had cast them from His sight. Here's what happened to Judah when they rejected the commandments of the Lord and began to follow the statutes which they made up themselves.

2 Kings 17:38 And the covenant that I have made with you, you shall not forget, nor shall you fear other gods. The Lord blessed His people when they feared Him and followed His commandments. On the other hand, He did not deliver them from their enemies when they followed the worship rituals of other gods.

2 Kings 19:7 Surely I will send a spirit upon him, and he shall hear a rumor and return to his own land; and I will cause him to fall by the sword in his own land. It's interesting that, in this case, the Lord allows a rumor to help accomplish his purposes. Note that the scripture does not say that the Lord caused the rumor or started it. It just says that the person would hear a rumor. Many scriptures advise us to be truthful and not to gossip (Ephesians 4:29; Exodus 23:1; James 1;26).

2 Kings 20:6 And I will add to your days fifteen years. Here's a case where a sick Hezekiah was told by Isaiah, the prophet, that the Lord told him he would die. Then after Hezekiah's prayers in which he said he had walked in truth with a loyal heart and done what was right in the Lord's sight, the Lord granted him healing and fifteen more years of life. Some people say that the LORD does not change His mind, but this situation does not seem to go along with that thought.

2 Kings 21:6 He did much evil in the sight of the LORD, to provoke *Him* to anger. This statement was made about Manasseh, who was a king in Judah. What evil had he done to provoke the Lord? There were many issues noted in this part of scripture. He allowed obscene images as altars for Baal. He practiced soothsaying. He was involved in witchcraft and consulted mediums. He also worshiped heavenly bodies. This was prohibited in the Law of God (Deuteronomy 4:19; 17:2-7). There doesn't seem to be anything in scripture to indicate that the Law of God has changed on this issue. As wicked as Manasseh was, God heard his prayer when he repented and did good (2 Chronicles 33:12-16). Nevertheless, some consequences came from these sins (17:18, 19; 24:26, 27).

13

1 Chronicles

1 CHRONICLES - History of the Israelites

Through the Davidic covenant, David's kingdom itself embodies the promise of the future kingdom whose ruler is the great Son of David, Jesus Christ." (NSB page 660) 1 Chronicles omits David's weaknesses, which are detailed in the book of Samuel.

1 Chronicles 2:3 The sons of Judah *were* Er, Onan, and Shelah. *These three were born to him by the daughter of Shua, the Canaanites. Er, the firstborn of Judah, was wicked in the sight of the Lord; so He killed him.* This appears to be a somewhat curt and shocking statement; simple and to the point. Er was wicked in the sight of the Lord and therefore was killed. That's about all we know about Er. However, judging by how patient the Lord is throughout scripture, Er must have been evil and deserved capital punishment.

1 Chronicles 3:3 Now these were the sons of David who were born

---

[13] NSB quotations are from the Nelsons Study Bible, copyright (c) 1997 by Thomas Nelson, Inc., Nashville, TN; used by permission; scripture taken from the New King James Version, Copyright (c) 1979, 1980, 1982 used by permission. All rights reserved.

to him in Hebron: The firstborn *was* Amnon, by Ahinoam the Jezreelitess; the second, Daniel, by Abigail the Carmelitess; Six sons of David born in Hebron by six different wives are mentioned in this chapter. Others were born in Jerusalem. David had fallen into the ancient custom among kings of marrying the daughters of neighboring kings to create allies. "Negative results inevitably followed such multiple marriages (NSB pg. 665)." See 2 Samuel 13:14. The fact that David had many wives does not mean that God condoned polygamy, nor does the scripture indicate that polygamy was acceptable. However, it was the custom of the nations in those days.

1 Chronicles 4:10 And Jabez called on the God of Israel saying, "Oh, that You would bless me indeed, and enlarge my territory, that Your hand would be with me, and that You would keep *me* from evil, that I may not cause pain!" So God granted him what he requested. Here is what appears to be an example of a good prayer to pray since God gave Jabez what he requested.

1 Chronicles 6:6 The sons of Levi *were* Gershon, Kohath, and Merari. In those days, per directions from God, all personnel involved in the Tabernacle or temple ministry had to be members of the tribe of Levi. Other things were also different in those times. For example, in the culture of those days, the Law of Moses did not prohibit first cousins from joining in marriage (see Genesis 11:29). Note that some things have changed since then from a cultural and scriptural perspective.

1 Chronicles 6:31 Now these are the men whom David appointed over the service of song in the house of the Lord, after the ark came to rest. There were musicians and worship in the house of the Lord in King David's time. At that time, the ones who served in this capacity were all Levites.

1 Chronicles 9:33 These are the singers, heads of the fathers' *houses*

of the Levites, *who lodged* in the chambers, *and were* free *from other duties;* for they were employed in *that* work day and night. In Jerusalem, the leaders of the singers stayed in the chambers of the house of God. Thus, they could be available at any time as needed. The statement that they **were employed at that work day and night** could mean that there was worship going on all the time or that they needed to be available (see 1 Chronicles 15:1-17:27).

There are many times throughout history that various groups instituted 24/7 worship and prayer. One current group is in Kansas City, Missouri. On September 19, 1999, the International House of Prayer started a worship-based prayer meeting that has continued for twenty-four hours a day "in the spirit of the tabernacle of David" since then.

Note that David's Levites were free from other duties because they had to be available at any time of the day or night to perform their ministerial duties. In Old Testament times the Israelites were chosen by God for a specific purpose, and the tribe of the Levites had a specific priestly ministry. Under the covenant of grace, these duties opened up to all who repent and believe in Christ. Christ paid the price for our sins so that we can have direct access through Him to God the Father (John 1:29; Luke 22:20; Romans 3:20; Romans 6:14-15; Ephesians 2:8-9; Romans 8:9-11; Hebrews 9:15). God saves by grace through faith, by grace through faith, by grace through faith…….. And, who is the author of that faith? God. We do not get to boast or take pride in doing something to save ourselves. These facts distinguish Christianity from any other belief system. Our salvation is a gift from God. There is nothing we can do to save ourselves. It is all a work of God.

1 Chronicles 10:13 So Saul died for his unfaithfulness which he had committed against the Lord, because he did not keep the word of the Lord, and also because he consulted a medium for guidance. 14 But *he* did not inquire of the Lord; therefore He killed him, and

turned the kingdom over to David the son of Jesse. Here's another case where the scripture tells us that the Lord kills a person. However, in this case, there is more explanation. Scripture tells us that the way Saul died was that he fell on his sword. In other words, he committed suicide. But, since this scripture states that the Lord killed him, how do we reconcile these two statements? Let's take it for what it says. It appears that the Lord let Saul pursue his selfish course, and that led to his death. Thus, "**He killed him** (10:14)."

Providing a poor analogy might be something like a father telling his obstinate and rebellious son to ask him for help if he needs it. Not listening to his father, the son joins a gang, begins drinking and taking illegal drugs all the time. In his arrogance and rebellion, the son gets drunk and decides to drive with the grandson. He soon runs the car into a tree which kills the grandson. The son is so distraught about the death of his son that he tells his father he is going to kill himself. The father is also distraught and does not intervene to stop his son from killing himself. It is challenging to come up with a good analogy that adequately addresses the sovereignty of God. However, you can get the picture from this scenario that there are times where a father may give up on a rebellious son who will not follow his counsel.

1 Chronicles 13:1 Then David consulted with the captains of thousands and hundreds, *and* **with every leader.** Here and elsewhere in scripture, we have examples and exhortations to consult with others, especially other godly, wise people and leaders, before embarking on a new major goal. Of course, we also need to consult with the great counselor, the Lord, in addition to consulting with people. In this case, it appeared that David wanted to make sure bringing the Ark of the Covenant to Jerusalem was of the Lord and supported by all the leaders and people.

1 Chronicles 13:8 Then David and all Israel played *music* **before**

God with all *their* might, with singing, on harps, on stringed instruments, on tambourines, on cymbals, and with trumpets. Note here that it was all of Israel playing music before God in this verse. It wasn't just the worship leaders who participated in this music. All the people participated in whatever way they could, whether singing or playing harps, other stringed instruments, tambourines, cymbals, or trumpets. And how did they participate? They participated with all their might. This was not a half-hearted effort. This should be an example for us to put our heart into worship and not do it half-heartedly.

1 Chronicles 14:15 ...And it shall be, when you hear a sound of marching in the tops of the mulberry trees, then you shall go out to battle, for God has gone out before you to strike the camp of the Philistines." Before going out against the Philistines, David asked God if he should do so and got the green light from the Lord, who told him they would be delivered into his hand (1 Chr. 14:10). Thus, here, David gives us an example again of seeking counsel from the Lord before going to battle. Also, this scripture demonstrates that God is the source of victories in battle.

1 Chronicles 15:22 Chenaniah, leader of the Levites, was instructor *in charge of* the music, because he *was* skillful; In this verse, we find out why a worship leader was selected. He was skillful. Thus, one of the prerequisites for a leader in charge of music is that the person is skillful.

1 Chronicles 16:4 And he appointed some of the Levites to minister before the ark of the Lord, to commemorate, to thank, and to praise the Lord God of Israel: Here are some goals of worship; to commemorate, to thank, and to praise. Further along in this paragraph of scripture, we find that stringed instruments, harps, cymbals, and trumpets facilitate this goal. This statement seems to include most, if not all, musical instruments and percussion instruments available to them.

1 Chronicles 16:9 Sing to Him, sing psalms to Him;
Talk of all His wondrous works!.....
23 Sing to the Lord, all the earth;
Proclaim the good news of His salvation from day to day.....
25 For the Lord *is* great and greatly to be praised;
He *is* also to be feared above all gods....
36 Blessed *be* the Lord God of Israel
From everlasting to everlasting!
And all the people said, "Amen!" and praised the Lord. These selected verses are from a psalm David delivered to thank the Lord. Note that the people are encouraged to sing to and talk about the Lord. The psalm also encourages proclaiming the good news of His salvation daily. Why? Because he is great and greatly to be praised. He is the living God above all false gods that the pagans believed in, which were not really "gods" in the first place. We should fear the living God, not the nonexistent or false gods.

1 Chronicles 16:41 ...and with them Heman and Jeduthun and the rest who were chosen, who were designated by name, to give thanks to the Lord, because His mercy *endures* forever; 42 and with them Heman and Jeduthun, to sound aloud with trumpets and cymbals and the musical instruments of God. Now the sons of Jeduthun *were* gatekeepers. Here we learn that musical instruments are "instruments of God." Of course, all instruments, the earth, and the universe belong to God, who made the earth and everything in it directly or indirectly through the workers (people) he made.

I agree with the commentators in the Nelson Study Bible when they say: "It is difficult to overemphasize the importance of music in Old Testament worship." Psalms and scripture testify that their statement is validated. It is also true that singing psalms, hymns, and spiritual songs continue in the New Testament (see Eph. 5:19 and Col. 3:16). The New Testament also mentions the sound of musical instruments.

The sound of a trumpet (Matthew 24:31) will occur when God gathers together His elect and "when the dead shall be raised incorruptible (1 Cor. 15:52)." Also, in heaven, every one of the twenty-four elders before the Lamb has a harp (Rev. 5:8). In Revelation 14, we read of "**harpers harping with their harps.**" Thus, there are musical instruments used for worship in heaven. The New Testament does not mention any change in direction regarding musical instruments in the worship of God. Thus, if there has been no change in scripture on this point, there has been no change. Therefore it is easy to conclude that the use of "instruments of God" should continue throughout the time of the covenant of grace.

1 Chronicles 17:13 ...I will be his Father, and he shall be My son; and I will not take My mercy away from him, as I took *it* **from** *him* **who was before you. 14 And I will establish him in My house and in My kingdom forever; and his throne shall be established forever.'"** This scripture, which appears to be speaking of Christ, comes to David from the prophet Nathan. It refers to God removing his mercy from Saul (**him who was before you**, 17:13) and establishing a dynasty ending with Christ (the son of David) who will rule forever (Luke 1:32-33).

1 Chronicles 17:20 O Lord, *there is* **none like You, nor** *is there any* **God besides You, according to all that we have heard with our ears.** There is only one living God. Other so-called gods are counterfeits or idols not worth any attention.

1 Chronicles 18:13 He also put garrisons in Edom, and all the Edomites became David's servants. And the Lord preserved David wherever he went. Notice who "preserved" David. It was the Lord. In verse 18:11, we learn that David dedicated the spoils of war to the Lord. Thus, it appears that David recognized who was making him successful in battle.

1 Chronicles 19:18 Then the Syrians fled before Israel; and David

killed seven thousand charioteers and forty thousand foot soldiers of the Syrians, and killed Shophach the commander of the army. Here is one scripture that, on first reading, appears to disagree with another part of scripture. In 2 Samuel 10:18, which speaks of the same battle, there is a reference to seven hundred charioteers being killed. Of course, this could be a translation error. However, even if it is not a translation error, the two statements are not contrary because they don't state the exact time the statement was made. If seven hundred charioteers were killed at one point in time, more could have been killed later. Thus, if this is not just a translation error, then both statements still could be correct. The Word of God is true (John 17:17).

1 Chronicles 21:10 ..."Go and tell David, saying, 'Thus says the Lord: "I offer you three *things;* choose one of them for yourself, that I may do *it* to you."'" This is one place in the Bible where the Lord offers alternative punishments. David admitted his sin in this situation but was still required to suffer some consequences of his sin. "The Lord requires certain conditions people must meet for Him to act one way or another (NSB page 695)." Specific prayer sometimes appears to be one of those conditions.

1 Chronicles 21:24 Then King David said to Ornan, "No, but I will surely buy *it* for the full price, for I will not take what is yours for the Lord, nor offer burnt offerings with *that which* costs *me* nothing." Here is a principle of giving that David practiced. He would not give something to the Lord that did not cost him anything. This is the principle of sacrificial giving practiced by David that serves as an example to us. For an offering to God to be a sacrifice to God, it has to be personally sacrificial.

1 Chronicles 22:12 Only may the Lord give you wisdom and understanding, and give you charge concerning Israel, that you may keep the law of the Lord your God. 13 Then you will prosper,

if you take care to fulfill the statutes and judgments with which the Lord charged Moses concerning Israel. Be strong and of good courage; do not fear nor be dismayed. This scripture reflects back to Joshua 1:8. The Lord tells specific leaders that they would prosper if they keep His law and how he told Moses to lead Israel. This is probably good instruction for leaders in all walks of life. Although from a human perspective, this may not always appear to be the case. It has been my experience that leaders who are honest, trustworthy, and wise generally do prosper.

1 Chronicles 23:4 Of these, twenty-four thousand *were* to look after the work of the house of the Lord, six thousand *were* officers and judges, 5 four thousand *were* gatekeepers, and four thousand praised the Lord with *musical* instruments, "which I made," said David, "for giving praise." Here again, we learn why David made musical instruments. They were made explicitly for "giving praise." Apparently, through other scriptures, it appears that the Levites usually entered service at age 25 (Numbers 8:24,25), although exceptions were made (Numbers 4:3). Perhaps when there were adequate numbers of older people, there was no need to call younger people into service. Musicians and singers were a specific division of the Levites, as were the gatekeepers.

1 Chronicles 23:30 ...to stand every morning to thank and praise the Lord, and likewise at evening; 31 and at every presentation of a burnt offering to the Lord on the Sabbaths and on the New Moons and on the set feasts, by number according to the ordinance governing them, regularly before the Lord;... It appears that thanksgiving and praise were offered multiple times each day at the temple in Jerusalem. This thanksgiving and praise were provided by the Levites who had been appointed to this duty. These Levites began their ministry when they were twenty years old, and no retirement age is specified except that in other parts of scripture, those over fifty years old were apparently exempted from doing the heavy lifting type of service (Numbers 8:25).

1 Chronicles 25:6 All these *were* under the direction of their father for the music *in* the house of the Lord, with cymbals, stringed instruments, and harps, for the service of the house of God. Asaph, Jeduthun, and Heman *were* under the authority of the king. 7 So the number of them, with their brethren who were instructed in the songs of the Lord, all who were skillful, *was* two hundred and eighty-eight. Here again, we see that cymbals, stringed instruments, and harps were used in temple worship. Also, the singers and musicians were instructed. The ones who were skillful were used to lead the worship.

1 Chronicles 25:25 Moreover David and the captains of the army separated for the service *some* of the sons of Asaph, of Heman, and of Jeduthun, who *should* prophesy with harps, stringed instruments, and cymbals. Per verse 3 of this paragraph, the prophecy had to do with giving thanks and praise to the Lord. Verse 6 notes that there was music in the house of the Lord with cymbals, stringed instruments, and harps. Verse 7 indicates that **"all who were skillful, was two hundred and eighty-eight."**

1 Chronicles 27:1 And the children of Israel, according to their number, the heads of fathers' *houses*, the captains of thousands and hundreds and their officers, served the king in every matter of the *military* divisions. *These divisions* came in and went out month by month throughout all the months of the year, each division *having* twenty-four thousand. It appears King David's military men served one month at a time. There were twelve divisions, one for each month of the year. Each division had twenty-four thousand capable men for a standing army of 288,000. Each man in the military had eleven months to work at his own business and one month to serve in the military.

1 Chronicles 27:31 ...and Jaziz the Hagrite *was* over the flocks. All these *were* the officials over King David's property. It appears that there wasn't much difference between the nation's assets and the state's assets. In other words, the assets of the state belonged to the King in those days. Individuals also appeared to have property rights within the kingdom and owned their assets.

1 Chronicles 28:4 However the Lord God of Israel chose me above all the house of my father to be king over Israel forever, for He has chosen Judah *to be* the ruler. And of the house of Judah, the house of my father, and among the sons of my father, He was pleased with me to make *me* king over all Israel. David makes a statement that God chose him to be the king of all Israel forever. David was in the line of Jesus Christ (Acts 13:33; Heb. 1:5).

1 Chronicles 29:9 Then the people rejoiced, for they had offered willingly, because with a loyal heart they had offered willingly to the Lord; and King David also rejoiced greatly. This statement comes after the mention of how much the tribes gave to the work of the house of God. They are said to have given willingly. In other words, there was no coercion to this giving. They wanted to provide, and they were pleased about giving to this project. King David modeled joyful worship for the people. His praise included praise for God's eternity, His control over the universe, His great power, and the fact that all things came from the Lord. David recognizes that we are aliens and pilgrims before the Lord and that in comparison to eternity, our lives here are just a shadow. Without the Lord, we are without hope.

1 Chronicles 29:17 I know also, my God, that You test the heart and have pleasure in uprightness... David realized that the Lord likes righteousness in His people. People who give to the Lord demonstrate their love for the Lord and trust in Him (1 Sam. 15:22). David also appeared to be happy that his people understood the principle of giving and that a righteous life produces a generous spirit.

1 Chronicles 29:28 So he died in a good old age, full of days and

riches and honor; and Solomon his son reigned in his place. David died at age 70, which in his time was considered old age. In Psalm 90:10, this is stated by Moses as a standard for reasonable longevity. Of course, over the generations, many people have lived much longer than this.

14

2 Chronicles

[14]**2 CHRONICLES** - The Great Message of Redemption

2 Chronicles 1:10 Now give me wisdom and knowledge, that I may go out and come in before this people; for who can judge this great people of Yours?" God had asked Solomon what He should give him. It pleased God that Solomon asked for wisdom and knowledge because He granted both to him along with the things he didn't ask for, such as riches, wealth, and honor. When Solomon asked for wisdom and knowledge, Solomon demonstrated that he was more concerned about ruling and judging the people as king than about his fortunes. Solomon was the king, but he demonstrated servanthood by asking for something to help him serve the people as their king. This is probably a good model for our actions and prayers. Christ established this same principle in serving us while here on earth, even to the extent of laying down His life for us.

2 Chronicles 1:3 Now Solomon began to build the house of the Lord at Jerusalem on Mount Moriah, where *the Lord* had appeared to his

---

[14] NSB quotations are from the Nelsons Study Bible, copyright (c) 1997 by Thomas Nelson, Inc., Nashville, TN; used by permission; scripture taken from the New King James Version, Copyright (c) 1979, 1980, 1982 used by permission. All rights reserved.

father David, at the place that David had prepared on the threshing floor of Ornan the Jebusite. This place is the land of Moriah where Abraham took Isaac for sacrifice, which is known today as the temple mount and the site of the Muslim Dome of the Rock. It is directly north of Mount Zion, which was the location of David's tabernacle.

2 Chronicles 5:12 ...and the Levites *who were* the singers, all those of Asaph and Heman and Jeduthun, with their sons and their brethren, stood at the east end of the altar, clothed in white linen, having cymbals, stringed instruments and harps, and with them one hundred and twenty priests sounding with trumpets— 13 indeed it came to pass, when the trumpeters and singers *were* as one, to make one sound to be heard in praising and thanking the Lord, and when they lifted up their voice with the trumpets and cymbals and instruments of music, and praised the Lord, *saying:*
"*For He is* **good,**
For His mercy *endures* forever,"
that the house, the house of the Lord, was filled with a cloud, 14 so that the priests could not continue ministering because of the cloud; for the glory of the Lord filled the house of God. One thing of interest here is that there were so many involved in worship at the house of God. We know from other scripture that this house could not contain God (6:18). The cloud was just a small manifestation of God for the benefit of the people. Verse 6:18 explains that the heaven of heavens cannot contain God. The cloud filled the temple after the singers and instrumentalists made one sound praising and thanking the Lord. The priest could not continue ministering because of the cloud from the glory of the Lord. We also know that God is separate from humanity (2:6). However, He does come down to our low position to fellowship with us (Genesis 2:8; 11:5; 18:1, 2). He also did this through Christ (John 1:14).

2 Chronicles 6:18 "But will God indeed dwell with men on the earth? Behold, heaven and the heaven of heavens cannot contain You. How

much less this temple which I have built! This makes sense. God cannot be contained in a little temple on earth since He is beyond our heaven and the heaven of this heaven. God, who created our universe, has to transcend its boundaries. To us, our world appears to be infinite, but it may not be to God.

2 Chronicles 7:1 When Solomon had finished praying, fire came down from heaven and consumed the burnt offering and the sacrifices; and the glory of the Lord filled the temple. God's glory was noted here. It appeared as a dark cloud. Since scripture tells us that God is light, it seems that the cloud of darkness may have been shielding the priests from actually seeing the light emitted by God because that would have been too much for them and may have killed them. When God ignited the fire that consumed the burnt offering and the sacrifices, this appeared to be an act of approval of Solomon's prayers by God.

2 Chronicles 7:14 ...if My people who are called by My name will humble themselves, and pray and seek My face, and turn from their wicked ways, then I will hear from heaven, and will forgive their sin and heal their land. Here's a great promise God made to the Israelites. It speaks of having the humility to confess sins and repent. At this, the Lord says he will forgive them and heal their land. God's response to humility, prayer, and repentance would be hearing them, forgiving them, and healing them. This is an excellent bargain for the people.

In verse 19, the converse of this is stated. If they turned away and didn't follow God's statutes and commandments and served other gods and worshiped them, He would uproot them from His land, which He gave to them, and the temple they had built would be cast out of His sight. In other words, it would be destroyed. Unfortunately, this is what happened to the Israelites. They were thrown out of the land, and the temple was destroyed. This type of prophecy is spread through the Bible and is a clear indication that God knows the future like no other, and He sometimes reveals the future to us through His Word.

There does not seem to be any other written document that can predict the future with the specificity and accuracy of the Bible. Now that archaeologists have dated some of the early examples of scriptures that have been found, it is clear that scripture preceded the predictions (Amos 9:14-15; Ezekiel 37:21-22). Some people do not want to accept that the Bible does accurately predict the future. That would mean that it is true and that they will be dying in their sins if they don't repent.

2 Chronicles 9:11 And the king made walkways *of* the algum wood for the house of the Lord and for the king's house, also harps and stringed instruments for singers; and there were none such *as these* seen before in the land of Judah. Some of the people who played instruments also sang since this scripture states that the musical instruments were for the singers. It looks pretty likely that some of the Levites played stringed instruments to accompany their singing. As is the case today, certain types of wood are highly valued for the tonal qualities produced when used to make guitars or other stringed instruments. In this case, algum was a good wood with which to make stringed instruments. Today, Brazilian rosewood or rosewood from East India has this desirability for making acoustic guitars.

2 Chronicles 12:12 When he humbled himself, the wrath of the Lord turned from him, so as not to destroy *him* completely; and things also went well in Judah. This passage of scripture illustrates a pattern for Judah repeated time after time, as noted in 2 Chronicles 11-36. Over these chapters, there were four leaders under which there were humility and reforms with associated blessings from God and five periods of rebellion during which the Lord forsook them. When they sought the Lord God with all their heart and soul, the Lord gave them rest all around (15:12-15). When they foolishly turned away from the

Lord, they had wars (16:9).

2 Chronicles 16:7 And at that time Hanani the seer came to Asa king of Judah, and said to him: "Because you have relied on the king of Syria, and have not relied on the Lord your God, therefore the army of the king of Syria has escaped from your hand. The Lord expects us to seek His guidance. When we just proceed on our own, sometimes He allows us to suffer the consequences. In another passage of this chapter, the scripture notes that Asa was diseased in his feet and sought only the physicians and not the Lord on this issue, and he died. Perhaps this is included in scripture to let us know not that it is a problem to seek out physicians but that it is a problem not to seek the Lord in every challenge we face.

We know from scripture that we are required to take action when we face a problem, but not until we seek the Lord's guidance and direction. When God parted the Red Sea, the Israelites still had to go across; they couldn't just sit there. When we have an illness or injury, we may need to pray about what doctor or hospital to go to. But, once we have done so, we need to take action and not just sit there. In an emergency, we may not choose where we are being taken in an ambulance, but we can still pray about the situation while we are in transport unless we are unconscious, and then our family and friends may need to pray about our treatment.

2 Chronicles 18:21 So he said, 'I will go out and be a lying spirit in the mouth of all his prophets.' And *the Lord* said, 'You shall persuade *him* and also prevail; go out and do so.' 22 Therefore look! The Lord has put a lying spirit in the mouth of these prophets of yours, and the Lord has declared disaster against you." Here is a verse that is easily subject to misinterpretation if one is not aware of or ignores the whole counsel of God. Other scriptures need to be remembered, saying that God cannot lie (Titus 1:2; Numbers 23:19). Knowing this, we should interpret this scripture as saying that God can allow a lying spirit to deceive even the prophets. Thus God does not lie, but He has given others the free will to do so.

Note that this scripture mentions his prophets in referring to the prophets of Ahab, the king of Israel. The scripture says God has put a lying spirit in the mouth of prophets of *yours (this refers to Ahab's prophets)*. Thus, the Lord allowed deceiving prophets to convince Ahab to go up against Syria, and Ahab was killed by one of their arrows in fulfillment of what the Lord's prophet said.

There are a couple of points to remember from this scripture. First, the king should have listened to the prophet of the Lord instead of his own deceived prophets who told him what he wanted to hear, and second, he should have made sure that he listened to wise counsel from the Lord's prophet. The take-home lesson for us might be that when we seek counsel, make sure the council is from a wise counselor, preferably one who is well acquainted with the wisdom in the Bible.

2 Chronicles 19:6 ...and said to the judges, "Take heed to what you are doing, for you do not judge for man but for the Lord, who *is* with you in the judgment. This is advice that Jehoshaphat gave to the judges he appointed. It would be great if our judges had this thinking in mind when they were doing their job.

2 Chronicles 19:9 And he commanded them, saying, "Thus you shall act in the fear of the Lord, faithfully and with a loyal heart: This advice was given to Jehoshaphat, and even though he was the king, he was advised that in all matters of the Lord, he was to be under the authority of the chief priest. Thus, here, we see an integration of the government with religion. The king was to be over administrative matters and the priest over moral, spiritual, and religious matters. Our forefathers appear to have established a similar arrangement by prohibiting the government of the United States from establishing any law promoting or restricting the free exercise of religion. The First Amendment of the United States Constitution prohibits the federal government from making a law "respecting an establishment of religion, or prohibiting the free exercise thereof." This law was extended to state and local governments through the Fourteenth Amendment. The courts, however, have demonstrated that this free exercise of religion is not absolute through prohibiting polygamy. Thus in the United States, the law cannot interfere with beliefs and opinions, but it may restrict certain practices. The same principle might hold for vampirism or the use of certain drugs.

2 Chronicles 20:3 And Jehoshaphat feared, and set himself to seek the Lord, and proclaimed a fast throughout all Judah. This is an example of praying and fasting. Jehoshaphat knew that their success in battle depended on the Lord's favor, and apparently fasting and prayer were done to focus on the Lord. Matthew 6:17 indicates that fasting is to be done in secret between a person and the Lord. It is not something to display to other people. Perhaps fasting helps us focus on the Lord and that without the food he causes to grow, we would not last long. The scripture does not say what type of food they were fasting from, whether it was one type of food or all food. There appear to be different types of fasts in the scriptures. For example, Daniel fasted from meat for some time, apparently during the Passover. "**At that time I, Daniel, mourned for three weeks. I ate no choice food; no meat or wine touched my lips; and I used no lotions at all until the three weeks were over.**" (Daniel 10:2-3)

2 Chronicles 20:19 Then the Levites of the children of the Kohathites and of the children of the Korahites stood up to praise the Lord God of Israel with voices loud and high. Here is an example to us regarding how we should praise the Lord. In this case, they were praising the Lord in preparation for a military battle. Later, the Lord set ambushes against their enemies so they would destroy each other (20:22-23). This is an excellent example for us to prepare for any battles we might be facing with prayer and praise. If you know you are going into a war, why not first do whatever you can to learn how the Lord would have you proceed and to gain His support. We don't want to go against the Lord (Matt. 12:30) since we know that is a recipe for ultimate disaster.

2 Chronicles 20:21 And when he had consulted with the people, he appointed those who should sing to the Lord, and who should praise the beauty of holiness, as they went out before the army and were saying:
  "Praise the Lord,
  For His mercy *endures* forever." If you are going to be in a battle, this is the kind of battle you want to be in. When the people sang and praised the beauty of holiness, their enemies fought against themselves and utterly destroyed each other. So the inhabitants of Judah and Jerusalem didn't have to lift a finger or lose any soldiers, and when they returned to Jerusalem with joy, they brought stringed instruments and harps and trumpets to the house of the Lord. They were singing and playing with joy in response to what the Lord had done with their enemies. Sometimes the Lord will let our enemies and His destroy themselves as we praise the Lord and focus on Him and His mercy.

2 Chronicles 21:4 Now when Jehoram was established over the kingdom of his father, he strengthened himself and killed all his brothers with the sword, and also *others* of the princes of Israel. This is an example of how evil a person can get in his quest to hold on to power. His lust for power was so intense it even motivated him to kill his brothers with the sword. That is how perverted a person who lusts for power can get. They will stop at nothing.

2 Chronicles 24:18 Therefore they left the house of the Lord God of their fathers, and served wooden images and idols; and wrath came upon Judah and Jerusalem because of their trespass. When Judah left the house of the Lord God and began to serve idols, wrath came upon them. It appears that this can also happen in modern-day times when a country turns its back on God.

America is an example of a country that began with many believers as citizens but now appears to be straying toward the worship of idols in various forms. We even have television programs devoted to American Idols and the country is definitely come way down from its lofty heights as a world leader and power in the years immediately after World War II. This downward spiral appears to be continuing with the American government spending more each year than it takes in and borrowing much of this money from foreign countries. Proverbs 22:7 warns us that the borrower is a servant to the lender. Thus, America is becoming a servant to the country to which it owes the most. That country may have very different rules regarding the freedoms we enjoy here and take for granted.

Many immigrants to America in the 1940s and 1950s know the blessings of the freedoms we enjoy because they have had first-hand experience with the type of oppression that can occur when a person like Lenin or Hitler becomes the supreme ruler and idol of a country. Many born Americans do not understand or appreciate what can happen in a country that turns its back on God.

2 Chronicles 24:24 For the army of the Syrians came with a small company of men; but the Lord delivered a very great army into their hand, because they had forsaken the Lord God of their fathers. So they executed judgment against Joash. When a nation forsakes the Lord, the Lord can allow its enemies to overtake them even with a smaller army. America is only 4.4 percent of the world's population now (2014), and after World War II was the world's superpower. However, as America turns away from its roots and its Judeo-Christian values, its position and dominance appear to be waning from the economic and even its military superiority.

At this point, we still seem to be a favored nation, and when disaster strikes, many citizens turn their focus to God, but as peace and comfort return, we again turn our focus to other things, people, and our capabilities. As the scripture states in 25:8, we need always to remember that "...**God has power to help and to overthrow**." We need God on our side before we go to battle, or the results can be disastrous even if we are against a seemingly weak foe. It is also interesting to note that God sometimes allows people of the same background to turn against each other and destroy each other when they turn against Him and worship other gods. An example of this is in 2 Chronicles 25, where we read how Israel defeated Judah.

2 Chronicles 25:20 But Amaziah would not heed, for it *came* from God, that He might give them into the hand *of their enemies*, because they sought the gods of Edom. Here is an example of how God will let people make their own decisions when they worship other gods. These decisions can result in the fulfillment of God's plan even when they are made without input from God. As a result of his decision to face Israel, Amaziah was defeated and captured.

2 Chronicles 26:5 He sought God in the days of Zechariah, who had understanding in the visions of God; and as long as he sought the Lord, God made him prosper. This scripture speaks about Uzziah, who became king at age 16 and ruled 52 years in Jerusalem. It is interesting to note that there is a condition to God's blessing on him. That condition was that he seeks the Lord. Some early manuscripts use the word "fear" for "visions" in this verse. Many other scriptures talk about fearing the Lord who can destroy the soul and the body instead of fearing man who can only destroy the physical body (Matt.10:28). Thus, we are commanded what to fear; the Lord, and not to fear; man.

There are many blessings associated with fear of the Lord, including long life (Prov. 10:27), wisdom (Psalm 111:10; Prov. 9:10), knowledge (Prov. 1:7), and life (Prov. 19:23). Therefore, it is a good thing to have visions or fear of God. And, if we fear Him, we will want to know what He wants us to do. Understanding what He wants us to do is straightforward and doesn't have to be mystical. He gave us the Bible for a purpose.

If I am your boss and write some instructions to you in a memo, do you wait until I also tell you verbally before you carry out the instructions, or do you take action based on the note? He is the boss. He has had His subordinates write 2202 pages of instructions (in the Bible I use), policies, procedures, history, justifications, commandments, and reasons to us. When we carry out all these instructions, we can expect that He might take some time to give us verbal instructions. These policies inform most decisions we have to make, and if we follow them, we will be obeying our boss, and He may cause us to prosper. Note: He does not have to make us prosper or do anything in our timing, but based on this scripture and many others, I believe He will make us prosper in His time.

2 Chronicles 26:16 But when he was strong his heart was lifted up, to *his* destruction, for he transgressed against the Lord his God by entering the temple of the Lord to burn incense on the altar of incense. Uzziah did well for a while, but then as he had great success, his pride got the best of him, and he also tried to do the consecrated priest's job of burning incense in the sanctuary. As a result, Uzziah instantly got leprosy. This is a familiar pattern.

A king gets power and sometimes starts out fine following the Lord and worshiping Him. This brings blessing and success. Then the king begins to take credit for the achievements and becomes prideful, thinking that he can take all the credit for his accomplishments. Then comes the downfall.

Often the Lord's way of dealing with a prideful society is to let their enemies defeat them. We need to keep this in mind as we stray further from relying on the Lord's guidance and direction and think our ingenuity can protect us from our enemies. Recently, we found out that just a few terrorists in our planes could take out our World Trade Center and attack our Pentagon.

In 2001, a few people overcame the pride in the United States military might. We never thought they could hurt us on our soil. Arrogance and pride can be self-destructive as we sit and think we cannot be touched. Hopefully, these events taught us something. Our real security comes not only from our military might but the Lord. When we turn from Him, He can and will withdraw His protection. In many situations, the Israelites brought judgment on themselves through worshiping idols (see 2 Kings 17:7, 18).

2 Chronicles 29:25 And he stationed the Levites in the house of the Lord with cymbals, with stringed instruments, and with harps, according to the commandment of David, of Gad the king's seer, and of Nathan the prophet; for thus *was* the commandment of the Lord by His prophets. We learned in 1 Chronicles 23:5 that King David made musical instruments for giving praise to God. Here we learn that the use of musical instruments in the house of the Lord was the commandment of the Lord by His prophets. In this situation, it is also noted in verse 29:28 that "**all the assembly worshiped;**" the singers sang, and the trumpets sounded, and they sang praises with gladness. I find nothing in the scriptures that changes this expectation from the Lord for modern-day believers.

2 Chronicles 30:12 Also the hand of God was on Judah to give them singleness of heart to obey the command of the king and the leaders, at the word of the Lord. It should be noted that the grace of God is always involved in any of our efforts to please Him. He gives us the singleness of heart to obey him, which works in concert with our openness to having him work in our hearts. We could say that our relationship with the Lord is symbiotic (1 Thessalonians 4:1-6). He uses and guides us as we open ourselves to being directed and obedient.

2 Chronicles 30:7 And do not be like your fathers and your brethren, who trespassed against the Lord God of their fathers, so that He gave them up to desolation, as you see. Those of us who are believers know that life here on earth is really like a pre-life to our eternal life. In this life and the life following this life, those who trespass against the Lord will experience desolation. From other scripture (Ecclesiastes 3:1; Acts 1:7; 2 Peter 3:8) we know that the timing of the desolation is not always immediate, but it is inevitable if the Lord says it. There is no need for us to try to take revenge to speed up the process of desolation. We have commands that revenge is the Lord's (Romans 12:19; 1 Peter 3:9; 1 Thessalonians 5:15).

2 Chronicles 30:21 So the children of Israel who were present at Jerusalem kept the Feast of Unleavened Bread seven days with great gladness; and the Levites and the priests praised the Lord day by day, *singing* to the Lord, accompanied by loud instruments. Here it is interesting to note that they sang to the Lord accompanied by "loud" instruments. This singing and playing do not seem to be of the sad variety you would expect to be accompanied by softer-sounding instruments. This scripture appears to be speaking about the joyous rejoicing that would be associated with praise and thanksgiving. Both types of worship are noted in the scriptures. The Passover and the Feast of Unleavened Bread were typically celebrated together over several days, so they had a lot to rejoice and be thankful about. Right after they celebrated Israel's deliverance from bondage, they celebrated the beginning of the barley harvest. In verse 30:25, the scripture notes that the whole assembly rejoiced, including the sojourners, the aliens who lived there and adhered to God and the Law (Deuteronomy 16:11, 26:11, 29:11, 31:12).

2 Chronicles 31:4 Moreover he commanded the people who dwelt in Jerusalem to contribute support for the priests and the Levites, that they might devote themselves to the Law of the Lord. The scripture says that in response to this command, the people tithed "abundantly" of everything. When they did this, God blessed them, and they had much to eat and plenty left. I have experienced this type of blessing from the Lord. However, I would not recommend taking the attitude of giving to get back. That attitude would probably backfire on the giver.

The Lord owns everything. We are just temporary stewards. Anything we "give" to the Lord or His institutions already belongs to Him. Therefore, when we tithe to our local church operation, we are transferring what the Lord has allowed us to control to an institution pursuing His agenda of spreading His Word. Then, the use of His resources applies to His people.

Those who are not believers are also allowed to achieve significant gains here on earth, but none will be able to take any of it with them when they leave (Matthew 6:19-21; 1 Timothy 6:7-10). In Malachi 3:8, we learn that failing to bring the tithe, generally viewed as a tenth of the annual produce, is the equivalent of robbing the Lord. Why would the Lord bless someone who is robbing Him? He might allow someone who says they don't believe in Him to get away with it for a while, but in the end, all unbelievers will stand before Him for judgment. Every knee will bow, and every tongue will confess that Jesus Christ is Lord (Romans 14:11).

2 Chronicles 31:21 And in every work that he began in the service of the house of God, in the law and in the commandment, to seek his God, he did *it* with all his heart. So he prospered. This scripture about Hezekiah shows a king how to prosper by putting all his heart into serving God. Without God, another scripture indicates that a king is just an arm of the flesh (Jeremiah 17:5; 2 Chronicles 32:8). With God, a king has the Lord who has an army of angels to help fight the battles.

2 Chronicles 32:25 But Hezekiah did not repay according to the favor *shown* him, for his heart was lifted up; therefore wrath was looming over him and over Judah and Jerusalem. Here's an example of what can happen to a king who becomes proud in his mind even though it was God who blessed his kingship. He became a showoff and indulged his pride. After this, God withdrew from him to test what was in his heart. This appears to have been for Hezekiah's benefit. He needed to remember where all his blessings came from and not take credit for that which was God's.

2 Chronicles 33:6 Also he caused his sons to pass through the fire in the Valley of the Son of Hinnom; he practiced soothsaying, used witchcraft and sorcery, and consulted mediums and spiritists. He did much evil in the sight of the Lord, to provoke Him to anger. These were things that Manasseh did in Judah that were prohibited by Saul (1 Samuel 28:3, 9). Soothsaying, witchcraft, sorcery mediums, and spiritists are all things to be strictly avoided by God's people (Isaiah 2:6; Jeremiah 27:9; Deuteronomy 13:1-6; 18:9-14). These things are evil in the sight of the Lord and, therefore, should be avoided by His people.

2 Chronicles 33:12 Now when he was in affliction, he implored the Lord his God, and humbled himself greatly before the God of his fathers, 13 and prayed to Him; and He received his entreaty, heard his supplication, and brought him back to Jerusalem into his kingdom. Then Manasseh knew that the Lord *was* God. Here is how Manasseh knew that the Lord was God. He prayed to Him, and God answered his prayers in the affirmative. The Lord answers prayers when they are in accord with His will. Prayers for anything outside the will of the Lord should not be made in the first place.

Notice how Christ prayed even when He was facing an excruciating death through crucifixion. In Matthew 26:39, He prayed **"O My Father, if it is possible, let this cup pass from Me; nevertheless, not as I will,**

but as You *will*." If we want our prayers answered, perhaps our ending prayer should be: "your will be done." For a believer, who knows who God is, why would we ever think that our desires could deserve more weight than that of the creator of the universe? That position would be incredibly arrogant. He is the one who holds all things together, and without whom, there would be no physical world in which we live. We are just the equivalent of a nanoparticle in this vast infinite universe. Why would we not humble ourselves in His sight (James 4:10)? That is the only proper and true position for us to take when addressing Him. To do anything else would be arrogant and full of pride.

Sometimes the Lord lets things happen to us that have to do with forces in the universe that are not about us. These are forces that we do not control. When we start to get prideful and to think we are in charge, these circumstances can overwhelm us so that we can get back to a more realistic position and think that we are not in charge of the universe. We merely occupy a small little space in the universe and should be grateful for any bit of peace we get to experience in our brief life spans here on this minute planet earth.

2 Chronicles 34:14 Now when they brought out the money that was brought into the house of the Lord, Hilkiah the priest found the Book of the Law of the Lord *given* by Moses. This was a great discovery and one that began a great revival in Israel. There was a reformation, and attention was focused on Jerusalem as the center of worship (see 2 Kings 23:4-20). Apparently, the Pentateuch was found. The Pentateuch is the first five books of the Bible (Exodus 24:4). It seems God orchestrated the preservation and discovery of these books. They contain long lists of blessings and curses attached to the covenant with Israel (Deuteronomy 28:29). When Josiah the king heard the words of the law, he listened to the scriptures and began to follow them himself and led the people. Very few of the kings of Judah promised to **follow the Lord** (34:31) as Josiah did (NSB). He re-instituted the day-long Passover feast, which included fellowship, praise and, music.

2 Chronicles 35:21 But he sent messengers to him, saying, "What have I to do with you, king of Judah? *I have* **not** *come* **against you this day, but against the house with which I have war; for God commanded me to make haste. Refrain** *from meddling with* **God, who** *is* **with me, lest He destroy you."** Here is a case where God spoke to a pagan leader to facilitate His purposes. Of course, God can talk to anyone He chooses, but we often think He would only communicate with believers. There are also other situations where God spoke to pagan leaders and others (36:22: see Genesis 20:6; 41:25; Daniel 2;28).

2 Chronicles 36:14 Moreover all the leaders of the priests and the people transgressed more and more, *according* **to all the abominations of the nations, and defiled the house of the Lord which He had consecrated in Jerusalem.** The abominations spoken of here appear to be primarily idolatry and the perverse actions that typically accompany idolatry. The concept of being separate from this practice is woven into scripture. The Israelites were set apart from these corrupt and perverse practices (Exodus 23:24; Leviticus 26:1; Deuteronomy 4:15-20, etcetera).

15

Ezra

[15]**EZRA** - God's Faithfulness to His People

Ezra 1:5 Then the heads of the fathers' *houses* **of Judah and Benjamin, and the priests and the Levites, with all whose spirits God had moved, arose to go up and build the house of the Lord which** *is* **in Jerusalem.** Note that God moved the spirits of individuals in the Old Testament days. Moved means "to rouse" or "to stir up."

Ezra 2:41 The singers: the sons of Asaph, one hundred and twenty-eight. At this point, there were 128 singers who would be returning to reestablish worship in Jerusalem. At one time in Solomon's temple, there had been as many as four thousand who "praised the Lord with musical instruments" (1 Chronicles 23:5). The singers were Levites who were responsible for praising God with singing, accompanied by instruments (1 Chronicles 15:16). In verse 2:64 of Ezra, there is mention of **two hundred men and women singers.** These were not the temple choir of verse 41. These may have been employed for banquets, feasts, or funerals

---

[15] NSB quotations are from the Nelsons Study Bible, copyright (c) 1997 by Thomas Nelson, Inc., Nashville, TN; used by permission; scripture taken from the New King James Version, Copyright (c) 1979, 1980, 1982 used by permission. All rights reserved.

(see 2 Chronicles 35:25 and Ecclesiastes 2:7, 8).

Ezra 3:11 And they sang responsively, praising and giving thanks to the Lord:
"**For** *He is* **good,**
For His mercy *endures* **forever toward Israel."**
Then all the people shouted with a great shout, when they praised the Lord, because the foundation of the house of the Lord was laid. Here's one of the few examples of how they sang praises and thanksgiving in those days. There were different singers (Nehemiah 12:24, 31), and one group would sing a line, and another would sing in response to what the first group sang. We still see this form in some of the worship music today. Note that all the people **shouted with a great shout when they praised the Lord.** They had great joy in building the temple for the Lord. Some of the older men who had been around when the first temple was still in existence were crying with emotion at the thought of a new temple being built. Some were weeping, and others were shouting with joy, and all of this noise could be heard from far away. It was the second temple that they were building. Note that the age at which the Levites could begin serving in the temple decreased as time went on. At first, it was 30, then 25, and finally, it was lowered by David to 20 (1 Chronicles 23:24, 27).

Ezra 5:12 But because our fathers provoked the God of heaven to wrath, He gave them into the hand of Nebuchadnezzar king of Babylon, the Chaldean, *who* **destroyed this temple and carried the people away to Babylon.** The Lord used a pagan king to punish Israel for turning away from and disobeying Him. This is not the only time where God uses unbelievers to punish and discipline His people. Ultimately, it was not the power of Nebuchadnezzar that allowed him to overtake Israel and destroy the first temple; it was the sin of the Israelites that led to their defeat which God implemented through using Nebuchadnezzar and the forces at his command.

Ezra 6:21 Then the children of Israel who had returned from the captivity ate together with all who had separated themselves from the filth of the nations of the land in order to seek the Lord God of Israel. There were times past when God's people had to separate themselves from the filth around them. The filth referred to here is probably some form of idolatry. It is no different today. In our culture of freedom, almost every depravity is available in some form or another. The only way to keep this filth from having an idolatrous effect on our lives is to separate ourselves from it.

Be careful where you go and what you view on the various options that are instantly available. Some of these things can quickly become addictive (addictive is one of our new terms for something that becomes an idol for us). We still have to separate ourselves both in mind and body from the filth that is all around us so that we can seek the Lord God. As we live in this corrupt world, we can take comfort that we can still have the Holy Spirit's help in this pursuit. It is a daily, hourly, minute-by-minute battle that goes on, not only with those struggling with a significant issue but also within those who may appear to have it all together but are battling on a different level to achieve higher levels of sanctification.

Ezra 7:10 For Ezra had prepared his heart to seek the Law of the Lord, and to do *it*, and to teach statutes and ordinances in Israel. Here it appears that "**his heart**" is referring to his whole being. Ezra studied the Word of God and was a scribe. Thus, he worked on knowing the scriptures and living by them. In return, the gracious hand of the Lord his God was upon him (v.9). It is a good thing to have the gracious hand of the Lord upon you. Ezra is a model for us. If we want to have the hand of the Lord our God upon us, we can do what Ezra did; study the scriptures, follow them and teach others to do the same. If we do this, perhaps that gracious hand of the Lord our God will be on us.

Ezra 7:15 ...and *whereas you are* to carry the silver and gold which

the king and his counselors have freely offered to the God of Israel, whose dwelling *is* in Jerusalem; 16 and *whereas* all the silver and gold that you may find in all the province of Babylon, along with the freewill offering of the people and the priests, *are to be* freely offered for the house of their God in Jerusalem. It appears that God accepts gifts from people who do not know him and gifts from people who know him. However, He does not accept gifts from people who act as if they know Him but whose hearts are far from Him (Isaiah 1:10-15).

Ezra 8:21 Then I proclaimed a fast there at the river of Ahava, that we might humble ourselves before our God, to seek from Him the right way for us and our little ones and all our possessions. Here Ezra proclaimed a fast so that the people could experience submitting to God in humility. He wanted the people to seek the right way for themselves and their children. He also wanted them to consider using their possessions in the right way. In other words, he wanted them to use their possessions in a way that honored God.

Ezra 9:5 At the evening sacrifice I arose from my fasting; and having torn my garment and my robe, I fell on my knees and spread out my hands to the Lord my God. There are various physical postures of humility mentioned in the scriptures. In this instance, Ezra got on his knees. This appears to be a posture of humble respect. Then he spread out his hands, which appears to be a sign of openness to God. Tearing his garment and robe appear to be signifying his grief over the sins of his people. His people incurred the wrath of God in the past and present. Ezra was confessing these sins to God and probably asking for His mercy.

Ezra 10:3 Now therefore, let us make a covenant with our God to put away all these wives and those who have been born to them, according to the advice of my master and of those who tremble at the commandment of our God; and let it be done according to the law. Many of the people had taken pagan wives and this was considered an abomination at that time because it would mix the holy seed with the people of those lands. This was prohibited by the law of Moses (Exodus 34:16; Deuteronomy 18:9-12). They had specific instructions to keep separate from those who practiced abominations which filled the land with impurity. So most of them separated themselves from these people and put away their pagan wives and the children if they had any. This drastic measure was apparently required based on the unlawful unions that had occurred. Sometimes the consequences of sin have a negative impact far beyond the people who perpetrate the corruption.

16

Nehemiah

[16]**NEHEMIAH** - Godly Leadership in Times of Trial

Nehemiah 1:4 So it was, when I heard these words, that I sat down and wept, and mourned *for many* days; I was fasting and praying before the God of heaven. Nehemiah was very sorrowful that the wall of Jerusalem was broken down. In those days, a city without walls was very vulnerable, and it might have been tempting for enemies to try to come in and rob the treasury in the temple. Nehemiah then prayed and confessed the sins of the Lord's people and his sins. Because of the sins of the people, the Lord had scattered them among the nations. Nevertheless, He left the door open for them to come back to the place He chose for them if they would return to the Lord and keep His commandments and do them.

Nehemiah 2:4 Then the king said to me, "What do you request?"
So I prayed to the God of heaven. 5 And I said to the king, "If it pleases the king, and if your servant has found favor in your sight,

---

[16] NSB quotations are from the Nelsons Study Bible, copyright (c) 1997 by Thomas Nelson, Inc., Nashville, TN; used by permission; scripture taken from the New King James Version, Copyright (c) 1979, 1980, 1982 used by permission. All rights reserved.

I ask that you send me to Judah, to the city of my fathers' tombs, that I may rebuild it." Note that Nehemiah first considered what might be important to the King before making his request. He then addressed the King with the proper respect and appealed to what might get the King's attention since the burial place of one's ancestors may have been significant in his culture. Note also that he prayed (apparently silently) before making his request of the King. In his mind, he may have said something like: **"Lord please give me the right words to say to the King."** It must have been a short prayer because he would not have wanted to keep the King waiting.

Nehemiah 2:19 But when Sanballat the Horonite, Tobiah the Ammonite official, and Geshem the Arab heard *of it,* **they laughed at us and despised us, and said, "What** *is* **this thing that you are doing? Will you rebel against the king?"** Here's something to remember: there will be mockers when you are doing work for the Lord. Nehemiah just told them that God would prosper this work because he knew he was following God's directions. They accused Nehemiah of false motives and rebellion. Nehemiah corrected them and informed them that he and the others building the wall were servants of the God of heaven. Of course, the accusations against him were false. Nehemiah also basically told his accusers that they had no business in Jerusalem. It is instructive to know that there are times when it is appropriate to put scoffers in their place and not let them hinder the work that the Lord has laid on your heart to do regardless of the accusations or threats from unbelievers.

Nehemiah 4:4 Hear, O our God, for we are despised; turn their reproach on their own heads, and give them as plunder to a land of captivity! Nehemiah faced those who despised what he was doing by praying that they would reap what they were sowing. Later, when these same angry people conspired to attack him, he set a watch against them day and night but kept building the wall. He didn't even let the threat of physical harm deter him from what he knew was the Lord's will for his life. He seemed to believe that an assault on people who were doing the work of God was an assault on God. He also encouraged the workers not to be afraid even though their enemies were spreading rumors that they would not know when they would be killed to stop the work on the wall. Nehemiah prayed and took action to have the workers armed to protect themselves. Nehemiah gave serious thought to each issue and then took the appropriate measures. When they made accusations against him, he denied them and refused to get distracted from his primary goal when his enemies offered to meet and talk things over. When he was directly threatened, he refused to go hide in the temple. He kept up the work.

Nehemiah 6:3 So I sent messengers to them, saying, "I *am* doing a great work, so that I cannot come down. Why should the work cease while I leave it and go down to you?" Nehemiah would not allow himself to be sidetracked by these enemies. We need to keep Nehemiah's actions in mind when we face opposition to what we know we should be doing. It is easy to get distracted in this world. Of course, there are times when the enemy will attack, and nothing can be done but battle. That is why Nehemiah had his workers armed. They were ready if the enemy brought the fight to them, but they were not going out of their way and stopping their essential work to go to the enemy's table to sit around and talk about their disagreements about the work they were involved in completing.

Note that although what Nehemiah told his enemies was true, it was not the whole story. He didn't tell them that they were dirty, no-good scoundrels for trying to get him to quit building the wall. They sent the same type of message four different times, and each time Nehemiah patiently answered them the same way. Then when they sent a letter saying that the rumors were that he was trying to be their king and rebel, Nehemiah sent word to them as follows: **"No such things as you say are being done, but you invent them in your own heart."** Nehemiah then perceived that they were trying to get him to sin and prayed that the Lord would remember them according to their works.

Nehemiah 7:66 Altogether the whole assembly *was* forty-two thousand three hundred and sixty, 67 besides their male and female servants, of whom *there were* seven thousand three hundred and thirty-seven; and they had two hundred and forty-five men and women singers. This scripture lists the people who came back to Judah from Persia in 536 B.C. under Zerubbabel's first return from captivity. Often in scripture, it is assumed that men and women are included in group gatherings though women are not explicitly mentioned. Here it is clear that men and women took part in singing worship to the Lord.

Nehemiah 8:8 So they read distinctly from the book, in the Law of God; and they gave the sense, and helped *them* to understand the reading. This is an example of the good teaching of the Word of God. The teacher provides a sense of meaning to help the people understand what is read to them. Thus, the people understood the meaning of the Law of God. Nehemiah also told them the well-known words: "**Do not sorrow, for the joy of the Lord is your strength**" (vs. 10). The people began to **rejoice greatly, because they understood the words that were declared to them** (vs. 12). There is gladness when we are in communion with God. This joy comes from our relationship with God. This joy seems to be a byproduct of having a goal to know the Lord. It is His joy experienced by us.

Nehemiah 9:2 Then those of Israelite lineage separated themselves from all foreigners; and they stood and confessed their sins and the iniquities of their fathers. When we understand what God does on our behalf, as the Israelites did here, it leads to confession of sins, worship, joy, and a deeper desire for more of the Word of God. The whole congregation responded by spending one-quarter of the day listening to the Book of the Law of the Lord being read and one-quarter of the day confessing and worshiping. The first verse of the Levites Psalm they used in part of their worship was: "**Stand up and bless the Lord your God Forever and ever!**" This psalm is about God's saving works and has four parts: (a) glorification of God, (b) statement of God's faithfulness, (c) God's righteousness and (d) confession. The psalm contains the phrase: "**you delivered them according to your mercies.**" This is an Old Testament statement that agrees with Ephesians 2:8, 9 that salvation has always been by grace through faith. The law did not save people in the Old Testament days. It was, as it is today, a guide to let us know what behavior pleases the Lord and to let us know where we fall, but only God's grace can save us (Ephesians 2:8-9).

Nehemiah 9:37 And it yields much increase to the kings
   You have set over us,
   Because of our sins;
   Also they have dominion over our bodies and our cattle
   At their pleasure;
   And we *are* in great distress. This is a section from the Levites' Psalm. In this poem, as with most poetry, there are uses of different methods of communicating concepts. These include hyperbole, metaphor, and irony. However, this particular passage is relatively easy to understand. It explains that God allows us to have certain kings (presidents in modern America), "**Because of our sins.**" We tend to forget that God is in control even when we select our ruler through our voting. No, it's more like God allows us to vote in the leader that we, as a nation, deserve. We are called to be servants of God, but we can wind up being servants of the people in our government that we chose. Thus, we have no one to blame but ourselves.

Nehemiah 10:35 And *we made ordinances* to bring the firstfruits of our ground and the firstfruits of all fruit of all trees, year by year, to the house of the Lord; It is important to keep in mind who made the land in the first place and gave it to the people. The Lord ultimately owns the ground producing all of the fruit, and will eventually take it away. We are just on earth for a short time as temporary stewards of His land.

Nehemiah 11:1 Now the leaders of the people dwelt at Jerusalem; the rest of the people cast lots to bring one out of ten to dwell in Jerusalem, the holy city, and nine-tenth *were to dwell* in *other* cities. In this case, it appears that Nehemiah cast lots to determine which of the people would repopulate Jerusalem. It seems that he was trying to discern the will of the Lord in this way. Proverbs 16:33 says: "The lot is cast into the lap, but its every decision is from the Lord." This seems to imply that the decision of the lot is from the Lord. Globally, this must be true. I'm not sure the concept holds for each decision.

There are other ways in scripture used to determine the will of the Lord. How about seeing what the scripture says about specific actions. For example, scripture says that a child who treats his mother or father with contempt is cursed (Deuteronomy 7:16). Regardless of what any lot might say, we can assume that the Lord does not like to see an offspring hold his mother or father in contempt. In other words, if an action goes against what the Lord tells us to do in scripture, it is probably not His will that we do it. If we know that a path is contrary to the ordinances and statutes of the Lord, casting lots is not going to make it in line with the will of the Lord in an individual's life.

Nehemiah 11:22 Also the overseer of the Levites at Jerusalem *was* Uzzi the son of Bani, the son of Hashabiah, the son of Mattaniah, the son of Micha, of the sons of Asaph, the singers in charge of the service of the house of God. This scripture makes it plain that the singers were in charge of the service in the temple. They also helped celebrate the wall's dedication with thanksgiving and singing (12:27) along with the use of cymbals, stringed instruments, and harps. In chapter 12, we learn that they also used trumpets in the worship and thanksgiving in the temple with two choirs; **group alternating with group** (12:24).

The scripture says that they **sang loudly with Jezrahiah as the director**. It wasn't only the men and choirs rejoicing, **the women and children also rejoiced so that the joy of Jerusalem was heard afar off** (43).

Nehemiah 13:10 I also realized that the portions for the Levites had not been given *them;* **for each of the Levites and the singers who did the work had gone back to his field.** At this point, Nehemiah was not happy that the people who were in charge had let Tobiah have a room in the courts of the house of God and that they had quit giving tithes to support the Levites and singers, and they had to go back to work in the fields. He got this straightened out and appointed treasurers to make sure this work was carried out faithfully.

Nehemiah 13:25 So I contended with them and cursed them, struck some of them and pulled out their hair, and made them swear by God, *saying,* **"You shall not give your daughters as wives to their sons, nor take their daughters for your sons or yourselves.** Nehemiah got very aggressive concerning this issue. He pointed out that pagan women caused even Solomon to sin. He cleansed them from all this pagan influence and assigned duties to keep this from happening again.

Nehemiah 13:31 Remember me, O my God, for good! These are Nehemiah's last recorded words and the last words in this book. These words would be a good prayer for any of us to pray.

17

Esther

[17]**ESTHER** - God's Protection of His People - The Book That Does Not Directly Mention God

Esther 6:1 That night the king could not sleep. So one was commanded to bring the book of the records of the chronicles; and they were read before the king. First, it is interesting that the king decided to have Chronicles read to him when he couldn't sleep. A good thing for any of us to do late at night when we can't sleep would be to read scripture. Perhaps reaffirming the knowledge that God is ultimately in control of what happens on earth would calm a person so that they could go back to sleep. Note that God led the king to specific scriptures that would influence his thinking in this instance. This reading put Mordecai in good standing and reputation with the king, which led to the king's retraction of his letter directing that the Jews be annihilated in all the king's provinces.

Esther 8:17 And in every province and city, wherever the king's

---

[17] NSB quotations are from the Nelsons Study Bible, copyright (c) 1997 by Thomas Nelson, Inc., Nashville, TN; used by permission; scripture taken from the New King James Version, Copyright (c) 1979, 1980, 1982 used by permission. All rights reserved.

command and decree came, the Jews had joy and gladness, a feast and a holiday. Then many of the people of the land became Jews, because fear of the Jews fell upon them. Esther had just convinced the King to revoke Haman's letters, which directed the destruction of the Jews in all the King Ahasuerus' 127 provinces from India to Ethiopia. Haman wound up hanged on the gallows because he tried to lay hands on the Jews. Jews were in all the cities. Mordecai was allowed to send letters, sealed with the king's ring, that permitted Jews to gather together on a specific day. They were allowed to protect their lives and to destroy, kill, and annihilate all the forces of any people or province that would assault them. On that day, the enemies of the Jews had hoped to overpower them, but the opposite occurred. Helped by all those doing the king's work, the Jews overcame those who hated them. In a couple of days, the Jews and those who helped them killed 800 men who were their enemies in Shushan. In the other provinces, the Jews killed seventy-five thousand of their enemies. The Jews celebrate these days of deliverance in the festival of Purim. Though these numbers were significant for the time, they are small compared to the numbers that resulted when a modern Haman (Hitler) tried to annihilate the Jews. In WWII, worldwide about 60,000,000 people lost their lives and over five and a half million were Germans; the ones who started the hostilities.

18

Job

[18]**JOB** - Submission and Faith is Our Proper Response - God is not obligated to bless the obedient; He is sovereign.

Job 1:8 Then the Lord said to Satan, "Have you considered My servant Job, that *there is* none like him on the earth, a blameless and upright man, one who fears God and shuns evil?" It appears here that Satan's final banishment from heaven had not yet occurred. The term "Satan" may have been more of a title than a name. Job is referred to as a servant. That is what we should all be for our creator. Our relationship with God should always be one of being a servant. Job seemed to take this role willingly and joyfully and without ulterior motives. Satan takes his usual role as the adversary in this story. Satan demeaned God and addressed Him directly, but Satan is still just a minor player in comparison. Satan asserted that Job would curse God if his prosperity and possessions were removed. Note that God limits Satan's power and that people may not always be the primary focus in the universe as we often like to think of ourselves as being.

---

[18] NSB quotations are from the Nelsons Study Bible, copyright (c) 1997 by Thomas Nelson, Inc., Nashville, TN; used by permission; scripture taken from the New King James Version, Copyright (c) 1979, 1980, 1982 used by permission. All rights reserved.

Job 1:21 And he said:
  "Naked I came from my mother's womb,
  And naked shall I return there.
  The Lord gave, and the Lord has taken away;
  Blessed be the name of the Lord." Here is the proper attitude toward God no matter what we have lost on earth. Job had just lost his sheep and servants who cared for them. His camels had been stolen, and the servants who looked after them killed. A hurricane killed his sons and daughters. What did Job do in response while he was mourning with a torn robe and shaved head? He forced himself to worship God with these words. Apparently, he was not serving God for the profit of all the blessings in his life as Satan had alleged. He didn't appear to blame God for his calamities. He mourned greatly, but he still recognized that God is sovereign. He accepted what had happened to him and **fell to the ground and worshiped**.

From our own experiences, we all know that this had to be a deliberate act of humility on Job's part. Once he humbled himself, he told it like it is. The truth was that he came into this life naked with nothing and would leave taking nothing. Then he repeatedly acknowledges that God is in control of his circumstances. He accepts that premise no matter what his circumstances are. Later, Job notes that when we accept good from God **shall we not accept adversity** (vs. 2:10)? God even affirmed that Job had maintained his integrity in this situation (vs. 1:3). He did not sin against God by what he said. God allowed Satan to test Job severely, but God restored Job and delivered him from his suffering in His time.

Job 3:3 "May the day perish on which I was born,
  And the night *in which* it was said,
  'A male child is conceived.' It got so bad for Job that he wished that he had never been born or died at birth due to the terrible sorrow he was experiencing. Here, in his suffering, Job did not understand the meaning of life as outlined in Ephesians 1:3-14. The book of Ephesians was not

written. Thus, Job was at a disadvantage in comparison to those of us living in these times. The mystery is revealed **that the Gentiles should be fellow heirs, of the same body, and partakers of His promise in Christ through the gospel** (Eph. 3:6). Our purpose is not just to be happy, but **to know the love of Christ which passes knowledge; that you may be filled with all the fullness of God** (Eph. 3:19). Ecclesiastes 12:13-14 puts it this way: "**Here is the conclusion of the matter: Fear God and keep his commandments, for this is the whole duty of man...**"

We do not appear to be the center of the universe nor the reason the universe was created. In our pride, we like to think of ourselves that way, but the earth is not the center of the universe, and neither are we. Nevertheless, we are important to God. Some of Job's friends concluded that because Job was suffering, he must have sinned. But you cannot always determine the cause by looking at an outcome. Though God may allow us to suffer or discipline us at times, that was not the case here.

We need to be careful not to condemn a person who is suffering, but instead, we should make allowances for the reactions to their pain (6:24-26). In the end, God commended Job for speaking what was right. Later in this book, Zophar interrogates Job and uses some sound doctrine in the process but appears to apply this doctrine without love which is against what the Lord directs us to do in 1 Corinthians 13. Job wishes that Zophar would have just remained silent rather than criticize and interrogate him (13:5).

Job 14:5 Since his days *are* determined,
  The number of his months *is* with You;
  You have appointed his limits, so that he cannot pass. God has set either the general global lifespan of men or the specific time of each man. Psalm 90:10-14 says:
  The days of our lives *are* seventy years;

And if by reason of strength *they are* **eighty years,**
Yet their boast *is* **only labor and sorrow;**

For it is soon cut off, and we fly away. Thus, this passage of scripture notes that God has set a general lifespan of 70 years, but some strong individuals may surpass this general limit. In modern days, a few people have lived over 120 years, but no one has lived much beyond that. The oldest was Jeanne Calment of France, who lived 122 years and 164 days. She died in 1997. Note that this scripture does not set a limit, just a general number. Thus, there is a general limit, but there may also be a specific time set for each individual, and some scriptures seem to indicate that this is also true (Job 14:5). However long an individual lives, in the overall scheme of the universe, it is very minute. As the scripture says about man: **He comes forth like a flower and fades away**. Our lifespan is described as a vapor (Psalm 39:5, 11; James 4:14). Thus, whatever our lifespan is on earth, in comparison to eternity, it is very, very short.

Job 16:21 Oh, that one might plead for a man with God,

As a man *pleads* **for his neighbor!** Here is a scripture that anticipates the work of Christ as our Intercessor (Hebrews 7:25) and Advocate (1 John 2:1). Note that Job's friends had some things to say that were theologically sound in the general sense. Still, when they applied these general principles to Job's specific situation, they went beyond their capacity to assess the bigger picture of the things that go on in heaven that can affect what happens on earth. One problem with their application of general principles was their lack of knowledge of the timing by which these principles would apply. The righteous can indeed expect God's blessing at some point (Deuteronomy 28), but to presume that one of us human beings knows when that will be is very presumptuous of us. Conversely, the wicked can expect to be punished, but we don't know when that punishment or curse will come either. We know that human suffering is not always a sign of God's judgment (John 9:3), and success here on earth is not always a sign of God's blessing.

God causes the wheat and chaff to grow together under the blessings of sunshine until the harvest (Matthew 3:12). We live in a fallen world. Often the innocent and the wicked suffer together in this world when the floods come. However, we can take comfort in the fact that God is still working, and His grace and justice will prevail in the end. In His time, He will reward the righteous and punish the wicked.

Job 19:25 For I know *that* my Redeemer lives,

And He shall stand at last on the earth; This powerful statement is the hope that we need to hang on even in the face of tremendous suffering and pain. Our Redeemer does live. Without this hope, there doesn't appear to be any good purpose for our existence. Other gurus claim to know something about life, but no others made the kind of claims Christ makes about Himself and then fulfilled those claims. Then He went on to fulfill the claims he made through dying on a cross and rising from the dead in three days.

C.S. Lewis has noted that Christ left no middle ground for interpretation. Based on what Christ said, He was either (a) whom He said he was (i.e., God incarnate), (b) mentally ill and having delusions of grandeur, or (c) a liar who had a fantastic ability to tell the future. Whom we decide that He is can impact our eternal destiny. This is the preeminent question of life. It is the question that Christ asked Peter (Mark 8:29). It is the question of the ages. We have to have an accurate perception of who He is before we can appropriately follow Him.

It doesn't matter who we think anyone else on earth is as long as we get this one right because Jesus Christ is our Redeemer and, according to the Bible, without Him, we are lost and utterly without any real hope. We are just floating in the vast material universe on this little speck of matter we call earth. But thankfully, we do have a redeemer, and we have hope, and we can have eternal life with our God.

Job 20:15 He swallows down riches
   And vomits them up again;
   God casts them out of his belly. I couldn't help but think of a person addicted to drugs or alcohol when reading this verse. Though the taste or feeling is sweet when first taken, over time, the experience turns sour. The addicted person can wind up vomiting, sick, and poor with terrors coming upon them. However, though this description may have been accurate for someone practicing this type of evil and oppressing others or forsaking the poor, Job did not fit this description. Therefore, these words do not explain Job's situation.

In Job's response to this criticism, he notes that the wicked deny God's existence so they can live in their houses without fear. Thus, there are loopholes in the retribution dogma. Suffering does not always indicate God's punishment of a person here on earth. Not to worry, God is still in control and will administer justice in the end (see Romans 8:28).

It may not be in our preferred timing, but all things will work out in God's timing, and we may have to suffer some in the interim period. It is essential to know that the righteous are not always blessed, and the wicked are not always punished here on earth in this fallen world. Job knew that he was being tested and that God knew what He was doing. Even after all he had been through, Job had the hope that he would "**come forth as gold**' after being tested. Job's attitude, which could be part of the message of this whole book, was that no matter what happens, people should still trust in God. Job knew that it was only through the breath of God that he was alive and said that as long as the breath was in him, he would not speak wickedness.

Job 25:13 "There are those who rebel against the light;
   They do not know its ways
   Nor abide in its paths. The scripture talks about the adulterer and thieves after this scripture. These are the type of people who don't like

the light shined on their activities.

Job 26:13 By His Spirit He adorned the heavens;
   His hand pierced the fleeing serpent.
   14 Indeed these *are* **the mere edges of His ways,**
   And how small a whisper we hear of Him!
   But the thunder of His power who can understand?" When you realize that some of the stars we can see from the earth are trillions of miles away, it is hard to comprehend that the universe we live in is just **the mere edges of God's ways**. We can't even understand our universe, which appears to be infinite to us. Thus, there is no way we are going to totally comprehend God. We hear just a small whisper but we know that, in comparison to what we hear, His power is like thunder. On earth, we can only stand the thunder if we are far from it. If we listened to the thunder of God, its power would surely destroy us. For this reason and others, the message of the Book of Job is that no matter what happens, we should trust God (40:8; 42:1-6). That message is also in many other scriptures throughout many books of the Bible.

Job 28:28 And to man He said,
   'Behold, the fear of the Lord, that *is* **wisdom,**
   And to depart from evil *is* **understanding.'"** It may be that Solomon gained some of his wisdom from reading this scripture. Solomon concluded the book of Ecclesiastes with the words: **"Fear God and keep His commandments, For this is man's all."** Solomon appeared to be reaffirming these concepts. We need to fear/respect the Lord by keeping His commandments. When we do this, we will be departing from evil.

Job 31:1 "I have made a covenant with my eyes;
   Why then should I look upon a young woman? Job knew that the eyes were where temptation could begin. So he made a deal with himself not to let his eyes even begin the process that could lead to sin. Several

scriptures speak of the eye and how it can cause you to sin (Mark 9:47 etc.). The eye is the lamp of the body (Luke 22:34). When it is good, the whole body is good, and the reverse is true when bad.

Job 31:9 "If my heart has been enticed by a woman,
　Or *if* I have lurked at my neighbor's door,
　10 *Then* let my wife grind for another,
　And let others bow down over her.
　11 For that *would be* wickedness;
　Yes, it *would be* iniquity *deserving of* judgment. This verse continues the theme started in verse one. Job notes that if his eye and heart should stray, then the same type of betrayal should happen to him. Often this is what eventually does happen in cases of adultery. Job is correct that this would be a sin worthy of judgment, but he is pointing out that he is not guilty of this sin and therefore is not worthy of judgment for adultery.

Job 32:2 Then the wrath of Elihu, the son of Barachel the Buzite, of the family of Ram, was aroused against Job; his wrath was aroused because he justified himself rather than God. Elihu did have the perception to know that Job had been elevating himself in some of the discourse as if he were equal to God. God is not under any obligation to any man for anything. For Job to talk to God as if he wanted to be in court with God was improper. The point is made later that everything under heaven is God's (41:11). Therefore, he can do anything He wants with what He owns.

Job 34:14 If He should set His heart on it,
　***If* He should gather to Himself His Spirit and His breath,**
　15 All flesh would perish together,
　And man would return to dust. This is a reality that we sometimes forget. We are not on equal footing with God. We should not even think in such a way as to diminish God's stature by acting as if we are equals in some way. If God decides to remove His spirit from us, we would

perish instantly and be just dust. Thus, the proper attitude toward God is always reverence, respect, and praise.

As verse 36:24 says, we should: "**Remember to magnify His work.**" We are to obey Him. It appears that He even provides winter for three specific reasons. One, for correction. In other words, sometimes winter provides storms that are a form of judgment for sins. The winter also provides the blessing of water nourishing the land as it is stored up in lakes and the ground. Three, the winter offers mercy for us based on His loyal love. We can stop our work for a while in the winter and recognize His mighty works and learn from Him. He truly is great, and we are not. Sometimes, He allows us to suffer or have nightmares to get our attention so that we can turn toward Him and begin to seek a meaningful life in His will. In other words, God does not owe us; we owe Him. What do we owe Him? Everything.

Job 38:4 "Where were you when I laid the foundations of the earth?
Tell *Me*, if you have understanding.
5 Who determined its measurements?
Surely you know!
Or who stretched the line upon it? Here's a couple of good questions for anyone who would dare to question God. There is a reason that we should be His servants. That is what He made us to be. God sometimes has to overwhelm us into submission to Him, which is our proper and correct role. We are His servants. When we fail to realize this fact, we go astray.

Job 40:8 "Would you indeed annul My judgment?
Would you condemn Me that you may be justified? Here God puts Job in his place. This is an area where Job was in error. Job had questioned how God ran the universe and implied that there wasn't social, moral order in it (24:1-17). This is not true, and Job has no position to impose his ideas of what is right and what should be done differently

on God. Suffering in this world is not always retribution for sin, just as Job's suffering was not the direct result of his sin. We are to be content wherever God places us (Phil. 4:10-12). That is sometimes very difficult to do, but that does seem to be what we should do.

Job 40:15 "Look now at the behemoth, which I made *along* with you; He eats grass like an ox. We are not sure exactly what animal the behemoth is, but as the description goes on, it seems to transcend any beast we now see on earth and could be a mythical monster representing chaos. One part of the description talks about the behemoth as being "**the first of the ways of God**" (v. 19). That sounds like it could be a dinosaur. Regardless, the point is that Job couldn't even approach a beast that God created, so he should not think himself qualified even to present his case to God. In other words, we are not in a position to question the creator of the universe regardless of our circumstances. We need to always keep in mind that God is rightly in control of happenings here on the earth He created and with the creatures He created, including man. We would not want to provoke a beast like a behemoth, nor would we want to provoke God.

Job 41:11 Who has preceded Me, that I should pay *him*? Everything under heaven is Mine. The reality is that no one or anything preceded God. He, therefore, owes nothing to anyone. Not only that, He owns everything and everyone that he created. God doesn't owe us anything for being righteous or any other way. He is not obligated to reward or punish. Job had implied that God owed him something in 34:5-8 for his righteousness. God corrected this misconception and put Job back in his place of being dependent on God for everything, even the breath that gave him life. God is the owner of everything that was taken from Job. God does not have to reward us for what we consider good works. Salvation is through the grace of God (Ephesians 2:8-10). Our salvation is not dependent on our works. It is apart from our works. When Job heard God's perspective, he repented and was restored to a right relationship with God.

**Job 42:5 "I have heard of You by the hearing of the ear,
But now my eye sees You.
6 Therefore I abhor** *myself,*
And repent in dust and ashes." In these verses, Job gets back the correct view of God. He repents of his words and accusations, he submits to the will of the Lord and his relationship is restored. He realizes he is in no position to accuse the Lord, or to expect anything from him. In essence, Job humbled himself before the Lord.

Job 42:7 And so it was, after the Lord had spoken these words to Job, that the Lord said to Eliphaz the Temanite, "My wrath is aroused against you and your two friends, for you have not spoken of Me *what is* **right, as My servant Job** *has.* Job had recanted his false statements about God and repented. Apparently, at this point, his friends had not done so. After Job repented, the Lord blessed him, and all that he lost was restored to him, and after he prayed for his friends, Job had all that was taken from him restored twofold. He lived one hundred and forty years and **saw his children and grandchildren for four generations**.

19

Psalms

[19]**PSALMS** (the deep passions of each individual's response to God in sometimes emotional, exaggerated, poetic, or figurative speech) - There are Psalms emphasizing that God is the King, Psalms focusing on Jerusalem, Psalms of confession, Psalms providing wisdom, Psalms asking God to deal with the wicked, Psalms expressing joy and Psalms expressing praise of God. In general, the Psalms appear to be for singing and public worship in the temple. They were written over thousands of years. They were in poetic language that uses many of the common emotional expressions of this type of prose, like dramatic exaggeration and figurative speech. Each Psalm appears to be based on an individual's response to a specific situation. Thus, there are many individual expressions represented in the Psalms. Taken together, the Psalms are the longest book of the Bible in the modern division into 66 books.

Psalms 1:2 But his delight *is* in the law of the LORD
And in His law he meditates day and night.

---

[19] NSB quotations are from the Nelsons Study Bible, copyright (c) 1997 by Thomas Nelson, Inc., Nashville, TN; used by permission; scripture taken from the New King James Version, Copyright (c) 1979, 1980, 1982 used by permission. All rights reserved.

**3 He shall be like a tree
Planted by the rivers of water,
That brings forth its fruit in its season,
Whose leaf also shall not wither
And whatever he does shall prosper.** This psalm speaks of the righteous person and what usually happens with them. People trust the person who has a reputation for dealing honestly with others. Thus in business, they may prosper. The story of Job shows us that this is not a guaranteed formula in the short run but is a general principle that will usually prove true over time.

However, this probably isn't the main point of these verses. When the word "prospers" is used, we need to ask whether this refers to prospering in the material or the spiritual. These are two different ways to prosper. If it means in the spiritual sense, which is what I think is the primary focus, it would mean that the person would be more productive and valuable to the Lord. This is something to ponder.

What is more important, that we are materially prosperous or that we are spiritually prosperous? There are two ways to go. Jesus said: "I am the way" (John 14:6). Did He mean that He was the way to material prosperity? Based on the Bible, I don't think so. He is the way to eternal life and spiritual prosperity (John 3:16; Matthew 25:46; John 11:25-26). Thus, it seems that, even though material prosperity can be a byproduct of following the law of the Lord, this Psalm is probably best interpreted to be speaking of the spiritual prosperity that comes from following the Lord.

**Psalms 2:2 Why do the nations rage,
And the people plot a vain thing?** Throughout history, sooner or later, many nations have turned against the God of the Bible. At the cross, this rage came out in dramatic action. Some people in power here on earth do not want to answer to anyone, including God. It's the same old

story that gets repeated century after century; man wants to take the place of God and do his own thing. Of course, this will never happen because, in the end, a man is just a man whether he wants to admit it or not. At the cross, the people's wrath was directed against Christ and to those who followed Christ. The Lord will hold them in **derision**, **wrath**, and **deep displeasure** (Psalm 2:4-5; 2 Chronicles 19:2). That will not be a good time for those who plotted against the Lord and His anointed. At that time, those who have put their trust in the Lord will be blessed (v. 2:12).

Psalms 3:5 I lay down and slept;
 I awoke, for the Lord sustained me.
 6 I will not be afraid of ten thousands of people
 Who have set *themselves* against me all around. As we go to sleep each night, the Lord will sustain us both here on earth and afterward, so there is no need to fret about people who may be against us, even if it is ten thousand people. The Lord made all those people, and if He chose to, He could instantly remove the breath of life from them. He holds off on doing so to give them all the chance to turn toward Him (Romans 9:22-24; 2 Peter 3:8). Nevertheless, they have the free will that He gave them to harden their hearts toward Him, in which case, they deserve His judgment.

Psalms 5:3 My voice You shall hear in the morning, O Lord;
 In the morning I will direct *it* to You,
 And I will look up. When should we start looking to the Lord regarding the activities of our day? Early in the morning is the answer. It is easy to get off track as soon as our life responsibilities start to hit us early in the day. Therefore, we need to get up early enough to spend some time in prayer, worship, and study to put ourselves in the right frame of mind to face the difficulties before the day starts. If we do not, life can get overwhelming quickly, and we can lose sight of what we are doing here. What are we doing here? We are getting ready for our eternal

life with the Lord. Why? Because that's the reason He made us. We are for His pleasure. We are to give glory and honor and praise to our maker. Understanding our purpose makes life easier because we are not trying to put a square peg in a round hole anymore. We can do what we were made to do.

Psalms 5:9 For *there is* no faithfulness in their mouth;
   Their inward part *is* destruction;
   Their throat *is* an open tomb;
   They flatter with their tongue. If you listen closely to the speech of an unbeliever, you will often hear some derogatory reference to God. This speech is a reflection of what they believe or do not believe in their heart. Often, they will use profanity and "God" or "Jesus" in anger, and they are angry a lot of the time. When a person rebels against the purpose they were created to fulfill, they can become bitter and angry and easily provoked to outbursts of expressing anger. This anger is often directed at God with what is said. Interestingly, people who profess disbelief in God can use the words "God" and "Jesus" more than believers. However, their use of these words in anger may wind up being an open tomb for them (Psalms 5:9). In other terms, their speech condemns them and reveals their heart (Matthew 12: 36-37; Matthew 15:10-11). Be careful when around these people. Their hearts may be hardened against the Lord.

Psalms 7:1 O Lord my God, in You I put my trust;
   Save me from all those who persecute me;
   And deliver me, This passage echoes a lot of scriptures. The Psalms and the book of Job, especially make the point absolutely clear that: 1. God is good and 2. life can be difficult. There is no escape from these two realities. For now, we live in this world where we make choices every day. We expect that if we make the right choices that we will not suffer, but in a fallen world, that is not always the case. Nevertheless, it is still important to make choices that are in line with God's commandments as we are called to do regardless of the consequences here on earth.

**Psalms 9:1 I will praise *You*, O Lord, with my whole heart;
I will tell of all Your marvelous works.
2 I will be glad and rejoice in You;
I will sing praise to Your name, O Most High.** Note that in Hebrew the first lines begin with consecutive letters in the alphabet forming an acrostic. It is obvious from these first words in this psalm that the psalmist is determined to praise God. Note that he states that he will praise with his whole heart. He does not want to give the Lord, who is the creator of the universe, half-hearted praise and he wants to tell others what the Lord has done. He obviously had faith in the Lord and that He would, in the end, make everything right.

**Psalm 11:5 The Lord tests the righteous,
But the wicked and the one who loves violence His soul hates.** We can expect to be refined and tested while here on earth. This testing is for our good and helps us see what we believe when it comes down to the basics. He allows trials to come into the believer's life, but He will be with us to help us through the trials and become strong in the faith as a result.

**Psalm 11:7 For the Lord *is* righteous,
He loves righteousness;
His countenance beholds the upright.** This is something to keep in mind. **The Lord is righteous**. If we can keep this thought in mind when undergoing troubles, this can help us get through those times and come out with a renewed strength to face the troubles of the world strengthened by the support from the righteous Lord. Through faith and the grace of God, we can learn through these troubles to put on the righteousness of God, which will sustain us until we finish our race here on earth.

**Psalms 12:4 Who have said,
"With our tongue we will prevail;**

Our lips *are* our own;

Who *is* lord over us?" Those who are filled with pride and believe they can be their own god may say "who is lord over us"? And if they think this way, they may say anything they feel like saying. Interestingly, some of them actually use the words "God" and "Jesus Christ" in a negative or blasphemous way more than believers use these names with a positive connotation. It is as if they are trying, in vain, repeatedly to convince themselves that these words and the persons they refer to do not matter. But, no matter how many times a person communicates a concept, if the concept is wrong, it is still wrong. As Shakespeare once wrote in Hamlet: "The lady doth protest too much, methinks."

The alternative for others who think this way is to lace much of their speech with profanity and vulgarities. They don't realize or care that what they say does have an effect on themselves and on others. Their lips are really not their own. Their lips and the rest of their bodies belong to the Lord who made them and gave them the breath of life and is Lord over them. The Lord will give them free rein for a time here so they have an opportunity to come to accept this truth. The Bible says that there will come a time when every knee will bow and every tongue will confess that "Jesus Christ is Lord" (Philippians 2:10-11).

God grants freedom to believe in something or nothing. The Lord allows us to see the truth, but at some point, there will be judgment separating the chaff (unbelievers) from the wheat (believers)(Luke 3:17). I am just the messenger here, but I do not want to soft-peddle what the scripture says and give the reader a false impression of the predicted judgment time.

Psalms 12:5 "For the oppression of the poor, for the sighing of the needy,
   Now I will arise," says the Lord;
   "I will set *him* in the safety for which he yearns."

6 The words of the Lord *are* pure words,
Like silver tried in a furnace of earth,
Purified seven times.
7 You shall keep them, O Lord,
You shall preserve them from this generation forever. Here, the Lord lets us know that those who have been oppressed by those who think they can be their own God will eventually receive the safety they desire and that what the Lord says is righteous. He gives everyone time to repent, not wanting any to perish, but eventually, the Lord will judge the speech of the wicked. Justice will be established. This part of the Psalm also lets us know the importance of the Word of God and how pure these words are. This earth will someday pass away, but the words of the Lord will last forever. God, who is eternal, stands behind these words.

Psalms 13:6 I will sing to the Lord,
Because He has dealt bountifully with me. There are a lot of instances in scripture about singing to the Lord. This is just one of many that gives one of many reasons why we should sing praises to the Lord in public and private settings. Here David resolves to sing before the people in worship, which will be an example to others. This is the essence of praise (see 40:1-3).

Psalms 14:14 The fool has said in his heart,
"*There is* no God."
They are corrupt,
They have done abominable works,
There is none who does good. This refers to the person who is practicing atheism. Atheism is the belief that if there is a God, it doesn't matter. To become "corrupt" is like the process of milk becoming sour. A person who does not believe that God matters can eventually degenerate into doing evil, as they come to think: "why not if I think I can get away with it?"

Psalms 15:1 Lord, who may abide in Your tabernacle?
Who may dwell in Your holy hill?
2 He who walks uprightly,
And works righteousness,
And speaks the truth in his heart;
3 He *who* does not backbite with his tongue,
Nor does evil to his neighbor,
Nor does he take up a reproach against his friend; This Psalm is instructive regarding criteria for being close to God. It is instructive to see that backbiting and saying bad things about a friend are right in there with lying and doing evil to a neighbor. Many people in a Church today, even pastors, can do reasonably well with some of these requirements but struggle with not backbiting or taking up a reproach against a friend if the friend is now viewed as no longer loyal to the friendship. This shows that everyone still needs the forgiveness that only faith in Christ can provide, even those who are viewed as religious leaders. Of course, no one is righteous compared to God (Mark 10:18) but may have a temporary form of righteousness or imputed righteousness from Christ.

Psalms 17:7 Show Your marvelous lovingkindness by Your right hand,
O You who save those who trust *in You*
From those who rise up *against them.*
8 Keep me as the apple of Your eye;
Hide me under the shadow of Your wings,
9 From the wicked who oppress me,
***From* my deadly enemies who surround me.** This psalm demonstrates that there will be enemies of those who trust in God. These enemies will fight against the believer, but God can be our shield and protector. Note that David is referring to God's "marvelous lovingkindness." In the Bible, the word marvelous is only used in relation to God. When we are under the protection of God's love, we find safety, warmth, and shielding from the enemies. In Psalm 18, David makes the

declaration that the Lord is his strength, his fortress, and his deliverer in whom he trusts. In addition, he states that God is worthy to be praised and that God will save him from his enemies. The believer has no reason to fear but still needs to take personal action just as David did when he hid in the mountains for security. God was the stronghold for David just as He can be our stronghold. And, no matter what happens to us on earth, we know that we have eternal life with God so, our time here on earth is just a very brief time of refining in preparation for eternity.

Psalms 18:17 He delivered me from my strong enemy,
From those who hated me,
For they were too strong for me. This verse goes along with Hebrews 13:6. Note that David knew that his enemies were too strong for him, but they were not too strong for the Lord. Even if the Lord decides to allow us to be taken out of this world, we are still in good shape with Him. When the Lord is our helper, we will still have problems on earth, but the result is good. Death has lost its sting for believers (1 Corinthians 15:55).

Psalms 18:40 You have also given me the necks of my enemies,
So that I destroyed those who hated me.
41 They cried out, but *there was* **none to save;**
***Even* to the Lord, but He did not answer them.** Note that David's enemies were even praying for deliverance, but it didn't do them any good because the Lord usually does not answer the prayers of the wicked unless it is a prayer of repentance. He did not answer their prayers, nor did their so-called gods.

Psalms 18:50 Great deliverance He gives to His king,
And shows mercy to His anointed,
To David and his descendants forevermore. Here David refers to himself as "anointed," but in the next line, he references his descendants, one of which is the savior, the true anointed one; Christ.

Psalms 19:19 The heavens declare the glory of God;
   And the firmament shows His handiwork.
   2 Day unto day utters speech,
   And night unto night reveals knowledge.
   3 *There is* no speech nor language
   ***Where* their voice is not heard.** This is the truth for anyone who wants to open their eyes and see it. God made it this way. We can't explain the heavens that reach eternity in any way that makes sense without reference to God, who is beyond our comprehension and finite abilities. He has to be supernatural when one realizes that something cannot come from nothing in the natural physical world. In God's realm, He can bring something into physical existence just by speaking. It makes sense that for there to be the natural, there has to be the supernatural that created it. There will always be those who try to explain the cosmos in other ways, but from the Biblical perspective, they will be as wrong when they finish as when they started. Believers don't have to explain it, the Bible does this for us, and it was inspired by the one who made the cosmos, so He knows how it came into existence. Every human being can experience the creation of God if they are open to doing so no matter what language they speak.

Psalms 21:2 You have given him his heart's desire,
   And have not withheld the request of his lips. *Selah* In general, people do get their desires fulfilled when these desires are in line with the will of God (20:4, 37:4, 145:19). This is how it should be. As the Lord's prayer states: "**Your will be done.**" (Matthew 6:9) He knows what He is doing with the world, and the outcome for the universe may not revolve around "me."

Psalms 22:22 I will declare Your name to My brethren;
   In the midst of the assembly I will praise You.
   23 You who fear the Lord, praise Him!
   All you descendants of Jacob, glorify Him,

And fear Him, all you offspring of Israel! Here David encourages people to praise and fear the Lord. Why should we fear Him? For one, the scripture encourages us to fear the Lord over and over. That is enough reason. Then what is the result? When we fear the Lord, we are more apt to follow his commandments and instruction and learn from the wisdom that He provides in His Word.

Just before this verse in the psalm, David describes how he suffered, and now he turns to how he is still determined to praise the Lord, his Deliverer. We need to keep in mind that Christ suffered for us and that suffering is part of the refining process of life here on earth. We still need to fear and praise the Lord as David did.

The Lord was always near David. He heard him, He answered Him and saved him. David recognized these facts and determined to continue to sing praises to the Lord and encourage people in his time and people born in the future through all time to do the same. In the Psalms, David repeats this theme of singing praises about the Lord and to the Lord.

Where we should praise the Lord is also mentioned. David suggests doing so "in the great assembly" (22:25) as one of the places. Also, David suggests doing so "In the congregations…" (26:12). I believe he is speaking of believers' congregations because just before this scripture, David asks that his soul not be gathered with sinners. Elsewhere, David speaks of singing praise to the Lord as "sacrifices of joy" (27:6). Seeking His face (His presence) seemed to be one of David's greatest desires. We should have a similar desire to keep in the presence of the Lord. He is always with us but will not come in unless we invite Him. Then, we can receive His Spirit. (1 Corinthians 12:13; Romans 8:9)

Psalms 27:14 Wait on the Lord;
  Be of good courage,
  And He shall strengthen your heart;

Wait, I say, on the Lord! One of the primary purposes of the Psalms seems to be to praise God. In doing this, the Psalms (a) use many names for the Lord, (b) use many descriptions for the Lord, and (c) speak of His many attributes. Some of the names are My King (5:2), God of my salvation (18:46), Mighty One (45:3), the Almighty (68:14), Holy One of Israel (71:22), our Maker (95:6), their Savior (106:21) and, God of heaven. Some of the descriptions include a shield for me (3:3), the one who lifts my head (3:3), a just judge (7:11), my strength (18:1), my shepherd (23:1), my hiding place (32:7), my exceeding joy (43:4), a father of the fatherless (68:5) and my high tower (144:2). In addition, the Psalms encourage us to wait on the Lord and to have hope in Him. If we do this in humility and truly recognize who He is, we will realize that His timing is far more important, appropriate, and righteous than our impatient wants.

Psalms 30:4 Sing praise to the Lord, you saints of His,
And give thanks at the remembrance of His holy name. After encouraging all believers to sing praise to the Lord, in the rest of this Psalm, David talks about not being moved from this position of thanksgiving even when we are prosperous. He also talks about how the Lord turned his mourning (sorrow) into dancing (joy). This is an acceptable type of boasting where David boasts that his countenance has been transformed and renewed by God's blessing. In the Old Testament, there were other sacrifices given to atone for sin in addition to the sacrifice of praise. In the New Testament, since Christ paid the ultimate price for sin, the only sacrifice remaining for us to give is the sacrifice of praise which will continue even in heaven (Hebrews 13:15).

Psalms 33:2 Praise the Lord with the harp;
Make melody to Him with an instrument of ten strings.
3 Sing to Him a new song;
Play skillfully with a shout of joy. In the last Psalm (150), everything that has breath is encouraged to praise the Lord. In the Psalms, many instruments are mentioned as having a place in praise to the extent it

appears every instrument was to be used in praising the Lord. In fact, it appears that David invented instruments for the very purpose of use in praise and worship (2 Chronicles 7:6). That makes sense to me. Since God created us for His pleasure (Revelation 4:11), it makes sense that He would give us the ability to make musical instruments that we could use in giving Him pleasure.

Psalm 33:1 suggests that one purpose of praise is for believers to rejoice in God, who has given us new life. This praise is described as "beautiful," as it seems that God enjoys praise from His people. David also says to play "skillfully" and "with a shout of joy," encouraging us not to approach the Lord with a casual attitude but to give the Lord our best effort and to do so joyfully even to the point of shouting for joy. It sounds like a lot of fun when we approach praise and worship as God tells us to.

Note also that this psalm encourages His people to sing new songs. We are not bound by scripture to always sing only old hymns. Many popular hymns composed in the eighteen hundreds have stood the test of time and still have value in worship, but we are encouraged to use at least some new songs. Singing a new song can also mean to sing with a new sense of all that the Lord has done.

Psalms 34:3 Oh, magnify the Lord with me,
And let us exalt His name together. Here, David encourages congregational worship where the group sings the praises of the Lord. One thing that happens when people exalt the name of the Lord together is that the humble hear of it and are glad (vs. 2). Why would the humble be glad? Maybe they like that the ruler over them believes in a higher moral power other than himself. The problem with a ruler who does not believe in God is that they only have themselves and other people decide what is right and wrong. Typically, when a person has this type of power, their lusts and wants corrupt their perception. When they think they are gods, their people can become slaves to their every evil desire. The

old saying that "power corrupts and absolute power corrupts absolutely" is not far off the mark. It is right to be wary of rulers, even those who say they are believers. History has shown that any ruler can become incredibly ruthless in maintaining their power regardless of what they say they believe. Power is very seductive. It's a good thing we have a two-term limit for our President in the United States.

Psalms 35:18 I will give You thanks in the great assembly;
I will praise You among many people. This passage indicates thanks we give the Lord should be offered publicly in the temple. When a person acknowledges God and gives him thanks, it may be harder for them to become as prideful and egotistical as those who see no reason to be thankful to God for anything.

Psalms 37:4 Delight yourself also in the Lord,
And He shall give you the desires of your heart. We really need to grasp a concept to understand what scripture tells us about prayer and getting what we want. That concept is that a narrow reading of scripture, which does not consider the whole counsel of God, can lead to disillusionment and disappointment. We need to understand completely what the scripture says about getting what we want. If you read only the second line of the above verse, you could have an incorrect interpretation of what is being communicated. The first line is the controlling concept that determines what desire of your heart will be fulfilled. In other words, when you have the attitude of "your will be done" toward anything you ask of the Lord, with His desires taking first place over yours, the desires of your heart will be fulfilled because you will desire what the Lord wants to do. When we put the Lord first in our lives, our wishes will be fulfilled because our wishes will be for what the Lord wills. In turn, we will be blessed when the Lord's will is done.

Psalms 37:8 Cease from anger, and forsake wrath;
Do not fret—*it* only *causes* harm. Here is some great advice. Most

of us have seen the end result of unrelenting anger both for the person who harbors anger and the object of the anger.

The Lord repeatedly says, "vengeance is mine" (Psalms 91:4; Romans 12:19; Hebrews 10:30). However, people do not want to accept this and take revenge on whoever they feel has offended them. Unfortunately, those who constantly try to hurt others to get back at them wind up getting the people they are trying to hurt more angry in response. Two angry people trying to hurt each other create massive amounts of emotional, and sometimes physical, harm to both parties and anyone around them, including their close relatives and friends. My advice when you encounter a person who cannot get past their anger for a brother or sister in the faith is to stay as distant from them as you can. Scripture supports this position. We are advised to keep a distance from angry people (Titus 3:9; Proverbs 22:24; 2 Timothy 3:1-5).

So be careful when you encounter an angry person. They will attempt to manipulate you into their desire to hurt the person with whom they are angry. Then you will also become a target for one side or the other. If you don't go along with the angry person in their vendetta, you may be seen as agreeing with their enemy because their accurate perception is blinded by their anger. The end result of anger and worry (fretting) is harm. This harm is not only for the object of the angry person but also for the person who is angry. Thus, again it is good to stay away from angry people.

Psalms 37:30 The mouth of the righteous speaks wisdom,
   And his tongue talks of justice.
   31 The law of his God *is* in his heart;
   None of his steps shall slide. Why do the righteous speak wisdom? It is because they know the law of God and base their actions on what the Word of God says as opposed to their ideas. Memorizing key scripture and continuing to study the Word daily is the way to keep the law of

God in our hearts and keep from backsliding, which will be the natural consequence if we start to lean on our understanding (Proverbs 3:5). There are ultimately only two ways to go. The way of righteousness or the way of evil. If we are not pursuing righteousness, we will begin to slide into evil.

Psalms 39:5 Indeed, You have made my days *as* handbreadths,
   And my age *is* as nothing before You;
   Certainly every man at his best state *is* but vapor. *Selah* This is something that we don't realize, especially when we are younger. We don't last long on the earth. Thankfully, our life on earth is not all there is. It appears that we are here for a while in a kind of test mode before we move on to the next phase. Therefore, our hope for the future needs to be in God, who is not bound by our tiny speck of a planet in the vast universe He created. This is a good place to put our hope because He is faithful and keeps his promises. Our life here on earth is a vapor, but we can have hope that covers all eternity.

Psalms 42:8 The Lord will command His lovingkindness in the daytime,
   And in the night His song *shall be* with me—
   A prayer to the God of my life. This psalm speaks of having His song with a person in the night. The song can be a prayer to the God of our life. Just as in modern times, there are many types of worship songs and hymns for different occasions and expressions. In Biblical times there were many types of Psalms and songs for different occasions and purposes. Here is a list of the types of Psalms they had in ancient Israel: individual lament, national lament, individual thanksgiving, national thanksgiving, general praise, specific praise, enthronement, ascent or pilgrimage, royal, didactic and imprecatory. Many of these types are self-explanatory, but some of these descriptors are not. For example, a royal psalm can compare the rule of an earthly king to that of the heavenly king. A didactic psalm may be teaching us something about how we should

live. An imprecatory psalm may be calling down divine judgment.

Psalms 41:9 Even my familiar friend in whom I trusted,
Who ate my bread,
Has lifted up *his* heel against me. This verse appears to be fulfilled by Judas, who ate with Christ (Matt. 26:25-25) and was called a friend (Matt. 26:50) by Christ. The verse was mentioned by Christ (John 13:18), and so it appears that Judas fulfilled this verse when he betrayed Christ.

Psalms 43:4 Then I will go to the altar of God,
To God my exceeding joy;
And on the harp I will praise You,
O God, my God. Here we note that the psalmist was determined to use the harp to praise the Lord. Often in the Psalms, in addition to using our voices to sing praises to the Lord, musical instruments of all types are mentioned as being used to praise the Lord, even cymbals, horns, flutes, stringed instruments, and the timbral (see Psalm 150). In other words, it appears that almost every instrument invented by that time was used in praise. David invented some of these instruments specifically to be used in worship, praise, and thanksgiving (2 Chronicles 7:6). I believe this is the primary reason God gave us voices that could sing and the ability to invent musical instruments. Like a lot of what God has given us, these instruments can be used for their intended and ordained purpose, or inappropriately. A hammer can be used to build a house as was its purpose (a good use), or it can be used to hit someone (a bad use). A voice or musical instrument can praise the Lord or aggrandize a human being (Proverbs 18:21; James 3:1-12).

Psalms 47:47 Oh, clap your hands, all you peoples!
Shout to God with the voice of triumph! In this verse, people are encouraged to even use the clapping of their hands as an instrument of praise. In the final verse of the Psalms, everything that has breath is encouraged to praise the Lord! This does not need much interpretation,

does it? It is as clear and straightforward as it can be. We just need to follow this direction.

Psalms 47:5 God has gone up with a shout,
   The Lord with the sound of a trumpet.
   6 Sing praises to God, sing praises!
   Sing praises to our King, sing praises!
   7 For God *is* the King of all the earth;
   Sing praises with understanding. It has been a criticism of modern worship songs that some of them are repetitious. When you hear criticism of worship practice, it is good to look to the Bible to determine whether the complaint is valid. This verse and many others prove that repetition can be appropriate in praise and worship songs. Here in just two verses, we have the words "sing praises" used five times. Hopefully, we get the message when it is in the scriptures one time. When it is in the scriptures five times in two verses, the message becomes unavoidably clear that we are to "sing praises" to the Lord. Many poetic techniques are used in the Bible (i.e., dramatic, exaggerated, and figurative prose), and repetition is just one of them. Repetitious prose is at least sometimes appropriate since examples can easily be found in the scriptures.

Psalms 50:10 For every beast of the forest *is* Mine,
   ***And* the cattle on a thousand hills.**
   11 I know all the birds of the mountains,
   And the wild beasts of the field *are* Mine. Note that everything belongs to the Lord even if he lets us have temporary stewardship of the things in our house. He does not need anything from us since He owns the universe. Our puny offerings are not required and do not appear to be pleasing to God. But He says, "**whoever offers praise glorifies Me**" (vs. 23). Our praise/worship does seem to please God. He also appears to like obedience: "**Whoever orders his conduct aright I will show the salvation of God.**" Obedience appears to be the beginning of worship that leads to God showing His salvation.

Psalms 51:10 Create in me a clean heart, O God,
   And renew a steadfast spirit within me.
11 Do not cast me away from Your presence,
   And do not take Your Holy Spirit from me. Here the psalmist is talking about a clean heart. What is a clean heart? One that doesn't think about evil things. The word "heart" seems to be related to our inner being. Proverbs 15:13,14 puts heart, knowledge, and emotions together. Thus, a clean heart would not have impure thoughts or desires. The hard heart would be the opposite and is the heart that produces all kinds of evil (Genesis 8:21). When the Holy Spirit is with us and in us, it affects our hearts in a good way. We need the Holy Spirit to keep us from having evil thoughts and desires.

Psalms 51:17 The sacrifices of God *are* a broken spirit,
   A broken and a contrite heart—
These, O God, You will not despise. Christ paid the price for our sins, and therefore, there is no longer a need for other sacrifices. It appears that God does not find pleasure in animal sacrifices. What he seems to find pleasure in is our humility before Him.

Psalms 55:16 As for me, I will call upon God,
   And the Lord shall save me.
17 Evening and morning and at noon
I will pray, and cry aloud,
And He shall hear my voice. This is a stance of faith from David. He remembers the great acts of deliverance the Lord instituted for him in the past and expects the same in the future. He also realizes that he needs to trust in God at all times of the day and pray. This is what we all need to do evening, morning, and at noon.

Psalms 56:3 Whenever I am afraid,
   I will trust in You.
   4 In God (I will praise His word),

In God I have put my trust;
I will not fear.
What can flesh do to me? Here are great verses of trust and faith. When we are afraid, who do we need to trust? We need to trust in the Lord and fear not. Ultimately, the flesh can only deal with flesh, but without the breath of life, the flesh is nothing but some water, chemicals, and elements. For those who trust in the Lord, our glorification is already imminent. No work of the flesh can change that. We may suffer here on earth, but the ending outcome of our eternity in heaven is already determined. The thought expressed in these verses is repeated in other verses. The basic idea is that we need to be more concerned about what God thinks than any man thinks. We are often urged to praise the Lord and His word and not to fear man or worry about what a man can do to us.

59:16 But I will sing of your strength,
   in the morning I will sing of your love;
   for you are my fortress,
   my refuge in times of trouble. This theme repeats several times in the Psalms and other scripture. Singing in the name of the Lord as an act of faith seems to be an essential behavior for believers. It appears to be required.

Psalms 61:5 For You, O God, have heard my vows;
   You have given *me* the heritage of those who fear Your name. What does it mean to "fear" the name of the Lord? The meaning in the Bible is sometimes a little different than how we usually interpret the word. In this context, it appears to mean holding the Lord in awe and worshiping and obeying Him. Psalm 147:11 says that the Lord takes pleasure in those who fear Him. It gives Him pleasure when we humble ourselves and hold Him in awe and wonder. Doing something that pleases the Lord is a good thing to do. Exodus 20:20 gives another perspective on fear of the Lord. It appears that a fear that keeps us from sinning is a good thing,

but we can keep in mind that we do not need to be afraid that the Lord will be arbitrary with us. He may test us but always wants us to pass the tests. (Psalms 26:2; 139:23).

Psalms 61:8 So I will sing praise to Your name forever,
That I may daily perform my vows. In a previous verse of this psalm, David had mentioned his vows, to praise the Lord. He had also said that he would declare the Lord to his brethren and that he would praise the Lord in the assembly (22:22). David was determined not only to praise the Lord forever but also to do so daily. In modern culture, we have relegated a time of praise to a 20-minute session on Sunday mornings. That is not how it should be. According to this and other scripture, our praise of the Lord should happen daily, and if David is an example, we should vow to do so.

Psalms 62:6 He only *is* my rock and my salvation;
  ***He is* my defense;**
  I shall not be moved. David, here for a second time in this psalm, declares his dependence on God. We know that David took actions based on this belief, he didn't just sit there and expect God to defend him. When confronted with what appeared to be hopeless odds to others, David simply picked up his sling and some smooth rocks, which was the weapon he had been prepared to use, and did what he believed he was called to do. He knew that with the Lord on his side, it didn't matter how large of an enemy he faced. The Lord would prevail.

Psalms 62:10 Do not trust in oppression,
  Nor vainly hope in robbery;
  If riches increase,
  Do not set *your* heart *on them*. This part of the psalm acknowledges that some believers will wind up rich. Those who do are advised not to set their heart on them. In other words, do not put your trust in money. It can be valuable today and worthless or gone tomorrow. There have

been countries where the inflation rate was so high that it would devalue the money to the point that it could take $900,000.00 to rent a room for the night. A millionaire in that country didn't have much. On the other hand, those who trust in the Lord are always rich in a different kind of way, and by setting their heart on the Lord they will always be in good shape.

Psalms 62:11 God has spoken once,
  Twice I have heard this:
  That power *belongs* to God. David is letting us know that he is very sure that power belongs to God. In other words, God's power is more than anyone else whether on earth or in the heavens.

Psalms 63:3 Because Your lovingkindness *is* better than life,
  My lips shall praise You.
  4 Thus I will bless You while I live;
  I will lift up my hands in Your name. Earlier in this Psalm, David states that God is his God and that he seeks God. He also shows us an example of how he praises the Lord with what he says, what he sings, and by lifting his hands to His name. He seems determined to praise God throughout his life and recognizes that the concern (loyal love) of the Lord is more important (better) than living. He is also determined to meditate on the Lord even at night. In this psalm, we learn that meditating is good when the focus is on the Lord. The opposite, which some gurus would propose, is to empty your mind. That is potentially a dangerous type of meditation because there is no telling what might come in if we empty our minds.

Psalms 64:10 The righteous shall be glad in the Lord, and trust in Him.
  And all the upright in heart shall glory. This is just a true statement. The righteous are simply glad in the Lord. When a person knows that they are in the Lord, it is something about which to be happy. That is

essentially fulfilling our best and highest destiny, and therefore, why wouldn't we be glad?

Psalms 65:1 Praise is awaiting You, O God, in Zion;
   And to You the vow shall be performed. The Lord will be praised for the good harvest and the good rain that comes from Him in the future. We can shout for joy and sing at the pleasure of this happening. This productivity will increase substantially during the coming new millennium. David wanted to live in the presence of the Lord. We should follow his example in this.

Psalms 66:1 Make a joyful shout to God, all the earth!
   2 Sing out the honor of His name;
   Make His praise glorious. We are encouraged (a) to recognize who God is, (b) be in awe of Him, (c) be joyful in our praise of Him, (d) to see His works, (e) make the voice of His praise heard and (f) to bless Him through all of this. At some point, the psalm predicts all who are on the earth will worship and praise God.

Interestingly, worship and singing are separated into two specific words in this psalm. It seems that the word submit may mean to "cringe" at His unfathomable power and immenseness. Once we pay attention to this aspect of God, it becomes a natural response to worship by kneeling or bowing down to Him. Those who don't are just not in very good touch with the actual reality of mankind's situation. The truth is that we are wholly dependent on God for maintaining our life and everything else. We just don't always recognize or pay attention to that fact.

Psalms 67:1 God be merciful to us and bless us,
   And cause His face to shine upon us, *Selah*
   2 That Your way may be known on earth,
   Your salvation among all nations.
   3 Let the peoples praise You, O God;

Let all the peoples praise You. The last sentence of verse 3 is repeated later in this psalm. The psalmist wanted to get this point across. He wanted all the people to praise God and the Lord's favor upon all the nations. That is still a great thing to ask for, and one day, it will be granted. When that happens, all people will be blessed. Since God created us and continues to provide for us (68:19) we should want to praise Him.

Psalms 68:3 But let the righteous be glad;
Let them rejoice before God;

Yes, let them rejoice exceedingly. We are to rejoice at what God is doing and what He will do, and what He has done. And, how should we rejoice? Exceedingly! How do we accomplish that? We "sing praises to His name" and extol Him. That means that we should praise and laud Him. He is a father to the fatherless and defender of widows. Only His mercy causes God to delay His judgment on all the earth (75:2; 2 Peter 3:9).

Psalms 68:25 The singers went before, the players on instruments *followed* after;

Among *them were* the maidens playing timbrels. Here is another case where a percussion instrument is mentioned in the Bible as used in some type of procession of God. The timbrel was something like a modern-day tambourine. They are often associated with dance and seem to suggest joy in their use.

Psalms 68:32 Sing to God, you kingdoms of the earth;

Oh, sing praises to the Lord, *Selah* Again, we are encouraged to "sing" to God. The Psalms provide examples of many different emotions along the spectrum, from great joy to deep depression. They let us know that we can pour our hearts out to God regardless of our mood, always remembering that He is in control and has a great love for us. Whatever comes our way, a Christian can believe that it has been filtered through God and that He has determined that we can handle it or need it or that it will help refine us or test us in a way that will help increase our faith.

It is said that there are no coincidences in a believer's life, even though it may seem that way. We always need to turn to God in faith to get through difficult situations. We should also turn to God in faith when everything is good in our lives. He allows us to go through both, and we should be thankful to Him for both even if going through diverse trials (see James 1:2-4). The psalmists repeatedly determined to sing praises to the Lord, magnify Him, and give thanks to Him (see 69:30-32 and many other verses).

Psalms 71:1 In You, O Lord, I put my trust;

Let me never be put to shame. With this psalm, we have an example and a model of dealing with difficult situations. We should put our complete trust in the Lord, but we can still ask for deliverance from these situations. Verse 14 goes on to say: "**But I will hope continually, And will praise You yet more and more.**" Then in verse 18, David talks about declaring the power of the Lord even when he is old and grey-headed. Later in Psalm 71, there is a declaration about praising the Lord with the lute. Thus, there is no mistaking David's intent to be a worshiper with singing and with instruments "more and more" and to trust the Lord with rejoicing and thanksgiving to the end of his life.

Psalms 72:12 For he will deliver the needy who cry out,

the afflicted who have no one to help. Here is a prophecy about what the Messiah will do. The Psalm goes on to state that He will "**save the souls of the needy**." This psalm ends with some great words of benediction where the words speak of the whole earth being filled with His glory and then it ends with Amen repeated two times. Some commentators believe that this ending indicates the end of book two of the Psalms and that the Psalm was used for the worship of God in His temple.

Psalms 73:25 Whom have I in heaven but you?
And earth has nothing I desire besides you. There is no one else in heaven who can or will help us. On earth, it is the same. Our real help comes from the Lord. The Lord may use people in the process, but still, their ability to help is God-given.

Psalms 74:2 Remember the nation you purchased long ago,
the people of your inheritance, whom you redeemed—
Mount Zion, where you dwelt. There are times when it will seem that the Lord has abandoned us to our own devices. It is alright to cry out to the Lord in these situations and ask Him to remember us and help us. For our part, we always need to remember what the Lord has done for His people in times past. He may allow us to experience the consequences of our actions, but He has purchased us. He has redeemed us, and He dwells with us. So, the bottom line is that He will take care of us and deliver us. However, He may not do so when and how we want. If we seek God's will in these situations and align our wants with His grand overarching plan, it *will* be done when and how we want it done. That is why we pray for His will to be done. He is infinitely more able to determine what is best in the grand scheme of life than we are. Thus, we need to trust that His way is the best way. Even if we are poor and needy, we need to praise His name. He has made a covenant with us and He will fulfill it.

Psalms 75:1 We give thanks to You, O God, we give thanks!
For Your wondrous works declare *that* Your name is near. All we have to do to know that God is near is look out our window and see the earth and all its wonders that He created. Not only is His name near, but He also goes on to say that at the time of His choosing, He will judge the earth and, at the appropriate time, the first heaven and the first earth will pass away (Revelation 21:1). In the proper time, there will be a new heaven and new earth (Isaiah 65:17). The Lord gives, and the Lord takes away, blessed be the name of the Lord (Job 1:29). The Lord will someday

take away the very strength the wicked use to boast that there will be no judgment. We should do as this psalm says and give thanks and sing praises to God, for He truly is the righteous judge.

Psalms 76:10 Surely the wrath of man shall praise You;
   With the remainder of wrath You shall gird Yourself. Scripture affirms many times that only God is to be feared. There is no escape from God for the wicked, and any anger they have against God is so obviously futile that those who oppose God in anger can be pitied.

Psalms 77:11 I will remember the works of the Lord;
   Surely I will remember Your wonders of old.
   12 I will also meditate on all Your work,
   And talk of Your deeds. Here is another place in the scriptures where we are encouraged to meditate. However, we are told what to meditate on. We are to meditate on the laws of God in the Bible (Joshua 1:8; Psalm 1:2) and on God and what He has done (Psalm 63:6; Psalm 77:12). The Bible does not tell us to empty our minds and let whatever comes in, come in. We know that out of the heart of man comes evil (Matthew 15:19; Mark 7:21) so, that would probably not be a good idea.

All of us probably have had to experience with our minds going places where it ought not to go. Controlling the direction of the mind is the first step in getting our behavior under control. The Bible tells us to think about these things (Philippians 4:8): "**whatsoever things are true, whatsoever things are just, whatsoever things are pure, whatsoever things are lovely, whatsoever things are of good report; if there be any virtue, and if there be any praise, think on these things**." That scripture gives us plenty of things to meditate on. So use this scripture as a guide to steer clear of meditation that does not fall into line with this guidance. Otherwise, we can easily fall into sin with our thought life.

Of course, we are not fully capable of altering our thought life or our behavior without faith and the help of the Holy Spirit within us. This psalmist is also declaring here that not only will he meditate on the works of the Lord, but that he will talk about them with others and, through doing so, spread the knowledge of the Lord.

Psalms 78:21 Therefore the Lord heard *this* and was furious;
So a fire was kindled against Jacob,
And anger also came up against Israel,
22 Because they did not believe in God,
And did not trust in His salvation. Here we find out what makes God angry. It is unbelief. They were not content with the food that God gave them but rather wanted the food of their fancy, and Israel spoke against God while in the wilderness. They provoked God with their rebellion. They were not grateful for what God had given them. They audaciously rejected the manna, the bread from heaven, that He gave them. They failed to seek God's will and ceased to praise Him for what He provided. They wanted their will to be done and acted like self-centered complainers. It is simply folly for a measly man to question God who gives him the very breath of life and can remove it just as easily. We need to be satisfied and thankful for whatever life He has given us and maintain that attitude of thankfulness (1 Corinthians 7:20-24).

Psalms 79:13 So we, Your people and sheep of Your pasture,
Will give You thanks forever;
We will show forth Your praise to all generations. This is the proper respect that man should always show toward God. And, we should teach the children of our generation to do the same.

Psalms 80:3 Restore us, O God;
Cause Your face to shine,
And we shall be saved! This seems to be an important element of Psalm 80 because it is repeated three times. It reminds us of the benediction of the priest in Numbers 6:25 which asks for the same thing

to happen. Also, it appears that being in the presence of the Lord as Moses was when the Lord spoke to him face to face (Ex. 33:11) caused Moses' face to shine. When Moses came down off the mountain with the two tablets of the Testimony, the skin of his face shone. It appears that his close association with the Lord transformed Moses and supernaturally caused the skin of his face to shine. The scripture doesn't say that the skin of his hands shone. After this, when Moses removed the veil that he was wearing, the people could see the glow of his face declining.

Paul taught that the people could not look steadily at the face of Moses because of the glory of his countenance, but the glow faded over time because this glory was imperfect (2 Cor. 3:7, 13). Paul calls the law engraved on stones the ministration of death that was passing away. The ministration of the Spirit is much more glorious. Paul puts it this way: **"For if the ministry of condemnation *had* glory, the ministry of righteousness exceeds much more in glory"** (2 Cor. 3:9). We have the great privilege of being under the ministry of righteousness rather than the ministry of death.

Psalms 81:1 Sing aloud to God our strength;
  Make a joyful shout to the God of Jacob.
  2 Raise a song and strike the timbrel,
  The pleasant harp with the lute. It is scripture like this, including Psalm 150, that makes it undeniably clear that we are to sing praises to the Lord accompanied by musical instruments. Loud singing with instruments is a standard element of joyful praise mentioned in many Psalms. Many of the words sang in the Old Testament days were the words in the Psalms which, when considered together, form the longest single Book of the Bible. This fact seems to bring even more credence that praise, worship, and thanksgiving are essential parts of the Christian life. Those Christians who forbid the use of instruments in worship appear to ignore the Psalms' directions. Thus, we need to be familiar with God's whole counsel if we want to be in harmony with what God

says.

Psalms 82:3 Defend the poor and fatherless;
Do justice to the afflicted and needy.
4 Deliver the poor and needy;
Free *them* from the hand of the wicked. These verses give us some guidance regarding how to treat the poor, the fatherless, the afflicted, and the needy. We are to help them and not let wicked people take advantage of them.

83:1 Do not keep silent, O God!
Do not hold Your peace,
And do not be still, O God!
2 For behold, Your enemies make a tumult;
And those who hate You have lifted up their head. Here the psalmist wants God to take action against His enemies, not realizing that God withholds His judgment as an act of mercy, giving people every possible chance to see the light. God's delayed judgment is an act of mercy from which many of us have benefited (2 Peter 3:9). The reality is that God's timing is right, and ours is impatient.

Psalms 84:12 O Lord of hosts,
Blessed *is* the man who trusts in You! In these final words of this Psalm, the Psalmist is addressing the Lord of hosts. The hosts are believed to refer to the armies of angels in heaven. So the sentence seems to be referring to God as the Lord of armies. This Psalm also says that good things will come to those who walk uprightly and that the Lord will give grace and glory. The Psalm speaks of the Lord God as being a sun and shield. In Malachi 4:2, the sun appears to be a biblical symbol associated with righteousness. That makes sense because we have many other scriptures demonstrating that the Lord is righteous (Psalm 119:137; Deuteronomy 32:4; etc.).

Psalms 85:2 You have forgiven the iniquity of Your people;
You have covered all their sin. Selah This psalm clarifies that God is a saving God though He does discipline sin (or allow the consequences to occur). God may forgive the sin, but most sin still has negative results. The Psalmist seems to understand that the sin of the people disciplined by God caused their troubles. The people had turned to God and prayed for revival and renewal after a catastrophe. They showed their trust in God by what they prayed for in this Psalm.

Psalms 86:2 Preserve my life, for I *am* holy;
You are my God;
Save Your servant who trusts in You! This Psalm has David's name in the title: "A Prayer of David." Thus, we can view it as his prayer to God. The first line of verse two could be considered to be a prideful statement, but in context, that is not what it is. Before this statement, David clarifies that he is viewed as "poor and needy." Thus, he was making a case that because he associated himself with God, by God's grace, David was living in accord with God's laws and therefore had the imputed holiness of God. The Psalms make it clear that God is happy with those who serve and obey Him, and in this context, even though David was poor and needy, he was holy because he was seeking to serve and obey God. He sought answers from His Lord and wanted to learn His ways so that he could walk in the truth of the Lord. Then he could glorify the name of the Lord. He knew that it was the Lord who delivered his soul from Sheol.

Psalms 87:7 Both the singers and the players on instruments *say*,
"All my springs *are* in you." This verse from Psalm 87 indicates that the singers and players will be coming to worship the Lord. The words in quotes seem to be providing an image of salvation. When people lack water, they thirst, and their focus gets more and more on obtaining the water they need. When found, a spring can satisfy what they need and want.

Similarly, we have a spiritual need. We will search to satisfy that need. Sometimes we look in the wrong places and don't find the clear, pure satisfaction of that need that only the Lord can supply. There is a clear and pure spiritual thirst quencher that everyone needs, but that not everyone accepts. There are imitations and false prophets, but only one Christ can fully satisfy the need and sustain life eternally. All others are just temporary counterfeits.

One other note about this psalm is that the singers and players on instruments are recognized separately, indicating that both singing and instrumentation were used in this worship.

Psalms 88:1 O Lord, God of my salvation,
I have cried out day and night before You. This Psalm is a contemplation of the Sons of Korah. In it, the salvation of the Lord is recognized, but the psalmists are loudly crying out to God in desperation and weeping while appealing for Him to listen. There does not seem to be a resolution to the psalmist's troubles in this psalm. He seems to know that the Lord hears and will answer at some point, but his troubles are not resolved in this psalm. That is the way it is in life here on earth sometimes. There are some problems for the believer that are only resolved through leaving this realm.

Psalms 89:1 I will sing of the mercies of the Lord forever;
With my mouth will I make known Your faithfulness to all generations. Mercies can be translated as "loyal love." In 2 Samuel 7:15, God had promised that His mercy would always be with David's son. Here the psalmist refers to "**all generations.**" The psalmist also notes that God is "**greatly to be feared**" and to be held in "**reverence**" by all those around Him. It appears here that singing is part of the way a believer communicates the message to others that God is faithful all the time. Not only is He faithful, He follows through every time and keeps His promises every time. He is not like us in these respects. His timing

may be different than ours, but He is always faithful. There is no one else like Him on earth or in heaven.

Psalms 90:4 For a thousand years in Your sight
  Are like yesterday when it is past,
  And like a watch in the night. God is eternal so His perception of time may be very different than ours while we are here on earth. Also, this verse seems to indicate that God does not perceive time passing as we do. This could be a poetic way of saying that God sees the past (and possibly the future) at the same time. Or, it could be saying that God has a memory that doesn't forget anything whereby something that happened a thousand years ago is as clear to Him as something that happened twenty-four of our hours ago.

In 2 Peter 3:8, Peter confirms that a thousand (of our) years is but a day to the Lord. The Bible does use poetic language, but these scriptures seem to be making it clear that in the realm of God, time is very different than in our realm and perception. Our whole lifespan may be like the span of a portion of 24 hours to the Lord. - In the poetic language of the Bible, our lifetime is compared to grass and to a vapor (1 Peter 1:24; Psalms 39:5; 39:11; 62:9). Neither of these lasts very long.

I believe that the accurate findings of science and scripture will one day be one hundred percent aligned. I don't think the time frame of creation in the Bible refers to seven literal 24-hour days in our way of marking time (i.e., roughly the time it takes the earth to rotate 360 degrees relative to the sun; I say "roughly" because the earth's rotation is actually slowing down). Thus, if a thousand years is like yesterday to the Lord, some scripture appears to be using poetic descriptions of the relative amount of time God spent on each segment of time to create the earth. Scientific evidence indicates our universe is about 13,800,000,000 years old and our earth is calculated to be about 4.54 billion years old. Note that science indicates a beginning, not an eternal existence.

It appears the creation of the universe occurred way before man. Thus, the scripture about the creation could easily be providing relative time frames in terms we could understand. Our reference is of 24-hour blocks of time have to do with our earth's speed of rotation. Our time does not have much meaning in the marking of time in the rest of the universe. Our day was not even possible until the planet was set on its axis and started spinning around at a reasonably constant speed so that one day was equal to one rotation.

Put in the context of poetic statements in the scriptures about how God perceives time, the creation of the earth could have taken the billions of our years that science indicates it took. Suppose a thousand years is a poetic statement giving us the idea that time is different for God who is eternal. In that case, the statement could just as easily have used a million in place of a thousand and communicated the same idea that time is different for the Lord and that we cannot restrict our thoughts about God by using our little concept of time when our whole lifespan hardly even moves the meter so to speak. A human lifespan in the context of eternity is probably just barely perceptible. And, the time it takes for our little earth to rotate 360 degrees just does not seem to rise to the level of importance to be the standard of time by which everything else in the universe is measured.

Psalms 90:12 So teach *us* to number our days,

That we may gain a heart of wisdom. What does "number our days" mean? Just preceding this sentence are verses that speak of our death and the fear we should have for the Lord. Thus, it appears that when we number our days, we should be using the brief time we have here on earth for eternal purposes rather than just focusing on our life here.

It is said that there are two important days in our life; the day that we are born and the day that we discover why. One why is in the Bible. We are here for God's pleasure (though we tend to think it is all about us). If we are in this life for the pleasure and *at* the pleasure of the Lord, maybe it would make sense to pay attention to what His pleasure is. The scriptures give us a clear picture. One crucial aspect is serving the Lord and recognizing Him for who He is. A child who would deny the existence of their earthly father would probably not make that father very happy. If they also refused to follow what he taught them, it would make their father even more unhappy.

The scripture indicates that God sees us as His children (John 1:12; 11:52; Romans 8:16). When through faith in Him, we recognize Him as our heavenly Father, He seems to like that. When He provides us with a measure of faith, He also provides for all our needs (Philippians 4:19; Matthew 6:31-32).

Psalms 91:4 He shall cover you with His feathers,
  And under His wings you shall take refuge;
  His truth *shall be your* shield and buckler. Here God is described as being like a mother hen who spreads out her wings for her chick to come under for protection and refuge. It is His truth that brings complete protection. In other words, God and His truth is a complete protector. That does not mean that anyone on earth will not have difficulties, trials, and temptations. It does seem to indicate that those who belong to the Lord will be preserved and protected for eternity. That is a truth that is worth remembering. This Psalm addresses "**He who dwells in the secret place of the Most High.**" That may be Christ. Later the Psalm speaks of "**His angels having charge over you.**" Either way, believers are covered.

Psalms 92:3 On an instrument of ten strings,
  On the lute,
  And on the harp,
  With harmonious sound. This psalm speaks of giving thanks and praise to the Lord with stringed instruments and harmonious sound in a

public setting. When we sing in harmony, everyone has their part to sing, and it sounds good. If we try to sing just a harmony part without the melody, it doesn't sound quite right. But when the melody part is present, even though the harmony note is different, it goes with the melody and adds to and supports it. Not just any note sang by the harmony singer or played on an instrument will work. The harmony notes need to be the exact right notes that harmonize with the melody note. It is analogous to how we need to be in line with what the Lord is doing and in harmony with Him, or our life doesn't work as well.

I think that one of the purposes of the Bible is to give us the melody that the Lord is singing so that we can get in tune with Him and sing our part in support of His melody. It is His song and His creation. God made music, and He created us for singing and playing it.

We are not the lead melody singer in the song of life, but we have a part to sing and play. This is our destiny. The sooner we understand that and get on board with our destiny of following the Lord, the better off we will be. Otherwise, we are kicking against the goads (Acts 26:14). It is like beating your head against the wall. In the end, it doesn't produce anything of value; it just makes your head hurt.

Psalms 92:14 They shall still bear fruit in old age;
   They shall be fresh and flourishing,... The older I get, the more I like the sound of this verse. It is speaking of the "**righteous**" who are "**planted in the house of the Lord.**" Is it not great to think that we can be "**fresh and flourishing**" even in our old age and in the life to come (Psalm 23). We all can take encouragement from this verse.

Psalms 93:1 The Lord reigns, He is clothed with majesty;
   The Lord is clothed,
   He has girded Himself with strength.
   Surely the world is established, so that it cannot be moved. There

is no man or another god who is even comparable to God. He created the universe and everything in it. He established our earth as a tiny part of His creation and makes it stable for now. Our current world will be removed (Revelation 21:1), but the Lord is everlasting. By the way, modern-day science agrees with the Bible that our earth is not eternal. Scientists have calculated that our sun is about halfway through its fuel supply. The world, as we know it, will no longer exist when the sun runs out of fuel and burns out.

Psalms 94:1 O Lord God, to whom vengeance belongs—
O God, to whom vengeance belongs, shine forth! Here is something that man often forgets: vengeance belongs to God. When we try to take revenge, we are overstepping our authority and rightful place, and it does not produce the results for which we had hoped. My advice is to leave it to the Lord. He is the only fair judge anyway, and He knows the intent of a man's actions better than we do. He knows whether a person had an evil plan or accidentally hurt someone. His judgments are fair. This psalm also lets us know that we can identify wicked people by their insolent speech and their boasting in themselves. The Psalm refers to them as fools because the Lord made ears and eyes. He hears what they say and sees what they do. He even knows their futile thoughts. Our thoughts pass quickly, but the Lord's endure.

Psalms 95:1 Oh come, let us sing to the Lord!
Let us shout joyfully to the Rock of our salvation. Here is another of the many calls to worship that is in the Psalms and the Bible. The word translated "worship" literally means to "prostrate oneself" before our mighty King in the original language. In other words, we should have humility before the Lord and recognize Him for who He is. Nevertheless, in this Psalm, we are encouraged to "shout joyfully" to our great God and King more than once. At first, we might think there is a conflict between the concept of humility and the concept of shouting joyfully. However, humility is having a correct attitude toward ourselves and God.

The proper attitude we should have toward God is that He is the great God and King. As His humble servants, we should shout that fact out joyfully because we are His people.

Psalms 96:1 Oh, sing to the Lord a new song!
Sing to the Lord, all the earth. This Psalm encourages the people that the Lord is great and greatly to be praised and points out that the other gods of the people are just idols and didn't make the heavens as our Lord did. We need to fear Him, worship Him and give glory and honor to Him. Another thing in this Psalm, we need to remember is that He is coming to judge the world with righteousness.

Psalms 97:1 The Lord reigns;
Let the earth rejoice;
Let the multitude of isles be glad! "The Lord reigns" is a crucial phrase of what is called the "royal" psalms. The words of this psalm let us know that the Lord is righteous and that the heavens declare this fact. We may not know exactly how this fact is declared by the heavens, but we know that it is based on this psalm. The psalm also lets us know that those who worship idols and other so-called gods will experience shame and terror at the final righteous judgment of God before He establishes His kingdom on earth. The psalm begins and ends with encouragement for us to rejoice because the righteous God does reign.

Psalms 98:1 Oh, sing to the Lord a new song!
For He has done marvelous things;
His right hand and His holy arm have gained Him the victory. This psalm contains encouragement to (a) praise God as the savior (98:2), then (b) as the King, and finishes with (c) praising God as the coming judge (98:9). It encourages followers to sing a "new song!" to the Lord, which seems to provide a license for musicians and singers to continue developing new songs of praise and thanksgiving. In the New Testament (Ephesians 5:18-19) we are encouraged as follows: "**18 And do not**

be drunk with wine, in which is dissipation; but be filled with the Spirit, 19 speaking to one another in psalms and hymns and spiritual songs, singing and making melody in your heart to the Lord,...".

Drunk people sometimes sing profane or obscene songs, but our joy should be expressed in songs of praise to God. We are encouraged in proper expression of our joy and gladness through singing, rejoicing, and thanksgiving. Our music should be designed to please God and promote His glory.

The scripture uses drunkenness in comparison to being filled with the Spirit. In each case, something other than our natural self contributes to how we act and feel. If we are drunk, there is no telling what we might do or say, but if we are filled/controlled by the Holy Spirit (the Word of God), we can do what God wants us to do. Under these situations, we would expect our worship to be bold, expressive, and exuberant under the control of the Spirit. It would probably not be lukewarm. In other words, we can allow ourselves to sing to the Lord with joy and rejoicing.

Psalm 99:8 You answered them, O Lord our God;
  You were to them God-Who-Forgives,
  Though You took vengeance on their deeds.
  9 Exalt the Lord our God,
  And worship at His holy hill;
  For the Lord our God *is* holy. Psalm 99 makes it clear that the Lord our God is holy. Three different times the psalm refers to the Lord as holy. Not only is the Lord holy, but He is holy, holy, holy as noted in Isaiah 6:3 and Revelation 4:8. Isaiah states that the whole earth is filled with His glory. That is an interesting statement and one that explains why no one will have an excuse on the day of judgment.

Psalms 100:1 Make a joyful shout to the Lord, all you lands!

2 Serve the Lord with gladness;
Come before His presence with singing. This sounds like joyful, loud, and exuberant praise.

100:3 Know that the Lord, He *is* God;
***It is* He *who* has made us, and not we ourselves;**
***We are* His people and the sheep of His pasture.** We have a maker who is God, no matter how much we do not want to acknowledge this fact or explain it away somehow. We belong to Him even though He gives us the freedom to run away. It is better to accept our destiny as His sheep and accept His loving care (Ezekiel 34:31).

Psalms 101:1 I will sing of mercy and justice;
To You, O Lord, I will sing praises. Here is something else the psalmist noted that was good to sing about.

Psalms 101:7 He who works deceit shall not dwell within my house;
He who tells lies shall not continue in my presence. The Lord does not sanction deceit or lies. He is truthful and righteous. Note: He is holy holy holy (Isaiah 6:3).

Psalm 102:18 This will be written for the generation to come,
That a people yet to be created may praise the Lord. We are one of those generations for whom these Psalms were written. Regardless of who or how later generations try to discredit these Psalms, they help us in later generations continue in praise to the Lord.

Psalms 102:19 For He looked down from the height of His sanctuary;
From heaven the Lord viewed the earth,
20 To hear the groaning of the prisoner,
To release those appointed to death, We are prisoners of sin (Galatians 3:22) until we are saved from this status by the grace of God through faith. After that, we are better able to win out over the sin in

our lives through the work of the Holy Spirit in us. We were previously appointed to death (Psalms 102:20). Now, believers have eternal life with God (John 3:15).

Psalms 103:1 Bless the Lord, O my soul;
   And all that is within me, *bless* **His holy name!**
   2 Bless the Lord, O my soul,
   And forget not all His benefits:
   3 Who forgives all your iniquities,
   Who heals all your diseases,... Forgiveness and healing are some of the benefits from the Lord. There are many others that stem from these, and we should not forget that fact.

Psalms 104:14 He causes the grass to grow for the cattle,
   And vegetation for the service of man,
   That he may bring forth food from the earth,
   15 And wine *that* **makes glad the heart of man,**
   Oil to make *his* **face shine,**
   And bread *which* **strengthens man's heart.** Here is some straightforward scripture, but in some respects, challenging to understand and, therefore, produces different compliance and interpretation. It tells us that God causes things to grow for the benefit of animals and our benefit because we eat both vegetation and the animals that eat vegetation. Thus, it appears that God makes these things grow for our use. All of these things can be enjoyed in moderation or abused in gluttony or overindulgence. It is clear from other scripture that just because a little is good does not mean that more is better. In some situations, even though believers have the freedom to partake of any of these items, they should not do so where they could cause someone else to stumble (1 Corinthians 8:13; Mark 9:42).

Psalms 104:33 I will sing to the Lord as long as I live;
   I will sing praise to my God while I have my being. Over and over

in the Psalms and in other scripture, we are encouraged to praise the Lord. This means to express our public commendation of God and His attributes and person along with thanksgiving.

Psalms 105 Oh, give thanks to the Lord!
   Call upon His name;
   Make known His deeds among the peoples!
   2 Sing to Him, sing psalms to Him;
   Talk of all His wondrous works! Here, we are encouraged to tell others about what the Lord has done.

Psalms 106:12 Then they believed His words;
   They sang His praise. The Israelites had ups and downs with their faith, just as we sometimes do today. At times they did not wait for the counsel of the Lord and lusted after their wants. God sometimes gave them their request, "**but sent leanness into their soul**" (vs. 15). I'm not sure exactly what that means, but it does not sound good. In this context, leanness could mean lacking in richness, fullness, or quality. It could also mean not having enough of something. Either way, it could be a problem.

Psalm 107:1 107 Oh, give thanks to the Lord, for He is good!
   For His mercy endures forever.
   2 Let the redeemed of the Lord say so, So we who are saved should say that the Lord is good and give Him thanks because He is good. We can and should celebrate God's continuing "loyal love" for His people. The great thing about God illustrated in this psalm is that His mercy endures forever. In other words, He is always ready and willing to forgive if we call on Him.

Psalms 107:8 Oh, that *men* would give thanks to the Lord *for* His goodness,
   And *for* His wonderful works to the children of men!

9 For He satisfies the longing soul,
And fills the hungry soul with goodness. Verse 8 is repeated three times in this Psalm so it is like a chorus in a modern-day song. It is the summation of the main point of the Psalm. The Psalm also provides many reasons for us to give thanks to the Lord. One of these reasons is that God satisfies the longing soul. Until a person realizes this, they can spend their whole life barking up the wrong tree. There is nothing else up there that can do for the soul what God can. We were created that way.

Some people do not want to acknowledge that we were created at all. They believe that no intelligent creator made the physical world or say that we cannot know whether there is or is not. For those who believe there is a creator, it makes sense that we should humbly recognize that fact and live in a way that pleases our creator.

If we are not created by God, we would get to decide what is right or wrong on our own. However, as scripture lets us know, eventually every knee will bow to our creator (Romans 14:11). Still, for the time being, people can believe that matter, the universe, and our very being came from nothing or was just some cosmic accident for no reason and with no organization. Even though this position seems to defy elementary logic, they can live a whole life with this understanding.

Logic and the heavens tell me that God created the universe and follows the laws of physics that He made. If there were no matter, there would be no universe. There would be no matter if there were no God. Since something cannot come from nothing in the natural world, it is logical that if there were no supernatural, there would be no natural.

Some will say that matter could have always existed or at least that gravity always existed, but this seems to be a desperate grasp at denying the obvious and even seems to defy reason and the scientific evidence that our universe began at some point in time. This is known as the big bang theory in some circles. It is known as creation to me. People have a longing in their soul for an explanation, but none will be as satisfying, as good, or as accurate as what the Lord provides.

Psalms 108:1 O God, my heart is steadfast;
  I will sing and give praise, even with my glory.
  2 Awake, lute and harp!
  I will awaken the dawn.
  3 I will praise You, O Lord, among the peoples,
  And I will sing praises to You among the nations. Here's a situation where the psalmist, David, apparently awoke before the sun came up and engaged in praise accompanied by instruments. Maybe he couldn't sleep well that night, and what better way to welcome the dawn than to sing praises to the one who created the dawn. This Psalm goes on to ascribe the words "**I will rejoice**" to the Lord. It appears that the Lord celebrates the deliverance He gives to His people.

Psalms 109:30 I will greatly praise the Lord with my mouth;
  Yes, I will praise Him among the multitude.
  31 For He shall stand at the right hand of the poor,
  To save *him* from those who condemn him. Here is the ending of another psalm where the psalmist vows to and praises the Lord. Praise of the Lord seems to be the general theme of all the psalms. It also appears from this Psalm that the Lord Himself will be defending the poor from those who condemn them.

Psalms 110:1 The Lord said to my Lord,
  "Sit at My right hand,
  Till I make Your enemies Your footstool." This is an interesting choice of words for David, who wrote this Psalm. When he says: "The Lord said to my Lord," he seems to be talking about God the Father in heaven speaking to Jesus the Messiah who would be coming to the earth.

According to the interpretation of Jesus (Matt. 22:41-45; Mark 12:35-37; Luke 20:41-44), this wording appears to refer to a heavenly conversation between God the Father and the Son of God who is David's Lord and our Savior Christ Jesus. Later the Psalm speaks of the Lord executing "**kings in the day of His wrath.**" This wording would also refer to the judgment that Christ will carry out (Rev. 19:19-21). When the Psalms were written, Jesus was the great king and judge to come, and He was the only one who could be judged based on the law and not condemned when He lived on the earth because He was righteous and He did not sin.

Psalms 111:1 Praise the Lord!
  I will praise the Lord with my whole heart,
  In the assembly of the upright and in the congregation. This is a Psalm of wisdom and praise where the psalmist is determined to wholeheartedly praise God in the midst of the congregation. The end of this psalm, says that the beginning of wisdom is "**The fear of the Lord...**"

As if for emphasis, this psalm and the next two also begin with the phrase: "**Praise the LORD!**" This is undoubtedly a central theme of the Psalms, which is repeated in different ways for many reasons. The psalms leave absolutely no room for error or misinterpretation or even different interpretations on this point. We are to "**Praise the LORD,**" and that is part of our purpose. When we let something usurp the rightful place of the LORD as the person to whom our praise is due, we are veering off track from our purpose and destiny.

When we veer off track, there is a probability for our lives to become a wreck. I'm not talking about a wreck in the world's assessment. I'm talking about a wreck in the Lord's assessment. Nevertheless, many do their own thing and act as if there is no God or God is dead. In reality, if God were dead, so would we be dead because it is Him who sustains our life. Without God, there would be no life for us, animals, or plants.

He made the elements that our physical bodies are composed of and gave the breath of life (Genesis 2:11; Job 33:4) that makes us sentient and intelligent natural men (living souls, carnal) and the Spirit of God that makes us spiritual beings. There is a natural body, and there is a spiritual body (1 Corinthians 15:44). Both come from the Lord.

Psalms 112:1 Praise the Lord!
Blessed is the man who fears the Lord,
Who delights greatly in His commandments. Later in this Psalm, we learn that righteousness endures forever, but the desire of the wicked will perish. So the spiritual man who fears the Lord will be blessed.

Psalms 113:3 From the rising of the sun to its going down
The Lord's name *is* to be praised. When should the name of the Lord be praised? Basically, any time when there is daylight appears to be a good time. Also, it seems fine to praise the Lord at night (Psalm 16:7-8).

Psalms 113:9 He grants the barren woman a home,
Like a joyful mother of children.
Praise the Lord! Note that God can bring a home into the life of a woman who has not had biological children. Perhaps some couples do not conceive children so that they will be available to provide respite to parents from the unending responsibility to feed, house, clothe, protect and teach their children everything they need to know.

Note that the psalm speaks of the woman being "**Like a joyful mother of children**" and not like one who has a problem child. Thus, there are different roles for different people. One of the aspects of being joyful is to accept God's plan for your life and embrace the abundant life He has for us. This is regardless of our current situation in the world. The idea is to grow where you are planted (1 Corinthians 7:14-24). It is not an absolute principle because Paul acknowledges exceptions to it, but generally, we should seek to grow morally and spiritually in whatever situation we are in when called rather than seeking the easier or more pleasant life situation.

Psalms 114:1 When Israel went out of Egypt,
The house of Jacob from a people of strange language, The people, never did adopt the language and culture of their captors, the Egyptians, even though they were their slaves. With this Psalm, the redemption of Israel from the Egyptians is celebrated at Passover.

Psalms 115:1 Not unto us, O Lord, not unto us,
But to Your name give glory,
Because of Your mercy,
Because of Your truth. We tend to let the flesh take glory unto ourselves. We need this Psalm to remind us that credit belongs to the Lord and not to us. The Psalm also notes that "**our God is in heaven**" and not like the idols that men make here on earth that can't do or say anything. The Psalm also notes that it is the work of the living to praise the Lord who made heaven and earth.

Psalms 116:6 The Lord preserves the simple;
I was brought low, and He saved me. In this context, it appears that the psalmist is saying that when he was innocent that the Lord humbled him and saved him from his problems. The book of Proverbs is said to give prudence to the simple. In the book of Proverbs, the word "simple" appears to be referring to people who are not viewed as smart (Proverbs 22:3).

Psalms 116:14 I will pay my vows to the Lord
Now in the presence of all His people. The psalmist asked what he should render to the Lord for all the benefits the Lord had bestowed upon him. He concluded that he should take up the "cup of salvation" and pay his vows to the Lord in a public setting in front of all the Lord's people. We can and should do the same when we are with the Lord's

people at church.

The Psalm ends with the emphatic exclamation and very common verse in the Psalms: "**Praise the Lord!**" Part of this psalm was a prophecy fulfilled by Jesus when he took up the "cup of salvation," and he may have sung the words of this psalm the night before His crucifixion (Matt. 26:30, Mark 14:26). We are not told what he sang on that Passover night so, it could have been this Psalm. Jesus also fulfills the role of chief worship leader by singing (Matthew 22:30; Mark 14:26; Hebrews 2:12; Romans 15:19).

Psalms 117:1 Praise the Lord, all you Gentiles!
Laud Him, all you peoples! This is the shortest psalm in the Bible. The point seems to be that Jerusalem and everyone else were to praise the Lord because of His merciful kindness and truth. In other words, everyone on earth should "**Praise the Lord!**"

Psalms 118:6 The Lord *is* on my side;
I will not fear.
What can man do to me? This is a concept that comes up more than once in the scriptures. Who we should fear is not man but the Lord. And, if we are doing right by the LORD, we don't need to fear a man who could take away the life of the body but after that can do no more. A man cannot cast your soul into hell (Hebrews 13:6; Luke 12:5).

God is our refuge (Psalm 46:1-3), and therefore, we do not need to fear no matter what is happening, whether it be an earthquake or a flood. "**There is no fear in love**" (1 John 4:18), and God is love (1 John 4:8). Thus, we need to fear God if we have not accepted His forgiveness and are not in His love. Once we are in this position with God, we have a different kind of fear defined by reverence and awe (Hebrews 12:28). If you are in His grace and mercy, it is a different situation, and you can rest in His care while still having reverence for Him.

Psalms 118:14 The Lord *is* my strength and song,
And He has become my salvation. The words "strength and song" are also used in the "Song of Moses" (Exodus 15:2) and in Isaiah 12:2. God is depicted as using His unlimited strength to save His people. But, what about the word "song"? Why is the Lord the psalmist's song? One definition of a song is a short musical composition with words. This does not seem to fit the meaning conveyed in combination with the word "strength."

Another definition of the word song is a distinctive or characteristic sound. That may be the meaning closer to what the psalmist was trying to convey. Some have tried to insert a different word here, but that is not a literal translation, so we are left to understand the concept of putting strength and song together.

Some commentators and translators suggest that the idea expressed by the psalmist is more along the lines of the Lord is my "strong song" or "my song of strength." In other words, the LORD's strength is distinctive, and if we were to hear the LORD singing, it would be unique, powerful, and strong. In comparison to us, the omnipotent God is all-powerful and distinctive. There is no other like the Lord.

Psalms 118:22 The stone *which* the builders rejected
Has become the chief cornerstone. Just like the stone in this verse, Jesus was rejected by many (Mark 8:31; Luke 9:22). He was put to death but then was elevated to the right hand of God (Acts 7). He has become the chief cornerstone. Jesus is the one who came in the name of the Lord and revealed God the Father (John 14:8-11). He is the One who can save now (Hosanna). "Save now" are the words that the rocks would have had to shout out if the children did not do so upon Jesus' triumphant entry into Jerusalem before He paid the price for all of our sins on the cross.

Psalms 119:4 You have commanded *us*

To keep Your precepts diligently. The law appears to be a gift from God, showing us what is right and at the same time showing us that we need forgiveness because we are not capable of obeying all of God's laws.

Most religions seem to have a "you can save yourself through your individual actions" mentality, which is the opposite of the Christian worldview. The Bible specifies that there is no personal work you can do to save yourself. Only the work of Christ in paying the price for your sin before a just and holy God can save you. The commandments are like a plumb line that shows us how perfectly straight and upright God is and how unlike Him we are. In Romans 5:22, we learn that the law came alongside to increase man's knowledge of sin already in existence (see Romans 7:7). The law is still valid but was explicitly given to a group of people at a specific time to help them in their relationship with God.

Only one person who has lived on the earth could fulfill every one of the Ten Commandments. He was the Messiah, and He took away our sins (John 1:29). He finished the old covenant and ushered in a new one when He said, "it is finished" (2 Cor. 3:13; Ephesians 2:15; Col. 2:14; Rom. 7:4; Rom. 7:6; Rom. 10:4).

The great news about all of this is that we are not under the law but under grace (Romans 6:14). Under the Old Covenant, though all the commandments are what we should be doing, God's blessing could appear to be based on what the people did. But, later, we learn that Abraham was saved by grace through faith just like we are (Romans 4:3). However, Christ has satisfied the need for justice, and He said: "**it is finished**." Under grace, our salvation is based on what Christ did for us, not on what we have done for Him. We do not want to be under the curse of the law (Galatians 3:10), which would bring death to us (2 Corinthians 3:6-7; Romans 7:10-11).

We need to remember that Christ was the end of the law for righteousness to those who believe (Romans 10:4). Those who believe, are not under the law but under grace (Rom. 6:14). That is a great place to be and a great blessing. Let's not forget that fact. It is crucial to experience God's grace and blessing as opposed to His punishment and condemnation.

Psalms 119:37 Turn away my eyes from looking at worthless things,
And revive me in Your way. This is a great preventative measure for sin. Unless we choose to sin spontaneously without thinking about it, there is often a process we go through before we do something we should not do. First, we look, then we linger, then we lust, then we imagine, then we act. If we can stop this process at the beginning, right at the fork in the road, that is the best place to keep from going down that path. Other scriptures support this position. The psalmist says, "**I will set no wicked thing before mine eyes**" in Psalm 101:3. This is more wisdom that God gave us long before psychologists figured it out.

Psalms 119:44 So shall I keep Your law continually,
Forever and ever.
45 And I will walk at liberty,
For I seek Your precepts. People who become addicted to drugs or alcohol can tell you what it is like not to have the liberty that comes from keeping God's law. Our natural tendency is to think that when we can do whatever we want, we have freedom. The opposite can be true when it comes to overindulging. The reality is that when we keep God's law, we can do what we want in freedom.

Overindulgence can often become a sin and take away freedom. Once it takes control and your heart is hardened, you no longer are free to choose whether you will participate. The activity, which initially seemed to be an exercise of freedom, becomes the enslaver. Overuse of any legal or illegal drugs or alcohol can take over not only your mind but also your body to the extent that they will eventually take all your freedom from you by taking your very life. Notice that it is excessive use that can do these things to you. It does not appear to be a sin for most people to partake of legal substances mildly. However, like a lot of things, an excess can become a sin. For people who have a genetic predisposition to overuse, any use can be a sin for them. Yes, what might be a sin for one person may not be a sin for another. Even for those who do not have a genetic predisposition for abuse problems, excessive use appears to be able to change or damage the brain chemistry of an otherwise healthy brain and cause addiction.

For the person who has a problem controlling the use of drugs or alcohol, it is like driving in a car that doesn't have any brakes. Once that person gets started, it is hard for them to stop. It can become a chronic problem, and just like diabetes; it will require regular treatment. Ephesians 5:18 and Galatians 5:16 encourage us not to be drunk with wine but to be filled with the Holy Spirit. Mark 9:42 and Romans 14:21 enable us not to cause someone else to stumble with our behavior. Proverbs 20:1 lets us know that wine is a mocker, and strong drink a brawler and that whoever is led astray by these drinks is not wise. I think the same can be said of mind-altering drugs that make a person act like they are drunk.

Psalms 119:66 Teach me good judgment and knowledge,
For I believe Your commandments.
67 Before I was afflicted I went astray,
But now I keep Your word. Note that the Psalmist says that before he was afflicted, he went astray. He now appears to recognize that whatever was afflicting him positively impacted his ability or motivation to keep God's word. This is a recognition that we can get off course and forget God's commandments when things are going well for us. So as the book of James encourages us to do, we should count it as a blessing when we fall into trials and let the trials have a positive outcome on us. We can let trials develop patience and perseverance which are two essential qualities for success in life.

The psalmist says that God's law is better for him than thousands of coins of gold and silver. In other words, the psalmist has figured out that his character is more important than riches or money. He is not saying there is anything wrong with having some gold, but it has little value compared to knowing God's law. Farther along, he states that God's commandments make him wiser than his enemies and that God's words give light.

It is nice to have an unchanging moral guide in a world filled with confusion, sin, and error. Man's worldview can and will change regularly, but the Word of God stands forever. The psalmist delights in the Word of God and states that he praises Him seven times a day. If we allow 8 hours a day for sleeping, that means that the psalmist is praising God about every 2 1/4 hours of the day. A schedule for that praise could be something like this: before breakfast, at mid-morning, before lunch, at mid-afternoon, before dinner, at mid-evening, and then before going to bed. That would appear to be a seriously committed schedule of praise.

Psalm 119 also outlines the many benefits that come from following God's law including (a) peace (v. 165), (b) the power to resist sin (v. 3, 11, 101, 165), (d) joy (many verses), (e) understanding (v. 99, 125, 130, 169), (f) strength (v. 28), (g) freedom (v. 45), (h) hope (v. 114, 147), (i) comfort (v. 50, 52), (j) no shame (v. 6, 31, 46, 80), (k) reverence for God (v. 120, 161), (l) a thankful heart (v. 62), (m) a worshipful heart (v. 164, 171, 175), (n) a clean life (various verses) and (o) personal revival (various verses).

Psalms 120:1 In my distress I cried to the Lord,

    And He heard me. This is a great comfort. When we call on the Lord, He always hears. He may not respond to a request in the affirmative, but He hears the appeal. There are requests that He does not grant, but it is a great comfort when a request is granted.

Psalms 121:2 My help *comes* from the Lord,

Who made heaven and earth. This psalmist is reaffirming who ultimately can provide the type of help he might need. It comes from the Lord, and He is always on duty.

Psalms 122:6 Pray for the peace of Jerusalem:
"**May they prosper who love you.** In those times, the pilgrim was happy and delighted when he arrived in Jerusalem to worship the Lord. Jerusalem was the central place of worship of the Lord and where civil judgments were made. The civil laws were closely intertwined with the Law of God. Laws had a moral foundation as revealed by God. They were not just man's feeble attempt at setting the rule of law. Man's laws can be subject to continual change based on the culture of the time. God's Laws have a strong foundation. They don't bend and change with the winds of public opinion. Note that the psalmist is asking for those who want the peace of Jerusalem to prosper. However, this peace will not be final until Christ returns.

Psalms 123:3 Have mercy on us, O Lord, have mercy on us!
For we are exceedingly filled with contempt. As a Christian believer, there will be times when other people hold you in contempt. In other words, they will despise, dishonor, and disrespect you. This verse seems to recognize that fact and asks the Lord for mercy when this occurs. Yes, even though Christianity is all about love, peace, harmony, and joy, people will turn that upside down and blame Christians for all that is bad in the world. In some sense, they will be right that many so-called "Christians" have done many bad things in the world. However, they will be wrong that anything that Christ taught is bad. What Christ taught is "all good." However, people can take any teaching and twist it or take it out of context for their purposes. This may have been what happened with the "crusades," and there are many other misapplications of Christian principles and teachings.

The moral of this story is not to judge Christianity by some people who profess it but don't exhibit the fruit of the Spirit. That fruit is love, joy, peace, longsuffering, kindness, goodness, faithfulness, gentleness, and self-control (Galatians 5:22). Judge Christianity by what its founder, Christ, says. His words are right there, usually in red, in any correctly translated Bible you pick up. You don't have to listen to misapplications or misinterpretations from some self-professed leader, pastor, apostle, or charlatan. You can read it for yourself, and that is what every believer should do so that they will not be influenced by every wind of doctrine that blows through (Matthew 16:12; Romans 16:12; Ephesians 4:14). In some countries, this is hard to do because the government has banned the Bible, but there is no such excuse in America.

Psalms 124:8 Our help *is* in the name of the Lord,

Who made heaven and earth. Where should we first turn in times of trouble? This verse tells us where our help is. We may not get the answer we want, but we will get the correct answer in harmony with God's purposes here on earth.

Psalms 125:1 Those who trust in the Lord

Are **like Mount Zion,**

Which **cannot be moved,** *but* **abides forever.** This psalm, also notes that the Lord **surrounds His people** in the present, in the future, and for all time. Thus, the psalmist is celebrating God's protection of righteousness.

Psalms 126:3 The Lord has done great things for us,

And **we are glad.** In this situation, the Lord had brought the people back from Babylonian captivity, and they were happy and joyful about that. The Lord does great things in our daily lives, but we don't always recognize what He does for us. He even supplies the air that we breathe that keeps us alive. However, we generally take that for granted. If He were to begin to remove the oxygen from the air, we would very quickly stop taking it for granted.

Psalms 127:1 Unless the Lord builds the house,
   They labor in vain who build it;
   Unless the Lord guards the city,
   The watchman stays awake in vain. Along with the book of Ecclesiastes, this verse reveals that what we do without the Lord's involvement is not worth much and is just vanity. In Ecclesiastes 12:13, we learn the opposite of vanity. The bottom line is that we should hold God in the highest esteem, worship only Him and follow His commandments. The rest is portrayed as worthless self-promotion and vanity. In the end, vanity won't be lasting, and there is no hope for eternity in vanity. The fact is that without God, for many of us, life can seem futile and meaningless. An irony is that some people who rebel against God are angry at the God they don't believe exists. That seems to be an exercise in futility.

Psalms 128:1 Blessed *is* every one who fears the Lord,
   Who walks in His ways. If we trust in the Lord and seek to do His will, we will be blessed. This is what fear the Lord seems to mean. It would not make sense to fear the Lord unless you believe He exists. Part of this sentence indicates that there is a God and He is to be feared. The other message is that those who follow the Lord and reverence Him are blessed (Hebrews 12:28,29). For unbelievers, the fear is entirely different (Luke 12:5; Hebrews 10:21). It is fear of His judgment and eternal separation (death). Until we learn who God is, we do not begin to know the truth (Proverbs 1:7). Our fear of God seems to form the basis for knowing, following, serving, and, yes, loving Him.

Psalms 129:5 Let all those who hate Zion
   Be put to shame and turned back. This is a request that those who hate Jerusalem would wither like grass growing on a rooftop when the sun gets warm. The intent seems to be that the wicked will end in shame (35:26). As the sun humiliates the grass on the rooftop, the Son will eventually completely humiliate the wicked, and every knee will bow

down to Him (Romans 14:11; Philippians 2:10).

Psalms 130:5 I wait for the Lord, my soul waits,

And in His word I do hope. The Lord does things in His timing, and therefore, we need to be patient in waiting for what He is going to do. We can keep hope in His word because, in fact, the promises in His word are the only real hope we have for what lies beyond the physical world we are now living in. If there is no spiritual world to which we will go, there isn't much hope. We will live our meager lives and pass away, never to have consciousness again. But, if our hope is in the Word of the Lord, we do have a reason for existing and a bright future (Afterlife), not just on this earth.

Psalms 131:1 Lord, my heart is not haughty,

Nor my eyes lofty.

Neither do I concern myself with significant matters,

Nor with things too profound for me. Some people who do concern themselves with great philosophies and profound issues become puffed up with their knowledge. They imagine that they have some understanding beyond what an average Christian has. They can be proud that they can reason and talk circles around less gifted people. The fact is that some are talking in circles; circular reasoning to be more precise. They do not have a plausible explanation for the creation of the expanding universe other than to explain that the scientific evidence supports a Big Bang from which our universe sprang in the distant past. They might try to convince you that because there is gravity, the universe could create itself. That does not explain it to me. From where did the gravity come? That leap is way beyond what it takes to believe that an all-knowing supernatural God created the universe. If someone puts himself above the one who made the heavens and the earth, that is a lot of self-esteem. However, even the simpler laws of physics, or a little common sense, cannot explain something that came from nothing outside of the supernatural explanation.

We are directed to be ready to defend our faith. We should do so when it is appropriate and does not lead to the sin of anger against another person. There are some brilliant people who have rejected the supernatural. They have studied and know so much that they have come to view themselves and their philosophies as a sort of god. When encountering intellectuals who appear to worship their intellect, it will probably not be of much value to debate theological issues. Instead, it might be best not to try to respond to a diatribe against "Christianity" and all of the supposed damage it has done in the world.

Psalms 132:7 Let us go into His tabernacle;

Let us worship at His footstool. In the Old Testament days, the tabernacle was viewed as a footstool for God as they recognized that there was no way that a tabernacle on earth could contain God. His dwelling is in heaven (99:5). However, He did come to earth as a man for a brief period to redeem us.

Psalms 133:1 Behold, how good and how pleasant *it is*

For brethren to dwell together in unity! It is a great thing when believers get together in unity of understanding about the scripture. It is a delight or like precious oil. We seldom see this type of unity on earth, but it is wonderful when we do. This psalm ends with a statement about the Lord commanding "**Life forevermore.**" Thus, it would seem to be pointing to the benefits of unity here on earth and the spiritual unity of the Kingdom of God in heaven throughout eternity.

Psalms 134:2 Lift up your hands *in* the sanctuary,

And bless the Lord. Lifting hands toward heaven was a typical posture of worship and prayer in those times (1 Timothy 2:8). In this way, the people blessed the Lord, which means that they identified Him as the source of all blessing (103:2).

Psalms 135:3 Praise the Lord, for the Lord *is* good;

Sing praises to His name, for *it is* pleasant. Many times in the Psalms, the psalmist notes that God is good. There are times in life when it appears that bad things are happening to people who are good in our eyes. We can ask why God didn't stop this from happening. We can think: He has the power, so why didn't He prevent a bad thing from happening. There are several problems with this attitude. First, it puts us in the position of judging the creator of the universe. We need to remember that He has a much larger perspective than we do and that we are to walk in His ways, not our ways (Deuteronomy 8:6; 1 Kings 2:3). His ways are better. Second, questioning God assumes that somehow we have a right to do so. This is ridiculous when you consider what a tiny insignificant speck our whole earth is in the vast universe that He created. Verse 135:6 notes that "**Whatever the Lord pleases He does, In heaven and in earth.**" Who are we to question the LORD when this is what it says in His word. Rather than having so much pride that we question Him, we should probably be grateful for all that He has given us.

136:1 Oh, give thanks to the Lord, for *He is* good!

For His mercy *endures* forever. This statement appears to be encouraging public acknowledgment that we should be thankful to the LORD and one of the reasons why. This is hard for most people to accept, but we have no standing to expect or demand anything from the LORD. Yet, He still gives us much, including the breath of life that makes us sentient beings and the very intelligence and consciousness that provides us the capacity for the grandiose arrogance to think about questioning Him. If He didn't have the loyal love (mercy) for us, it would make sense for Him to extinguish humans. The second part of this verse is repeated 26 times in this one Chapter. It seems that the message is made indisputably clear that: "His mercy endures forever."

Psalms 138:1 I will praise You with my whole heart; Before the gods I will sing praises to You. [2] I will worship toward Your holy temple, And praise Your name For Your lovingkindness and Your

truth; For You have magnified Your word above all Your name. As in other Psalms, here David states his intent to praise God with everything he has. Interestingly, David makes mention of "other gods." We don't know what he thought about these "other gods," but we do know that he was making a specific effort to praise the God of the Bible and perhaps to do so even when many were worshiping other gods. There are other god's, mentioned several times in the Bible (Psalms 86:8; 96:4; 135:5; 97:7; Exodus 12:12; Number 33:4; Exodus 20:3; Exodus 23:32-33; Deuteronomy 4:19). These gods appear to have rebelled against God and will eventually have to suffer the consequences. For now, the real battles on earth are between what Paul calls "principalities and powers." These spiritual powers appear to be behind the wars and other cultural battles on the earth. The Psalm also provides more encouragement to praise the Lord. Interestingly, the Psalm indicates that His Word is magnified even above His name. The "Word" is often a metaphor for Christ in the scriptures (John 1:14). That may be the case here.

Psalms 139:8 If I ascend into heaven, You *are* there;
If I make my bed in hell, behold, You *are there.* It appears that the psalmist believed that God is everywhere. This fact seems to be the teaching of the Bible. That can be a comforting fact, especially in difficult times.

Psalms 139:13-14 For You formed my inward parts;
You covered me in my mother's womb.
14 I will praise You, for I am fearfully *and* wonderfully made;
Marvelous are Your works,
And *that* my soul knows very well. When does God's involvement with us start? From the psalmist's perspective, it began in the womb with the formation of everything that makes our bodies function. It is complex and amazing how all our organs and tissues are put together and work.

139:23-24 Search me, O God, and know my heart;
Try me, and know my anxieties;
24 And see if *there is any* wicked way in me,
And lead me in the way everlasting. This is a bold statement since we all know that there are times when what is in our hearts is not what we want anyone, let alone God, to know. We know that there are wicked thoughts (Jeremiah 17:9).

Psalms 141:2 Let my prayer be set before You *as* incense,
The lifting up of my hands *as* the evening sacrifice. He wanted his prayers to be pleasing to the Lord. It appears he wanted his prayers to be sweet and pleasant to the Lord so that they might be accepted. David was desperate at this time and was crying out for the Lord to hear his prayers.

Psalms 142:7 Bring my soul out of prison,
That I may praise Your name; Here David asks to be set free from the sanctuary of the cave that had become his prison so he could be free to praise the Lord in the open. In failure, we can become self-focused and down on ourselves. In victory, we can become self-focused and prideful. A better approach is to focus on the Lord, whether in failure or success (2 Corinthians 3:18,19; Hebrews 12:2). Then we will know that whatever happens on this earth, we have a hope for an abundant life after this life is over (Ecclesiastes 12:7; John 11:25; 1 Corinthians 15:51-54).

Psalms 143:2 Do not enter into judgment with Your servant,
For in Your sight no one living is righteous. This is a true statement. Until we understand the ramifications of this fact, we do not understand our need for forgiveness and a Savior who can provide that forgiveness. Only the imputed righteousness can allow us to have a relationship with the living God who is holy holy holy. With this imputed righteousness, we are seen as righteous by God. Our sins are as far as the East is from the West in His sight (Psalms 103:12).

Psalms 143:8 Cause me to hear Your lovingkindness in the morning,
For in You do I trust;
Cause me to know the way in which I should walk,
For I lift up my soul to You. Interestingly, the psalmist sometimes apparently goes to sleep with an expectation and trust that an answer from the Lord will come in the morning. I have noticed that when we need to make a big decision, it is best not to make it hastily, but rather to pray about it and then sleep on it, and in the morning, the correct answer is often more apparent.

Psalms 143:12 In Your mercy cut off my enemies,
And destroy all those who afflict my soul;
For I *am* Your servant. Here is a prayer from David for God to cut off his enemies. His enemies were trying to kill him at the time, so this seems like a rational prayer. But then he gives God a reason to destroy them. He says that he is God's servant. The implication is that his enemies were not serving God. We do not talk much about this type of prayer, but if you have enemies not serving the LORD, you might feel like following David's example.

Earlier in this psalm, David asks that he be revived for God's namesake and God's righteousness' sake. Thus, David reasoned with God to answer his prayers to preserve His name and righteousness. He seemed to be reasoning that since David was God's servant, it would not look good for the Lord, by association, if David were to be destroyed by his nonbelieving enemies.

Psalms 144:4 Man is like a breath;
His days *are* like a passing shadow. Wow, that is not very long. Even without believing in an afterlife, our life seems like a long time when we are young. Then as we age and we eventually see some of our contemporaries die, we start to realize that life on earth is not very

long. Compared to the almost 14 billion years that scientists tell us our universe has existed, our lifespan is entirely insignificant (120 years would be .0000000086 % of the total).

If a person lives to be 120 years old, I calculate the percentage a lifespan is of the time our universe may have existed at .0000000086 percent. No matter how you cut it, that isn't much. To us, our life can seem long, but in reality, its length is insignificant. However, even though our lives are short, they are significant to us and God.

Psalms 144:9 I will sing a new song to You, O God;
On a harp of ten strings I will sing praises to You,... Here again, there is a commitment from the psalmist to sing a new song of praise to God and accompany the song on a ten-stringed harp. This is confirmation that the use of instruments in worship is wholly acceptable and even desirable.

Psalms 144:15 Happy *are* the people who are in such a state;
Happy *are* the people whose God *is* the Lord! Of course, people whose God is the Lord cannot be happy one hundred percent of their time on earth. Nevertheless, in general, they should be happier than a person who has no hope for an afterlife.

Psalms 145:2-3 Every day I will bless You,
And I will praise Your name forever and ever.
3 Great *is* the Lord, and greatly to be praised;
And His greatness *is* unsearchable. Here the psalmist is committing to bless the Lord and praise Him every day. How many of us praise the name of the Lord daily? When this psalmist says that the Lord is great, he is stating an obvious fact.

Psalms 145:7 They shall utter the memory of Your great goodness,
And sing of His righteousness. Here David commits to singing

praises to the Lord for his goodness and righteousness.

Psalms 145:18 The Lord is near to those who call upon him. This is excellent news. It is good to have the Lord near to us at any time.

Psalms 145:20-21 The Lord preserves all who love Him,
But all the wicked, He will destroy. That the Lord will destroy the wicked is a sobering thought. That is not a category in which anyone should want to be.

Psalms 146:1-2 Praise the Lord!
Praise the Lord, O my soul!
2 While I live I will praise the Lord;
I will sing praises to my God while I have my being. This is a commitment by King David to praise the Lord for the rest of his life. He is an example for all of us.

Psalms 146:3 Do not put your trust in princes,
Nor in a son of man, in whom *there is* no help. Don't put your trust even in good people seems to be the message of this psalm. Stated in another way, we may not be able to turn to the best of mortal people for help in the most difficult of times. The Lord is the only one who has the answer to the most difficult of eternal questions. Better go to the one who had the power to create the heavens and the earth for help.

Psalms 147:1 Praise the Lord!
For *it is* good to sing praises to our God;
For *it is* pleasant, *and* praise is beautiful. Here are some other reasons to spend time in praise of the Lord. This verse explains it very simply. It is good, pleasant, and beautiful in addition to being the right thing to do.

147:5 Great *is* our Lord, and mighty in power;
His understanding *is* infinite. How many of us human beings can be

said to have an infinite understanding? I would guess, none. Our Lord is great, mighty, powerful, and has infinite understanding. No one on earth can even come close to this.

Psalms 147:7 Sing to the Lord with thanksgiving;
Sing praises on the harp to our God, Repeatedly, Psalms encourage us to praise the Lord in song. The Lord knows how dense we can be and that for us to comprehend something and remember it fully, we need to have it repeated multiple times.

Psalms 147:11 The Lord takes pleasure in those who fear Him,
In those who hope in His mercy. The simple message here is that fear/respect for the Lord pleases Him. This Psalm takes two lines to let us know part of what fear of the Lord means. Here the fear of the Lord is directly followed by an explanation that these are the people who hope in His mercy. Thus, I believe the meaning of the word translated fear in this verse is reverence or awe.

Psalms 148:5 Let them praise the name of the Lord,
For He commanded and they were created. This would apply to all of us. God commanded, and humans were created. He is our creator, and therefore, we should give Him the respect and praise that He deserves.

Psalms 149:1 Sing to the Lord a new song,
***And* His praise in the assembly of saints.** Many of the hymns from the 16 and 1700s are still popular today, but when they were written, they were new songs far removed from the time when the psalms were written. There is nothing in the Bible that encourages us only to sing songs from a certain period of history though some Christians act as if there is because they are hostile against any songs that were not composed in the 16 or 1700's.

In this psalm (149), we are encouraged to continue writing "new" worship songs. There is nothing wrong with old songs, but we should not get stuck in a particular century as our resource for all songs to be used in worship. Charles Wesley is said to have written 8989 hymns in the seventeen hundreds. That is probably enough songs for anyone to sing in a lifetime, but it is not enough for the Lord because He wants and deserves "new" songs.

Psalms 149:4. For the Lord takes pleasure in His people;
He will beautify the humble with salvation. This is excellent news. We can do some things that the Lord takes pleasure in, and He will grant these with salvation. These believers are humble enough to recognize the Lord for who He is and give Him the praise and respect that He deserves.

150:1-6 Praise the Lord!
Praise God in His sanctuary;
Praise Him in His mighty firmament!
2 Praise Him for His mighty acts;
Praise Him according to His excellent greatness!
3 Praise Him with the sound of the trumpet;
Praise Him with the lute and harp!
4 Praise Him with the timbrel and dance;
Praise Him with stringed instruments and flutes!
5 Praise Him with loud cymbals;
Praise Him with clashing cymbals!
6 Let everything that has breath praise the Lord.
Praise the Lord! The message here is simple and profound. We should praise God with our voices and all instruments at our disposal for all our lives (146:1, 2). This is the culmination of all the psalms, which is the book of praises. It is the longest book in the Bible which I take as another indication of how important it is to recognize God through singing His praises. What an honor and privilege He has given us to use songs and music in a way that gives pleasure to our creator.

20

Proverbs

[20]**PROVERBS** - This book is composed of a type of Hebrew poetry that uses parallelism to repeat thoughts. Often the second line repeats the first in different terms. This is synonymous parallelism. Antiparallelism is also used where the second line expresses the thought in negative terms. In other proverbs, the second line completes the thought in the first line. These proverbs are different from other books of wisdom in that this wisdom appears to be based on faith in God.

Proverbs 1:7 The fear of the Lord *is* the beginning of knowledge, *But* fools despise wisdom and instruction. In this first chapter of Proverbs, we learn a knowledge prerequisite. I think this means that knowledge gained without a correct foundation can quickly come to incorrect conclusions and understanding. These first proverbs are from Solomon and, according to the introduction, are for gaining wisdom and understanding, which is helpful for prudence and discretion. Proverbs 1:5 says that "**a man of understanding will attain wise counsel.**" Proverbs is part of the wise counsel that a man of understanding is

---

[20] NSB quotations are from the Nelsons Study Bible, copyright (c) 1997 by Thomas Nelson, Inc., Nashville, TN; used by permission; scripture taken from the New King James Version, Copyright (c) 1979, 1980, 1982 used by permission. All rights reserved.

expected to attain. The word "instruction" can also be translated as "discipline," so that is something to keep in mind. Part of what this introduction appears to be implying is that wisdom does not involve just knowledge. It involves knowledge and intelligence, but also moral integrity. Without moral integrity, knowledge is not worth much and can be dangerous.

Proverbs 1:19 So *are* the ways of everyone who is greedy for gain; It takes away the life of its owners. Here's a sobering thought against greed. In other words, it appears that greed can become so all-consuming when it is allowed to fester that it kills the real life of the person who has it.

Greed is not simply a bad thing; it is a matter of life and death. A television show called American Greed highlights many people whose greed caused them to steal and deceive others, and when they were caught, they wound up in prison. Thus, even in our current culture, freedom is taken away from greedy lawbreakers, just as the proverb predicts.

Proverbs 2:3 Yes, if you cry out for discernment,
   ***And* lift up your voice for understanding,**
   4 If you seek her as silver,
   And search for her as *for* hidden treasures;
   5 Then you will understand the fear of the Lord,
   And find the knowledge of God. Many people would say, I don't want to fear God. They don't want to be afraid of anything. There are at least two different meanings for fear of the Lord. For those who have accepted the forgiveness that the Lord offers, the fear would be the definition that has to do with "reverential awe," especially for God. Synonyms for this type of fear are respect, reverence, awe, and veneration. I believe that this type of "fear" of the LORD is what the scripture means much of the time when "fear" is the word used in the English translation.

Others may be thinking of the standard definition of the word that connotes a feeling of anxiety and doom. In the next part of chapter 2, the Proverbs provide wisdom regarding those who participate with an immoral woman whose house the proverb asserts "leads down to death." The chapter goes on to say that these wicked and unfaithful will eventually be "cut off from the earth." So here, for those described in these proverbs, the common definition of "fear" would be appropriate.

Proverbs 3:5-6 Trust in the Lord with all your heart
   and lean not on your own understanding;
   6 in all your ways submit to him,
   and he will make your paths straight. Here is a very well-known proverb. We are encouraged not to forget God's law or commandments. We are to continue to pursue mercy and truth. If we trust the Lord, we will also honor Him by tithing from the first of our income and possessions. When we do this, the proverbs let us know that we will still have plenty. This is true because it is in God's word, and that is all the proof we need, but you can also prove this proverb through your own experience.

Proverbs 3:13 Blessed are those who find wisdom,
   those who gain understanding, Here are two things that are more important than money or fine gold or rubies: wisdom and understanding. All the other material things do not even compare to these. These things generally lead to a long and peaceful life. By wisdom and understanding, the Lord established the earth, the heavens, and the land on which we live (Proverbs 3:19). Wisdom is strongly associated with creation. Chapter 8 of Proverbs makes this abundantly clear. This wisdom will cause us to do good to our neighbors and realize that God will bless the home of the just. He will also correct and discipline those He loves (the just) and curse the house of the wicked in His due time.

Proverbs 5:15 Drink water from your own cistern,
   And running water from your own well. In the context of this

proverb, we understand that we are to maintain absolute marital fidelity. A wise man will stay far away from an immoral woman and even from the door of her house. The proverbs do not allow a shred of misunderstanding regarding a husband's responsibility to his wife with this wording: "Let her breasts satisfy you at all times; And always be enraptured by her love" (Proverbs 5:19).

Proverbs 6:16 These six *things* the Lord hates,
 Yes, seven *are* an abomination to Him:
 17 A proud look,
 A lying tongue,
 Hands that shed innocent blood,
 18 A heart that devises wicked plans,
 Feet that are swift in running to evil,
 19 A false witness *who* speaks lies,
 And one who sows discord among brethren. I have been told that some Universalists believe God is so full of grace, love, and kindness that He doesn't hate anything. Based on this scripture, that position is a different gospel than what is in the Bible. This part of Proverbs clearly states that there are at least seven things that the Lord hates. Other scriptures site many more things that are an abomination to Him. Thus, according to the Christian Bible, the Lord hates many things. All of the things listed in this parable are things the Lord hates. Some of us are guilty of several of these offenses. Hence, to satisfy justice, there is a need for punishment. Christ took on this punishment on our behalf. He paid the price that justice demanded for our sins.

Most alternative gospels say that you have to do some kind of work to be good enough to obtain favor from God and be saved. The Christian Bible says you cannot be good enough. Do not misinterpret what I am saying. I am not saying anything negative about doing good works. The person who has accepted the gift of salvation through faith in what Christ did for us will wind up demonstrating that faith through their good works.

So faith and works are intertwined. However, we need to understand that good works cannot earn anyone salvation.

Salvation in the Bible is through faith by the grace of God. In this same chapter, adultery and thievery are condemned. Other verses of this chapter make it clear that the man who allows himself to be seduced into adultery is "**descending to the chambers of death**." He should not even think about her, or he is in danger of being reduced **to a crust of bread**. It sure sounds like this adulterous behavior is not innocent. Nevertheless, we need to remember that even a person who has done all of these sins can be forgiven. However, it does not appear that God will force forgiveness on anyone if they do not want it from Him.

Proverbs 6:30-31 *People* do not despise a thief
   If he steals to satisfy himself when he is starving.
   31 Yet *when* he is found, he must restore sevenfold;
   He may have to give up all the substance of his house. The preceding verse is about adultery. Whereas, though it is still wrong to steal, the person who steals food to keep from starving can be understood. However, the adulterer should not be given the same understanding and cannot restore what they have taken. A thief shall restore sevenfold and be exonerated, but what is taken cannot be restored with adultery.

Proverbs 7:2 Keep my commands and live,
   And my law as the apple of your eye.
   3 Bind them on your fingers;
   Write them on the tablet of your heart. In the Hebrew idiom, the apple of the eye meant the pupil. This begs the question: to what lengths will you go to protect the pupil of your eye? The answer is that most of us would do a lot to protect the window to the visual world around us, the pupil of the eye. I think this proverb is saying we should memorize as much as we can of the commandments of God. To bind them on your fingers could mean to keep the commands and law as close as being at

your fingertips at any time. In our modern-day world, keeping a copy of the Bible on our phones would seem to be an excellent way to keep the commands and law at our fingertips.

Proverbs 8:14-18 Counsel *is* mine, and sound wisdom;
I *am* understanding, I have strength.
15 By me kings reign,
And rulers decree justice.
16 By me princes rule, and nobles,
All the judges of the earth. Translation: God is ultimately in control. He set our world up and gave us free will to do as we please, but in the end, God's plan will be fulfilled. All rulers and anyone else would benefit when obtaining counsel and wisdom from God. If God chose to, He could remove any ruler from their position immediately. Still, God is incredibly patient with us in giving us time to decide to follow Him.

Proverbs 8:17 I love those who love me,
And those who seek me diligently will find me.
18 Riches and honor *are* with me,
Enduring riches and righteousness. For those who love and follow the Lord, they will end up with riches and honor in eternity. Even in this world, following the precepts of God generally leads to success. However, success in this world is not the most important issue, nor is it guaranteed for anyone. What is far more important is an eternal success with God. Life here is just a vapor compared to eternity (James 4:14).

Proverbs 8:21 That I may cause those who love me to inherit wealth,
That I may fill their treasuries. The Lord may bless those who love Him with inherited wealth. He does not have to and may not. But, when He does, inherited wealth should be viewed as a gift from God. After all, He made the person from whom the wealth is being inherited.

Proverbs 8:25-26 Before the mountains were settled,

**Before the hills, I was brought forth;
26 While as yet He had not made the earth or the fields,
Or the primal dust of the world.** This seems to be about Christ. The following proverb says that before the heavens were prepared, "I was there." Thus, if this is Christ speaking, it confirms that He always existed and was God.

**Proverbs 9:7 "He who corrects a scoffer gets shame for himself,
And he who rebukes a wicked *man only* harms himself.** Sometimes we don't need any response to a scoffer or a wicked man. Notice that this proverb appears to be specific to an adult. Once a "man" is set in his ways, the correction you might provide to a young person is no longer appropriate. When this proverb mentions a scoffer, it may also apply to a mocker. These people are usually not humble and do not even accept constructive criticism (1:22) instead of a wise person who may welcome it. Thus, the advice provided here is that if someone is mocking your belief in God, this may not warrant any kind of response. If you have an adult-to-adult discussion, that is a different situation.

**Proverbs 9:10-12 "The fear of the Lord *is* the beginning of wisdom,
And the knowledge of the Holy One *is* understanding.
11 For by me your days will be multiplied,
And years of life will be added to you.
12 If you are wise, you are wise for yourself,
And *if* you scoff, you will bear *it* alone."** Here, it is fairly clear that each person develops wisdom and understanding individually. Those who fear the Lord will have their days multiplied. Their days will be eternal. That is an infinite amount of multiplication.

This may also apply to years on earth since it appears that the person who follows the Lord and His ways will also generally have a longer life on earth if for no other reason than better health through moderation. This proverb points out that fear, which in this instance appears to mean reverence for the Lord, is central to the life of a believer. The proverbs point this out over and over. This proverb also points out that you will experience either the effects of your wisdom or your foolishness individually. There are temporal and eternal consequences both here and in the afterlife.

Proverbs 10:12 Hatred stirs up strife,
But love covers all sins. Love covers all sins. What a great thought! It was the love of Christ that paid the price (i.e., covered) all of our sins. On the other hand, hatred causes the opposite to happen. If you hate, there is no quarter given; there is no forgiveness; there is no love; only fighting and strife. When you think about it, we have to have a prideful opinion of ourselves to hate someone, and pride is a root of evil. Thus, it is not reasonable to expect any good to come from hatred. Love and understanding are generally the much better course of action.

Proverbs 11:1 Dishonest scales *are* an abomination to the Lord,
But a just weight *is* His delight. Dishonest scales are also disliked by almost everyone else.

Proverbs 11:2 When pride comes, then comes shame;
But with the humble *is* wisdom. The word pride here means the arrogant, insolent type of pride. That is the type of pride that has the person saying or doing things that do not flatter the person when they come to light.

Proverbs 11:4 Riches do not profit in the day of wrath,
But righteousness delivers from death. Part of the problem with spending too much time accumulating riches is that you do not take it with you. Those who focus on righteousness can be the ones who gain eternal life. Upon our physical death, only righteousness matters. How much you had before you died does not help you in the afterlife.

Proverbs 11:14 Where *there is* no counsel, the people fall;
But in the multitude of counselors *there is* safety. This is a clear recommendation for us to talk to others before making big decisions. But who are the best people with whom to talk? Suppose a couple is having problems with their marriage and wants to keep it together. In that case, they should probably seek counsel from people who have had success keeping their marriages together rather than a person who has had multiple failures in this area. Or, if you are having problems managing your finances, it might be good to seek counsel from people who are well off in this area instead of a person who has had multiple bankruptcies. It is best to get several opinions from mature, wise, and godly counselors.

Proverbs 11:15 He who is surety for a stranger will suffer,
But one who hates being surety is secure. A surety is making a pledge or guarantee for someone else. Co-signing a loan for someone is an example. It certainly is not a good idea to provide surety for someone you do not know. Generally, it is not a good idea to provide surety for anyone who does not have a good reputation on their own. If a person needs surety from someone else, it may be a sign that they are not a good risk on their own. Nevertheless, to balance this thought, it is good to be generous to those in need, but do not be generous to the point of putting your reputation in jeopardy due to the inability of someone to make good on their promise.

Proverbs 11:22 *As* a ring of gold in a swine's snout,
***So is* a lovely woman who lacks discretion.** A ring of gold and a lovely woman are both nice, but a pig is still a pig even if it has a gold ring in its snout. Lack of discretion is still a lack of discretion even when practiced by someone who looks good.

Proverbs 11:25 The generous soul will be made rich,
And he who waters will also be watered himself. The generous

person will be rich one way or another, either spiritually or materially.

Proverbs 11:28 He who trusts in his riches will fall,
   But the righteous will flourish like foliage. Riches can come and go with the rising and falling of the stock market. However, the one who is given righteousness through faith generally grows in that righteousness.

Proverbs 11:30. The fruit of the righteous *is a* tree of life,
   And he who wins souls *is* wise. What is the tree of life? Eternal life. Why does righteousness produce more life? The righteous inherit eternal life. Recovering the lost tree of life appears to be comparable to winning souls.

Proverbs 12:4 An excellent wife *is* the crown of her husband,
   But she who causes shame *is* like rottenness in his bones. It is a tremendous benefit for a husband to have a good wife. Everything in life is impacted. She can make him look good, and this explains the reference to a crown. On the other hand, because the two are as one, if a wife (or husband for that matter) causes shame, it deeply negatively affects the non-offending spouse.

Proverbs 12:5 The thoughts of the righteous *are* right,
   ***But* the counsels of the wicked *are* deceitful.** It is good to get a multitude of counsel but do not get it from wicked people. Instead, always obtain your counsel from righteous people.

Proverbs 12:25 Anxiety in the heart of man causes depression,
   But a good word makes it glad. The depression that is caused by anxiety can be reduced by an encouraging word from someone, especially when the encouragement comes at the appropriate time.

Proverbs 13:3 He who guards his mouth preserves his life,
   ***But* he who opens wide his lips shall have destruction.** It is wise

to control the tongue and not say everything you are feeling, thinking, or know. There was a war-time saying that "loose lips sink ships." This slogan reminded people not to discuss ship movements because if the information got into enemy hands, it might sink the ships. It is also clear that what we say can be very destructive, so it is good to use discretion.

Proverbs 13:20 He who walks with wise *men* will be wise,
But the companion of fools will be destroyed. Associate with wise people is the message here. If you want to be wise, it helps a lot to associate with wise people. Part of the reason is the influence of peer pressure. Peers have a tremendous influence. Therefore, it is good to spend time with wise people who can influence us in good ways and provide wise counsel. Another advantage of associating with wise people is that they can be trusted. Fools cannot be trusted and may use and abuse their so-called friends. Of course, we were also probably foolish at some point in our lives and needed to be around wise people. Thus, though we need to walk with wise people, we should not isolate ourselves from others as they also need wise influences to avoid destruction.

Proverbs 13:24 He who spares his rod hates his son,
But he who loves him disciplines him promptly. Discipline helps a young person to know where the limits are. When there are limits with appropriate consequences attached, the young person develops self-control through living within limits. If there are no limits or the limits are not stable, it becomes difficult for the developing person to learn self-control. Without some self-control, everything in life is harder or impossible to accomplish. What children need is compassionate but firm authority. The balance is between love and discipline. A good parent does not discipline out of anger but rather because they want the best for their child. This parent knows how difficult it will be for the child when they get to adulthood if they have not been taught to live within appropriate limits and have developed self-control in the process.

There are several reasons to discipline from a Biblical perspective. First, discipline can prevent or deter destruction. It is better for a child to get an appropriate spanking than to be allowed to run into the street and get run over by a car. Second, for discipline to be complete, it needs to involve words of instruction and consequences for failure to meet the mark. Third, keep in mind that discipline shows the child that they are loved enough for the parent to discipline them to do the right thing (Hebrews 12:6-9). Fourth, the goal of discipline is to help the child learn self-control and obedience (Hebrews 12:9). Fifth, it is recognized that there may not be gain without some pain. However, the pain is generally short-term, but the gains can be life-long. Also, the parent needs to have a long-term perspective on giving discipline because it is usually painful in the short term. Years later, a child may finally recognize the love it took for the parent to discipline them and how beneficial it was for them to learn self-control. The idea here is not to give in to a short-sighted approach. Discipline your child, and, in the long run, you and your child will be happier.

Proverbs 14:7 Go from the presence of a foolish man,
When you do not perceive *in him* the lips of knowledge. This proverb says not to hang out with foolish people. It does not appear to be talking about a person who made a few bad decisions. For a person to be a foolish man would probably involve a long string of bad choices. We are advised to depart from these people when we encounter them.

Proverbs 14:15 The simple believes every word,
But the prudent considers well his steps. Do not believe everything you hear. In the fallen world in which we live, it makes sense to have a healthy level of skepticism and hear both sides of an issue before forming an opinion. Even as we watch the news and listen to stories that are later proved to be incorrect, we know that we should not form opinions until we have a chance to ponder what we have been told and check it out with multiple sources. We need to be careful about being too gullible.

Proverbs 14:26-27 In the fear of the Lord *there is* strong confidence, And His children will have a place of refuge.
27 The fear of the Lord *is* a fountain of life,
To turn *one* away from the snares of death. Fear of the Lord brings strong confidence and life. As noted elsewhere in this commentary, fear in this context may be translated as a positive reverence or respect for the LORD. It can be described as not wanting to displease Him. When we have a healthy respect for the Lord's commandments and follow them, we avoid a lot of negative consequences.

Proverbs 14:29 *He who is* slow to wrath has great understanding,
But *he who is* impulsive exalts folly. This is a short proverb that speaks of what can be called emotional intelligence. A person who has it does not let anger get the best of them. They take time to get all the facts before making a decision and obtain a multitude of godly counsel before making big decisions.

Proverbs 14:34 Righteousness exalts a nation,
But sin *is* a reproach to *any* people. Sin does not exalt a nation. When our leaders are honest, just, and righteous, it has a positive impact on the nation's reputation. Also, the collective individual actions of its citizens affect the overall reputation of a country.

Proverbs 15:3 The eyes of the Lord *are* in every place,
Keeping watch on the evil and the good. The Lord sees everything and knows what is going on 24/7. This is a good thing. The cover of darkness does not get you anonymity with the LORD.

Proverbs 15:8 The sacrifice of the wicked *is* an abomination to the Lord,
But the prayer of the upright *is* His delight. It is good to know that the Lord delights in our prayers. That is one good reason to keep praying. On the other hand, the LORD does not like anything coming His way

from someone wicked. The Bible describes the wicked as oppressive, arrogant, and proud (Psalm 10:2). They are also aggressive and violent (Psalms 10:7). The LORD does not like these people coming to Him with hypocrisy as if they cared.

Proverbs 15:22 Without counsel, plans go awry,
But in the multitude of counselors they are established. For big decisions, counsel is even more important and should not be from just one source. Other scripture, advises that the best counsel comes from wise people (see 15:33).

Proverbs 15:33 The fear of the Lord *is* the instruction of wisdom,
And before honor *is* humility. Knowledge alone may not be that valuable if it is not put in the correct context of reverence for the LORD.

Proverbs 16:1 The preparations of the heart *belong* to man,
But the answer of the tongue *is* from the Lord. We can make plans but what happens is ultimately determined by the LORD.

Proverbs 16:4 The Lord has made all for Himself,
Yes, even the wicked for the day of doom. Interestingly, the LORD made the wicked for the day of doom. This puts a different perspective on those who we think are wicked. They were part of God's plan for the world. He made the world and everything in it for Himself and therefore can do whatever He wants with all of His creation.

When you think about it, how would we know what is good unless there was something bad? If every car were 100 percent dependable, there would be no meaning to the statement: "the car is a lemon." Nor would there be any meaning to saying that a car is 100 percent dependable if all cars were 100 percent dependable.

Also, how would it be if you did not have a choice to do something wrong?

That would mean that you had no free will. You would do what you were programmed to do. In that case, would you be a human being? The answer is that if you were still a human being, it would be a very different kind of human being. This is an example of an issue that shows us we have a creator who has a lot more intelligence and understanding than any human being.

Note also that this proverb tells us why God created us. He made us for Himself. In other words, He made us because that is what He wanted to do.

Proverbs 16:16 How much better to get wisdom than gold!
   And to get understanding is to be chosen rather than silver. Wisdom and understanding are more important than riches.

Proverbs 16:31 The silver-haired head *is* a crown of glory,
   ***If* it is found in the way of righteousness.** It is good to know that silver hair can be a crown of glory since if we live long enough, most of us will wind up with silver hair if we still have hair. Note that there is a caveat that the glory depends on the person being in the way of righteousness.

Proverbs 16:33 The lot is cast into the lap,
   But its every decision *is* from the Lord. In general, under the dispensation of grace in which we are currently in, it may not be a good idea to try to determine the LORD's direction by casting lots. However, in the Old Testament days, when this was part of the culture, it appears that they needed to take it as the LORD's will. I don't think this is the way to determine the LORD's will in our time. Also, if you did, you might cast lots with the questions structured for your will as opposed to the LORD's, in which case, you may be fooling yourself.

Proverbs 17:15 He who justifies the wicked, and he who condemns

the just,

Both of them alike *are* an abomination to the Lord. In the last days, men will say that good is bad and bad is good (Isaiah 5:20; 2 Timothy 3:1-5). The LORD does not like this scenario. We know that the LORD loves justice (Isaiah 61:8), so this backward scenario would be detestable to the LORD.

Proverbs 17:27 He who has knowledge spares his words,

***And* a man of understanding is of a calm spirit.** Sometimes it is wise not to say everything you know.

Proverbs 18:6 A fool's lips enter into contention,

And his mouth calls for blows. Many of us have run across someone who fits this description in our lives. It is probably best to stay away from this kind of person.

Proverbs 18:10 The name of the Lord *is* a strong tower;

The righteous run to it and are safe. When we have difficult times, believers rely on the LORD for comfort and safety. There is no other name as strong to whom we can go for comfort.

Proverbs 18:15 The heart of the prudent acquires knowledge,

And the ear of the wise seeks knowledge. So, rather than diminishing the quest for knowledge, the Bible recommends it and says that the pursuit of knowledge is prudent and wise. Some think that the Bible discourages pursuing science, but this proverb refutes that thinking. It encourages science and higher levels of knowledge about the universe.

Proverbs 18:21 Death and life *are* in the power of the tongue,

And those who love it will eat its fruit. James 3:2 says that if you can control the tongue, you probably can control the whole body. The tongue is small but has tremendous power even over life and death. A judge pronouncing a death sentence or a president making a declaration of war are examples of the power of the tongue over life and death.

Proverbs 19:1 Better *is* the poor who walks in his integrity
Than *one who is* perverse in his lips, and is a fool. Here again, we see that integrity is more important than wealth. Integrity is consistently given high regard in the proverbs.

Proverbs 19:20 Listen to counsel and receive instruction,
That you may be wise in your latter days. Here again, we are encouraged to get a multitude of counsel and be open to teaching. Of course, from other scripture, we know that the council needs to come from wise sources. What does this wise counsel do for us? It makes us wise in our senior years.

Proverbs 19:21 There are many plans in a man's heart,
Nevertheless the Lord's counsel—that will stand. This is a different way of saying, "man makes his plans, but the LORD directs his path." I can remember planning my career and having it take a totally different direction. That direction turned out to have a much better outcome than what I had been planning. This proverb is helpful when we think things are not going our way. They may be going a better way in the long run. Here are five words starting with the letter "P" that might help a person decide what direction to take: Providence (open doors), Prayer (do this first), Patience (wait for direction), Passion (What do you like and what are you good at?), Perspective (always get a multitude of godly counsel). If all of these line up, it could indicate that you are headed in the right direction.

Proverbs 20:1 Wine *is* a mocker,
  Strong drink *is* a brawler,
  And whoever is led astray by it is not wise. We have all probably seen the negative effects of too much wine or more potent mixed drinks. Some people have a Dr. Jekyll/Mr. Hyde reaction when they drink

too much alcohol. A generally considerate person can become angry, belligerent, or violent under the influence of alcohol or drugs.

Government statistics show that 26 to 32 percent of people in prison were under the influence of some mind-altering drug when they committed the crime that led to their incarceration. Obviously, in conjunction with other advice in the scripture against drunkenness, Christians should not drink to excess or to the point of losing control. The amount of alcohol in the blood allowed for driving would be one standard to keep in mind. If you have had too much to drive, you probably have had too much.

Some people seem to have a biological predisposition to be unable to control the consumption of alcohol or drugs. These people cannot imbibe at all without terrible consequences for themselves and their family and friends. Even if you are one of the people who can drink without overindulging, the "one and done" approach might be a good standard to keep in mind.

Proverbs 20:3 *It is* honorable for a man to stop striving,
Since any fool can start a quarrel. This is true. The person who pursues peace is honorable, but some people appear to be itching for a fight. It might be a good idea to avoid these people.

Proverbs 20:5 Counsel in the heart of man *is like* deep water,
But a man of understanding will draw it out. Again we have the advice to seek counsel. Over and over, we are advised to seek out wise counsel.

Proverbs 20:13 Do not love sleep, lest you come to poverty;
Open your eyes, *and* you will be satisfied with bread. This appears to be a recommendation to get up, get out, and work to be able to buy food. Employers expect employees to show up at the specified day and time, rested and ready to work. Those who do not comply with these

expectations are usually let go because the employer cannot depend on them.

Proverbs 20:18 Plans are established by counsel; By wise counsel wage war. Hopefully, our leaders will not go to war without getting a lot of counsel about why it is necessary. War is so destructive it usually needs to be a last resort.

Proverbs 20:19 He who goes about as a talebearer reveals secrets; Therefore do not associate with one who flatters with his lips. It is potentially damaging to associate with someone who cannot keep confidence. Therefore, it might be prudent to avoid being around this type of person.

Proverbs 20:22 Do not say, "I will recompense evil"; Wait for the LORD, and He will save you. The LORD says that vengeance is His (Matthew 5:38,39). One of the problems, if we were to attempt to repay evil, is that we are not perfect judges and do not know the heart of a man like the LORD does. His justice will be just. Ours may not.

Proverbs 20:27 The spirit of a man *is* the lamp of the LORD,
   Searching all the inner depths of his heart. A lamp provides light so things can be seen. This proverb compares a lamp to the spirit of man. Thus, our spirit illuminates the depths of our hearts to the LORD.

Proverbs 21:1 The king's heart *is* in the hand of the Lord,
   ***Like* the rivers of water;**
   He turns it wherever He wishes. God is in control. We may not like the direction that things are flowing at the moment, but we need to accept that it may not flow the direction we want, especially in the short run.

Proverbs 21:5 The plans of the diligent *lead* surely to plenty,

But *those of* everyone *who is* hasty, surely to poverty. In whatever endeavor we are engaged, it helps to be diligent, patient, and persistent. Those who do not take the time to develop good plans and diligently apply them can go from one get-rich-quick scheme to the next and will probably not have plenty but instead end up in poverty.

Proverbs 21:17 He who loves pleasure *will be* a poor man;
He who loves wine and oil will not be rich. This is just stating that if you focus too much on pleasure, wine, and oil, you will probably end up poor. Not that being rich should be our goal, but neither should pleasure, wine, and oil. We need a balance between work and leisure that will lead us to a productive and satisfying life.

Proverbs 21:19 Better to dwell in the wilderness,
Than with a contentious and angry woman. If a man (or a woman, for that matter) only has a contentious angry person to consider as a spouse, it would be better for you to go to the wilderness and wait than to become tied to such a person.

Proverbs 21:20 *There is* desirable treasure,
And oil in the dwelling of the wise,
But a foolish man squanders it. Even when a gambler's ship comes in, so to speak, it usually does not stay for very long. The old saying: "come easy, go easy," is probably true. Wise people typically work over long periods to become successful. Those who have easy gains, such as gambling winnings, tend to let it go as quickly as it came. However, those who work hard for their money are not as comfortable letting that hard-earned money slip through their hands.

Proverbs 21:21 He who follows righteousness and mercy
Finds life, righteousness, and honor. Proverbs 15:9 says that the LORD loves the person who follows righteousness. Matthew 5:7 says that the merciful will receive mercy. From James 2:13, we know that

mercy triumphs over judgment. Put all this together, and good things are the result.

Proverbs 21:23 Whoever guards his mouth and tongue
Keeps his soul from troubles. We know that the tongue and mouth are small but incredibly powerful for good or destructive actions. The tongue is like the rudder of a ship or the bit in a horse's mouth. It can control the direction of something much larger. The person who can keep control of what they say generally can control what they do and avoid big troubles.

Proverbs 22:9 He who has a generous eye will be blessed,
For he gives of his bread to the poor. It is good to give to the poor as they are in need. At the same time, it can be destructive to give to the non-disabled individual who simply refuses to work and begins to expect someone else to take care of them (2 Thessalonians 3:10). The difficulty is in separating the needs from the wants. A person may want to have you take care of them, but if they are non-disabled, they may not need you to do so. And, if you do so, you may be fostering what can be called learned helplessness. That is not a good thing for the giver or the receiver. Individual discretion is needed in these situations.

Proverbs 22:10 Cast out the scoffer, and contention will leave;
Yes, strife and reproach will cease. Sometimes a divisive person just needs to be removed from the group, or very little will be accomplished. Strife and reproach are generally counterproductive to any kind of progress.

Proverbs 22:15 Foolishness *is* bound up in the heart of a child;
The rod of correction will drive it far from him. Discipline should not be delivered with anger or destructive force. However, the child who never receives appropriate discipline can fail to develop self-control and, therefore, can become self-destructive and other-destructive. The child

without limits can grow into an adult without limits who will sooner or later violate the laws of society and end up incarcerated behind iron bars that will limit their behavior.

Proverbs 22:16 He who oppresses the poor to increase his *riches*,
   And he who gives to the rich, *will* surely *come* to poverty. This seems to be a warning that giving to the rich is not a good idea. They do not need us to provide for them anyway. Too much of this activity and you may become poor yourself. Also, there is more than one kind of poverty. There is financial poverty and spiritual poverty. The person who oppresses the poor may increase his riches while at the same time becoming spiritually poor.

Proverbs 23:1-3 When you sit down to eat with a ruler,
   Consider carefully what *is* before you;
   2 And put a knife to your throat
   If you *are* a man given to appetite.
   3 Do not desire his delicacies,
   For they *are* deceptive food. Wow! This seems pretty dramatic. It advises those who dine with a ruler not to desire all the fine food they have. Why is it deceptive food? Maybe overindulgence in this rich food will make a person who is not accustomed to it sick.

Proverbs 23:4 Do not overwork to be rich;
   Because of your own understanding, cease! We all have heard of the "workaholic" who does not have a balanced life. This proverb seems to be saying not to become so involved in working to make more money that you miss living. What good is money if you don't take any time to enjoy life, family, and friends? On the other hand, the proverbs discourage laziness (Proverbs 6:9-11 and others). There is an appropriate balance in the Bible.

Proverbs 23:9 Do not speak in the hearing of a fool,

For he will despise the wisdom of your words. There are times when it is best not to share all the wisdom you know with someone who does not want to hear it or is not ready to hear it. They will just hold it against you. Of course, as with all proverbs, a general principle of a specific proverb needs to be balanced with what other scriptures may say about potential exceptions or clarifications to a general rule presented.

Proverbs 23:10-11 Do not remove the ancient landmark,
Nor enter the fields of the fatherless;
11 For their Redeemer *is* mighty;
He will plead their cause against you. Who is the Redeemer spoken of in this proverb? It is God who is mighty. Those who take advantage of the poor fatherless children by taking their food are going against the will of God, and, in the end, it will not go well for them.

Proverbs 23:12 Apply your heart to instruction,
And your ears to words of knowledge. Sometimes, atheists will mock Christians as dumb for believing in God. Here we find that Christians are implored to be instructed and become knowledgeable. Disciples of Christ are encouraged here and elsewhere to increase learning (Proverbs 1:1-33). It appears that the Bible is encouraging Christians to be smart. Those who know the science are often considered to be smart.

Interestingly, scientific measurements and findings are validating a beginning of our universe. This thinking is in agreement with the Bible. Some scientists refer to the hot and dense spot of the beginning as singularity. From here, as I understand it, the scientific explanation for the expanding universe is that there was an unimaginably gigantic explosion called the Big Bang, which formed the entire universe within a fraction of a second. But what caused the Big Bang if there was nothing before the Big Bang occurred? The Bible explains the resulting question demanded by the Big Bang theory. The believer answers that the "unimaginable power" who created our universe is not unimaginable. It is God. Since God is spirit and, therefore, outside the dimension of science, it is appropriate that science is wholly inadequate in explaining how the universe could come from nothing.

Proverbs 23:17-18 Do not let your heart envy sinners
But *be zealous* for the fear of the Lord all the day;
18 For surely there is a hereafter,
And your hope will not be cut off. Sometimes it can seem that people who do not observe moral standards get ahead. They often do get ahead. On earth, God causes the sun to shine on everyone. However, there is a hereafter. Those who are forgiven will have a glorious future in that time.

Proverbs 23:26-27 My son, give me your heart,
And let your eyes observe my ways.
27 For a harlot *is* a deep pit,
And a seductress *is* a narrow well. A deep pit or a narrow well is not something into which you would want to fall. If you did, it would not be easy to get out of either. Better to focus on the LORD and stay away from harlots.

Proverbs 23:29-35 Who has woe?
Who has sorrow?
Who has contentions?
Who has complaints?
Who has wounds without cause?
Who has redness of eyes?
30 Those who linger long at the wine,
Those who go in search of mixed wine.
31 Do not look on the wine when it is red,
When it sparkles in the cup,
***When* it swirls around smoothly;**

32 At the last it bites like a serpent,
And stings like a viper.
33 Your eyes will see strange things,
And your heart will utter perverse things.
34 Yes, you will be like one who lies down in the midst of the sea,
Or like one who lies at the top of the mast, *saying:*
35 "They have struck me, *but* **I was not hurt;**
They have beaten me, but I did not feel *it.*
When shall I awake, that I may seek another *drink?"* Here is a stark picture of what it is like to be a drunkard or, using modern-day terminology, an alcoholic (or drug-addicted person). It was not a pretty picture way back then and is still not a pretty picture. It is incredible how little the life of someone addicted to a mind-altering substance has changed over the centuries. All of these substances still bite like a serpent and sting like a viper in the end. Unfortunately, there have been many new substances developed that are even more devastating than the old ones. These substances often have some great medical uses in restricted quantities, but using too much is like swimming in a river above a waterfall. As you swim closer to where the water goes over the cliff, it gets faster and faster. At a certain point, your capability to swim upstream diminishes, and you can't keep from going over the falls to your demise.

Proverbs 24:6 For by wise counsel you will wage your own war,
And in a multitude of counselors *there is* **safety.** Here again, a multitude of counselors is recommended. This is a regular theme in the Bible. When the Bible says something one time, it is important. When it says the same thing numerous times, it seems even more important, and it probably is.

Proverbs 24:16 For a righteous *man* **may fall seven times**
And rise again,
But the wicked shall fall by calamity. The righteous are persistent

if they fall seven times and rise again. This calamity for the wicked may not come soon, but it will eventually come.

Proverbs 24:17 Do not rejoice when your enemy falls,
And do not let your heart be glad when he stumbles; It is clear that the LORD does not want us to gloat when something negative happens to one of our enemies. Even rejoicing at our enemy's failure appears to be a type of punishment for them that the LORD reserves for himself as the righteous and fair judge.

Proverbs 24:21 My son, fear the Lord and the king;
Do not associate with those given to change; This is an interesting proverb given the goal of many politicians that what we need is change, change, change.

Proverbs 24:25 But those who rebuke *the wicked* will have delight,
And a good blessing will come upon them. So, it is not acceptable to take any kind of personal vengeance on the wicked or even to be happy with their failures. However, it is fine and even preferable for the wicked to be rebuked for their wickedness.

Proverbs 24:29 Do not say, "I will do to him just as he has done to me;
I will render to the man according to his work." Here again, we are to leave vengeance to the LORD. In Old Testament days, an eye for an eye and a tooth for a tooth restricted the revenge to a degree, but under the covenant of grace, even that restricted level of revenge is no longer acceptable (Romans 12:19-21).

Proverbs 25:8 Do not go hastily to court;
For what will you do in the end,
When your neighbor has put you to shame? If at all possible, we should resolve our disputes without the involvement of a court. Another

scripture advises settling our differences before we get to court or even on the way before we get there (Luke 12:57-59). This is wise counsel.

Proverbs 25:17 Seldom set foot in your neighbor's house,
   Lest he become weary of you and hate you. It is great to be a good neighbor, but it is also good to have a little distance between you and your neighbor, or it can put a damper on the relationship. You do not want your neighbor to become weary of you. It is generally better if your neighbor would like to see more of you than less. The way to accomplish this balance is not to visit your neighbor's house too often, especially if not invited or welcome. Because of the proximity, neighbors need to value each other's privacy a little more than non-neighbors.

Proverbs 25:20 *Like* one who takes away a garment in cold weather,
   And *like* vinegar on soda,
   ***Is* one who sings songs to a heavy heart.** There are times when singing upbeat songs is not appropriate due to the circumstances. This proverb advises us to be considerate and take the other person's countenance and feelings in mind before singing around them. They may not be in the best frame of mind to hear an upbeat, cheerful song.

25:21-22 If your enemy is hungry, give him bread to eat;
   And if he is thirsty, give him water to drink;
   22 For *so* you will heap coals of fire on his head,
   And the Lord will reward you. Here is advice to treat your enemies with compassion. Perhaps, if you do, you will make them into friends. Also, you will be leaving their judgment to the LORD, which is what we need to do. Vengeance is the LORD's, so if you back off and leave vengeance to Him, as He tells us to do, you will be rewarded (Romans 12:19-21).

Proverbs 25:26 A righteous *man* who falters before the wicked
   ***Is like* a murky spring and a polluted well.** A righteous man needs to

keep a pure heart. If he loses his principles when pressured by a wicked person, his heart becomes impure like the water in a murky spring or polluted well.

Proverbs 26:5 Answer a fool according to his folly,
Lest he be wise in his own eyes. There are times when it is better not to engage in a debate that can devolve into anger or arguments at a lower level of discourse. You do not want to get on the same level as a foolish person in a debate with them. Remember that a fool does not want to hear your wisdom, nor will they accept it. They will try to draw you into their kind of argument, which will probably include deceit, scoffing, becoming angry, or abusive. We do not want to become like him and argue "according to his folly." Thus, for an unimportant issue, we may want to ignore a foolish discourse or debate. With more essential matters, we may need to respond. In other words, there are times when reproof is appropriate but not digression into a foolish argument.

Proverbs 26:12 Do you see a man wise in his own eyes?
***There is* more hope for a fool than for him.** We have heard the statement that "he was a legend in his own mind." This proverb does not provide much hope for the person with this kind of pride.

Proverbs 26:17 He who passes by *and* meddles in a quarrel not his own
***Is like* one who takes a dog by the ears.** When you grab a dog by the ears, he may not like it and could bite you. Similarly, if you insert yourself in someone's dispute, you could have both parties turn against you.

Proverbs 26:24-26 He who hates, disguises *it* with his lips,
    And lays up deceit within himself;
    25 When he speaks kindly, do not believe him,
    For *there are* seven abominations in his heart;

26 Though his hatred is covered by deceit,
His wickedness will be revealed before the assembly. These are strong words for someone who hates. The proverb does not tell us the object of the hatred, but perhaps it does not make much difference. Hate is a strong emotion that can harm to the person who harbors it more than to the person who is the object of the hatred. It is so much better to forgive and move on with life. If it is revenge that you seek, leave it to the just judge who knows the heart of man and will provide appropriate justice (Romans 12:19-21).

Proverbs 27:1 Do not boast about tomorrow,
For you do not know what a day may bring forth. This is so true. There may be a major fire or an earthquake, or a hurricane tomorrow. We can and should make our plans but need to realize that our plans are in God's hands and may never come to fruition. Our plans should be couched in the attitude that "If the LORD wills, we shall live and do this or that" (James 4:15). Also, we should not worry too much about what is going to happen tomorrow. Today has enough trouble to be concerned about (Matthew 6:25-34). Seek first the kingdom of God (Matthew 6:33).

Proverbs 27:9 Ointment and perfume delight the heart,
And the sweetness of a man's friend *gives delight* by hearty counsel. If we have good friends, they are a great source of pleasure and good counsel. They generally know you better and may be able to see the truth of a situation better. Knowing the truth helps a person give accurate and more beneficial counsel.

Proverbs 27:15-16 A continual dripping on a very rainy day
And a contentious woman are alike;
16 Whoever restrains her restrains the wind,
And grasps oil with his right hand. A nagging wife, or husband for that matter, can truly be like a continual irritating dripping. It is hard to restrain the wind, and it is hard to grasp oil even with a strong right

hand, just as it is hard to tame a contentious woman (or man).

Proverbs 27:19 As in water face *reflects* face,

So a man's heart *reveals* the man. This sounds like it is saying that a man's heart accurately reflects who he really is. Perhaps this proverb also means that we see in others what we recognize in ourselves. We may be in harmony with those who reflect character traits that we see in ourselves.

Proverbs 27:20 Hell and Destruction are never full;

So the eyes of man are never satisfied. Unfortunately, this is how it is. We are always looking for something better. Once we have what we thought we wanted, we start thinking about the next new thing. The constant dissatisfaction can lead to many problems in life. It is better to be content with where we are and what we have (Philippians 4:12-13; Hebrews 13:5). Of course, to provide balance to this statement, it is not wrong to seek the LORD's will for our life, to have realistic goals, and to work to achieve those goals (Proverbs 15:9; 21:5; Philippians 3:12-14; Psalms 37:14; John 4:34).

Proverbs 27:23 Be diligent to know the state of your flocks,

***And* attend to your herds;** We should be diligent about our flocks and herds if we are ranchers and diligent about our work responsibilities if something else is our life work. Rewards will generally come to the one who applies themselves to their work. Whatever we do, let's do it diligently or do something else.

Proverbs 28:1 The wicked flee when no one pursues,

But the righteous are bold as a lion. The righteous should be bold since they have the LORD on their side. The person who knows they are doing wrong has both man and God to answer to, so they know they are guilty and have good reason to flee. Sometimes they run even though no one has discovered their crime because they are trying to keep from being caught when their offense is discovered.

**Proverbs 28:5 Evil men do not understand justice,
But those who seek the Lord understand all.** What is justice? In general, it means to cause to receive appropriate punishment for misdeeds. Those who seek the Lord understand that justice is proper, and we all deserve punishment for our transgressions. Therefore, we appreciate forgiveness and mercy from the LORD. Evil people just want to get away with their misdeeds and give no thought that justice is morally righteous and correct. A lot of people give a lot of lip service to the need for justice. However, when they are caught in a misdeed, they generally want mercy and forgiveness rather than justice.

**Proverbs 28:9 one who turns away his ear from hearing the law,
Even his prayer *is* an abomination.** When one turns his ear from hearing the law, they ignore God's rules for our existence. It appears God does not like this approach and finds the prayers of these people an abomination.

**Proverbs 28:12 When the righteous rejoice, *there is* great glory;
But when the wicked arise, men hide themselves.** Most people have an innate sense that when bad people are around doing their thing, bad things can come of it. Often they arise to a party, which may involve getting drunk or loaded on drugs. They may also arise to do some crime or intimidate someone. These are not pleasant people to relax around. You never know what is going to happen, and what does happen is usually not good.

**Proverbs 28:13 He who covers his sins will not prosper,
But whoever confesses and forsakes *them* will have mercy.** When we try to hide our sins from God, it takes its toll on us. We have a hard time making progress when trying to hide things. On the other hand, God appears to like it when we agree with Him about our sin and confess

it to Him. He is a God of mercy and forgiveness.

Proverbs 28:20 A faithful man will abound with blessings,
But he who hastens to be rich will not go unpunished. This proverb gives us the idea that being faithful to God is much better than trying to get rich. In other words, it does not make sense to forget moral standards to get rich. We will pay the price for putting too much emphasis on material prosperity (i.e., greed).

Proverbs 28:25 He who is of a proud heart stirs up strife,
But he who trusts in the Lord will be prospered. This is a nice thought. Humility and trust in the LORD will lead to success, whereby pride can lead to strife.

Proverbs 29:6 By transgression an evil man is snared,
But the righteous sings and rejoices. Someone said that you do not have to have as good of a memory if you tell the truth. If you tell a lie, you have to remember what you said and then make sure that anything said lines up with the lie. Over time, this process can become difficult to manage and cause the lie to be uncovered. It is much easier to sing and rejoice when you do not stress trying to remember lies and the anxiety of realizing that you might get caught in the lie and have your reputation destroyed.

Proverbs 29:7 The righteous considers the cause of the poor,
***But* the wicked does not understand *such* knowledge.** The righteous consider the poor because they care about them and want them to have a better life and get out of poverty. The wicked could care less about the poor unless they could somehow exploit them.

Proverbs 29:11 A fool vents all his feelings,
But a wise *man* holds them back. There are times when it is much better to hold off on saying everything you are feeling at the moment.

Feelings are often off base and not based on all the facts of a situation. To express those feelings all the time can cause unnecessary harm to others. Thus, discretion is the better option. It is wise not to express all your initial feelings immediately. Those feelings may be wrong, and they may hurt someone else or yourself or your relationships. It is a sign of emotional intelligence to control the expression of your feelings until you are sure that it is wise to do so.

Proverbs 29:15 The rod and rebuke give wisdom,
   But a child left *to himself* brings shame to his mother. This is so true. The child raised without limits does not have a chance to develop self-control. When they get older, the lack of self-control is devastating. It negatively impacts all aspects of their life. The parent who loves their child wants them to grow up with self-control.

Proverbs 29:27 An unjust man *is* an abomination to the righteous,
   And *he who is* upright in the way *is* an abomination to the wicked.
Abomination means something abhorred or loathed. The unjust and upright have the same opinion of each other.

Proverbs 30:3-4 I neither learned wisdom
   Nor have knowledge of the Holy One.
   4 Who has ascended into heaven, or descended?
   Who has gathered the wind in His fists?
   Who has bound the waters in a garment?
   Who has established all the ends of the earth?
   What *is* His name, and what *is* His Son's name,
   If you know? John 3:13 says: **"No one has ascended to heaven but He who came down from heaven, *that is,* the Son of Man who is in heaven."** Thus, this messianic riddle is answered in the New Testament. It is Jesus who ascended and who came down from heaven. In Old Testament times, they may not have known the answer to this riddle. It took many years for the answer to come. Now, we know the answer.

Proverbs 30:5-6 Every word of God *is* pure;
  He *is* a shield to those who put their trust in Him.
  6 Do not add to His words,
  Lest He rebuke you, and you be found a liar. This is a sobering statement. There have been a few self-described "prophets" who have tried to add to these words. One of them started a religion in the United States that continues to this day. Make no mistake, the canon of scripture was settled long ago, and no one should add to them.

Proverbs 30:8-9 Remove falsehood and lies far from me;
  Give me neither poverty nor riches—
  Feed me with the food allotted to me;
  9 Lest I be full and deny *You*,
  And say, "Who *is* the Lord?"
  Or lest I be poor and steal,
  And profane the name of my God. This proverb suggests that it is best to be at the middle-income level, not rich and not poor. The rich can forget the LORD as they trust in their riches, and the poor can try to justify stealing because they are poor. Just being poor does not make stealing okay. The moral rules appear to apply to the poor as they do to the rich.

Proverbs 30:15 The leech has two daughters—
  Give *and* Give!
  There are three *things that* are never satisfied,
  Four never say, "Enough!": Unfortunately, when people become dependent on others for their sustenance, it can become a vicious circle where there is never enough to satisfy their desires. This proverb is not directed at the disabled person who needs assistance but to those who are non-disabled but have learned that living off the work of others is an easier way. Unfortunately for them, the old saying: "come easy, go easy" seems true. When a person does not have to work for what they have, they place a lot less value on it, and it is often wasted and gone.

Proverbs 30:24-25 There are four *things which* **are little on the earth, But they** *are* **exceedingly wise:**
25 The ants *are* **a people not strong,**
Yet they prepare their food in the summer; The point here seems to be that even tiny insects can be wise in planning. We can learn something from these tiny insects. It is wise to store up food for when it will be scarce.

Proverbs 30:32 If you have been foolish in exalting yourself,
Or if you have devised evil, *put your* **hand on** *your* **mouth.** Sometimes even generally good people make mistakes. If they can, it is good for them to keep it to themselves and repent of these thoughts before the thoughts become public.

Proverbs 31:4-7 *It is* **not for kings, O Lemuel,**
It is **not for kings to drink wine,**
Nor for princes intoxicating drink;
5 Lest they drink and forget the law,
And pervert the justice of all the afflicted.
6 Give strong drink to him who is perishing,
And wine to those who are bitter of heart.
7 Let him drink and forget his poverty,
And remember his misery no more. There were several things to note in these verses. First, kings should remain sober at all times to fairly administer justice with a clear head. They need to have all their faculties to remember the law and how to apply it. However, there are some situations where a strong drink can be beneficial. One would be for a person who is in the process of dying. It may help them ease the transition and diminish the pain. I think this would also apply to pain medication for extreme pain. The other appears to be a situation where a person is in misery and bitter due to their poverty. It may not make matters any better, but it seems they should still be allowed to use alcohol. Of course, that permissive attitude would not apply to a person driving a

car and could hurt someone with it.

Proverbs 31:8 Open your mouth for the speechless,
  In the cause of all *who are* appointed to die.
  9 Open your mouth, judge righteously,
  And plead the cause of the poor and needy. It is our responsibility to help the speechless, poor and needy.

Proverbs 31:20 She extends her hand to poor,
  Yes, she reaches out her hands to the needy. Here is another example of encouragement to help the poor and needy. From other scripture, we know that those who are non-disabled but refuse to work should be excluded from the help offered for the poor and needy (2 Thessalonians 3:10).

Proverbs 31:30 Charm *is* deceitful and beauty *is* passing,
  But a woman *who* fears the Lord, she shall be praised. This passage tells us about the Proverbs 31 woman who runs the household very well. It is not her outward appearance that is most important but her faith in the LORD.

21

Ecclesiastes

[21]**ECCLESIASTES** - This book clarifies that life can be utterly futile if viewed as just what is in the material world. Though this earthly life is short and passes quickly, it is not meaningless to those who have an eternal focus and accept that life would not exist in this material world if not for the spirit of God giving it to us.

If we skip to the end of this book, we find the conclusion: "Fear God and keep His commandments, for this is Man's all." Most of us have a concern about eternity which comes from what God put in our hearts (3:11). If we search for true meaning only in this short life on earth, we will wind up lacking. The end of the matter has to do with the eternal God and not just the temporary natural or material world in which we live.

Ecclesiastes focuses on the fact that this life is quickly passing (38 times). Life here can be difficult, but we can still have joy if we have a heart for the eternal future that God is providing. Ecclesiastes lets us know

---

[21] NSB quotations are from the Nelsons Study Bible, copyright (c) 1997 by Thomas Nelson, Inc., Nashville, TN; used by permission; scripture taken from the New King James Version, Copyright (c) 1979, 1980, 1982 used by permission. All rights reserved.

that even though much of our short life here is vanity, there can still be meaning in it.

Ecclesiastes 1:2 "Vanity of vanities," says the Preacher; "Vanity of vanities, all is vanity." What does this mean? The word translated vanity means "breath" or "vapor," which passes quickly. At my current age, it is easier for me to believe that this verse means our life here on earth is quickly passing. Not only is life here disappearing like a vapor, but it also disappears like the shortest of vapors.

I was outside in about 50-degree weather the other day, and the vapor I could create by breathing out went away in a fraction of a second. Compared to eternity, that is how fast our earthly lifespan ends. But, even though it passes quickly, that doesn't mean it is without meaning.

Though some things are more important than others, most of what humanity spends time and effort on is just vanity. The point appears to be that our time here is a fleeting gift from God. In verse 14, all the works that we do are described as "**grasping for the wind**" which is futile. Even gaining more wisdom and knowledge can seem superfluous. Life on earth is temporary. We will come to the end of this life.

Ecclesiastes 3:1 To everything there is a season, A time for every purpose under heaven: This verse enumerates things of life that have a time. The phrase "**under the heavens**" appears to imply everything that is under our sun.

Ecclesiastes 3:22 So I perceived that nothing is better than that a man should rejoice in his own works, for that is his heritage. For who can bring him to see what will happen after him? We don't know what is going to happen after we are finished, and someone else takes over. We need to enjoy what we are doing while doing it and not worry about what comes after.

Ecclesiastes 4:4 Again, I saw that for all toil and every skillful work a man is envied by his neighbor. This also is vanity and grasping for the wind. Envy is a waste of time and like chasing the wind.

Ecclesiastes 4:10 For if they fall, one will lift up his companion. But woe to him who is alone when he falls, For he has no one to help him up. Here is a verse that speaks of the value of friendship. It has been said that "no man is an island." That is true, and it is also true that it is not good for man to be alone. One of the first statements about something not being good in the Bible is that "**It is not good that man should be alone;…**" Modern research has confirmed this declaration with findings that both loneliness and social isolation can shorten a person's lifespan. Maybe the old saying that "God does not subtract from a person's lifespan the time they spend fishing" should be modified to "God does not subtract from a person's lifespan the time they spend fishing with a companion." Of course, it is as essential to be a good friend as it is to have a good friend, and those who are good friends probably have good friends.

Ecclesiastes 4:10 He who loves silver will not be satisfied with silver; Nor he who loves abundance, with increase. This also is vanity. This is the third time that an insatiable appetite is addressed. No matter how much some people have, if they love silver, it will not be enough. The scripture clearly states that this is vanity. When we understand that the work we have to do is a gift from God and that we can't take anything with us out of this world, we have a better chance of living a contented and valuable life.

Ecclesiastes 6:9 Better is the sight of the eyes than the wandering of desire. This also is vanity and grasping for the wind. This appears to be another way of saying that we need to be happy with what we have as opposed to desiring more and more all the time. Fantasizing about things that are beyond our reach is like grasping for the wind. It is a waste of time and energy.

Ecclesiastes 7:10 Do not say, "Why were the former days better than these?" For you do not inquire wisely concerning this. We should not spend our time overthinking about the "good old days" at the expense of living in the present. It may be that the past was not near as good as our selective memory tells us anyway.

Ecclesiastes 7:16 Do not be overly righteous, Nor be overly wise: Why should you destroy yourself? This seems to be speaking of being excessively righteous or wise in your own eyes. We know that it is good to be righteous and wise, but apparently it is not good to be so in your own opinion. And the reality stated in verse 20 is that no one on earth is just and sinless. If a person does believe that they are righteous and wise, that will make them prideful, which is a sin. Then they would be deceitful, prideful, and still not righteous or wise. They would be a mess.

Ecclesiastes 7:21 Also do not take to heart everything people say, Lest you hear your servant cursing you. If you overhear someone saying something negative about you, realize that it may be true. However, even if it is not, the person could just be blowing off steam at the expense of your reputation. Or they could be speaking about you as you have talked about others. Note that even if what someone says is accurate, we should always be more concerned about what God thinks than what a human being thinks.

Ecclesiastes 8:15 So I commended enjoyment, because a man has nothing better under the sun than to eat, drink, and be merry; for this will remain with him in his labor all the days of his life which God gives him under the sun. Well, this sounds good. Those who are blessed with employment are encouraged to eat, drink, and be merry. The righteous person knows that God has provided what we have and can be thankful and enjoy life rather than continually be dissatisfied and unhappy. This is one of the main themes of this book. Life is short and can be hard in this fallen world, so we don't want to make it any more difficult by not enjoying what we can in line with the appropriate limits God sets to protect us from sin.

Ecclesiastes 11:2 Give a serving to seven, and also to eight, For you do not know what evil will be on the earth. Here we are encouraged to be generous if we have more than we need (see Psalms 41:1; 112:9). So if we are generous seven times, maybe we can go the extra mile and be generous to eight. But what about the next part of this verse? Well, that seems to be a warning that we could also fall on hard times and need some help. If we have given when we need help, we may receive it (see Luke 6:38). Other scriptures provide balance by advising us not to be a patsy by giving food to able people who refuse to provide for themselves (2 Thessalonians 3:10).

Ecclesiastes 11:10 Therefore remove sorrow from your heart, And put away evil from your flesh, For childhood and youth are vanity. This chapter encourages youth to rejoice in their youth without doing things that will bring them God's judgment. Why should the youth enjoy it while they can? You guessed it. Because adolescence is also here today and gone tomorrow like a vapor, remember vanity can mean brief.

Ecclesiastes 11:7 Then the dust will return to the earth as it was, And the spirit will return to God who gave it. Notice who gives the spirit that enlivens the elements from which our bodies are made. Some people, like the Sadducees of biblical times, do not believe there is a spiritual dimension. They do not recognize that when the God-given spirit leaves the body, that produces death. In other words, life provides evidence against their belief and for the existence of the spiritual dimension of sentient beings. When we are dead, the elements previously animated by the spirit decompose and become dust.

Ecclesiastes 11:13 Let us hear the conclusion of the whole matter: Fear God and keep His commandments, For this is man's all. Here is the "fear God" phrase one of the 19 or so times that these two words are used in the Bible. As noted elsewhere in this commentary, fearing God usually means having awe and respect for Him. It also would mean that we have faith in Him. If we do that, we will want to follow His commandments. That faith is all we need. Without faith, life is insignificant vanity that is here today and gone tomorrow.

22

Song of Solomon

[22]**SONG OF SOLOMON** - Oh my, this book encourages sexual relations between married Christians for pleasure. It appears that this is God's design for marriage. There was a time when this book was not allowed to be read until a person was an adult since it has adult-oriented content. One main theme seems to be that sexual intimacy within a marriage is great, pleasurable, and designed by God as a beautiful guilt-free experience. It can provide physical, emotional, and spiritual bonding. Per Genesis 2:24, in marriage, we become one flesh. Per Hebrews 13:4, we learn that the marriage bed is undefiled. Thus, whereas sexual intimacy outside of marriage is discouraged, it is celebrated and encouraged within marriage. Of course, through the sacrifice of Christ, God can and does forgive the sexual sins of believers along with other sins.

Song of Solomon 1:2 Let him kiss me with the kisses of his mouth— For your love is better than wine. Here the setting is noted as emotional and sensual.

---

[22] NSB quotations are from the Nelsons Study Bible, copyright (c) 1997 by Thomas Nelson, Inc., Nashville, TN; used by permission; scripture taken from the New King James Version, Copyright (c) 1979, 1980, 1982 used by permission. All rights reserved.

Song of Solomon 2:7 I charge you, O daughters of Jerusalem, By the gazelles or by the does of the field, Do not stir up nor awaken love Until it pleases. It pleases when it is sanctioned as in marriage. These verses appear to instruct the young maidens to keep from awakening love until the proper time within the marriage relationship (see 3:5 and 8:4). "Love" in this context appears to refer to sexual intimacy.

Song of Solomon 8:7 Many waters cannot quench love, Nor can the floods drown it. If a man would give for love All the wealth of his house, It would be utterly despised. This verse lets us know two things. One, true love cannot be extinguished, and two, you cannot buy love. It must be freely given and freely received.

Song of Solomon 8:10 I am a wall, And my breasts like towers; Then I became in his eyes As one who found peace. Here, in poetic language, the writer appears to be letting her fiance know that she has been waiting for their marriage before becoming intimately involved. Then, when they are married, she will be faithful to the one in whose eyes she has found peace through their intimate relationship.

23

Isaiah

[23]**ISAIAH** - These are God's words spoken through the vision of one of the great prophets of the Old Testament. He faced much opposition but stood up for the truth. Note that the name Isaiah means "The Lord Saves."

Isaiah 1:2 Hear, O heavens, and give ear, O earth! For the Lord has spoken: "I have nourished and brought up children, And they have rebelled against Me;... Here the Lord states that His children have turned against Him even though He has provided for them and taught them. They were heading down a path that led to destruction. Even a dumb animal would act more in line with the wishes of a master who feeds them and trains them.

Isaiah 1:5 Why should you be stricken again? You will revolt more and more. The whole head is sick, And the whole heart faints. Sometimes it does not make sense to keep telling people something because they will only reject it more. This was the case in Isaiah's time.

---

[23] NSB quotations are from the Nelsons Study Bible, copyright (c) 1997 by Thomas Nelson, Inc., Nashville, TN; used by permission; scripture taken from the New King James Version, Copyright (c) 1979, 1980, 1982 used by permission. All rights reserved.

Isaiah 1:11 "To what purpose is the multitude of your sacrifices to Me?"

Says the Lord. "I have had enough of burnt offerings of rams And the fat of fed cattle.

I do not delight in the blood of bulls,

Or of lambs or goats. It appears the Lord was rejecting the ritualistic worship. In the next verse, the Lord says to bring no more futile sacrifices to Him and that incense is an abomination. This is in the context of the attempt by the people to obtain forgiveness through ritualistic sacrifices without repenting.

Isaiah 1:17 Learn to do good; Seek justice, Rebuke the oppressor; Defend the fatherless; Plead for the widow. This appears to be more of what the Lord would like from the people instead of their ritualistic pseudo-religious practices. He wants the people to do good by calling out the oppressor and taking care of the fatherless and women whose husbands have died.

Isaiah 1:28 The destruction of transgressors and of sinners shall be together, And those who forsake the Lord shall be consumed. This is very clear and does not need much interpretation. The only question I have is what the word "consumed" means in this context. When someone is consumed, they are destroyed by decomposition, dissipation, waste, or fire. Under any of these processes, the person will be substantially different than before being consumed.

Isaiah 2:4 He shall judge between the nations, And rebuke many people; They shall beat their swords into plowshares, And their spears into pruning hooks; Nation shall not lift up sword against nation, Neither shall they learn war anymore. This encouraging scripture looks forward to when there is no more war. Since war is so destructive to all countries involved, this is excellent news. This situation can only occur when Christ comes back to the earth and exercises His authority in judging the nations.

Isaiah 2:12 For the day of the Lord of hosts Shall come upon everything proud and lofty, Upon everything lifted up—And it shall be brought low— There will come a time when idols and other things lifted (exalted) above God will be brought down low where they deserve to be. Idols will be abolished at the appropriate time, and only the Lord will be exalted.

Isaiah 5:5 And now, please let Me tell you what I will do to My vineyard: I will take away its hedge, and it shall be burned; And break down its wall, and it shall be trampled down. God's vineyard was Israel at that time. Since they turned against Him, they would no longer receive God's protection.

Isaiah 5:11 Woe to those who rise early in the morning, That they may follow intoxicating drink; Who continue until night, till wine inflames them! Here is yet another admonition about drinking too much alcohol. When a person's drinking gets to the point where they have to get up early to drink some more, they are in bad shape and probably addicted. That is not a good position to be in. Later in this book, the scripture says, "**Woe to men valiant for mixing intoxicating drink,…**".

Isaiah 5:12 The harp and the strings, The tambourine and flute, And wine are in their feasts; But they do not regard the work of the Lord, Nor consider the operation of His hands. It seems that having music and wine at feasts (which are really just drinking parties) without any concern for the work of the Lord will bring woe to these partiers. The woe that these people will experience is defined as distress, affliction, and trouble. The anger of the Lord will eventually be aroused against these people.

Isaiah 6:3 And one cried to another and said: "Holy, holy, holy is the Lord of hosts; The whole earth is full of His glory!" The holiness of God can be regarded as beyond mere words, but in this passage, an attempt is made to capture the concept by repeating the word holy three times. His holiness seems to be transcendent and beyond our understanding.

Isaiah 7:14 Therefore the Lord Himself will give you a sign: Behold, the virgin shall conceive and bear a Son, and shall call His name Immanuel. Here is a clear prophesy of Jesus' birth from a virgin. Immanuel means "God with us," which is what Jesus was. He was Mighty God incarnate (9:6).

Isaiah 8:13 The Lord of hosts, Him you shall hallow; Let Him be your fear, And let Him be your dread. Rather than fear a human being, the appropriate person we should fear (revere), praise and worship is God. Hallow means to honor as holy or sacred.

Isaiah 10:1 "Woe to those who decree unrighteous decrees,
  Who write misfortune,
  ***Which* they have prescribed**
  To rob the needy of justice,... This is terrible news for the politicians who write laws that result in injustice on the needy.

Isaiah 10:5 "Woe to Assyria, the rod of My anger
  And the staff in whose hand is My indignation. This is interesting. It notes that even though God used Assyria to accomplish His will (7:17), they will still have to pay for their sins (13:5). God is sovereign over people who believe in Him and over those who do not.

Isaiah 10:22 For though your people, O Israel, be as the sand of the sea,
  A remnant of them will return;

The destruction decreed shall overflow with righteousness. Here is an opportunity to see a prophecy from thousands of years ago appear to come true in our time. In 1948, the nation of Israel was reestablished, and the remnant of Israel repopulated the country. It is amazing that remnants of Israel survived as a cohesive group over all of those years and then gathered to form a new government called Israel (66:8).

Isaiah 11:1 There shall come forth a Rod from the stem of Jesse,
And a Branch shall grow out of his roots. This Rod appears to be Christ the Messiah (Matthew 1:17). The Messiah would be empowered by the Holy Spirit (11:2). He would honor and obey God (Exodus 20:20).

Isaiah 11:6 "The wolf also shall dwell with the lamb,
The leopard shall lie down with the young goat,
The calf and the young lion and the fatling together;
And a little child shall lead them. This verse is speaking of the time after Christ returns when all animals will be herbivores. I wonder if human beings will also wind up being herbivores. It seems like that might be the case. The coming kingdom will not have the same level of concern about animals hurting children or other animals.

Isaiah 12:1 And in that day you will say:
"O Lord, I will praise You;
Though You were angry with me,
Your anger is turned away, and You comfort me.
2 Behold, God *is* my salvation,
I will trust and not be afraid;
'For Yah, the Lord, *is* my strength and song;
He also has become my salvation.'" This is part of a great hymn of praise. Notice that salvation from God is mentioned in each verse. The next verse also mentions salvation. So this hymn has a lot of focus on the one who can provide salvation.

Isaiah 12:6 Cry out and shout, O inhabitant of Zion,

For great *is* the Holy One of Israel in your midst!" Here's another encouragement to be exuberant in our worship. In other words, there is a time to let the joy of the Lord come out, even if it involves loud shouting.

Isaiah 13:9 Behold, the day of the Lord comes,

Cruel, with both wrath and fierce anger,

To lay the land desolate;

And He will destroy its sinners from it. This talks of the anger of the Lord against Babylon. Babylon is viewed as the enemy of God's kingdom in those days (Revelation 14:8).

Isaiah 13:11 "I will punish the world for *its* evil,

And the wicked for their iniquity;

I will halt the arrogance of the proud,

And will lay low the haughtiness of the terrible. Here is a terrifying prediction for the proud. The big issue here appears to be pride. This verse confirms the old saying that "pride comes before a fall." After this verse, there are proclamations against Syria, Israel, Ethiopia, Egypt, Edom, Arabia, Jerusalem. Tyre, and the whole earth. There are also some blessings along the way. Later there will be salvation for those who trust in the Lord (26:4) and the restoration of Israel (27:6).

Isaiah 28:7 But they also have erred through wine,

And through intoxicating drink are out of the way;

The priest and the prophet have erred through intoxicating drink,

They are swallowed up by wine,

They are out of the way through intoxicating drink;

They err in vision, they stumble *in* judgment. Here again, is a description of the negative aspects of drunkenness. This theme is repeated numerous times in the Bible. Drinking a little wine is not prohibited, but excessive use is never approved. A one-and-done philosophy appears to be the best plan when it comes to intoxicating beverages. I assume a similar principle applies to other substances that can alter the mental state of a person. Some substances should be avoided because one little dose can have devastating consequences. Just two milligrams of one of these substances will result in certain death. Some also appear to be so potent that they can induce addiction-like behavior for some people after just a single dose. With these powerful drugs, a person can risk negatively altering their whole life path with a single exposure.

Isaiah 29:16 Surely you have things turned around!
   Shall the potter be esteemed as the clay;
   For shall the thing made say of him who made it,
   "He did not make me"?
   Or shall the thing formed say of him who formed it,
   "He has no understanding"? In our life here on earth, who is the potter? The potter is God, and this part of scripture clarifies that the vase has no standing to question the potter. That would be backward from the order of things that God set up. He is the potter, we are the clay, and we have no standing whatsoever to question God. The person who denies God is essentially saying to God, "you did not make me." That is the kind of unwarranted unmerited pride it takes for the thing formed to criticize the one who formed it. It would be nonsensical, but many people will deny that they have a Maker.

Isaiah 29:19 The humble also shall increase *their* **joy in the Lord,**
   And the poor among men shall rejoice
   In the Holy One of Israel.
   20 For the terrible one is brought to nothing,
   The scornful one is consumed,
   And all who watch for iniquity are cut off— Humility is a virtue in God's economy, and this scripture again reaffirms that fact.

Isaiah 30:1 "Woe to the rebellious children," says the Lord,

"Who take counsel, but not of Me,
And who devise plans, but not of My Spirit,
That they may add sin to sin;** Again, planning without consulting God is discouraged. We need to take counsel from the Word of God and the Holy Spirit before setting our plans in motion. Those who rebel will experience woe.

**Isaiah 30:21 Your ears shall hear a word behind you, saying,
"This *is* the way, walk in it,"
Whenever you turn to the right hand
Or whenever you turn to the left.** You may have heard that God can speak in a still small voice (1 Kings 18:20-40 19:12). This can be translated as a "gentle whisper." Keep in mind that though God can communicate to a person this way, He can also communicate in any number of other ways like a whirlwind (Job 38:1), an earthquake (Exodus 19:18), or thunder (1 Samuel 2:10). He also has spoken through the scriptures in the Bible. In Old Testament days, He spoke through the prophets, and in the last days in which we live, He has spoken to us by His Son. Perhaps the most explicit way He speaks to us now is through His Word. Of course, how He speaks to us is not as important as how we respond to what He says. Do we listen and follow, or ignore?

**Isaiah 31:1 Woe to those who go down to Egypt for help,
And rely on horses,
Who trust in chariots because *they are* many,
And in horsemen because they are very strong,
But who do not look to the Holy One of Israel,
Nor seek the Lord!** So, it is vital to seek the Lord in matters of state that involve conflict. How do we do that? Through prayer and searching the scriptures. We need to ask, seek, and knock (Matthew 7:7-8). That does not mean that a state should not prepare for conflict. History has shown that very few countries can avoid conflict altogether without being overrun by some other country at some point. When certain despots

gain power, they cannot get enough of it and will generally expand their area of influence.

Isaiah 31:5 Like birds flying about,
　So will the Lord of hosts defend Jerusalem.
　Defending, He will also deliver *it;*
　Passing over, He will preserve *it.*" Interestingly, thousands of years before the invention of the airplane, the scripture talks of God defending Jerusalem "**Like birds flying about,**…" I believe God can see our past, present, and future at the same time. It is not a problem for God to talk about airplanes way before there was such a word in the vernacular of the person through whom the Lord was communicating.

Isaiah 34:4 All the host of heaven shall be dissolved,
　And the heavens shall be rolled up like a scroll;… At some point, what we see in the sky will be dissolved and rolled up. The "host of heaven" may be speaking of pagan deities. The rolling up is an interesting picture that makes me think of black holes that our physicists have identified. Maybe what we see in our heavens will be rolled up into a black hole. Regardless, from Revelation 6:13-14, we know that our old cosmos will be replaced by the new at the appropriate time.

Isaiah 35:10 And the ransomed of the Lord shall return,
　And come to Zion with singing,
　With everlasting joy on their heads.
　They shall obtain joy and gladness,
　And sorrow and sighing shall flee away. At some point, believers (the ransomed) will happily return to Zion (a symbol of Jerusalem). They will be everlastingly joyous. That is a nice thought.

Isaiah 37:21 Then Isaiah the son of Amoz sent to Hezekiah, saying, "Thus says the Lord God of Israel, 'Because you have prayed to Me against Sennacherib king of Assyria, 22 this *is* **the word which the**

Lord has spoken concerning him: Here is an example of God taking action "because" of a prayer of a king. God can take action whenever He wants but, it appears that there are times that prayer has a bearing on His actions. In this case, Jerusalem overcame her attackers.

Isaiah 38:4 And the word of the Lord came to Isaiah, saying, 5 "Go and tell Hezekiah, 'Thus says the Lord, the God of David your father: "I have heard your prayer, I have seen your tears; surely I will add to your days fifteen years. Hezekiah was sick and near death. Isaiah, the prophet, had told him that the Lord says to get your house in order because you will die. Hezekiah prayed to the Lord. The scripture does not say that he prayed for longer life, but it makes sense. This is one of the few situations in the Bible where God appears to have changed His mind. After Hezekiah's prayer, Isaiah was told to tell Hezekiah that he would live 15 more years. Now, some say God does not change His mind. Scripture does say that God does not change (Malachi 3:6; James 1:17). However, it does not say that He will not change His mind (see scripture cited below). Someone may not change in many respects but could still change their mind. However, another way of looking at this situation is that God could have already decided that only if Hezekiah prayed would He be granted 15 more years. Based on what Isaiah told Hezekiah, it makes this situation appear that God changed His mind.

Nevertheless, it could be that God always had in mind that if Hezekiah humbled himself and prayed that he would receive a longer life, but if he did not, he would die soon. If this is what happened, God did not change His mind. The actions of Hezekiah caused a different outcome. In Jeremiah 26:3, after giving Israel a judgment message, God says: **"I will change my mind concerning the calamity that I intend to bring on them because of their evil deed."** Thus, even though God may not change, He may change His mind according to this scripture.

Isaiah 40:8 The grass withers, the flower fades,

But the word of our God stands forever. This scripture can be put on a plaque to make a statement about the word of God. The word of our God can mean the Bible (2 Timothy 3:16). It can also mean Jesus Christ (John 1:14). Under either meaning, this scripture is correct. The Bible and Jesus Christ are forever.

Isaiah 40:26 **Lift up your eyes on high,**
  And see who has created these *things,*
  Who brings out their host by number;
  He calls them all by name,
  By the greatness of His might
  And the strength of *His* **power;**
Not one is missing. My opinion: it is obvious that our universe demands a creator. There is too much order for it to be the result of random chance over time. Even if this was a reasonable theory, the question of where matter came from in the first place is still unanswered. Recent scientific findings regarding the age and expansion of our universe indicate a beginning. They call it "the big bang." And then there is the DNA in all living cells that contains all the intelligence to guide and direct the cells to form living beings and plant life. Unfortunately, for those who deny the existence of God, we are responsible for seeing the universe as evidence of God's creation (Romans 1:18-32). We are guilty when we ignore or deny the creation. Also, there are many prophecies in the book of Isaiah regarding the Messiah (52:13; 53:2; 53:4; 53:5; 53:6; 53:7; 53:9; 53:10; 53:12).

Isaiah 42:5 **Thus says God the Lord,**
  Who created the heavens and stretched them out,
  Who spread forth the earth and that which comes from it,
  Who gives breath to the people on it,
  And spirit to those who walk on it: Here the Lord makes note of the fact that He is the one who made our universe and earth. He also gives us the breath and spirit that makes us alive.

Isaiah 42:10 Sing to the Lord a new song,
  And His praise from the ends of the earth,
  You who go down to the sea, and all that is in it,
  You coastlands and you inhabitants of them! This is another example of a scripture imploring us to sing a new song to the Lord. Another is in Psalm 98:1 and another in Psalm 96:1. We can get the idea from these scriptures that we should seek to compose some new worship songs instead of singing the same songs that were written in the 1500s or 1600s all the time. There are also other commands to sing in this book (54:1).

Isaiah 43:1 Everyone who is called by My name,
  Whom I have created for My glory;
  I have formed him, yes, I have made him." Here is a scripture that tells us why we are here. We are here for God's glory. That is our purpose. So, when we go off in another direction in opposition to our purpose, we can expect that it may not work out well. So, what is for His glory? It is dignity, honor, praise, and worship.

Isaiah 43:10 "You _are_ My witnesses," says the Lord,
  "And My servant whom I have chosen,
  That you may know and believe Me,
  And understand that I _am_ He.
  Before Me there was no God formed,
  Nor shall there be after Me.
  11 I, _even_ I, _am_ the Lord,
  And besides Me _there is_ no savior. This is a key scripture. Much wisdom starts from knowing this truth. For believers, it puts to rest any speculation about who God is. There was no god before Him, and there will not be any after. He is eternal and always existed. He is the savior. He is God, and He is the incarnate Jesus Christ (John 14:9). Later in this chapter, He says, "I am God." To make such a statement, you are either God, a liar, or mentally ill. I believe He is who He says He is. This

scripture also makes it clear that there is no other savior. Thus, all the others who claim to be saviors are incorrect. We need to be discerning when we contact someone else who is making this kind of claim. He also says, more than once, that there is no other God (44:6; 45:5). In the forty-fourth chapter, He notes that He made the heavens and the earth and formed us from the womb (44:24). This book supports that salvation for the world will come through Israel (14:1, 2; 19:23-24; 49:23,26; 54:3; 60:11).

Isaiah 45:23 I have sworn by Myself;
The word has gone out of My mouth *in* righteousness,
And shall not return,
That to Me every knee shall bow,
Every tongue shall take an oath. It appears that even though we can currently deny and ignore God, that will not always be the case. At some point, every knee will bow to the God of the Bible. That is a comforting thought for Christians who are ridiculed and sometimes executed for their beliefs.

Isaiah 47:10 "For you have trusted in your wickedness;
You have said, 'No one sees me';
Your wisdom and your knowledge have warped you;
And you have said in your heart,
'I *am*, and *there is* no one else besides me.' The person who rejects the God of the Bible is noted as warped and as a person who thinks they are the great "I am." In other words, they are filled with so much pride that they are blind to the fact that they are not God and never will be. Not only that, but they think no one sees what they are doing and that therefore, no one will ever judge them. The unfortunate reality for them is that there is an all-knowing and all-seeing God who is the great "I am" and who will judge them when the time is right. Over and over in the Bible, God clarifies that He is the one responsible for creating the earth and all that is in it (48:13).

Isaiah 48:12 "Listen to Me, O Jacob,
   And Israel, My called:
   I *am* He, I *am* the First,
   I *am* also the Last." In this verse, the Lord makes it clear that He called Israel to fulfill what they were called to do. For one, salvation for the world would come through Israel.

Isaiah 48:20 Go forth from Babylon!
   Flee from the Chaldeans!
   With a voice of singing
   Declare, proclaim this,
   Utter it to the end of the earth;
   Say, "The Lord has redeemed
   His servant Jacob!" Interestingly, this part of scripture is that singing about the Lord's redemption of Jacob is commanded. Singing to the Lord, about the Lord, and about the great things He has done is a part of the Christian life.

Isaiah 49:13 Sing, O heavens!
   Be joyful, O earth!
   And break out in singing, O mountains!
   For the Lord has comforted His people,
   And will have mercy on His afflicted. The Lord's mercy is something to rejoice about. He appears to have given us music to use in worship, and He commands that we use it that way. Of course, music, as with many other communication tools we have today, can be used appropriately for worship and even for our pleasure (52:8,9). However, it can also be misused.

Isaiah 51:7 "Listen to Me, you who know righteousness,
   You people in whose heart *is* My law:
   Do not fear the reproach of men,
   Nor be afraid of their insults. Note that the following verse indicates

that people who reproach and insult believers will be eaten up like a moth on a garment. Not a pretty picture. So, if a believer is insulted, they can feel sorry for the one doing the insulting. They will have problems, but the Lord's righteousness will last forever.

Isaiah 53:2 For He shall grow up before Him as a tender plant,
   And as a root out of dry ground.
   He has no form or comeliness;
   And when we see Him,
   There is **no beauty that we should desire Him.** This appears to be an Old Testament prophecy of Christ. According to this and the following scriptures, He would not stand out as a handsome person. He would bear our sorrows and griefs and be wounded for our transgressions and iniquities. That is exactly what He did. He was despised and rejected. The Lord laid the iniquity of us all on Him. Thus, He paid the righteous price demanded by justice for our sin. Verse 11 says that He will justify many. Note that it does not say that He will justify "all," just "many."

Isaiah 54:8 With a little wrath I hid My face from you for a moment;
   But with everlasting kindness I will have mercy on you,"
   Says the Lord, your Redeemer. At the appropriate time, the Lord, our Redeemer, will have mercy on us.

Isaiah 55:8 "For My thoughts *are* **not your thoughts**
   Nor *are* **your ways My ways," says the Lord.**
   9 "For *as* **the heavens are higher than the earth,**
   So are My ways higher than your ways,
   And My thoughts than your thoughts. It is clear from this verse that we do not have the same thoughts or actions of the Lord. It is also clear that our thoughts and actions are very rudimentary in comparison to the Lord's. Maybe that is why it is better for us to mold our thoughts and actions to go along with the Lord's rather than get Him to come along with us. In prayer, we need to align with God's plans by praying for "His"

will to be done.

Isaiah 59:2 But your iniquities have separated you from your God; And your sins have hidden *His* face from you,

So that He will not hear. Why are we separated from God? Here is the answer. When we disobey, sin, and go our own way, He will not listen to us. God is holy, holy, holy (Isaiah 6:3; Rev. 4:8), and if a sinner were in His presence, they would probably be undone (Isa. 6:5). What does that mean? Undone means ruined, destroyed, or annulled.

Isaiah 62:10 Go through,
Go through the gates!
Prepare the way for the people;
Build up,
Build up the highway!
Take out the stones,
Lift up a banner for the peoples! This appears to be an admonition to take out the impediments (stones) to worship (Lift up a banner; 11:10). Jesus Christ can be viewed at the banner to the gentiles (11:10). Preparing the way seems to be an encouragement for the people to come to the temple and worship.

Isaiah 64:6 All of us have become like one who is unclean,
and all our righteous acts are like filthy rags;... When we do something we think is good or righteous, that may not be the case at all. God will look at our motives and provide a correct assessment. In many cases, what we think is righteous is not. In fact, in this verse, some of what we believe is righteous is actually like filthy rags. Filthy rags would not be considered very righteous.

Isaiah 64:7 And *there is* no one who calls on Your name,
Who stirs himself up to take hold of You;
For You have hidden Your face from us,

And have consumed us because of our iniquities. When we continue to sin and reject God's mercy and grace, we are hiding our faces from Him. Eventually, our earthly bodies will be consumed back into the earth—dust to dust.

Isaiah 65:17 "For behold, I create new heavens and a new earth;
And the former shall not be remembered or come to mind.
18 But be glad and rejoice forever in what I create;
For behold, I create Jerusalem *as* **a rejoicing,**
And her people a joy. Here we learn that at some point, our heavens and earth will be no more but will be replaced with something better. Scientists also understand that our current earth cannot endure as it is forever because the sun will run out of fuel in about five billion years. This scripture lets us know what our earth and system will be replaced, and there will be a new city of Jerusalem, a place of rejoicing. The lion will eat straw like an ox, and the wolf and the lamb will feed together (65:25).

24

Jeremiah

JEREMIAH - Jeremiah was one of the great prophets of the Old Testament who remained faithful to God even through various hardships.

**Jeremiah 1:5 "Before I formed you in the womb I knew you,
before you were born I set you apart;
I appointed you as a prophet to the nations."** It appears that God selected Jeremiah before he was even conceived and sanctified him and ordained him. Thus, he was well prepared to be a prophet.

**Jeremiah 3:12 Go, proclaim this message toward the north:
"'Return, faithless Israel,' declares the Lord,
'I will frown on you no longer,
for I am faithful,' declares the Lord,
'I will not be angry forever.** The Lord is forgiving and full of mercy for His children. If we simply return to Him, He is faithful to forgive.

Jeremiah 4:13 Look! He advances like the clouds,

---

[24] NSB quotations are from the Nelsons Study Bible, copyright (c) 1997 by Thomas Nelson, Inc., Nashville, TN; used by permission; scripture taken from the New King James Version, Copyright (c) 1979, 1980, 1982 used by permission. All rights reserved.

his chariots come like a whirlwind,
his horses are swifter than eagles.
Woe to us! We are ruined! This text is speaking of Judah. They had become foes of the Lord, and He would use international foes to deal with them as a result. They would wind up ruined.

Jeremiah 5:15 People of Israel," declares the Lord,
  "I am bringing a distant nation against you—
  an ancient and enduring nation,
  a people whose language you do not know,
  whose speech you do not understand. When was this prophecy to be implemented and was it to happen just once or multiple times. There have been several nations that have come against Israel in times of old and in modern times. Many of them spoke a different language. The five most ancient and enduring nations include Iran, Egypt, South Korea, China, and Armenia. Now that Israel (as of 1948) has been re-established as a country, we will see what the future brings.

Jeremiah 6:13 "From the least to the greatest,
  all are greedy for gain;
  prophets and priests alike,
  all practice deceit. It looks like an indictment of even the prophets and priests. Apparently, at this time, even the religious leaders had defrauded God and man. Everyone was dealing falsely. It was not a good situation. A complete transformation was needed. At this time, Judah's society needed to be transformed from top to bottom. The people had rejected God's law, and therefore, He brought calamity upon them (6:19). There was a price to pay for rejecting God's law. God says not to pray for these disobedient people because he will not hear prayers for them (7:16). Judah was indeed in a depraved state at this time and had committed abominations. So God allowed others to take their wives and their land (8:10). Judah wasn't even ashamed of what they had done (8:12). There is no healing for people intent on rebelling against God (8:20-22). Ethical

standards had fallen (9:4), and the people refused to know the Lord (9:6).

Jeremiah 9:24 ...but let the one who boasts boast about this: that they have the understanding to know me, that I am the Lord, who exercises kindness, justice and righteousness on earth, for in these I delight,"
declares the Lord. This is what Judah needed to do. They needed to know the Lord and understand Him. Then, He would exercise kindness, justice, and righteousness, which He would like to do. The people called by the Lord's name should demonstrate loving-kindness, justice, and righteousness.

Jeremiah 10:10 But the Lord is the true God; he is the living God, the eternal King. When he is angry, the earth trembles; the nations cannot endure his wrath. This verse was contrasting idols made by man who can't do any good or any evil and have to be carried around because they cannot go anywhere by themselves (10:5). There is only one true and everlasting God. **He is the Maker of all things** (10:16).

Jeremiah 12:17 But if they do not obey, I will utterly pluck up and destroy that nation," says the Lord. Here's what will happen to the nations who will not obey the Lord. Regarding Judah, even though they had been removed from the promised land, at some point, God would have compassion on them and bring them back to Israel (12:15). It looks like that happened in 1948, but we shall see if that is the return to the land that God was predicting. It is amazing that after so many years of exile, the Jewish state of Israel was re-established. People from all over the world moved back to this land and formed a country.

Jeremiah 13:10 This evil people, who refuse to hear My words, who

follow the dictates of their hearts, and walk after other gods to serve them and worship them, shall be just like this sash which is profitable for nothing. The very first commandment says, "You shall have no other gods before Me." Just about everyone violates this one at times. Some can put power, cheap labor, or conservatism as their god. Pastors can have congregation size or contributions as theirs. Others can have self, government, sex, race, or liberalism as their god. False gods can even be deadly like uncontrolled alcoholism, drug addiction, other unhealthy behavior. Then there are the more subtle ones. The point is that any of these false gods will disappoint us in the end. The fact is that we don't want any of these false gods to capture our hearts and take the place of the real God of the Bible. Beware of following your heart as is so often recommended in modern entertainment. There are times when your desires should be a part of the consideration, but usually, these desires should be tempered with reality and guidance from the Word of God. From what I've seen, the person who blindly follows their selfish desires usually winds up alone and in a bad situation.

Jeremiah 13:16 Give glory to the Lord your God
  Before He causes darkness,
  And before your feet stumble
  On the dark mountains,
  And while you are looking for light,
  He turns it into the shadow of death
  And **makes** *it* **dense darkness.** Here the Lord spoke to a specific group of people (Judah), but the general principle is probably still applicable. The people God made are responsible for exalting and worshiping Him, which is what it means to give Him glory. We were made to give Him glory (Isaiah 43:7). That is our primary purpose. If we don't do this and darkness comes, we have only ourselves to blame. We have been forewarned.

Jeremiah 16:15 ...but, 'The Lord lives who brought up the children

of Israel from the land of the north and from all the lands where He had driven them.' For I will bring them back into their land which I gave to their fathers. The Lord had said that He would punish Judah's sins (14:10). Now we find a prediction that the children of Israel would come back to the lands from which they had been driven out. So what happened in 1948? Israel was re-established in the same ground from which they had been driven out.

Jeremiah 17:5 Thus says the Lord:
  "Cursed *is* the man who trusts in man
  And makes flesh his strength,
  Whose heart departs from the Lord. How often have people been disappointed when they put their faith in a man? All men are flawed, and none have the capability of saving us from our sins as Jesus Christ can do. This verse makes it even worse to trust in man. It says the person who does so is cursed. That does not sound like something anyone would want. Thus, the moral of this story is to put your trust in God. His spirit needs to be our strength, not a corruptible man.

Jeremiah 18:7 The instant I speak concerning a nation and concerning a kingdom, to pluck up, to pull down, and to destroy *it*, 8 if that nation against whom I have spoken turns from its evil, I will relent of the disaster that I thought to bring upon it. Here's another situation whereby the actions of men will produce a different result from God. God has different results prearranged depending on the decisions of man. The people of the time did not like what Jeremiah was saying and planned to persecute him (18:18). Nevertheless, he didn't stop letting the people know what the Lord had said about bringing catastrophe on the place (19:3). It was so bad for Jeremiah that the chief governor (Pashhur) had him beaten and put in stocks (20:2). Still, Jeremiah told Pashhur he would go into captivity and die in Babylon (20:6). Poor Jeremiah was imprisoned, rejected, and persecuted, but he remained steadfast in his calling.

Jeremiah 19:11 For I know the thoughts that I think toward you, says the Lord, thoughts of peace and not of evil, to give you a future and a hope. This is an excellent thought. God's thoughts toward the people were to provide them with a future and hope. We do have hope because He gives it to us. He goes on to say that if we search for Him with all our heart, we will find Him. Not everyone who is a non-believer will do that. I think it was C.S. Lewis who said searching for God as an atheist is like a criminal searching for a policeman. It is probably not going to be a very full-fledged effort.

Jeremiah 21:12 O house of David! Thus says the Lord:
  "Execute judgment in the morning;
  And deliver *him who is* plundered
  Out of the hand of the oppressor,
  Lest My fury go forth like fire
  And burn so that no one can quench *it*,
  Because of the evil of your doings. This message and others lets us know how a nation will fare that does not deliver the plundered person. The Lord's fury will be kindled against them.

Jeremiah 22:3 Thus says the Lord: "Execute judgment and righteousness, and deliver the plundered out of the hand of the oppressor. Do no wrong and do no violence to the stranger, the fatherless, or the widow, nor shed innocent blood in this place. Here is more on how a nation should behave and appears to indicate how God judges a nation. Note that a nation is expected to deliver the plundered out of the hand of the oppressor. Strangers, the fatherless and widows, are probably unable to fend for themselves and, therefore, should have no wrong or violence done to them. This is basic decency. If Judah did not practice this basic decency, they would become a desolation (22:5). As we know, Judah and Israel ceased to be a nation for many centuries, but in modern times Israel was re-established as foretold by Jeremiah (23:3).

Jeremiah 23:3 "But I will gather the remnant of My flock out of all countries where I have driven them, and bring them back to their folds; and they shall be fruitful and increase. Since 1948 when Israel was re-established, and remnants from many parts of the world moved to the new country, Israel has flourished and won several wars against countries that wanted to put them out of existence. The Lord had driven them out of the Land of Israel but said they would be brought back to dwell in their land again as foretold through Jeremiah some 2500 years ago. From what I know, only God can predict what will happen 2,500 years into the future. I believe a true prophet sent by God is always correct in their predictions. It may take a long time in our understanding of time, but the predictions will always come to pass.

Jeremiah 26:3 Perhaps everyone will listen and turn from his evil way, that I may relent concerning the calamity which I purpose to bring on them because of the evil of their doings.' Here is another example of scripture from the Lord that indicates that the Lord would treat people differently if they cease doing evil. This verse also again demonstrates the free will of man. He can go one way or another, and the consequences of each choice are different.

Jeremiah 27:4 And command them to say to their masters, "Thus says the Lord of hosts, the God of Israel—thus you shall say to your masters: 5 'I have made the earth, the man and the beast that *are* on the ground, by My great power and by My outstretched arm, and have given it to whom it seemed proper to Me. This verse clarifies that God made the earth, man, and animals by His great power. Since He made us and the universe we inhabit, He has every right to do with us as he pleases. But wait, you say. What if I don't believe that God did all that. Well then, what logical, reasonable explanation do you have for the existence of all these things and the universe? I don't see anyone else or any other explanation that even comes close to explaining everything we see and everything there is in our universe. No other explanation appears to pass the alpha and omega test. Random accidents over time do not answer the origin question. If not God, who or what is the uncaused cause? A "big bang" simply does not answer the question regarding how matter came into existence.

Jeremiah 29:4 Thus says the Lord of hosts, the God of Israel, to all who were carried away captive, whom I have caused to be carried away from Jerusalem to Babylon: Note that even though Nebuchadnezzar carried out the dispersion of Israel as captives to Babylon, it was ultimately by God's hand that it was done. He also promised to bring them back from the places they had been carried away as captives (29:14).

Jeremiah 30:11 For I *am* with you,' says the Lord, 'to save you;
  Though I make a full end of all nations where I have scattered you,
  Yet I will not make a complete end of you.
  But I will correct you in justice,
  And will not let you go altogether unpunished.' Here the Lord says that He will make a complete end to the nations that had captured Judah and taken them away from their land. He also says that he will not make a complete end of Judah but that they would be punished. He explains in a following verse that they were punished for the multitude of iniquities.

Jeremiah 31:31 "Behold, the days are coming, says the Lord, when I will make a new covenant with the house of Israel and with the house of Judah— This new covenant would be the covenant of grace. The old covenant (called the Mosaic or Deuteronomic) required complying with laws and commandments. The people were unable to keep these laws and commandments. That was part of what the commandments taught us. We cannot follow all the commandments. They are like a mirror that shows us just how bad we look. Following the law did not save people then, nor does it now. The law was a tutor for us to show us our need for a savior (Galatians 3:24).

Jeremiah 31:33 But this *is* the covenant that I will make with the house of Israel after those days, says the Lord: I will put My law in their minds, and write it on their hearts; and I will be their God, and they shall be My people. We are under the covenant of grace (Hebrews 9:11; Galatians 3:8) at this time, and those who have God's law in their minds and in their hearts are His people.

Jeremiah 31:35 Thus says the Lord,
   Who gives the sun for a light by day,
   The ordinances of the moon and the stars for a light by night,
   Who disturbs the sea,
   And its waves roar
(The Lord of hosts *is* His name): Without the Lord, we would not have the sun. Without the sun, life on earth would be impossible. He also provided for the moon and the stars, which affect the tides of the sea. One of the main things to be learned from the book of Jeremiah seems to be that God is sovereign over what happens with all the nations of the earth.

Jeremiah 32:41 Yes, I will rejoice over them to do them good, and I will assuredly plant them in this land, with all My heart and with all My soul.' This scripture is interesting in that it makes mention of God's heart and soul. We can relate to these concepts because we have an idea of what our hearts and soul are. The reference to heart and soul seems to imply that God can understand our heart, will, and emotions since He also has these qualities.

Jeremiah 48:42 And Moab shall be destroyed as a people,
   Because he exalted *himself* against the Lord. Doesn't sound too good for Moab. Not a good idea to exalt yourself against the Lord. Moab's primary sin seemed to be pride. They put themselves above God.

25

Lamentations

[25]**LAMENTATIONS** - This is a book of grief, suffering, hope, pain, and remembrance.

Lamentations 1:17 Zion stretches out her hands,
  but there is no one to comfort her.
  The Lord has decreed for Jacob
  that his neighbors become his foes;
  Jerusalem has become
  an unclean thing among them. Jerusalem had strayed from their God, so they suffered the consequences of their neighbors turning against them. These people were selected by God and then turned on Him and became worse than their pagan neighbors.

Lamentations 3:22 Because of the Lord's great love we are not consumed,
  for his compassions never fail.
  23 They are new every morning;

---

[25] NSB quotations are from the Nelsons Study Bible, copyright (c) 1997 by Thomas Nelson, Inc., Nashville, TN; used by permission; scripture taken from the New King James Version, Copyright (c) 1979, 1980, 1982 used by permission. All rights reserved.

great is your faithfulness. This verse may be the key to this book. Even though we have challenges, trials, and tribulations, God can comfort us through them and will be faithful and compassionate. He may not take us out of the trials because we need to be refined, but He is still faithful. He is full of grace (John 1:14).

Lamentations 3:39 Why should the living complain when punished for their sins? That is a good question, but that is what we do. Even when we receive punishment as a natural and logical consequence of our actions, we still do not want to accept it.

Lamentations 3:58 You, Lord, took up my case;
   you redeemed my life. Here is an Old Testament verse that portends the future of Christ paying the price for our sins.

Lamentations 4:9 Those killed by the sword are better off
   than those who die of famine;
   racked with hunger, they waste away
   for lack of food from the field. In difficult times of famine caused by war, it can be easier to die quicker in battle than to starve to death. When people are starving, who do not have strict moral standards to follow, they can even get to the point where they will rationalize eating their children (4:10).

Lamentations 4:13 But it happened because of the sins of her prophets
   and the iniquities of her priests,
   who shed within her
   the blood of the righteous. Note that priests can turn bad and lead the people astray. People often hold their "religious leaders" in high esteem and follow what they say. This scripture lets us know that these leaders are not infallible. Modern priests in the Catholic church have proven this scripture correct many times through their abuse of children in the

churches. Though it may be a tiny percentage of the priests who abuse their congregations' children, it is evident that priests can go astray and need to be monitored and supervised and immediately held accountable for their actions if they fall into sin. No one is above question.

Lamentations 5:14 The elders are gone from the city gate; the young men have stopped their music. 15 Joy is gone from our hearts; our dancing has turned to mourning. This is where Zion would wind up through turning away from God. People would cease to take pleasure in normal things like music and dancing. Instead, they would be in mourning. But wait. In one of the last verses of the book, hope is expressed. See verse 5:21 below.

Lamentations 5:21 Restore us to yourself, Lord, that we may return; renew our days as of old... Here is the answer to the mourning of the people. The people needed to turn back to God and then He could restore them. God had a message for His rebellious people: turn. Jeremiah tells the people to "turn" many times (Jeremiah 3:1, 7, 12, 14, 22). To turn can be a life or death matter, and God is the one who can make things new when the people turn toward Him (Ezekiel 11:19; 18:31).

26

Ezekiel

[26]**EZEKIEL** - This book contains literary techniques, including puns, poetry, allegories, parables, lamentations, and proverbs. Without understanding these techniques, it can be easy to misunderstand what is said. It appears that God wanted it that way. This book helps us understand why God must judge sin in His righteousness and justice. The ultimate aim of God's judgment is our repentance and knowledge that He is the Lord.

Ezekiel 2:2 And He said to me, "Son of man, stand on your feet, and I will speak to you." 2 Then the Spirit entered me when He spoke to me, and set me on my feet; and I heard Him who spoke to me. Here we learn that Ezekiel is indwelt by the Holy Spirit of the living God. Thus, he is speaking for God, so the people should listen to him. However, God knew that Israel would be hard-hearted and not listen to Ezekiel as they would not listen to Him (3:7).

Ezekiel 2:7 You shall speak My words to them, whether they hear or

---

[26] NSB quotations are from the Nelsons Study Bible, copyright (c) 1997 by Thomas Nelson, Inc., Nashville, TN; used by permission; scripture taken from the New King James Version, Copyright (c) 1979, 1980, 1982 used by permission. All rights reserved.

whether they refuse, for they *are* rebellious. God, of course, knows that many people will refuse to listen to what He says to them. He gave us the free will to oppose Him. Still, many people do not recognize from where this freedom came. Ezekiel was to tell these people what God told him to say whether the people listened or not.

Ezekiel 3:27 But when I speak with you, I will open your mouth, and you shall say to them, 'Thus says the Lord God.' He who hears, let him hear; and he who refuses, let him refuse; for they *are* a rebellious house. Freedom is alive and well with the Lord. However, consequences for bad decisions are a natural and logical outcome. Those who listen and turn from sin shall live, and those who do not shall die (3:20-21). Still, the choice is up to the person.

Ezekiel 4:17 ...that they may lack bread and water, and be dismayed with one another, and waste away because of their iniquity. One interesting point of this passage is that wasting away would be an outcome of iniquity. Such a slow demise would be very difficult. God had made promises to the people for their disobedience and therefore, could not fail to implement this promise (Leviticus 26:14-29; Deuteronomy 28:47-53).

Ezekiel 5:12 One-third of you shall die of the pestilence, and be consumed with famine in your midst; and one-third shall fall by the sword all around you; and I will scatter another third to all the winds, and I will draw out a sword after them. God says that their abominations would be repaid (7:8). They would get what they deserved (7:27). Some will judge God and say that this punishment is too harsh. This is the position of a person who views themselves and their opinions above the creator of the universe. This level of pride would only be possible from a person who has no respect or belief in God.

Ezekiel 6:8 "Yet I will leave a remnant, so that you may have *some* who escape the sword among the nations, when you are scattered

through the countries. This is precisely what happened to Israel. A remnant of Israel was scattered through many other countries, and over hundreds of years, they still maintain their identity. Many of their descendants eventually came back to Jerusalem. This fact alone should give unbelievers pause in considering the credibility of the Bible as the Word of God.

Ezekiel 9:9 Then He said to me, "The iniquity of the house of Israel and Judah *is* exceedingly great, and the land is full of bloodshed, and the city full of perversity; for they say, 'The Lord has forsaken the land, and the Lord does not see!' This is one of those difficult passages for unbelievers and believers to understand. God had ordered that all men, women, and children of those participating in the abominations of idolatry be killed. Those who were marked as being repentant and who showed remorse were spared. This judgment is shocking to most of us; however, we are not God, and we only see things from our perspective. God knows the past, present, and future, and He is just. Who are we to judge God? We do not have the status to judge God. We are not the creator of all things as He is. He is the potter; we are the clay (Isaiah 64:8, 45:9; Romans 9:21; Jeremiah 18:6; Isaiah 29:16; Romans 9:20-21).

Over and over, the scriptures make it clear that God is like a potter. The potter has the right to do whatever he wants with his creations. Some creations He may mold into a different vessel. Some, he may destroy, and some he may make for honorable use. We may not like it because we are not the potter who decides which is which. But know this, God is just (Isaiah 61:8; 30:18; Deuteronomy 32), and all His decisions are just. So, if there is something we don't understand or doesn't look good from our perspective, we may have to take it on faith and live with it until we go to heaven. Then we will understand much more (1 Corinthians 13:12). Note that we still will not know everything. We will not be omniscient as God is, but we will better understand many things when we see Him face to face.

Ezekiel 11:17 Therefore say, 'Thus says the Lord God: "I will gather you from the peoples, assemble you from the countries where you have been scattered, and I will give you the land of Israel." ' Here is a real clear prophecy that the Israelites would be returning from various countries to the land of Israel. Amazing when you consider how long ago this prophecy was made. Note that the covenant regarding this land goes back a couple of thousand years to Abraham's time (Genesis 12:1-3).

Ezekiel 13:3 Thus says the Lord God: "Woe to the foolish prophets, who follow their own spirit and have seen nothing! This scripture recognizes that there were false prophets and there still are. Since early times, these prophets have been making predictions and often get notoriety when they do, but are disgraced when their prophecies fail to happen.

Ezekiel 14:12 The word of the Lord came again to me, saying: 13 "Son of man, when a land sins against Me by persistent unfaithfulness, I will stretch out My hand against it; I will cut off its supply of bread, send famine on it, and cut off man and beast from it. The thing about this prophecy is that the Word goes on to say that even if Noah, Daniel, or Job were in the land that is persistently unfaithful to the LORD, they would be the only ones who would be delivered from the famine (14:14). Nevertheless, if Jerusalem experiences disaster, they will know that the LORD does nothing without cause (14:23). This is a heavy prophecy for a country that is persistently unfaithful. Possibly, some of the treaties Jerusalem was making involved Jerusalem worshipping other gods as part of their ceremonies, and some of these countries may have practiced infanticide (16:20,21, 26). It appears that the nations that obey will be blessed, and the ones that disobey will be cursed. Even with all of this, there is a ray of hope that a remnant will still be brought out of these situations (14:22).

Ezekiel 18:4 "Behold, all souls are Mine;

The soul of the father
As well as the soul of the son is Mine;
The soul who sins shall die. Not only is all the material world owned by the LORD, but also our very souls belong to Him. What we need to understand is our bodies, and our souls cannot be separated except at death. The body without the soul is about 99 percent water, carbon, hydrogen, nitrogen, calcium, and phosphorus. Only .85 percent is composed of another five elements. Without the life of the soul, these elements can't do much.

Ezekiel 18:20 The soul who sins shall die. The son shall not bear the guilt of the father, nor the father bear the guilt of the son. The righteousness of the righteous shall be upon himself, and the wickedness of the wicked shall be upon himself. This verse is admonishing us that personal responsibility for sin is essential. God will be just and righteous in dispensing His judgments fairly and individually.

Ezekiel 20:12 Moreover I also gave them My Sabbaths, to be a sign between them and Me, that they might know that I *am* the Lord who sanctifies them. Here, the reason for the Sabbath is explained. They were a sign that the Israelites could know who the Lord was and what He did. He sanctified them.

Ezekiel 20:23 Also I raised My hand in an oath to those in the wilderness, that I would scatter them among the Gentiles and disperse them throughout the countries, 24 because they had not executed My judgments, but had despised My statutes, profaned My Sabbaths, and their eyes were fixed on their fathers' idols. Here, as in 20:41, is another prophecy about the Israelites made over a thousand years ago that appears to have been fulfilled in our time. In 1948 Israel was re-established. This is phenomenal. Those who do not accept the Bible as the inspired Word of God might have a hard time explaining these prophecies, but they will give it their best.

Ezekiel 20:41 I will accept you as a sweet aroma when I bring you out from the peoples and gather you out of the countries where you have been scattered; and I will be hallowed in you before the Gentiles. In conjunction with the scripture above, this prophecy says that the Lord will bring Israel back to their land from countries to which they had been scattered. It appears that this prophecy was fulfilled over a thousand years later in 1948. That is amazing. It is also amazing that Israelites kept their identity over all these years. Note that in general, God grants each individual the absolute right to have a destiny in line with the decisions they make.

Ezekiel 22:22 As silver is melted in the midst of a furnace, so shall you be melted in its midst; then you shall know that I, the Lord, have poured out My fury on you.' " In Deuteronomy 28:12 and 24, the amount of rain that came was associated with the amount of obedience. This verse is similar in that the sins of Jerusalem would result in her desecration and destruction by the Babylonians. God would judge Jerusalem by allowing the Babylonians to make them cease the lewdness, harlotry (23:7), and bloodshed (24:7, 8) that they imported from Egypt. After the Babylonians and others destroyed Israel, they wound up being destroyed themselves (25:7-11).

Ezekiel 29:6 'Thus says the Lord:
   "Those who uphold Egypt shall fall,
   And the pride of her power shall come down.
   From Migdol *to* **Syene**
   Those within her shall fall by the sword,"
   Says the Lord God. In this book, the LORD makes various negative proclamations against multiple people and groups (Ammon, Moab Edom Philistia, Tyre, Sidon, Egypt, Pharaoh). In most of them, the proclamation is explained by the phrase **"they shall know that I am the Lord GOD."** It appears that the LORD would let them know what was going to happen to them, and then when it happened, they would realize that the LORD

had followed through on his proclamations and, therefore, they would know who He was.

Ezekiel 33:9 Nevertheless if you warn the wicked to turn from his way, and he does not turn from his way, he shall die in his iniquity; but you have delivered your soul. There is a principle here that applied to Ezekiel, the prophet. If he did not warn the house of Israel for the Lord, he would experience something negative for his soul.

Ezekiel 33:11 Say to them: 'As I live,' says the Lord God, 'I have no pleasure in the death of the wicked, but that the wicked turn from his way and live. Turn, turn from your evil ways! For why should you die, O house of Israel?' God's judgment is always fair, and He indicates that He wants people to turn and be saved. How does a wicked person turn? The example given is the thief who gives back what they have stolen. In other words, they can make restitution. People will say that the Lord is not fair, but He is. He says: "I will judge every one of you according to his own ways." (33:20).

Ezekiel 36:24 For I will take you from among the nations, gather you out of all countries, and bring you into your own land. Here is a promise from the Lord that He would renew Israel to their land. Note that this does not say that Israel's possession of the land would not be continued without interruptions. At least one of the times where Israelites have come back from other countries to the land of Canaan happened in 1948 when the country of Israel was reestablished.

Ezekiel 40:44 Outside the inner gate *were* the chambers for the singers in the inner court, one facing south at the side of the northern gateway, and the other facing north at the side of the southern gateway. Note that singers in the inner court would inhabit the temple to be built. These singers were to celebrate, worship, thank, and praise the LORD.

Ezekiel 44:20 "They shall neither shave their heads nor let their hair grow long, but they shall keep their hair well trimmed. 21 No priest shall drink wine when he enters the inner court. Here, it is interesting that the priests were practicing some behaviors that might set them apart from the rest of society. A couple of things are mentioned here. At the time, if a male let his hair grow long, it could be a sign of taking some vow like abstinence from wine (Numbers 6:3, 4).

On the other hand, shaving the head could signify mourning. The priests were not to stand out for either of these extremes but were to maintain hair well-trimmed. Regarding drinking wine, it appears that the priests could on occasion drink wine but were not allowed to drink any before ministering for the LORD. In conjunction with other scripture on drinking wine (Ephesians 5:18), it is clear that believers can drink wine in moderation but should never drink to excess, nor should they drink before any ministry activities. Christians should remain clear-headed and abstinent whenever the Holy Spirit is working in and through them for any ministry activities or worship services.

Ezekiel 47:21 "Thus you shall divide this land among yourselves according to the tribes of Israel. 22 It shall be that you will divide it by lot as an inheritance for yourselves, and for the strangers who dwell among you and who bear children among you. They shall be to you as native-born among the children of Israel; they shall have an inheritance with you among the tribes of Israel. 23 And it shall be *that* in whatever tribe the stranger dwells, there you shall give *him* his inheritance," says the Lord God. This is the direction to the Israelites that the strangers dwelling among them who married Israelites and bore children should receive the same inheritance as the native-born. In other words, these non-Israelites were to be completely accepted as if they were native-born when it came to inheriting land.

Ezekiel 48:35 All the way around *shall be* eighteen thousand *cubits*;

and the name of the city from *that* **day** *shall be:* **THE LORD** *IS* **THERE."** This is the last sentence of the book of Ezekiel. What a great name for a city. Ezekiel had foreseen that God would regather the Israelites in the land, and God would return to His temple.

27

Daniel

[27]**DANIEL** - This book demonstrates that God's plans will come to pass and that He will use the pagans to facilitate His plans if He wants.

Daniel 2:26 The king answered and said to Daniel, whose name *was* Belteshazzar, "Are you able to make known to me the dream which I have seen, and its interpretation?" Daniel explains to King Nebuchadnezzar that God would make known to him what would happen in the latter days even though all of the King's other advisors could not interpret the dream. After many kingdoms, Daniel predicted that God would establish a kingdom that would stand forever. There are a couple of different views on the interpretation of what this kingdom will be like, but I'll say it will be great. Nebuchadnezzar's dream interpretation was revealed to Daniel in a night vision (vs. 2:19). Before Daniel interpreted the King's dream, he enlisted the help of his companions to **seek mercies from God** as one of his first steps in this crisis. Thus, he wasn't praying alone but getting his friends involved in the prayer for enlightenment. This was a crisis for the wise men of the community, including Daniel

---

[27] NSB quotations are from the Nelsons Study Bible, copyright (c) 1997 by Thomas Nelson, Inc., Nashville, TN; used by permission; scripture taken from the New King James Version, Copyright (c) 1979, 1980, 1982 used by permission. All rights reserved.

and his friends, if they could not interpret the dream because the King had issued a decree that they were to be killed if they could not interpret the dream.

Daniel 3:21 Then these men were bound in their coats, their trousers, their turbans, and their *other* garments, and were cast into the midst of the burning fiery furnace. This relates to the story of Shadrach, Meshack, and Abed-Nego, who were thrown into a fire by the King because they would not worship a gold image that he had set up. The men who threw them into the furnace got too close and were killed, yet Shadrach, Meshack, and Abed-Nego walked into the fire and were seen with a fourth person. The three emerged unscathed, not even smelling like smoke. At this miracle, the King decreed that if any people, nation, or language said anything amiss about the God of Shadrach, Meshack, and Abed-Nego they were to be cut into pieces and have their houses made an ash heap. This is not a very pleasant outcome. Note that Nebuchadnezzar was a pagan king.

Daniel 4:17 'This decision *is* by the decree of the watchers,
  And the sentence by the word of the holy ones,
  In order that the living may know
  That the Most High rules in the kingdom of men,
  Gives it to whomever He will,
  And sets over it the lowest of men.' Some of what is in the Old Testament will sound authoritarian and, we seem to have an innate tendency to rebel against authority. Sometimes God allows a lowly person to be a governing authority over us. This verse makes it clear that it is bad news for the subjects in the countries ruled by these lowly rulers.

Note that of the approximately 195 countries in the world, in 2013 only 88 (40%) were designated by the *Freedom in the World* group as free. The others have various levels of freedom from authoritarian rule. Some may have what could be called benevolent dictators that allow some freedoms for their subjects. For others, the ruling class has very little tolerance for any dissent. Twenty-five percent of these countries are rated as not free at all.

Those who advocate for socialism in America may not realize what implementation of socialism could mean for them in terms of their freedoms and "rights." If they do realize what an authoritarian government system does to freedoms and rights, then they must like the idea of being told what you will do and what you cannot do all the time.

In countries that are not free, government rulers or dictators determine what is right and wrong. They implement punishment for anyone who does not go along with the collective good as determined by them. My preference is to live under a government that governs least and provides the highest level of freedom.

I have been fortunate to live at a time in America where there has been a general level of freedom exceeding that in most other countries. America has even been viewed as the beacon of freedom in the world. However, I'm not sure how long the American experiment with self-governance will last. Nevertheless, I'm thankful that it has lasted as long as it has.

At this time (2019), there appear to be signs that many of our citizens are now willing to vote for a higher government control of more aspects of daily life in America. At least we still get to vote and dissent, but that could change quicker than many people realize. Freedom of speech, for example, at one time, included almost everything that would not cause potential physical harm, like shouting "fire" in a crowded theater. There are many other controls on what can and cannot be said if not because of laws then because of social mores. I hear there is a lack of free speech at California State University at Berkeley, which once was the birthplace of the student free speech movement in the 1960s. Now, many students will not let those speak who will not tell them what they want to hear.

Daniel 6:5 Then these men said, "We shall not find any charge against this Daniel unless we find *it* against him concerning the law of his God." Here people wanted to do harm to Daniel. To get him, they knew that he would follow all of the rules unless there was something that his beliefs contradicted. It is interesting that in this culture, once a king made a decree, even he could not revoke it. So, they got the King to decree that anyone who petitioned any god or man except the King in the next thirty days would be thrown into the lion's den. With his windows open, Daniel defied the order and prayed to God. This brought him the punishment of being thrown into the lion's den for a night from which he emerged the following day unscathed. It didn't work out so well for Daniel's accusers. The King had them and their families thrown into the lion's den, and all of their bones were broken into pieces quickly. After this, the King held Daniel's God in high esteem and decreed that all the kingdom should recognize the God of Daniel. So Daniel prospered in the kingdom.

Daniel 8:27 ...Then the kingdom and dominion,
And the greatness of the kingdoms under the whole heaven,
Shall be given to the people, the saints of the Most High.
His kingdom *is* an everlasting kingdom,
And all dominions shall serve and obey Him.' Here's an interesting prediction for the future. God's saints are given the kingdoms under the whole heaven and will exercise rule over them. There are sections in the New Testament that talk about God ruling kingdoms on earth through His saints (Revelation 2:26, 27: 20:4-6). Who are these saints? That would be those who through faith believe in and follow the God of the Bible and are granted salvation through His grace. These prophecies appear to be taking place many days in the future.

Daniel 9:27 ...Then he shall confirm a covenant with many for one week;
But in the middle of the week

He shall bring an end to sacrifice and offering.

And on the wing of abominations shall be one who makes desolate,

Even until the consummation, which is determined,

Is poured out on the desolate." According to history, one of the events referred to as the abomination of desolation occurred in 167 B.C. when king Antiochus Epiphanies set up an altar to Zeus over the altar of burnt offerings in the Jewish Temple in Jerusalem and sacrificed a pig on the altar in that Temple. Putting this verse together with Matthew 24:15 and other scripture, it appears to be a reasonable conclusion that Daniel, though he may not have understood what he was saying, is predicting something in the future similar to what Antiochus Epiphanies did. The thinking is that in the end times of our dispensation, the Antichrist will establish a covenant with Israel for seven years and then set up the abomination standing in the holy place in the Jewish Temple. This individual will exalt themselves above every so-called god or another object of worship. After this, Jesus says there will be great tribulation in the world before He returns to the earth. So, the Temple in Jerusalem will someday be rebuilt. There are groups in Israel that have plans to do this when they can. The Antichrist will make a deal with Israel and rule for three and a half years before setting up the abomination of desolation in the Temple. He will declare that he is God and must be worshiped (Revelation 19:20).

Daniel 13:13 "As *it is* written in the Law of Moses, all this disaster has come upon us; yet we have not made our prayer before the Lord our God, that we might turn from our iniquities and understand Your truth. Many people do not like to think that God has anything to do with how things turn out here on earth. For those who do not believe that there is a God, it makes perfect sense that those who think God has anything to do with what happens here are delusional. Yet here in Old Testament days, men realized that disaster could come upon them due to their iniquities. One might wonder how long God will continue to allow America to prosper in our postmodern age of disrespect, disbelief, and iniquities. God who does not show favoritism (Romans 2:11; 2 Chronicles 19:7; Acts 10:34; 1 Peter 1:17).

28

Hosea

[28]**HOSEA** - Hosea was a prophet of judgment and salvation during the eighth century before the Common Era (BCE).

Hosea 3:3 Then the Lord said to me, "Go again, love a woman *who is* loved by a lover and is committing adultery, just like the love of the Lord for the children of Israel, who look to other gods and love *the* raisin cakes *of the pagans.*" Hosea's wife had left him and became a prostitute just as Israel had left the LORD and worshiped other gods. Hosea repurchased his wife and retook her to be his wife. God took Israel back after she went off and worshiped pagan gods just as Hosea had been encouraged to take his wife back. The LORD talked about Israel's unfaithfulness but still reconciled with them just as Hosea reconciled with his unfaithful wife. It appears that the LORD was letting Hosea get a good idea of what it was like to have someone you love be unfaithful and then forgiving and reconciling with them. This process may have given the prophet a better understanding of how the LORD dealt with Israel. In the end, it appears that as Hosea redeemed and restored his

---

[28] NSB quotations are from the Nelsons Study Bible, copyright (c) 1997 by Thomas Nelson, Inc., Nashville, TN; used by permission; scripture taken from the New King James Version, Copyright (c) 1979, 1980, 1982 used by permission. All rights reserved.

unfaithful wife, the LORD will redeem and restore His unfaithful nation.

Hosea 6:6 Come, and let us return to the Lord;
For He has torn, but He will heal us;
He has stricken, but He will bind us up. Here Israel is being called to repentance. When they do repent, God will be quick to forgive and restore His relationship with them. On the other hand, God's judgments can be **like the light that goes forth** (6:5). We were in a lightning storm at our house the other day, and a bolt struck a huge old oak tree and blew off the bark where it carved a path down the trunk to the ground within about 100 feet of our home. It produced a brief but incredibly bright light and a loud and dramatic explosive sound. The light that went forth seemed instantaneous, but according to science, we know that light travels at approximately 186,000 miles per second which may be as fast as anything in the physical world can go but is not instantaneous. God's judgments can go that fast.

Hosea 7:2 They do not consider in their hearts
That **I remember all their wickedness;**
Now their own deeds have surrounded them;
They are before My face. People who do not believe in God can convince themselves that there is no judgment. In the Bible, this is called a hardened heart (Romans 2:5; Mark 8:13; Mark 6:22). But, according to the Bible, there is a judgment day (Matthew 12:36; Hebrews 9:27; Psalm 73:11). God holds unbelievers responsible for their misdeeds and rewards believers for their good deeds (Matthew 6:1-4; Galatians 6:9; Ephesians 2:8-9). Note that believers have also sinned/transgressed, but through God's gift of grace they are forgiven. Their transgressions are as far as the East is from the West in God's eyes (Psalm 103:12).

Hosea 9:17 My God will cast them away,
Because they did not obey Him;
And they shall be wanderers among the nations. Here is another

prophecy that appears to have come to pass. The Israelites were dispersed among many countries, and many still are. Also, many came back to the new state of Israel which was formed in 1948, after hundreds of years of dispersion. This seems to have been predicted in the scriptures (Isaiah 66:8; Ezra 1:2). There are different explanations regarding these predictions and whether the new Israel actually fulfills these predictions, but it is interesting.

Hosea 10:12 Sow for yourselves righteousness;
   Reap in mercy;
   Break up your fallow ground,
   For *it is* time to seek the Lord,
   Till He comes and rains righteousness on you. Here Hosea is encouraging Israel to repent and obtain mercy from the LORD. It was not too late, and God would probably still bless them if they did repent.

Hosea 13:4 "Yet I *am* the Lord your God
   Ever since the land of Egypt,
   And you shall know no God but Me;
   For *there is* no savior besides Me. The LORD tells Israel who He is and what He has done for them and will do with them. He is God, and He directs Israel to relate to Him as such. He also clarifies that He is their savior and their only savior. Those of us who have accepted what the Bible says as the truth also believe that He is our savior, and He is the only one who can save us in the sense that the Bible describes.

This salvation carries special spiritual significance in addition to the other related dimensions. A crucial aspect of the term has to do with the spiritual salvation that comes from God. In this sense, salvation is a spiritual birth from above without which one cannot enter the kingdom of heaven (John 3:1-11). It is also much more detailed in many other scriptures. It is a process whereby Christ paid the ultimate price for our sins and transgressions (Romans 4:25; Matthew 20:28; 1 Corinthians

15:3). There are other dimensions of salvation waiting to be revealed (1 Peter 1:5; Romans 8:23). I'm sure it will be glorious.

Hosea 13:12 "The iniquity of Ephraim *is* bound up;
His sin *is* stored up. This could be bad news for America if God still keeps records of a nation's iniquity as He did regarding Ephraim. From a Biblical perspective, we sure do seem to have escalating iniquity in our country. It depends on your point of view, but probably most people who have lived a while could point to areas where our American culture has gone downhill in their lifetimes.

Hosea 14:2 Take words with you,
   And return to the Lord.
   Say to Him,
   "Take away all iniquity;
   Receive *us* graciously,
   For we will offer the sacrifices of our lips. Well, at the end of Hosea's prophecy, it looks like Israel will have its relationship with God restored. In general, what God demands of Israel, or us for that matter, are just repentance and faith. The thing about repentance and faith is that they go together. Perhaps it would be better to write them this way: repentance-faith. It is hard to have one without the other. Repentance describes the believer's attitude toward sin, and faith describes the same believer's attitude toward God. The words appear to be different perspectives on the same process, twin graces that are difficult or impossible to separate in the spiritual context. There is a word for this: synecdoche - a figure of speech in which a part is used for the whole or the whole for a part. In other words, regarding salvation conversion, both words are permeated by the other and inseparable.

29

Joel

[29]**JOEL** - The book of Joel appears to be set at about 600 B.C. and deals with the judgments and blessings of nations.

Joel 2:24 The threshing floors shall be full of wheat,
  And the vats shall overflow with new wine and oil.
  25 "So I will restore to you the years that the swarming locust has eaten,
  The crawling locust,
  The consuming locust,
  And the chewing locust,
  My great army which I sent among you. Before this blessing, the land had been laid waste by the Day of the Lord in which God brought down wrath and judgment for the wicked and salvation to the righteous.

Joel 2:28 "And it shall come to pass afterward
  That I will pour out My Spirit on all flesh;
  Your sons and your daughters shall prophesy,

---

[29] NSB quotations are from the Nelsons Study Bible, copyright (c) 1997 by Thomas Nelson, Inc., Nashville, TN; used by permission; scripture taken from the New King James Version, Copyright (c) 1979, 1980, 1982 used by permission. All rights reserved.

Your old men shall dream dreams,
Your young men shall see visions.
29 And also on *My* menservants and on *My* maidservants
I will pour out My Spirit in those days. According to the New Testament, this is a major prophecy that came to pass at Pentecost (the day the Holy Spirit came upon the disciples who were waiting in the upper room per this prophecy in Joel). The whole of the book of Joel was summed up by Nathan D. Holsteen and Michael J. Svigel in *Exploring Christian Theology: Volume 1: Revelation, Scripture, and the Triune God* (*2014,* Bethany House Publishers) as follows: "with repentance, judgment gives way to blessing…and, in the future, *ultimate* judgment will usher in *ultimate* blessing." I can't summarize the book any better than that. There are different opinions regarding the fulfillment of this prophecy, and it could have more than one fulfillment. On a related issue, I agree with many of the commentators that Pentecost was the beginning of what the Bible calls "the last days." The next big event appears to be the Tribulation period of seven years which could begin at any time.

Joel 3:20 But Judah shall abide forever,
    And Jerusalem from generation to generation.
    21 For I will acquit them of the guilt of bloodshed, whom I had not acquitted;
    For the Lord dwells in Zion." Just before this prophecy, there is a prophecy about Egypt which says that it will be a "**desolation.**" The prophecy indicates that at some point Judah will be re-established and continue "**forever.**" That is an interesting thought considering the nation of Israel was re-established in 1948. It will be interesting to see if that is the Judah about which this prophecy is talking.

30

Amos

[30]**AMOS** - This book by the minor prophet Amos is all about justice, injustice, and the relationship issues that proceed from both of these. It is said to have been written somewhere around 755 B.C.

Amos 1:3 Thus says the Lord:
  "For three transgressions of Damascus, and for four,
  I will not turn away its *punishment,*
  Because they have threshed Gilead with implements of iron. I do not question who made this pronouncement. It was the Lord. So, what were the transgressions of Damascus? The scripture does not say what they did to deserve the punishment. Since they were not a nation that was given direct revelation from God of the Ten Commandments, it appears that they may have violated what can be called the "law of nature." What is that? It is the regularly occurring or inevitable phenomenon observable in human society. These phenomena are similar across many cultures, and come from general revelation. Anyway, apparently, the Damascus people had violated what they knew to be right and, therefore,

---

[30] NSB quotations are from the Nelsons Study Bible, copyright (c) 1997 by Thomas Nelson, Inc., Nashville, TN; used by permission; scripture taken from the New King James Version, Copyright (c) 1979, 1980, 1982 used by permission. All rights reserved.

were going to receive punishment for what they had done.

Amos 3:6 "Also I gave you cleanness of teeth in all your cities,
And lack of bread in all your places;
Yet you have not returned to Me,"
Says the Lord. Clean teeth are not a good thing if they are clean because you don't have enough food to eat. The Lord says He was allowing Israel to have negative consequences for their behavior. Another scripture in Amos criticizes them for oppressing the poor, taxing grain taxes from the poor, afflicting the just and taking bribes, idolatry, violence, robbery, extravagant living, pride, and not accepting correction. As a result, they would suffer earthquakes and destruction. However, He would not utterly destroy them (9:8).

Amos 9:12 That they may possess the remnant of Edom,
And all the Gentiles who are called by My name,"
Says the Lord who does this thing. In the Old Testament, note that way before Christ came to the earth, Gentile believers are mentioned as being called by His name. These people would appear to be the gentiles who became Believers. The remnant of Edom referred to in this scripture seems to be the Tabernacle of David which had been repaired and raised from its ruins (9:11). This appears to be a metaphor for Judah being restored. God punishes, and He restores.

Amos 9:14 I will bring back the captives of My people Israel;
They shall build the waste cities and inhabit *them;*
They shall plant vineyards and drink wine from them;
They shall also make gardens and eat fruit from them.
15 I will plant them in their land,
And no longer shall they be pulled up
From the land I have given them,"
Says the Lord your God. Here the prophecy says that Israel will come back to the land that God gave them. Could it be that this prophecy has

been fulfilled when the nation of Israel was re-established in 1948? If so, verse 15 states that they will no longer be pulled up. Interesting.

31

Obadiah

³¹**OBADIAH** - Most scholars appear to date this book around 586 B.C., immediately after the Babylonian destruction of Jerusalem.

Obadiah 1:15 "For the day of the Lord upon all the nations *is* near; As you have done, it shall be done to you;
Your reprisal shall return upon your own head. This scripture makes it known that the day of the Lord is not just related to Israel. All nations, at some point, will reap what they sew.

Obadiah 1:21 Then saviors shall come to Mount Zion
To judge the mountains of Esau,
And the kingdom shall be the Lord's. This book seems to predict that someday in the future, the Lord will own and rule justly over all nations. Perhaps this is a reference to the Millennial one-thousand-year period that comes after Christ returns to the earth. I take this to predict that God will eventually humble the proud and lift up the humble of the earth.

---

[31] NSB quotations are from the Nelsons Study Bible, copyright (c) 1997 by Thomas Nelson, Inc., Nashville, TN; used by permission; scripture taken from the New King James Version, Copyright (c) 1979, 1980, 1982 used by permission. All rights reserved.

32

Jonah

[32]JONAH - Many people have heard the story of Jonah. Jesus used the story as an analogy to His death and resurrection, so we can consider it an important book. Every book of the Bible is important, but maybe some books are more important than others. Anyway, the book seems to affirm that God can do whatever He wants to do. He is sovereign over everything in our universe and illustrates that in this story of the great fish. Note; the words used describe a fish, not a whale. I tend to view this book as a prophetic parable with historical and prophetic meaning.

Jonah 2:4 Then I said, 'I have been cast out of Your sight;
  Yet I will look again toward Your holy temple.'
  5 The waters surrounded me, *even* to my soul;
  The deep closed around me;
  Weeds were wrapped around my head. So the story goes that the Lord chose Jonah to warn Nineveh of their impending overthrow due to their wickedness. Instead of following God's direction, Jonah heads out on a boat to a different city, at which point God caused a mighty storm

---

[32] NSB quotations are from the Nelsons Study Bible, copyright (c) 1997 by Thomas Nelson, Inc., Nashville, TN; used by permission; scripture taken from the New King James Version, Copyright (c) 1979, 1980, 1982 used by permission. All rights reserved.

on the sea. The people Jonah was with eventually threw him overboard because they thought he was the reason they were going to perish. He had previously shared his story with them. He did not want to share the Lord's message with the people of Nineveh, which could cause them to repent and be spared from destruction. The scripture says that Jonah was thrown into the sea and was in the **fish's belly three days and three nights**. A succeeding verse, says that he cried out from the **belly of Sheol** (2:2). Then in verse 2:4, Jonah says he would **look again toward Your holy temple**. Thus, I'm not sure how he could look toward God's holy temple from inside the belly of a fish. Thus, maybe the "belly of the fish" is an analogy for being in the sea. I don't know, but the rest of the story is that after getting out of this situation, Jonah did go to Nineveh and warned them, and they repented, and God spared about 120,000 people from disaster. And so, that is the story of Jonah, who has been called the anti-missionary because he initially resisted God's call. God accomplished what he wanted to do even though Jonah initially resisted what he was called to do.

33

Micah

[33]**MICAH** - Thankfully, Micah seems to relieve some of the doom and gloom of other Old Testament prophets. From one perspective, the most pleasing and encouraging aspect of Micah is where he predicts the Messiah will be born in Bethlehem. This prediction was made some 700 plus years before the event happened. Micah is viewed as being written sometime in the last third of the eighth century B.C. As with many scriptures in the Bible, Micah reveals digressions and offers cleansing/forgiveness.

Micah 2:12 "**I will surely assemble all of you, O Jacob,**
  I will surely gather the remnant of Israel;
  I will put them together like sheep of the fold,
  Like a flock in the midst of their pasture;
  They shall make a loud noise because of *so many* **people.** Here is an encouraging prophecy about Israel. It says that God will put the remnant of Israel back together. Remember this was written over 2,700 years ago. Amazingly, there are ancestors of Israelites still identifiable,

---

[33] NSB quotations are from the Nelsons Study Bible, copyright (c) 1997 by Thomas Nelson, Inc., Nashville, TN; used by permission; scripture taken from the New King James Version, Copyright (c) 1979, 1980, 1982 used by permission. All rights reserved.

and they have been brought back together into a country.

Micah 3:6 "Therefore you shall have night without vision,
And you shall have darkness without divination;
The sun shall go down on the prophets,
And the day shall be dark for them. What is interesting about this passage is that it seems to predict that false prophets would stop prophesying. That does appear to be what happened after God provided the written canon of scripture that we have today. I guess that is enough for us because none of us seem to fully comprehend what is in the Bible. If we were able to master all that is in the written Word of God (the Bible), then we might need more prophets.

Micah 4:2 ...For out of Zion the law shall go forth,
And the word of the Lord from Jerusalem.
3 He shall judge between many peoples,
And rebuke strong nations afar off;
They shall beat their swords into plowshares,
And their spears into pruning hooks;
Nation shall not lift up sword against nation,
Neither shall they learn war anymore. Here's a prophecy that looks many years ahead to a time when there will not be any more war. This appears to possibly be looking forward to the 1,000-year millennial period when Christ rules the world.

Micah 5:2 "But you, Bethlehem Ephrathah,
Though **you are little among the thousands of Judah,**
Yet **out of you shall come forth to Me**
The One to be Ruler in Israel,
Whose goings forth *are* **from of old,**
From everlasting." This is a prophecy that the Messiah would come out of Bethlehem and be the Ruler in Israel one day. Of course, Christ is everlasting and always existed, so his birth would be unlike any other.

The story of His birth and the wise men visiting is prominent in the New Testament. Verse 2 of this section of scripture appears to be related to the first coming of Christ, and the following few verses appear to be related to His second coming.

34

Nahum

[34]**NAHUM** - This book was written in the seventh century B.C. and is the second book about Nineveh. Nahum the prophet is sent to preach to Nineveh, but Nineveh does not listen this time.

Nahum 1:14 The Lord has given a command concerning you:
"Your name shall be perpetuated no longer.
Out of the house of your gods
I will cut off the carved image and the molded image.
I will dig your grave,
For you are vile." Nineveh had reverted to its idolatrous and violent past. It was full of lies and robbery. In the book, it is described as the mistress of sorceries. Therefore, the prophecy came true, and the city was destroyed. It was so devastated that it couldn't even be found for thousands of years until the nineteenth century when archaeologists found it in modern-day northern Iraq. For about fifty years, some think it was the largest city globally, and then it became nothing.

---

[34] NSB quotations are from the Nelsons Study Bible, copyright (c) 1997 by Thomas Nelson, Inc., Nashville, TN; used by permission; scripture taken from the New King James Version, Copyright (c) 1979, 1980, 1982 used by permission. All rights reserved.

35

Habakkuk

[35]**HABAKKUK** - Habakkuk was another of the so-called minor prophets. He was different in that he questioned God. He seemed to prophesy between 605 and 612 B.C. Habakkuk indicates that in the end, all wrongs will be made right, judgments will occur, and believers can look forward to this day.

Habakkuk 2:4 "Behold the proud,
  His soul is not upright in him;
  But the just shall live by his faith. The Babylonians were proud and boasted about what they had accomplished. They did not believe in God and didn't care about Him or His commandments. The reality presented in the Bible is that there is no true righteousness without God, and it comes through humble faith. The book of Habakkuk ends with a Hymn of Faith and a note to the Chief Musician indicating that the hymn is to be accompanied by stringed instruments. In this hymn, the writer says that he will rejoice and have joy in the LORD even in an adverse situation. That is what true faith can do.

---

[35] NSB quotations are from the Nelsons Study Bible, copyright (c) 1997 by Thomas Nelson, Inc., Nashville, TN; used by permission; scripture taken from the New King James Version, Copyright (c) 1979, 1980, 1982 used by permission. All rights reserved.

36

Zephaniah

ZEPHANIAH - I will start with the end of the book of the minor prophet Zephaniah because it ends with a promise of future blessing with even the LORD rejoicing over Jerusalem with singing. That is a good ending. Of course, there is a warning of impending judgment and a call to repentance before the ending.[36]

Zephaniah 1:4 "I will stretch out My hand against Judah,
  And against all the inhabitants of Jerusalem.
  I will cut off every trace of Baal from this place,
  The names of the idolatrous priests with the *pagan* priests— Here is the judgment part of the book where God says that He will cut off Baal and the idolatrous and pagan priests. Baal was a deity of the Ammonites whose worship had infiltrated Jerusalem. The worship of Baal included acts of infant sacrifice per 2 Kings 23:10 and Jeremiah 32:35. If human life begins at conception or the start of the heartbeat, or any other time before birth, one could be concerned about the modern-day acceptance of abortion. Recent news has reported that it is now the single leading

---

[36] NSB quotations are from the Nelsons Study Bible, copyright (c) 1997 by Thomas Nelson, Inc., Nashville, TN; used by permission; scripture taken from the New King James Version, Copyright (c) 1979, 1980, 1982 used by permission. All rights reserved.

cause of death worldwide.

Zephaniah 1:17 "I will bring distress upon men,
 And they shall walk like blind men,
 Because they have sinned against the Lord;
 Their blood shall be poured out like dust,
 And their flesh like refuse." Here is another part of the judgment mentioned in Zephaniah. It appears that the judgment would come on so fast that people left would be in a state of shock and wandering around like blind men. The next verse speaks of the fire of His jealousy. That makes it sound like the destruction would come from fire or heat. A subsequent verse in the book says "…**All the earth shall be devoured With the fire of My jealousy**" (3:8). Thus, it looks like a worldwide judgment is predicted.

Zephaniah 3:20 At that time I will bring you back,
 Even at the time I gather you;
 For I will give you fame and praise
 Among all the peoples of the earth,
 When I return your captives before your eyes,"
Says the Lord. Now, here is the good news that has even the LORD singing. He had taken away their judgments and cast out the enemies of Jerusalem and promises that they will see disaster no more. The book begins and ends with a statement that these words are from the LORD. Zephaniah is just the guy who the words came through.

37

Haggai

[37] **HAGGAI** - Haggai is another of the minor prophets. He admonishes the people to rebuild the temple to which they initially seem indifferent but then repent and receive God's encouragement and blessing.

Haggai 1:4 "*Is it* time for you yourselves to dwell in your paneled houses, and this temple *to lie* in ruins?" Haggai gets right down to the issue at hand. The people were spending all their time and resources on their houses as the temple of God sat in ruins. In other words, their priorities needed adjustment. There may not have been anything wrong with having a nice house, but not at the expense of leaving the temple in ruins.

Haggai 1:13 Then Haggai, the Lord's messenger, spoke the Lord's message to the people, saying, "I *am* with you, says the Lord." This is the good news that God would be with them. The same promise is recorded in Isaiah 7:14, where Immanuel's coming meaning "God is with us," is prophesied. That is an encouraging statement. When Israel came

---

[37] NSB quotations are from the Nelsons Study Bible, copyright (c) 1997 by Thomas Nelson, Inc., Nashville, TN; used by permission; scripture taken from the New King James Version, Copyright (c) 1979, 1980, 1982 used by permission. All rights reserved.

out of slavery in Egypt, the LORD told them that His spirit would stay with them, so they did not need to fear. Christ also promised that when He left the earth, He would leave the Holy Spirit with His people and came through on that promise at Pentecost (John 14:15-17).

Haggai 2:8 'The silver *is* Mine, and the gold *is* Mine,' says the Lord of hosts. If you ever wondered who owns everything, here is the answer. It is God. He made it, and he owns it. We are very temporary stewards of what we think we own. What we own is just on loan. So maybe we should honor the one who owns what we have temporary control of with the things we think we own.

Haggai 2:19 Is the seed still in the barn? As yet the vine, the fig tree, the pomegranate, and the olive tree have not yielded *fruit*. *But* from this day I will bless *you*. In the end, the LORD blesses the people as they change their priorities and lay the foundation for the temple. They became productive because God blessed them, and their seed would continue to grow as the vine, the fig tree, the pomegranate, and the olive tree.

38

Zechariah

[38]**ZECHARIAH** - This is a minor prophet who brings encouragement and hope. Some of the chapters of Zechariah are the most frequently quoted section of the Old Testament in the New Testament. Zechariah preached righteousness and called the people to practice righteousness. The word Zechariah means "Yahweh Remembers."

Zechariah 2:3 And there *was* the angel who talked with me, going out; and another angel was coming out to meet him, 4 who said to him, "Run, speak to this young man, saying: 'Jerusalem shall be inhabited *as* towns without walls, because of the multitude of men and livestock in it. 5 For I,' says the Lord, 'will be a wall of fire all around her, and I will be the glory in her midst.'" This seems to be talking about a future Jerusalem (Zephaniah 3:15-19). Another section of scripture in Revelation talks about a New Jerusalem. I'm not sure how these two prophecies interact.

Zechariah 4:4 Then He answered and spoke to those who stood

---

[38] NSB quotations are from the Nelsons Study Bible, copyright (c) 1997 by Thomas Nelson, Inc., Nashville, TN; used by permission; scripture taken from the New King James Version, Copyright (c) 1979, 1980, 1982 used by permission. All rights reserved.

before Him, saying, "Take away the filthy garments from him." And to him He said, "See, I have removed your iniquity from you, and I will clothe you with rich robes." This section of prophecy from the Old Testament seems to point to grace. In this situation, God is replacing dirty clothes with clean clothes. It is similar to the gift of God's righteousness on us when we are transgressors. Christ's righteousness is placed/imputed on us, and God sees us as clean (Romans 5:18-19; 2 Corinthians 5:21). It is God's grace!

Zechariah 8:7 "Thus says the Lord of hosts:
   'Behold, I will save My people from the land of the east
   And from the land of the west;
   8 I will bring them *back*,
   And they shall dwell in the midst of Jerusalem.
   They shall be My people
   And I will be their God,
   In truth and righteousness.' Here again, is a prediction that Israelites would come back to Jerusalem over 2,000 years ago. As noted before, Israel was re-established in 1948, and many Jews from the east and west went back there. There was the first temple in Jerusalem that was destroyed and then a second temple was begun in 536 B.C. and was destroyed in 70 A.D. Now, many people expect a third temple to be built sometime in the future. There are people in Jerusalem who are currently making equipment and furniture for the next temple. We will see if a new temple in Jerusalem is started in our lifetimes.

Zechariah 8:17 ...Let none of you think evil in your heart against your neighbor;
   And do not love a false oath.
   For all these *are things* **that I hate,'**
   Says the Lord." We can have a hard time thinking that the LORD can hate, but here in black and white is a verse that says He hates a false oath. Note that this verse does not say that the LORD hates the person who

gives a false oath. It only says that He hates the false oath. He also does not like us to think evil of our neighbor. The following verses encourage a love for truth and peace.

Zechariah 9:9 "Rejoice greatly, O daughter of Zion!
  Shout, O daughter of Jerusalem!
  Behold, your King is coming to you;
  He *is* just and having salvation,
  Lowly and riding on a donkey,
  A colt, the foal of a donkey. This prophecy was made hundreds of years before Jesus fulfilled it through riding on a donkey into Jerusalem. He was just and had salvation. Eventually, at His second coming, He will assume His rightful place as a King in the governmental sense in addition to the spiritual sense.

Zechariah 11:9 Then I said, "I will not feed you. Let what is dying die, and what is perishing perish. Let those that are left eat each other's flesh." Here is a principle that is hard to fathom but is something that has happened and will happen in the future. There will be times when, due to people's actions or governments, God's judgment will result in people starving to the point of eating the flesh of those who die. There may be things that are going to happen that we will have no control over and may have to accept as part of life in a fallen world.

Zechariah 12:9 It shall be in that day *that* I will seek to destroy all the nations that come against Jerusalem. So, we may not know exactly when "that day" will be, but it is clear here that when "that day" comes, the LORD will be against any nation that goes against Jerusalem. That is not the side on which we want to be. So far, America has generally seemed to be on the side of Israel/Jerusalem, but that could easily change with one election. According to this verse, if it does change, it may not bode well for America.

Zechariah 14:2 For I will gather all the nations to battle against Jerusalem;
  The city shall be taken,
  The houses rifled,
  And the women ravished.
  Half of the city shall go into captivity,
  But the remnant of the people shall not be cut off from the city. This verse describes an absolutely terrible time in the history of Jerusalem. According to the previous verses, the one-third of the people who survive the battle will be refined and then will be the ones who say: **"The LORD is my God."** The end of the battle turns to a victory for Jerusalem when the LORD takes up the fight against all those nations which came against Jerusalem. This battle is referred to as the day of the LORD. However, other days in the Bible are also referred to as the day of the LORD. So, this is not the only one.

Zechariah 14:12 And this shall be the plague with which the Lord will strike all the people who fought against Jerusalem:
  Their flesh shall dissolve while they stand on their feet,
  Their eyes shall dissolve in their sockets,
  And their tongues shall dissolve in their mouths. This prediction is not pleasant for any nation contemplating going against Jerusalem. I don't know how or when this event will occur, but no one would want to be part of this group fighting against Jerusalem.

Zechariah 14:20 In that day "HOLINESS TO THE LORD" shall be *engraved* on the bells of the horses. The pots in the Lord's house shall be like the bowls before the altar. There will come a day of the LORD when the people of Jerusalem will complete their destiny of being a holy and priestly nation with "HOLINESS TO THE LORD" even engraved on the horse's bells and pots they use. The same statement was inscribed on a plate of pure gold worn on the front of the high priest's turban in Exodus 28:36, so this is an inscription that has been used for a long time. This all may be something that will take place when the Messiah is ruling over Jerusalem. The dispensationalists believe there will be a period where Christ will rule the earth for one thousand years (The Millennium) and that this may be what Zechariah chapter 14 is addressing. Whatever or whenever it does take place, it should be a great time for believers. In reality, what I believe or don't believe about the Millennium will not affect what is going to happen. Thus, I consider what someone thinks about this period as a nonessential belief. In other words, there are some essential beliefs to the Christian faith, but what you believe about the when and where of the Millennium is not one of them. Nevertheless, it is encouraging to think about when Christ is the ruler of the earth.

39

Malachi

[39]**MALACHI** - This is the final book of the 39 books that make up the Old Testament. It encourages readers not to forget about the love of God. In it, he seems to speak of John the Baptist, who will come to prepare the way for the Messiah, Jesus Christ. The general thinking seems to be that this book was written some 400 plus years B.C. The book talks about the second exodus of the Israelites. The first exodus was from Egypt. The second was from Babylon.

Malachi 1:3 But Esau I have hated,
  And laid waste his mountains and his heritage
  For the jackals of the wilderness." It appears that the word translated "hate" here may be more appropriately translated "not to choose." Esau was not chosen by God for blessing and love. For his part, Esau appeared to be spiritually insensitive as he despised his birthright (Genesis 25:29-34) and married wives from Canaan (25:34-35). Thus, the bottom line interpretation appears to be that God blessed Jacob but did not choose Esau for blessing.

---

[39] NSB quotations are from the Nelsons Study Bible, copyright (c) 1997 by Thomas Nelson, Inc., Nashville, TN; used by permission; scripture taken from the New King James Version, Copyright (c) 1979, 1980, 1982 used by permission. All rights reserved.

Malachi 1:11 For from the rising of the sun, even to its going down,
  My name *shall be* **great among the Gentiles;**
  In every place incense *shall be* **offered to My name,**
  And a pure offering;
  For My name shall be great among the nations,"
  Says the Lord of hosts. This prediction in the Old Testament that His name would be great among the Gentiles seems to have been fulfilled since there are many more gentile Christians than Messianic Jews.

Malachi 2:10 Have we not all one Father?
  Has not one God created us?
  Why do we deal treacherously with one another
  By profaning the covenant of the fathers? We all have one Father who created us. Therefore, we should treat each other well and not lie, cheat or steal from each other.

Malachi 3:1 "Behold, I send My messenger,
  And he will prepare the way before Me.
  And the Lord, whom you seek,
  Will suddenly come to His temple,
  Even the Messenger of the covenant,
  In whom you delight.
  Behold, He is coming,"
  Says the Lord of hosts. According to Matthew 11:10 and Mark 1:2, 3, this is a prediction regarding John the Baptist and Jesus about 400 years later. Christ appears to be the Messenger of the covenant. He brought a new covenant of grace. In the next verse, Malachi talks about the Messiah's second coming when He will come as a judge (Joel 2:11; Amos 5:18; Luke 21:36; Revelation 19:11-21).

Malachi 3:10 Bring all the tithes into the storehouse,
  That there may be food in My house,
  And try Me now in this,"

Says the Lord of hosts,
"If I will not open for you the windows of heaven
And pour out for you *such* blessing
That *there will* not *be room* enough *to receive it.* Here is the only place I know of in the Bible where we are invited to test the Lord. The wording appears to be speaking to the whole congregation of people bringing tithes into the Lord's storehouse. Getting the principle down to the individual level our experience has been that the more we tithed, the more we earned.

Malachi 4:6 And he will turn
   The hearts of the fathers to the children,
   And the hearts of the children to their fathers,
   Lest I come and strike the earth with a curse." In general, when the Lord offers judgment, there is also an offer of mercy.

40

Matthew - HIGHLIGHTS of the BIBLE - THE GOSPELS COMMENTARY - VOLUME II

[40] **MATTHEW** - The Fulfillment of Old Testament Prophecies

Matthew 1:18 Now the birth of Jesus Christ was as follows: After His mother Mary was betrothed to Joseph, before they came together, she was found with child of the Holy Spirit. The fundamental element of a marriage is a contract. There was a betrothal period in the Jewish culture like an engagement before the couple consummated the marriage.

Thus, the order of events was the betrothal (engagement), then the wedding, and then the marriage consummation. Before Joseph and Mary consummated the marriage through sexual relations, "**she was found with child through the Holy Spirit.**" In other words, it was the Holy Spirit that made her pregnant, not a man. During this period, an angel

---

[40] NSB quotations are from the Nelsons Study Bible, copyright (c) 1997 by Thomas Nelson, Inc., Nashville, TN; used by permission; scripture taken from the New King James Version, Copyright (c) 1979, 1980, 1982 used by permission. All rights reserved.

of the Lord spoke to Joseph and told him that Mary was pregnant by the Holy Spirit's action, implying that he did not need to break off the impending marriage due to infidelity. Thus, through the marriage, Jesus (Yeshua, "The Lord Shall Save" or "to deliver" in Hebrew) became the legal son of Joseph though Joseph was not his biological father.

The virgin birth will not make sense to one who does not believe a spiritual dimension (i.e., the Holy Spirit) can interact with and make things happen in the physical world. Since the Bible says that God is Spirit (John 4:24), to deny that there are spirits is to deny that there is a god as the Bible portrays God. The fact that there is a spiritual world is of utmost importance. Without it, in my understanding, belief, and reasoning, the physical world and man would not exist. As a rational skeptic who respects science's legitimate findings and laws, there must be a supernatural/spiritual dimension, or there would be no physical dimension. See other parts of this commentary for more on these beliefs/findings.

Matthew 2:12 Then, being divinely warned in a dream that they should not return to Herod, they departed for their own country another way. There are times when the Lord speaks to people through dreams. This scripture says that they were "**divinely warned**." Had they not listened, we can assume that the Lord would have taken other actions to accomplish His will.

Matthew 3:11 I indeed baptize you with water unto repentance, but He who is coming after me is mightier than I, whose sandals I am not worthy to carry. He will baptize you with the Holy Spirit and fire. This is a statement by John the Baptist. Upon this advent, Christ ushered in widespread baptism of the Holy Spirit in the lives of His people. His apostles demonstrated the Holy Spirit's power through many things accomplished by the Spirit through them. Note that at Christ's actual baptism, we have God the Father speaking, the Holy Spirit of God coming down like a dove, and God the Son involved (Matthew 3:13-17). The baptism by fire may reference the judgment that will come upon the next advent of Christ. This is what I think, but there are other views. In the following verse 12, there is an agricultural analogy stating that Jesus will "gather His wheat into the barn; but He will burn up the chaff with unquenchable fire." This appears to be the baptism by fire spoken of in verse 11. Second Peter 3:10-12 and Revelation 31:8 also appear to refer to this event.

Matthew 4:1 Then Jesus was led up by the Spirit into the wilderness to be tempted by the devil. Interestingly, the Holy Spirit led Jesus into the wilderness to be tempted. Note that it is not the Holy Spirit that was doing the tempting. However, the process was necessary because it was the Holy Spirit that led Jesus to be tempted. This temptation was immediately after the baptism. Thus, often temptations and trials come after great spiritual experiences. In response to these situations, it's good to do what Christ did, that is, quoting the Word of God. But, according to my friend Jan, "This is where most people run into trouble believing what we read in the scripture! How do we know it is the word of God?"

Well, I could say: I know because I know. However, that is not a very satisfying answer. But, in reality, it is part of the answer. The facts appear to be that (a) there is no other book that makes the credible claims about itself that the Bible makes, (b) there is no other book that has three of the major world religions accept at least part of it as God inspired, (c) there does not appear to be any other book that makes verifiable prophecies about the future that have come to pass (like the reformation of the nation of Israel after hundreds of years), and (d) there is no other book that has the number of historic versions documenting the accuracy of translation over the years.

Many theologians provide a lot more evidence than I can, but that may not be what will convince anyone of the Bible's veracity. This knowledge and faith is a gift from God (Hebrews 12:2; Ephesians 2:8). Part of the gift of faith is the knowledge that the Bible is the Word of God. Thus, no one can take credit for their faith or belief that the Bible as the Word of God. We cannot do anything to earn this gift. It is free for acceptance. We have no right to boast (Romans 3:27). Any faith we have results from what God has done for us (Ephesians 2:6, 16).

So, you can see that even though I believe faith in the integrity of the Bible is rational and, when fully understood, will align with completed scientific findings, this faith is a gift from God. This is why I said at the beginning of this section that I know because I know. I don't fully understand why I was open to this belief because, for many years, I was opposed to it but open to considering all the options. During this consideration, I began reading the Bible, and the faith came from hearing the message as the Bible notes can happen (Romans 10:17). Of course, it can help to ask for understanding since God, based on my personal experience, can give it to you (Luke 11:9–12) and give you more (Luke 17:5; Mark 9:24). Jesus prayed for Peter's faith to be strengthened (Luke 22:32). When we receive the gift of faith, it makes sense to use it (Romans 12:1–2, 6–8).

There is great power in the Word of God to help us avoid giving in to temptation. When we are tempted, we need to trust God and remain in His will. We have a choice in each of these situations. In other words, we have free will. If there were no viable choices, what good would our free will be? Thus, it seems that God allows there to be a possible choice for members of His creation. When we think deeply about the concept of love, we may realize the concept dies on the vine, so to speak, without the freedom not to love. My heart goes out to those who reject the gift of faith.

Matthew 4:23 And Jesus went about all Galilee, teaching in their synagogues, preaching the gospel of the kingdom, and healing all

kinds of sickness and all kinds of disease among the people. This is what Jesus did once he started His earthly ministry. He taught, preached, and healed. He taught through many illustrations and parables about spiritual issues. He preached that the kingdom of heaven was at hand, and He was involved with many miracles of healing. To quote my friend Jan: "Jesus was the earthly manifestation of God; an example of the spiritual dimension that can interact with the physical world."

Matthew 5:10 Blessed *are* those who are persecuted for righteousness' sake,

For theirs is the kingdom of heaven. Here's a thought that is difficult to appreciate unless we have a grander scale of consideration than our small immediate world. In other words, this statement seems to apply to people who are believers. It is not a message of salvation but instruction for believers.

Not everyone will repent and accept the gift of salvation that is offered. For these people, any of the Lord's light reflected on them can make them painfully aware of their choice to reject the gift. They can become jealous or angry at those who have accepted the gift. As a result, they may try to persecute those they perceive as shining this light on them to keep this from happening. Or, according to my friend Jan: "maybe they just tire of people that believe they are the chosen ones trying to push their ideas on others."

Not to worry, the Lord has the kingdom of heaven for those who are persecuted for reflecting His light on a dark world. Thus, for every little bit of persecution a believer suffers here on earth, we can be happy about the result of having the kingdom of heaven.

Great are the rewards of the prophets and the persecuted saints in heaven (Matthew 5:12; Luke 6:23, 35; 1 Corinthians 3:14; 9:18). In the beatitudes and elsewhere, Jesus provided insight into the nature of true religion and what the law was set in place to accomplish (see Matthew 5).

Matthew 5:14, "You are the light of the world. A city that is set on a hill cannot be hidden. Note that we would not have any good light in us to reflect if not for the Lord. Any good light coming from us is the light of the Lord. Though the light is in us, we are also like a mirror reflecting the light from another source.

It is like the light that the moon provides. The moon reflects the light of the sun. It has no source light of its own to give. Without the sun's light reflecting off of it, the moon is dark and hard to see. But when the sun's light reflects off of it, we can see it. Any good works that appear to come from us are actually the work of God in and through us.

Matthew 5:22 But I say to you that whoever is angry with his brother without a cause shall be in danger of the judgment... Here and in other places, Jesus teaches us that sin starts with thoughts, and He encourages us to bring our thoughts under control (Matthew 15:19-20; Proverbs 15:26). We need to repent of evil thoughts and behavior. He says that if a man looks on a woman who is not his wife with lust in his heart, he has already committed the sin of adultery with her in his heart (5:27-28). This is where the transgression starts, and if we nip it in the bud, it will not bloom into a full-blown sin that hurts not only the one who first thought about the transgression but also others.

Sin is like the Ebola virus; it is better to stop it before others are exposed to its dangerous effects. The seed of evil can grow exponentially into a huge crop. Jesus uses hyperbole (exaggerated saying) to emphasize that we need to be very diligent in doing what we can to remove the temptation to do evil no matter the cost. When we take the whole counsel of God (the Bible) into consideration, it makes sense that He is not telling us to literally pluck out an eye or cut off a hand. For example, Leviticus 19:28 says, "**You shall not make any cuttings in your flesh for the dead,**

nor tattoo any marks on you: I am the LORD." See the commentary on verse 5:28 for more on this issue.

The Bible uses many aspects of language to communicate and get points across, including hyperbole, exaggeration, anthropomorphism, and poetic language. That's one reason we need to study the entire Bible. When we take the entire Bible into account, this part of scripture uses hyperbole to emphasize how important it is to get our thoughts under control. It is not directing someone to cut off a hand or pluck out an eye.

Matthew 5:28 But I say to you that whoever looks at a woman to lust for her has already committed adultery with her in his heart. 29 If your right eye causes you to sin, pluck it out and cast *it* from you; for it is more profitable for you that one of your members perish, than for your whole body to be cast into hell. Generally, most people would probably agree that human behavior follows thought. (Many psychologists would probably also agree with this idea.) Here we see that students of the Bible will know that even the thought of sinning is a sin. It seems that our thought life is where the battle against sin begins and where it can end with help from the power of the Holy Spirit.

Even our legal system recognizes the difference between an intentional act and an accidental or impulsive act. Increasing punishment levels are generally provided depending on how much premeditation was involved, whether it be homicide or some other crime/sin like stealing. The greater the premeditation, the greater the opportunity to repent, and this is the level where repenting needs to take place: in the mind.

Regarding Christ's words about plucking out an eye, in light of God's whole counsel, I believe, as in other scripture, Christ is using an exaggerated saying (hyperbole) in this passage to make a point. Other scripture speaks against self-harm of this sort and must be taken into consideration. Leviticus 19:28 says, **"You shall not make any cuttings**

in your flesh for the dead, nor tattoo any marks on you: I am the LORD."

In the New Testament, cutting oneself in one instance was associated with possession by an "unclean spirit" (demons) (Mark 5:2-5). From my perspective, cutting behavior can also result from mental illness (disruption of neural circuits or a biochemical imbalance in the brain). When this is the case, it may not have to do with demons. The Bible does not say that "all" cutting of oneself is due to possession by demons. The scripture here refers to this one man who had an unclean spirit.

First Corinthians 6:19 tells us we belong to Christ, who purchased us at a high price. The price he paid for us was death on the cross as the propitiation for our sins. It is like we went to court before the judge for a crime we committed, and someone else paid the fine so the judge set us free. He was sinless but stepped in and took the righteous legitimate punishment on our behalf to redeem us. Thus, we should not damage our bodies, which are now to be viewed as the property of Christ.

Matthew 5:34 But I say to you, do not swear at all: neither by heaven, for it is God's throne; 35 nor by the earth, for it is His footstool; nor by Jerusalem, for it is the city of the great King. In other words, the everyday words of a believer should be trusted. It should not be necessary to swear at all. This doesn't seem to prohibit making an oath on a solemn occasion. However, the point is not that we should not lie under oath; we should not lie at all (Colossians 3:8-9). Nevertheless, we probably all lie (Psalm 116:11), and therefore, it is good that those who trust in the Lord and confess their sins are forgiven.

Matthew 5:44 But I say to you, love your enemies,... Now here's a concept that separates Christians from others. How many can pray for their enemies and do good to them? This process is not from our natural tendencies. In so doing, we are imitating God, who sends His sun to rise on the evil and the good and sends rain on the just and unjust. Not only that, He died for our sins while we were still sinners and standing by the great sin of unbelief.

Matthew 6.6 But you, when you pray, go into your room, and when you have shut your door, pray to your Father who *is* in the secret *place;* and your Father who sees in secret will reward you openly. In other words, it is not for us to be making a big show of our prayers, especially out in the open, to appear righteous. Our motives for prayer should not have anything to do with others seeing us. It should have to do with our private relationship with God and to help us get in line with His will for our lives and the lives of others. From other scripture and examples, we know that public prayer can be acceptable (1 Timothy 2:8; Psalm 141:2; Daniel 6:10; 9:3). It appears that only public prayer to appear righteous to other people is the problem.

Matthew 6.14 "For if you forgive men their trespasses, your heavenly Father will also forgive you. 15 But if you do not forgive men their trespasses, neither will your Father forgive your trespasses. I think forgiveness is one of the most essential concepts for human beings! Without God's forgiveness and mercy, we are doomed. Here we are encouraged to forgive others. This sounds good, but it is difficult. It may be easier for someone who has accepted the gift of forgiveness that comes through what Christ did for us on the cross.

It is still difficult to forgive others who have done mean things to us. But, the Lord makes it undeniably clear that vengeance is His and His alone. He will repay (Rom. 12:19 et al.). Maybe forgiveness is easier than I make it sound if you believe it is the right thing to do.

Matthew 6.17 But you, when you fast, anoint your head and wash your face,... As with prayer, fasting is not something to be done so that others can see what you are doing. The scripture says that your Father, who is in the secret place, will see in secret but will reward openly.

John 4:24 says that "**God is Spirit, and those who worship Him must worship in spirit and truth.**" We'll cover more on that issue later, but as relates to Matthew 6:17, it appears that some things do need to be just between the Lord and us. If other people get involved, we can be distracted by our pride in the wrong (earthly or non-spiritual) focus of our prayers or our fasting.

Matthew 6:33 But seek first the kingdom of God and His righteousness, and all these things shall be added to you. According to the preceding verses, these things are material things like food, water, and clothes. For some people, the material world is all they seek. God says that if we seek His kingdom first, He will still give us the material things we need. Thus, we don't lose anything by putting His kingdom first in our lives. Seeking His kingdom is to desire God's righteous rule on the earth.

Matthew 7:1 "Judge not, that you be not judged." Generally, we are not appointed to be a judge, and therefore should not act like a judge pronouncing punishment. Especially to those who are enemies of the gospel, we should leave them alone (14:15) and refrain from sharing wisdom from the Bible with them or telling them where we think they are headed. That is God's job through His Spirit!

This does not mean that we should not share with unbelievers. They need to hear the gospel. This scripture appears to be about judgment toward those who seem to have decided to oppose the gospel. Thus, we are to use discernment to determine who we are speaking to and withhold information about judgment and wisdom from those opposed to or indifferent to it and have made it clear that they do not want to receive it.

This scripture does *not* appear to be a direction to never judge other issues. For example, we are directed and provided examples of correcting the behavior of believers (1 Timothy 5:1-2). How do we do this? We do not rebuke. We exhort an older man as a father, an older woman as a mother, and a younger woman as a sister in all purity. Your objective should be to help the person (Matthew 18:15).

Matthew 7:12 Therefore, whatever you want men to do to you, do also to them, for this is the Law and the Prophets. This is incredible wisdom, so simple yet so profound! If everyone on earth lived this way, it would be great. This is a different way of stating what is in Leviticus 19:18: **"You shall love your neighbor as yourself."** This "Golden Rule" can help anyone decide how to treat someone else. As my friend Jan puts it: "You just love everyone and do the next best thing."

Matthew 7:14 Because narrow *is* the gate and difficult *is* the way which leads to life, and there are few who find it. The Christian life of trusting in God is not easy and will seem lonely at times, but it leads to eternal life. Many easy ways lead to destruction, but one narrow way leads to life. Many cannot accept this truth and will try to convince others that it is not true and all we may be able to do is pray for them. They may try to find enlightenment elsewhere, but that does not change the facts presented in the Bible. We can wish with all our hearts that it is a wide gate, but; the Bible says it is not. Some other writings contradict this teaching, but none I know of is authoritative or even claims to be authoritative.

Matthew 7:28 And so it was, when Jesus had ended these sayings, that the people were astonished at His teaching, 29 for He taught them as one having authority, and not as the scribes. Christ does not just have some authority; He has *all* authority. He is God. Two people may look the same on the outside, and both appear to be righteous, but their foundations may be very different, and the life founded on the right relationship with Christ (the Rock) will be the one that endures the floods and the winds. Those who have a right relationship with Christ hear His sayings and do them, not those who just talk about it. Big talk and no action is just talk. Also, Jesus made it clear that being a physical descendant of Abraham does not guarantee entrance into His kingdom (see Ephesians 2:11, 12).

Matthew 8:31 So the demons begged Him, saying, "If You cast us out, permit us to go away into the herd of swine." Jesus then told them to go, and they went into the swine, demonstrating that animals can possess demons. These demons recognized the deity of Christ and asked Him if He came to torment them before the time. Many of them were in one man. It was almost like they had to have a host and, like a fish out of water, couldn't just survive in the air. It is also interesting to note that there is an appointed time that demons expect to be tormented.

Matthew 9:30 And their eyes were opened. And Jesus sternly warned them, saying, "See *that* no one knows *it*. " Here it appears that Christ did not want too many people coming to Him just for physical healing alone, perhaps because spiritual healing was His primary purpose.

Matthew 10:1 And when He had called His twelve disciples to *Him*, He gave them power *over* unclean spirits, to cast them out, and to heal all kinds of sickness and all kinds of disease. After Christ gave the twelve disciples authority over unclean spirits, they were called apostles. Some preachers today think and act like they have this kind of authority. It appears that when Christ was walking the earth, it was only the twelve apostles who were given this authority. It makes me wonder if those who currently claim this authority are legitimate. It may not be appropriate to judge others' motives, but we can and should use discernment based on what the Bible teaches.

So what does the Bible teach about apostles? They had all seen the LORD themselves (Acts 1:22; 22:14; 1 Corinthians 9:1). They were selected by the Lord or the Holy Spirit (Matthew 10:5; Mark 3:13-14; Luke 6:13; Acts 1:26; 9:15; 22:14-15,21; 26:16). They were able to implement miracles (Mark 3:15; 16:17-20; Luke 9:1-2; John 14:12,26; 15:24-27; 16:13; Acts 2:43; 4:29-31,33; 5:12,15-16; 6:6; 8:14-18; 19:6; 2 etcetera). Using these criteria (there are others), it is easy to discern who is and is not a real apostle from the Biblical perspective. This is the kind of judgment we need to use, or we can wind up deceived. Many do not realize that the famous verse cited as forbidding judgment (Matthew 7:2) forbids hypocrisy in judging right from wrong instead of forbidding any judgment. Please see Matthew 13:30 for more on the issue of appropriate and inappropriate judgment.

Matthew 10:16 "Behold, I send you out as sheep in the midst of wolves. Therefore be wise as serpents and harmless as doves. This is excellent advice. Though He spoke specifically to His twelve Apostles in this passage, it seems applicable to those who preach the gospel even today. He had advised them to let their peace come upon the worthy households and depart from the households or cities that would not listen to them. He also told them that the cities that did not listen to them would have a hard time on the day of judgment. Perhaps even though they were sent to save people, they would be perceived as a snake trying to hurt people and, therefore, would need the cunning of a snake but not the venom (i.e., harmless as doves) to avoid being diverted from their mission.

Modern-day Christians may need to remember and practice this verse because many see Christians as hypocritical, judgmental pains with unrealistic expectations. As presented by Jesus in parables in the book of Matthew, the reality is that there are many "tares" (counterfeit Christians) growing alongside authentic believers. Based on the interpretation of parables, there may be as many or more counterfeits who go to church and refer to themselves as Christians as there are authentic believers. It may be hard to tell the difference. Even genuine believers are nowhere near perfect in their behavior, which contributes to our difficulty in judging motives. Generally, I don't think it is within our ability to judge motives correctly, but we sometimes need to judge behaviors. At the end of this age, God will separate the wheat (authentic believers) from the tares, and He is immensely qualified to do so because he knows the heart of people, not just the behavior. Thus, His judgment will be fair. For now, we all grow together.

Matthew 10:28 And do not fear those who kill the body but cannot kill the soul. But rather fear Him who is able to destroy both soul and body in hell. We think of God as loving, merciful, and forgiving, and He is all of these, but here we see the justice side of His personality. This verse can be taken as a caution to keep an eternal perspective. What happens here in our life on earth, which is a mere vapor compared to eternity (Psalm 39:5; James 4:14), is not what we should be most concerned about regarding who we fear.

We should have a healthy respect for the Lord of the universe, who controls where our souls will go for eternity. This verse demonstrates that our souls continue to exist even after our earthly bodies die. The word "destroy" in this verse is translated from a word that means ruination instead of annihilation. Some souls will still exist but will be separated from God ("**in hell**").

Though we may want to believe that everyone will wind up in heaven, that is not what the Bible says will happen. According to this scripture, God will respect your choice to reject being with Him through eternity. God is loving, merciful, and forgiving, but it does not appear that He will force people to love Him. Since love has to be and can only be through free will, it would not be love if it were forced anyway.

Matthew 10:32 "Therefore whoever confesses Me before men, him I

will also confess before My Father who is in heaven. 33 But whoever denies Me before men, him I will also deny before My Father who is in heaven. Here's a good reason to be open about our beliefs. Romans 8:17 says that if we suffer with Him, we will also be glorified with Him and other parts of scripture say that we will reign with Him (Revelation 20:4). He is who He says He is. If we believe He is, we need to confess this fact. In verse 10:39, Christ says that **"he who loses his life for My sake shall find it."** What life do we find? The life He intended for us to have when He made us. In 10:38, He says: **"And he who does not take his cross and follow after Me is not worthy of Me."** Taking up the cross seems to mean being willing to die for Him. This is a big commitment and one which many of the apostles fulfilled. The question is: Would we be ready to fulfill this level of commitment?

For most of us, we may be able to take some verbal abuse but may not handle the ultimate commitment of physically dying for our beliefs. The person making guns is involved in the process and has a level of commitment, but the soldier who goes to war with the gun is committed.

Matthew 11:30 "For My yoke *is* easy and My burden is light." With this statement, Christ was contrasting His way with the way specified by the scribes, rabbis, and Pharisees. They had come up with 39 categories of actions to be forbidden on the Sabbath, and they thought Jesus' disciples were "harvesting" and therefore breaking the Sabbath. They were also trying to implicate Jesus in breaking the Mosaic covenant. He might have been against their rules, but obviously, He was not breaking His law (God's law).

For those who believed in Christ, He provided rest (and still does to this day) from all of the rules that religious leaders had added to God's law regarding the Sabbath. This concept appears to also apply to any other day of the week. It can be viewed as a critical distinction that Christianity has from all other religions. I hesitate to use the word "all" because it is absolute and absolutes are usually wrong but this one may be correct. All other religions seem to add individual effort for their members to obtain salvation (or whatever the religion pursues).

In other words, followers of other religions (and even many who call themselves Christian) add human effort to what God does. From my understanding of counsel in the Bible, a Christian is saved by what God did. Good works will come from being saved (a believer and follower), but according to the Bible, do not produce salvation, nor does failure to follow superfluous human-made rules negate salvation.

Thus, the Christian's yoke is easy, and the burden is light because Christ (the eternal God) paid the price, past, present, and future, for all of our transgressions. From God's perspective, our transgressions are as far as the East is from the West (Psalm 103:12). It is joyous not to be guilt-ridden. Nevertheless, God does not appear to force anyone to accept this gift.

Note: It is interesting that religions other than Christianity also accept parts of the Christian Bible (i.e., Islam and Judaism). However, they have different interpretations and conclusions.

Matthew 12:31 "Therefore I say to you, every sin and blasphemy will be forgiven men, but the blasphemy *against* the Spirit will not be forgiven men. 32 Anyone who speaks a word against the Son of Man, it will be forgiven him; but whoever speaks against the Holy Spirit, it will not be forgiven him, either in this age or in the *age* to come. Here's what is essential. For someone who stubbornly refuses to yield to the Holy Spirit's invitation to accept the forgiveness of sins by God's grace through faith, this sin will not be forgiven. Many proofs have been given, and no more is needed. There have been (a) the prophecies in the Old Testament, (b) the ministry of John and, (c) Christ's testimony, His death, and resurrection, which was observed and reported by many. The Bible records and documents these firsthand reports by the people there. Note that there are many fragments, documents, and transcripts of the Old and New Testament attesting to the resurrection of Christ. There is also a secular text from the time that mentions Jesus Christ (Flavius Josephus A.D. 93 or 94). Some people who observed the resurrection died for their belief in Christ. It is unlikely that someone would go to the grave because of their faith if they knew the one they believed in was a charlatan. People will die for their beliefs, but probably not for something they know is a false belief.

There is also the Holy Spirit's ongoing testimony with us, and for those who believe, the Spirit is in us and then upon us. In this scripture, speaking against the Holy Spirit is the one sin that in Jesus' words: **"will not be forgiven him."** He also makes it very clear how important our words are concerning the Holy Spirit when he says in verse 37: **"By your words you will be justified, and by your words, you will be condemned."** Of course, it is not just saying certain words that would condemn or save a person. It is saying the words and believing the meaning or interpretation of those words.

A counterfeit can easily say some words and not mean them. Words are critical in God's economy and appear to be interconnected with the Holy Spirit. Christ himself is even called The Word of God. We seem to be created with a void that needs to be filled with the Holy Spirit. If we don't allow the Holy Spirit in, the void may be filled with wicked spirits (vs. 12:43-45). Because of the importance of words, we get a good idea of what a person believes by the words they use.

A person who uses many vile and profane words probably has a different spirit than the person who uses kind and non-profane words. Those who say that words are just words and not important might indicate that they do not believe in what the Bible says about words. What a person says can be a life-and-death issue. The old saying that "loose lips sink ships" is true. The bottom line is that words matter and *the* Word matters. How do we tell if a person's words are what they believe? We check their actions.

Matthew 13:30 ...Let both grow together until the harvest, and at the time of harvest I will say to the reapers, "First gather together the tares and bind them in bundles to burn them, but gather the wheat into my barn." Some people who appear to be believers are intermingled with the genuine believers, and it will be that way until the "Harvest" (Christ's return). Tares (now thought to be darnel or Lolium Temulentum; this is called false wheat by some) look similar to wheat until their fruit appears but are not suitable to eat because its fruit, their black seeds, contain a narcotic drug that causes slumber. They are like a counterfeit. They will not be separated until the Harvest when the counterfeits can be distinguished from the genuine. Some of the genuine might be uprooted with the tares if the separation occurred too early.

Scripture says that the tares are "**sons of the wicked one**" (vs. 37). When the Harvest comes, angels will come forth, **separate the wicked from among the just and cast them into the furnace of fire** (vs. 49). It is important to note that this job was not for the disciples. It is left to the angels at the Harvest. Thus, it does not appear that this is our job to do either, nor would we have the correct discernment to do this job properly. We would probably damage some of the genuine if we tried to do so. Thus, the counterfeits are free to enjoy the advantages of growing with the genuine until the Harvest, and we are directed to allow them to do so.

Of course, another scripture encourages us to deal with sin in our congregations. This is a different issue. The sin may be engaged in by a genuine believer or a counterfeit, so even in this situation, we are not judging the person's soul or motives, but only their actions (Matthew 7:1-5). There are two types of judgment, one focused on motives and the other based on actions. When we are judging actions, we are to judge our actions before even trying to look at the actions of others. Scripture implies that it is hypocritical to judge the speck of sin in someone else before judging the log of sin in our actions. Only God has the right and power to judge someone's heart appropriately (1 Samuel 16:7). Also, we have no business judging outsiders other than to remove them from a congregation if they claim to be a believer and their sinful actions are ongoing, and they are unrepentant (1 Corinthians 5:12-13). In other words, our only allowed judgment would be toward the actions, not the motives, of a professing believer who refuses to repent of an ongoing sin (Proverbs 9:8; 2 Timothy 2:22; Romans 16:17).

Matthew 14:23 And when He had sent the multitudes away, He went up on the mountain by Himself to pray. Now when evening came, He was alone there. This is an excellent example for us. Sometimes we need to get away from other people and go up on a mountain to pray. There are fewer distractions up there, and with a good view, it is hard not to recognize the glory of God in His creation.

Matthew 15:18 But those things which proceed out of the mouth come from the heart, and they defile a man. It is what comes out of us that defiles us. We need to put our thoughts into captivity. In other words, we need the Word of God to be in our thoughts (2 Corinthians 10:5). And then what comes out of us will not defile us. David said that he put the Word in his heart to not sin against the Lord. We also need to be careful about what we let into our minds. David said that he would set nothing wicked before his eyes because he knew that if the wicked thoughts got into his head, they might influence what would come out through his words and actions (Psalm 101:3; 119:11). He knew firsthand how what you look at can corrupt your actions.

Matthew 16:27 For the Son of Man will come in the glory of His Father with His angels, and then He will reward each according to

his works. To be clear, salvation is always a gift of God's grace through faith. Nevertheless, per this scripture, our works do influence rewards for believers when Christ returns.

Matthew 18:5 Whoever receives one little child like this in My name receives Me. This could refer to children or those young in the faith. The basic idea is that we should help children and those young in the faith grow and not sin or stumble. If we are the one who causes them to stumble, that is not good for them or us. Verse 10 also advises us not to despise them and that they have angels in heaven watching over them. That's a nice thought and good to know since there are many challenges and tests they will face while here on earth where the wheat (real believers) grows side by side with the tares (counterfeits). Note: it is not our job to separate or judge the tares from the wheat. That will be accomplished in the presence of angels when the Lord returns (Revelation 14:10).

Matthew 18:22 Jesus said to him, "I do not say to you, up to seven times, but up to seventy times seven..." This statement answered Peter's question about if we should forgive someone who sinned against us up to seven times. The answer implies that we should always be willing to forgive. This is an excellent use of exaggeration to make a point! It is not likely that someone would need our forgiveness 490 times. However, if they did, we are directed by the Lord to continue forgiving them that many times. He is not saying that we should keep count and stop at 490. He points out that we should always be willing to forgive by using this high number. We are to forgive others for their trespasses. After all, haven't we been forgiven all of our trespasses by God? The Lord explains this further with a parable which poses this question (18:33): **"Should you not also have had compassion on your fellow servant, just as I had pity on you?"**

Matthew 19:4 And He answered and said to them, "Have you not

read that He who made *them* at the beginning *'made them male and female,'* 5 and said, *'For this reason a man shall leave his father and mother and be joined to his wife, and the two shall become one flesh'*? This is God's plan for marriage: one man and one woman joined together. It appears that in God's view, married couples are one. We should have the same view. Married couples should act as one, and their married life will be much better. What married people need to realize is that whatever they do that harms their spouse is also self-destructive. It's bad enough if one person in the marriage is trying to hurt the other, but if both spouses are trying to hurt each other, a quadruple dose of harm is inflicted. As we know, this quadruple dose of the harm often breaks the oneness, and the couple winds up with a marriage broken into pieces that can't be put back together again (except for a miracle from God).

Matthew 19:17 So He said to him, "Why do you call Me good? No one *is* good but One, *that is,* God. But if you want to enter into life, keep the commandments." My understanding is that this passage could be translated as "Why are you asking me concerning what is good?" Then He answers the question showing subtly that He is God.

Matthew 20:13 But he answered one of them and said, 'Friend, I am doing you no wrong. Did you not agree with me for a denarius? This passage seems to indicate that it is not wrong for an employer to be more generous with one worker than another, especially when he was fulfilling the agreement he made with both workers. Even though the employer was criticized, he gave each worker the agreed-upon wages.

Matthew 20:19 ...and deliver Him to the Gentiles to mock and to scourge and to crucify. And the third day He will rise again." As predicted by Christ himself, here's the best thing to happen in all of human history about His own resurrection. This fact is so essential that if Christ did not rise from the dead, my comments here are useless, and so is my faith. But, He did rise from the dead. Therefore, we do have hope (1 Corinthians 15:17-20). You can search and search, but you will not find anyone who has done what Christ has done for you.

Matthew 20:27 And whoever desires to be first among you, let him be your slave— 28 just as the Son of Man did not come to be served, but to serve, and to give His life a ransom for many." Thus, we are to follow Christ's example by serving others even to the point of functioning as if we are their slave. This passage shows that the measure of greatness is not possessions, money, or power but rather service.

Matthew 21:21 So Jesus answered and said to them, "Assuredly, I say to you, if you have faith and do not doubt, you will not only do what was done to the fig tree, but also if you say to this mountain, 'Be removed and be cast into the sea,' it will be done. 22 And whatever things you ask in prayer, believing, you will receive." Faith is the basis for prayer, where the answer is yes. When we pray, if our prayer is in the will of the Lord, it will be answered in the affirmative. However, we often pray in our own will, and sometimes the answer to these prayers is "no" (James 4:3). We may be asking with the wrong motives. The area of prayer is one in which it is especially important to know the whole counsel of God and the examples given to us. If we look at only one scripture, we can easily obtain an incorrect understanding. I like what Bill Hybels wrote about this subject: 'If the request is wrong God says "No." If the timing is wrong God says "Slow." If you are wrong, God says "Grow."But if the request is right and the timing is right, and you are right, God says, "Go."

Matthew 21:44 And whoever falls on this stone will be broken; but on whomever it falls, it will grind him to powder." Christ, whom some had rejected, is the chief cornerstone. We need to humble ourselves and fall on Christ for His forgiveness. We can be broken with repentance by falling on Christ or be ground to powder if Christ's judgment falls on us because we fail to repent. This is not what we may want to hear, but here it is in the scripture.

Matthew 22:10 So those servants went out into the highways and gathered together all whom they found, both bad and good. And the wedding *hall* was filled with guests. This is a summary of the Parable of the Wedding Feast. God invited special guests (the Israelites), but most of them declined and were destroyed. He then invited all of us (both Jews and Gentiles), and many accepted the invitation. It appears that the invited guests have free will to accept or decline the invitation for salvation. Still, there are consequences (the destruction of Jerusalem in A.D. 70 is an example) or rewards depending on whether the invitation is accepted or not. At the end of this scripture are the famous words (vs. 14), "**For many are called, but few are chosen.**" This had to do with a guest who was not prepared with the correct garments (i.e., the righteousness from Christ, which comes by grace through faith). Belief in Christ's sacrifice for our sins is necessary (John 3:16 ...**Whoever believes in Him should not perish but have everlasting life.**) We need to believe in Him to be granted His righteousness.

Matthew 22:30 For in the resurrection they neither marry nor are given in marriage, but are like angels of God in heaven. It is interesting that in heaven, there is no marriage. It appears that the spiritual realm is different from the physical realm regarding marriage. This is just one difference. We can look forward to a better understanding of the other differences.

Matthew 22:37 Jesus said to him, " *You shall love the LORD your God with all your heart, with all your soul, and with all your mind.'* 38 This is *the* first and great commandment. 39 And *the* second *is* like it: *You shall love your neighbor as yourself."* 40 On these two commandments hang all the Law and the Prophets." These are critical words. How great it would be if we could follow these commandments completely. Jesus quotes from the Jewish confession of faith. The two main aspects of these great commandments are the love for God and love for other human beings. We are to love others with the same love that we have for ourselves. The ten commandments are similarly divided between those having to do with our responsibilities to God (the first four) and our responsibilities to other human beings (the next six; see Exodus 20).

Matthew 23:8 But you, do not be called 'Rabbi'; for One is your Teacher, the Christ, and you are all brethren. Do not call anyone on earth your father; for One is your Father, He who is in heaven. Here's an excellent example of the need to consider all scripture when interpreting any one section's meaning. If we take this section by itself, we might think it had a universal application. In fact, in light of other scripture and the context of this particular scripture, we will understand that the application of these statements is much more narrow. There are many examples in scripture, even in this book, where the word father is used to refer to an earthly father (15:4-6; 19:5; 29:2). Thus, we know that this prohibition on calling people 'Father' or 'Rabbi' probably only applies to those hypocrites who sought these titles for their purposes of pride, prestige, or power. There are hierarchies of authority sanctioned in scripture, but the leadership is to be performed with humility and an attitude of servant leadership. In other words, I believe this scripture is telling us that if we are teaching or leading a group of leaders, do not let people put you on a pedestal and call you 'Rabbi' or father.

Matthew 23:11 But he who is greatest among you shall be your servant. This is the biblical type of leadership that all leaders should practice. It is the leader who recognizes that God has allowed them to be in their position, and therefore, they should handle their responsibilities with humbleness and a servant's attitude rather than trying to lord it over others. This leadership can be referred to as servant leadership.

Matthew 23:23 "Woe to you, scribes and Pharisees, hypocrites! For you pay tithe of mint and anise and cummin, and have neglected the

weightier *matters* of the law: justice and mercy and faith. These you ought to have done, without leaving the others undone. It appears that the scribes and Pharisees were very knowledgeable about specific aspects of the law but were neglecting justice, mercy, and faith. These concepts appear to summarize important parts of the law. Christ calls the scribes and Pharisees hypocrites, which designates that they pretend they believe one way, but their actions say something else. This is a truth of scripture that can easily be observed and proven. Some people protest about others' sins and crimes when they are guilty of secretly being involved in those same sins or crimes for which they are criticizing others. This process is something like a firefighter who personally sets fires.

You would think that the leaders like the scribes and Pharisees would practice all aspects of the law, including justice, mercy, and faith, but that was not always the case. Sometimes leaders preach one concept but do the opposite. In modern times, some of the most notorious of this type of hypocrisy occurs when a church pastor has an affair, steals money from the church, or treats church employees like personal servants. Instead, a pastor should practice servant leadership, loyalty, and trustworthiness as Christ taught and modeled. If a pastor or church leader is involved in ongoing sin or treats members unkindly or with anger instead of love, the members need to question their qualifications to be in a high position in the church.

Matthew 24:14 And this gospel of the kingdom will be preached in all the world as a witness to all the nations, and then the end will come. In other words, the Good News of Christ's life, ministry, death, and resurrection will be preached all over the world before the end of time, as we know it, will come. The good news found in John 3:16 is part of the gospel that "**whoever believes in Him should not perish but have everlasting life.**" Part of this good news is that we are saved through faith and not by our works. A believer's works will have a bearing on their rewards, but the grace of God saves them through faith (Ephesians 2:8).

Matthew 24:15 "Therefore when you see the 'abomination of desolation,' spoken of by Daniel the prophet, standing in the holy place" (whoever reads, let him understand), 16 "then let those who are in Judea flee to the mountains. The abomination of desolation can be translated: "the abomination that makes desolate." This language seems to be speaking of something in the future similar to when Antiochus IV desecrated the Jewish temple and set up an idol to Zeus a couple of hundred years earlier. The Nelson Study Bible (1997) says, "Paul speaks of the Antichrist at the end times setting himself up as god (see 2 Thessalonians 2:3, 4; Revelation 13:14, 15; Daniel 9:27)." Revelation prophecy interpreters indicate that the Antichrist may set up a covenant with Israel that he will break by doing something similar to what Antiochus IV did. Thus, we need to **"Be always on the watch, and pray that you may be able to escape all that is about to happen, and that you may be able to stand before the Son of Man"** (Luke 21:36).

Matthew 24:22 And unless those days were shortened, no flesh would be saved; but for the elect's sake those days will be shortened. Note that at least some of the elect will go through the tribulation period. It doesn't matter much whether a person thinks the church will be removed from the earth before, during, or after the tribulation. What will be will be. What matters is whether a person is one of the elect because the result for the elect is eternal life with the Lord.

While here on earth, there will be problems. Some of these problems and trials will test and refine us, while others will just be problems. With an eternal perspective, all of what happens here does not seem quite as important or as difficult. Thus, it is better to keep an eternal perspective on things that happen. The sun shines on the wheat, and the chaff and rain falls on the wheat and the chaff. The end result is all good for the elect, whether they go through the tribulation or are removed. If the church is removed before the tribulation some new converts are made during the tribulation because scripture says that the days will be shortened for the elect's sake.

Matthew 24:24 For false christs and false prophets will rise and show great signs and wonders to deceive, if possible, even the elect. From this scripture, it appears that there will be false prophets who will also be able to perform what appear to be miracles, especially during the tribulation. What they do and say must still meet the test of scripture (Deuteronomy 13:1-5; 1 John 4:1-3). If they are from God, they will "confess that Jesus Christ has come in the flesh…" When Christ returns, it will be as dramatic as when the lightning flashes from the East to the West (Matthew 24:27-31). He will come on the clouds of heaven with power and great glory.

Matthew 24:34 Assuredly, I say to you, this generation will by no means pass away till all these things take place. Once the events that usher in the coming of the Son of Man start, that generation will not pass away until the process is completed. Some will be taken, and some will be left. Of two men in a field or two women grinding at a mill, one may be taken and the other left. This sounds like a rapture scenario. The point is spelled out in verse 24:42, which says: **"Watch therefore, for you do not know what hour your Lord is coming."** We also might want to watch out for people who, through their predictions, indicate they think they know when the Lord is coming. I consider this prediction contrary to scripture, which says that we do not know when the Lord is coming. Nevertheless, we are to be ready anytime for He **"is coming at an hour you do not expect"** (Matthew 24:44).

Matthew 25:29 'For to everyone who has, more will be given, and he will have abundance; but from him who does not have, even what he has will be taken away. This is a summary of the Parable of the Talents. Thus, we need to use the abilities, spiritual gifts, and material possessions God has given us in His service, or they may be taken away from us (Hebrews 5:11, 12). We can rely on the strength and ability that God supplies in using these gifts (1 Peter 4:11).

Matthew 25:46 And these will go away into everlasting punishment, but the righteous into eternal life." Those who are righteous are the ones who have the righteousness of Christ. This righteousness is imputed to us by the grace of God through faith (John 3:16). People say that there is no free lunch, but even though this concept may generally be pretty accurate, salvation is free, by the grace of God. We should rejoice that there is free salvation because it would be impossible for us to be good enough on our own to be in the presence of the holy, holy, holy God. We need His provision of forgiveness of our sins. The cursed will go with the Devil and his angels into the everlasting fire (25:41). That's the bottom line, or as they say, "where the rubber meets the road."

Matthew 26:25 Then Judas, who was betraying Him, answered and said, "Rabbi, is it I?"
He said to him, "You have said it." Here we have even from Christ's inner circle of disciples a person who was willing to betray Him for money. Judas was a trusted member of the group who appeared to have integrity enough to be the treasurer.

Matthew 26:30 And when they had sung a hymn, they went out to the Mount of Olives. Here's a clear indication that Christ and the disciples sang hymns in New Testament times. Some take that musical instruments are not explicitly mentioned in the NewTestament scripture on worship that something changed between the New Testament and the Old Testament. One church bans musical instruments from use in worship. Nowhere in either Testament does the Bible say to do this.

The Psalms, and especially Psalm 150, encourage the use of various instruments in worship, and there is no teaching to the contrary that I have found. Thus, it seems to me that musical instruments should be used in worship because there is no legitimate authority to ban them. The idea to ban instruments appears to have originated from a man rather than from God. If musical instruments (a) were used extensively in the Old Testament times (see the Psalms), (b) are used in heaven (Revelation 5:8 and 15:2; 1 Corinthians 15:52), and (c) there is no scripture to indicate that instruments should not be used on earth in New Testament times, I don't see any valid justification not to use instruments in worship now.

Matthew 26:39 He went a little farther and fell on His face, and prayed, saying, "O My Father, if it is possible, let this cup pass from Me; nevertheless, not as I will, but as You *will*." Here it appears that even Christ had difficulty following what His Father wanted Him to do. Nevertheless, He obeyed and followed. We know that the right thing to do can often be difficult. That does not mean we should not do it. If we know that it is the will of God, we should continue regardless of the difficulty, opposition, or adverse consequences for us personally.

Christ prayed more than once for "the cup" to be taken from Him, but he accepted God's will anyway, regardless of the cost. In so doing, He paid the price for our sins. There is no greater love than this. During this visit to earth in physical form, Christ came as the humble spiritual Savior and not the conquering political ruler. Later (per Matthew 24:30; 26:64), He will come with great power and glory. He said: **"hereafter you will see the Son of Man sitting at the right hand of the Power and coming on the clouds of heaven."** Everyone will see Him, and all mockery will cease as He rules the nations with a rod of iron (Psalm 2:9).

Matthew 26:74 Then he began to curse and swear, *saying*, "I do not know the Man!"
Immediately a rooster crowed. Here Peter lied about knowing Christ when Christ was being arrested, mocked, and abused. It appears that

Peter did not have the Holy Spirit's power at this time to keep him from letting his flesh control his actions. Later, he received great power to preach the gospel. The difference in how Peter responded without and with the Spirit is an excellent example that we need the power of the Holy Spirit to keep us on the right track and doing the next right thing. Peter appeared remorseful and wept about this when he realized his weakness. In the very next chapter, we have information about another disciple who was remorseful. It was Judas who confessed that he had sinned by betraying innocent blood.

Matthew 27:25 And all the people answered and said, "His blood *be* on us and on our children." Here the people of unbelief and pride told Pilate that they would take responsibility for the death sentence on Jesus. Thus, per 23:31 and 32, the people were witnesses against themselves, and they would inherit the guilt of their forefathers. One aspect of this situation that we can glean is to note that there are times when the people who are most adamant about punishing someone else are the same who protest the behavior of others the most. They may be looking for a scapegoat without even realizing it because they have repressed acknowledging their behavior to the point that the subconscious guilt causes them to want someone other than themselves to be punished for that behavior. And, of course, that is what happened. Christ took the punishment for their behavior/sin even though He was completely innocent. That's amazing grace.

Matthew 27:52 ...and the graves were opened; and many bodies of the saints who had fallen asleep were raised; 53 and coming out of the graves after His resurrection, they went into the holy city and appeared to many. Here's a phenomenal event that appeared to signal that Christ's work of paying the price for our sins had an incredible immediate effect on the world and humanity. Not only was the veil of the temple torn from top to bottom; the earth quaked, the rocks split, and saints who had died came out of their graves. Then they went to

Jerusalem and appeared to many. This convinced the centurions who had been guarding Jesus to say, **"Truly, this was the Son of God (27:54).** This was their conclusion. You will come to a personal conclusion on this issue. God demonstrated that access was opened to Him, and truly, this was the Son of God!

One other point about this raising of the bodies of saints is that per Colossians 1:18 and Revelation 1:5, Christ was the firstborn from the dead. Thus, these people raised from their graves probably were raised as Lazarus was, to ordinary physical life instead of being raised with a "resurrection or spiritual" body (1 Corinthians 15:44). In another way of putting it, they did not rise with their glorified bodies.

It is also interesting that the chief priests and Pharisees had described Jesus as **that deceiver** when they were the deceivers (26:4). This often happens when people make too much of an issue about someone else's words or actions. If the truth is known, they may have the same issue but have denied it in their own life, which compounds the problem.

Matthew 28:7 And go quickly and tell His disciples that He is risen from the dead, and indeed He is going before you into Galilee; there you will see Him. Behold, I have told you." This is the main issue that divides the Christian faith from other religions. Christ paid the price for our sins and then demonstrated that He had conquered death by rising from the dead.

Matthew 28:18 And Jesus came and spoke to them, saying, "All authority has been given to Me in heaven and on earth. 19 Go therefore and make disciples of all the nations, baptizing them in the name of the Father and of the Son and of the Holy Spirit, 20 teaching them to observe all things that I have commanded you; and lo, I am with you always, *even* **to the end of the age." Amen.** Jesus has "**all authority.**" How much authority is that? All. Thus, the great commission, that is "**making disciples,**" is based on Christ's authority. Also, note that this baptism is in the name (a singular noun) "**of the Father and of the Son and of the Holy Spirit.**" This section of scripture captures the essence of the difficult to comprehend; the concept that God is three in one (i.e., the Trinity).

41

Mark

[41]**MARK** - Jesus Actions and Achievements

Mark 1:1 The beginning of the gospel of Jesus Christ, the Son of God. Here is a summary of three aspects of the Messiah. Jesus means "Yahweh saves" (God saves), which is the translation to English of the earthly name of Jesus that He is thought to have received at birth. Early translations translated His name as Joshua or Yoshua, and there is no "J" sound in Hebrew. Joshua was a prevalent name at the time of Jesus' birth, and perhaps this is why later translators used Jesus, which is a much less common name in English, although it is a common spelling for a Spanish name.

Now, it would be rare for someone to be named Jesus. However, what set Him apart from the every day Joe has always been who He was and His titles (Christ or the Messiah), not His name. Some prefer to stay with the name in Greek. In late Biblical Hebrew, Yeshua is used. Later, this was transliterated in English to Jesus. However, Jesus may have spoken

---

[41] NSB quotations are from the Nelsons Study Bible, copyright (c) 1997 by Thomas Nelson, Inc., Nashville, TN; used by permission; scripture taken from the New King James Version, Copyright (c) 1979, 1980, 1982 used by permission. All rights reserved.

Aramaic though most scholars believe the New Testament was written in Greek. (A small minority think it was originally written in Aramaic.)

Anyway, in Hebrew/Aramaic, the name of Jesus was Yeshu'a. This was translated into Greek, then Latin, then German, and in English, it became Jesus. Whatever translation of the common name is used does not alter the fact that Christ or Messiah are the Old Testament titles that designate Him as God's chosen servant. The additional description of "Son of God" explains that this text is referring to the deity with a unique relationship to and status with God the Father.

Mark 1:9 It came to pass in those days *that* Jesus came from Nazareth of Galilee, and was baptized by John in the Jordan. John's baptism in water was for the repentance of sins as a ceremonial cleansing that prepared Christ's baptism, which followed conversion and symbolizes the spiritual death, burial, and resurrection with Christ for a believer in Christ (Acts 19:1-5). Later there is a baptism by fire. Baptism does not save a person. It is only a symbol that they are saved. One thief on the cross with Christ was told that he would be with Christ in paradise. He had not been through a formal baptism ceremony. He was saved by the grace of God through his belief, just as everyone else on earth can be saved. Even Abraham was saved in this manner. He believed God, and it was accounted to him as righteousness (Romans 4:3; Galatians 3:6). Though he was looking forward to the salvation of the Messiah, and we look back to the salvation of the Messiah, it is the same grace of Jesus Christ who saved Abraham as saves us. Salvation is always by God's grace through faith. Our only part in the salvation of our souls is to accept the gift of salvation through faith that Christ can save us, and He even supplies the faith, lest any man should boast about it (Ephesians 2:9).

Mark 1:15 ...and saying, "The time is fulfilled, and the kingdom of God is at hand. Repent, and believe in the gospel." In this verse, Christ is encouraging people to exercise faith through repenting and believing, and He proclaimed the Kingdom of God, which was the subject of much Old Testament prophecy. Note: Christ's teaching was different than others that leaned on the wisdom of other teachers. He had the wisdom and authority Himself and taught based on His wisdom and authority (1:23).

Mark 1:35 Now in the morning, having risen a long while before daylight, He went out and departed to a solitary place; and there He prayed. This scripture presents Christ's model for prayer. He planned His day ahead of time so that He would get up early enough to have time. He got away to have private uninterrupted time, and He kept at it long enough. He was out there so long that others got concerned about Him and started to look for Him.

Mark 1:38 But He said to them, "Let us go into the next towns, that I may preach there also, because for this purpose I have come forth." Here Christ models for us His singleness of purpose and dedication to His mission. He didn't let His friends derail Him from His mission to preach.

Mark 2:17 On hearing this, Jesus said to them, "It is not the healthy who need a doctor but the sick. I have not come to call the righteous, but sinners." This is an example of Christ using a tongue-in-cheek kind of comment. Some of the people He was talking to thought of themselves as righteous and not in need of salvation, but it is clear from scripture that all people (yes, all people) are sinners and in need of salvation (Romans 3:23). It is probably also true that most of us do not want to accept this fact and will fight against it for some time in our lives even though, deep down, we know that in comparison to the Holy, Holy, Holy God, in our unredeemed state, we are anything but righteous. I am just reporting what the scripture says here, so you do not need to get angry at me. However, if you do, please read further to see what the scripture says about doing that.

Mark 2:27 Then he said to them, "The Sabbath was made for man, not man for the Sabbath. Here we find that the Sabbath was made for man. In other words, it was for our good, but it was still under the authority of Christ. The Sabbath, based on man-made rules (human tradition), did not have a higher status than God's laws and principles. Can you imagine any of the people who would criticize Jesus for healing on the Sabbath approving the closure of an emergency room on the Sabbath if they were the one with a broken arm or a bleeding gash? Christ simply exposed their hypocrisy.

Mark 3:5 And when He had looked around at them with anger, being grieved by the hardness of their hearts, He said to the man, "Stretch out your hand." And he stretched *it* out, and his hand was restored as whole as the other. This is one of the few times in scripture where Christ is described as having anger. Paul exhorts (Ephesians 4:26) that it is possible to have anger and not sin. Jesus demonstrates this type of anger in this passage. We can call this righteous anger. It is the type that does not result in retaliation or even losing control of the emotions. Generally, our anger does not fall into this category. It is usually related to something we selfishly want our way, and we are not getting what we want. Our actions should usually result in kindness, humbleness of mind, meekness, longsuffering (Colossians 3:12-16), forgiveness, and peace. Our anger often does not result in these characteristics.

Anger is usually destructive to the target of our rage and ourselves. "**Vengeance is mine, I will repay, says the Lord**" (Romans 12:19) is a saying we need to remember when we are tempted to become angry with one of God's created beings. He will repay (Deuteronomy 7:10; Psalms 54:5; Isaiah 59:18). This is essential for all Christians to know. We should rarely be angry with our brothers and should not let our anger get beyond the day (Ephesians 4:26). We need to remember that "**anger**

rests in the bosom of fools" (Ecclesiastes 7:9) and try not to be in this category.

In high school, I got angry, resulting in a fistfight with one of my classmates over who was responsible for a fender bender in the school parking lot. This fellow thought it was my fault and said he would beat up a friend who testified on my behalf at the small claims court hearing against me. The judge ruled we were both moving and would be responsible for fixing our respective damages.

Neither of us felt very good after this fight. The chances are that nothing would have come of it if I had not become angry. However, looking back at the situation, maybe I did have a little bit of righteous anger because this guy was threatening to beat up my friend for just reporting what he saw to the court. Our fight was the end of it, and the fellow I fought never confronted my witness about his testimony. Neither of us was hurt very much.

Mark 3:28 "Assuredly, I say to you, all sins will be forgiven the sons of men, and whatever blasphemies they may utter; 29 but he who blasphemes against the Holy Spirit never has forgiveness, but is subject to eternal condemnation"— 30 because they said, "He has an unclean spirit." This scripture is about the one unforgivable thing. If you continually blaspheme the Holy Spirit, you are placing yourself outside the redeeming grace of God. This seems to be referring to a continual state of willfully opposing God. It appears that the tense of **"They said"** indicates continued action, not just a one-time event. What Christ said and did was through the power of the Holy Spirit. Thus, to say that these sayings and actions were from Satan would be to attribute God's good things to Satan. It would be calling good evil and evil good, which will happen more in the end times (Matthew 12:31, 32; Isaiah 5:20; 2 Timothy 3:1-5). It seems to be happening in our times more and more in the political scene where both sides call the other liars.

Mark 3:34 And He looked around in a circle at those who sat about Him, and said, "Here are My mother and My brothers! 35 For whoever does the will of God is My brother and My sister and mother." Here we find that spiritual allegiance includes obedience to God's will surpassing loyalty to family. We know that family loyalty is essential, and this scripture does not change that fact. It just means that spiritual kinship for the believer has greater importance.

Mark 4:11 And He said to them, "To you it has been given to know the mystery of the kingdom of God; but to those who are outside, all things come in parables,... Some truths are not for everyone to know and will continue to be "mysteries" to unbelievers. Also, many things will continue to be mysteries to believers. However, it appears that some spiritual truths are only for believers at this time in our history. Some of these spiritual truths are revealed to believers through parables that some people (those who are not believers) cannot understand.

Parables can reveal and conceal at the same time. With parables, you have to have a key to understanding them, and the key to understanding some parables is faith. Without the key, you cannot fully understand the parable. Those without faith appear to be spiritually blind to the meanings of these parables (see Matthew 21:45,46). In the following parable of the Sower (4:20), only one soil bears fruit, the soil (person) who hears the Word and accepts it. I will not say a lot about the interpretation of the parables. You can read them yourself and understand them if you have the key.

Mark 5:5 Night and day among the tombs and in the hills he would cry out and cut himself with stones. The scripture says this man had an **"unclean spirit"** (5:2). This is an example of demon possession causing cutting behavior. Note: this does not mean that all cutting behavior is caused by demon possession. It just means that in this case, it was. It could result from mental illness, disease, or extreme, irrational thinking of some sort in other situations.

Mark 5:34 And He said to her, "Daughter, your faith has made you well. Go in peace, and be healed of your affliction." This is another scripture having to do with the power of faith. It is said to make a person well in this case. Through her faith, it was Christ's divine will to heal her. Her faith is what motivated her to seek healing from Christ. Also, her faith was in Him. What we put our faith in makes all the difference. Faith is to trust and believe. It is to relinquish faith or trust in ourselves and put it in another. In this case, that faith was put in Christ.

Mark 6:4 But Jesus said to them, "A prophet is not without honor except in his own country, among his own relatives, and in his own house." 5 Now He could do no mighty work there, except that He laid His hands on a few sick people and healed *them*. Here's a scripture that illustrates the incredible synchrony between Christ and His followers through our faith and prayers (Luke 1:37; Psalm 18:6). The Word says that even Christ could do "**no mighty work**" in His hometown because of their unbelief - lack of faith. It appears there is a connection between God and human beings such that our lack of belief could keep Christ from doing mighty works while He was here on earth. God set it up this way, but it is still hard to comprehend that our unbelief here on earth could have any impact whatsoever on what He did or didn't do. This is hard to fathom. Just before this section of scripture, Christ had healed a woman and restored a girl to life. Of course, the girl would die again, in contrast to Christ, who was restored to life after He died an earthly death and had His body transformed so that He would never again face death. With God, all things are possible.

Mark 6:31 And He said to them, "Come aside by yourselves to a deserted place and rest a while." For there were many coming and going, and they did not even have time to eat. This is good advice for all of us, even in our time. We can get caught up in living and miss the essence of life if we don't get out **"to a deserted place and rest for a while"** from time to time. We need time to rest, pray, collect our thoughts, and recharge our energy. Note that the scripture goes on to say that they **"departed to a deserted place in the boat by themselves."**

Scripture records several times where Christ got into a boat and once where He ordered his disciples to get into a boat to go to the other side of a body of water. In a boat, you are surrounded by water, which can be a peaceful and tranquil place. They were getting away from all the other people as soon as they shoved off. They could then go to a deserted place that would be hard to access over land. Christ also provides an example of getting away to spend blocks of time praying before big decisions are made. For example: before He selected 12 disciples to be His apostles, He spent all night praying (Luke 6:12).

Mark 7:6 He answered and said to them, "Well did Isaiah prophesy of you hypocrites, as it is written:
 This people honors Me with their lips,
 But their heart is far from Me.
 7 And in vain they worship Me,
 Teaching as doctrines the commandments of men.' Here Christ teaches us the difference between God's laws and the doctrines of men. Violating God's law produces real moral defilement. Violating man's rules is ceremonial defilement. God's law is always superior to human-made tradition. Written commentaries on God's law should never be given greater status than the Word of God, including the commentaries in this book. When in doubt, always go with the **bold** print that is scripture from the Bible.

Mark 8:30 Then He strictly warned them that they should tell no one about Him. It is interesting that at this time, Christ told His disciples not to tell others what they knew about Him. The Jewish leaders of the time, and some still today, expected the Messiah (the Christ) to be a political leader and liberator. Instead, He had come to release (liberate) them from slavery to sin (John 8:34) and its eternal consequences. Thus at that time, if they told others that He was the Christ, it would have been misunderstood by the Jewish leaders and by the Roman authorities because of what they thought the Messiah would do. Note that sin still can have earthy consequences even when God forgives eternal consequences.

Mark 8:33 But when He had turned around and looked at His disciples, He rebuked Peter, saying, "Get behind Me, Satan! For you are not mindful of the things of God, but the things of men." It appears that Christ is rebuking Peter here for presenting thoughts from a Satanic point of view, contrary to God's will. God's will was for Christ to pay the price for our sins and rise on the third day conquering death once and for all. Peter was rebuking Christ for telling the disciples what would happen as he was arrogant enough not to agree with Christ. Note that Peter's disagreement with Christ on this point did not keep Christ from using Peter in a powerful way after this dispute. Peter took the rebuke and continued to follow Christ. Christ ignored Peter's rebuke and continued with his mission to provide a way of salvation for all of us. Eventually, He will **"come in the glory of His father with His angels, and then he will reward each according to his works"** (Matthew 16:27).

Mark 8:34 When He had called the people to *Himself*, with His disciples also, He said to them, "Whoever desires to come after Me, let him deny himself, and take up his cross, and follow Me. 35 For whoever desires to save his life will lose it, but whoever loses his life for My sake and the gospel's will save it. We are reminded here that becoming a Christian can be a difficult road. We may wind up losing friends. We could wind up losing our lives for our beliefs. Earthly things are not important compared to the future of one's soul.

Mark 9:23 Jesus said to him, "If you can believe, all things *are*

possible to him who believes." .... 9:29 So He said to them, "This kind can come out by nothing but prayer and fasting." [NU-Text omits *and fasting*.] Thus, it appears that all things are possible to him who believes, but there are some qualifiers to this statement in other scriptures. One of the qualifiers is in the same chapter, where it is noted that prayer and fasting are needed in some situations. We might want to ask what "all things" means because another qualifier in other parts of scripture is that things we ask that are in the will of God will be done (James 4:3). Herein lies the danger of not taking in the whole counsel of God.

Over the centuries, people have taken parts of scripture out of context to support their ideas about meaning. Without the whole context, diverse and inappropriate conclusions can be drawn. Don't just read what is written here. I implore you to read the entire Bible to understand all that God has for you. In 11:23, Christ again points out that the impossible can be accomplished with faith in God. Another scripture clarifies that what we ask for needs to be in the will of the Lord. If we have faith in God, our instruction is to pray for His will to be done. This should be one of the first few requests we make in our prayers per the teachings of Christ (Matthew 6:9-13).

Mark 9:35 And He sat down, called the twelve, and said to them, "If anyone desires to be first, he shall be last of all and servant of all." This is excellent advice for a leader. If a leader takes this attitude, it will help keep them from getting pumped up with pride. In God's kingdom, to be great, one must have a servant's perspective just as Christ had when he served all of us by paying the price for our transgressions.

Mark 9:40 For he who is not against us is on our side. This is a good thought to keep in mind. If someone is not actively against you, you could consider them on your side.

Mark 9:42 "But whoever causes one of these little ones who believe in Me to stumble, it would be better for him if a millstone were hung around his neck, and he were thrown into the sea. Causing others to stumble is not a good thing, especially if the one you are causing to stumble is a "little one who believes in Christ." Christ says it would be better to enter into life maimed than to go unmaimed to hell (Mark 9:43).

Mark 10:7 *For this reason a man shall leave his father and mother and be joined to his wife, 8 and the two shall become one flesh*'; so then they are no longer two, but one flesh. The bond in marriage is comparable to a blood relationship. And when a married couple has children, the children are a combination representing a blood relationship with both parents. God's original purpose for marriage appears to be that the bond would not be broken. He allows it to be broken in situations of sexual immorality (Matt. 5:32). Of course, as with most other bad behavior, the price for divorce without an acceptable reason was paid by Christ's death on the cross for those who believe.

Mark 10:24 The disciples were amazed at his words. But Jesus said again, "Children, how hard it is to enter the kingdom of God! 25 It is easier for a camel to go through the eye of a needle than for someone who is rich to enter the kingdom of God." 26 The disciples were even more amazed, and said to each other, "Who then can be saved?" 27 But Jesus looked at them and said, "With men *it is* impossible, but not with God; for with God all things are possible." This is the great news about all our sins and for the rich. Our reward for being with God is eternal life in His presence in the age to come (10:30). It is impossible to save ourselves. We can only be saved by the work of Christ in paying the price for our transgressions. It is a gift. It is by the grace of God through faith.

Mark 12:25 For when they rise from the dead, they neither marry

nor are given in marriage, but are like angels in heaven. There is no marriage, as we know it, in heaven. It makes me think that our interrelations may be much closer to all souls, and we may feel united with others on a spiritual plane that is different from how we feel united here on earth. Now we see dimly. Maybe marriage on earth is a small representation of a spiritual connection that is experienced in heaven. God is still **"the God of Abraham, the God of Isaac, and the God of Jacob"** (11:26). Their souls are still all alive in heaven, and their bodies will eventually be raised anew as well. At this time, we may not be capable of fully understanding life in heaven. We do not have to know or understand everything right now.

Mark 12:29 Jesus answered him, "The first of all the commandments is: 'Hear, O Israel, the LORD our God, the LORD is one. 30 And you shall love the LORD your God with all your heart, with all your soul, with all your mind, and with all your strength.' This *is* the first commandment. 31 And the second, like *it*, is this: 'You shall love your neighbor as yourself.' There is no other commandment greater than these." For a Christian, it would be hard to overemphasize these two commandments. The first commandment here summarizes the first four commandments in Exodus 20, having to do with our relation to God. The second summarizes the final six regarding our relationships with other people.

Mark 12:43 So He called His disciples to *Himself* and said to them, "Assuredly, I say to you that this poor widow has put in more than all those who have given to the treasury;... It appears God measures generosity by how much is retained rather than how much is given.

Mark 13:20 And unless the Lord had shortened those days, no flesh would be saved; but for the elect's sake, whom He chose, He shortened the days. When the tribulation comes, there will be sorrows for all people, and those who believe the Gospel will be hated for Christ's namesake by those opposed to the Gospel. There will be false Christs and false prophets who even show signs and wonders to deceive. However, we have been warned, and these will not overcome the elect. When Christ does return, the sun will be darkened. The moon will not give forth its light, and stars will fall from heaven (13:24). Thus, it will be unmistakable, and everyone will see. He will come in the clouds with great power and glory and send His angels to gather the glorified bodies of His elect (Mark 13:26).

Mark 13:32 "But of that day and hour no one knows, not even the angels in heaven, nor the Son, but only the Father. This statement regarding the return of Christ seems very clear. Therefore, when we see people saying that they know when these things will take place or start to happen, it would seem that they are false prophets, to put it bluntly. We are to watch and pray; not make speculative, inappropriate predictions. This type of speculation only makes the person doing the predicting look uninformed.

Mark 14:10 Then Judas Iscariot, one of the twelve, went to the chief priests to betray Him to them. Of course, the "Him" that Judas betrayed was Jesus Christ. There is often a Judas in a group of believers of over ten people. Christ was probably not easily recognizable in those days when there were no cameras, televisions, or videos. Apparently, Christ's looks were not that different from other people, so it would be difficult for Him to be easily identified. Thus, they needed someone to identify Him to make the arrest. Judas was already profiting from his association with Christ but was greedy for more.

Mark 14:26 And when they had sung a hymn, they went out to the Mount of Olives. Here's one of the places in the new testament that mentions singing. The scripture does not say they had any musical instruments accompanying them, nor does it say they did not have musical instruments accompanying them. Old Testament scripture, especially the psalms, has many references to worship accompanied by all kinds of musical instruments (see Psalm 150). The scripture even mentions musical instruments used in heaven (Revelation 5:8 et al.). Thus, it seems that the preponderance of scriptural evidence points to support for the use of musical instruments in worship. Some Christians believe that because musical instruments in worship are not explicitly mentioned in the New Testament, we should not use musical instruments in worship. Note that there is no prohibition of using musical instruments in the New Testament that I can see. The Old Testament seems to indicate that the primary reason musical instruments were invented by David was for worship. Thus, it does not make sense to conclude that New Testament times are the only times during which musical instruments are not to be used to facilitate worship. Still, I encourage those who do not wish to include musical instruments to worship in a way they deem acceptable.

Mark 14:32 Then they came to a place which was named Gethsemane; and He said to His disciples, "Sit here while I pray." Many times Christ got away from others to pray. He is an example to us in this. We need regular alone time to talk to and listen to the Lord. It seems Christ wanted uninterrupted privacy when He got away to pray (6:46; Matt. 14:22, 23; John 6:14, 15). He praised God (Luke 10:21), He thanked the Father (8:6, 7), and He made petitions (14:36) and intercessions. Note that at times He took a few of His closest disciples with Him part of the way when He went away to pray. In this passage, He took Peter, James, and John part of the way and then left them to go a little further and fell on the ground and prayed, and when he came back to them, He found them sleeping. He is an example to us in this also. We all need friends to support us. We are not meant to live in isolation.

Mark 14:38 Watch and pray, lest you enter into temptation. The spirit indeed *is* willing, but the flesh *is* weak." This passage highlights the internal battle between the Spirit and the flesh that all experience daily. This battle takes constant vigilance. Our fallen human nature, even after conversion, wars against the work of God. However, we can now win this war by walking in the Spirit (Galatians 15:16-18). We are no longer under the control of the flesh. When we walk by the Spirit, we can have victory over the dwindling resistance movement of the flesh. When we walk in the Spirit, the fruit is love, and love fulfills the law (Galatians 5:22). The great news is that when the Holy Spirit leads us, we are not even under the law (Galatians 5:18). How do we walk in the Spirit? We are doing so when we believe in the promises of God. Our faith in what Christ did for us allows us to believe that He *works* everything together for our good.

The way to walk by the Spirit is to have faith, and then we can be happy with God's promises, which brings us into harmony with the Spirit. We live in the flesh by faith in the Son of God (Galatians 2:20). A nice thing about focusing on walking by the Spirit is that it diminishes guilt, fear, and greed, which can enslave us and keep us thinking about worldly things rather than being heavenly-minded. The secret to walking in the Spirit can be consistently meditating on the Word of God. I have been encouraged to provide some personal examples in this commentary. That is difficult because I am uncomfortable with appearing to be exalting myself.

Thus, I will preface this example by saying something I believe: "This is what the Lord did." I worked full-time for a nonprofit social service agency for over thirty-nine years. The last 31 years were spent as the Chief Executive Officer (CEO). Over the years, many difficult decisions were made. Some of those decisions had significant consequences for program participants and staff members, creating angst and difficulty. I wasn't sure how long I would be able to continue with this level of stress. According to research I've seen, the average tenure of CEOs/Executive Directors of nonprofit agencies is between 4.2 and 7.79 years. About ten years into my career, I began walking in faith and believing that everything would work together for good. After that, the decisions were still difficult, but focusing on God's promises allowed me to hope for the best outcomes and happily continue for over twenty more years. Over those years, I came to view this work not as just a career but as a calling. It was a calling I had never even imagined or pursued. Over those years, the agency continued to have good outcomes and grew from less than 100 to over 600 staff members serving tens of thousands of program participants.

Mark 14:62 "I am," said Jesus. "And you will see the Son of Man sitting at the right hand of the Mighty One and coming on the clouds of heaven." This statement cannot be reconciled easily by anyone who does not believe in Christ. Either Jesus was (a) who He said He was, (b) a liar, or (c) delusional/mentally ill. He did not leave many options for those who want to make Him out to be something else. Any other choice is intellectually untenable. His statements about Himself make it difficult for those who want to make Him out to be just a great moral leader but not God in the flesh. How could He be a great moral leader if He is lying about His deity? Nevertheless, these facts will probably not turn a soul toward God. A person needs to recognize their transgressions and be convinced that they need God's salvation.

Mark 15:34 And at the ninth hour Jesus cried out with a loud voice, saying, "Eloi, Eloi, lama sabachthani?" which is translated, *"My God, My God, why have You forsaken Me?"* Here just before His death, Christ quotes Psalm 22:1 while in intense spiritual and physical agony. He had been beaten, hung on the cross, and abandoned by His Father for a time to bear the sins of the world. Note: He still refers to His Father as My God even in this difficult time. We may have difficulty understanding the Trinity in this situation, but that appears to be our problem and not for us to know about while we are here on earth so I won't attempt any more explanation.

Mark 15:38 Then the veil of the temple was torn in two from top to

bottom. Many interpret the temple's veil tearing as a symbol that access to God is now open to all. This appears to be a correct interpretation based on the totality of scripture (Hebrews 10:19-20). The Gospel could now be preached as the Good News of Salvation to all people on earth.

Mark 16:14 Later He appeared to the eleven as they sat at the table; and He rebuked their unbelief and hardness of heart, because they did not believe those who had seen Him after He had risen. After rebuking the apostles, the risen Christ gave them the great commission to **"Go into the world and preach the gospel to every creature"** (16:15). That is what they did. We should do the same in how the Holy Spirit leads us. There are many parts of the body of Christ, and as scripture teaches us, they are all essential to getting the job done just as all the parts of our physical body help us function (Romans 12:5,1; 1 Corinthians 12:12-27; Ephesians 3:6 and 5:23; Colossians 1;24). The vocal cords have their function, and the hands have different functions. It can take both to get things done.

42

Luke

[42]**LUKE - A Unique Perspective**

Luke 1:15 For he will be great in the sight of the Lord, and shall drink neither wine nor strong drink. He will also be filled with the Holy Spirit, even from his mother's womb. This passage is about John the Baptist. Note that God gave John, Zacharias' son, his name, and when God gives anyone a new name, the person is generally used by Him. This verse also says that John was filled with the Holy Spirit, which means that he was directed by and obedient to the Holy Spirit (see Ephesians 5:18). It can also be observed that John was not to drink wine nor strong drink. On the other hand, Christ apparently drank some wine on occasion (John 2:1-11; Matthew 26:9) and once turned water into wine (John 2:11). Nevertheless, since He never sinned (2 Corinthians 5:21; Hebrews 4:15; 1 Peter 2:22; 1 John 3:5; Luke 23:41), we can be sure that he never drank so much wine that He got drunk. Thus, we can reason that making wine is not a sin, even though some people might abuse it.

---

[42] NSB quotations are from the Nelsons Study Bible, copyright (c) 1997 by Thomas Nelson, Inc., Nashville, TN; used by permission; scripture taken from the New King James Version, Copyright (c) 1979, 1980, 1982 used by permission. All rights reserved.

This fundamental principle could also be applied to other products. For example, some people might overeat ice cream and become gluttonous by doing so, which could be considered a problem. The person who made the ice cream did not sin. How about the people who make ropes? Some people commit suicide with ropes. The people who made the ropes did not transgress by doing so. What about people who make knives? Some people murder with knives. In my opinion, the people who made the knives did not transgress. Note that there is a legitimate and potential illegitimate use of the product in all of these examples. If there was no legitimate use, this basic principle might not apply.

Luke 1:37 For with God nothing will be impossible." This statement explains how Elizabeth could conceive John in her old age and how Mary could conceive God's Son without knowing a man. Indeed, for God, who spoke the vast universe into existence, these are minor accomplishments but of universal significance.

Luke 1:50 And His mercy *is* on those who fear Him

From generation to generation. This statement comes from the Song of Mary. She came humbly before the Lord as His maidservant who was ready for faithful and obedient service. Justice is getting the punishment you deserve. Mercy is not getting the punishment you deserve. Grace is getting what you don't deserve, or in another way of looking at it, it is having someone else receive the punishment you deserved. To fear the Lord is to look respectfully on Him and honor him. It is keeping faith with Him (Psalm 147:11). To fear Him is to appropriately respond to Him in awe and wonder as the one who spoke our universe into existence. We cannot even imagine this kind of power. God seems to bless and enjoy people who respond rightly to Him, although He tests them and disciplines them to refine them (Jeremiah 17:10). For those who fear (honor/respect) Him, He removes our transgressions from us as far as the East is from the West (Psalm 103;12).

Luke 1:79 To give light to those who sit in darkness and the shadow of death,

To guide our feet into the way of peace." To those blinded by the darkness of their sins, the Messiah (Dayspring from on high) provides the light of truth and forgiveness. Forgiveness is the way for us to see the light which will guide us to peace. What a great concept!

Luke 2:26 And it had been revealed to him by the Holy Spirit that he would not see death before he had seen the Lord's Christ. There are times when the Holy Spirit reveals things to people who are listening. In this case, the Holy Spirit revealed to Simeon **"that he would not see death before he had seen the Lord's Christ."** Simeon was a just and devout man who was waiting for Christ to come. He had studied the scriptures so that he knew that, as he put it, the Consolation of Israel would be coming (Luke 2:25).

Luke 2:40 And the Child grew and became strong in spirit, filled with wisdom; and the grace of God was upon Him. It is interesting that Christ "grew" and became strong in spirit. We are not told how He started but that he **"became strong in spirit with wisdom and the grace of God."** The story does not pick back up in the scriptures until He is about twelve years old in verse 41. At this time, He already astonished the teachers in the temple with His questions, understanding, and answers. His response to them when they found Him in the temple indicates that He already knew (the Holy Spirit may have communicated this to Him) that He had to be about His Father's business. Talking to the teachers in the temple was part of His Father's business. They appeared to be studying the scriptures and trying to discern the meaning among themselves. Jesus joined in this process and demonstrated an understanding that amazed them coming from a twelve-year-old boy. So, He already had learned enough to know that He had to be about His Heavenly Father's business. As we found out, this business was living a sinless life and then paying the price for our transgressions so that we could be reconciled to God per His plan.

Luke 3:3 And he went into all the region around the Jordan, preaching a baptism of repentance for the remission of sins, 4 as it is written in the book of the words of Isaiah the prophet, saying: This scripture refers us back to the old covenant from Isaiah. John fulfilled this prophecy. Baptism is the process of identifying with something. When John preached, people were baptized by him as a sign of identifying with his message. It was an outward sign of their inward repentance from their transgressions. Once they identified with John's message, they were expected to act differently. They were to help the needy, work with integrity, refrain from abusing their power, and generally be content. When John was asked if he was the Christ, he told them that he baptized with water, but that one was coming who would baptize with the Holy Spirit and fire, which pointed to and prepared the way for Christ's baptism. The baptism of the Holy Spirit appears to relate to His first coming. The baptism by fire seems to apply to His second coming when He separates the wheat from the chaff, and **"He will burn up the chaff with unquenchable fire"** (Matthew 3:12). The chaff is the portion of the wheat that is the useless shell of the grain. It may be much more comforting to think that everyone will get to heaven, but that thinking is not taught in the Bible that I can find.

Luke 4:8 And Jesus answered and said to him, "Get behind Me, Satan! For it is written, *You shall worship the LORD your God, and Him only you shall serve.*" So here we have one of Christ's responses to His temptation by Satan. Note that each of His three responses reported by Luke involves usage of the ideas from the book of Deuteronomy. The words may have been slightly different, but the message is the same. Also, notice that there is an element of truth in what Satan has to say to Christ, but not the whole truth. He is crafty in this way.

By including an element of truth, someone telling a lie can get your mind in an accepting mode so that it is more difficult to discern which part is truth and which part is not. In the message from Satan that preceded the statement from Christ, Satan said that authority had been given to him and that he would give it to whomever he wished. The nuance here is that Satan has been allowed to have authority for a time here on earth, but the lie is in the exaggeration. He does not have the authority to deliver kingdoms. He was trying to get Christ to bypass the Cross and take the easy way by not depending on and following the Father's path. He was trying to derail Christ by offering him power by the wrong means. Only God is worthy of worship, and we are to serve Him and Him only. This chapter of scripture also reveals that the mere use of Biblical words does not always reveal God's will. Satan used God's words in an inappropriate context. Thus, we need to learn at least three things from this chapter.

1. Use God's word to combat temptation.

2. Beware of lies cloaked in a bit of truth to make them more palatable.

3. Beware of the Word of God taken out of context to tempt you down the wrong path.

Luke 4:33 Now in the synagogue there was a man who had a spirit of an unclean demon. And he cried out with a loud voice, 34 saying, "Let *us* alone! What have we to do with You, Jesus of Nazareth? Did You come to destroy us? I know who You are—the Holy One of God!" This scripture demonstrates that the demons know who Christ is. Just knowing who He is does not save a person. Accepting the gift of salvation through faith and *following* Him is the key. Many individuals know who He is and choose not to accept the gift and follow Him. He gives us that free will.

Luke 4:43 ...but He said to them, "I must preach the kingdom of God to the other cities also, because for this purpose I have been sent." Here we are told why Christ came. He was sent here to earth to preach the kingdom of God. He announced the rule of God through His person (24:47), He distributed the Spirit (24:49), and He will reign with

His followers according to the promises (see Psalm 2:7-12; Acts 3:18-22).

Luke 5:16 So He Himself *often* withdrew into the wilderness and prayed. If we want to follow Christ, here is something to consider; periodically, He withdrew from the hustle and bustle of life into the wilderness and prayed. What better way is there to recharge ourselves and get perspective from the Lord than to get out in His creation and speak with Him? Christ got into a boat to withdraw from the multitudes in other passages. It may not matter how we withdraw to get away and pray, but it does appear to be essential to do so for those of us who want to follow Christ's example.

Luke 5:39 And no one, having drunk old *wine*, immediately desires new; for he says, 'The old is better.'" This scripture explains why those involved in Judaism may have a difficult time accepting Christ. If they are satisfied with the old way, they may resist change. This analogy explains why some people in Israel at the time were not turning to Jesus. He brought in a fulfillment of the old that some could not accept. Also, note in verse 32, Jesus says that He has "**not come to call the righteous, but sinners, to repentance.**" He was criticized for socializing with sinners, and, indeed, he did not quarantine Himself from them (1 Corinthians 9:5-13). How could He have had much influence with them if He had no contact with them? We might want to ask ourselves this same question.

Luke 6:12 Now it came to pass in those days that He went out to the mountain to pray, and continued all night in prayer to God. This is another excellent example for us. After Jesus healed a man's withered hand on the Sabbath, the Pharisees were filled with rage against Him. What He did then was to go to the mountains to pray all night. The night is an excellent time to pray because there are fewer distractions, especially in the mountains away from the city's hustle and bustle, where even at night, there can be many distracting activities going on. In the mountains, it can be peaceful and quiet. When not in the mountains, I have found the most peaceful, quiet, and interruption-free time is in the middle of the night. There are very few interruptions, and if there is one, it will probably be a subject for Prayer.

Luke 6:20 Then He lifted up His eyes toward His disciples, and said: " Blessed *are you poor,*

For yours is the kingdom of God. These words of Christ to His disciples seem to carry both a direct and spiritual meaning. Most of the disciples were lacking in terms of money and possessions. However, they were also previously poor in spirit before they came to follow Christ. From other scripture, we know that the kingdom of God belongs to followers of Christ. Thus, a financially poor person can, at the same time, be spiritually rich. Conversely, a wealthy person can easily be spiritually poor.

Luke 6:30 Give to everyone who asks of you. And from him who takes away your goods do not ask *them* back. Here are some instructions directly from Christ that most Christians will find hard to implement. Basically, in the context of statements on loving your enemies, Christ says that we should forgive and forget it and not ask for it back if someone takes something from us. It does not say to refuse to receive the item back if offered, but it does say not to ask for it back. This is a big contrast to what we would typically want to do in the face of such an injustice. Not only would we like the item back, but we would want the offender punished to the full extent of the law. Is Christ possibly saying that if an offender wished to have something enough to steal it, we should have enough compassion to offer it to them? It seems that this might be the case because, in the following sentence, Christ recites the golden rule: 31 "**And just as you want men to do to you, you also do to them likewise.**"

If we got so desperate that we stole something from someone else, what would we want; mercy, forgiveness, restoration or punishment, retribution, and judgment? This kind of command is a lot easier to impose on other people than ourselves. Verse 37 below is how we can do what this command tells us to do. It all starts with not judging others. The government, in subjection to God, has that role (Romans 13:1). As individuals, we are told not to get involved in judging the intentions of those who do not believe in God (Matthew 7:1). Still, we are to judge the behavior and actions of believers that contradict God's principles (1 Corinthians 2:15). We can leave the job of judging the heart of a man to the only one who can do it fairly and justly; that is God.

One of the great things about the Bible is that it provides balance when you take in the whole counsel of God. Thus, we should not give to strangers to the point of neglecting our first responsibility, which is to take care of our relatives. 1 Timothy 5:8 makes this clear: **"But if any provide not for his own, and specially for those of his own house, he hath denied the faith, and is worse than an infidel."** Also, we need to look beyond what a person is asking for and see what they need. Becoming an accomplice to some sort of transgression or illegal behavior is not a good idea. For example, it may not be good to loan your car to someone who wants to rob the corner liquor store or loan money to someone who wants to use it to buy illegal drugs or even legal alcohol. It also may not be good to give money for food to a non-disabled person, so they do not have to work for their food as others do. That could create an unnecessary dependency. 2 Thessalonians 3:10 instructs, **"For even when we were with you, this we commanded you, that if any would not work, neither should he eat."** We are to be generous to those in need but not to the point of supporting laziness or to those who simply do not want to take advantage of other resources available to them.

Should we give everyone on the street corner asking for help when they may qualify for food stamps? Unfortunately, we do not know what the person is going to buy. Thus, we can say "no thank you" if we do not feel led to give money or food. Those who have other ideas for using the cash may not like an offer of food. This is an individual decision for which you can pray. I heard that a Rescue Mission implied that when you give without discretion, you could be helping someone stay homeless rather than get the help they need. I would not want to be the one who provided the resources for an overdose.

Of course, many homeless people are mentally ill and unable to support themselves in our free society. Thus, this does not allow for exact determinations in all cases. Someone I know had a healthy young stranger ask for money to buy a movie ticket. They did not provide the funds for the ticket as it seemed that the person could easily earn money for a ticket like others do. The bottom line is that we need to be generous but with discernment. Be as shrewd as a serpent but as harmless as a dove (Matthew 10:16) and listen to the Holy Spirit. A friend wrote to me that: "I for one would rather give to one not needy than withhold a meal from one who is really hungry. That is a risk I'm willing to take. All of us can spare a dollar or two!!" That generous response is certainly good to consider as you ponder these issues. Deuteronomy 15:11 says: **"For the poor will never cease from the land; therefore I command you, saying, 'You shall open your hand wide to your brother, to your poor and your needy, in your land.'"** And Christ said, '**Truly, I say to you, as you did it to one of the least of these my brothers, you did it to me.**' Thus, we may also want to consider this verse before deciding how to help the hungry, thirsty, strangers, the sick, and prisoners.

Luke 6:37 "Judge not, and you shall not be judged. Condemn not, and you shall not be condemned. Forgive, and you will be forgiven. 38 Give, and it will be given to you: good measure, pressed down, shaken together, and running over will be put into your bosom. For with the same measure that you use, it will be measured back to you." For many Christians, this is where their flesh gets the best of them. In other words, it is very hard not to judge and condemn others even when it is not our responsibility nor even optional. There are a few areas in scripture (like 1 Corinthians 5:12) where we are expected to address the sin of other church members. Generally, this is the exception to the "judge not" rule. We are to let God or government authorities do almost all judging.

The government authorities are to judge regarding adherence to laws of the society. Note that there is a real negative to judging, condemning, or even failing to forgive others. It comes back on you. On the other hand, there are blessings to being gracious to others. This scripture does not say that we should ignore sin (see: 11:39-52 and Gal. 6:1-2), but it is saying that we should always be gracious and quick to forgive. And what a great blessing for the one who is giving in these areas of life. That is what we should want. The next time you feel judgemental, think about the fact that you are not in that other person's shoes and that if you can resist the temptation to be judgemental, your own shortcomings may also be forgiven.

It is possible that when Christians are not controlled by the Holy Spirit, they might tend to boast by comparing themselves to a fallen believer instead of trying to restore the fallen person to a Holy Spirit-filled life. They might be trying to justify their fleshly behavior by making it seem that the other person is more carnal. Outbursts of wrath, contention, hatred, jealousies, and selfish ambition all fall under the heading of works of the flesh (Galatians 5:19). When you see these responses from a person, you know that they are operating under the works of the flesh, even though they may be a high-ranking official in a church. Seeing this behavior in a high-ranking official may be a good thing for us. We never want a person who is being used by God as a messenger to become an idol to us. Even the highest-ranking official in any church is only a human being and a sinner who, hopefully, has received Christ and is generally predominantly controlled by the Holy Spirit instead of their own flesh. Having said that, we know that they will not be one hundred percent controlled by the Holy Spirit in this fallen world, so we need to have forgiveness in our hearts, even for them.

Luke 6:42 Or how can you say to your brother, 'Brother, let me remove the speck that *is* in your eye,' when you yourself do not see the plank that *is* in your own eye? Hypocrite! First remove the plank from your own eye, and then you will see clearly to remove the speck that is in your brother's eye. Here again, Christ expresses a negative aspect of judging others. We cannot clearly see the transgressions in someone else because the denial of our own transgressions clouds our vision. When we deny our wrongdoings and seek to hide them from others, we can be even harsher in judging others' transgressions as we expect them to be as perfect as we think we are. We can even be more negative toward those who have the same sins that we are hiding, perhaps because we are upset with them because they are not as good at hiding their sin as we are.

Immediately after this scripture, in verses 43-45, we find that actions indicate where a person's heart is, and thus, we can see from the fruit of a person's actions whether they are acting based on the Holy Spirit's control of their life or out of their flesh. If the result of interpersonal interaction is anger or hatred, the person experiencing these feelings is probably responding to their flesh. There are rare occasions where righteous anger may be present on the part of a Christian, but our anger is typically the result of personal (i.e., fleshly) issues. Even Christ exhibited rare righteous anger on behalf of His Father (Matthew 21:12-13; Mark 11:15-18; John 2:13-22; Mark 3:5), but the vastly predominant effect of His interactions with people was the fruit of the Spirit (Galatians 5:22-23) and never the flesh (Galatians 5:20-21).

Unfortunately, many of us are too smart for our own good in justifying our fleshly interactions. Smart people can justify their behavior even if their words were hurtful and expressed name-calling, gossip, denigration, or talk about the other person's past sins. A smart person may even bring up things supposedly long-ago forgiven to justify their behavior. This justification can occur, especially if another person questions their responsibility as Christians to be gracious to everyone. And it does not matter what status the person acting in the flesh has. In fact, for a person of high position in a church, it may be easier for them to justify their inappropriate judgment of others (remember the Pharisees and Sadducees).

The higher status person may feel that a lower status person has no business questioning anything they say or do. They can tend to think: "How dare they question me?" This type of pride has led to many pastors and teachers' downfall as they do not allow themselves to see the truth of their anger and judgment of others because of the "plank" in their eye. This can also be devastating to people who hold them in high esteem. We sometimes get to see that some of these high-level people are no better than the average person with controlling the flesh.

Perhaps this is one of the ways God keeps us from letting a person take His place as the one we worship. Those in the inner circles of churches are perhaps the ones who have the best vantage point on these issues. We learn through scripture about the great patriarchs in the Bible that almost all of them who God used still let the flesh take control at times and participated in great sins. Christ is the only one who had no sin, and He never even put himself above others in an earthly governing institution though He had every right to do so and someday will take His rightful place.

Luke 7:33 For John the Baptist came neither eating bread nor drinking wine, and you say, 'He has a demon.' The point here seems that the religious leaders dismissed John as demon-possessed. They dismissed Christ as living loosely and associating with sinners. In other words, God's messenger would have been rejected by the religious leaders no matter what style in which He came, possibly because they became jealous of His successes. Those who responded to John or Christ were vindicated because they received the blessing of justification. Jesus' open association with sinners was a repeated theme by Pharisee's (Luke 34; 5:8, 30,32; 13:2; 15:1, 2, 7,10; 18:13; 19:7; 27:7). A Pharisee would reject associations with people they considered unrighteous. We need to be more like Christ and less like the Pharisees.

Luke 7:47 Therefore I say to you, her sins, *which are* many, are forgiven, for she loved much. But to whom little is forgiven, *the same* loves little." The concept here seems that those who have been forgiven much will love the Lord more. Those who have been forgiven little will not love the Lord as much. Jesus told the woman that her faith had saved her (7:50; Ephesians 2:8-9). Note: faith is the channel, not the cause of salvation. Salvation is a gift of God! It is of the Lord (Jonah 2:9). It does not originate from anything a person does. The grace of God is the source of our salvation. The gift of salvation was accomplished on the cross for past, present, and future generations. Salvation is always by grace through faith!

Luke 8:10 And He said, "To you it has been given to know the mysteries of the kingdom of God, but to the rest *it is given* in parables, that
   'Seeing they may not see,
   And hearing they may not understand.' From this scripture, it is clear that not everyone will know the mysteries of God's kingdom and that God does not want everyone to know certain things or understand these things. This scripture speaks specifically about the parables that Jesus communicated. They both revealed and concealed truths. From the parable of the sower, we learn that the cares, riches, and pleasures of this life can be significant obstacles to spiritual fruitfulness. We need to meditate on the truths of scripture to establish them as internal principles so that we can withstand the trials and temptations that come with life.

Luke 8:25 But He said to them, "Where is your faith?" Here, Christ has just demonstrated His command of the weather and could be asking them why they did not trust Him to protect them because He had the power to control the wind and the waves. (One other option is that they should have trusted that whatever happened, even if they perished, they were in good hands because they knew Christ and would have eternal life with Him once their time on earth was finished.)

8:30 Jesus asked him, saying, "What is your name?" And he said, "Legion," because many demons had entered him. 31 And they begged Him that He would not command them to go out into the abyss. The abyss is the underworld, which is associated with judgment. Even these demons did not want to be sent to the place of judgment and asked to be sent into unclean animals, and this is what was granted; unclean spirits went into unclean animals.

Luke 8:46 But Jesus said, "Somebody touched Me, for I perceived power going out from Me." It makes sense that healing takes power. Nevertheless, Christ called out this woman and declared that her faith made her well. It seems that the power to heal the woman came from Christ, but the key to unleashing that power was the woman's faith, and she was commended publicly for exercising her faith. Note: this does not say nor does it appear to mean that every person who has faith will be healed. There are examples in the Bible of faithful people who earnestly prayed and were not healed. The Apostle Paul is one of them (2 Corinthians 12:9). This fact seems to contradict the "name it and claim it" approach. Prayer always needs to be couched in a "your will be done" context.

Luke 8:52 Now all wept and mourned for her; but He said, "Do not weep; she is not dead, but sleeping." 53 And they ridiculed Him, knowing that she was dead. Note that Christ said that the girl's death was not permanent, and He was ridiculed for making that statement. Thus, even before Christ suffered in preparation for the Cross, He was ridiculed much as Christians continue to be ridiculed in many situations. The lesson is that we need to understand that this is part of the Christian life. We should probably be encouraged by it rather than discouraged as long as we are secure that we are acting from a spiritual (nonmaterial/divine/heavenly focused) perspective.

Luke 9:1 Then He called His twelve disciples together and gave them power and authority over all demons, and to cure diseases. Here, Christ specifically gave the *twelve* disciples power and authority over all demons and cured diseases. Over the centuries, some people have thought that they also have been given these powers. Though I firmly believe that God can and does sometimes miraculously heal people, I'm skeptical about some modern-day *self-proclaimed* faith healers. Jesus specifically commissioned the apostles to preach and heal. Later, he gave seventy others the ability to heal the sick (Luke 10). I'm just not sure that gift is still operative in the same way today. Of course, God can still heal whenever and whomever He wants. However, it does not appear that He heals one person through another in the same way. It seems that the apostles had the healing gift to affirm that their message was from God.

Luke 9:23 Then He said to *them* all, "If anyone desires to come after Me, let him deny himself, and take up his cross daily, and follow Me. In conjunction with other scriptures, here is a scripture that may have resulted in the saying, "you have to lose your life to find it." Jesus goes on to say that: **"whoever loses his life for My sake will save it."** Salvation is a gift based on scripture (John 1:12; 3:16-18; Ephesians 2:8,9). However, Christ clarifies that believers will endure suffering and hardship here on earth (John 16:33) along with others who live in this fallen world (Matthew 15:19; Romans 5:12). Gaining the whole world is not worth anything if, in the end, a person is destroyed or lost (9:25). Thus, we need to keep ourselves mindful of the eternal as we go about our day-to-day lives. Thankfully, we can take heart because Christ has overcome the world (John 16:33)!

Luke 9:28 Now it came to pass, about eight days after these sayings, that He took Peter, John, and James and went up on the mountain to pray. This is another example of Christ going up on a mountain to pray. This time, He took some friends along, and they were privileged to see Him with Moses and Elijah. They spoke of Jesus' departure, which was about to happen. He would go to the side of God, but will someday return with authority and judgment (Acts 10:42; 17:31). Jesus is the new prophet after Moses who would lead a new group of people into salvation (Matthew 21:43; Romans 11:1-36; 1 Peter 2:9-10). Christ was the one to reveal another part of God's plan to His people.

Luke 9:50 But Jesus said to him, "Do not forbid *him*, for he who is not against us is on our side." Here, Jesus seems to dissuade sectarianism (excessive attachment to a particular sect). He said not to be against this person who was casting out demons in Christ's name just because he did not appear to be following the same path as they were. The message seems to be that if someone does not appear to be against you, you don't need to be in the business of trying to keep them from doing what they are doing.

Luke 9:62 But Jesus said to him, "No one, having put his hand to the plow, and looking back, is fit for the kingdom of God." When we choose to follow Christ, we don't need to be waiting to get earthly things done first. Following Him should be our priority, and we don't need to be looking back. We need to keep looking forward. Looking back would make it difficult to plow straight furloughs in the analogy. Unfortunately, even in churches, we can spend a lot of time looking backward instead of forward.

Luke 10:5 But whatever house you enter, first say, 'Peace to this house.' Here's a great scripture that comes with a blessing. When seventy were sent out two by two to various cities and places where Christ would go, He told them to say 'Peace to this house.' The blessing seemed to be that if peace did not rest on the house because there was no Son of peace in the house, it would rest on the two who pronounced the blessing. I assume that the "Son of peace" description could be substituted by a "daughter of peace" and have the same result. There was no downside to blessing the houses to which they were going. It was a win-win direction and prediction from Christ. These seventy that He appointed were also given directions and the power, in His name, to "**heal the sick there.**"

Luke 10:20 Nevertheless do not rejoice in this, that the spirits are subject to you, but rather rejoice because your names are written in heaven." Even after Christ gave the seventy authority not to be hurt by snakes or scorpions and power over the spirits, He warned them to keep focused on the heaven where their **names are written**. We need to keep ourselves from losing the proper focus also. Even when ministering the gospel, our pride can get in the way if we don't keep heavenly-minded. Also, note that this authority over spirits was granted to specific people (His immediate circle of disciples in this case), in specific circumstances. As previously reported, I am wary of modern-day self-proclaimed prophets who tell us they have this kind of authority. Also, note that the authority given to the eleven (Matthew 28:16-20) was not the most important issue. It seems that the more critical issue was that their names were **written in heaven**.

Luke 10:27 So he answered and said, " *You shall love the LORD your God with all your heart, with all your soul, with all your strength, and with all your mind,' and 'your neighbor as yourself.'"*

28 And He said to him, "You have answered rightly; do this and you will live." The statement originally comes from Deuteronomy 6:5. The faithful Jews of the time are reported to have recited this often. It summarizes the central ethical standard of the law. We know from other scripture regarding faith that Christ's statement here did not indicate that their works could save a person. He was more likely saying that if a person did all of the above, they would probably have had faith since their heart, soul, strength, and mind were all involved in their actions. He appears to be saying here that if we put our faith in Christ and follow Him, we will receive eternal rewards (Matthew 19:27-30).

Luke 11:4 And forgive us our sins,

For we also forgive everyone who is indebted to us. Here is a part of the model prayer Christ gave us that we can tend to forget or ignore. Some translations have wording to the effect that we should be forgiven as we forgive those who *sin* against us. Those who pray this prayer and don't forgive those who have sinned against them should not be surprised if their sins are not forgiven. In other words, we need to adopt the same standard that we expect others to follow. If mercy is sought from God, it must be given by us.

Luke 11:13 If you then, being evil, know how to give good gifts to your children, how much more will *your* heavenly Father give the Holy Spirit to those who ask Him!" Now, this is something we need: the Holy Spirit. We need to ask for the Holy Spirit in our lives. How do we know we have it since we can't see the Holy Spirit and cannot understand how something outside of our physical world and laws operates? We can look for what is called the "fruit of the Spirit" in ourselves and in others (Galatians 5:22,23) that is: **love, joy, peace, forbearance, kindness, goodness, faithfulness, gentleness and self-control.** It is not that hard to identify these character traits (and the opposite) in people.

Luke 11:17 But He, knowing their thoughts, said to them: "Every kingdom divided against itself is brought to desolation, and a house *divided* against a house falls. These are the famous words of Christ which he used to demonstrate that the attribution of His miracles to Satan was illogical. These are words that appear to be confirmed by history. In his famous "House Divided" speech, Abe Lincoln paraphrased these words.

Luke 11:23 He who is not with Me is against Me, and he who does not gather with Me scatters. These words of Christ demonstrate that there is no middle ground with Him. Others have also made a good case that logic does not allow a middle ground position concerning Christ. As C.S. Lewis demonstrated, either He is who He said He is, or you have to conclude He was a liar or mentally ill. Based on what He said about Himself, these are the only intellectually and logically valid conclusions. He said things like: "**He who has seen Me, has seen the Father**" (John 14:9). Some say that He was a great prophet and others say He was a great moral teacher. However, it is not very logical to classify Christ as either of these if, with His own words, He was lying about Himself. Thus, He gives us all an obvious choice concerning what to believe about Him. There is no other like Him. He is unique, and He says that He is *the* way to the Father (John 14:6). Note that He does not say He is one of many ways to God the Father. He says: "**No one comes to the father but through Me**" (John 14:6). He does not leave it to interpretation. He makes it undeniably clear. For the Christian, He closes the door with finality regarding other paths to God, such as good works, meditation, other religious leaders, pastors, gurus, or self-actualization.

(A personal note: In my early adulthood, I was a theist and did not like the abrupt way this passage's content was presented to me. I immediately rejected it. Therefore, I understand why many people have the same reaction I did. I was angry about it and rebelled against it. Still, my reasoning told me there had to be a god, and I keep searching. After searching through many avenues, I came to faith that Christ is who He says He is. In the Christian paradigm, salvation is a gift from Him. Now, I accept this belief. He paid the price to redeem us, and all we need to do is accept His gift and begin to follow Him (1 John 5:11-12)).

Luke 11:24 "When an unclean spirit goes out of a man, he goes through dry places, seeking rest; and finding none, he says, 'I will return to my house from which I came.' 25 And when he comes, he finds *it* swept and put in order. 26 Then he goes and takes with *him* seven other spirits more wicked than himself, and they enter and dwell there; and the last *state* of that man is worse than the first." The point here seems to be that when we remove evil from our lives, we need to replace it with good. Space is subject to being filled with something. If we are filled with something unclean that gets cleaned out, we need to continue filling that space with something clean. For example, we can replace evil thoughts of anger and rebellion with the good Word of God. If we don't fill the space with the Word of God, it is easy for evil thoughts to come back.

Jesus said to those Jews who believed Him, **"If you abide in My word, you are My disciples indeed. And you shall know the truth, and the truth shall make you free"** (John 8:31,32). I do not think we really understand exactly how spiritual forces work within us. However, this scripture gives us an indication of how we can conceptualize what happens if we don't get the Word of God into our hearts and minds through continual reading, studying, and meditating on it. Yes, meditation is part of the Christian life. However, this meditation does not focus on first emptying your mind as practiced in some types of meditation. The scripture advises us to meditate on the Word of God (Joshua 1:8). Thus, we are filling any space in our mind with something good that will lead to good thoughts and behaviors rather than to the lust of the flesh (1 John 2:16, James 1:14-15). When we experience God's forgiveness, we don't want to ignore His Word. We want to continue in it. **"But He said, 'More than that, blessed are those who hear the word of God and keep it!'"** (11:28)

Luke 11:34 The lamp of the body is the eye. Therefore, when your eye is good, your whole body also is full of light. But when *your eye* is bad, your body also *is* full of darkness. We need to be very careful about what we allow to get into our minds through our eyes. King David, in Psalm 101:3, put it this way: **"I will put nothing wicked before my eyes."** Through first-hand experience, David knew how allowing himself to look and then lust led to sin. I take this to mean that we need to focus on what is good, the Word of God rather than the false teaching of the world. Other beliefs often come down to a works orientation toward salvation or the thought that you can be or become your own god. The idea is that you can earn your way into heaven through something you do or how good you are (works). We don't need to delve a lot into these systems to know the basic ideas since they are pointed out in many scriptures in the Bible (Ephesians 2:6-9; Romans 11:6; Romans 3:20-30; et al.).

I am not saying we should ignore other beliefs, but we should spend the bulk of our time knowing what the Bible says if we are Christians. Works-based systems can be tempting to our flesh/pride, which wants to buy into some kind of works-based salvation to take pride in what *we* have accomplished. This is not what the Bible says we should be doing. By the way, Christianity is unique in this concept of salvation through grace as a gift. From what I know, other religions are works-based in one way or another. By "works-based," I mean that you have to earn your salvation in some way by what *you* do. Why not take the gift? To balance this out, if you take the gift, the evidence that you have done so will be your behavior/works. But you did not earn your salvation through these efforts. These efforts are the result of receiving the gift of salvation.

So, what about the Ten Commandments? The commandments were given for the people's well-being because they are good for us to the extent that we follow them, but no man can be saved by keeping them (Galatians 3:24). They show us that we cannot save ourselves by following them (Galatians 2:16). As it says in Galatians 3:24, **"The law has become our tutor to lead us to Christ, so that we may be justified by faith."** In other words, the purpose of the commandments is to teach us how much we need the forgiveness that Jesus Christ offers.

Luke 11:42 "But woe to you Pharisees! For you tithe mint and rue and all manner of herbs, and pass by justice and the love of God. These you ought to have done, without leaving the others undone. Christ had just told the Pharisees that they made the outside of the cup clean, but the inward part was full of greed and wickedness. They reportedly tithed down to the smallest item but neglected love and justice (Micah 6.8; Zechariah 7:8-10).

Luke 12:2 For there is nothing covered that will not be revealed, nor hidden that will not be known. Here's a warning that should make us stop and think before practicing any hypocrisy. When we think we are fooling someone, we need to remember that any lies or deception will eventually be disclosed; both the good and the bad. Eventually, all the things we whispered into someone's ear in a private room will be "**proclaimed on the housetops.**" That will be a very embarrassing time for anyone prone to gossiping and anyone who said terrible things about others that were not true. It will also be bad for any lawyers who prevented others from drawing near to God by telling them they must bear many burdens and hindering them from gaining the key of knowledge (the knowledge of the Messiah).

Luke 12:7 But the very hairs of your head are all numbered. Do not fear therefore; you are of more value than many sparrows. Here again, we are told not to fear because we are valuable to the Lord, and He knows all about us, even how many hairs are on our heads. As noted in other sections of this commentary, the type of fear we should have for the LORD is reverential awe and respect because He cares about each one of us. Even though God is the one **who is able to destroy both soul and body in hell** (Matthew 10:28), He is also the one who can provide us with eternal life. While on earth, we will be persecuted (2 Corinthians 4:9) but need to be more concerned about eternity than with this short lifespan on earth.

Luke 12:11,12 "Now when they bring you to the synagogues and magistrates and authorities, do not worry about how or what you should answer, or what you should say. 12 For the Holy Spirit will teach you in that very hour what you ought to say." This is another case of being encouraged to be filled with and listening to the Holy Spirit. Luke refers to being controlled by the Holy Spirit as being "filled with the Holy Spirit." At least ten times, Luke refers to the Holy Spirit. In the book of Acts, the disciples waited for the Holy Spirit's empowering on the Day of Pentecost. Before this event, the Holy Spirit was working in the lives of those connected with Jesus, John the Baptist, Mary, Elizabeth, and Simeon. Even Christ is said to be filled with the power of the Holy Spirit (Luke 4:1-13). The Old Testament prophets spoke of One who the Spirit of God would empower.

It appears that the ministry of the Holy Spirit is widespread and generally centers on Christ. The takeaway seems to be that it is good to be filled with the Spirit. How do we know if we are? The scripture tells us this too. When our actions produce what the scripture calls the fruit of the Spirit, this is a good indication that we might be filled with the Spirit (Galatians 5:22,23). When our actions and words lead to the opposite of the fruit of the Spirit (Galatians 5:19-21), that would be a good indication that we are not filled with the Spirit. For example: if someone is involved in ongoing adultery, sorcery, hatred, wrath, murder, drunkenness, and the like, they are probably not under the influence of the Holy Spirit. Interestingly, a lot of these activities that are not influenced by the Holy Spirit often involve excess liquid "spirits" of a different type (i.e., alcohol).

Luke 12:15 And He said to them, "Take heed and beware of covetousness, for one's life does not consist in the abundance of the things he possesses." They asked Christ to be a judge over an inheritance dispute between two brothers. He refused and used the event as an opportunity to teach them about an inheritance that is far more important. The conclusion is that we are to be "rich toward God" rather than concerned about storing up treasures here on earth since we do not know how long we will live. We might spend all our time building bigger barns to store our earthly treasures and then die. Then all that we have worked for will go to someone else. On the other hand, if we store our treasures in heaven through following and obeying Christ, we will enjoy the fruits of our efforts for eternity.

The things we control here on earth do not belong to us anyway. The Lord owns the earth and everything that is on it. He made it. We are just temporary stewards. Things on earth are all temporary and ultimately worthless. In other words, we are advised not to focus solely on ourselves and what earthly riches can buy. We do not get to take it with us on the day we die, and we become immediately poor but spiritually rich. "**But seek the kingdom of God, and all these things shall be added to you**" (12:31). So, do not worry. Worry is useless and appears to show a lack of faith in God's plan for our lives. We do not need to worry about getting the best possessions on this earth ship that will be destroyed. We are better served by keeping our hearts focused on heaven and storing treasures there.

Luke 12:51 Do *you* suppose that I came to give peace on earth? I tell you, not at all, but rather division. This is something we need to understand. Christ will separate the wheat from the chaff (Luke 3:17); believers from unbelievers. Now, He brings division between believers and unbelievers. It does not take much investigation to find the unbelievers' animosity, and sometimes hatred, toward believers. And unfortunately, some people who call themselves Christians seem to reciprocate this animosity contrary to instructions in the Bible that we should do good to those who hate us (Luke 6:27). To those who respond to God, He brings peace (see 2:13; 7:50; 8:48; 10:5; Acts 10:36; Ephesians 2:13-17). Thus, He brings division and peace at the same time.

Luke 12:58 When you go with your adversary to the magistrate, make every effort along the way to settle with him, lest he drag you to the judge, the judge deliver you to the officer, and the officer throw you into prison. This is good advice. Unfortunately, we can let our flesh get in the way of following this advice due to our emotions and pride. In the same way, we need to become reconciled to God before we get to the judgment. There is a saying about making peace with God. That is what we need to do, and it is not hard. It merely involves recognizing Him for who He is and accepting the gift of salvation. It's as easy as that. Then, once we are justified, we can begin to follow and obey Him and continue in the process of sanctification.

Luke 13:5 I tell you, no; but unless you repent you will all likewise perish." This response to a situation where some Galileans were killed and Christ asked the people there if they thought those killed were worse sinners than other Galileans. Apparently, the way they were allowed to die here on earth had nothing to do with their sins. The takeaway from this part of scripture seems to be that the important thing is whether we have repented of our sins before we die, not the level or type of our sins. All sin leads to death and separation from God unless we repent and accept the gift of salvation through our belief that Christ came, paid the price for our sins, and rose from the dead, conquering death (2 Timothy 1:10, 1 Corinthians 15:54, John 3:16, etc.). Put another way; we do not want to die outside of God's grace.

Luke 13:23 Then one said to Him, "Lord, are there few who are saved?"

And He said to them, 24 "Strive to enter through the narrow gate, for many, I say to you, will seek to enter and will not be able. One of the ideas here seems to be that we do not set the parameters for salvation; God does. It is not a situation where we get to choose any number of people to pay the price for our sins or decide that we can earn our way to heaven through our efforts or some other works-based system. God sets the parameters, and He chose to have Christ pay the price for our sins. All we have to do is accept a gift, lest any man should boast of how they saved themselves (Ephesians 2:8-9). None of us can save ourselves. But God can save any of us and wants to. However, he will not force us to accept His gift. God provides us the free will to choose.

Jesus explains that knowing His actions, sitting down to a meal with Him, or listening to His message is different from Him knowing you. He needs to know you, or you will not be able to enter the gates of heaven. You will be outside and even be able to see the prophets inside but will not pass through the gates. He apparently will only own us as His if we accept the forgiveness of sin and salvation He freely offers. It does not appear that God, who is Holy, Holy, Holy, will adopt someone into His family against their will. Those who are not forgiven in a way that allows them to enter heaven and be in His presence cannot go there. This makes sense as it appears that unforgiven sinners (i.e., people referred to as **the workers of iniquity**) are prohibited from entering through the gates of heaven and being there with God. As unforgiven sinners, maybe they could not survive being in the intensely Holy light of His presence anyway.

The Lord at the door appears to be Jesus (v. 26). We have to come to God on His terms, not on ours. Also, there may be many surprises in heaven. Some who are despised on earth may be in heaven, and some honored on earth may not be there. It all depends on whether a person has accepted Christ's atonement for their sins or not. No one is forced to accept the forgiveness of Christ, and therefore, no one will be in heaven who has not chosen to go there. I have one rare point of disagreement with C.S. Lewis's statement that "All that are in hell choose it" (The Great Divorce 1945). Yes, those who are there will have chosen sin and rejected God. There are always consequences to unforgiven sin, but I do not think many fully believe they will ever receive the consequences. Unfortunately, God eventually judges, passes sentences, and throws people into the lake of fire (Revelation 20:15; Mark 9:27; Matthew 13:42;25:30).

Luke 14:2 And behold, there was a certain man before Him who had dropsy. 3 And Jesus, answering, spoke to the lawyers and Pharisees, saying, "Is it lawful to heal on the Sabbath?" Here, Christ lets the people know that God never intended for the Sabbath to be observed in such a legalistic manner that good could not be done on it. Thus, he reveals the hypocrisy of the rabbis' with an example of an ox falling into a pit. They would allow the owner to get the ox out of the pit but wanted to prohibit Jesus from rescuing a human being. They had misinterpreted perfect obedience to their additions to the law demonstrating love for God when it had become a prideful digression from an attitude of submission to the Lord. They were trying in vain to earn salvation through their work, which is not possible (Galatians 2:16).

Luke 14:11 For whoever exalts himself will be humbled, and he who humbles himself will be exalted." Just before making this statement, Christ advises people who are invited to a wedding feast not to sit down in the best place, lest one more honorable comes, and you are asked to give up your place for them. Then He tells them that whoever exalts himself will be humbled and the converse that whoever humbles himself will be exalted. Then later in this same section of scripture, He says to invite the poor, the maimed, the lame, and the blind when you have a feast and says you will be blessed if you do so.

Luke 14:33 So likewise, whoever of you does not forsake all that he has cannot be My disciple. This is clear. We should not decide to follow Christ lightly. There is a cost here on earth. Repayment comes at the resurrection of the just. When we decide to follow Christ, we need to be willing to forsake everything else. In other words, we need to be willing to give Christ first place even concerning family members or our own life and all our possessions.

Luke 15:7 I say to you that likewise there will be more joy in heaven over one sinner who repents than over ninety-nine just persons

who need no repentance. Who are the people who think they need no repentance? It appears to be a way of describing the Scribes and Pharisees. Apparently, they did not believe they needed to repent because they were not lost. They did not understand the great holiness of God, and they greatly inflated their opinion of themselves to the point that they thought they could achieve their own salvation through their self-imposed righteousness. In comparison to the righteousness of the Lord, their deeds could be compared to filthy rags, according to the scripture (Isaiah 64:6).

Luke 15:31 "And he said to him, 'Son, you are always with me, and all that I have is yours. 32 It was right that we should make merry and be glad, for your brother was dead and is alive again, and was lost and is found.'" Here, after the story known as the Prodigal son's story. The father tells the son who had stayed home why he forgave the Prodigal son and rejoiced that he had returned even after all that he had done. This is an example of how our Father in Heaven treats repentant sinners when they return to him. This seems to be the more important aspect of this story. The Father is full of grace. He gives us what we don't deserve. All we have to do is repent and humbly return to His care. He is ready to forgive based on what He has done for us, not what we have done for Him.

Not only did the Father in this story accept his wayward son, but he also ran to him and kissed him, illustrating his immediate acceptance, just like our Father in heaven accepts a sinner who turns to Him. This parable also shows how God allows people to go their own way. At this time in history, He invites everyone, but He is not forcing anyone to follow Him. We need to realize that we bring nothing to Him that He needs, and we don't deserve anything from Him. We must rely entirely on His mercy and grace.

Luke 15:32 It was right that we should make merry and be glad,

for your brother was dead and is alive again, and was lost and is found.'" This appears to be the inspiration for the Amazing Grace song lyrics: "I was lost, but now I'm found." When the lost person is found, it is a reason to celebrate. When a sinner repents and turns to his heavenly Father, it is a reason to celebrate.

Luke 16:13 "No servant can serve two masters; for either he will hate the one and love the other, or else he will be loyal to the one and despise the other. You cannot serve God and mammon." This scripture comes from the Parable of the Unjust Steward. The parable demonstrates that a person who cannot handle money cannot handle spiritual matters either. The parable also indicates that small examples of selfishness lead to larger examples; conversely, small examples of generosity can also lead to larger examples.

Luke 16:16 "The law and the prophets *were* until John. Since that time the kingdom of God has been preached, and everyone is pressing into it..." The goal of the law was reached when John came. First, there was a time of promise. "Now the promise of God's Kingdom is preached" (The Nelson Study Bible, pg. 1731). The new era came in, and all are urged to come into it.

Luke 16:25 But Abraham said, 'Son, remember that in your lifetime you received your good things, and likewise Lazarus evil things; but now he is comforted, and you are tormented. Here is hope for any believer in Christ who does not receive good things in life here on earth. At the time of our death on earth, we know our fate. The souls of the unrighteous dead appear to be gathered in Hades. The standard of how we treat others may be applied to us in this place. If we lacked compassion in this life, we might not receive compassion in the afterlife. Once we have died in this sphere in an unrighteous state, it does not appear to be possible for us to enter into the sphere of the righteous (Nelson's Study Bible 1731), nor is it possible for the righteous to then enter the sphere of unrighteousness.

Luke 16:31 But he said to him, 'If they do not hear Moses and the prophets, neither will they be persuaded though one rise from the dead.'" This is a true statement. Many who did not listen to Moses and many people were not persuaded when Christ rose from the dead.

Luke 17:3 Take heed to yourselves. If your brother sins against you, rebuke him; and if he repents, forgive him. What if your brother is also a person who has authority over you? What should you do in this case? Paul was in this type of situation and apologized for criticizing the ruler, citing Old Testament scripture (Exodus 22:28; Acts 23:5). Thus, though we sometimes are aware of a ruler's sins, it can be challenging to deal with this type of situation. When are Christians to disobey a ruler? Answer: when the ruler demands us to disobey God. For example, in Acts 5:29, we see: **"Then Peter and the other apostles answered and said, we ought to obey God rather than men."** They said this in response to being questioned about why they had disobeyed the ruling authority. Thus, I understand that we are to obey the ruling or governing authorities' laws unless they direct us to do something against God's law.

Luke 17:20 Now when He was asked by the Pharisees when the kingdom of God would come, He answered them and said, "The kingdom of God does not come with observation; 21 nor will they say, 'See here!' or 'See there!' For indeed, the kingdom of God is within you." This is very interesting. The kingdom of God is within us. This can be interpreted to mean that the Holy Spirit is in his children, the ones who have received Christ as their savior. He and His kingdom are within us. Christ left us the Comforter (the Holy Spirit) to be in us until His glorious return to rule on earth. In His day, His coming will be unmistakable. It is compared to lightning flashing from one part to another part under heaven. We don't need to follow people who tell us to be looking here or there for Christ. His second coming will be dramatic and unmistakable (17:22-24). (Check Romans 14:17, 1 Corinthians 4:20)

Luke 17:33 Whoever seeks to save his life will lose it, and whoever loses his life will preserve it. Those who invest their lives in advancing Christ's kingdom while they are on the earth will often experience difficulties and suffering, just as Christ did when He was on the earth. Some will even suffer death for their faith. However, when Christ comes to reign on the earth, they will receive great privilege, responsibility, and glory (Revelation 5:10; Matthew 20; 2 Peter 3:9). Some will be taken, and some will be left on His day. "Each person stands before God alone" (the Nelson Study Bible p. 1734). Now, we can have the kingdom of God within us. At His second coming, He will take over the earth and vanquish all rival kingdoms, and His Kingdom will be within us and outside of us.

Luke 18:9 Also He spoke this parable to some who trusted in themselves that they were righteous, and despised others: ...14 I tell you, this man went down to his house justified *rather* than the other; for everyone who exalts himself will be humbled, and he who humbles himself will be exalted." This scripture is from the Parable of the Pharisee and the Tax Collector. It makes a point very clear. Those who exalt themselves and judge others will be humbled (1:52, 14;11). Only God's mercy and grace can deliver us, not any works that we do. Thus, we have no justification or reason to exalt ourselves. We can all probably think of examples of people, even leaders in the church, who have exalted themselves and been humbled.

Luke 18:26 And those who heard it said, "Who then can be saved?" 27 But He said, "The things which are impossible with men are possible with God." This question and answer were concerning a statement from Christ about how difficult it was for a rich man to be saved and enter the kingdom of God. Unfortunately for a rich person, it is much easier for them to trust what they have than trust in God. It is hard to turn from wealth to a life of faith. However, in the next chapter of this book, Christ provides an example of a rich tax collector. Zacchaeus finds salvation through his faith in Christ and putting Christ first rather than his riches. Christ said that He came to "seek and save that which is lost." Thus, a rich man can be saved, not through his efforts or works but in the same way everyone else can be saved; through Christ by the grace of God (see John 3:3). This salvation can be referred to as being born of the Spirit.

Luke 18:42 Then Jesus said to him, "Receive your sight; your faith has made you well." This blind man could see who Jesus was more clearly than the sighted people around him. He cried out for mercy from Christ. This demonstrated his faith that Christ had the power to heal him. The healing led to praise from the blind man and others who saw what had happened.

Luke 19:26 'For I say to you, that to everyone who has will be given; and from him who does not have, even what he has will be taken away from him. This statement from Christ demonstrates that unfaithfulness leads to a loss of reward (see Revelation 3:11). The Minas parable also demonstrates that we are expected to do something with what God has given us. Our abilities and talents need to be used to multiply the gospel even if in a small way. Using our skills in this way is similar to putting money entrusted to your care in an interest-bearing account. The bank gains from loaning the money out, but there is also interest in the money earned for the one who entrusted you with overseeing their money.

Lending our talents and skills to your church is one way we can leverage what we have been given and be a part of something bigger than ourselves. This honors our Father in heaven, who gave us our abilities. Thus, it makes sense to use some of what He has given us to honor Him.

According to the Urban Institute, religious organizations in America received about 11.68 billion dollars in donations in 2014, so many Americans give generously to their religious institutions. Other research indicates that about 17 percent of Christians tithe 10 percent or more of their income. Muslims and Jews also give generously to their mosques and temples.

Luke 19:37 Then, as He was now drawing near the descent of the Mount of Olives, the whole multitude of the disciples began to rejoice and praise God with a loud voice for all the mighty works they had seen, 38 saying:

 " 'Blessed *is* the King who comes in the name of the Lord!'
Peace in heaven and glory in the highest!" By this time, the disciples knew Jesus was the Messiah and recited a section of Psalms 118:26 with a slight change in wording. Instead of saying "Blessed is He," they sang, "Blessed is the King." They now recognized that Christ was the promised King. They also seemed to recognize that Christ came to bring peace between man and God, which is implied by the second line. When the Pharisees called on Christ to rebuke His disciples for implying that He was the King, Christ pointed out to them that if they kept silent, **"the stones would immediately cry out."** That is an amazing statement. We can't understand a lot about the universe and if this was a figure of speech or if the stones would cry out. Whatever the interpretation, He appeared to be pointing out that the people were correct to refer to Him as the King. Thus, even though He humbled Himself while He was here on earth, He accepted the exaltation that was His due.

Luke 19:45 Then He went into the temple and began to drive out those who bought and sold in it, 46 saying to them, "It is written, 'My house is a house of prayer,' but you have made it a 'den of thieves.'" So here we have a scripture that could be one of the most misapplied in the Bible to justify anger. Numerous verses speak of the dangers of being angry (Psalm 37:8; Romans 12:19; Hebrews 10:30; Colossians 3:8;

Ecclesiastes 7:9; Colossians 3:21; 1 Timothy 3:2-3; Ephesians 4:26; James 1:26; James 1:19; Matthew 5:22; 2 Timothy 2:14; James 4:11; 2 Timothy 2:14; James 1:20; Titus 3:9; Matthew 5:22; Ephesians 4:31-32; Titus 3:2; James 1:26; James 4:11). But, here we see that Christ did get angry about this situation. We need to realize that His anger was justified where ours is usually not. John also records a temple cleaning which may not have been the same event that Luke is reporting here.

Christ was not happy with having the house of prayer/worship become a site for taking economic advantage of people. We should not take this as an excuse for our anger, which is generally not the result of some abuse of God's Holy place but rather our petty, selfish desire to have things our way rather than how things are. Unfortunately, most of our anger is not about situations where there is idolatry or irreverence for that which is holy, but rather because we are not getting what we want when we want it.

In other words, our anger usually has to do selfish desire to have things our way or in our time. Our excuses for anger are not usually righteous. From this scripture and others, we know that there is righteous and unrighteous anger and that we need to avoid the unrighteous type. The number of scriptures urging us not to let our anger get the best of us far outweigh the couple of examples we are given of righteous anger. Additionally, we are not to miss-characterize our anger as coming from God.

Luke 20:13"Then the owner of the vineyard said, 'What shall I do? I will send my beloved son. Probably they will respect *him* when they see him.' This statement comes from the parable of the Wicked Vinedressers. It explains how God feels about those who killed His son and those who reject His message. It's not a pretty picture for those people. The Vinedressers conspired to kill the Vineyard owner's son so that they could take the vineyard for themselves. This is what men tried to do with the killing of Christ. They were trying to take His world for themselves, but He rose from the dead and spoiled their plan.

Luke 20:25 And He said to them, "Render therefore to Caesar the things that are Caesar's, and to God the things that are God's." Here is an important scripture that applies to many situations where Christians sometimes get off track. The basic principle captured in this statement seems to be that believing in God does not let the believer off the hook for following their government's rules if those rules are not contrary to God's. It appears that Caesar, as the ruler, had the right to collect taxes. At the same time, He makes the point that God should be honored above a ruler. In Romans 13:1-7, we learn that we are to follow our government and God simultaneously. Thus, the only time when we might have a problem is when there is a specific conflict between what the two authorities direct us to do, at which point, the higher of the two authorities (God) should be followed.

Luke 20:34 Jesus answered and said to them, "The sons of this age marry and are given in marriage. 35 But those who are counted worthy to attain that age, and the resurrection from the dead, neither marry nor are given in marriage; 36 nor can they die anymore, for they are equal to the angels and are sons of God, being sons of the resurrection. There is no marriage nor death in the resurrection age. This scripture indicates that those who are counted worthy to attain that age (i.e., go to heaven) will be sons of God like the angels. How can we "be counted worthy?" According to scripture, it appears we can only be counted worthy by receiving God's gracious forgiveness. We receive that forgiveness through faith that Christ paid the price for our sins. Those who believed in Old Testament times had faith in what God would do for them through Christ, and we have faith in what God did for us in the past through Christ. Salvation has always been, by grace through faith (Romans 4:3). We cannot, through our work, save ourselves.

Luke 21:6 "These things which you see—the days will come in which not *one* stone shall be left upon another that shall not be thrown down." Here Christ predicts the destruction of the temple. This prediction was fulfilled in A.D. 70. This place of worship was temporary, just as other places of worship will be in the last days.

Luke 21:9 But when you hear of wars and commotions, do not be terrified; for these things must come to pass first, but the end *will* not *come* immediately." Scripture lets us know that there will be counterfeits who come and say they are Christ but who are not. When Christ comes back in the clouds, everyone will know it for sure (Mark 13:26; Matthew 24:27).

Luke 21:12 But before all these things, they will lay their hands on you and persecute *you*, delivering *you* up to the synagogues and prisons. You will be brought before kings and rulers for My name's sake. 13 But it will turn out for you as an occasion for testimony. Here is the reason for some of the persecution the disciples of Christ faced. At times this persecution would result in an occasion for testimony. And when the time came to testify, Christ Himself said that He would supply the words which their adversaries would not be able to contradict or resist. This section of scripture warns the disciples that they may even be betrayed by parents and brothers, relatives and friends, and some would be put to death for what they believed. Matthew 5:10-12 calls those who endure suffering blessed. The last sentence in this paragraph of scripture says: "B**y your patience possess your souls**." That is interesting statement and seems to imply that they would get to keep possession of their souls through their steadfast faith. Some of this instruction to the disciples may also apply to us in the times we live.

Luke 21:20 "But when you see Jerusalem surrounded by armies, then know that its desolation is near. We know that Jerusalem was destroyed in A.D. 70 by the Romans, but it will be destroyed again.

Luke 21:27 Then they will see the Son of Man coming in a cloud with power and great glory. When Christ comes the second time to earth, He will come in a cloud in power and glory. Everyone will see who He is. This will be a glorious day (Matthew 24:27).

Luke 21:36 Watch therefore, and pray always that you may be counted worthy to escape all these things that will come to pass, and to stand before the Son of Man." Christ says not to let your hearts be weighed down with carousing, drunkenness, and the cares of this life. If you do, that Day could come upon you unexpectedly. That Day is the Day of Jesus' return. We need to be looking for that Day all the time, even though it may not come in our lifetime here on earth. We should still live as if it is imminent (Nelson's Study Bible p. 1743).

How would it be if you were drunk when the Lord returned or involved in some other kind of sin. We need to keep an eternal focus. What do our cares on this earth matter in comparison to eternity? Our whole life here is but a brief spec of time, if that, in contrast to eternity. How can we be counted worthy to escape the bad things that are coming to pass here? We can accept the forgiveness of our sins that Christ offers us. He took on the punishment for our sins on Himself on our behalf through His death on the cross. It *is* that simple. Forgiveness is a gift from God. It is not something we can earn. It is humbly accepting this gift based on God's grace.

Luke 22:3 Then Satan entered Judas, surnamed Iscariot, who was numbered among the twelve. The name Satan means the adversary. The fact that Satan is said to enter Judas shows us that these events were part of cosmic forces at work against the work of Christ. We are not told exactly how Satan enters a person. However, we know that the Holy Spirit enters believers when saved (1 Corinthians 12:13; Romans 8:9; Ephesians 1:12-14). This happens when we believe, and there appears to be an ongoing filling process. Scripture talks about being "in" Christ

(Colossians 2:10; Galatians 3:27; 1 Corinthians 6:19) or "united" with Him (1 Corinthians 6:17).

Sometimes I think about our life as being in a bubble with the Holy Spirit all around us, and when we come to faith, our little bubble becomes permeable, and we are then in the Spirit, or the Spirit is in us (Ephesians 5:18; Exodus 31:3). When we sin after we become believers, the bubble becomes less permeable again, removing some of the Spirit, and when we confess, the bubble becomes permeable again. It is like the Holy Spirit always surrounds us, but we are not always fully permeated.

In other words, we can put up barriers to being filled by the Spirit. The barrier that can surround us is analogous to a lead balloon, and the Spirit is like an x-ray. When the lead balloon is all around us, the x-ray does not penetrate completely. When the lead balloon is removed, the ex-ray can see all through us and in us even though we can't see it. We know from this scripture and others that spirits can come into a person or an animal and have a negative or a positive effect.

How do we tell which spirit is in control? We can look at the fruit. Scripture tells us what the fruit of the Holy Spirit is, and we can surmise that the fruit of Satan's demons is somewhat the opposite. So, the good fruit (Galatians 5:22-23) is love, peace, patience, kindness, goodness, faithfulness, gentleness, and self-control. The opposites could be anger/hate, uproar, impatience, cruelty/meanness, evil/wickedness, dishonesty, cruelty/harshness, or lack of self-control. Can anger ever be considered good fruit? Yes, but in limited circumstances that are generally beyond our capabilities. Yes, Christ appeared angry when He drove the moneychangers out of the temple. That would be an example of righteous anger. However, even in that situation, it was probably not the kind of hatred or self-fulfillment that characterizes unrighteous anger that we might have.

Luke 22:20 Likewise He also *took* the cup after supper, saying, "This cup *is* the new covenant in My blood, which is shed for you. This is where Christ tells His disciples and all of us about the new covenant for those who respond (Hebrews 8:8, 13; 9:11-28), whereby he pays the price for our sins so that we can have direct fellowship with Him. This is the substitutionary image of Christ dying in our place on the cross for our sins (Acts 20:28).

Luke 22:26 But not so *among* you; on the contrary, he who is greatest among you, let him be as the younger, and he who governs as he who serves. Here Christ talks about the concept of servant leadership that He so convincingly displayed through His example to us of serving. This is the opposite of the traditional worldview of leadership which involves a leader lording it over their subjects.

Luke 22:43 Then an angel appeared to Him from heaven, strengthening Him. Sometimes God removes difficulties before us. Other times, He strengthens us to get through these difficulties. Christ was strengthened by an angel but still had to go to the cross to facilitate our salvation. Christ prayed for this cup to be removed if possible. However, that was not possible in God's plan, so the answer to this prayer was "no." Note that Christ also prayed for the will of the Lord to be done, and that is what was done. That prayer was answered "yes."

Luke 22:65 And many other things they blasphemously spoke against Him. Just as they spoke against Christ and made accusations about Him, people still talk against Christians and make accusations against them. Unfortunately, some of the charges against Christians, no matter how high their status, are true even though they were not true about Christ. True Christians are forgiven but still subject to failures/sin (Romans 3:10; Romans 3:23).

**Luke 23:18 And they all cried out at once, saying, "Away with this

Man, and release to us Barabbas"— 19 who had been thrown into prison for a certain rebellion made in the city, and for murder. Interestingly, Christ was substituted for Barabbas just as He substituted for all of us. As with Barabbas, we are also worthy of death for our sins against our Creator, who is holy, holy, holy. Realizing this can be the first step toward repentance and belief in Christ.

Luke 23:41 And we indeed justly, for we receive the due reward of our deeds; but this Man has done nothing wrong." 42 Then he said to Jesus, "Lord, remember me when You come into Your kingdom." 43 And Jesus said to him, "Assuredly, I say to you, today you will be with Me in Paradise." There are a few crucial truths in these verses. First, the thief who said these words was perceptive in speaking the truth about Christ that He had done nothing wrong. Second, the thief recognized and believed in Christ. Third, the thief didn't have time to get baptized. Fourth, Christ told the thief he would see Him in Paradise that day. Note that the thief didn't have any time to earn his way into heaven. He wasn't even able to be baptized, but he was still going to Paradise that very day.

This situation demonstrates that it only takes faith and God's grace for someone to be saved and go to heaven. There is nothing we have to do other than receive the gift of salvation through faith. Of course, a change of heart like this will result in a change of behavior and attitude. Yes, according to my understanding of the scriptures, that is all there is to it.

Luke 24:38 And He said to them, "Why are you troubled? And why do doubts arise in your hearts? 39 Behold My hands and My feet, that it is I Myself. Handle Me and see, for a spirit does not have flesh and bones as you see I have." After Christ rose from the dead, he had a body that was more than only spirit. He had flesh and bones, and he ate some broiled fish and honeycomb, confirming the physical nature of His resurrected body. The disciples could touch Him at this point. Christ made it clear that He had been raised bodily and was not a hallucination or only spirit. He had a body that looked similar with the difference being that His raised body was spirit but also solid and not corruptible or subject to death (1 Cor. 15:35-58). How could this be? We don't know.

Luke 24:44 Then He said to them, "These *are* the words which I spoke to you while I was still with you, that all things must be fulfilled which were written in the Law of Moses and *the* Prophets and *the* Psalms concerning Me." 45 And He opened their understanding, that they might comprehend the Scriptures. Now we know how God's plan fits together. The Law of Moses, the Prophets, and the Psalms all point to Christ. The patriarchs and saints of the Old Testament were saved through their faith in God. It appears that when they believed God, it was accounted to them for righteousness (Galatians 3:6, 3:14; Romans 3:30). As Christ was to pay the price for their sins after they walked on the earth, He paid the price for our sins before we walked on the earth. For God's chosen people, the Israelites were imputed righteousness through their faith looking forward. For present-day gentiles and messianic Jews, righteousness is imputed through faith, looking back. What a great God!

Luke 24:46 Then He said to them, "Thus it is written, and thus it was necessary for the Christ to suffer and to rise from the dead the third day, 47 and that repentance and remission of sins should be preached in His name to all nations, beginning at Jerusalem. The Lord graciously offers remission of sins for all who repent and believe (Acts 2:38; 10:43). People of all countries are asked to turn from their selfish ways and follow Christ. Christ suffered and rose from the dead fulfilling two parts of God's plan as predicted in Psalms 22 and 118:22. Note that the offer of salvation (remission of sins) is now to everyone who will receive it; Jews and gentiles (everyone other than Jews).

Interestingly, Christ told the disciples to tarry in Jerusalem until they were endued with power from on high. On the day of Pentecost, they received the power of the Holy Spirit and were able to go out and spread the gospel. I know that God is omniscient, omnipresent, righteous, and just. Thus, He is fair, and He created all people, so He can do whatever He wants with us, and we have no business trying to judge whatever He does. He is the potter; we are the clay (Isaiah 64:8).

43

John

⁴³JOHN - Introduction: The book of John is significant and could be recommended as the first book of the Bible that you read because it contains the key to eternal life (20:31).

John 1:1-3 In the beginning, was the Word, and the Word was with God, and the Word was God. 2 He was with God in the beginning. 3 Through him all things were made; without him nothing was made that has been made. This scripture starts a little like Genesis. It makes it abundantly clear that the Word (Christ; John 1:14) is God. He is not *a* god or *a* prophet or just *a* great teacher. He and God are one and the same. It is also made clear that He is the one who made everything in our universe. We probably will not completely understand how the Father, Son, and Holy Spirit can be one and the same until we get to heaven and better understand the spiritual. However, that is what the scripture says. There are three in one, and it has always been that way.

Apparently, being face-to-face was important for people of equal stature

---

[43] NSB quotations are from the Nelsons Study Bible, copyright (c) 1997 by Thomas Nelson, Inc., Nashville, TN; used by permission; scripture taken from the New King James Version, Copyright (c) 1979, 1980, 1982 used by permission. All rights reserved.

in the ancient world. In this scripture, John uses the Word to refer to Jesus Christ. Thus, in the spiritual realm, Christ can be with God and be God simultaneously. In the physical domain of our bodies, it is hard to grasp this kind of concept. How oxygen interacts with other elements might give a little understanding. Oxygen, when combined with Hydrogen, is water. When mixed with other molecules, we call it air. I don't think there is a good explanation for the spiritual realm in the physical world. However, some aspects of the physical world may give us a glimmer of the spiritual. For example, we know that x-rays can go right through our physical bodies. Similarly, the Holy Spirit can indwell our physical bodies.

These are crude examples but offer some rudimentary idea of how even something in the natural world can be with and in something else or someone. We can't understand it, but it appears that Christ, the Holy Spirit, and God have always existed. None were created, and God, the Father, created the world (Genesis 1:1) through God the Son (Colossians 1:16; Hebrews 1:2; NSB). Also, note that life was not created. It always existed in Christ (5:26; 6:57; 10:10; 11:25; 14:6; 17:3; 20:31). Our life comes from God. It was breathed into us (Genesis 2:7).

John 1:4 In Him was life, and the life was the light of men. This verse clarifies that we are utterly and completely dependent on God for our very life. Without Him, we would not have life. It's that simple. We depend on God not only for our physical life but also for our spiritual life. In contrast, Christ always had life. The scripture does not say that life was created. In other words, Christ does not depend on life being given to Him. In the words of scripture, "**In Him was life.**" We don't create our own life. It comes from Him and exists in Him (5:26; 6:57; 10:10; 11:25; 14:6; 17:3; 20:31). He is our light. If we did not have His life-giving light, we would be in darkness and death. We would just be some water and some common matter that decays rather quickly without the life and light that God supplies. As stated in the Nelson Study Bible, "As the creation of light was the beginning of the original creation (Genesis 1:3), so when believers receive the light, they become part of the new creation (2 Corinthians 4:3-6)".

It is also interesting to note that the light from Christ exposes both sin and God to us (see Psalms 36:9). The life, which comes from Christ, is the light we have. Somehow, the life that we enjoy comes from Christ. In John 8:12, Christ says that "**I am the light of the world**." I take this to mean that the life in the world comes from Him and is part of Him. In John 12:36, Christ goes on to say: "**While you have the light, believe in the light, that you may become sons of light**." Christ appears to be using "light" as interchangeable with Himself. We know from other scripture that He is the light (1:4; 8:12; 9:5). That makes sense because, without His light, there would be no life in the world.

This is a simple but difficult to comprehend concept in the Bible. If we grasp the meaning and believe it, it changes how we view everything. We become a new creation when we receive His light (2 Corinthians 4:3-6). We are new. Many people do not acknowledge that they are dependent on God for the very life they have been granted. It's like a child saying to his biological father: "you are not my father." No matter how many times the child says it or how strong the child's belief is, it doesn't change the reality of the situation. And it does not change the fact that the very life that allows a person to understand the concept of life and deny the giver of life is the life that came from God. He is the life (11:25) and the light (8:12) that allows us to see a little bit of the concept of life. When we receive the light, we become part of the new creation (2 Corinthians 4:3-6).

John 1:12 Yet to all who did receive him, to those who believed in his name, he gave the right to become children of God. Here is a "right" we definitely do not want to miss. Today, we talk about many rights. In our society, we theoretically have unalienable rights (granted by our creator - God) that cannot be taken away by our government. Our particular form of republic government even has a bill of rights for its citizens. However, many of these supposed rights have been diminished substantially.

Nevertheless, here is a "right" laid out in the Bible that should not be ignored. This right comes as a gift to all those who believe in His name. To believe in His name means to trust in Him and what His name stands for, which is the Lord is Salvation (Exodus 3:14, 15). Based on this right, we can become a child of God. As a child of God, we believe Jesus Christ is the eternal Son of God and have faith in Him as Savior and seek to follow and obey Him. As a result, we are granted eternal life with God after our current life here on earth has ended. It is an incredible blessing to be a child of God. Even though we are undeserving, we can be entitled to full membership in God's family. That is the most important right a human being can have, and it is a gift to be received, not something we can work to earn.

In other words, when we believe in what His name stands for, that is: the Lord is salvation (Exodus 3:14, 15), it means to believe that Jesus is the Christ, the Word, the life, and the light. **"The right"** means the legitimate entitlement to the position as **children of God**. Amazingly, we can become full-fledged members of God's family just by believing. It is a gift granted through the grace of God as opposed to anything we could earn through our works (4:10, 14). When we trust Christ, we are born of God.

John 1:17 For the law was given through Moses; grace and truth came through Jesus Christ. As noted before, the law shows us that we cannot completely follow it and need grace. That grace comes through what Jesus Christ did for us. He took our place in receiving the just punishment for our transgressions. Now, we can be forgiven and appear just as if we had never broken the law because our debt is paid in full

(Titus 3:7; Galatians 3:24; Galatians 2:16-17; Romans 5:1-21; Roman 3:28; Philippians 3:9; Romans 4:25).

John 1:23 He said: "I *am*
  'The voice of one crying in the wilderness:
  "Make straight the way of the Lord,"'
  as the prophet Isaiah said." John the Baptist identifies himself here as the one spoken of in Isaiah 40:3 as the voice calling people to **make straight the way of the Lord**. Apparently, in those days, they didn't have roads everywhere as we do, and when a king was to go someplace, they had to cut new roads so that there would be a smooth road for the King to go over and not get stuck.

John 1:33 And I myself did not know him, but the one who sent me to baptize with water told me, 'The man on whom you see the Spirit come down and remain is the one who will baptize with the Holy Spirit.' 34 I have seen and I testify that this is God's Chosen One." So, John, the Baptist said that Jesus would baptize with the Holy Spirit, and that is what He did. John's mission was given to him by God, and he fulfilled it by baptizing Christ and seeing the Spirit descend from heaven like a dove and remain on Him. After this, John called Jesus the Lamb of God.

John 1:51 And He said to him, "Most assuredly, I say to you, hereafter you shall see heaven and the angels of God ascending and descending upon the Son of Man." The **Son of Man** expression was used in Daniel 7:13, about a heavenly being. Jesus used this phrase often when referring to Himself (Matt. 8:20; Mark 2:10). In Genesis 28:12, Jacob had a vision of angels descending and ascending a ladder from heaven.

John 2:9 When the master of the feast had tasted the water that was made wine, and did not know where it came from (but the servants

who had drawn the water knew), the master of the feast called the bridegroom. Here is one of the first demonstrations of Jesus' power, He turned water into good tasting wine. Some people have difficulty understanding how Christ could perform such a miracle, given all of the trouble and destruction from people who drink too much wine. Others use this scripture to justify their overindulgence in drinking alcoholic beverages but have to ignore the clear teaching against getting drunk in other scriptures in using this scripture in this way.

Many should not drink alcohol because they cannot keep from drinking too much. Their friends are guided not to drink in front of those who cannot control their drinking because it may cause them to stumble (Romans 14:13-23). If everyone practiced what the scripture tells us to do regarding alcohol, there would not be the amount of death and destruction from people overindulging.

John 2:11 What Jesus did here in Cana of Galilee was the first of the signs through which he revealed his glory; and his disciples believed in him. The first sign of Christ's glory was that at the request of his mother, He turned water into good wine for a wedding feast. This act indicated His supernatural power. The fact that Christ made wine does not condone using it to excess. Many scriptures warn against the overuse of wine. Ephesians 5:8 says: **"be not drunk with wine, in which is dissipation."** Proverbs 20:1 says: **"Wine is a mocker, Strong drink is a brawler, And whoever is led astray by it is not wise."** Romans 14:21 says: **"It is good neither to eat meat nor drink wine nor do anything by which your brother stumbles or is offended or is made weak."** Proverbs 23:29-30 says: **"Who has woe? Who has sorrow? Who has strife? Who has complaints? Who has needless bruises? Who has bloodshot eyes? 30 Those who linger over wine, who go to sample bowls of mixed wine."** Thus, it is clear that a Christian (or anyone else) who drinks alcoholic beverages should be cautious about where, when, and how much they consume.

Out of love for others, it appears that there are times when Christians should abstain from drinking alcoholic beverages. This is so that they will not negatively influence a believer who does not have the freedom to drink due to their lack of self-control in this area.

Regarding secular information on alcohol use, the International Agency for Research on Cancer of the World Health Organization has alcohol classified as a Group 1 carcinogen. Thus, there is also research that agrees with Biblical directions to use moderation when it comes to alcohol use. It is also interesting that as far back in the Bible as Judges 13:7, a pregnant woman was advised not to drink wine or other fermented drinks. This was centuries before scientists connected alcohol use and fetal alcohol syndrome. Of course, it is not surprising that God's knowledge is centuries ahead of man's knowledge.

John 2:16 To those who sold doves he said, "Get these out of here! Stop turning my Father's house into a market!" With this statement, Christ seems to claim His messiahship and authority. He sought to purify the temple as one of the first public acts, and He was upset that the temple had become a market. This is one of the very few times where we have an example of Jesus getting angry.

John 3:3 Jesus replied, "Very truly I tell you, no one can see the kingdom of God unless they are born again." Here is a concept that is hard to accept for anyone who does not recognize a spiritual and physical dimension. Jesus further clarified that a person has to be born of water (physical birth) and of the spirit (spiritual birth) to enter the Kingdom of God. How are we born of the spirit? We simply believe in Christ, and God imparts spiritual and eternal life to us. The spirit is like the wind, we cannot see where it comes from or where it goes, but we know it is there. To understand the things of God, it appears that we have to believe (1 Corinthians 2:11). John 3:14, which states: **"Just as Moses lifted up the snake in the wilderness, so the Son of Man must be lifted up, 15**

that everyone who believes may have eternal life in him" clarifies that to have eternal life in God's kingdom requires belief in Christ.

This scripture gives unbelievers a lot of grief. The Greek word translated in this scripture as *"again"* can also be translated "from above." Jesus later used the wind analogy in describing this heavenly birth, so it seems like He was talking about the new spiritual birth from above. Like the wind, we cannot tell where the Holy Spirit comes from or where it goes, but that does not mean it is not there. In verses 3:6-8, Christ further contrasts being born of the flesh with being born of the Spirit. These two births are very different. It appears that even before we accept this new birth from above, the Spirit is with us. Once we accept the truth and are born from above, the Holy Spirit comes in us. When we allow the Holy Spirit to control us, the power to minister is also provided.

John 3:5 Jesus answered, "Most assuredly, I say to you, unless one is born of water and the Spirit, he cannot enter the kingdom of God. What is this "born again" concept? Here the idea is described as being born of **the spirit**. The word "again" can be translated to mean "from above" or "anew." In Titus 3:5 the concept is referred to as the **"washing of regeneration and renewing of the Holy Spirit."** The Holy Spirit makes a person spiritually new in the moment of belief. Then it is the Holy Spirit, working and enabling in the believer's life, allowing the Christian life and the performance of good deeds. As this process continues, the Christian grows in character and good works. These activities are thus the work of God's mercy in delivering us from our sin.

Our good works, stated differently, are simply evidence of God's work in our life. They have no value in our salvation. The Holy Spirit working in us also allows us to treat others the way God treated us when we were involved in sins. He paid the price for us. This is something that, except for the closest of relations, is impossible for the natural man without the empowering of the Holy Spirit. Christ paid the price for our sins while we were his enemies, not his close family member. His sacrifice for us is like one of us stepping in to serve the prison sentence for a burglar caught in the act of burglarizing our house. I don't think that has ever happened in humanity's history, yet that is what Christ did for us. He stepped in and paid the price for our sins.

John 3:8 The wind blows where it wishes, and you hear the sound of it, but cannot tell where it comes from and where it goes. So is everyone who is born of the Spirit." Interestingly, Christ uses the wind to illustrate how the Holy Spirit comes into and influences our lives. We can't tell what direction it comes from, but we know it is there if we pay attention. Immediately after this scripture, Christ discusses "heavenly things" in contrast to "earthly things." The heavenly things come from **the Son**, by the cross (v. 14) and faith (v. 15). If we believe (have faith), we are not condemned and have heavenly things (the Holy Spirit). We are condemned if we don't have faith (v. 18). These people are in rebellion against their maker: God. They don't want anything to do with Christ. They want to do their own thing. It is like a child saying to his father, I do not recognize that you are my father or even that you exist nor that you have any say over me or what I do.

John 3:27 John answered and said, "A man can receive nothing unless it has been given to him from heaven. Of course, even with faith, a man receives nothing "heavenly" **unless it is given to him from heaven** (v. 27). The people wanted John the Baptist to take on more authority than had been given to him from heaven. With his statement, he set them right. He wasn't about to take on more authority than had been granted to him from heaven. Some pastors seem to have a difficult time with this issue when their congregations expect more authority from their pastor than has been given to them from heaven. It can be difficult for the pastor to set their pride aside and work against the tendency for some in the congregation to figuratively put them on a pedestal and begin to treat them as if they are Christ. The fact is that the pastor is merely a vessel through which the Word of God is distributed. All pastors need to keep this in mind. Unfortunately, the old saying that "power corrupts and absolute power corrupts absolutely" sometimes comes into play when a pastor begins to view themselves as something more than they are. It would be better if all had the attitude of John, who said: **"He must increase, but I must decrease."** We can't even accept Jesus' testimony without God's work in drawing us (6:44).

John 3:33 He who has received His testimony has certified that God is true. 34 For He whom God has sent speaks the words of God, for God does not give the Spirit by measure. Apart from God's work in us, we cannot accept Jesus Christ as Lord (6:44). The Father has to draw us. When we receive Christ's testimony, we certify that God is true regarding what He has sealed. Many could not read in the time when Christ was on the earth, and a seal was the certification of a clear message to those who could not read. A seal certified that a document was the true official document instead of a fabrication. Now we use notarized signatures in this same way to document that a signature is the real signature of a person on an approved document. When we believe the testimony about Christ, we certify that He is the real deal; **the way, the truth and the life** (John 14:6).

John 3:36 Whoever believes in the Son has eternal life, but whoever rejects the Son will not see life, for God's wrath remains on them. It is hard to parse or sugar coat this direct uncompromising statement. It is what it is. My opinion is that you do not want God's wrath on you. How do you believe? You let God work in you.

John 4:13 Jesus answered and said to her, "Whoever drinks of this water will thirst again, 14 but whoever drinks of the water that I shall give him will never thirst. But the water that I shall give him will become in him a fountain of water springing up into everlasting life." In other words, this sounds like the "water" that Jesus gives suggests a divine life for believers. We receive eternal life when we drink in the Holy Spirit that Jesus gives. Once we have eternal life, we no longer have to thirst for it from external sources. The fountain (the Holy Spirit) provides a constant spring of refreshment from within our bodies, which have become a temple.

John 4:23 Yet a time is coming and has now come when the true worshipers will worship the Father in the Spirit and in truth, for they are the kind of worshipers the Father seeks. So, what does this mean? How do we worship in spirit and truth? We know that God is spirit, and spirit is not something physical that we can see. But to have the spirit of God in us, we have to believe in Him. When we believe, He imparts His Spirit to us. We also know that, per John 6:62, the words that Jesus Christ spoke are spirit. Therefore, to worship in His Spirit, we have to believe in Him and use words in harmony with what He said. That is the first thing. Then there is the issue that we are in the Spirit as a matter of position but may not be as a matter of practice.

Nevertheless, the Spirit stays with us through our post-conversion sin. This grieves the Spirit (Ephesians 4:30). Of course, if we are involved in corruption, we will not feel like worshiping. In this situation, we need to repent of the sin and confess it to get back into a right relationship with God (John 1:9). When we repent and pray for forgiveness (Acts 8:22), we open the door to worshiping in spirit. Then we can worship with an eye toward God with every word we sing.

Once we understand the spiritual aspect of worship, we need to understand the truth? Christ is the truth, the way, and the life (John 14:6). Since Christ is truth and His Word is truth, our worship always needs to be in harmony with the words and truth that are in the Bible. The truth is that our worship needs to glorify and focus on God and His principles and concepts. If we look at the Psalms as an example, there is a great focus on pouring out our hearts in praise, thanksgiving, and worship of God.

After urging us to praise the Lord with (a) all the instruments, (b) with dancing, (c) with rejoicing, (d) with loud voices and instruments, (e) with new songs, (f) with exaltation, (g) with singing, (h) with gratitude and (i) with what is essentially our whole being, the final Psalm 150 puts it this way: "**Let everything that has breath praise the LORD. Praise the LORD.**" Since Psalms is the longest book in the Bible, I think I get the message that praise and worship should be a significant part of the Christian life and probably not just on Sundays.

John 4:24 God *is* Spirit, and those who worship Him must worship in spirit and truth." This scripture comes shortly after the scripture above about drinking from the water that Christ gives. The water He gives provides eternal life and continues to be a fountain in the person who receives it. The Holy Spirit fulfills this process in the believer. Together, these statements let us know that we need the Holy Spirit to worship **in spirit**. Notice that this scripture singles out **true worshipers**. We could just go through the motions without having the spirit in us and appear to be worshipers. To be a **true worshiper**, we had to have previously drunk the water Jesus gave. A **true worshiper** has the Holy Spirit in them and knows and has accepted **the truth** (John 3:16; 14:6). Note that spirit is the opposite of material and earthly things and is not bound by space or time. The truth is what is in harmony with the nature and will of God. It is the opposite of what is false. When we worship in spirit and truth, our worship is a spiritual matter of the heart, and we worship in harmony with the Word, which is the truth (John 1:1; John 17:17). Worship is part of the intimate relationship between man and God.

John 4:25 The woman said, "I know that Messiah" (called Christ) "is coming. When he comes, he will explain everything to us." 26 Then Jesus declared, "I, the one speaking to you—I am he." Here is another claim made by Jesus that He was the Messiah. By what He says about Himself, there is no mistaking that He claims to be God in the flesh. He also said that if you have seen Him, you have seen the Father (John 14:9). Thus, He leaves no room for viewing Him as just a great prophet or a great moral teacher from an intellectually valid perspective. That would not make sense. Based on what He said about Himself, He only left a few intellectually valid conclusions available. He was either (a) mentally ill, (b) a liar, or (c) who He said he was. If He was (a) a mentally ill delusional person thinking that He was God when He was not or (b) lying about it, He could not, at the same time, be a great prophet or great moral teacher. Those characteristics do not logically go together.

John 4:34 Jesus said to them, "My food is to do the will of Him who sent Me, and to finish His work. Here is an example for us. Christ knew that what he was to do and what would ultimately sustain and nourish Him was to do the will of His Father in heaven. He was heavenly-minded and would let His Heavenly Father guide and direct what He did on earth regardless of the cost to Himself. If Christ is our example, we should do the same.

How do we know what the specific will of God is for our lives? Here are some questions related to five words beginning with the letter "P" to ask yourself to help you determine the answer to that question. I don't know exactly where this originally came from, but there are numerous other "Five P's" related to Bible study. The words for this example are Providence, Prayer, Patience, Passion, and Perspective. Appropriate questions to ask are (a) where is the open door (providence); (b) have you prayed about the correct direction (prayer); (c) are you being patient in waiting for an answer (patience); (d)what do you want to do (passion); and (e) what advice have you received from multiple godly counselors (perspective)?

The idea is that when all five P's line up, we are probably going in the right direction. From the scriptures, we learn a lot about God's will for our lives and that He has a plan for each of us (Ephesians 2:8) if we choose to accept it. He wants us to believe in Jesus Christ, whom He sent (John 6:29). He wants us to keep his commandments (John 14:15). He wants us to love one another (John 15:12). He wants us to do the good works He has prepared for us (Ephesians 4:16). If that is not enough to keep us busy (very unlikely), we can search the scriptures and find more direction.

John 4:46 So Jesus came again to Cana of Galilee where He had made the water wine. And there was a certain nobleman whose son was sick at Capernaum. This scripture refers back to John 2:1-11. It appears that what was produced by this and many other miracles performed by Christ was the best of its kind. Though Christ produced wine for its proper use, this in no way does away with His caution not to get drunk (Luke 21:34).

We need to always keep in mind the warning in Proverbs 20:1: "**Wine is a mocker, Strong Drink is a brawler, And whoever is led astray by it is not wise.**" Also, Proverbs 23:29 gives us the indication that those who linger long at the wine and go in search of mixed wine will experience woe, sorrow, contentions, complaints, wounds without cause, and redness of eyes. These don't sound like good things to have.

Romans 13:13 tells us not to walk in revelry and drunkenness. Certain authorities are encouraged to be careful about how they present themselves and not become involved in drinking, which can cloud their decision-making ability (Proverbs 31:4). And, all of us are encouraged not to become a stumbling block to others in Mark 9:42. In Romans 14:21, we are encouraged not to "**drink wine nor do anything by which your brother stumbles or is offended or is made weak.** "

In Ephesians 5:18, we are told not to be drunk with wine, but instead to be filled with the Spirit singing and making melody in your heart to the Lord. This is a much healthier, edifying, and spiritual alternative to the artificial numbing of our mental and physical capabilities through excessive consumption of wine (or other chemicals that produce similar effects on the mind). It is much safer to have a Holy Spirit-filled sober driver available. Almost everyone is equipped with the ability to pilot a two-ton missile made of steel with a tank full of explosive liquid (i.e., a car with gasoline) whether they are safe to do so or not.

Suppose we take all that the Word has to say about the consumption of wine. In that case, it appears that for people who are not leaders or judges, moderate consumption of wine is okay in situations where the person who drinks will not be a stumbling block to anyone who has demonstrated that they cannot keep from overindulging. Based on my reading of other Proverbs and scriptures, it is probably best for everyone to avoid strong or mixed drinks (i.e., whiskey, vodka, rum, etc.). It is too easy to go overboard and get drunk with just a little of these strong "spirits." I believe the same principle could be applied to other potent mind-altering drugs (i.e., heroin, fentanyl, etc.).

John 5:21 For just as the Father raises the dead and gives them life, even so the Son gives life to whom he is pleased to give it. Clearly, God the Son (Jesus Christ) has authority even over life, as does God the Father.

John 5:22 Moreover, the Father judges no one, but has entrusted all judgment to the Son, 23 that all may honor the Son just as they honor the Father. Whoever does not honor the Son does not honor the Father, who sent him. So, even though the Father and Son are one, they have different responsibilities. However, action by the Son apart from the Father does not seem possible because of the unity of the two (John 5:19). This verse also clarifies that those who try to worship and honor only the Father are not honoring Him if they are denying His Son. Note that there appears to be a judgment of the people in the Old Testament. Since this scripture says that all judgment has been entrusted to the Son, Christ must have been involved in these judgments.

As I have said before, we are not in a position to judge God in any way. Therefore, we need to understand God's righteous judgment in the context of the whole of scripture, which is a hopeful message of freedom, forgiveness, and salvation. We should be careful about taking one scripture out of context without considering the whole Word of God. We also need to consider the culture in which scripture was written instead of viewing it only through our cultural lens. Physical discipline may be viewed negatively in our culture, even though modern-day governments and nations use it.

In the Old Testament, where almost all cultures practiced slavery, the Bible indicates special concern for the oppressed, slaves, widowed, the orphaned, poor, and homeless. The death penalty was sanctioned in those days and may have been necessary. Now, it may not be.

Regarding one story of judgment from the Old Testament, God facilitated many Egyptians' death to free the Israelite slaves from bondage. Thus, this judgment was necessary. Other situations of violence had to do with protecting the chosen people from pagan practices of idolatry. Just as we are aroused to righteous anger when our own family is threatened by violence or injustice, God seems to have the same protective attitude toward His people. I have to keep in mind that whatever God does is just and true. I am not His judge: He is mine. Therefore, I need to change my thinking if I have a problem with God's judgments. He is the ultimate righteous judge who made everything and has every right to do what He wants with what He has created.

The Son can also give life just like the Father can. In a prior verse, Christ points out that, He **can do nothing by Himself** (5:19). Thus, the Father and Son are one and always work together in unity and deity.

John 5:24 "Very truly I tell you, whoever hears my word and believes him who sent me has eternal life and will not be judged but has

crossed over from death to life." Here is all it takes to pass from death into life. It is that simple. No works can get you there. No effort is required on your part. Salvation is simply by the grace of God through faith (Ephesians 2:8). The essential concept is not what we can do for God but what He has done for us. Salvation is a gift, and all we do is receive the gift through faith. Our natural tendency seems to be that we want to make it challenging and complex to be saved, but the Lord didn't want it that way. We are dependent on Him for our life now and in the future. That's just the way it is.

Believers already have eternal life, so deciding this point is unnecessary. We will only be judged regarding rewards (our inheritance) that we may receive in the kingdom (Romans 14:10; 2 Corinthians 5;10). Later in this book, we learn that the one who has **done good, to the resurrection of life**, is the one who believes in Christ (6:28,29). That is the work of God. This is an excellent promise for believers. We have eternal life and will not be judged regarding our eternal destiny. We will only be judged regarding our inheritance and rewards (Matthew 19:28-29; Matthew 5:11-12; Matthew 16:27).

John 5:28 "Do not be amazed at this, for a time is coming when all who are in their graves will hear his voice 29 and come out—those who have done what is good will rise to live, and those who have done what is evil will rise to be condemned. Note that those who have done what is good are those who have believed in Christ. Their sins do not count against them regarding this resurrection of glorified bodies.

John 5:43 I have come in My Father's name, and you do not receive Me; if another comes in his own name, him you will receive. This is interesting. Christ tells us that if someone proudly came in their own name, the very people who did not believe what He was telling them would follow that person. Not only do we have to be on guard for pride in our own lives, but we have to be on guard for believing a prideful person who is setting themselves up as a god. Perhaps this is why God often allows leaders to have serious character flaws, even in the church and in the government (Moses, David, etc.). He knows our tendency to set a person on a pedestal/throne/podium and worship them rather than who we should be worshiping; the one true everlasting God.

John 5:46 For if you believed Moses, you would believe Me; for he wrote about Me. Here Christ lets us know that Moses wrote about Him. Christ also says that Old Testament prophecies are fulfilled by Him (Luke 24:25-27). Commentators say that over 300 of these prophecies are fulfilled by His first coming.

John 6:15 Jesus, knowing that they intended to come and make him king by force, withdrew again to a mountain by himself. This was a time of testing for Jesus. The people were trying to make Him king, but He knew there was a different plan for Him from God. He gives us an example of what to do in times of testing; withdraw. From other examples, we can assume that He retreated to the mountain and prayed. There are times when that is what we need to do.

John 6:21 Then they were willing to take him into the boat, and immediately the boat reached the shore where they were heading. Here the disciples took Christ into the boat they were in after seeing Him walking on water, and apparently, they were all then supernaturally transported to where they were going. This is the fifth sign/miracle reported in John's gospel. The signs that John reports point to Christ's deity.

Isn't it interesting that they were immediately at their destination when Christ got into the boat with them? This is the same as when we get into the boat with Christ. We have reached our goal. This is our destiny. This is where we belong. There is still much to do when we reach the shore.

From many scriptures, it appears to please the Lord when we are in the same boat with Him, and He is at the helm directing what we will do and where we will go from there. When you are on a boat, you are going where the boat is going unless you want to swim, and you won't get far swimming in the deep water out there. It won't be long, and you will run out of energy and probably sink. Getting on board with the Lord seems to be the best way to get supernaturally transported to your destination.

John 6:27 Do not labor for the food which perishes, but for the food which endures to everlasting life, which the Son of Man will give you, because God the Father has set His seal on Him." This scripture says we can't work our way to heaven. Shortly after this scripture (6:33) it is made clear that Christ is the bread of life who **"gives life to the world."** This life is provided as a gift (4:10). Thus, just like with any other gift, the definition is that we didn't work for it, or it wouldn't be a gift. Our salvation is based on what Christ has done for us, not what we have done for Him. This can be a hard truth to accept in a prideful mindset, but it is the truth.

Christ makes it very clear that it is the will of the Father **"that everyone who sees the Son and believes in Him may have everlasting life; and I will raise him up at the last day** (6:40)." Even the drawing of a person to believe is not our own doing as noted in verse 6:44, where Christ states: **"No one can come to me unless the Father who sent me draws him..."** Thus, we can't even take credit for having the sense to move toward belief in Christ.

John 6:40 For my Father's will is that everyone who looks to the Son and believes in him shall have eternal life, and I will raise them up at the last day." We know that to be absent from the body for believers is to be present with the Lord (2 Corinthians 5:6-8). Thus, our spirit will immediately be with the Lord, from what I can tell. Later, our bodies will be resurrected in an incorruptible eternal form (1 Corinthians

15:51-54) and reunited with our spirits. Further along in chapter 6, we have the words: **6:44 "No one can come to me unless the Father who sent me draws them, and I will raise them up at the last day."** This scripture clarifies that God has drawn anyone who comes to believe in Christ. Thus, even our faith comes from God. Herein is the balance that everyone who sees the Son and believes in Him will have everlasting life (6:40), but some will not believe (6:64) even though they are invited and drawn. We humans still appear to have free will.

John 6:53 Then Jesus said to them, "Most assuredly, I say to you, unless you eat the flesh of the Son of Man and drink His blood, you have no life in you. From other scriptures that define the meaning of the words used here, we know that Christ is not speaking of literally eating His flesh. He is speaking symbolically. Eternal life is available to us because Christ shed His blood, paying the price for our sins. A person can achieve the benefit of eternal life through faith, which is symbolically referred to as eating His flesh and drinking His blood.

This is a strong statement and one that Christ does not want us to forget. It is the essence of taking communion that we are encouraged to do so that we will not forget (1 Corinthians 11:26). The symbolism of these scriptures seems to be that we have to take in His words and believe them. Elsewhere in the book of John, Christ is called the bread of life (6:48). He gives His flesh for the life of the world (6:51). He tells us in 6:63 that His words are spirit. To have His life, we have to take in His words (His Spirit) and believe in Him. When we do, we have everlasting life. We have arrived at our destiny.

When we take Communion, eating the bread is a synonym for faith (v. 35, 48-50). Thus, dramatically, Christ lets us know how important it is for us to take in His words (His Spirit) and believe that He paid the price for our sins through dying on the cross for us. When we take in His words, we can worship in His Spirit. When we do this, we are using words that agree with or are quoted from the words of Christ. Thus, to have eternal life, we have to have His Spirit or put another way, His Spirit in us. He put it symbolically in this scripture by saying we have to eat his flesh and drink his blood.

John 6:63 It is the Spirit who gives life; the flesh profits nothing. The words that I speak to you are spirit, and *they* are life. Interestingly, Christ is referred to as the Word in the first part of John's gospel, and then here, Christ states that the words He spoke are spirit. Obviously, words and *the* Word are important in the economy of God. Not only are Christ's words spirit, but they are also life. I take this to mean that belief in Christ and His words are very important and can result in eternal life. That is how powerful words are. God's words are incredibly powerful. The scripture says that God spoke our universe into existence (Genesis 1:3-26). That is an unimaginable amount of power from the words of God. God's words are so powerful that they were used to create our vast universe. Thus, God's words that can bring you eternal life are just a small example of what His words can do.

I don't view the creation of the universe by God as eliminating the possibility that the universe evolves as it expands and that God is continuing to be creative. I went to a dinosaur museum a while ago and was struck by the fact that 99 percent of the species that have been on earth are already extinct. Some people who study this stuff say it is more like 99.999 percent. That makes me think that God continues to create new species. Every known living thing has genetic information coded in its DNA double helix molecule, which gives instructions for development, functioning, growth, and reproduction. It is compelling evidence to me that a supernatural writer wrote this code. When I read a book, I think that there was an author. When I see a building, I think there was a builder. Scientists have discovered that they can read the DNA sequence and use letters to designate each nucleobase (C, G, A, or T). It would take one thousand 200-page books to contain the genome of a human being. This genome is about 3 billion letters in a precise sequence. When I see DNA code, I think there was an author of that code. It would seem an unimaginable stretch of the imagination to believe that this precise code resulted from chance occurrence.

If I show you a book full of words that make sense, there is no way you would believe that the book wrote itself or was a chance occurrence.. I see DNA the same way. There is no way that this incredibly complex code in every cell of every living being that is long enough to fill 1000 books could write itself. The code tells every cell in a living being how to grow and replicate to do its correct function. I don't need any proof because I am a person of faith, but this sure appears to be proof positive that the code had to be written by an intelligent being who implemented an intelligent design. For me, that someone is the supernatural God of the Bible, who claims that He *is* the author and creator of our world and the universe in which we live. I believe the DNA code had to have an author just as any book had to have a writer. I do not usually talk in absolutes, but it seems to be an *absolute* impossibility for 3 billion letters of code to create themselves in the correct sequence to be the blueprint to direct life.

John 6:70 Jesus answered them, "Did I not choose you, the twelve, and one of you is a devil?" Interestingly, even Judas was chosen by Christ to be one of the twelve disciples. However, scripture does not say that Judas ever believed. Thus, a person can be called/chosen but still has the free will not to believe. This short scripture seems to explain a lot about the concept of election. Judas appears to have been called (elected) by Christ but does not believe. We can also be called but choose not to believe. This explains how many can be called, but few are chosen (Matthew 22:14). Even Jesus' brothers did not believe in Him at this point in His ministry (7:5).

John 7:15 And the Jews marveled, saying, "How does this Man know

letters, having never studied?" When God calls a person into a specific teaching ministry, the Holy Spirit can give them a supernatural ability to learn, understand and remember the scriptures even when they haven't attended a school that taught them these things.

John 7:24 Do not judge according to appearance, but judge with righteous judgment." This is a commandment directly from the mouth of Christ. It is one command that most of us fail to follow though it doesn't even need any interpretation because it is so clear; "**Do not judge according to appearance…**" It couldn't be any more simple. We need to remember this scripture the next time our flesh tries to take over and influence our opinion of someone because of how they look before we even get to know them. We need to resist this temptation, which is obviously against the command of Christ.

John 7:38 He who believes in Me, as the Scripture has said, out of his heart will flow rivers of living water." The phrase "**as the Scripture has said**" seems to be a reference to various scriptures such as Deuteronomy 18:15, Isaiah 58:11 and Zechariah 14:8. The believers are overflowing so that not only will their thirst for the Holy Spirit (v. 39) be satisfied, but the thirst of others will also be satisfied. After He taught on this subject, some said that Jesus was the Christ (v. 40).

John 8:7 So when they continued asking Him, He raised Himself up and said to them, "He who is without sin among you, let him throw a stone at her first." In this situation, the scribes and Pharisees tested Christ, asking if an adulteress should be stoned per Moses' command in the law. Jesus somewhat ignored them at first while writing on the ground with His finger. We don't know what He was writing, but it is interesting that after He told them His answer, they began leaving **one by one, beginning with the oldest**.

This story doesn't tell what was being written in the dirt by Christ, but it tells us that the accusers began to leave the area. It seems like something Christ wrote in the dirt convicted them so that they were ashamed to test Christ anymore and therefore just left the area. He could have named their undisclosed sins (dirt), starting with the oldest person. If this is what Christ was writing, it is interesting that their dirt was written in the dirt. Note: after His writing in the dirt, no one condemned her, nor did Christ condemn her, but He did tell her to "**go and sin no more.**"

Shortly after this, Christ says that He is **the light of the world**. Jesus exposes sin (v. 1-11) and gives light (9:1-7). The light He seems to have shed on this situation is that people who want to hold others accountable for their exposed sin may have hidden sins that make them hypocrites when they condemn others.

John 8:12 Then Jesus spoke to them again, saying, "I am the light of the world. He who follows Me shall not walk in darkness, but have the light of life." What is this light of life that Jesus speaks about here? He seems to be declaring that He is the spiritual source of enlightenment. We can perceive two lights in the world: physical light and spiritual light. Here, Jesus appears to be speaking allegorically about the spiritual light that lights up His truth, words, and eternal life. Those who perceive this light will never walk in spiritual darkness. When we follow Christ, we have this spiritual light that illuminates the spiritual aspect of eternal life. This is one reason I think that faith comes before understanding when reading the Bible. No matter how many times a person reads the Bible, spiritual understanding will be lacking without faith. To understand the spiritual, we have to have the light of life that Christ provides.

John 8:24 Therefore I said to you that you will die in your sins; for if you do not believe that I am *He*, you will die in your sins." When this quote refers to "I am *He*" Jesus is making another "I am" statement that is how God referred to Himself in the Old Testament (Exodus 3:14). In other words, Christ was equating Himself with God as he does several times in the book of John. This is the fact that many will not accept, no matter what. Humanity has been given that free will option. I hope that anyone who reads this does not choose unbelief. Note that belief in Christ is the central issue in being saved (born again). That is it. There are no elaborate rituals or works to be performed so that a person could boast in their accomplishment. God made it very simple yet profound.

Thus, Christ clarifies that those who do not believe in Him for the remission of sins will die in their sins. Jesus claimed to be God with the "**I AM**" statement here and in verse 58 (see Exodus 3:14). This one statement exerts eternal preexistence and deity. All of us have a beginning in time. God always existed and is not bound by time as we who have had a beginning.

John 8:31 Then Jesus said to those Jews who believed Him, "If you abide in My word, you are My disciples indeed. 32 And you shall know the truth, and the truth shall make you free." To know the truth and be free is a great thought. When I read this, it made an impression. I wanted to know the truth and be free. One might ask from what are we to be free? Free from the bondage of sin. We already think we are free in America, but we are not. We have many habits in behavior and thought that enslave us to repeat what we are in the habit of doing and thinking. The promise here is that if we listen to and abide in what Jesus says, we will know the truth, and the truth will make us free.

So we need to abide in His Word if we want to know the truth and be set free. Abide means to continue or remain. Free from what? We are free from our hopeless thoughts about life and destructive behaviors that result from these thoughts. We can quickly become a slave to those damaging thoughts and actions. Or we can follow the advice in this passage and be free from the bondage of bad thoughts and behaviors that may be hurting ourselves and others. That sounds good and can motivate a seeker of the truth who also wants release from bad habits.

However, we will not be 100 percent free of undesirable thoughts and actions until we get to heaven. There will still be confession and forgiveness needed as we progress in sanctification (a process of being increasingly set apart to God for His use).

John 8:50 And I do not seek My *own* glory; there is One who seeks and judges. 51 Most assuredly, I say to you, if anyone keeps My word he shall never see death." This appears to be referring to spiritual death, which is separation from God. We are encouraged to keep His Word, enjoy another great reward, and be set free from sin.

John 8:51 Most assuredly, I say to you, if anyone keeps My word he shall never see death." Here Jesus appears to be saying not that a person will not experience physical death because other scripture says that it is appointed for man to die once (Hebrews 9:27). Thus, at least half of the old saying that nothing is certain in life but death and taxes is true. Therefore, this scripture has to be about spiritual death. Their spirits will have eternal life (Philippians 1:22) and, at the appropriate time, will be reunited with an incorruptible body that will be eternal (Romans 8:23; Philippians 3:20-21).

John 9:1 Now as *Jesus* passed by, He saw a man who was blind from birth. 2 And His disciples asked Him, saying, "Rabbi, who sinned, this man or his parents, that he was born blind?" In answer, Jesus explained that neither sinned to cause blindness. He was blind **"that the works of God should be revealed in him"** (9:3). Jesus then anointed the man's eyes and sent him to wash them out. When the man came back, he could see. This is one of the seven specific signs of Jesus in the Gospel of John. Others include: turning water into wine (2:1-11), healing of the nobleman's son (4:46-54), healing a man who had been sick for a long time (5:8), the feeding of the five thousand (6:1-15), walking on water (6:16-21), this passage where a man blind from birth is given his sight and the raising of Lazarus from the dead (11:1-44). Jesus also performed many other signs and wonders (21:25) that John did not single out to report in his gospel. He seemed to be saying if these people didn't believe after seeing all these, they were not going to believe. These seven should have been enough to convince anyone.

John 9:38 Then he said, "Lord, I believe!" And he worshiped Him. This is the type of faith in the One who can save that results in salvation. "Faith is only a channel to the worthy object, the Lord Jesus Christ" (NSB pg. 1782). This man, who said to Jesus: "**Lord, I believe,**" went through a progression. First, he called Jesus "**a man**" (v. 11); then "**a prophet**" (v. 17); and then the "**Son of God**" (v. 35-38).

John 10:7 Then Jesus said to them again, "Most assuredly, I say to you, I am the door of the sheep. The door or gate is something that we can go through, or it can be something that can keep out what might hurt us and keep us safe inside, protected from what could hurt us on the outside. We have to enter the sheepfold through the door (Christ) (vs. 10:1). When we enter by the right door (Christ), we are called by His name (Christians), and we hear His voice (vs. 10:3,4), and we follow Him because we know his voice (the scriptures). Continuing the metaphor, He also refers to Himself as the good shepherd who gives His life for the sheep. He is not a hireling who runs away when danger comes. He is not a thief who takes away life, but the giver of life; eternal life.

John 10:27 My sheep hear My voice, and I know them, and they follow Me. 28 And I give them eternal life, and they shall never perish; neither shall anyone snatch them out of My hand. Here is another example of a metaphor for faith in the scripture. There are three things noted in this metaphor. One, Christians hear the voice of Christ. Two, Christ knows those who believe in Him. Three, He gives believers eternal life that can not be taken away. Other metaphors for faith in the Gospel of John include "drinking water" (John 4:10-15; John 7:37-39) and "eating bread."

John 11:4 When Jesus heard *that,* **He said, "This sickness is not unto death, but for the glory of God, that the Son of God may be glorified through it."** This passage is about Lazarus, the brother of Mary and Martha. Lazarus had gotten sick and died. Lazarus had been in the tomb for four days. Yet Jesus said: "Your brother will rise again," which is what happened, demonstrating Christ's deity. After all, the sickness did not have death as a final result, and this miracle glorified God.

John 11:25 Jesus said to her, "I am the resurrection and the life. He who believes in Me, though he may die, he shall live. "Christ is the resurrection for those who believe and are physically dead. He is the life for those who believe and have not yet died (NSB p. 1786)." In other words, we must believe in Christ to have eternal life with Him. Our physical bodies will die once, but we will live on spiritually and even will receive new "glorified" spiritual bodies (Philippians 3:20-21; John 20:19, 26; Luke 24:39). We will enjoy food but may not have to have it. These bodies will be solid to the touch but offer no hindrance when traveling. We don't know what this will be like because our main reference point is the physical world we live in.

John 12:7 But Jesus said, "Let her alone; she has kept this for the day of My burial. 8 For the poor you have with you always, but Me you do not have always." Note that Judas Iscariot asked the question before Christ gave this answer. Scripture explains that the reason Judas asked why fragrant oil wasn't sold and proceeds given to the poor was so he could steal the money from the money box in his possession. Thus, Christ, knowing Judas' real reason for asking the question, used the opportunity to teach two lessons. One was a lesson to Judas that he would not get a chance to steal this money. Second, it demonstrated that Christ's anointing for burial was a higher priority at this time than giving to the poor, which could always be a need. Mary anticipated His death by anointing Christ at this time, which would come within a week.

John 12:14 Then Jesus, when He had found a young donkey, sat on it; as it is written: It had been written hundreds of years earlier that the King would come riding on a donkey's colt (Zechariah 9:9). Thus, this is another Old Testament prophecy that Jesus fulfilled.

John 12:27 "Now My soul is troubled, and what shall I say? 'Father, save Me from this hour'? But for this purpose I came to this hour. 28 Father, glorify Your name."

Then a voice came from heaven, *saying,* **"I have both glorified** *it* **and will glorify** *it* **again."** Here we learn that Christ had similar emotions to what we might have if faced with dying a painful death to save someone else. He knew His purpose and was determined to fulfill it no matter what because He knew that it was the Father's will. He knew that He had to suffer for a time to be lifted up later and draw people to Himself and be their light.

John 12:39 Therefore they could not believe, because Isaiah said again: 40 "He has blinded their eyes and hardened their hearts,

  Lest they should see with *their* **eyes,**

  Lest they should understand with *their* **hearts and turn,**

  So that I should heal them." Unfortunately, those who repeatedly refuse to believe what is written in the Bible may wind up having that option taken from them. They will not see the truth, and their hearts will be hardened to it.

How could God participate in the hardening of a heart when scripture says that He wants all men to be saved (1 Timothy 2:4)? The scripture also clearly states that God did harden some hearts (see Exodus 4:21; Exodus 11:10; Isaiah 63:17; et al.). First, note that in these situations, the hearts were already hard. God is simply giving them what they want. When these scriptures say that God "hardened their hearts," it seems to be saying that God is accepting that the person is definitely against Him. These people have already decided to be hard. God is accepting their decision. Of course, God knows that they are not going to change, so at some point, He accepts that they are not going to change. Usually, He has given them several opportunities before leaving them to their hard hearts.

I know no instance where God takes a person without a hard heart and turns him into one with a hard heart. Since God is not bound by space and time like we are, He probably already knows what choices these people will make now and in the future. Note that just because God knows what we may do in the future does not mean that we do not have free will. This is another one of those mysteries that we probably will not fully understand on this side of heaven.

Isaiah 12:40 is a scripture from the Old Testament (Isaiah 6:10). It explains that after the repeated rejection of the truth in the face of irrefutable evidence, the Lord hardened their hearts so that they could not believe.

John 13:2 And supper being ended, the Devil having already put it into the heart of Judas Iscariot, Simon's *son*, to betray Him, 3 Jesus, knowing that the Father had given all things into His hands, and that He had come from God and was going to God, 4 rose from supper and laid aside His garments, took a towel and girded Himself. Notice that Satan put it into Judas's heart to betray Christ. We've all heard the saying: the Devil made me do it. That is probably an exaggeration since, though the idea could have come from the Devil as it did in this case, Judas had to be willing and had to take action actually to carry out the betrayal. So, in the end, the Devil didn't "make" him do it, he just gave him the idea, and it was his sinful nature, including greed, pride, and self-direction, that allowed him to carry out the deeds. In this case, the Devil put the idea in Judas' head, but most of the time, when we sin, the idea probably just came out of our own flesh, which has its sinful nature, including greed, pride, and will self-direction.

John 13:10 Jesus said to him, "He who is bathed needs only to wash *his* feet, but is completely clean; and you are clean, but not all of you." 11 For He knew who would betray Him; therefore He said, "You are not all clean." Here is a scripture that appears to be a metaphor for the forgiveness of sins. When we believe in Christ, His payment for our sins is accepted as complete payment, and it is just as if we had never sinned in the first place. Our transgressions are all washed away when we believe and are saved. After that, we only need forgiveness of new daily transgressions through confession. That is good news.

Our confession of these transgressions to God is a process of agreeing with Him about things we should or should not do. The thing is that after we become believers (Christians), we all continue to fall short of the perfection mark and still sin. When we confess these new sins, He forgives them, and we are again clean (1 John 1:9). In this situation, one of the disciples was not a believer and eventually betrayed Christ. This is why Christ says, "**You are not all clean.**" The others were, but not this one (Judas Iscariot).

John 13:27 Now after the piece of bread, Satan entered him. Then Jesus said to him, "What you do, do quickly." Here is something that happened to one who was very close to Christ; in His inner circle. Note that in previous scripture, we are told that Satan put into Judas's heart to betray Christ. Once that idea gained traction and was accepted by Judas, Satan could go the next step and enter Judas. Once Satan entered Judas, he immediately went out into the darkness of the night and spiritual darkness.

John 13:35 By this all will know that you are My disciples, if you have love for one another." Here's an important little statement. This statement follows a new commandment directly from Christ for people to **love one another**. Why did He say this when Moses had already said to "Love your neighbor as yourself" (see Leviticus 19:18)? Jesus said it was a new commandment apparently because He set a new standard by which this commandment would be measured. The new standard was **as I have loved you.**

Previously in this chapter, He gave them the example of serving one another by washing the Apostles' feet. So what should people use to determine who is following Christ today? Should they look at the doctrine of the church? Should they look at miracles performed by the leaders of their group? Should they be recognized by how they treat unbelievers? Maybe these issues have some importance, but the standard that Christ set was their deeds of love for one another.

When you think about it, if we cannot love people who believe as we do, how would we love those who do not even agree with us? This is what we are called to do; to love our family and friends and even our enemies as much as is possible. Christians are expected to show love for one another within the church. And, what is meant by "the church" is not the building. The church is every Christian in the world. It is a big brotherhood. (Note from my friend Jan: "Just because someone disagrees does not make them an enemy." I agree with this comment.)

John 14:2 In My Father's house are many mansions; if *it were* not *so*, I would have told you. I go to prepare a place for you. It is nice to know that we will have mansions in heaven.

John 14:6 Jesus said to him, "I am the way, the truth, and the life. No one comes to the Father except through Me. 7 If you had known Me, you would have known My Father also; and from now on you know Him and have seen Him." This famous scripture reveals some major truths. First, He is the way. He was the way in the past, and He is the way in the future. Before His death, burial and resurrection, people were saved by grace through faith (Eph. 2:8). Their faith appears to have looked forward to Christ paying the price for their sins. After His resurrection, people are saved by grace through faith, looking back to Christ, paying the price for their sins. He always existed (Genesis 1:26), and salvation has always been by grace through faith. Abraham was saved through faith (James 2:23). Christ was always the way.

John 14:9 Jesus said to him, "Have I been with you so long, and yet you have not known Me, Philip? He who has seen Me has seen the Father; so how can you say, 'Show us the Father'? 10 Do you not believe that I am in the Father, and the Father in Me? The words that I speak to you I do not speak on My own *authority*; but the Father who dwells in Me does the works. This is as straightforward as you can get regarding the deity of Christ. Those who saw Him on earth were seeing God the Father. He revealed God the Father to them to the extent that they could see Him in a human incarnation. They could see Him in His human incarnation without perishing. In Exodus 33:20, God declares, "You cannot see my face, for no one may see me and live." To know Christ was to know the Father (1 John 2:23).

Interestingly, Christ refers to the Father as dwelling in Him. Before we are believers, the Holy Spirit is with us. When we believe, He lives in us, and then as we receive the Spirit, He overflows from us. We are said to be the temple of the Holy Spirit (1 Corinthians 6:19-20). Speaking of God, Christ also says that **"from now on you know Him and have seen Him."** Thus, it is clear that the Father, Son, and Holy Spirit are personalities or attributes of one God. We call it the Trinity. This concept appears to be as close as we can get in the realm in which we live. Concepts in the spiritual realm do not always translate well to the dual realm in which we live, physical and spiritual.

John 14:16 And I will pray the Father, and He will give you another Helper, that He may abide with you forever— 17 the Spirit of truth, whom the world cannot receive, because it neither sees Him nor knows Him; but you know Him, for He dwells with you and will be

in you. 18 I will not leave you orphans; I will come to you. This is a great promise. In the Old Testament, the Spirit sometimes was given by God. In Ezekiel 11:5, Ezekiel says that "**the Spirit of the Lord fell upon me**"... From John 14:16, we know that the Spirit was with the disciples and would come into them at some point. In the Ezekiel passage, the Spirit tells Ezekiel to speak specific words to the House of Israel. In other words, Ezekiel was used by the Spirit to be a spokesperson for God. The Holy Spirit was overflowing from him. A rudimentary example of how this might work is to imagine a cup of water sitting beside an empty cup. That cup of water is with the empty cup. If you pour it into the empty cup, the water is *in* the cup. If you keep pouring water into the empty cup, once it is full, the water overflows the cup. This would be like what was happening with Ezekiel. The Spirit came into him and then overflowed from him to influence others. When we study God's Word as believers and memorize some of these words and concepts, we take in words from the Holy Spirit. When we quote these words to others, I believe we are overflowing. It is beautiful to know that there will not be any orphans of God and that the Holy Spirit continues to be active in believers.

John 14:19 "A little while longer and the world will see Me no more, but you will see Me. Because I live, you will live also. Because Christ paid the price for our sins and rose from the dead concurring death, we can live through him. The disciples saw Jesus in the flesh and later in a spiritual sense. We "see" Him in a spiritual sense. The world would not see Him in the physical sense anymore after He ascended to heaven after the crucifixion, but we continue to see Him in the spiritual sense.

John 14:21 He who has My commandments and keeps them, it is he who loves Me. And he who loves Me will be loved by My Father, and I will love him and manifest Myself to him." Here we find that faith that does not result in some action may not really be faith. In other words, real faith will result in obedience to the commandments of Christ. (Another note from my friend Jan: "In other words, do unto others as you would have them do unto you.")

John 14:23 Jesus answered and said to him, "If anyone loves Me, he will keep My word; and My Father will love him, and We will come to him and make Our home with him. Note that this scripture indicates that God, the Father, and the Son will be with those who love Christ and that those who do will keep His word. Of course, we know that we cannot keep His word all the time while we are in this fallen world, as scripture indicates (Romans 7:20). However, that is the goal we move toward through the sanctification process. When we are initially saved, we are justified with our sins forgiven. When we sin after we are justified and confess these sins, they are also forgiven through sanctification (Galatians 5:16; 1 John 1:9).

John 15:4 Abide in Me, and I in you. As the branch cannot bear fruit of itself, unless it abides in the vine, neither can you, unless you abide in Me. Here is another metaphor indicating that just as a branch cannot bear fruit unless it obtains nourishment through the vine, we cannot bear fruit unless we obey the teachings of Christ. Christ is our vine in this illustration. Note that just like a vine separated from the branch, we wither and die if we are separated from Christ, who is the source of food and nourishment for our souls.

John 15:10 If you keep My commandments, you will abide in My love, just as I have kept My Father's commandments and abide in His love. Though Christ loves us, it appears that we need to keep His commandments to experience and more fully understand His love (Ephesians 3:14-19). This love of Christ surpasses all understanding and can reside in our hearts as we keep His commandments and abide in His love.

John 15:16 You did not choose Me, but I chose you and appointed you that you should go and bear fruit, and *that* your fruit should remain,

that whatever you ask the Father in My name He may give you. Note the context of this text is that Christ spoke specifically to His disciples in response to a question from Judas (not Judas Iscariot). However, some of this passage seems to have more widespread application. It appears that He initiates the relationship with us and draws us to himself even though we seem to have the free will to decline His offer of fellowship. Also, note that Christ specifically chose and appointed these disciples to **go and bear fruit.** These disciples were allowed to ask for things (in his will) and receive them. Asking for the Lord's will should probably always be a part of our prayer life. He made us and gave us life. Why would we not want to keep all that we ask according to what He wants?

John 15:18 "If the world hates you, you know that it hated Me before *it hated* you. 19 If you were of the world, the world would love its own. Yet because you are not of the world, but I chose you out of the world, therefore the world hates you. This scripture lets us know what to expect from some people so we will not be surprised when we run into hatred based solely on our beliefs. Look what the government did to Christ at the behest of the religious leaders. Thus, it is not surprising that the world will have a similar attitude toward His current-day followers. We are very fortunate in America to live in a country that at least says it provides religious freedom. However, even in America, this freedom is eroding. Christians in some other countries have a very different experience and in a few countries, acting on your Christian faith (or some other faith) can be punishable by a death sentence. This is predicted in verse 16:2 where the scripture states: **"They will put you out of the synagogues; yes, the time is coming that whoever kills you will think that he offers God service."** This is what members of some religious groups think about Christians. By some religions, we are referred to as infidels. It is true that in the world, we will have tribulation, but Christ has overcome the world (16:33).

John 15:21 But all these things they will do to you for My name's

sake, because they do not know Him who sent Me. 22 If I had not come and spoken to them, they would have no sin, but now they have no excuse for their sin. This is a frightening statement for an unbeliever because it says they **have no excuse for their sin.** Before Christ came and spoke to these people, they had more of an excuse for their sin. A child may be innocent of accountability for sin because they are before the *age* of accountability. In other words, if the child is not mature enough to comprehend the concept of a particular sin, they may not be accountable for that sin. The same concept may apply to a person who has limited intellectual capacity. We know that God is fair and just (Psalm 25:8-14), so we don't have to worry about it. He will judge fairly based on his grace, mercy, and justice.

John 16:2 They will put you out of the synagogues; yes, the time is coming that whoever kills you will think that he offers God service. 3 And these things they will do to you because they have not known the Father nor Me. Those who do not know God will be very angry toward those who do and will even think they are doing their god a service when they kill a Christian. We see this prophecy being fulfilled throughout history and to this day. So many prophecies in the Bible are fulfilled, it is hard to imagine that anyone reading it with their heart open will not see the truth in these words, but some hearts are hardened to these words.

John 16:7 Nevertheless I tell you the truth. It is to your advantage that I go away; for if I do not go away, the Helper will not come to you; but if I depart, I will send Him to you. 8 And when He has come, He will convict the world of sin, and of righteousness, and of judgment: It was a great advantage for us for Christ to pay the price for our sins and then send the Holy Spirit to convict the world of the sin of unbelief in Christ. The Holy Spirit uses believers in this process of convincing unbelievers of the truth (15:26,27). When the Holy Spirit speaks through us, we witness what God has done in our lives. So, as a result of Christ coming and leaving the earth, we have the Holy Spirit to comfort and help us. We have the potential for joy and greater knowledge, and peace. The Holy Spirit indwells all believers at the same time. When Christ was here in physical form, it appears that His physical presence was not as beneficial for believers as the indwelling of the Holy Spirit would be after He paid the price for our sins and ascended to heaven. Note that the spirit of this world can influence the hearts of unbelievers (1 Corinthians 2:12). Believers can and should let the Holy Spirit be their guide and influence. **The natural man does not receive the things of the Spirit of God** (1 Corinthians 2:14). With the Holy Spirit, we can have Christ's **mind,** which we always need to have. We have been given the Spirit of God to know the things of God (1 Corinthians 2:11).

John 16:13 However, when He, the Spirit of truth, has come, He will guide you into all truth; for He will not speak on His own *authority*, but whatever He hears He will speak; and He will tell you things to come. The Bible is inspired by the Holy Spirit (Mark 12:36; Acts 1:16; 2 Peter 1:20-21; John 14:26; 2 Timothy 3:16-17) and is one way the Holy Spirit communicates to us. Things to come are one thing the Bible talks about. We often don't know when the prophecies will be fulfilled, but we do know what will happen from reading the scriptures.

John 16:23 "And in that day you will ask Me nothing. Most assuredly, I say to you, whatever you ask the Father in My name He will give you. In the paragraph before this verse, Jesus is speaking of His post-resurrection appearances and the joy of forgiven sins (1 Peter 1:8) that no one can take away. At that time, the disciples would not need to ask Him questions because many things would then be clarified for them by Christ's resurrection. When they did ask for something, it would be asking for something "in His will," and therefore, it would be done. This section of scripture is often misunderstood. Pridefully asking the ultimate creator of the universe for something outside of His will would show a complete lack of humility and understanding about who He is and an elevation of ourselves way beyond where we should stand in relation to our creator and savior.

John 16:33 These things I have spoken to you, that in Me you may have peace. In the world you will have tribulation; but be of good cheer, I have overcome the world." Pressure, affliction, and distress will come our way while we are on earth. That is the world's way, but we are not ultimately of the world in a spiritual sense. We are here for a while and will partake of these issues just as Christ did when he walked on the earth (vs. 14-16). He is glorified (revealed) in us (vs. 10), so we need to be here and communicate Christ's words through the power of the Holy Spirit. We can be at peace and have joy amid difficulties when we keep our ultimate purpose in mind.

John 17:17 Sanctify them by Your truth. Your word is truth. Most everything else is subject to change, and people's opinions and experiences are unreliable and untrustworthy, but the Word of God remains the same and is reliable and trustworthy.

John 17:20 "I do not pray for these alone, but also for those who will believe in Me through their word; 21 that they all may be one, as You, Father, *are* in Me, and I in You; that they also may be one in Us, that the world may believe that You sent Me. Here, Christ is praying for us to be one with Him and the Father. I do not know what that means in the spiritual realm, but I imagine it will be quite amazing to be one in God in heaven.

John 17:21 ...that they all may be one, as You, Father, *are* in Me, and I in You; that they also may be one in Us, that the world may believe that You sent Me. Even high-level people in churches may come up with ways to justify being in disharmony with each other and being disparaging about one another. Still, the Word of God takes a different approach. Christ prays that the unity of believers here on earth will be like the unity between Him and the Father. The two are one. When we bring up the sins of other believers and speak negatively about them or gossip about them or try to get others to cut them off or retaliate against them, even in "private," we are going against what Christ has commanded us to do. Suppose the fruit of God's love brings unity among all believers. In that case, an easy way to determine if some statement about another person who professes to be a believer is with love is to ask the question: Did what was said bring unity or strife?

John 17:22 And the glory which You gave Me I have given them, that they may be one just as We are one: This is important. Christ was talking to the Father and asking that we would have the same revelation that the Father gave to him that we could be as one with Him. He was asking to be in us as the Father was in Him. Then we could be one just as the Father and Christ are one. Jesus prays for and commands unity among believers. The Father gave Christ His glory. In other words, the Father revealed His plans to Christ when He was here on the earth, and Christ has, in turn, given us the revelation of Himself. We now know something of what He knows about His mission on earth, and as a result, as we experience sanctification, we become more one with Christ. This should create unity among those who are chosen to believe this gospel. We are to love each other. When we don't see this love, which scripture says is the greatest witness of Jesus Christ, there is something wrong. Correct belief will produce unity among believers. If there is no unity, perhaps there is no correct belief, sanctification, or justification on either side of the disunity.

John 17:25 O righteous Father! The world has not known You, but I have known You; and these have known that You sent Me. 26 And I have declared to them Your name, and will declare *it,* **that the love with which You loved Me may be in them, and I in them."** We need to know the love of God so it can be replicated in us. Then, the world can be drawn to Christ.

John 18:11 So Jesus said to Peter, "Put your sword into the sheath. Shall I not drink the cup which My Father has given Me?" Here Christ provides an example of following what God has given us even if it results in our death. The difficulty here is knowing what God's will is for our lives. How do we find out? One way is to read the Bible, with prayer and supplication, and glean what it says about how we should proceed with our lives. Once we have mastered following and obeying the written instructions (not likely, but this is the goal) that He has provided, then we should continue to pray and do more of the same. We need to read, understand, delight, and exemplify the Word. Put together the first letters of these three words, and it spells rude, but that is the opposite of what you will be if you practice this advice daily (Joshua 1:8).

There are times when following the will of the Lord is not what we want to do and may cause us to have to pick up a cross and bear some great burden for the sake of benefiting someone else. Note that Christ restored the ear (Luke 22:51) that Peter cut off. When we take things into our own hands and try to change God's plan, He can do the same for us. He can restore what has been taken away. We tend to be egocentric, thinking that we are more than what we are. The reality is that the world does not revolve around us, and there are times when we simply play a small insignificant part in a more cosmic spiritual event.

Notice how Job played a part in communication between God and Satan. Even though Job was faithful, God was not obligated to bless him. In the end, God had a good plan for Job, but in between, Job had an unpleasant job to do in exercising his faith and obedience. The reality is that God is sovereign. He has free will and is not bound by anyone's preconceived expectations of what He has to do based on any theological system that a man may have invented. With the story of Job, we learn that our prosperity is not dependent on our goodness. God can restore and reverse the results of any of our actions that are not in accord with His will.

John 18:37 Pilate therefore said to Him, "Are You a king then?"

Jesus answered, "You say *rightly* that I am a king. For this cause I was born, and for this cause I have come into the world, that I should bear witness to the truth. Everyone who is of the truth hears My voice." It appears that Pilate did not want to know the truth, or He would have listened to Christ. After Christ makes this statement, Pilate asks a cynical question about truth as if to say; no one can know the truth. Then he pronounced Jesus as not guilty and said, "**I find no fault in Him at all.**" This was the truth. There was no fault in Him.

John 19:11 Jesus answered, "You could have no power at all against Me unless it had been given you from above. Therefore the one who delivered Me to you has the greater sin." There are a couple of points in this scripture of great importance. First, God is in charge, even in this situation, where Christ would suffer great torture and pain. When we are in situations where we feel we are suffering even though we think we didn't do anything to deserve the suffering, we should remember that this is the very situation that Christ was in to pay the price for our sins. Maybe that will give us more empathy for what He went through on our behalf. Our suffering probably is nowhere near what He went through. In other words, our cross to bear is probably a lot lighter. Second, Caiaphas was the one who had the greater sin (18:24, 28). (Note that this passage implies different grades of sins.) He was a religious leader and should have recognized the Messiah.

John 19:17 And He, bearing His cross, went out to a place called *the Place* of a Skull, which is called in Hebrew, Golgotha, 18 where they crucified Him, and two others with Him, one on either side, and Jesus in the center. Note that one of the others crucified with Christ was given eternal life and went to Paradise to be with Christ (Luke 23:43). He didn't even go to church. He didn't get baptized. He didn't prove he was worthy. He didn't do any good works or any works at all, for that matter. He just believed in Christ and went to heaven. It's the same process for us who believe when we leave this earth. We are saved by grace through faith (Ephesians 2:8).

John 19:27 Then He said to the disciple, "Behold your mother!" And from that hour that disciple took her to his own *home.* Jesus placed his mother in the care of John. Thus, He made arrangements for her well-being after He left the earth.

John 19:41 Now in the place where He was crucified there was a garden, and in the garden a new tomb in which no one had yet been laid. This scripture notes the fulfillment of another prophecy from Isaiah 53:9 that Christ would be buried in a rich man's grave.

John 20:17 Jesus said to her, "Do not cling to Me, for I have not yet ascended to My Father; but go to My brethren and say to them, 'I am ascending to My Father and your Father, and *to* My God and your God.'" This took place after Jesus rose from the dead and, through doing so, conquered death once and for all. He did not want Mary to cling to Him because He knew that he needed to ascend to heaven soon.

John 20:22 And when He had said this, He breathed on *them,* and said to them, "Receive the Holy Spirit. 23 If you forgive the sins of any, they are forgiven them; if you retain the *sins* of any, they are retained." This is important. Here, Jesus was talking to His Apostles and gave them the Holy Spirit and what appears to be a representative authority. I say "representative authority" because I understand that it is actually by God's authority that transgressions can be forgiven (Acts 8:22; Mark 2:7). As God had sent Him, Jesus was sending them out to proclaim the gospel. The Holy Spirit would empower their testimony. They were given spiritual power. Later at Pentecost, the Spirit unified the body of Christ and empowered people to testify of Jesus (1 Corinthians 1:13). The Holy Spirit is not the human spirit of natural life: it is the Spirit of God that produces eternal life.

The disciples were called to a specific ministry. They could not perform this ministry without the Holy Spirit. Thus, Christ gave them the power of the Holy Spirit that they needed. "At Pentecost, the Spirit unified the believers into one body and empowered them to testify of Jesus (see 1 Corinthian 12:13)" (NSB p. 1808). Here the Holy Spirit is breathed on the disciples like when Adam was given a spiritual life in Genesis 2:7, except that the spirit given here was the Spirit of God, not a human spirit of life. Thus, the Holy Spirit was given to the disciples, giving them abilities far beyond the spirit of life that all humans need. We need the spirit of life to have the kind of life we live.

Our life is different from the type of life that the animals have. The spirit of life that God gave man is a spirit that allows us to go farther beyond what is built into our instinct. We have an intellectual and spiritual capacity that animals don't have, though some "soulish" animals have aspects of emotion and the ability to learn similar to what we have. Even with emotion and learning, the most human-like animals have a rudimentary capacity in these areas. Nevertheless, the physical abilities of some animals far surpass ours. A big difference is that animals seem to have little capacity for the knowledge of morality. They apply reason in certain situations, and they can certainly experience emotions like joy and anger. The bottom line is that animals are part of God's creation and deserve our respect.

John 20:29 Jesus said to him, "Thomas, because you have seen Me, you have believed. Blessed *are* those who have not seen and *yet* have believed." Jesus is God in the flesh. Believing in Him results in the right to have eternal life with Him. It is a too-good-to-be-true offer that is true. Believers are blessed. Hallelujah and Amen!

John 20:30 And truly Jesus did many other signs in the presence of His disciples, which are not written in this book; 31 but these are written that you may believe that Jesus is the Christ, the Son

of God, and that believing you may have life in His name. In other words, we have enough evidence in the Bible. If someone doesn't believe with all of this evidence, their hearts may be hardened. More evidence will probably not make any difference. The scripture is straightforward. To have life eternal, we simply believe in His name. Of course, if we do believe in His name, we would want to follow and obey what He wants of us in our life here on earth.

John 21:16 He said to him again a second time, "Simon, *son* of Jonah, do you love Me?"

He said to Him, "Yes, Lord; You know that I love You."

He said to him, "Tend My sheep." Here's what Christ told Peter to do with his life. The people need to be fed the Word of God and guided in their application of the Word. Peter had denied the Lord three times, and in this chapter, he affirms his love for the Lord three times. Peter was now empowered to carry out his ministry and focus on that. He was to follow Christ and not worry about what the Lord had in store for others. When Peter said he loved the Lord, he received a duty to fulfill. Peter could be a model for us. If we love the Lord, we might ask the Lord for guidance regarding what responsibility He would like us to fulfill. The scriptures are full of options and examples. Each person is different and has their place in the body of Christ. We don't need to be concerned about someone else's place. We need to be concerned about finding our place. Like Peter, we are ready for service with the Lord's complete forgiveness and empowerment. As a fitting end to this commentary on the Gospels, we can now be prepared for service.

44

Acts - HIGHLIGHTS of the BIBLE - ACTS to REVELATION COMMENTARY - VOLUME III

[44] **ACTS** - This book tells how the gospel spread through people who knew Christ and saw Him with His glorified body after the resurrection.

Acts 1:4 And being assembled together with *them,* **He commanded them not to depart from Jerusalem, but to wait for the Promise of the Father, "which,"** *He said,* **"you have heard from Me; 5 for John truly baptized with water, but you shall be baptized with the Holy Spirit not many days from now."** Christ's words were spoken to the disciples after the resurrection over 40 days before His ascension. Once the disciples received the Holy Spirit, they went and testified all over the place and spread the gospel. They were doing more testifying than convincing. They had a spirit of uniformity and power to witness locally and **to the ends of the earth**. They were to tell others about the truth of

---

[44] NSB quotations are from the Nelsons Study Bible, copyright (c) 1997 by Thomas Nelson, Inc., Nashville, TN; used by permission; scripture taken from the New King James Version, Copyright (c) 1979, 1980, 1982 used by permission. All rights reserved.

the gospel. Note that witnessing is different than convincing. Convincing is more like what a salesperson would do. They were more like witnesses reporting what they believed than salespeople.

Acts 1:11 This *same* Jesus, who was taken up from you into heaven, will so come in like manner as you saw Him go into heaven." This verse is speaking of the "second coming" when Jesus returns to the earth in the same way that He ascended from it.

Acts 1:20 "For it is written in the Book of Psalms:
   'Let his dwelling place be desolate,
   And let no one live in it';
   and,
'Let another take his office.' This scripture has to do with the selection of Judas Iscariot's replacement as an apostle. Two people had gone in and out among the other apostles. They had witnessed the miracles and teachings of Jesus. They had also witnessed His resurrection. They prayed to choose between the two proposed individuals, asking the Lord which of the two to number with the eleven apostles. They cast lots, and Matthias was the one chosen.

Acts 2:5 And there were dwelling in Jerusalem Jews, devout men, from every nation under heaven. 6 And when this sound occurred, the multitude came together, and were confused, because everyone heard them speak in his own language. The sound referred to here was the people speaking in other tongues. Tongues in Greek is the usual word for languages. So the people were speaking in different languages that they did not know, and the people who spoke heard them. The Holy Spirit had given these people the ability to speak in tongues they did not know. The foreigners who spoke different languages could understand what they were saying. Thus, this was amazing to the people who were there. Based on other scriptures (10:46; 1 Corinthians 14:16), the apostles praised God's mighty works when speaking other languages.

Also, these scriptures appear to provide an example to us that there should be understanding when anyone else is speaking in a different tongue or language if what they say is from God. If there is no understanding or interpretation, ten thousand words would not be very edifying; five words with understanding would be better.

Acts 2:21 *And it shall come to pass*
That whoever calls upon the name of the LORD
Shall be saved.' This verse is a quote from the prophet Joel in the Old Testament, which is another sign that the New Testament is following along and is in harmony with the Old Testament. Before this text, Peter notes that in the last days (Acts 2:17), God would pour out His Spirit on all people. His Holy Spirit would no longer be limited to prophets and a few others, as was His practice in Old Testament days. This event where God poured out His Spirit on many people is called Pentecost and appears to be the beginning of the period referred to as the last days.

It is interesting that even as believers who have the Holy Spirit residing in us, we still have the free will to resist the influence of the Spirit. Of course, there may be negative consequences for us. Most of the guidance we receive from the Holy Spirit, whether it be from the Word of God (the Bible), visions, dreams, or prophecy, in the long run, will be to our benefit even though it may not seem that way in the short term.

Immediately after this verse, Peter talks about how Jesus of Nazareth did miracles, wonders, and signs that they had observed (2:22-24). They also saw Him be put to death and raised by God. King David had previously spoken of Christ's resurrection (2:31) and that Christ would be exalted to God's right hand. Peter then told them to **repent** (of their unbelief in Christ and what He had done for them) and **be baptized in the name of Jesus Christ for the remission of sins, and you shall receive the gift of the Holy Spirit** (2:38). Note that the baptism was not what saved them; it was their belief in Christ (10:34-43). Baptism is simply an outward sign of a belief. Remember the thief on the cross? He did not have a chance to be baptized, but Christ told him that he would be in paradise with Him that very day (Luke 23:43). Both the Holy Spirit and Salvation are a gift. As many as **the Lord our God will call** will receive the Holy Spirit (2:39). Some people think they know who is saved by God. I think these people have a little too high of an opinion of their abilities.

Acts 2:38 Then Peter said to them, "Repent, and let every one of you be baptized in the name of Jesus Christ for the remission of sins; and you shall receive the gift of the Holy Spirit. These days, we generally think of repenting as an act of turning away from doing some inappropriate action. In this scripture, "repent" appears to mean turning away from inappropriate and wrong beliefs about Christ. It seems to mean going from disbelief to believing that Christ was who He said He was. That is, Jesus Christ is God incarnate. He was the Messiah. He was the one who was resurrected and ascended. He is the one in whom our faith can provide salvation and eternal life. To become a Christian involves repenting of our unbelief in Christ and turning to belief. We are justified through this faith and this faith alone by God's grace (Romans 4:1-8; Ephesians 2:8,9). Through this faith, we are declared righteous in the sight of God. Of course, if we do repent of our unbelief, our behavior will generally change.

Acts 2:42 And they continued steadfastly in the apostles' doctrine and fellowship, in the breaking of bread, and in prayers. The fellowship is essential. It has to do with the close association and sharing with other believers. We learn from others and support each other in the Christian walk. Part of this fellowship involves eating together and participating in corporate prayer. All of these activities serve to bond believers together in pursuing shared interests.

Acts 3:6 Then Peter said, "Silver and gold I do not have, but what I do have I give you: In the name of Jesus Christ of Nazareth, rise

up and walk." So Peter, the Apostle, was given the power to heal this gentleman. That does not mean that anyone else could simply speak these words and heal someone. From my perspective, God's power was granted to the apostles and a few others, but I don't think any of these people are currently on earth.

Acts 3:19 Repent therefore and be converted, that your sins may be blotted out, so that times of refreshing may come from the presence of the Lord, There is that word repent again. Does it mean something else this time? I don't think so. The scripture appears to be encouraging us to repent of unbelief. Then, our sins would be forgiven (blotted out). Once this happens, **times of refreshing may come from the presence of the LORD.**

Acts 3:21 ...whom heaven must receive until the times of restoration of all things, which God has spoken by the mouth of all His holy prophets since the world began. Here is a mention of **"the times of restoration of all things."** When is that time coming? I don't know, and I don't think anyone else knows precisely when that time is coming, either. We know that Christ is currently in heaven and that when He comes back to the earth, it will be a great time. I believe that, and it is something to which to look forward. This would be when Christ establishes His Kingdom on the earth (Joel 2:29; 3:1; Jeremiah 33:15).

Acts 4:12 Nor is there salvation in any other, for there is no other name under heaven given among men by which we must be saved." This verse clarifies that there is no other name by which people can be saved. The verse is speaking about Jesus Christ of Nazareth. It makes sense to know who this person/man/God is. Who else could fill these shoes? Noone. How many biological earthly fathers do you have? Well, it appears you also only have one heavenly spiritual father. I once thought there could not be just one way to salvation and was upset with those who maintained that position. Now, I agree that this is the truth. Based on my experience, I know it is hard to fathom that only one God can redeem you. However, that *is* the message of the Bible. Those who want it to be different will have to find another good book. I've looked at some work-based belief systems, and none of them come close to explaining God as does the Christian Bible.

Acts 4:19 But Peter and John answered and said to them, "Whether it is right in the sight of God to listen to you more than to God, you judge. 20 For we cannot but speak the things which we have seen and heard." Here is a case where we find out who has priority when there is a discrepancy between what a government says to do and what the Lord says to do. We are to follow the Lord. There are government authorities that reject the sovereignty of God. If they direct us to do something we know is contrary to God's will, this is the one time that we should disobey. Other scriptures say that we should obey God rather than men (5:29).

Acts 4:31 And when they had prayed, the place where they were assembled together was shaken; and they were all filled with the Holy Spirit, and they spoke the word of God with boldness. Here we find out what can empower someone to talk about the word of God boldly. It is the Holy Spirit. Note that God gives the Holy Spirit to those who obey Him (5:32).

Acts 4:32 Now the multitude of those who believed were of one heart and one soul; neither did anyone say that any of the things he possessed was his own, but they had all things in common. Interestingly, the early Christians shared and viewed their possessions as not their own. That is appropriate because, according to the scriptures, all things on earth belong to the Lord. We are just temporary stewards. Note that other scriptures encourage Christians to help the poor among us. However, keep in mind that the first people who are to be supported when they are in need are immediate family members (1 Timothy 5:8;

Ephesians 6:1-2). After those needs are met, other conditions should be generously considered (Acts 20:35; Proverbs 19:17; Deuteronomy 15:11, etc.). It appears that just as when an oxygen mask is needed on an airplane, you put it on yourself first. You have to have your financial health before you can help others. You can't help others if you are unconscious due to a lack of financial oxygen.

Acts 5:12 And through the hands of the apostles many signs and wonders were done among the people. And they were all with one accord in Solomon's Porch. Signs are supernatural events. The signs and wonders helped convince people of what the Apostles told them. Solomon's Porch is thought to be an open-aired triple aisled entrance; this was a gathering place for early Christians.

Acts 5:41 So they departed from the presence of the council, rejoicing that they were counted worthy to suffer shame for His name. At the direction of the religious leaders of the day, the Apostles had just been beaten and rejoiced. That is amazing. After being beaten, they were rejoicing. Why? Because they felt in harmony with Christ and empathized with Him. This begs the question: how many of us could be beaten and threatened and rejoice about it?

Acts 6:8 And Stephen, full of faith and power, did great wonders and signs among the people. Even though Stephen had spoken the truth and recited the history of how God had delivered Israel by Moses, the religious leaders and people stoned him to death. Some of his last words were: "**Lord, do not charge them with this sin**" (7:60). That shows a great deal of forgiveness on Stephen's part.

Saul, who later became Paul, was present and participated in the stoning of Stephen. He did not forget Stephen's request to God for mercy for the people who stoned him. In Romans 8:28, God promises, "**And we know that all things work together for good to those who love God, to**

those who are the called according to *His* purpose." One of Stephen's persecutors became Paul, who wrote about half of the New Testament. That shows how forgiving God can be. Paul participated in killing one of Christ's apostles and later became a great apostle himself.

Acts 8:17 Then they laid hands on them, and they received the Holy Spirit. Later, Peter preached to the Gentiles, and they were said to have received the Holy Spirit without the laying on of hands. Once the Holy Spirit was received, the believers were apparently in greater harmony (1 Corinthians 12:12-13). When you think about it, how could Jews and Samaritans get along and agree very much without the Holy Spirit's work?

Peter admonished Simon for trying to pay money to be given the ability to lay on hands and transmit the Holy Spirit to someone. Peter clarifies that God's gift cannot be purchased with money and tells Simon to pray to God for forgiveness. Then Simon asked Peter to pray for him.

Acts 8:30 So Philip ran to him, and heard him reading the prophet Isaiah, and said, "Do you understand what you are reading?" Here we have a further indication that we need to study and have others guide us after becoming believers. The Holy Spirit does not eliminate the need to be taught by more mature people in the faith. It helps us better understand what we are taught and read in the scriptures.

Acts 8:36 Now as they went down the road, they came to some water. And the eunuch said, "See, *here is* water. What hinders me from being baptized?" 37 Then Philip said, "If you believe with all your heart, you may." Thus, there does appear to be a prerequisite to being baptized. That prerequisite is believing with all your heart. Is this prerequisite always fulfilled? Probably not. But, it is still a requirement without which the baptism would not be as significant.

Acts 9:13 Then Ananias answered, "Lord, I have heard from many about this man, how much harm he has done to Your saints in Jerusalem. This appears to be the first time in Acts where people previously called believers or disciples are now called saints. What is a saint? It is a person who is recognized as having an unusual degree of holiness, likeness, or closeness to God. Human beings, on their own, are not saints. However, we can be designated saints if our transgressions have been forgiven through what Christ did on our behalf. God thus sees us as saints. "Christ did for us what we could not do for ourselves" (*How Can I Explain the Gospel?* Vaneetha Rendall Risner, April 11, 2019).

Acts 10:28 But God has shown me that I should not call any man common or unclean. Here Cornelius recognizes that God had shown Him that he should not regard gentiles as unclean, which God had cleansed. He revealed that the gift of the Holy Spirit was poured out on the gentiles as well as the Jews who believed. All they had to do was believe; nothing more and nothing less. Once the Gentiles had faith, they were the same as the believing Jews in God's eyes (11:18).

Acts 11:26 And the disciples were first called Christians in Antioch. Before being called Christians, the word of God needed to be written. Before that, the followers of Christ were called The Way (19:9). In a history written by Josephus, they were called the tribe of Christians. A Roman historian also referred to them as Christians.

Acts 13:39 and by Him everyone who believes is justified from all things from which you could not be justified by the law of Moses. In a court of law, if someone else pays your fine, you could be set free. Then it would be as if you had not committed the crime in the first place. Christ paid the price for our crimes against God so that we could be forgiven. We could not follow the laws of Moses well enough to be justified. No human being can. These laws show us that we cannot live sinless life and are in great need of forgiveness.

Acts 13:46 Then Paul and Barnabus grew bold and said, "It was necessary that the word of God should be spoken to you first; but since you reject it, and judge yourself unworthy of everlasting life, behold, we turn to the gentiles. How could someone judge themselves unworthy of eternal life? Well, it appears that the Jews at that time were full of envy about the fact that Paul and Barnabus had also invited the Gentiles to be taught the word of God. The Jews started disagreeing with what Paul was teaching. They even contradicted him and blasphemed. Thus, by rejecting the gospel, they determined they did not need forgiveness from God. By thinking that they did not need forgiveness, they were condemning themselves. Clarification: everyone needs forgiveness (Romans 3:23). At this time, the Gentiles who **had been appointed to eternal life believed** (13:48). Note that scripture says that many are called, but obviously, not all are chosen (Matthew 22:14).

Acts 15:11 But we believe that through the grace of the Lord Jesus Christ we shall be saved in the same manner as they. The scripture leading up to this conclusion had to do with whether Gentile converts should follow the Jewish tradition of being circumcised. Peter intimated that this yoke should not be put around their necks. He seemed to be saying that this tradition of Moses should not be required of the Gentile converts. As with the Jews who were saved, the Gentiles were saved the same way; through faith by God's grace. They could not be saved by keeping the laws and traditions of Moses. The law shows us that we need forgiveness because no flesh can be justified by the law (Romans 3:20). We all fall short of following all the law (Romans 3:23). We are in the dispensation of grace in which those who become believers will want to follow God's laws and be in His will, but we know that following the law is not what provides salvation. Again, salvation is through faith by God's grace toward us. No more, no less.

Acts 19:11 Now God worked unusual miracles by the hands of Paul,

12 so that even handkerchiefs or aprons were brought from his body to the sick, and the diseases left them and the evil spirits went out of them. According to Hebrews 2:3 and 4, these unusual miracles resulted from God confirming and bearing witness that the apostles were telling the truth about the gospel they were teaching. God confirmed Paul's authority through the miracles that verified he and the other Apostles spoke for God.

Acts 19:19 Also, many of those who had practiced magic brought their books together and burned *them* in the sight of all. And they counted up the value of them, and *it* totaled fifty thousand *pieces* of silver. This event took place after an evil spirit said that he knew who Jesus and Paul were but did not know some of the exorcists were using the Lord Jesus's name for their selfish purposes. These people were driven out of the house naked and wounded by the man with the evil spirit. This magnified the name of the Lord Jesus and resulted in the burning of the books on magic as the people following these practices repented. People who do not believe in Christ and do not have His Spirit in them should not use His name to get what they want.

Acts 20:29 For I know this, that after my departure savage wolves will come in among you, not sparing the flock. There are both external and internal threats to the church. The wheat and the weeds grow together, and believers and counterfeits (savage wolves) will go to church. Thus, there will be those who speak perverse ideas from inside and outside the church to draw people away.

Acts 20:35 I have shown you in every way, by laboring like this, that you must support the weak. And remember the words of the Lord Jesus, that He said, 'It is more blessed to give than to receive.' It appears that though Paul had a right to be supported by the church, he worked with his hands to support himself and the weak. Paul practiced what he preached, even when not required to do so.

Acts 21:9 Now this man had four virgin daughters who prophesied. This fulfills what Peter said in chapter 2:17 about how God would pour out His Spirit on all flesh, and sons and daughters would prophesy. It was probably not expected in the male-dominated culture that daughters would receive the Spirit of God and prophecy.

Acts 23:5 Then Paul said, "I did not know, brethren, that he was the high priest; for it is written, 'You shall not speak evil of a ruler of your people.' In this situation, Paul was given a chance to speak for himself, and he criticized the High Priest because the High Priest had Paul struck on the mouth for saying that he lived in all good conscience.

We do not know why Paul did not know the High Priest's identity until told, but it does appear that he immediately repented. That was appropriate. They made accusations against him that he was a plague and creator of dissension (24:5). In his defense, he told them what he believed and about his hope in God and **"that there will be a resurrection of the dead, both of the just and the unjust"** (24:15).

Earlier in my life, this statement would have been a revelation because I thought we just ceased to exist when we died. Now, I accept that though our physical bodies die, our spirit lives on, and later believers will receive glorified eternal spiritual bodies (1 Corinthians 15:42-44; Philippians 3:21, etc.). If you believe what the Bible says, it changes everything. If we are just an accident of biological processes over a long time and no more or less important than an amoeba, what difference does anything in life make? What basis is there for any particular behavior? Why isn't survival of the fittest the highest or the only value? Who has the authority to determine what has value? Would it be the strongest, most ruthless, or most compassionate? Why would it be any of these?

It seems that throughout history, some countries have attempted to abolish religion of any type. These countries can wind up with a charismatic dictator who can convince people with the most lethal weapons to do their bidding and consolidate power by wiping out anyone who opposes them (democide). Considering the history, if you put together the seven countries, you would have democide of approximately 128,000,000 people. The Khmer Rouge was possibly the worst. As described in Chapter 9 of Death by Government, from 1975-1978, they killed about 31 percent of the men, women, and children in the country.

You might think that a dictatorship could not happen in America because of our three branches in the government system. Nevertheless, some people have called at least one American president a Nazi. If that were true, the right to bear arms would be the most important civil right and possibly the first right he would attempt to abolish. Those who wrote the Constitution knew that the risk of having a government turn against the citizens was real and therefore instituted the Second Amendment. Its primary purpose is to keep a dictator from taking power, confiscating the citizens' guns, and using the military to control or wipe out anyone who opposes them. History has shown this scenario has happened more than once and that coups are not uncommon.

Acts 27:23 For there stood by me this night an angel of the God to whom I belong and whom I serve, 24 saying, 'Do not be afraid, Paul; you must be brought before Caesar; and indeed God has granted you all those who sail with you.' Sometimes it is good to be close to a person who belongs to God. In this case, all the people on the ship with Paul were kept alive even though the ship was destroyed. During a severe storm and the ship's breakup, Paul had asked the Lord for their lives to be spared, and it pleased the Lord to preserve all 276 persons. According to an Angel of God who appeared to Paul, he was to be brought before Caesar. He was (a) a Jew, (b) a Roman Citizen, (c) originally a Pharisee, (d) the son of a Pharisee, and (e) probably a relative of Agrippa.

Acts 28:22 But we desire to hear from you what you think; for

concerning this sect, we know that it is spoken against everywhere." Here we find out that Christianity was spoken against even in the beginning, and this has not changed. It is still spoken against today by those opposed to the Gospel.

45

Romans

[45] **ROMANS** - This is a critical book written by Paul that covers much of the important theology. The book makes it abundantly clear that humanity needs to be set free from sin and rescued. We all fall short of the glory of God. It reasserts that salvation for both Jews and Gentiles is by God's grace through faith.

Romans 1:16 For I am not ashamed of the gospel of Christ, for it is the power of God to salvation for everyone who believes, for the Jew first and also for the Greek. What is this salvation spoken about in this verse? According to John 3:16, it is **"everlasting life."** According to Ephesians 3:8, it is **"by grace you have been saved through faith."** It is not something that can be earned through works **"lest anyone should boast."** According to Hebrews 12:2, Jesus is **"the author and finisher of our faith."** Faith leads to salvation, whereby we no longer have the penalty of sin. Christ has paid the penalty for our past, present, and future sins, so we are no longer God's enemies (Matthew 1:21). We are His children (John 1:12).

---

[45] NSB quotations are from the Nelsons Study Bible, copyright (c) 1997 by Thomas Nelson, Inc., Nashville, TN; used by permission; scripture taken from the New King James Version, Copyright (c) 1979, 1980, 1982 used by permission. All rights reserved.

Romans 1:18 For the wrath of God is revealed from heaven against all ungodliness and unrighteousness of men, who suppress the truth in unrighteousness, 19 because what may be known of God is manifest in them, for God has shown *it* to them. This is terrible news for unbelievers. It more than implies that God has shown everyone the truth about Himself, but many people don't want to hear it and suppress what He has shown them. The verse after this one explains that although God is invisible, the world He created is visible. His creation makes His attributes seen by those who open their eyes (1:20). The design of the world makes it so evident that He is the Godhead with eternal power that those who suppress this truth are "**without excuse**" (1:20). The bottom line of this verse is that God is the Creator and is worthy of our worship. A person has to suppress this observable truth not to see it. God's wrath will be revealed against those who suppress this truth.

Romans 1:24 Therefore God also gave them up to uncleanness, in the lusts of their hearts, to dishonor their bodies among themselves, 25 who exchanged the truth of God for the lie, and worshiped and served the creature rather than the Creator, who is blessed forever. Amen. This verse covers what happens when some of God's created beings deny He exists. That would be the equivalent of a son or daughter denying their mother or father. When you look around the world, it is evident how evil people can be. For example, it is relatively well established that governments have killed over 100,000,000 people over the last century. That fact alone is good evidence that many dictators have lusted for power to the point of being willing to eliminate their opposition through democide and any other means.

Romans 1:26 For this reason God gave them up to vile passions. For even their women exchanged the natural use for what is against nature. I will leave it to the reader to figure out the definition of "vile passions." The term "**against nature**" appears to mean something contrary to how God created us to be. The interesting thing about this verse is that the Lord seems to have given them up to their vile passions as **"the penalty for their error which was due"** (1:27). When we are given up to these passions, we become slaves. This is most evident in those who have a passion for certain drugs. Once you use enough of them, these drugs have a hold on you that you cannot ignore. You become a slave to the drug.

With other sins, slavery is not obviously controlling the person's life. This slavery is much more subtle, but it is still like being a slave (Romans 6:16). Being a slave to sin leads to death. Being a slave to obedience to God (Romans 6:22) leads to righteousness. Either way, we are going to be a slave to something. Of course, the sexual sin mentioned in verse 1:26 is not the only sin deserving of a penalty. There are many more that some of us were involved in before repenting (1 Corinthians 6:11). For those who **did not like to retain God in their knowledge"** (1:28), they may be or pursue: **"..., wickedness, covetousness, maliciousness; full of envy, murder, strife, deceit, evil-mindedness;** *they are* **whisperers, 30 backbiters, haters of God, violent, proud, boasters, inventors of evil things, disobedient to parents, 31 undiscerning, untrustworthy, unloving, unforgiving, unmerciful; 32 who, knowing the righteous judgment of God, that those who practice such things are deserving of death, not only do the same but also approve of those who practice them"** (1:29). This is one of the most complete lists of sins in the Bible. If we look them over, it is evident that most of us fit in one or many categories. We tend to rationalize some of these sins as worse than others. Still, we probably should not feel any self-righteousness if we only were involved in a couple of these sins because, in God's economy, any one of them deserves the death penalty. We need to be forgiven to have any hope of having righteousness imputed to us. Thankfully, God has provided the means to have all of these sins forgiven by grace through faith, as noted many times in the scriptures. This forgiveness is available to all of us as a gift from God.

Romans 2:11 For there is no partiality with God. This is good to know. God doesn't care about our position, race, gender, money, etcetera. He is impartial and a righteous judge. God does not judge according to external appearance but knows the heart (2:25-29; 1 Samuel 16:7).

Romans 3:9 What then? Are we better *than they*? Not at all. For we have previously charged both Jews and Greeks that they are all under sin. The Jews hoped that there was some exception for them, but there was not. They are in sin, just like everyone else.

Romans 3:20 Therefore by the deeds of the law no flesh will be justified in His sight, for by the law *is* the knowledge of sin. This is one of the verses that let us know the purpose of the law (the first five books of the Old Testament). Its purpose is to show us that we are sinners. We are incapable of following all of the laws. We fall far short (3:22)—justified means to be declared righteous. So, no one will be declared righteous by following the law. No one is capable of following all the commandments. The commandments expose sin.

Romans 3:23 ...for all have sinned and fall short of the glory of God, 24 being justified freely by His grace through the redemption that is in Christ Jesus, 25 whom God set forth *as* a propitiation by His blood, through faith, to demonstrate His righteousness, because in His forbearance God had passed over the sins that were previously committed, 26 to demonstrate at the present time His righteousness, that He might be just and the justifier of the one who has faith in Jesus. There is a lot in these verses. It is noted that everyone falls short of the glory of God. Then the verse describes how God sent Christ to pay the price for our sins. He was a propitiation. What is that? It is an action meant to regain God's favor and make up for our transgressions. It is as if we broke the law, went to court, and someone else paid our fine. We would be set free because someone else paid the price for our crime. Christ paid the price for all our transgressions so that God no longer sees them. Justification is God's act of imputing righteousness to a person. There are some differences of opinion regarding this definition. Still, in a rough translation, my opinion is that it makes a believer just as if they had never sinned in God's eyes. It is the process whereby He declares us righteous. Through this process, we come to peace with God. We were previously His enemies (Romans 5:10).

Romans 4:3 For what does the Scripture say? "Abraham believed God, and it was accounted to him for righteousness." Based on this scripture, we find that Abraham was saved the same way that we are, by God's grace through faith. The way I look at it, Christ paid the price for the sins of all who have faith, past, present, and future. Abraham believed. In other words, he had faith. Verse 3:25 and 26 put it this way: **"in His forbearance God had passed over the sins that were previously committed, 26 to demonstrate at the present time His righteousness, that He might be just and the justifier of the one who has faith in Jesus."** God is still just and holy even though he passes over and forgives sins. Christ satisfied God's justice by paying the price for all our transgressions, the transgressions of those who came before us, and those who will come after us. Righteousness is a gift to those who believe (4:5). A prideful person may want to work to earn their own salvation so they can boast about it, but, unfortunately, that effort is doomed to failure.

Romans 5:8 But God demonstrates His own love toward us, in that while we were still sinners, Christ died for us. Dying for you is something most people would not do. Therefore, it is appropriate to rejoice (5:11) and declare that Christ is the Messiah and Savior of humanity.

Romans 5:13 (For until the law sin was in the world, but sin is not imputed when there is no law. We know that God is just (Hebrews 6:10, et al.). So without a standard of behavior, the people did not have their sin imputed to their account. Even though sin was present in the world from Adam to Moses, God did not keep account of it in the same way because the law had not been given yet. That seems fair. When there is the law, people know what is expected and choose to follow it or not. Then when they have a choice, it is appropriate for them to suffer the consequences of choosing not to follow it. Without the law, people would not know what right and wrong behavior was. The same principle seems to apply to children before the age of accountability. Children may not be held responsible for everything they do in the early years because they cannot understand right from wrong. Thus, it is not fair to hold them accountable for everything.

Romans 6 What shall we say then? Shall we continue in sin that grace may abound? 2 Certainly not! How shall we who died to sin live any longer in it? 3 Or do you not know that as many of us as were baptized into Christ Jesus were baptized into His death? These verses clarify that we should consider ourselves dead to sin and alive to God. When Christ died on the cross, our sins died too. If we were to continue in sin, we would deny that we identify with Christ. Also, we would be a bad example of the life-changing aspect of our conversion. Our behavior does not save us, but when we are saved, our behavior will change. Some of our indiscretions may change immediately. Others may take years to overcome and correct, but there will be a different attitude about sin and a new desire not to be continually involved in it. One pastor I listened to said: "if there is no change, there has been no change." In other words, when we become a believer, our attitude toward continuing in transgressions should change. We no longer should want to let sin reign in our **mortal bodies (6:12).** We should no longer present ourselves to be slaves to sin. We should be slaves of obedience to God, leading to righteousness (6:16). We should consider ourselves slaves of righteousness (6:18).

Romans 6:23 For the wages of sin *is* death, but the gift of God *is*

eternal life in Christ Jesus our Lord. This verse says it all on this subject.

Romans 7:5 For when we were in the flesh, the sinful passions which were aroused by the law were at work in our members to bear fruit to death. Interestingly, the law arouses sinful passions. What we are forbidden based on the law is what we want to do. When we fulfill these passions, it leads to death. Being in the flesh is not a long-term recipe for heavenly life. It appears to be a recipe for death and destruction.

Romans 7:20 Now if I do what I will not *to do*, it is no longer I who do it, but sin that dwells in me. Unfortunately, when we become believers, we still have our flesh with us. It battles with our spirit. Sometimes the flesh wins out, and we get involved in sin. We have the power to live in the power of the Holy Spirit, but we don't always do so. We hope to align with our new nature, but sometimes we get off track.

Romans 8:6 For to be carnally minded *is* death, but to be spiritually minded *is* life and peace. This scripture speaks about the two warring factions in each believer. There is the carnal and the spiritual. To be carnally minded is to be in the flesh. We should be in the spirit of Christ. Our carnal bodies are dead, but the spirit is life. The Holy Spirit can overcome the death of the carnal body.

Romans 8:9 But you are not in the flesh but in the Spirit if indeed the Spirit of God dwells in you. Now if anyone does not have the Spirit of Christ, he is not His. This statement is monumental. It tells us that we no longer have to be subject to following every lust of the flesh, assuming we "indeed" have the Spirit of God. Being in the flesh means following the lust of the flesh. The Spirit of God trumps the flesh for those purchased by and belonging to Christ.

Romans 8:16 The Spirit Himself bears witness with our spirit that we are children of God, 17 and if children, then heirs—heirs of God and joint heirs with Christ, if indeed we suffer with *Him*, that we may also be glorified together. The part that we don't like about this scripture is the part regarding suffering with Him. That does not sound like any fun. However, that is what the scriptures say, and another scripture indicates that we should count it as joy when we fall into divers trials (James 1:2). Why? So we can test our faith and gain patience, which is a great virtue (James 1:3) because we will join Christ in His suffering for us (Romans 8:27: 2 Corinthians 1:5-7).

Romans 8:27 Now He who searches the hearts knows what the mind of the Spirit *is*, because He makes intercession for the saints according to *the will of* God. Isn't that great news! The Holy Spirit is making intercessory prayers on our behalf. God has an overarching plan, and we are involved in that plan though we don't always know what part we are to play and when. Nor do we know what we should pray for, because we may not know God's overarching plan and how we might fit in. We have our selfish desires, but those desires may be contrary to God's plan. Therefore, we need to pray that *His will* be done (Matthew 6:10) rather than ours.

Romans 8:28 And we know that all things work together for good to those who love God, to those who are the called according to *His* purpose. 29 For whom He foreknew, He also predestined *to be* conformed to the image of His Son, that He might be the firstborn among many brethren. This scripture gets into the fascinating issues of "predestination" and "election." What is hard to fathom and understand is that God can see our past, present, and future. We are stuck in the time dimension and can only be in the present, which instantly becomes the past and never quite gets into the future. God does not seem to have the same limits in the time dimension, such that He can only be in the present. Thus, He knows who will be His believers even before they become believers.

This scripture speaks of this process as being predestined. The Arminians (those who follow the position of the seventeenth century Jacobus Arminius) have battled the Calvinist (those who follow the position of John Calvin, the French reformer) for many decades. I suspect that there may be a bit of truth on both sides of the argument about election and predestination. The Bible seems to teach about man's responsibility and God's sovereignty (control). I conclude that we may not be able to unravel these apparent difficulties and differences of opinion in the earthly realm. We don't have to unravel it. There are some things that we are not able to, nor are we required to understand with our current limited intellect. When the time is appropriate (perhaps in the spiritual realm), these issues and problems will seem rudimentary. The bottom line is that God is just and fair. God will reveal what we need to know when the time is right.

Romans 8:38 For I am persuaded that neither death nor life, nor angels nor principalities nor powers, nor things present nor things to come, 39 nor height nor depth, nor any other created thing, shall be able to separate us from the love of God which is in Christ Jesus our Lord. Paul is very sure that we cannot be separated from the love of God. If Paul was sure that nothing could separate us from God's love, maybe we should have some of that same assurance.

Romans 9:18 Therefore He has mercy on whom He wills, and whom He wills He hardens. Back in Exodus is the story about how God hardened Pharaoh's heart. The Pharaoh did not want to let the Israelite slaves leave his land even though God made it abundantly clear that He wanted them to go. Thus, God allowed the Pharaoh to harden his heart even more on this issue until he couldn't handle it anymore and let them go, only to change his mind and try to bring them back by force. This didn't work out very well for the Egyptian's. Check it out in the Old Testament.

Anyway, it is evident from this verse, and other preceding verses, that God is sovereign over all that happens, and even though we don't deserve His mercy, He gives it freely. He has the same power that a potter when he makes a lump of clay into something. He can make one vessel for great value and another as a piece to be destroyed. This reality may be hard to accept, but that's just the way it is. If we try to apply our standards based on our myopic perspective, we might not understand this fact of life, but that does not change the facts nor make us right.

If, at any time, little human beings try to judge God, we are immediately wrong because we have no status whatsoever to even think about putting ourselves in a position to judge God (James 4:11-12; John 5:22; Matthew 10:28). We are vessels of mercy through faith by the grace of God. We may not understand all of what that means, but we know that it is a great position in which to be.

Romans 9:33 As it is written:
"Behold, I lay in Zion a stumbling stone and rock of offense,
And whoever believes on Him will not be put to shame." The "stumbling stone" referred to in this Old Testament verse from Isaiah 28:16 is Christ (Ephesians 2:20; 1 Peter 2:6-7). Israel was pursuing righteousness by the works of the law and not by faith (9:32). Unfortunately for them, no flesh can be justified by the works of the law (Galatians 2:16). No matter how hard you try, you can't establish your own righteousness. Salvation has to be by grace. It cannot be by works (11:5-6). A person has to have faith to be saved through the grace of God. They have to believe in their heart that God has raised Christ from the dead, whether they be a Jew or Gentile (1:16; 10:9).

Romans 10:17 So then faith *comes* by hearing, and hearing by the word of God. So this is how we gain faith. We hear the gospel and the word of God.

Romans 11:29 For the gifts and the calling of God *are* irrevocable. Here is some good news. Some people feel God's calling can be revoked, but this scripture contradicts that thinking. God has a plan for this earth, which will happen in His time (2 Peter 2:13; Galatians 4:4-5). Some examples of the gifts are prophesying, ministry, teaching, exhortation, giving, leadership, and mercy (12:6-8). The gifts differ for each person **according to the grace that is given to us** (12:6).

Romans 12:17 Repay no one evil for evil. Have regard for good things in the sight of all men. There are two sides to this recommendation. First, don't try to get back at someone who has done evil to you. As my mother used to say: "Two wrongs don't make a right." Two evils would not make things better. It would make it worse and probably escalate the evil. Also, that would be trying to take over God's role. He says: **"Vengeance is mine, I will repay"** (12:19). On the other side, we should recognize the good in others and try to emulate it. There is no problem with escalating good things. The more we do that, the better.

Romans 13:1 Let every soul be subject to the governing authorities. For there is no authority except from God, and the authorities that exist are appointed by God. This can be a difficult policy to follow. Of course, as with most scripture, it should not be considered in isolation from other scripture. In this case, especially, there are clarifying statements elsewhere. For example, another statement says that we should obey God rather than men (Acts 5:29). The governing authorities told the apostles not to teach in Christ's name. Thus, my takeaway is that we should follow our governing authorities unless they direct us to do something against what God tells us to do. That seems relatively straightforward.

Romans 13:9 For the commandments, "You shall not commit adultery," "You shall not murder," "You shall not steal," "You shall not bear false witness," "You shall not covet," and if *there is* any other

commandment, are *all* summed up in this saying, namely, "You shall love your neighbor as yourself." Wouldn't the world be a better place if everyone implemented these commandments? Unfortunately, that is not going to happen universally in our fallen world. However, we can follow this principle in our lives, making things better, which is a start. If you love your neighbor, you will not do the things to your neighbor that are prohibited by the commandments.

The fact that we can't follow the law on our own points us to the need for something different. In other words, the law is the instructor that tells us we need a different path. That different path is the grace of God. The interesting thing about accepting grace through faith is that when you do that, you will wind up following the law more than before, not because you have to, but because you want to. Under grace, we would not be inclined to murder, commit adultery, covet things that belong to our neighbors, or steal from them. These are some of the same things prohibited by the law.

Romans 14:1 Receive one who is weak in the faith, *but* not to disputes over doubtful things. What are the doubtful things over which there could be disputes? Well, people can find many things to argue about. What is proper to eat? What day should we consider the sabbath? Should instruments be used in worship, or should all worship be acapella? People can have their own opinions on these and many other issues, but we shouldn't make a big deal out of it, especially if we are more mature believers who understand liberties. Some things are forbidden by tradition or personal beliefs but not in scripture. "**For you, brethren, have been called to liberty; only do not *use* liberty as an opportunity for the flesh, but through love serve one another**" (Galatians 5:13).

Romans 14:11 For it is written:
  "***As* I live, says the Lord,**
  Every knee shall bow to Me,

And every tongue shall confess to God." I love this verse. It tells us, along with Genesis 6:3, that God will not always put up with humankind. God currently allows humanity to do whatever we want, but it will not always be that way. At some point, it appears God will require people to bow to Him and confess that He is God. I admit that it gives me a sense of comfort in that God will administer justice appropriately.

Romans 14:14 I know and am convinced by the Lord Jesus that *there is* nothing unclean of itself; but to him who considers anything to be unclean, to him *it is* unclean. Thus, if a person thinks something is improper for a Christian to do, for that person, it is improper.

Romans 14:16 Therefore do not let your good be spoken of as evil; 17 for the kingdom of God is not eating and drinking, but righteousness and peace and joy in the Holy Spirit. We live in the physical world of eating and drinking and consider these things necessary, but this verse lets us know that righteousness, peace, and joy in the Holy Spirit are the more critical issues in the realm of the kingdom of God. Mature Christians understand that they have some liberty but should not implement that liberty if it causes a weak person in the faith to falter. In other words, there are times when we should not implement our desires if someone else does not think they have the liberty that we do.

Romans 14:23 But he who doubts is condemned if he eats, because *he does* not *eat* from faith; for whatever *is* not from faith is sin. Thus, if you are not sure whether eating something is a sin, you should avoid eating it. What does "from faith" mean? If we have faith that we have the liberty to eat meat but someone we are with thinks that it is a sin, we may want to "**bear with the scruples of the weak**" when we are with them (15:1). We can exercise our liberty in private.

Romans 15:8 Now I say that Jesus Christ has become a servant to the circumcision for the truth of God, to confirm the promises

***made* to the fathers, 9 and that the Gentiles might glorify God for *His* mercy, as it is written:...** It appears that God had a plan for the Gentiles from the beginning. He came to the world as an Israelite to redeem all humanity. He wants Jews and Gentiles to come to faith and sing praise to the Lord. So God planned to bring the Gentiles in through the Israelites. Paul played a significant part in ministering to the Gentiles, so the Holy Spirit could sanctify them for service to God (15:16).

Romans 16:5 Likewise *greet* the church that is in their house.
  Greet my beloved Epaenetus, who is the firstfruits of Achaia to Christ. Priscilla and Aquila had a church in their house. Currently, house churches are common in some countries where larger Christian churches are persecuted. In past centuries, there have been severe persecutions of Christians by adherents of other religions.

Romans 16:17 Now I urge you, brethren, note those who cause divisions and offenses, contrary to the doctrine which you learned, and avoid them. Well, if you wanted a reason to avoid people who teach a different doctrine, this is it. The Bible tells us to avoid them. Of course, there are situations where you may not be able to avoid these people, and in those situations, we need to do our best to diminish the negative consequences. In talking with divisive people, we should discern what is essential and non-essential. On non-essential issues, we should be able to agree to disagree without falling into the sin of anger (Titus 3:9; Ephesians 4:26). In essential matters, we may need to implement the guidance of this verse and avoid these people if it is not possible to agree with them.

46

1 Corinthians

[46]**1 CORINTHIANS** - The Corinthians had many problems addressed by the two letters to them in the Bible. Paul encourages them to focus on the Lord as a means of addressing their problems.

1 Corinthians 1:18 For the message of the cross is foolishness to those who are perishing, but to us who are being saved it is the power of God. Here is a sad truth. According to the Bible, those who reject Christ don't have any hope to offer. I was a non-Christian for many years, so I know something about this thinking. What I thought was very pessimistic. We live and enjoy life as much as possible, and then we die. When we die, I thought that we ceased to exist as a sentient being. The phrase "ashes to ashes and dust to dust" was my limited immature thought. Life didn't have much real hope. The reasoning I had, which I now realize was faulty, was that there did not have to be anything after death.

With faulty thinking, I started seeking answers to some hard questions

---

[46] NSB quotations are from the Nelsons Study Bible, copyright (c) 1997 by Thomas Nelson, Inc., Nashville, TN; used by permission; scripture taken from the New King James Version, Copyright (c) 1979, 1980, 1982 used by permission. All rights reserved.

like how could there be anything in the material world if there was nothing to create it? Per my rational scientific thinking from what I had been taught and observed, everything required a cause. Therefore, I could not answer this question satisfactorily.

If you take causation back to the beginning, there must be an uncaused cause. There had to be something outside of the natural world. There had to be something supernatural. If there were nothing, there would be nothing. From a rational perspective, there is no way nothing could create everything. That would be a scientific and logical impossibility. To believe that everything came from nothing would not make any sense at all. That thinking is not rational. If there were no supernatural creator, there would be no creation.

I started searching for answers. After about ten years of sporadic searching, I finally wound up looking back in the Bible. There, I found the solution for which I had been looking. The answer is that there *is* a supernatural creator. He is God. Previously, I thought believers were the foolish ones and then realized that my previous thinking was irrational. I was going to perish without knowing why I had lived in the first place. Now there is much more reason and hope in life. We were created by God, the Creator, for His pleasure. He is supernatural and can give us eternal life through faith by His grace. That is much more satisfying than thinking that life is just some accidental chemical reaction that comes and goes with no meaning.

1 Corinthians 1:21 For since, in the wisdom of God, the world through wisdom did not know God, it pleased God through the foolishness of the message preached to save those who believe. There are scientists, philosophers, scholars, and other geniuses who are stumped by the universe's existence but think that God's Gospel is foolish. They come up with endless "theories" but don't know.

Who is foolish? Is it the one who has no real answers or the one who created everything and knows all the answers? I'll go with the one who has all the answers.

1 Corinthians 1:22 For Jews request a sign, and Greeks seek after wisdom; 23 but we preach Christ crucified, to the Jews a stumbling block and to the Greeks foolishness, 24 but to those who are called, both Jews and Greeks, Christ the power of God and the wisdom of God. What a great thing it is to be numbered among those who are called: **"Because the foolishness of God is wiser than men, and the weakness of God is stronger than men"** (1:25). Not surprisingly, God sets things up to shame those who think they are wise (1:26) but who are not. He has also chosen the weak of the world to put to shame the mighty (1:27). God does not tolerate a prideful man, no matter how smart or mighty he thinks he is. These people who are the rulers and wise of this age are really "**coming to nothing**" (2:6).

1 Corinthians 2:14 But the natural man does not receive the things of the Spirit of God, for they are foolishness to him; nor can he know *them,* **because they are spiritually discerned.** My experience is that it takes faith to open up the spiritual discernment required to partially understand what is written in the Bible. I read many parts of the Bible before believing that it was the word of God. Without faith, I did not understand a lot of what I read. Per this verse, the belief that the 66 books of the Christian Bible are God's word is a spiritual determination that will seem foolish to those who do not have faith. Experience validates this text.

1 Corinthians 3:3 for you are still carnal. For where *there are* **envy, strife, and divisions among you, are you not carnal and behaving like** *mere* **men?** The answer is yes. Interestingly, when there is envy, strife, and divisions, that is an indication that Christians are like babies who cannot take solid food yet. They still are trying to follow the messenger rather than the Lord. They said things like "I am of Paul" or "I am of Apollos." Paul was telling them that they had not matured to the point of realizing that Paul and Apollos were men like them, and they were just the messengers and should not be put on a pedestal and followed. All should be following only the Gospel that the messengers were preaching.

1 Corinthians 3:16 Do you not know that you are the temple of God and *that* the Spirit of God dwells in you? 17 If anyone defiles the temple of God, God will destroy him. For the temple of God is holy, which *temple* you are. If you are reading this, you now know that you are the temple of God as a believer. That means God Himself will deal with anyone who desecrates or defames you. He will give an appropriate disciplinary response in His time. That may not be when you want it to happen. Before you start thinking that you are something special, remember that God's presence makes anything holy. Even dirt is called holy when God is near it (Exodus 3:5).

1 Corinthians 5:11 But now I have written to you not to keep company with anyone named a brother, who is sexually immoral, or covetous, or an idolater, or a reviler, or a drunkard, or an extortioner—not even to eat with such a person. Before this statement, the scripture tells us that we should *not* avoid "**people of this world**" engaged in these things. After all, they do not have the Holy Spirit to help them. We are not to judge them. God does that, and we should not try to take His place. However, if someone in the church who calls themselves a believer is engaged in these activities, we should avoid them. They set a hypocritical example for everyone by talking the talk but not walking the walk. The church should be involved in judging its members in line with prescriptions for how this is to be done (Hebrews 13:17; Galatians 6:1; Matthew 7:3-5, 18:15; 1 Thessalonians 5:14; 2 Thessalonians 3:15; Titus 1:3).

1 Corinthians 6:11 And such were some of you. But you were washed, but you were sanctified, but you were justified in the name of the Lord Jesus and by the Spirit of our God. The preceding verse lists sins in which many of us previously participated. But through faith, by the grace of God, we are relieved of the just punishment for these sins. God's justice was fulfilled when Christ paid the price for our transgressions on our behalf and gave us the right to become children of God (John 1:12). That is good news.

Nevertheless, though we are forgiven, we will not want to continue these sins if we are true believers. Paul indicates that many sins are outside the body, but sexual immorality is against a person's own body (6:18), and we should glorify God in our body rather than commit sin with it. The body cannot be viewed as separate from the spirit and to operate independently (6:12-20).

1 Corinthians 7:2 Nevertheless, because of sexual immorality, let each man have his own wife and let each woman have her own husband. This verse recognizes the reality that human beings are sexual creatures. The verse provides an appropriate venue for sexual relations within a marriage. The following scriptures encourage married couples to have sexual relations so they will not be tempted to go outside of their marriage to satisfy their desires. Spouses are to give themselves to each other. **"It is better to marry than to burn with passion"** (7:9).

Unbelievers might find it surprising that the Bible encourages sex, but not only does the Bible promote sex, it requires it within marriage. However, it is *only* allowed within marriage. That is a restriction that many worldly people cannot accept. The interesting thing is that the Bible does not appear to expect believers to try to regulate nonbelievers' sexual behavior. There is a recognition that people of the world (unbelievers) do not have the ability to control their behavior. Governments may regulate the conduct of all citizens, but it is not a Christian's job to judge the behavior of those outside the church. Their government will somewhat control everyone under the threat of punishment, and eventually, we will answer to God for all that has not been forgiven. Nevertheless, Christians are discouraged from judging people of this world for this type of behavior (5:9). Clearly, that is God's purview.

1 Corinthians 2:14 For the unbelieving husband is sanctified by the wife, and the unbelieving wife is sanctified by the husband; otherwise your children would be unclean, but now they are holy. Isn't this interesting. What does it mean? It appears that it is a good influence to have at least one believer in marriage. Sanctified in this context means that the unbelieving spouse benefits from being set apart from some of the world's influence because of their spouse. Likewise, it is positive for children to have at least one parent who is a believer. This parent can help the children learn about God and help keep them from the world's negative influences.

1 Corinthians 7:20 Let each one remain in the same calling in which he was called. Whatever calling you are in when you come to faith, it may be good to continue in that calling. You will see things differently, but there is no necessity to make big changes. This is the "grow where you are planted" kind of idea. Apart from being in Christ, any other status doesn't make that much difference anyway. We all are called to be in harmony with the will of God in our lives.

1 Corinthians 7:31 For the form of this world is passing away. We don't know when the form of this world will pass away, but we know from this scripture and another that it will pass away. Scientists can also confirm that this is a true statement when they calculate how much fuel our sun has before it extinguishes. I have heard that this calculation gives the sun about four billion more years. Granted, that is a long time, but it is not everlasting. When the sun burns out, it should be obvious that our world will no longer be in its same form, and life as we know it will not exist. Of course, Christians who believe what the Bible says know that the earth will be reformed (Revelation 21:1).

1 Corinthians 7:39 A wife is bound by law as long as her husband lives; but if her husband dies, she is at liberty to be married to whom she wishes, only in the Lord. Most marriage vows have an "until death do us part" statement. This verse substantiates that idea and adds one caveat: the remaining spouse should marry another believer if they marry again.

1 Corinthians 8:9 But beware lest somehow this liberty of yours become a stumbling block to those who are weak. The idea here is that those who have the liberty to eat or drink whatever they want may not always want to exercise this liberty, especially when in the company of some who do not believe they have that same liberty. The reason is that if someone sees you exercising your liberty, it might influence them to do the same, contrary to what they think their conscience is telling them to do.

1 Corinthians 9:14 Even so the Lord has commanded that those who preach the gospel should live from the gospel. This is a direction from Paul that ministers of the gospel should be paid for doing so.

1 Corinthians 10:13 No temptation has overtaken you except such as is common to man; but God *is* faithful, who will not allow you to be tempted beyond what you are able, but with the temptation will also make the way of escape, that you may be able to bear *it*. When you think about it, there is generally a way of escaping when tempted. All we have to do is use it. Make no mistake about this. You will be tempted to do what you know you should not as long as you are alive on earth. That is part of life that is allowed by God. If we take the way of escape, we can become stronger in withstanding temptations. Of course, our enemy would like to see us fall and feel guilty about it. We are not perfect and will fall from time to time. When we do, we can confess to God and move on. He is faithful to forgive (1 John 1:9: James 5:16; Psalm 32:5).

1 Corinthians 10:23 All things are lawful for me, but not all things are helpful; all things are lawful for me, but not all things edify. 24 Let no one seek his own, but each one the other's *well-being*. Christians are to seek the well-being of others, especially when it comes to things that might be lawful for someone strong in the faith but not for someone who is weak. As we grow up, we generally gain more freedom and the responsibility that comes with this freedom. This verse encourages us to be careful about exercising our freedoms and make sure that what we do is edifying and helpful.

1 Corinthians 10:31 Therefore, whether you eat or drink, or whatever you do, do all to the glory of God. In other words, whatever we do should bring honor, praise, dignity, and/or worship to God (Chronicles 16:28-29). Why? Because He deserves it.

1 Corinthians 11:10 For this reason the woman ought to have *a symbol of* authority on *her* head, because of the angels. Here is a curious verse. It comes within a discussion of prayer and head coverings. I don't know if the head covering refers to a hat or hair, but the interesting aspect of the verse is that it references angels. Apparently, angels are listening to or learning something from the prayer. Other verses also speak of angels being involved with people (Matthew 18:10; Daniel 6:20-23; 2 Kings 6:13-17; Acts 7:52-53; Acts 8:26; etc). Always, they seem to have their eye on God, who is directing their assignments. I have no idea what the symbol of authority would be other than hair or a hat. A queen might have a crown, but this verse is not talking about a queen. Nevertheless, it is comforting that God has His angels looking out for us.

1 Corinthians 11:26 For as often as you eat this bread and drink this cup, you proclaim the Lord's death till He comes. This verse speaks of communion, a process whereby these elements symbolize Christ's death on our behalf and His coming return (11:24-25). Through this ceremony, we remember what Christ did for us on the cross and that we are under the New Covenant of grace by which we are redeemed (Luke 22:20; Hebrews 14-15).

1 Corinthians 12:3 Therefore I make known to you that no one speaking by the Spirit of God calls Jesus accursed, and no one can say that Jesus is Lord except by the Holy Spirit. An actor can make a statement without believing it, but those speaking by the Spirit of God would not be able to call Jesus accursed. What is accursed? It means doomed, ill-fated, damnable, or detestable under a curse. That is not a good thing to call Jesus and definitely would not be said under the influence of the Spirit of God. On the other hand, it would be difficult to honestly testify that Jesus is Lord if not under the influence of the Holy Spirit.

1 Corinthians 12:18 But now God has set the members, each one of them, in the body just as He pleased. The body of Christ has many members, and each has its own function. If we are part of that body, we have been given certain gifts and God Himself has a plan for how He wants us to use these gifts. It is comforting to know that God uses us to carry out His purposes. Yes, you could say that we are like pawns in the game, but what high-class pawns we are to be used by the almighty God. It is an immense honor to be that kind of pawn. Hopefully, we are accomplishing the mission God has given us here on earth.

1 Corinthians 13:3 And though I bestow all my goods to feed *the poor*, and though I give my body to be burned, but have not love, it profits me nothing. This verse comes after a recitation of many spiritual gifts. If you have all kinds of gifts without having love, the gifts you have are worthless. So, what is love as defined by the Bible? The next verse tells us something about it.

1 Corinthians 13:4 Love suffers long *and* is kind; love does not envy; love does not parade itself, is not puffed up; 5 does not behave rudely, does not seek its own, is not provoked, thinks no evil; 6 does not rejoice in iniquity, but rejoices in the truth; 7 bears all things, believes all things, hopes all things, endures all things. In stark contrast to the worldly idea about what love is, this definition seems mature and self-sacrificial. Notice that the Biblical definition doesn't speak as much about what love is as it does about what it is not. Thus, no matter what a person says about their feelings, these standards will tell us if they really have love. If a person says they love someone but treats them disrespectfully and thinks bad things about them, they may not be telling the truth. They may be trying to manipulate the person. It has been said that three things are important in life. The first is to be kind. The second is to be kind. And, the third is to punch them if they offend you. Just kidding. The third is also to be kind. Another verse says that "**Love never fails**" (13:8). The scripture says that prophecies will fail, tongues will cease, and knowledge will vanish. For now, we only see part of the overall picture. Paul puts it this way: "**For now we see in a mirror, dimly, but then face to face**" (13:12).

1 Corinthians 13:13 And now abide faith, hope, love, these three; but the greatest of these *is* love. This verse tells us how important love is by comparing it to other important concepts. It is preeminent. When we implement love toward other people, we follow what God empowers us to do through faith.

1 Corinthians 14:9 So likewise you, unless you utter by the tongue words easy to understand, how will it be known what is spoken? For you will be speaking into the air. The bottom line here is that if someone speaks in tongues, there needs to be an interpretation of what they said, or their speaking is not worth much. For example, Paul says that five words with understanding are worth ten thousand words in a tongue (14:19). Thus, my conclusion is that unless there is an interpretation, speaking in tongues is speaking into the air.

1 Corinthians 14:12 Even so you, since you are zealous for spiritual gifts, *let it be* for the edification of the church *that* you seek to excel. Here we have the reason for spiritual gifts. They are for the edification of the church. Earlier, we learned that love was more important, but there is also a place for spiritual gifts. They are important, just not as important as love (1 Corinthians 13:13).

1 Corinthians 14:40 Let all things be done decently and in order. This verse is good advice about how to run a church. Whatever a church does, it should be done for edification (14:26).

1 Corinthians 15:6 After that He was seen by over five hundred brethren at once, of whom the greater part remain to the present, but some have fallen asleep. This is what happened after Christ died for our sins, was buried, and rose the third day, thereby conquering death. Over five hundred witnesses saw Christ after He rose from the dead. He was in His glorified spiritual body, which later rose to the heavens.

1 Corinthians 15:14 And if Christ is not risen, then our preaching *is* empty and your faith *is* also empty. This verse clarifies that the resurrection is key to the Christian faith. If Christ did not rise from the dead, we would be pitied (15:19). Thus, every hope we have rests on the fact that Christ rose from the dead. If He did not, we would be without hope. But, the good news of the gospel is that Christ did rise from the dead, and there were many witnesses.

1 Corinthians 15:33 Do not be deceived: "Evil company corrupts good habits." This verse makes a statement that many parents know intuitively as they try to steer their children toward good friends. I can remember one friend I had when I was a freshman in high school. He didn't live too far away, and it was clear my parents did not like him.

Consequently, he wasn't asked to go with my family anywhere. They saw something at the time that I didn't see until later.

I found out that he didn't mind lying if it suited him, and he thought he could get away with it. I could get in bigger trouble by lying to my parents than just about anything else. When I saw this friend lying, his status went down in my eyes. I never developed a very close relationship with him. However, looking back, he may have had a bad influence on me, or maybe we had a bad influence on each other.

Somehow, we came up with the crazy idea to drop water balloons on cars from the partially-built walking bridge over the freeway. We hit one 1957 Chevy, and the driver promptly put on the brakes and parked at the bottom of the bridge. It was dark where we were, but we could see the driver open his trunk and bring out a tire iron. He then started heading up the walkway, and we were terrified that he was going to beat us to a pulp.

There was no place to get away, so we tried to hide in the rebar of the construction. That didn't work. It seemed like it took him a long time to walk up the ramp, and we imagined he was very mad. We realized he was an older kid from the neighborhood at the last minute. He gave us a stern warning and let us go. We never did that again, and the whole experience made me realize it was a very dumb thing to do. Later my accomplice in the water balloon dropping incident dropped out of high school and was said to be using heavy drugs. I lost contact with him.

Thinking back, I should have learned the lesson not to throw things at cars when I was 6 or 7 years old. At that time, I got into trouble trying to hit cars going by with dirt clods. I did learn not to throw dirt clods at cars, but that apparently didn't carry over to water balloons. This reminds me of a major overarching lesson for life; you have to learn from your mistakes and, preferably, from the mistakes of others. None of us can afford to make all the mistakes ourselves, or we may wind up in prison.

1 Corinthians 15:46 However, the spiritual is not first, but the natural, and afterward the spiritual. 47 The first man *was* of the earth, *made* of dust; the second Man *is* the Lord from heaven. Here we find that Adam (the first man) was of the earth, but Christ (the second Man) is spiritual and the Lord from heaven. I believe Christ is the last Adam referred to in this verse. Adam did not originally have a sinful nature, and Christ was the last man who did not sin. Christ (the last Adam) became a life-giving spirit (15:45).

1 Corinthians 15:51 Listen, I tell you a mystery: We will not all sleep, but we will all be changed— 52 in a flash, in the twinkling of an eye, at the last trumpet. For the trumpet will sound, the dead will be raised imperishable, and we will be changed. 53 For the perishable must clothe itself with the imperishable, and the mortal with immortality. 54 When the perishable has been clothed with the imperishable, and the mortal with immortality, then the saying that is written will come true: "Death has been swallowed up in victory." This is what will happen when Christ returns. Those alive at the time will instantly receive new glorified bodies and the faithful who have died will also be raised and receive glorified immortal bodies. We don't know how this happens. It will be miraculous. God will demonstrate His authority over life and death in a dramatic way.

1 Corinthians 15:56 The sting of death *is* sin, and the strength of sin *is* the law. The reality is that sin without forgiveness does lead to death. An appropriate response to this truth is that Christ died to remove the sin that led to death. Justice is served through what He did, and we can be forgiven. He made atonement for the sin. What would be the standard by which to gauge sin without the law? With no standard, the knowledge of sin would be minimal. With the law, sin is known and thus is strong to convict

1 Corinthians 16:9 For a great and effective door has opened to me, and *there* are many adversaries. It is interesting that Paul, immediately after saying the door is open for him, states there are many adversaries. It is as if the adversaries were an expected part of the door being opened. Thus, when a door is opened to us, we should not expect all smooth sailing ahead. You might get on the Olympic team, but you still have to compete to win. Make no mistake, if you are following God's plan for your life on earth, there will be opposition, and sometimes that opposition will come from people very close to you (Acts 15:36-41).

1 Corinthians 16:13 Watch, stand fast in the faith, be brave, be strong. Let all that you do be done with love. Love in everything we do is a tall order, but one for which we should strive. The last sentence of this verse balances out the other strong directions to basically be a mature, fair, firm, and friendly Christian.

1 Corinthians 16:22 If anyone does not love the Lord Jesus Christ, let him be accursed. O Lord, come! Wow. That sure sounds harsh, doesn't it? It is harsh, but this is about life or death issues. Therefore, Paul does not mince words or attempt to sugarcoat the truth. It is what it is. To be accursed is to be doomed as an enemy of God.

47

2 Corinthians

[47]**2 CORINTHIANS** - Many accusations had been made about Paul. In this book, he defends himself and his apostleship.

2 Corinthians 1:3 Blessed be the God and Father of our Lord Jesus Christ, the Father of mercies and God of all comfort, who comforts us in all our tribulation, that we may be able to comfort those who are in any trouble, with the comfort with which we ourselves are comforted by God. So, there is a good reason to go through some trials. We will know what it is like and have credibility with anyone else going through something similar.

2 Corinthians 1:21 Now He who establishes us with you in Christ and has anointed us *is* God, who also has sealed us and given us the spirit in our hearts as a guarantee. So God established, anointed, and sealed Paul and the apostles. He also gave them the Spirit. The Spirit in their hearts was like a partial payment that would be completed later through eternity.

---

[47] NSB quotations are from the Nelsons Study Bible, copyright (c) 1997 by Thomas Nelson, Inc., Nashville, TN; used by permission; scripture taken from the New King James Version, Copyright (c) 1979, 1980, 1982 used by permission. All rights reserved.

2 Corinthians 2:6 This punishment which *was inflicted* by the majority *is* sufficient for such a man, so that, on the contrary, you *ought* rather to forgive and comfort *him*. This situation resulted from the church discipline of a man. The goal was not to destroy him, but rather to see him correct his behavior and be restored. Apparently, the man repented. This is an example of how forgiveness should follow correction (Matthew 18:15-35).

2 Corinthians 2:16 To one we are the aroma of death leading to death, and to the other the aroma of life leading to life. We might ask why some people seem angry toward Christians? One answer to this question is that some people who call themselves Christian are extremely obnoxious. Whether they are real believers or counterfeits, we may not know. Maybe they are not counterfeits but have carried over an obnoxious personality into their Christian life. That is one reason, but the other is that real Christians can make people realize that they will die someday. This appears to be the **fragrance of His knowledge** (2:14). This aroma of death is not pleasant for anyone who doesn't have hope for a pleasant afterlife. The thought that you are totally gone at death is not pleasant even for a person who does not believe they will be spending time in hell. Therefore, they may not want to be around believers who are a reminder of their hopelessness when death comes, which it surely will. A few will be actively confrontational, aggressive, belittling, or occasionally violent toward Christians. In other words, the Gospel is a bright message of joy and hope to some, but a message of death and judgment to others. Thus, it is not surprising that those who smell death and judgment don't like it. It doesn't smell good at all. Therefore, we should be as considerate as possible while not compromising the gospel because it is the only way to smell a different aroma of hope.

2 Corinthians 3:5 Not that we are sufficient of ourselves to think of anything as being from ourselves, but our sufficiency is from God, who also made us sufficient as ministers of the new covenant,

not of the letter but of the Spirit; for the letter kills, but the Spirit gives life. That is a big statement from Paul indicating where his and the Apostle's competencies came from. They came from God. What is the letter mentioned? It is the Ten Commandments. Why do they kill? Because we all violate them and thereby are worthy of the death sentence (Romans 4:15; Romans 5:9-11). But God can counteract this sentence and give life.

2 Corinthians 3:11 For if what is passing away *was* glorious, what remains *is* much more glorious. What is passing away? It is the ministry of condemnation that Moses revealed when he brought down the Ten Commandments. It was this old covenant that was passing away. But, the new covenant of grace and righteousness is much more glorious. God is merciful toward us and will make those who believe in Christ's righteousness glorious. The new covenant has superseded the old.

2 Corinthians 3:17 Now the Lord is the Spirit; and where the Spirit of the Lord *is*, there *is* liberty. Here we see the trinity again. The Lord, the Holy Spirit, and God are all one. Each is a different personality of God. We wind up being free from sin, free from the condemnation of the law and entitled to live forever.

2 Corinthians 4:3 But even if our gospel is veiled, it is veiled to those who are perishing, 4 whose minds the god of this age has blinded, who do not believe, lest the light of the gospel of the glory of Christ, who is the image of God, should shine on them. This is incredible in the sense that the god of this age has blinded some people to the truth of the gospel. Who is the god of this age with a small "g" in this context? Well, I believe it is the one who is blinding unbelievers to the truth. That would be Satan and his demons. Here is the risk of denying Christ for too long. You can come under the influence of Satan and be blinded to the truth. You can wind up with a hard heart toward God.

You can see this process in the committed atheists. Not only will their heart be hardened, but they will also often be angry toward those who are believers. They appear to want everyone else to support their position. However, they seldom have any better explanation for life in our universe than some theory that does not support any intelligent design or afterlife.

2 Corinthians 4:13 And since we have the same spirit of faith, according to what is written, "I believed and therefore I spoke," we also believe and therefore speak, 14 knowing that He who raised up the Lord Jesus will also raise us up with Jesus, and will present *us* with you. Paul took a lot of risks to bring the Gospel to the Corinthians. His mission was to share the Gospel with them, so he did at great risk to himself. He was no longer living for his own goals but was dedicated to God's plan for his life. Paul knew that God raised Christ from the dead and believed that God would also raise him and others at the appropriate time.

2 Corinthians 5:7 For we walk by faith, not by sight. Here is a short statement with a lot of meaning. We do not see Jesus Christ like the apostles did since He is no longer walking on the earth. Still, we believe through faith. We hear the Gospel, and the Holy Spirit draws us into believing what we hear or read in the Bible.

2 Corinthians 5:10 For we must all appear before the judgment seat of Christ, that each one may receive the things *done* in the body, according to what he has done, whether good or bad. What happens at the judgment? All will be judged. Forgiven believers will be judged for rewards based on the good that they have done (Romans 8:1; Matthew 6:19-20). The unbelievers will be judged for punishment (Isaiah 66:24; Daniel 12:2; Matthew 7:13).

2 Corinthians 5:14 For the love of Christ compels us, because we judge thus: that if One died for all, then all died; 15 and He died for

all, that those who live should live no longer for themselves, but for Him who died for them and rose again. This is a verse that makes it clear that Christ died for all of us. Thus, the way we can look at it is that we owe Him our lives. He is giving us eternal life. What is that worth? A lot considering that we have no hope for the future or any real meaning to our life without His sacrifice.

2 Corinthians 5:17 Therefore, if anyone *is* in Christ, *he is* a new creation; old things have passed away; behold, all things have become new. Here we learn how we should view ourselves after believing in Christ. Spiritually, we are new. The old man has died. We have a new spirit that can help us battle evil spirits in heavenly places (Ephesians 6:12). In other words, we wrestle with principalities and powers in the heavens around the earth, not in the highest heavenly place where God, angels, and saints are. The highest heavens are sometimes referred to as the third heaven (Genesis 28:12; Deuteronomy 10:14; 1 Kings 8:27). Therefore, no one should be evaluated according to the flesh (v. 5:16).

2 Corinthians 5:21 For He made Him who knew no sin *to be* sin for us, that we might become the righteousness of God in Him. This is what Christ did for us. He stepped in and took the just punishment on our behalf. If we go to court and someone else pays the fine, the judge can free us because our debt has been paid. We have all broken the commandments of God and deserve punishment. But you say, "I'm not that bad. Others do a lot worse than I do." Well, let's ask ourselves a few questions based on a few of the ten commandments. Have you ever told a lie? Have you ever taken something that is not yours? Have you ever taken the Lord's name in vain? Have you ever looked upon a member of the opposite sex to whom you are not married (or same-sex) with lust? That is just four questions, and no one I know could answer "no" to all of those questions.

If you break one of the commandments, it is as bad as breaking them all (James 2:10). If you break one of the laws, it is like breaking one link of a chain. With one link broken, the chain is useless. With one law broken, your attempt at righteousness through living by the law is doomed. It would help if you had a savior with a means of getting your transgressions forgiven. We very much need to be reconciled to God (v. 20) and then be ambassadors encouraging others to be reconciled.

2 Corinthians 6:14 Do not be unequally yoked together with unbelievers. For what fellowship has righteousness with lawlessness? And what communion has light with darkness? This statement can be taken too literally. We are not to remove ourselves from contact with unbelievers, but it is wise not to get legally connected with them. If we are in business with an unbeliever, we will naturally disagree on some critical issues having to do with running the business. We are God's dwelling place (Leviticus 26:11; Jerimiah 32:38). When we are in a legal relationship with an unbeliever, how do you think they will get along with you when you smell like the aroma of death to them (2 Corinthians 2:16). They will try to get us to compromise with their values which will be different than ours. It will be hard to maintain our integrity if we are in a legal arrangement with an unbeliever. This is not saying that we should not interact with unbelievers. In fact, the opposite is the case. We will not have any influence unless we have interaction. However, we do need to try not to get legally bound to people who think differently than we do and could be good at justifying their actions based on worldly reasoning.

2 Corinthians 6:16 And what agreement has the temple of God with idols? For you are the temple of the living God. As God has said:
   "I will dwell in them
   And walk among *them*.
   I will be their God,
   And they shall be My people." This verse makes it clear that believers

are the temple of God. The Spirit of the Lord dwells in believers. When the living God dwells in you, everything is different. This is all the more reason to maintain integrity in our actions.

2 Corinthians 7:10 For godly sorrow produces repentance *leading* to salvation, not to be regretted; but the sorrow of the world produces death. Paul seemed to regret coming down on the Corinthians but was happy when they were sorrowful and repented of their transgressions. This kind of sorrow is not to be regretted because it leads to salvation.

2 Corinthians 8:9 For you know the grace of our Lord Jesus Christ, that though He was rich, yet for your sakes He became poor, that you through His poverty might become rich. Christ gave up a lot to come down to earth and die for our sins. From the creator of the universe to a poor sacrificial lamb for people's sins. With His sacrifice, we gain the richness of eternal life. That is phenomenal. No other religion that I know of provides salvation with no effort from the person saved. The Christian is saved by the actions of Christ, who paid the price for our transgressions. We cannot be good enough to accomplish perfect compliance with the law to be 100 percent holy, which would be the requirement.

2 Corinthians 9:15 Thanks *be* to God for His indescribable gift! What is this indescribable gift? It is Jesus Christ. Why is it indescribable? Well, partly because it is so great that words cannot adequately describe what Christ means to believers. Also, we don't know and are not currently knowledgeable about everything coming. We get a little taste from some of the scriptures describing heaven, but overall, we cannot describe what it will be like in the spiritual realm with a glorified body. We can say that it will be amazing to use an overused word.

2 Corinthians 10:4 For the weapons of our warfare *are* not carnal but mighty in God for pulling down strongholds, 5 casting down

arguments and every high thing that exalts itself against the knowledge of God, bringing every thought into captivity to the obedience of Christ, 6 and being ready to punish all disobedience when your obedience is fulfilled. There is a lot said in these verses. It is profound yet simple. Jesus says that the words He speaks to us are spirit. First, we might ask, what are non-carnal weapons? That would be that which is not about the flesh or the body. Thus, it is spiritual. Okay, what is spiritual? It is not material or physical. It has to do with character and moral quality. You cannot see it. God is spirit (John 4:24). If the natural is the physical world that we can see, touch, or measure somehow, the spiritual can be said to be supernatural.

We are currently in a natural body but will someday have a spiritual body (1 Corinthians 15:44). Actually, I'm not sure we will adequately describe or define the spiritual until we break free from the natural world.

Our words are also spirit (John 6:63). God's words are a manifestation of the spirit. What is the primary job of a believer? It is to speak or write God's truth. This is a spiritual process. Words are not the spirit, but the words in the Bible are the manifestation of the Holy Spirit. They may be as close as we can get to the spirit while in the natural world.

The way of God comes down to ideas, and the way we communicate and understand ideas is through words. We cannot understand these ideas without words. In Revelation, we have the final testimony of the two witnesses. They use words to provide evidence for God (Revelation 11:1-14).

2 Corinthians 10:17 But *"he who glories, let him glory in the LORD."* 18 For not he who commends himself is approved, but whom the Lord commends. Paul did not want to be commanded by anyone but the Lord. He did not want to commend himself. He wanted to be commended by God. Paul wanted to make sure that the only boasting that he did was about the Lord and what He did.

2 Corinthians 11:14. And no wonder! For Satan himself transforms himself into an angel of light. This verse comes right after Paul's exhortation about false apostles and deceitful workers who themselves boast of being apostles. Then, he lets us know that Satan himself will pose as an angel. His demons can do the same thing and disguise themselves as if they are apostles. The scripture says that their end will be according to their works (11:15). That is not what you want to be judged by. Those judged by their works will come up short and not be granted eternal life with God. No flesh can be justified by works (Romans 3:20; Galatians 2:16), so these imposters will not have a pleasant end.

2 Corinthians 11:30 If I must boast, I will boast in the things which concern my infirmity. Paul has all kinds of physical problems. He also was beaten, stoned three times, shipwrecked, imprisoned, and had other perils. This is not exactly an easy life like many people expect when they become believers. In reality, the Christian life is not the easy way to go, at least not while we are still on earth. This kind of destroys the health and wealth gospel that some people preach. When someone starts talking about the health and wealth gospel, I become wary. That is not the self-sacrificial, others-centered, humble gospel in the Bible.

2 Corinthians 12:19 Again, do you think that we excuse ourselves to you? We speak before God in Christ. But *we do* all things, beloved, for your edification. Even though Paul had to discipline and correct the Corinthians, he did it for their own good. We often suffer natural and logical consequences when violating God's principles and laws. We should not be surprised when bad things happen to us when we do bad things.

On the other hand, neither should we be surprised when bad things happen that we had nothing to do with. We live in a rebellious fallen world in which bad things are routine. God will establish a new heaven and new earth at the appropriate time. However, now we have free will to rebel and follow Satan or our own lusts. Doing either has consequences in the here and now from which we will not be rescued. It's like a parent telling a kid not to touch the hot stove. We have the freedom to touch the hot stove, and we do so on a grand scale. Then we wonder why God didn't keep us from burning even though we purposefully, in violation of what we were told, touched the hot stove and got burnt. We are a stubborn lot. Some of us will even blame God for burning our hands in this scenario. In some ultimate sense, He is responsible for giving us the free will to disobey, but we would be just like robots without that free will.

God apparently did not want us to be robots incapable of love since love cannot be forced. He wanted us to have the capacity to love, which can only be present in a life that also has the capacity to hate and disobey. So, if you had your choice to be a sentient, self-aware being with free will or a simple automaton with no free will to do wrong, what would you rather be? Now you know one of the reasons it is evil in the world. Yes, God made it that way, but you would be more like a machine than an independent person if He had not made it that way.

Give this some thought: From a rational perspective, there has to be a viable choice to do right or wrong for humankind to have free will. Some think if they abdicate enough power to the government, "they" will control people and keep everyone in line with coercive control and punishment. I don't think that will ever work long-term. The people at the government's top will become the ruling class, and everyone else will be their slaves. Bob Dylan sang, "you're gonna have to serve somebody" and he was right. Do you want to serve the governing elite or the Lord? Make no mistake, when the government gets big enough and strong enough, most of your freedom of choice may be gone. By the people, of the people, and for the people could become a fond memory when the government becomes ruled by a one-party system as it is in some other countries.

2 Corinthians 13:4 For though He was crucified in weakness, yet He lives by the power of God. For we also are weak in Him, but we shall live with Him by the power of God toward you. Note that Christ was crucified, which would indicate weakness but was raised from the dead through the power of God. We, as believers, also have the power of God (Jesus Christ) within us. We need to examine whether we are walking in the faith we express (13:5).

48

Galatians

[48]**GALATIANS** - The Magna Carta of Christian Liberty - Galatians is a concise yet comprehensive Gospel statement. The truth of this gospel summarizes the message of Galatians. The book clearly spells out that salvation is by the grace of God, through faith in Jesus Christ plus nothing else. That is it. We cannot earn salvation through our work or anything we do. It is a gift. All we do is receive the gift through faith.

Paul made it clear that he would let anyone who adds to this gospel be accursed. That is a serious statement. Unfortunately, our natural tendency is to want to earn our salvation and encourage others to earn theirs. If God allowed us to do that, we could take pride in it. He knew that and apparently, determined not to allow us to be prideful about earning our salvation. He set things up so we can't "earn" our salvation. You might ask: what about the ten commandments? According to Paul, they have the purpose of convicting us of our sin and showing us our urgent need for the forgiveness and salvation that Jesus Christ provides. Yes, it is one narrow road. Unfortunately, according to the Bible, not all

---

[48] NSB quotations are from the Nelsons Study Bible, copyright (c) 1997 by Thomas Nelson, Inc., Nashville, TN; used by permission; scripture taken from the New King James Version, Copyright (c) 1979, 1980, 1982 used by permission. All rights reserved.

roads lead to salvation. My opinion on this does not matter. What God says is all that matters, and His words tell us repeatedly that in these last days, faith in Jesus Christ is the way to salvation, period. Some people will decide that they don't believe what is in the Bible or that the Christian Bible is the inspired Word of God. The irony is that it is the one who inspired the words in the Bible who gave them life and the free will not to believe in Him or His Word.

Faith is believing God. In Abraham's day, he was responsible for what he knew, not what he didn't know. He didn't have all the revelation we do, nor had the Messiah come to the earth yet. But Abraham had faith in God and acted in faith. It was faith then, as it is now, that produces salvation through the grace of God. However, back then, the work of Christ to save had not yet been completely revealed. Now, there is more clarity about how God's grace has been provided through Christ, which perfectly fulfills God's plan for all of us who choose to believe through the free will He gave us.

Of course, many people will exercise their free will to reject the Bible as God's inspired Word. That is not something we control. For them, it appears to be true that any road they choose will lead them to where they are going.

It is simple for those who accept what the Bible says; there is nothing more and nothing less. Yet, we still struggle to accept this truth. It seems too easy. Paul goes even further in Galatians to let us know that salvation and sanctification (the process of being set apart) are both by grace through faith. Paul described this process as walking in the Spirit (5:22,23), being "led by the Spirit" (5:18), and sowing "to the Spirit" (6:8). My interpretation/translation is as follows: works are only worthwhile if motivated by the Holy Spirit and, even then, not to justify a person, but merely as an outcome of their justification. It is good to keep in mind that scripture clearly states: "**But if you are led by the Spirit, you are**

not under the law" (Galatians 5:18).

Galatians 1:11 But I make known to you, brethren, that the gospel which was preached by me is not according to man. 12 For I neither received it from man, nor was I taught *it*, but *it came* through the revelation of Jesus Christ. Paul clarifies that he had a unique call to be an apostle. It was direct from God. He received no instruction from the other Apostles, but his teaching agreed exactly with theirs. Paul had previously tried to earn his salvation like other Judaizers in Galatia through works. Now he knew and preached that salvation was only based on the grace of "**God the Father and our Lord Jesus Christ, who gave Himself for our sins, that He might deliver us from this present evil age, according to the will of our God and Father, to whom be glory forever and ever Amen**" (1:3). He was serious about this teaching and would let anyone who presented a different gospel be accursed (condemned to destruction). He was concerned that some were teaching that the law had to be added to the gospel. Paul clearly and unequivocally let people know that the offer of salvation from Christ was free and nothing else needed to be added, no works needed to be performed, or other laws kept to receive this gift.

Galatians 2:4 And *this occurred* because of false brethren secretly brought in (who came in by stealth to spy out our liberty which we have in Christ Jesus, that they might bring us into bondage),... People always seem to be trying to bring others into bondage one way or another. In this situation, people called themselves Christians but were trying to add aspects of the law to the gospel. Paul clearly rebuked that approach. He would not allow himself or his converts to be placed back into the bondage of Jewish legalism. They apparently would not accept that salvation was through faith alone and simply a gift of God. Because of this, it appears that Paul did not even recognize them as true Christians.

Galatians 2:16 knowing that a man is not justified by the works of the law but by faith in Jesus Christ, even we have believed in Christ Jesus, that we might be justified by faith in Christ and not by the works of the law; for by the works of the law no flesh shall be justified. Here Paul again clarifies that we are justified by faith in Christ. The scripture makes it indisputable for anyone who can read and understand what he is saying that keeping the law will not justify the person even if they were 100 percent successful. These passages clarify that it is not the law but faith in Christ that justifies the flesh. Faith is believing in God. In Abraham's day, he was responsible for what he knew, not what he didn't know. He didn't have all the revelation we do, nor had the Messiah come to the earth yet. But he had faith in God and acted in faith. Now we know that God and Christ are one. It was faith then, as it is now, that produces salvation through the grace of God. They didn't understand the whole revelation of how God would come to the earth and pay the price for our sins. Back then, the work of Christ to save humanity had not yet been fully revealed, but faith (i.e., believing God) was still how Abraham was justified. Now, there is more clarity about how God's grace has been provided through Christ, which perfectly fulfills God's plan for all of us who choose to believe through the free will He gave us.

Galatians 2:20 I have been crucified with Christ; it is no longer I who live, but Christ lives in me; and the *life* which I now live in the flesh I live by faith in the Son of God, who loved me and gave Himself for me. This is an important verse for any Christian to know and understand. It is good for us to live as if our old nature has died. We know that our old nature is a dead-end and that it does not profit us to continue to let sin rule in our lives. In the spiritual sense, we were "crucified with Christ," and Christ lives in us through this process. Our flesh was spiritually dead and will eventually also die physically, but the life of Christ in us will live forever. To put this concept in different terms, being united with Christ is life eternal; being separate from Christ is death.

Galatians 3:6 ...just as Abraham "believed God, and it was accounted to him for righteousness."7 Therefore know that *only* those who are of faith are sons of Abraham. Here we find out that salvation was through faith even before Christ came to earth and died for our sins. Christ apparently died for their sins after they lived on earth, and He died for our sins before we lived on earth (Romans 3:25-26). Any righteousness we have is not what we earn through the law but what we receive through belief in Christ (Philippians, 3:9).

The time dimension seems to be different for God. That makes sense because time, like the other dimensions that we experience, was created by God. It seems that He can see the past, present, and future simultaneously. Because He created the dimensions, the time dimension is under His authority and control even though we cannot understand it with our limited abilities and intellect. From this scripture, we learn that it was not by following the ten commandments that Abraham was saved. It was because he "believed God." Faith is believing God.

Many people who exercise their freedom to reject the New Testament teaching do not understand the grace of God and are still vainly trying to earn their salvation in one way or another. Some will even think that they can earn a place in heaven by hurting those who disagree with them. Those who understand what this book of the Bible says in conjunction with all the other scripture will understand that salvation is only for those of faith. Verse 11 goes on to clarify: **But that no one is justified by the law in the sight of God is evident, for "the just shall live by faith."** This is a quote by Paul of Habakkuk 2:4. Paul also cites Leviticus 18:5 to show us that trying to keep the law is incompatible with faith. It is one or the other. Since no one can keep all of the law, we are much better off with faith. Those who are of faith are not under the curse of the law. To please our loving savior, we will not want to violate His law, but it is not through keeping the law that we are saved. It is through faith.

Galatians 3:19 What purpose then *does* the law *serve?* It was added because of transgressions, till the Seed should come to whom the promise was made; *and it was* appointed through angels by the hand of a mediator. This is a fundamental concept to grasp. As with most believers, I did not understand the law's true purpose for many years. It is to help us understand our sin. We need to be forgiven, and Christ paid the price for our sin/transgressions so that God could see us as not having any transgressions at all. What a great message!

The law was given not to save us but to show us that we could not save ourselves and need a savior. God provided our savior in Christ, who paid the just price for our sins on our behalf and gave us eternal life through faith.

Paul gives two functions of the law. Before Christ came, it functioned to keep a man under guard (Galatians 3:24). What does that mean? The law was a tutor to prepare humankind for Christ so that we could be **justified by faith.** Now we don't need the law to tutor us. "**For you are sons of God through faith in Jesus Christ.**" What could be better than a system of faith that saves a soul for eternity? This is the defining issue of humanity, whether we know it or not. It distinguishes Christianity from every other religious system in that we cannot do anything to earn our salvation or good favor or anything else that other religions promise.

Our salvation is simply a gift, no matter how much we try to earn our salvation. We cannot be good enough or committed enough or innocent enough to connect with a God who is holy, holy, holy. We have to have a righteous savior. When we have faith in our Savior, we are not only sons of Abraham but sons of God and His heirs. Yes, we are His adopted children. We deserved judgment for our sins but have been redeemed. Someone else, Christ, took on the punishment for our transgressions.

It is too simple for some to accept. Doesn't it have to be more complex or difficult? With this system, an imbecile could be saved. That's right. All your intellectual capability, self-reliance, and efforts are all unproductive. Everyone's the same. No one can be good enough, and all of us human beings must humbly rely on Christ to save us. No one can boast that they were good enough, wise, or spiritual enough to be saved.

These beliefs are like no other belief system, and no others seem to want to entertain the possibility that we cannot save ourselves. We want to be our own god and be able to accomplish salvation or enlightenment or nirvana or self-actualization or whatever we call the highest spiritual accomplishment through our own efforts. These efforts are all ultimately futile and unproductive. The good news is that it has all been done for us, and this is one of the great mysteries of life that is now revealed. Yes, it takes humility to accept the gift of salvation, but that is exactly what we need to do.

Galatians 4:6 And because you are sons, God has sent forth the Spirit of His Son into your hearts, crying out, "Abba, Father!" 7 Therefore you are no longer a slave but a son, and if a son, then an heir of God through Christ. Those who believe are different. They have the indwelling Spirit of God. You could say that it is like having some of God in ourselves, just like we have our earthly fathers' DNA in us. With the Spirit of His Son, we are directly descended, family members. This status appears to be more than just being adopted. The Spirit is actually in us. As we are not our earthly father just because we have some of his DNA in us, we are not God just because we have His Spirit in us (see Romans 8:1-17). However, it does make us God's sons and daughters and direct heirs who inherit eternal life from Him.

The divine compensation package is immense. Not only will we receive a hundredfold according to Matthew (19:29), but we will also receive eternal life. Our brief span of years here on earth hardly registers on the scale of eternity. We are redeemed, which means we were bought from the slave market of this short-term life and set free for eternity. That is an amazing difference, and it did not cost us anything. It is a gift for those who chose faith in Christ over slavery to the law.

Rules and regulations should not limit the gospel. Grace and the law are dramatically different approaches to God and have opposite results. Grace is based on faith (2:16), and the law is based on works. Grace justifies sinful men; the law cannot produce salvation (2:16, 17). Grace is the way of the Spirit toward perfection; the law is the way of the flesh that cannot make perfect (3:3). Grace is a blessing (3:14); the law is a curse (3:13). Grace is God's end for His people (3:23-25); the law was intended only as a means to an end. Grace brings liberty (5:1); the law results in bondage (5:1). Grace depends on the power of the Holy Spirit (5:16-18); the law depends on human effort (5:19-21). Grace is motivated by love (5:13,14); the law is motivated by pride (6:3, 13, 14). Grace centers on the cross of Christ (6:12-14); the law is centered on circumcision (5:11; 6:12-15).

Galatians 4:16 Have I therefore become your enemy because I tell you the truth? Here it appears that Paul recognized that some of the Galatians did not want to hear what he had to tell them. Sometimes we should say things to our friends even though they may not like what we say. Paul realized that some of them would become his enemies because they disagreed with what he had to say, but he needed to be straight with them and make sure they understood exactly what he was telling them. Since what he told them is recorded in the New Testament, we also need to understand it. He had to tell them and us the truth even if it meant that some of them and some of us would not agree and fight against this message. A real friend may need to confront us with the truth, even if we don't want to hear it.

Galatians 4:23 But he *who was* of the bondwoman was born according to the flesh, and he of the freewoman through promise, 24 which things are symbolic. For these are the two covenants: the one from Mount Sinai which gives birth to bondage, which is Hagar— These verses explain a lot about the world's largest belief systems; one based on grace and most of the others based on works. Hagar, the bond-woman, was the mother of Ishmael. Isaac was the son of Sarah, a freewoman, and became the father of Jacob, who was one of the three great patriarchs of the nation of the Israelites. To be free is to follow Abraham's example of faith.

Galatians 5:1 It is for freedom that Christ has set us free. Stand firm, then, and do not let yourselves be burdened again by a yoke of slavery. It is clear. Christ set us free. He paid the price for our freedom, so why would we want to go back under bondage to the law? We absolutely do not have to keep the law of Moses to be saved. We are under God's grace, and to go back to trying to follow the law to be saved is acting as if Christ died on the cross for no reason. We would have to keep every bit of the law to be saved, and none of us can do that (Romans 3:10-18). There does not appear to be any place in God's plan of salvation for people's good works. We do not deserve this grace, but it is offered as a gift to receive anyway. The gospel is about forgiveness for sins. It is free for us.

The cross is offensive to some because they want to earn their own salvation or save themselves and thereby take pride in their accomplishment. That glory belongs to God and only God. We do not get to take any responsibility for it. We now live under the law of Christ (Mark 12:28-31), which has to do with loving God with all of our being and loving our neighbors as we love ourselves. According to Christ, these are the two most important commandments. The Old Testament law was fulfilled by Christ (Romans 10:4; Galatians 3:23-25; Ephesians 2:15). Rather than follow the over 600 individual commandments in the Old Testament, we just have a few under Christ. If we abide by those two, we will be fulfilling what God requires of us. Paul points out that this is not an excuse to sin (Romans 6:15). Our actions may be similar under both systems, but there is a different motivation.

Galatians 5:19 Now the works of the flesh are evident, which are: adultery, fornication, uncleanness, lewdness, 20 idolatry, sorcery, hatred, contentions, jealousies, outbursts of wrath, selfish ambitions, dissensions, heresies, 21 envy, murders, drunkenness, revelries, and the like; of which I tell you beforehand, just as I also told *you* in time past, that those who practice such things will not inherit the kingdom of God. This important scripture can serve as somewhat of a litmus test regarding human behavior. If you see jealousy contentions and other works of the flesh, where is that coming from? Clearly, it is coming from the flesh. It is as plain as day. How do we tell when something is not of the Spirit. It is right here and in the next scripture.

Galatians 5:22 But the fruit of the Spirit is love, joy, peace, longsuffering, kindness, goodness, faithfulness, 23 gentleness, self-control. Against such there is no law. It is, therefore, not very hard to discern between the works of the Spirit and the works of the flesh. These scriptures in Galatians don't leave much doubt about where an action or feeling falls among these two options: flesh or Spirit.

Galatians 6:7 Do not be deceived, God is not mocked; for whatever a man sows, that he will also reap. This seems to be a foundational principle in the Bible. If we give in to the flesh, we will reap corruption. If we give way to the spirit, we will reap everlasting life. Based on other scripture, this does not mean that you can earn eternal life by working to sow to the spirit. Rather, following the Holy Spirit will naturally lead to this end (Romans 6:22). As the scripture puts it, this is the result of having been set free from sin and becoming slaves to God. Part of why Christ came is so we could have a more abundant (eternal) life (John

10:10).

Galatians 6:10 Therefore, as we have opportunity, let us do good to all, especially to those who are of the household of faith. This verse tells us that, as an outcome of following the Spirit, we should do good to everyone. These works do not justify (2:16) or sanctify (3:3); they are the fruit or outcome of following the Spirit. We should also be doing good to non-Christians. That can be the harder aspect of following the Spirit.

Galatians 6:14 But God forbid that I should boast except in the cross of our Lord Jesus Christ, by whom the world has been crucified to me, and I to the world. Paul seems to be saying that if he were to boast, the only thing worth boasting about is what Christ did for us. Everything we are is a result of His grace, so taking credit for it would be like stealing it from the one it belongs to.

49

Ephesians

⁴⁹**EPHESIANS** - In this book, Paul continues his normal emphasis on justification by faith alone. He provides us with the central doctrines of the faith and certain armor that will help us withstand the forces of evil. He also clarifies that all Christians are united in one body through Christ (Ephesians 2:16). In Christ, we are joined together with people with whom we may have previously been divided. When he wrote this letter, Paul was apparently under house arrest status in Rome. At that time, Christians met in houses in various places over the Mediterranean world to which this letter could have been circulated. The letter emphasizes that we all need to play our part to build up the body. The church in Christ is the one body. People who were previously divided can be unified through Christ into one body. In other words, we can be joined together through Christ, and it is Christ's love, patience, humility, and gentleness that builds up the Church. Paul also talks about one of our life's purposes: **to the praise of the glory of His grace** (1:6).

Ephesians 1:4 ...just as He chose us in Him before the foundation of

---

[49] NSB quotations are from the Nelsons Study Bible, copyright (c) 1997 by Thomas Nelson, Inc., Nashville, TN; used by permission; scripture taken from the New King James Version, Copyright (c) 1979, 1980, 1982 used by permission. All rights reserved.

the world, that we should be holy and without blame before Him in love, 5 having predestined us to adoption as sons by Jesus Christ to Himself, according to the good pleasure of His will, 6 to the praise of the glory of His grace, by which He made us accepted in the Beloved. Wow, this is amazing that He chose us before the foundation of the world. It is obvious from this statement that God had a plan before He made this speck of a planet that we occupy in the vast universe. He determined that He would have people on it who had free will and that He would provide a way for people with free will to be reconciled to Him and be adopted as sons by Jesus Christ. This is all for His pleasure, as it says in this verse.

Why was our world made? It says it right here. It was "according to the good pleasure of His will." So, in the opening of this book, we find out the why and the what of human existence. The why is: God made us for His good pleasure. Then what does "to the praise of the glory of His grace" mean. He apparently wanted us to show the glory of His grace, and every time someone exercises the free will that He gave them to accept the gift of salvation, that is exactly what happens. We are saved to the praise of His glory, not ours. It is His grace that deserves the glory, not anything we did.

Why did He set it up this way? Because He is God, and that is the way He wanted to set it up. Though some men will argue about this, it doesn't make any difference. It is what it is, and God is who He is and always will be. Some things don't change, regardless of how many men try to change them.

I imagine God laughs at some of the things humankind comes up with to develop their own gods and/or idols. It would seem that it would have to be some tragic comedy of pride from God's perspective when humankind tries to act as if God doesn't exist and says that time, chance, or gravity can explain the workings and laws of the universe. If I were

Him, I would probably be having a belly roll of laughter regarding some of the explanations of the universe that the smartest men on the planet come up with.

How thoroughly man can deceive himself into believing something that is patently full of error when he doesn't want to accept the inevitable conclusion that matter is not all that there is or ever was. It can be difficult for some people to accept that there has to be an uncaused cause and that the material world had to have a supernatural creator (God), or it would not exist.

Ephesians 1:11 In Him also we have obtained an inheritance, being predestined according to the purpose of Him who works all things according to the counsel of His will,12 that we who first trusted in Christ should be to the praise of His glory. Notice that we who first trusted in Christ are spoken of as being to the praise of His glory. Here again, we see our purpose laid out clearly. We are to trust in Christ. That is our meaning and goal in life. In so doing, we bring praise to God's grace in saving us. If we don't fulfill our primary purpose, how can we ever enter into the peace (Isa. 57:2) or life (Matt. 19:17), or joy (Matt. 25:21) that He wants us to have. This is what we were "predestined" to do according to the purpose of God. He always wants the best for us but does not force us to have the best He has to offer. You can still go your own prideful way if you want.

Jeremiah states that when the Lord saves us, the Lord is our praise (Jeremiah 17:14). This appears to be a different way of saying that it is all about God and His purposes, not about what we do. Therefore, He should always be the focus of our praise, and we should keep our eyes on Him. God has now made known the mystery of His will, that at the proper time, He will **gather together in one all things in Christ, both which are in heaven and on earth - in Him** (1:10). All of us can know this. It is not just for a select few to know that all of our world is according to His good pleasure.

Ephesians 1:13 In Him you also *trusted,* **after you heard the word of truth, the gospel of your salvation; in whom also, having believed, you were sealed with the Holy Spirit of promise, 14 who is the guarantee of our inheritance until the redemption of the purchased possession, to the praise of His glory.** Interestingly, the Holy Spirit is the "guarantee" of our inheritance. We have been purchased by Christ, paying the price of our sins on the Cross. However, we have not yet received our full inheritance as sons (and daughters) of God. In the meantime, we have the Holy Spirit in us as a sort of down payment or good faith deposit that the best is yet to come. Later, we will receive our full inheritance. This will come when we are gathered together (in Him), which entails much more inheritance and unity than we have now. It's kind of like being engaged and receiving an engagement ring as an indication that more unity and togetherness are to come, but until that time, the engagement ring signifies that more is planned.

Ephesians 2:8 For by grace you have been saved through faith, and that not of yourselves; *it is* **the gift of God, 9 not of works, lest anyone should boast. 10 For we are His workmanship, created in Christ Jesus for good works, which God prepared beforehand that we should walk in them.** Here is one of the most important concepts to understand. We are saved by grace through faith. It is a gift, no matter how much we want to earn it somehow and take credit for our own salvation. All we do is accept a gift. There is no reason for us to take pride in ourselves for our salvation. On the contrary, it is all in God's plan.

The other interesting part of this scripture is that it explains why we were created and saved: "**for good works**." So what should we be doing while we are here on earth? Good works. We previously were spiritually dead, but now we can put aside our lust for fame, power, and riches and not let those desires take over our life. Another way to express all that is in this verse is that it was God's desire based on His heart of love, to have a blueprint or plan for our life that contains good works for us to do.

Since God made us, His plan for our life would be the best. He knows what He made us for. God's plan is the right road to take. Who else could provide a better direction? We might desire something different, but if our way is not in God's plan, it could wind up being a rocky road to a dead end.

God obviously wants the best for us and has given us the gift of a sixty-six book operator's manual (the Bible) to help us determine the best road to take. We just have to accept it and follow it. Even our faith is a gift of God. We truly are His workmanship. Note that we could not fulfill the law ourselves. We were saved when Christ paid the price for our sins in our place. Now, if we turn to the right channel (faith), we are saved by His grace through accepting the gift. The gift is that He paid the price for our sins. We owed the debt, but He paid it off once and for all. All we have to do is agree to be one of those for whom the debt is paid. It's kind of like a class action situation. Only those who accept being part of the class get to benefit from the class action.

Ephesians 2:3 For this reason I, Paul, the prisoner of Christ Jesus for you Gentiles— 2 if indeed you have heard of the dispensation of the grace of God which was given to me for you, 3 how that by revelation He made known to me the mystery (as I have briefly written already, 4 by which, when you read, you may understand my knowledge in the mystery of Christ), 5 which in other ages was not made known to the sons of men, as it has now been revealed by the Spirit to His holy apostles and prophets: 6 that the Gentiles should be fellow heirs, of the same body, and partakers of His promise in Christ through the gospel, 7 of which I became a minister according to the gift of the grace of God given to me by

the effective working of His power. What an incredible sentence. We have so much revelation in this one sentence that it is hard to grasp it all. Unless we understand that there are different "dispensations," it is difficult to reconcile what seem to be conflicting parts of scripture.

A dispensation is a time in history in which God deals with man in a specific way and reveals a specific part of Himself. It is clear from this statement that certain things were mysteries before this dispensation but now is revealed through His apostles and prophets. He has now revealed to us that gentiles are grafted into the family of believers as part of the same body as the Israelites through the gospel of Christ.

The good news is that we live in the dispensation of grace, as this particular scripture points out. We get to know some things that humanity was not privy to before in this period. We are also held accountable for what is going on in our short section of history. We are told why Christ came to the earth and what He did while here, and why it is of ultimate importance to our salvation. The mystery revealed is that we gentiles have an equal status in the body of Christ with the original chosen people. Paul's job was to enlighten gentiles about God's grace in Christ which was previously not fully revealed or understood even though it was predicted (Genesis 12:3).

Ephesians 3:10 ...to the intent that now the manifold wisdom of God might be made known by the church to the principalities and powers in the heavenly *places,* **11 according to the eternal purpose which He accomplished in Christ Jesus our Lord, 12 in whom we have boldness and access with confidence through faith in Him. 13 Therefore I ask that you do not lose heart at my tribulations for you, which is your glory.** It appears that God's plan of salvation had been hidden through the ages. It says right here that God created all things through Jesus Christ. When He says "all things," I assume He means all the physical universe that we can see. Sometimes we don't realize the extent of the universe He is talking about here. Compared to the size of our galaxy and the many others, our little world is but a speck of dust floating in a vast space.

We now have been able, through the Hubble telescope, to see the eXtreme Deep Field. With this, the most distant object we have seen so far is calculated to be over 13.2 billion light-years away. That means that the light we see coming from this distant galaxy is 13.2 billion years old because it took that long to get to our eyes.

Scientists are now working on a bigger space telescope that will probably allow us to see even more distant galaxies. So to figure out how far away the light we are seeing is coming from, multiply 13.2 billion years times 6 trillion miles. Light travels at about 186,000 miles per second. Thus, light could travel about 7 times around the earth in a second.

So, how powerful is a God who could create a universe that big and spread out? It is beyond our imagination. Truly, God's power cannot be understood by even our greatest imagination. Still, something is happening here on our little earth that God wants the powers in the heavens to see; that is the grace of God through faith in Jesus Christ. It appears that even the angels are learning things from how God is working with us. That is amazing, considering the small part of the universe we occupy.

Ephesians 3:17... that Christ may dwell in your hearts through faith; that you, being rooted and grounded in love, 18 may be able to comprehend with all the saints what *is* the width and length and depth and height— 19 to know the love of Christ which passes knowledge; that you may be filled with all the fullness of God. To be filled with the fullness of God sounds good, but what does that mean? It does appear to have to do with Christ residing in our hearts and the abundant gifts that come from God. The word "dwell" suggests that the

Spirit of Christ is settling in and being at home in the heart of a believer.

How do we know that this has happened? First, the believer will tell you that they now believe that Christ came to earth in the flesh. Second, there would be some change in their actions, feelings, and behavior based on the fruit of the Spirit. As the sanctification process occurs in them, the fruit should begin to surface. This is the fruit mentioned in Galatians 5:20, which is: love, joy, peace, patience, kindness, long-suffering, goodness, faithfulness, gentleness, and self-control. This evidence will not be perfect as we apparently will not achieve all of these attributes while here on earth. Nevertheless, there should be some movement in this direction and away from the opposites of these attributes. It has been said that "if there is no change, there has been no change." Also, if they do not confess that Jesus Christ has come in the flesh, that is an indication that they are not really believers in Christ (1 John 4:2).

Ephesians 4:1 I, therefore, the prisoner of the Lord, beseech you to walk worthy of the calling with which you were called, 2 with all lowliness and gentleness, with longsuffering, bearing with one another in love, 3 endeavoring to keep the unity of the Spirit in the bond of peace. Here again, we see the fruit of the Spirit emphasized with a recognition of how we will act under the control of the Spirit. If we believe the scripture, there should be an effect on our actions. That effect is summarized in the rest of the book of Ephesians.

In this particular verse, we learn that we will be humble, gentle, long-suffering, loving, and in unity with other believers. We are not running or standing still, but walking. Christ's life exhibited these traits for us. These traits do not come naturally to us but must be cultivated through a change in our beliefs and actions that follow. We need to remember that we are really one in the spirit with all actual believers. Of course, some put on a sheep's clothing but are actually wolves inside. We cannot always identify who these counterfeits are, but we should treat them the same as others anyway. When they show who they really are, a different approach may be appropriate if they are not repentant.

We should make every effort to maintain the unity of the spirit with other Christians who believe in the essentials of the faith even if we disagree on nonessential issues. All of us are given some spiritual gift or gifts to help the body of believers maintain unity. Unlike the physical world, where systems break down over time, we are endowed with the ability to build up parts of the body to maintain their function and not wear out.

50

Philippians

[50]**PHILIPPIANS** - Paul learned to be content in whatever situation he was in. This is a good character trait to have. He believed that God was continuing to work in him through various trials. Many of these trials were more difficult than any we are likely to face. Jesus was Paul's model and can also be for us.

Philippians 1:3 I thank my God upon every remembrance of you, 4 always in every prayer of mine making request for you all with joy, 5 for your fellowship in the gospel from the first day until now, 6 being confident of this very thing, that He who has begun a good work in you will complete it until the day of Jesus Christ; 7 just as it is right for me to think this of you all, because I have you in my heart, inasmuch as both in my chains and in the defense and confirmation of the gospel, you all are partakers with me of grace. There is a lot in this passage, so it is worth looking at the whole thing. Paul was obviously thankful for the Philippians. He expected God to continue working with them until the day of Jesus Christ. That would

---

[50] NSB quotations are from the Nelsons Study Bible, copyright (c) 1997 by Thomas Nelson, Inc., Nashville, TN; used by permission; scripture taken from the New King James Version, Copyright (c) 1979, 1980, 1982 used by permission. All rights reserved.

be the day that Christ returns to the earth.

Philippians 1:12 But I want you to know, brethren, that the things *which happened* to me have actually turned out for the furtherance of the gospel, 13 so that it has become evident to the whole palace guard, and to all the rest, that my chains are in Christ; 14 and most of the brethren in the Lord, having become confident by my chains, are much more bold to speak the word without fear. Paul was aware that God could use all the things that happened to him to further the gospel. Even when he was in prison, Paul positively influenced the prison guards. He was not going to be silenced about speaking the word of God. He followed what the governing authorities told him to do unless it conflicted with Christ's direction.

Philippians 1:16 The former preach Christ from selfish ambition, not sincerely, supposing to add affliction to my chains; 17 but the latter out of love, knowing that I am appointed for the defense of the gospel. Who are the former preachers? They are the ones who do not preach the gospel out of love. Who are the latter? They are the ones who are trying to build themselves up or make money through the gospel.

Philippians 1:19 For I know that this will turn out for my deliverance through your prayer and the supply of the Spirit of Jesus Christ, 20 according to my earnest expectation and hope that in nothing I shall be ashamed, but with all boldness, as always, so now also Christ will be magnified in my body, whether by life or by death. Paul knew what his mission was and knew that God was with him in whatever happened. Therefore, he rested and trusted in the Lord.

Philippians 1:21 For to me, to live *is* Christ, and to die *is* gain. Paul knew where he was going when he died and was not afraid of death. In fact, in this verse, he calls dying "gain." This was his attitude. When he died, he knew his struggles, trials, and tribulations would be over and he would receive his reward for his faithful service in spreading the Gospel.

Philippians 1:27 Only let your conduct be worthy of the gospel of Christ, so that whether I come and see you or am absent, I may hear of your affairs, that you stand fast in one spirit, with one mind striving together for the faith of the gospel, 28 and not in any way terrified by your adversaries, which is to them a proof of perdition, but to you of salvation, and that from God. We should not be afraid of people who do not believe the Gospel. Their severe opposition to the Gospel is proof that it has power. It would not warrant the level of opposition if it were merely fiction. You will notice that dictators often think that they will not have total control if they allow their citizens to read the Bible. About 200 years ago, Heinrich Heine wrote this about book burning: "Where they have burned books, they will end in burning human beings." Obviously, he made an accurate prediction that came true many years later. In conjunction with protests and riots, a group recently burned a Bible and an American Flag in an American city. This act shows how important the Bible is. If it meant nothing, it would not be burnt by these people alongside an American flag. Ironically, the fact that these people hate the Bible and the flag enough to burn them as a symbolic act of desecration demonstrates just how important they are.

Philippians 1:29 For to you it has been granted on behalf of Christ, not only to believe in Him but also to suffer for His sake, 30 having the same conflict which you saw in me and now hear *is* in me. It is a great gift to be granted to believe in Christ. It is also to be treasured if we are counted worthy to suffer for Him. It turns out that the Christian life is not all peaches and cream.

Philippians 2:3 *Let* nothing *be done* through selfish ambition or conceit, but in lowliness of mind let each esteem others better than himself. Even for those preaching the Gospel, it should not be done to build up yourself or gain status. Preachers of the gospel should be humble and hold the needs of others to be more important than their own needs.

Philippians 2:5 Let this mind be in you which was also in Christ Jesus, 6 who, being in the form of God, did not consider it robbery to be equal with God, 7 but made Himself of no reputation, taking the form of a bondservant, *and* coming in the likeness of men. 8 And being found in appearance as a man, He humbled Himself and became obedient to *the point of* death, even the death of the cross. God came to earth in the form of a man. This is a very important passage in the New Testament. It reveals that Christ was both a man and God. Though He looked like a man on the outside, He was God on the inside. The verse also explains how He could not know everything since He was God. He emptied Himself (**in the likeness of men**). He temporarily gave up some of this knowledge (Matthew 24:35-36, Luke (2:52).

Philippians 2:9 Therefore God also has highly exalted Him and given Him the name which is above every name, 10 that at the name of Jesus every knee should bow, of those in heaven, and of those on earth, and of those under the earth, 11 and *that* I urge you also, true companion, help these women who labored with me in the gospel, with Clement also, and the rest of my fellow workers, whose names *are* in the Book of Life. In our culture, many misuse the name of Jesus as a swear word. That is blasphemy. They also blaspheme God. Why would they use these names if they do not believe in Jesus or God? In fact, some of the most adamantly anti-Christian people may use the name Jesus Christ or God far more than Christians do. For some people, much of their verbalization is angry swearing. Just as Jesus could forgive those who were crucifying Him, he will forgive even these people if they repent of their unbelief and turn toward God. However, there is a limit to God's patience, and at some point, all in heaven and on earth will bow before Him.

Those whose names are written in the book of life will have no problem bowing before Christ, but those who have consistently ridiculed Him and used any of His names in vain will have a very hard time bowing before Him. The shame will be unbearable for them when they have to submit to Him when He returns in power in the clouds (Revelation 7:1).

Philippians 2:14 Do all things without complaining and disputing, 15 that you may become blameless and harmless, children of God without fault in the midst of a crooked and perverse generation, among whom you shine as lights in the world, 16 holding fast the word of life, so that I may rejoice in the day of Christ that I have not run in vain or labored in vain. Generally, it appears that Christians are to accept their situation rather than complain and dispute about it. We are to live righteously even though the people around us may be the opposite. We are to be an example to others of righteous living. Then we can rejoice when Christ returns. It will be an absolutely glorious day.

Philippians 2:27 For indeed he was sick almost unto death; but God had mercy on him, and not only on him but on me also, lest I should have sorrow upon sorrow. Paul had the power of an apostle but still needed those powers to be exercised in God's timing and will for those powers to be effective.

Philippians 3:3 For we are the circumcision, who worship God in the Spirit, rejoice in Christ Jesus, and have no confidence in the flesh, 4 though I also might have confidence in the flesh. If anyone else thinks he may have confidence in the flesh, I more so: Paul had all the credentials for having pride in the flesh. Nevertheless, he did not believe that those credentials could provide the righteousness required. Paul seems to be saying that the circumcision of the flesh is of little value, but the worship of God in the Spirit is what is needed and is far more beneficial and comes through faith in Christ.

Philippians 3:8 Yet indeed I also count all things loss for the excellence of the knowledge of Christ Jesus my Lord, for whom I have suffered the loss of all things, and count them as rubbish, that I may gain Christ 9 and be found in Him, not having my own righteousness, which *is* from the law, but that which *is* through faith in Christ, the righteousness which is from God by faith; 10 that I may know Him and the power of His resurrection, and the fellowship of His sufferings, being conformed to His death, 11 if, by any means, I may attain to the resurrection from the dead. Paul had great faith and righteousness through that faith in Christ. For Christians, this faith is the most important thing in life. It is the key to eternal life. What could be more important than that? We really need this kind of righteousness. He wanted to attain the resurrection of a glorified body at the appropriate time as decided by God.

Philippians 3:14 I press toward the goal for the prize of the upward call of God in Christ Jesus. I like the sound of the upward call. It sounds like a call from God Himself. We have a goal at the end of the race. It is a great prize. It is the abundant and eternal life that comes through Christ Jesus.

Philippians 4:4 Rejoice in the Lord always. Again I will say, rejoice! In the book of James, we are given information about why we should rejoice even when we wind up having difficulties and trials. We are to count it as joy (James 1:2-4). How can we do that when things are not going our way? We have to understand that God has told us that in a fallen world, there will be trials. However, we do not have to go through them alone. He will be with us through those trials. Apparently, trials present us with a unique opportunity to develop patience, perseverance and to draw us closer to God. They help us realize how much we need His constant presence in our lives. It makes it easier to forget how much we need God's help to get through this life when things are going well. We are to embrace patience to **be perfect and complete, lacking nothing**

(James 1:4).

A couple of important questions to ask about a trial are; how can I learn from this trial, and how can I use it to help others learn more about God? I don't totally understand this, but it makes sense that if we are in a situation we don't want to be in, we can use that situation to develop patience. Knowing that there can be some positive outcomes from our trials can help somewhat. Nevertheless, some trials do not go away no matter how much we want them to and how much we pray for that to happen. These situations are the most difficult and test our faith the most. These trials can encourage us to maintain a heavenly-minded or eternal perspective. Hopefully, we can reduce the current anxiety and pain by keeping focused on the eternal plan of God, which is for us to wind up in a place where there are no more tears and no more pain.

Philippians 4:5 Let your gentleness be known to all men. The Lord *is* at hand. Kindness and gentleness are fruits of the Spirit (Galatians 5:22-23). Interestingly, this verse ends with the statement that the **Lord is at hand**. What does that mean? It indicates that the Lord may not be happy if we are not kind to the other people that He made. We are directed to love everyone, even our enemies. Hard to do? Yes. So, who said that the Christian life was going to be easy. God did not say that. It will have rewards, some now and many others through eternity.

Philippians 4:6 Be anxious for nothing, but in everything by prayer and supplication, with thanksgiving, let your requests be made known to God; 7 and the peace of God, which surpasses all understanding, will guard your hearts and minds through Christ Jesus. To be anxious for nothing is hard to do. It is somewhat easier when you know that God is ultimately in charge and all things work to the good who trust in Him. It is better to pray about issues than to worry over them. Generally, we have a lot to be thankful for even when we have some problems. Even if everything on earth seems dark, we can be thankful for the coming afterlife. Many times, our problems are in our minds.

Anxiety is one of those problems that can and should be helped by focusing on prayer and thanksgiving. Supplication is like prayer in that it means a request or petition. It appears that our prayers and supplications are a kind of defense in the battle raging in our minds against anxiety when we know that God is ultimately in charge of our lives and what happens on earth. When the anxiety is coming from external issues, if the peace of God can replace it, that is a good thing.

Philippians 4:8 Finally, brethren, whatever things are true, whatever things *are* noble, whatever things *are* just, whatever things *are* pure, whatever things *are* lovely, whatever things *are* of good report if *there is* any virtue and if *there is* anything praiseworthy—meditate on these things. Here is where we are directed to meditate. We are not to just open our minds to whatever might come in. We are to meditate on things true, noble, just, pure, lovely, of good report, virtuous, and praiseworthy. We can also meditate on the word of God if those things are not enough. Coming out of this meditation should put us in a great frame of mind, ready for what comes our way.

Philippians 4:11 Not that I speak in regard to need, for I have learned in whatever state I am, to be content: 12 I know how to be abased, and I know how to abound. Everywhere and in all things, I have learned both to be full and to be hungry, both to abound and to suffer need. Paul had been in all of these situations and had learned to keep a heavenly focus in good and bad environments. He flourished and witnessed no matter where he was, whether free or in jail. That must have been very hard to do, but it is a good goal in all situations.

51

Colossians

[51]**COLOSSIANS** - Problems in the Church at Colossae

Colossians 1:2 To the saints and faithful brethren in Christ *who are* in Colosse: Grace to you and peace from God our Father and the Lord Jesus Christ. This letter starts with a statement about the intended audience. Here, as elsewhere in the Bible, believers are referred to as saints. How could we be saints when we know we still sin even though we are believers? We are told and learn through experience that when we become believers, we are changed spiritually. However, we still have our sinful bodies (the flesh) to deal with, and a battle starts for which side will control what we do (Galatians 5:16-21; Romans 8:13; 6:8; 1 Peter 2:11). Sometimes the flesh wins the internal battle. Hopefully, through the process of sanctification, our spiritual side will win more and more. However, we know that we will not achieve perfection as long as we are here on earth in these bodies.

Colossians 1:9 For this reason we also, since the day we heard it, do

---

[51] NSB quotations are from the Nelsons Study Bible, copyright (c) 1997 by Thomas Nelson, Inc., Nashville, TN; used by permission; scripture taken from the New King James Version, Copyright (c) 1979, 1980, 1982 used by permission. All rights reserved.

not cease to pray for you, and to ask that you may be filled with the knowledge of His will in all wisdom and spiritual understanding; 10 that you may walk worthy of the Lord, fully pleasing *Him,* **being fruitful in every good work and increasing in the knowledge of God; 11 strengthened with all might, according to His glorious power, for all patience and longsuffering with joy; 12 giving thanks to the Father who has qualified us to be partakers of the inheritance of the saints in the light.** Every tongue will confess that Jesus Christ *is* Lord, to the glory of God the Father (Romans 14:11). According to the scriptures, we don't know exactly when this will happen, but it will happen.

Colossians 1:16 For by Him all things were created that are in heaven and that are on earth, visible and invisible, whether thrones or dominions or principalities or powers. All things were created through Him and for Him. 17 And He is before all things, and in Him all things consist. 18 And He is the head of the body, the church, who is the beginning, the firstborn from the dead, that in all things He may have the preeminence. This scripture appears to be the words of a praise song inserted by Paul into this book. It attributes all creation, visible and invisible, to Jesus Christ. He is preeminent in all things. That is pretty simple. If we get this concept right, everything else flows from it. This idea goes against the gnostic ideas that Christ was just one among many angels.

Colossians 1:24 I now rejoice in my sufferings for you, and fill up in my flesh what is lacking in the afflictions of Christ, for the sake of His body, which is the church, 25 of which I became a minister according to the stewardship from God which was given to me for you, to fulfill the word of God, 26 the mystery which has been hidden from ages and from generations, but now has been revealed to His saints. 27 To them God willed to make known what are the riches of the glory of this mystery among the Gentiles: which

is Christ in you, the hope of glory. Here we see Paul rejoicing in sufferings because he was suffering for the sake of the Church, which is Christ's body here on earth. Then he talks about the mystery that is now revealed: believers have Christ within them, and collectively, they are His body on earth. This mystery was revealed at the time Colossians was written and communicated.

Colossians 2:23 These things indeed have an appearance of wisdom in self-imposed religion, *false* humility, and neglect of the body, *but are* of no value against the indulgence of the flesh. Here is a prime scripture against legalism. It talks about self-imposed regulations about what you can touch, what you can taste, or what you can handle. These things all perish and give the appearance of religion or humility but are just false humility. Christ freed us from this nonsense, but many people have difficulty accepting that freedom. These activities, called works, are of no value concerning salvation.

Colossians 3:2 Set your mind on things above, not on things on the earth. 3 For you died, and your life is hidden with Christ in God. 4 When Christ *who is* our life appears, then you also will appear with Him in glory. This is an essential concept for believers. Why should we focus our minds on what is perishing? The earth and all that is in it are not permanent, but the Word of God lasts forever. Without the work of Christ, no one would even be alive. He supplies the breath of life that makes us sentient beings. He is truly our life. Also, to appear with Him in glory, at the appropriate time, we will be granted glorified spiritual bodies that will last forever and that are incorruptible (1 Corinthians 15:42-44; Philippians 3:20-21).

Colossians 3:5 Therefore put to death your members which are on the earth: fornication, uncleanness, passion, evil desire, and covetousness, which is idolatry. If we have been saved and have the Spirit of God within us, we now can avoid the sins mentioned in this verse. Will we be perfect in avoiding all of these sins all of the time? No, because we are in a battle that rages within our bodies, and sometimes the Spirit does not triumph over the flesh. The good thing is that the price for our sins (past, present, and future) has been paid by Jesus Christ. We should be doing less and less of these types of activities through sanctification, but we will not be perfect in doing so. The encouraging thing is that our failures will not reverse the fact that our sins have been forgiven.

Colossians 3:8 But now you yourselves are to put off all these: anger, wrath, malice, blasphemy, filthy language out of your mouth. As with the Colossians 3:5 verse, this verse goes over more behaviors that should decrease in the lives of authentic believers. As one or more pastors have said, "if there is no change, there has been no change." In other words, there should be a change in a believer's life, not to make them a believer, but as a result of becoming a believer in Jesus Christ. If the behaviors mentioned in these verses continue to increase, there probably has not actually been repentance of unbelief. If the person is still in a position of unbelief in Christ, their flesh will continue to win when trying to avoid the behaviors mentioned in this verse.

Colossians 3:16 Let the word of Christ dwell in you richly in all wisdom, teaching and admonishing one another in psalms and hymns and spiritual songs, singing with grace in your hearts to the Lord. Here is a behavior that will replace some of the transgressions believers engaged in before their conversion. We are to teach and confront each other when our old flesh starts to get the better of us, and we fall into things in which we should no longer participate. There are a lot of psalms in the Bible, as well as hymns and new spiritual songs that we use to reinforce the mutual faith that has come to inhabit our new lives.

Colossians 3:18 Wives, submit to your own husbands, as is fitting

in the Lord.

19 Husbands, love your wives and do not be bitter toward them. Some people take issue with this verse indicating that wives should submit to their husbands. But then the scripture says that husbands should love their wives. So how should husbands love their wives? The scripture says that they should love their wives as Christ loved the Church. That is a love to the death as Christ did for all of us (John 3:16). We might ask what is the taller order; to submit or to love to the death? By the way, mutual submission is specified in other scriptures (Ephesians 5:21; Philippians 2:3).

Colossians 3:20 Children, obey your parents in all things, for this is well pleasing to the Lord. When children follow the directions in this scripture, I think they are generally happier, healthier, safer, and better adjusted. Not only that, but they also please the Lord when they do. Thus, it is a win-win situation.

Colossians 3:21 Fathers, do not provoke your children, lest they become discouraged. There seems to be a bit of a natural tendency for fathers, who are in a power position with their children, to use that status to inappropriately tease their children to the point of driving them to anger and discouragement. This verse encourages fathers not to do that.

Colossians 3:25 But he who does wrong will be repaid for what he has done, and there is no partiality. Also, those who do good will be rewarded. Thus, everyone receives their just deserts without favoritism.

Colossians 4:5 Walk in wisdom toward those *who are* outside, redeeming the time. 6 *Let* your speech always *be* with grace, seasoned with salt, that you may know how you ought to answer each one. There were many misconceptions about what Christians did in those days, so the Christians needed not to provide legitimate reasons to criticize them. Speech with grace seasoned with salt would appear to be gracious speech and speech that is acceptable because it is even more pleasant. We should be able to answer questions about our faith, which will require some study and meditation to be ready to answer.

52

1 Thessalonians

[52] **1 THESSALONIANS** - This book covers a lot of essential doctrines of the Christian faith.

1 Thessalonians 1:2 We give thanks to God always for you all, making mention of you in our prayers, 3 remembering without ceasing your work of faith, labor of love, and patience of hope in our Lord Jesus Christ in the sight of our God and Father, 4 knowing, beloved brethren, your election by God. This is a clear statement about the election of God. Of course, we know that God prefers that everyone is saved (1 Timothy 2:4; 2 Peter 3:9; Ezekiel 18:23; Matthew 23:37). However, some people are referred to as being elected by God as is the case in this passage (Matthew 22:14; John 6:37, 44, 65; 8:47; 10;26-29; Romans 8:29-30; 9:6-23; 11:5-10; 1 Corinthians 1:26-30). At the same time, free will appears to be communicated in the scriptures (Genesis 1:26; Deuteronomy 30:19; Isaiah 48:18; Proverbs 21:5).

Theologians have tried to understand these seemingly conflicting and

---

[52] NSB quotations are from the Nelsons Study Bible, copyright (c) 1997 by Thomas Nelson, Inc., Nashville, TN; used by permission; scripture taken from the New King James Version, Copyright (c) 1979, 1980, 1982 used by permission. All rights reserved.

paradoxical ideas for ages, so I don't plan to solve the questions in this commentary. However, I will say that God is sovereign over all things (1 Chronicles 29:11-12; Romans 9:18) and elects some to be saved at the same time that man appears to have free will and individual responsibility for making choices (Deuteronomy 30:19; Galatians 5:13; Ezekiel 18:30-32).

I do not anticipate fully reconciling these truths until I get to heaven. If you want to study this issue further, you might look at John Piper's book, *Does God Desire All to Be Saved?* We can worship God based on what He has revealed about His love and remain in awe of the complexity of His ways. The unfortunate truth is that some of His ways are way beyond our meager abilities to understand.

1 Thessalonians 2:10 You *are* witnesses, and God *also,* how devoutly and justly and blamelessly we behaved ourselves among you who believe; 11 as you know how we exhorted, and comforted, and charged every one of you, as a father *does* his own children, 12 that you would walk worthy of God who calls you into His own kingdom and glory. I believe that God calls everyone, but not everyone follows the call (Ezekiel 18:30-32). God does not want anyone to perish (2 Peter 3:9). However, He does not force anyone who is not willing to come to faith (Matthew 23:37).

To be called is to be invited. Just because you are invited to a party does not mean you will go (Matthew 22:14). To be chosen is a little different. It is to accept the invitation and its conditions. It is not easy to lay down your life for your belief in Christ (Matthew 7:13-14). The gate is narrow (Matthew 7:13-14), and the way is hard (Matthew 7:14). We do give up many things in this world. That is why many choose not to become believers.

1 Thessalonians 2:14 For you, brethren, became imitators of the

churches of God which are in Judea in Christ Jesus. For you also suffered the same things from your own countrymen, just as they *did* from the Judeans, 15 who killed both the Lord Jesus and their own prophets, and have persecuted us; and they do not please God and are contrary to all men,... The Thessalonians were suffering because they were believers and criticized by both the Jews and the Gentiles. Those who persecute Christians are not pleasing God (Revelation 20:10; 21:8).

1 Thessalonians 4:4 For, in fact, we told you before when we were with you that we would suffer tribulation, just as it happened, and you know. Some people think that if they become Christian, all their difficulties will be behind them. The opposite is actually true. There will probably be more tribulations but of a different kind. However, God will be with them and help them get through the trials and tests. Their faith will be tested, which will be difficult, and they will need the Comforter to help get them through.

1 Thessalonians 4:10 But we urge you, brethren, that you increase more and more; 11 that you also aspire to lead a quiet life, to mind your own business, and to work with your own hands, as we commanded you,... Interestingly, the Thessalonian believers were encouraged to lead a quiet life. I think this is good advice. The older I get, the better a quiet life sounds.

1 Thessalonians 4:16 For the Lord Himself will descend from heaven with a shout, with the voice of an archangel, and with the trumpet of God. And the dead in Christ will rise first. This appears to be a statement about when Christ returns to the earth. He will come in the clouds, and everyone will see it and hear Him come, and the dead in Christ will get their new glorified spiritual bodies. These new bodies of Christians will be incredible, incorruptible (1 John 3:2), immortal flesh and bone (Luke 24:39, 40; John 20:20, 25, 27) bodies. How can that be?

We do not know. We'll have to wait and see.

1 Thessalonians 5:8 But let us who are of the day be sober, putting on the breastplate of faith and love, and *as* a helmet the hope of salvation. 9 For God did not appoint us to wrath, but to obtain salvation through our Lord Jesus Christ, 10 who died for us, that whether we wake or sleep, we should live together with Him. This verse sounds a bit like verses in the book of Ephesians, but with a twist. I think the people "of the day" is referring to Christians. They are encouraged to be sober as they deal with the issues of life. The armor of God in Ephesians includes the "**breastplate of righteousness:** and the "**helmet of salvation**" (Ephesians 6:14-16). So the analogies are similar, but not exactly the same.

Here the helmet is referred to as the "hope" of salvation. The good news is that God did not appoint us to wrath. At some point, Christ will be coming back to earth and will come as a judge. Some will then experience His wrath, but not those "**of the day**." We will live through eternity with Him, and others will be separated. Notice that the verse includes faith, love, and hope, which are the basic building blocks of the Christian life. We continue to hope for Christ's return which will be a glorious day. Non-Christians, on the other hand, are repulsed by the thought of Jesus Christ returning.

1 Thessalonians 5:15 See that no one renders evil for evil to anyone, but always pursue what is good both for yourselves and for all. Here is a difficult task to endorse. We are not to get back at someone who wrongs us. That is contrary to our nature. Nevertheless, we are encouraged to seek what is best, even for our enemies. How's that for a life verse to live by?

1 Thessalonians 5:23 Now may the God of peace Himself sanctify you completely; and may your whole spirit, soul, and body be

preserved blameless at the coming of our Lord Jesus Christ. So what is this process of sanctification? It is becoming progressively more righteous in our behavior through the help and guidance of the Holy Spirit. It is a great thought to be preserved blameless at the coming of our Lord. As noted elsewhere in this commentary, we can be as if we have not sinned if through faith we accept the grace of God to forgive all of our sins; past, present, and future. As we continue in the faith, we will know the truth and be preserved blameless (John 8:31-32).

53

2 Thessalonians

[53] **2 THESSALONIANS** - This book highlights some events before Christ comes back to earth.

2 Thessalonians 2:7 For the mystery of lawlessness is already at work; only He who now restrains *will do so* until He is taken out of the way. 8 And then the lawless one will be revealed, whom the Lord will consume with the breath of His mouth and destroy with the brightness of His coming. There will be a falling away that comes first before the return of Christ (2:3). The evil (lawlessness) that will be evident is already in the world (Note: there are and will be many Antichrists.) (1 John 2:18). It appears that the current restrainer (probably the Holy Spirit who works in and through believers) will be removed at some point.

Antichrist is an entity that encourages others to deny Christ and instead worship some other false god. This could be some world leader or politician. The leader of these entities is the lawless one who will be

---

[53] NSB quotations are from the Nelsons Study Bible, copyright (c) 1997 by Thomas Nelson, Inc., Nashville, TN; used by permission; scripture taken from the New King James Version, Copyright (c) 1979, 1980, 1982 used by permission. All rights reserved.

revealed and be destroyed by Christ when He comes back to earth. There are other interpretations, but I think the believers will be removed from the earth at the appropriate time. The Holy Spirit will also temporarily be out of the way to fulfill the prophecy regarding the lawless one. This is called the pre-tribulation position.

2 Thessalonians 2:9 The coming of the *lawless one* is according to the working of Satan, with all power, signs, and lying wonders, 10 and with all unrighteous deception among those who perish, because they did not receive the love of the truth, that they might be saved. The lawless one will deceive many people because he will have similar power, signs, and wonders that the apostles had in the early years of Christianity. However, these will all be counterfeit imitations. They will deceive many unbelievers who will be convinced to follow him and reject the true God of the universe.

2 Thessalonians 3:10 For even when we were with you, we commanded you this: If anyone will not work, neither shall he eat. This appears to be speaking about non-disabled people who can work for their food but refuse to do so because they are lazy and don't care about having other hapless people do the work while they partake of the rewards without lifting a finger. The verse tells us not to let this happen.

There are good reasons not to let people who will not work partake of what others have earned. First, it is unfair for those willing to work to supply a lazy person who does not work. Second, it discourages self-reliance. Third, it allows the freeloader to learn to be helpless. The longer others support this person, the more dependent and lacking in self-dignity the person will become. Being in this status too long, a sense of entitlement might settle in, and the person could develop what can be called learned helplessness. That is not a good thing.

One more reminder: it is a different situation for a disabled or sick person. This person should be taken care of by the church and not have to work beyond their capacity. That is called charity and is a good thing.

2 Thessalonians 3:14 And if anyone does not obey our word in this epistle, note that person and do not keep company with him, that he may be ashamed. This is interesting. It appears to encourage avoidance of unrepentant idle members who do not do what we are directed to do in this book. This direction from Paul was prudent because having disobedient people around could be both disruptive and counterproductive. They were to be avoided. Nevertheless, this separation appears to be to encourage restoration. If they became ashamed, perhaps they could be restored to fellowship if they changed their minds and behavior.

54

1 Timothy

[54]**1 TIMOTHY** - The structure of authority in the church is covered in 1 Timothy.

1 Timothy 1:3 As I urged you when I went into Macedonia—remain in Ephesus that you may charge some that they teach no other doctrine, 4 nor give heed to fables and endless genealogies, which cause disputes rather than godly edification which is in faith. It appears that arguing over fables and genealogies is not the best thing because it does not lead to godly edification (spiritual improvement). In this verse, edification seems to imply the stewardship of the Gospel. We should be focused on the clear presentation of the Gospel found in the scriptures rather than the vain speculations of men that can cause disputes.

1 Timothy 1:8 But we know that the law *is* good if one uses it lawfully, 9 knowing this: that the law is not made for a righteous person, but for *the* lawless and insubordinate, for *the* ungodly and

---

[54] NSB quotations are from the Nelsons Study Bible, copyright (c) 1997 by Thomas Nelson, Inc., Nashville, TN; used by permission; scripture taken from the New King James Version, Copyright (c) 1979, 1980, 1982 used by permission. All rights reserved.

for sinners, for *the* unholy and profane, for murderers of fathers and murderers of mothers, for manslayers, 10 for fornicators, for sodomites, for kidnappers, for liars, for perjurers, and if there is any other thing that is contrary to sound doctrine, 11 according to the glorious gospel of the blessed God which was committed to my trust. So, who is the law for? It is for a lot of people doing bad things. And, it is specifically not for the righteous person. What gives with that? Well, the only righteous person, other than Jesus Christ, is the one who has been forgiven. No one else qualifies. The law is good because it points out what is bad and can hurt other people. It is a teacher. It also condemns us when we break it unless we are forgiven. The only way to be forgiven is the main message of the Bible. It is through faith by the grace of God.

1 Timothy 1:15 This *is* a faithful saying and worthy of all acceptance, that Christ Jesus came into the world to save sinners, of whom I am chief. Here Paul confesses his sin. Before his conversion, he was complicit in persecuting Christians even to death by stoning. That may be why he called himself the chief of sinners. Nevertheless, God elected and saved Paul and gave him a mission to spread the Gospel to the gentiles. A very simplified presentation of the Gospel is found in 1 John 3:23. It says to believe in Christ and love others due to this belief. Another is in John 3:16 as follows: **For God so loved the world that He gave His only begotten Son, that whoever believes in Him should not perish but have everlasting life.** The essential good news is that God, who is holy, provided a way for human beings to be forgiven for their transgressions. Christ paid the just price for all our sins by living a sinless life, dying on the cross, being buried, and rising the third-day conquering death. A simple concept of salvation is faith alone in Christ alone.

1 Timothy 2:2 Therefore I exhort first of all that supplications, prayers, intercessions, *and* giving of thanks be made for all men, 2 for kings and all who are in authority, that we may lead a quiet and

peaceable life in all godliness and reverence. 3 For this *is* good and acceptable in the sight of God our Savior, 4 who desires all men to be saved and to come to the knowledge of the truth. Paul encourages prayers for everyone and all those in authority regarding having a quiet life. If all men were believers, we would have a peaceable life, which is what God our Savior desires. However, here on earth, that is not the way it is in the present dispensation. Our free will allows us to reject the knowledge of the truth.

1 Timothy 2:5 For *there is* one God and one Mediator between God and men, *the* Man Christ Jesus, 6 who gave Himself a ransom for all, to be testified in due time, 7 for which I was appointed a preacher and an apostle—I am speaking the truth in Christ *and* not lying—a teacher of the Gentiles in faith and truth. Even in those days, some people thought other gods could provide salvation. This is not the case according to the Bible. There is only one God and one Mediator. That Mediator is Jesus Christ, and He is God Incarnate. Incarnate means made flesh. Jesus Christ is God in human form.

He is the only one who paid the price for our sins. No one else comes even close to paying the price for all our sins so we could be reconciled to God. That is a big deal and goes against the Universalist idea that Jesus Christ was just another prophet of many that have walked the earth. I wouldn't say I liked it the first time I heard there is only one way to salvation. Nevertheless, I know now that whether I like something has no bearing on the discernment of truth. I now know the Bible says Christ is God the Son, the one Mediator.

1 Timothy 3:3 This *is* a faithful saying: If a man desires the position of a bishop, he desires a good work. 2 A bishop then must be blameless, the husband of one wife, temperate, sober-minded, of good behavior, hospitable, able to teach; 3 not given to wine, not violent, not greedy for money, but gentle, not quarrelsome, not

covetous; 4 one who rules his own house well, having *his* children in submission with all reverence 5 (for if a man does not know how to rule his own house, how will he take care of the church of God?; 6, not a novice, lest being puffed up with pride he fall into the *same* condemnation as the devil. There is a high bar to meet for bishops. The qualifications are in this scripture. If all of these qualifications are met, the person can serve as a bishop. In this context, a bishop is an overseer in the church.

1 Timothy 3:8 Likewise deacons *must be* reverent, not double-tongued, not given to much wine, not greedy for money, 9 holding the mystery of the faith with a pure conscience. Here are the qualifications for deacons. The word deacon in Greek means servant. Thus, they seem to be servants in the church under the bishops who carry out some of the necessary internal work. They have the same prerequisites as the bishops and some of their own. Of course, we know that neither bishops nor deacons are perfect, and they may have had problems in the past as all of us have had, but they should not be continuing in these activities if they are a bishop or deacon.

1 Timothy 4:1 Now the Spirit expressly says that in latter times some will depart from the faith, giving heed to deceiving spirits and doctrines of demons, 2 speaking lies in hypocrisy, having their own conscience seared with a hot iron, 3 forbidding to marry, *and commanding* to abstain from foods which God created to be received with thanksgiving by those who believe and know the truth. This verse gives us some things to watch for in the latter days. Since it appears that we are in the latter times now (Hosea 3:4,5), we need to be wary of liars and people forbidding us to marry. Who does this in our time? One major church forbids its leaders from marriage. Others have strict rules about what their members cannot eat. Many are departing from the faith and speaking lies in hypocrisy. It sounds like what the scriptures predict in the latter times.

1 Timothy 5:5 Do not rebuke an older man, but exhort *him* as a father, younger men as brothers, 2 older women as mothers, younger women as sisters, with all purity. This verse encourages general hospitality to people with the appropriate respect, kindness, and purity that is their due.

1 Timothy 5:8 But if anyone does not provide for his own, and especially for those of his household, he has denied the faith and is worse than an unbeliever. It is clear from this scripture that we are to provide for our family members, especially in our own household. Unfortunately, many have abdicated this responsibility in our culture. Even though parents often leave their children, the government tries to make the parents pay to raise their children, but that is not enough. Children need parents in their lives, teaching them and caring for them. It is not just the financial support that children need.

A society that disincentivizes stable two-parent families through policies of their welfare system cannot expect all their children to become productive citizens. Some do well despite their circumstances, but many fall into drugs and crime as a way of life. Even good parenting by two parents does not guarantee successful, productive children, but it can help. The warning in this verse professes a vital truth for parents and other family members. We need to provide for our families if we call ourselves believers in the Gospel.

1 Timothy 5:11 But refuse *the* younger widows; for when they have begun to grow wanton against Christ, they desire to marry, 12 having condemnation because they have cast off their first faith. This has to do with putting a widow on the list for being supported by the church. The younger widows (presumably those under 60) could desire to become married again. That might be better for them as opposed to being supported by the church. They might not have enough to do and fall into idleness, gossiping, and other negative habits. If we take a principle from this verse, it might be, idle hands are the devil's workshop. When we are young, we need some productive responsibility or might develop negative behaviors that are bad for us and society.

1 Timothy 5:23 No longer drink only water, but use a little wine for your stomach's sake and your frequent infirmities. Timothy is encouraged to take a little wine as a medicine for frequent stomach problems. Thus, he would not be a teetotaler. Some might find this surprising, given the warnings in other scriptures against getting drunk and against causing others to stumble by our behavior. Those who know some people with substance abuse problems (alcohol or some other drug) see that they have great difficulty controlling their overindulgence and, therefore, usually need to refrain entirely.

1 Timothy 6:3 If anyone teaches otherwise and does not consent to wholesome words, *even* the words of our Lord Jesus Christ, and to the doctrine which accords with godliness, 4 he is proud, knowing nothing, but is obsessed with disputes and arguments over words, from which come envy, strife, reviling, evil suspicions, 5 useless wranglings of men of corrupt minds and destitute of the truth, who suppose that godliness is a *means of* gain. From such withdraw yourself. This verse seems to be saying to withdraw from people talking a good game and are not really followers of the faith. They can often exhibit pride and be involved in disputes and arguments over words. If they act like believers to obtain money, we should withdraw from these people.

1 Timothy 6:10 For the love of money is a root of all *kinds of* evil, for which some have strayed from the faith in their greediness, and pierced themselves through with many sorrows. First, note that this verse does not say that money, but rather the *love* of money is the root of all kinds of evil. Some people are blessed with the ability to make more money than others. There is nothing inherently wrong with that. But, if the love of money is a person's consuming feeling, it is a problem and will lead to evil. This love can cause a believer to stray from the truth into greed which typically does not lead to faithful living.

1 Timothy 6:11 But you, O man of God, flee these things and pursue righteousness, godliness, faith, love, patience, gentleness. This is what a believer should pursue instead of materialism. These pursuits are all a better alternative to materialism and will lead to a better life.

1 Timothy 6:18 *Let them* do good, that they be rich in good works, ready to give, willing to share, 19 storing up for themselves a good foundation for the time to come, that they may lay hold on eternal life. If we have wealth, who allowed us to gain it? It was God. Wealthy people need to recognize that whatever abilities or skills allowed them to generate this wealth were a gift from God. Of course, those who do not believe in God usually become prideful because they begin to think they are better than other people because of their successes. Those who are wealthy should be generous with what they have.

55

2 Timothy

[55] **2 TIMOTHY** - Perseverance Amid Difficulties.

2 Timothy 1:8 Therefore do not be ashamed of the testimony of our Lord, nor of me His prisoner, but share with me in the sufferings for the gospel according to the power of God, 9 who has saved us and called *us* with a holy calling, not according to our works, but according to His own purpose and grace which was given to us in Christ Jesus before time began, 10 but has now been revealed by the appearing of our Savior Jesus Christ, *who* has abolished death and brought life and immortality to light through the gospel, 11 to which I was appointed a preacher, an apostle, and a teacher of the Gentiles. There is a lot in this verse. First, Timothy is encouraged not to be ashamed of his testimony nor of Paul. Paul is forewarning him that there will be suffering. Next, Paul reminds Timothy of his holy calling, not due to his works, but because of God's purposes and grace. God had these things in mind before time began. I assume the time discussed here is our time because God existed before our universe, and its time

---

[55] NSB quotations are from the Nelsons Study Bible, copyright (c) 1997 by Thomas Nelson, Inc., Nashville, TN; used by permission; scripture taken from the New King James Version, Copyright (c) 1979, 1980, 1982 used by permission. All rights reserved.

dimension was created. Then Paul talks about how Christ brought life and immortality through the Gospel. Paul was selected by God and appointed to preach this Gospel to the Gentiles

2 Timothy 2:4 No one engaged in warfare entangles himself with the affairs of *this* life, that he may please him who enlisted him as a soldier. Believers are enlisted as soldiers in an internal battle between the flesh and the spirit, and an external battle with the fallen carnal world. Therefore, we may want to keep from getting weighed down by too much other stuff that will distract us from our primary mission and potentially cause us to lose or be ineffective. The battles we are in are not against flesh and blood but against the principalities of this world (Ephesians 6:12), which includes spiritual wickedness in high places.

2 Timothy 2:8 Remember that Jesus Christ, of the seed of David, was raised from the dead according to my gospel, 9 for which I suffer trouble as an evildoer, *even* to the point of chains; but the word of God is not chained. Paul got himself in trouble with the governing authorities because of his outspoken preaching of the Gospel. He suffered imprisonment and many other hardships as a result. Nevertheless, Paul was an influential and persistent apostle for Christ who did not give up when facing adversity. Instead, he turned the difficult situations in which he found himself into opportunities to spread the Gospel.

2 Timothy 2:12
   If we endure,
   We shall also reign with *Him*.
   If we deny *Him*,
   He also will deny us. The message here is: don't deny the Lord. In the end, it will not go well for you if you do.

2 Timothy 2:16 But shun profane *and* idle babblings, for they will increase to more ungodliness. Unfortunately, our culture has become incredibly profane. Profane means not sacred or Biblical. It is secular rather than religious. Not only is our culture profane, but it is also becoming more profane. Profanity that would have never been used in front of women or children just 50 years ago is now commonplace.

One of the most overused words is a slang term for sexual intercourse. Often this word is used with incestual connotation. Even young children use this kind of language in public and think nothing about it because this is the language they hear daily in movies, music, and even by their parents. They may not even know the meaning of the words they are using. Nevertheless, believers are directed to avoid idle profane babbling, so we should avoid this part of our culture.

We don't have to be like those who like to use a lot of profanity. We can be different. Not puritanical, but different. We have to understand that the tongue is the hardest thing to control. And for an unbeliever, they have no reason even to attempt to use less profane language. It feels good to them to get it out. They may not even be thinking about the meaning of the words.

Note that a believer's primary concern should be about their behavior and the behavior of people in their congregations (2 Corinthians 4:16). We are not responsible for taking action regarding everyone's behavior. We can leave them to the Government and God. It is specifically not our job to judge anyone's spiritual state, but we may need to judge what people do and say. In some cases, it may be our responsibility to take action based on this judgment, and in others, it will not. For example, if we observe an illegal activity, we may need to report it to the government authorities. If we observe someone in our church doing something immoral, but not illegal, we are responsible for taking appropriate action within the church. If we observe someone outside of our church doing the same thing, we should probably do no more than pray for them.

2 Timothy 3:12 Yes, and all who desire to live godly in Christ Jesus will suffer persecution. In scripture, we are often reminded that the Christian life will be difficult. We will suffer persecution at the minimum. In some places today, Christians can suffer persecution to death for their beliefs. Many communist regimes have killed off Christians who they considered a threat to how they wanted to govern.

2 Timothy 3:16 All Scripture *is* given by inspiration of God, and *is* profitable for doctrine, for reproof, for correction, for instruction in righteousness, 17 that the man of God may be complete, thoroughly equipped for every good work. This verse tells us why we have the Bible. It is profitable for us. It was inspired by God and instructs us in everything we need to know for a righteous life. It also equips us to stand up for the Gospel and do good works.

2 Timothy 4:14 Alexander the coppersmith did me much harm. May the Lord repay him according to his works. I assume Alexander was a nonbeliever because he was harming Paul, the apostle of Christ. This is a specific warning about a specific person. Other scriptures warn the apostles that they could expect opposition to their message (John 15:18-21).

56

Titus

[56]**TITUS** - It's all about grace.

Titus 1:5, For this reason I left you in Crete, that you should set in order the things that are lacking, and appoint elders in every city as I commanded you— 6 if a man is blameless, the husband of one wife, having faithful children not accused of dissipation or insubordination. Here are some prerequisites for elders. Paul gave many qualifications for elders, overseers, and bishops. I assume that the faithful children's qualifications would apply when the children were still children. Once children become adults, the parents would not influence them and the parents would no longer be responsible for their behavior.

Titus 1:16 They profess to know God, but in works they deny *Him*, being abominable, disobedient, and disqualified for every good work. It is recognized in this verse that people can say anything. What they do is the true measure of what they believe. Of course, any of us can make a mistake and have a temporary lapse of judgment. I think this

---

[56] NSB quotations are from the Nelsons Study Bible, copyright (c) 1997 by Thomas Nelson, Inc., Nashville, TN; used by permission; scripture taken from the New King James Version, Copyright (c) 1979, 1980, 1982 used by permission. All rights reserved.

verse is referring to people who consistently do abominable things.

Titus 2:2 But as for you, speak the things which are proper for sound doctrine: 2 that the older men be sober, reverent, temperate, sound in faith, in love, in patience; 3 the older women likewise, that they be reverent in behavior, not slanderers, not given to much wine, teachers of good things— 4 that they admonish the young women to love their husbands, to love their children, 5 *to be* **discreet, chaste, homemakers, good, obedient to their own husbands, that the word of God may not be blasphemed.** This is all great advice. What does the last line mean? Blasphemed means to show insult, contempt, or lack of reverence. So, this scripture is saying that if we speak, teach, and practice sound doctrine we will not be blaspheming the word of God.

Titus 3:3 For we ourselves were also once foolish, disobedient, deceived, serving various lusts and pleasures, living in malice and envy, hateful and hating one another. Before we get too proud of ourselves, we must continually be reminded that we once did some of the things mentioned in this verse. Note how God treated us while we were disobedient and had many of these character flaws. He paid the price for our transgressions and forgave us. Then, how should we treat those who are involved in these flaws? We should forgive them and help them to see what Christ did for all of us through the cross.

Titus 3:9 But avoid foolish disputes, genealogies, contentions, and strivings about the law; for they are unprofitable and useless. Psalm 37:8 agrees with this verse. It encourages us to cease anger and forsake wrath. Christians should not be involved in anger, wrath, malice, blasphemy, or even filthy language (Colossians 3:8). Anger is apparently to be avoided by believers (Ephesians 4:31). We are not to strive over words to no benefit (2 Timothy 2:14). We are also told to avoid foolish questions, genealogies, and contentions about the law in this very verse, and there are other similar admonitions elsewhere. Therefore, the conclusion is that we should seek to avoid getting involved in any of these activities that can lead to the sin of anger or worse behavior.

Titus 3:10 Reject a divisive man after the first and second admonition, 11 knowing that such a person is warped and sinning, being self-condemned. When we have done what we can to avoid contention with a divisive person within the church, the church can and should reject the person who will not correct their behavior after two warnings. I guess it really is three strikes, and you're out. On the other hand, how often should someone be forgiven if they repent? Christ says seventy times seven (Matthew 18:21-22). Thus, the goal is to restore the wayward person to good behavior and fellowship. Sometimes you will run into those whose heart is hardened and who will not be restored. These are the ones who will need to be rejected. They have condemned themselves by their insubordination.

57

Philemon

[57]**PHILEMON** - When we were slaves to sin, our just sentence was death, but we were redeemed from that fate.

Philemon 1:8 Therefore, though I might be very bold in Christ to command you what is fitting, 9 *yet* **for love's sake I rather appeal** *to you*—**being such a one as Paul, the aged, and now also a prisoner of Jesus Christ**— Here is a good example of how we should treat people who we supervise. Paul had the authority to issue orders, but instead, he made requests. The good thing about taking this approach, it that the dignity of the person receiving the request is preserved. People sometimes react negatively when given orders. However, when requested to do something, they always know they can choose not to follow through with the request. There still may be consequences, but they have a choice.

Philemon 1:18 But if he has wronged you or owes anything, put that on my account. Onesimus owed something or had stolen something, and Paul was willing to make it right on his behalf. That is a model of

---

[57] NSB quotations are from the Nelsons Study Bible, copyright (c) 1997 by Thomas Nelson, Inc., Nashville, TN; used by permission; scripture taken from the New King James Version, Copyright (c) 1979, 1980, 1982 used by permission. All rights reserved.

what Christ did for us. We were guilty, and Christ paid the fine on our behalf to set us free.

58

Hebrews

[58]**HEBREWS** - Christ is superior.

Hebrews 1:14 Are they not all ministering spirits sent forth to minister for those who will inherit salvation? This verse speaks about angels who are ministering to believers. Angels have a variety of assignments, including delivering messages, comforting the lonely, protecting, and in some instances, fighting battles (Psalm 34:7; Hebrews 1:14; Hebrews 13:2; Revelation 22:8-9). They go incognito most of the time, but sometimes they appear in human form. It's a comforting thought to think that angels are looking out for us.

Hebrews 2:9 But we see Jesus, who was made a little lower than the angels, for the suffering of death crowned with glory and honor, that He, by the grace of God, might taste death for everyone. When Adam was on earth, he had a job to do. He ruled over the earth. However, due to his fall into sin, he gave up that status. It appears, through what Jesus Christ has done, humankind will someday rule over the earth again

---

[58] NSB quotations are from the Nelsons Study Bible, copyright (c) 1997 by Thomas Nelson, Inc., Nashville, TN; used by permission; scripture taken from the New King James Version, Copyright (c) 1979, 1980, 1982 used by permission. All rights reserved.

(Philippians 2:6-11; Revelation 5:1-14). This verse also lets us know that when Christ came down to earth, he was in a position a little lower than the angels.

Hebrews 2:14 Inasmuch then as the children have partaken of flesh and blood, He Himself likewise shared in the same, that through death He might destroy him who had the power of death, that is, the devil, 15 and release those who through fear of death were all their lifetime subject to bondage. Jesus Christ humbled Himself to come down to earth and become flesh and blood just like we are. When Jesus died on the cross, He took away the power of Satan over death because Satan could no longer entice people to sin and then be fearful of death which would keep them in bondage to sin. It is a bit complex, so let's just say that we are now free from the just punishment for our sins through what Christ did. He paid the appropriate price on our behalf, so we do not have to pay the price. The old covenant is now obsolete due to the new covenant, the Gospel.

Hebrews 4:2 For indeed the gospel was preached to us as well as to them; but the word which they heard did not profit them, not being mixed with faith in those who heard *it*. The good news was announced so that the people could gain faith and the grace of God. However, their unbelief hindered them from profiting from the message. They had no faith, which is a prerequisite for benefiting from the Gospel.

Hebrews 4:12 For the word of God *is* living and powerful, and sharper than any two-edged sword, piercing even to the division of soul and spirit, and of joints and marrow, and is a discerner of the thoughts and intents of the heart. The word of God is the standard by which we will be judged (2 Corinthians 5:12). It tells us what is natural and what is spiritual. God knows how we think and uses His word to give us insights into the intent of our hearts.

Hebrews 6:10 For God *is* not unjust to forget your work and labor of love which you have shown toward His name, *in that* you have ministered to the saints, and do minister. It is comforting to know that God will not forget our efforts on His behalf.

Hebrews 7:18 For on the one hand there is an annulling of the former commandment because of its weakness and unprofitableness, 19 for the law made nothing perfect; on the other hand, *there is the bringing in of a better hope, through which we draw near to God.* We need to understand what is said here. The law cannot make anything perfect. It cannot forgive. It is a teacher that shows us our faults and needs. If we are honest with ourselves, we are doomed under the law (the Ten Commandments). Christ's Gospel is superior to the dispensation of the law because no flesh can be saved by the law (Galatians 2:16). It takes faith in Jesus Christ. Without that faith, we are lost. That is the unvarnished truth presented in the Bible.

Hebrews 9:15 And for this reason He is the Mediator of the new covenant, by means of death, for the redemption of the transgressions under the first covenant, that those who are called may receive the promise of the eternal inheritance. In other words, we can be saved by Christ. He is the Mediator between God and us. He redeemed us to satisfy justice. The called people experience eternal life as our inheritance from God as His children.

Hebrews 9:22 And according to the law almost all things are purified with blood, and without shedding of blood there is no remission. Christ's sacrifice for us was much better than the old way. He wound up in heaven with God.

Hebrews 10:10 For the law, having a shadow of the good things to come, *and* not the very image of the things, can never with these same sacrifices, which they offer continually year by year, make

those who approach perfect. Here we have the direct message that the law cannot make anyone perfect. We would have to be perfect to approach the holy, holy, holy God. The law teaches us to know how imperfect we are and, thus, can be a motivation for us to take a different approach because we can see that we will fail under the law. We need massive amounts of forgiveness which God provided through what Christ did for us. Through faith by the grace of God, He has removed our sins as far as the East is from the West (Psalm 103:12).

Hebrews 10:24 And let us consider one another in order to stir up love and good works, 25 not forsaking the assembling of ourselves together, as *is* the manner of some, but exhorting *one another*, and so much the more as you see the Day approaching. What day is approaching? From what I have read, I don't think this refers to a weekly church service, but you can come up with your own thinking on this. I believe the gathering here refers to gathering to Christ. For various reasons, I think the Day approaching is the second coming of Christ to the earth. At His return, we will go to Him. We have hope for this day and are encouraged to share this hope more and more.

Hebrews 11:1 Now faith is the substance of things hoped for, the evidence of things not seen. This is the Biblical explanation of the outcome of faith. We expect good things even though we cannot know where this hope comes from. The substance is the essence of the product of the faith. For the person of faith, the thing hoped for is the reality.

Hebrews 11:13 These all died in faith, not having received the promises, but having seen them afar off were assured of them, embraced *them* and confessed that they were strangers and pilgrims on the earth. This verse is speaking about the faith of Abraham, Isaac, Jacob, and Sarah. Modern-day believers are still pilgrims and strangers on the earth. Our eternal home is with God. Even modern-day scientists know that the ability of our earth to sustain life as we know it is time-limited. They can calculate how much fuel the sun has before it burns out, and the earth's source of light and warmth will be gone. At that time, life on earth will be extinguished.

The scientists may not be in agreement with the Bible regarding the timing of the earth's demise, but they are in agreement that the current earth cannot be eternal. I do not think the importance of faith in the Old and New Testaments can be overstated. Faith is essential for believers to receive the rewards waiting for them in heaven. All there is without faith is the physical world in which we live. When our life ends, we end. By faith, we overcome.

Hebrews 12:7 If you endure chastening, God deals with you as with sons; for what son is there whom a father does not chasten? When I was disciplined by my parents when growing up, I knew they would do so because they cared about me. They did it out of love knowing that if I grew up with discipline, I would not be out of control when I got older. God is the same way. He disciplines us because He cares and loves us.

Hebrews 12:11 Now no chastening seems to be joyful for the present, but painful; nevertheless, afterward it yields the peaceable fruit of righteousness to those who have been trained by it. If we learn from the chastening we receive and enjoy the fruit of righteousness, we should become mature people of high character. That peaceable fruit of righteousness can include kindness, honesty, truth, charity, and goodness.

Hebrews 12:14 Pursue peace with all *people*, and holiness, without which no one will see the Lord: We may not be able to be at peace with all people because it somewhat depends on them and we can't control them. Nevertheless, we are to do what we can on our side to keep our relationships with them peaceable.

Hebrews 13:4 Marriage *is* honorable among all, and the bed undefiled; but fornicators and adulterers God will judge. When this verse explains that within marriage, the bed is not defiled, the bottom line appears to be that it is up to the married couple to determine what sexual relations they wish to have. Whatever they decide is good, pure, moral, holy, and even encouraged by God.

On the other hand, sexual intercourse between two people who are unmarried will be judged by God. The terms used for the defiling activity (that is fornication and adultery) imply that the judgment will not be for reward but rather a punishment. So, in the Biblical narrative, sex within marriage is good and without is bad. It is that simple. Liberal thinkers will probably disagree with this interpretation, but it appears to be fairly clear here.

Hebrews 13:8 Jesus Christ *is* the same yesterday, today, and forever. 9 Do not be carried about with various and strange doctrines. For *it is* good that the heart be established by grace, not with foods which have not profited those who have been occupied with them. Jesus Christ is the same. This does not say that he is static. It means that His basic character does not change. He is dynamic and takes actions every day, and could change direction if He wanted to do so.

Strange doctrines appear to reference doctrines that stray from the Gospel. They come around from time to time, and we should resist them if they are strange.

Grace is to be a guiding principle for everything we do. Through God's grace, we are redeemed.

Hebrews 13:15 Therefore by Him let us continually offer the sacrifice of praise to God, that is, the fruit of *our* lips, giving thanks to His name. 16 But do not forget to do good and to share, for with

such sacrifices God is well pleased. We are no longer required to offer the sacrifices as required in the Old Testament as we are under a new covenant (Matthew 26:28; Luke 22:20; 2 Corinthians 3:6). Under this covenant, we offer a sacrifice of praise and thanksgiving. God also likes to see us do good and be generous. Truly, He has given to us, and to follow His example, we will be generous as well, first to our immediate family and then, as we can, to others. How we live our lives can also be viewed as part of our spiritual sacrifice.

Hebrews 13:17 Obey those who rule over you, and be submissive, for they watch out for your souls, as those who must give account. Let them do so with joy and not with grief, for that would be unprofitable for you. If the people who rule over you feel that you follow their directions and are a good and trustworthy worker, they generally will treat you better, and you will bring them joy. That is the way to get things done and make the boss happy.

59

James

[59]**JAMES** - This is the "how-to" book of the Christian life. It helps us with the practical aspects of dealing with problems. We are advised to put our trust in Christ and thereby endure trials. James covers prejudice, offensive speech, judging one another, leaving God out of our plans, and bitterness.

James, the half-brother of Jesus, seems to be the most probable author of this book. His sole claim to any authority came from his spiritual servanthood to the Lord Jesus Christ. This is one of the earliest books written as part of the New Testament. Perhaps Galatians was written first. The historian Josephus mentions the martyrdom of James in A.D. 46. James appears to have taken Peter's place as the head of the church in Jerusalem.

The major theological issue underscores faith and works. He discusses "dead" faith (i.e., faith that does not produce anything) and live faith that results in works as the natural outcome of that faith. This does not change

---

[59] NSB quotations are from the Nelsons Study Bible, copyright (c) 1997 by Thomas Nelson, Inc., Nashville, TN; used by permission; scripture taken from the New King James Version, Copyright (c) 1979, 1980, 1982 used by permission. All rights reserved.

the doctrine of salvation through faith by the grace of God. However, when we believe (have faith) in something, we will act on that belief. He is calling Christians to live their lives in line with their beliefs.

One critical section of James is in the first few verses of chapter four, where we learn to solve conflicts through humility.

James 1:2 My brethren, count it all joy when you fall into various trials, 3 knowing that the testing of your faith produces patience. Wow; now there is a statement that goes totally against the response of the flesh. Count it *all* as Joy? Really? Yes, that is what James says. How do we possibly do that? One help is to keep focused on the result, which is patience. How would we develop patience any other way than to experience trials and get through them and realize, when the next one comes, that we will get through them if we can have the patience not to do things that will extend the trial or keep the trial from ever getting resolved

We need patience and endurance when we are in a trial. Since trials are how we develop patience and perseverance, we should rejoice that our character is improving. We need to remember that the testing is not to destroy but rather to improve and refine us and purge us of impurities. We need to keep a heavenly focus in mind and know that our time on earth is just the beginning of our fellowship with saints.

We need to stand fast under pressure and not blow up emotionally or physically. These adversities can and probably should be viewed as opportunities to demonstrate our faith which will keep us calm even amid raging seas all around. The scripture says that when we let this process proceed, we may become perfect and complete, lacking nothing. What a great promise! That is what we need. It would be wonderful for us to be perfect and complete in our faith.

Do we want to be perfect and complete in our faith? Then we need a different attitude toward trials. We need to embrace trials as an opportunity to demonstrate and increase our faith rather than something to be avoided at all costs. The reality is that our faith needs to be tested and refined. Without testing and refinement, our faith still has a lot of impurities that cling to us like some excess super glue on the finger. It can hang on until it wears off through abrasion over time. We need to let the sandpaper of trials sand off our impurities so that what is left is a pure faith with no doubts; a faith that will not be diminished by trials.

James 1:5 If any of you lacks wisdom, let him ask of God, who gives to all liberally and without reproach, and it will be given to him. The wisdom God gives is not always about getting out of troubles but rather learning from them and gaining character from them. As is noted in Proverb 29:15, it is the rod and rebuke that bring wisdom. We are being encouraged to have a new perspective on trials. More information on avoiding trials is not provided for all potential trials. Some trials come from sin, as when a person commits a crime, gets caught, and has to go to prison. But other trials just come from living in a fallen world that we can't avoid. In this kind of trial, it helps to keep in mind that God has allowed these circumstances and, in the end, will further His good purposes (see Romans 8:28).

All of us, rich or poor, will suffer death unless the rapture comes before our appointed time. When we endure trials, we demonstrate our love for the Lord as we understand that even the Crown of Life will be received by people who endure trials in the end times (Revelation 2:10). What is the Crown of Life? We may not know exactly what this term means, but I think it signifies a winner of the ultimate enjoyment of eternal life in God's kingdom.

James 1:13 Let no one say when he is tempted, "I am tempted by God"; for God cannot be tempted by evil, nor does He Himself tempt

anyone. Here the focus changes from trials to temptations. These are two different things, and we need to recognize them as such. The Lord allows us to go through trials, but He does not tempt us to do evil. This scripture makes this point very clear. Seemingly, it is against God's nature to tempt someone to sin. However, He will allow us to be in adverse situations to help us build our character.

It is our desires that can cause us to sin. We all have them. We have to nip them in the bud. That means that we have to cut them off at the pass before they can get through to causing actions we will regret. The place where we can do that is at the thinking stage or the level of desire before we are drawn away from what we should be doing and enticed into taking action on these sinful desires. Scripture goes on to say that **"when desire is conceived, it gives birth to sin."** This sounds like the process of committing a premeditated crime. First is the desire for money or to hurt someone. If that desire is extinguished, there is no crime. However, when desire turns into action, theft, violence and crime happen.

James 1:19 So then, my beloved brethren, let every man be swift to hear, slow to speak, slow to wrath; This verse forms the outline for the rest of the book of James. The great news is that enduring trials lead to the crown of life, whereas yielding to temptation leads to death. Thus we need to listen, focus on the long-term benefits of enduring trials, and keep from getting angry. That is easier said than done, but with the proper perspective, our chances are a lot better of enduring without venting our wrath on some poor person that happens to get in the way of our anger.

James 1:22 But be doers of the word, and not hearers only, deceiving yourselves. We need "the implanted word, which is able to save our souls" (vs. 21). This paragraph clarifies that the doer of the word will be blessed in what they do. The scripture encourages us to visit widows and orphans in their trouble and keep ourselves unspotted from the world. Unspotted, in this context, means without a moral lapse or blemish on our record. It means to have a good reputation. The following paragraph of this book notes that a person who cannot control what they say deceives their own heart, and their religion is useless.

James 2:2 My brethren, do not hold the faith of our Lord Jesus Christ, *the Lord* of glory, with partiality. Regardless of the clothes, a congregant is wearing or the wealth they appear to have, members of the church are not to treat people coming in with any preference or partiality. This is a type of judgment that should not take place with Christians. The scripture tells of how God has chosen the poor of the world to have faith and be heirs of the kingdom. The implication is that the poor should be treated just as well when they come to church as the rich. The partiality of this type is sin. We are encouraged to uphold the royal law, *"You shall love your neighbor as yourself."*

This chapter also lets us know that if we break one part of the law, we are guilty of all the law. God does not allow selective obedience to the law. In other words, if we violate just one commandment, we are separated from God. The law of liberty, which is love, is what we need to practice toward all of God's children, whether rich or poor and regardless of their race or gender. Our judgment of either does not demonstrate mercy, and it is apparent in scripture that *"Mercy triumphs over judgment"* (vs. 13).

James 2:19 You believe that there is one God. You do well. Even the demons believe—and tremble! 20 But do you want to know, O foolish man, that faith without works is dead? This particular scripture is the one that cements the concept that faith cannot and should not be separated from works. The statement is made that even the demons believe — and tremble. But they don't follow. In other words, they don't have any works that demonstrate their faith and obedience. Their works demonstrate the opposite. If God says not to commit adultery or murder, this is what they would do.

Scripture asks if the kind of faith that doesn't have any works can save a person. The implied answer is that if a person says they have faith, but do not demonstrate that this faith makes any difference in their works/actions, they really do not have saving faith. They are just giving lip service to the concept of faith. It's like saying: "I smell smoke and believe that the building is on fire," but then just sitting there and perishing while the building burns down. Getting up and leaving the building would demonstrate that you believe that the building is on fire and not that someone was just burning some toast while saying they believed it was on fire.

The Bible uses a different illustration, but the point is the same: "**faith by itself, if it does not have works, is dead**" (vs. 17). The scripture makes the point that works makes faith perfect. "**Abraham believed God, and it was accounted to him for righteousness**" based on the faith that he demonstrated by what he was willing to do. He was justified by his faith which he demonstrated by his actions and his statements of faith. He obeyed God and showed his complete trust.

Rahab sending the messengers out another way demonstrated her faith. "**For as the body without the spirit is dead, so faith without works is dead also**" (vs. 26). This point is made multiple times in the book of James. Confessing to having faith in words is not saving faith unless it accompanied by actions. Actions that follow faith demonstrate that the faith is real. We need real faith that influences our behavior, not pseudo faith which is only words.

James 3:10 Out of the same mouth proceed blessing and cursing. My brethren, these things ought not to be so. The scripture advises that only a few should become teachers because they will be held to a higher standard of stricter judgment and that all men stumble with regard to what they say at times. If a teacher loses control of their tongue, they will be judged not only by God but also by people. Unfortunately, what we say with can defile our whole bodies, and the scripture also states that: "**it** (the tongue) **is set on fire by hell** (vs. 6). Wow! That cannot be a good thing.

The times that we lose control of what we say usually have to do with anger on our part, and anger usually has to do with the pride of not getting our way or not getting the "respect" we demand. Thus, hell (Satan) uses our pride against us and causes friction among families, friends, and believers in a very clever way by encouraging us in our pride to sin. It appears that only the work of the Holy Spirit can bring this destructive pride under control, and then only if we get beyond the denial that pride instills in our hearts.

James 3:17 But the wisdom that is from above is first pure, then peaceable, gentle, willing to yield, full of mercy and good fruits, without partiality and without hypocrisy. 18 Now the fruit of righteousness is sown in peace by those who make peace. This is a great scripture that demonstrates how we should proceed in wisdom from the Holy Spirit instead of our angry flesh guiding us. The wisdom spoken of here is the kind of wisdom that is the fruit of the Holy Spirit. When relationships with people degrade into arguments and strife, it is usually an indication that the fruit of the spirit is not evident in one or both of the people. The fruit as described in Galatians is love, peace, patience, kindness, goodness, faithfulness, gentleness, and self-control. With these characteristics in play by at least one of the people in an interaction, it is hard to imagine a big blow up in the relationship.

Unfortunately, some people cannot yield when their authority is challenged. They get caught up in their own unloving, self-centered, uncaring, unkind reactions. There is little possibility for peaceful interaction when there is a difference of opinion with this type of person. A person who possesses Godly wisdom will show it in their interactions with other people. They will be slow to speak.

James 4:3 You ask and do not receive, because you ask amiss, that you may spend *it* on your pleasures. With this scripture, we learn why the answer to many of our prayers is "no." Often we are *not* concerned with the will of God. We are just concerned about what we want. Often what we want is not suitable for us, and of course, God knows that (see Philippians 4:19). When we ask for personal desires through prayer, we are not asking the right question (see Matthew 6:33). As the Lord's prayer indicates, we need to focus on the Lord's will, not ours.

James also lets us know why there is a lot of conflict among believers. It comes from materialism, the desire for material things in this world. Immediately after this verse, the scripture addresses adulterers and adulteresses. These are powerful words to describe those who want to be a friend of the world. The implication is that if you desire to be a friend of the world, these are the kinds of sins in which you will get involved. Note that God resists the proud person who elevates their desires above the Lord's. We do not want to be in a situation where God is fighting against our plans.

James 4:10 Humble yourselves in the sight of the Lord, and He will lift you up. I was once in a heated discussion on some issues of disagreement with a fellow Christian. This discussion took place in a church sanctuary after everyone left the service. I began to get angry and became unkind on my side of the debate. The other person was doing the same thing, and the debate started to turn into an argument. The fellowship was going downhill fast as anger began to rise. Thankfully, before the argument went further, I realized this would end badly. Both of us could leave angry and never want to speak again. In my mind, I briefly prayed: "Lord help me."

What came from that prayer was the first part of this verse. I immediately changed my approach. I couldn't say that we agreed because we did not, but I did apologize for bringing any grief to the person I was talking to and asked for their forgiveness. After repeating these statements a few times, the conversation changed dramatically and ended positively. I did not win the argument, but I did keep something far more valuable, peace, fellowship, and harmony. We are probably still not in agreement, but we can maintain a relationship. This is one of the great side benefits of humbling yourself; not only will the Lord lift you up, but your relationships with people will be much better.

James 4:11 Do not speak evil of one another, brethren. He who speaks evil of a brother and judges his brother, speaks evil of the law and judges the law. But if you judge the law, you are not a doer of the law but a judge. This is a scripture that most people ignore at times. Even pastors, who know this scripture, can find it hard not to step into the judge role and justify themselves by rationalizing that they need to be the ones who protect the flock from anyone who disagrees with their view.

The reality is that a pastor can exercise their responsibility without trying to discredit others. In the secular world, employers better have a signed Release of Consent Form in their file before sharing any negative information about a former employee or they could be held accountable for violating the former employee's privacy rights. In churches, the government enforcers usually take a "hands-off" approach, which leaves church parishioners or former employees open to character assassination by a judgmental pastor who wants to "speak evil" about them.

This scripture in conjunction with verse 5:9 lets us know that the person who grumbles against another may be condemned: **"Do not grumble against one another, brethren, lest you be condemned. ..."** It appears that we will reap what we sow (Galatians 6:7) regardless of our position, and a teacher will be held to an even higher standard as we have seen in previous scriptures in the book of James (Chapter 3). There are four types of wars/disagreements mentioned in the book of James; class wars (2:1-9), employment wars (5:1-6), church fights (1:19-20; 3:13-18), and personal wars (4:11-12).

Christians should "**speak the truth in love**" (Ephesians 4:15). If what we feel like saying will be harmful to another, maybe we should think about not saying it (1 Peter 4:8). We should have discernment without offense (Philippians 1:9-10) and should not try to put ourselves in place of God and pass judgment, even if we are a pastor (Matthew 7:1-6). Why are we at war with others? James tells us they come from selfishness (4:1). This is the essence of sin. However, we are to righteously judge our sin and the sin of other Christians in our church (John 7:24; 1 Corinthians 2:15).

James 5:12 But above all, my brethren, do not swear, either by heaven or by earth or with any other oath. The reality is that if we are honest people, we don't need to swear by anything to strengthen what we are saying. Our history and reputation will be evidence enough that we will tell the truth. Also, if we were to swear by some object to confirm our integrity, that would be a type of idolatry in which a Christian should not be involved.

This scripture does not appear to prohibit involving God as a witness to some specific important statement (see 1 Thessalonians 2:5) or making an oath in a court of law per customary practices. If a person has a problem swearing to the veracity of their statements in court, they may be allowed to "affirm" that the statements they make will be truthful to the best of their ability.

James 5:15 And the prayer of faith will save the sick, and the Lord will raise him up. And if he has committed sins, he will be forgiven. This is another scripture about prayer that can easily be misinterpreted if not viewed with the whole counsel of God. For example, in chapter four of James, we learn about when our prayers requests are not granted because we ask for our will to be done instead of trusting God and asking for His will to be done. The Lord does have the capacity to heal a person miraculously or through the skill of doctors. Either way, it is the Lord who provides the healing.

Saying I'm waiting for the Lord to heal when the Lord has already supplied a doctor with the skills to fix the problem is putting the Lord to a foolish test or just being foolish. We cannot act foolishly and expect the Lord to bail us out every time. He expects us to take appropriate actions in conjunction with His provision, and it is apparent in scripture that the Lord often works through people to accomplish His will. He even uses unbelievers to facilitate His will (Habakkuk 1:6)

Sickness can be the result of sin, but it also can just be the result of living in a fallen world (John 9:1-3). If sin is involved with a particular sickness, it would appear that confession is a part of the healing process and when we trespass against someone, we need to confess this **to one another and pray for one another that we may be healed** (5:16).

James 5:19 Brethren, if anyone among you wanders from the truth, and someone turns him back, 20 let him know that he who turns a sinner from the error of his way will save a soul from death and cover a multitude of sins. Here are some encouraging final words for those who help people learn about and follow the truth. They can **save a soul from death and cover a multitude of sins**. It sounds like a good thing to do and an excellent way to end the book of James.

60

1 Peter

[60]**1 PETER** - This book is about something hard to do for anyone; returning good for evil. Christians are told why they will suffer and that there will be eternal rewards at the end of their life on earth. These rewards will more than compensate for this suffering. Troubles here can come from many sources. They often come from other people, employers or the government. The book encourages believers to keep in mind the spiritual realities of the persecution they may face.

The suffering, the act of paying the price for our sins, and then rising from the dead was a pivotal event in Christianity. In other words, suffering is intimately connected with everything that matters in achieving eternal life. There had to be a price paid to satisfy the justice of God.

The oppression of Christians began with the crucifixion and will continue until the end of this age. We need to remember that we are just pilgrims in this world, passing through to a glorious home in heaven. In other words, suffering is a natural outcome of a life dedicated to the one who

---

[60] NSB quotations are from the Nelsons Study Bible, copyright (c) 1997 by Thomas Nelson, Inc., Nashville, TN; used by permission; scripture taken from the New King James Version, Copyright (c) 1979, 1980, 1982 used by permission. All rights reserved.

took on the supreme level of suffering to the point of death for us. Even now, suffering is a part of our service to God.

1 Peter 1:3 Blessed *be* the God and Father of our Lord Jesus Christ, who according to His abundant mercy has begotten us again to a living hope through the resurrection of Jesus Christ from the dead, 4 to an inheritance incorruptible and undefiled and that does not fade away, reserved in heaven for you, 5 who are kept by the power of God through faith for salvation ready to be revealed in the last time. There is a lot in these few verses. Salvation is based on God's mercy despite our sinfulness. We are born again into a continuing hope because Christ rose from the dead. Therefore, we know that there is a spiritual world that is eternal and that we will be part of this world in heaven through faith. Our initial birth was into the physical world, which is corruptible, defiled, and perishing. In the spiritual world, our second birth is none of those things. We can rejoice in these facts even though grief and trials will continue while we are on earth. That's just the way it is. It is part of the testing process, which lets us know if our faith is genuine and if we will still "**praise, honor, and glory at the revelation of Jesus Christ,...**" (vs. 6). Scripture says that the end of this faith is the salvation of our souls. That is worth anything we have to go through here on earth. In other words, we are to continue to trust God through all the difficulties of life.

1 Peter 1:12 To them it was revealed that, not to themselves, but to us they were ministering the things which now have been reported to you through those who have preached the gospel to you by the Holy Spirit sent from heaven—things which angels desire to look into. This passage appears to be referring to the Old Testament prophets. They were speaking the words of the Holy Spirit but may not have known that at least some of the words they spoke were for our benefit. Note that it says the gospel is preached to us by the Holy Spirit. The Holy Spirit proclaims these truths even though they may come through a human being. We need to keep this in mind and not put the preacher on a pedestal on which they do not belong. Preachers are just the messengers. They didn't write the words. Also, even the angels are interested in this process of salvation that the Lord set up for us.

1 Peter 1:13 Therefore gird up the loins of your mind, be sober, and rest *your* hope fully upon the grace that is to be brought to you at the revelation of Jesus Christ; 14 as obedient children, not conforming yourselves to the former lusts, *as* in your ignorance;... When we were ignorant of the truth, we did think and do things we should not have. We need to think differently and especially control our thought life because sin begins there. We need to think *and* act holy, not just act holy. We need to be holy, not only in our conduct but also in our minds. Our minds need to be protected from improper thoughts, just as our body needs to be covered by the correct type of armor if we were to go into battle.

The armor for the mind is outlined in the book of Ephesians Chapter 6. As you read through these protections, you will notice they have to do with how we think and what we believe. If a person starts with the wrong belief, that can lead to the wrong (unholy) action because action usually follows thinking. Thus, we need armor for our thoughts. The armor for our thoughts and actions is truth, righteousness, the gospel of peace, faith, salvation, the Spirit of God, and prayer (Ephesians 6:10-20). Our actions can follow the right path with this armor for our minds. We are to live holy in all our conduct which means set apart from the sin in the world. We are in the world, but we don't need to be of it.

1 Peter 1:20 He indeed was foreordained before the foundation of the world, but was manifest in these last times for you 21 who through Him believe in God, who raised Him from the dead and gave Him glory, so that your faith and hope are in God. There are a couple of things to note about this scripture. One is that God had a plan for our salvation even before the world was formed. Another is that the times we live in are called the "**last times**." We believe in God through Christ, whom God raised from the dead and glorified as an example to us of the power of God over life and death.

Now we know what only God knew before. We are His elect according to the election of grace, and we have been granted to know these things. And grace is what sets Christianity apart from all other religions. This grace is free to us, but it is not cheap. It cost Christ His life, and because of this grace, we have hope now and for the rest of eternity.

Peter had denied Christ three times, but later, he experienced the grace of God and wrote this book knowing the hope that comes from that grace. Scriptures like 1 Peter 2:11-12 and Hebrews 13:14 remind us that this earth is not our permanent home. The reality is that our flesh perishes, "**But the word of the Lord endures forever**" (1:25). So, we have a choice. Are we going to focus on what lasts for a little while? Or, are we going to focus on eternity and put our hope in that reality?

1 Peter 1:22 Since you have purified your souls in obeying the truth through the Spirit[a] in sincere love of the brethren, love one another fervently with a pure heart, 23 having been born again, not of corruptible seed but incorruptible, through the word of God which lives and abides forever,... There is a lot in this part of the sentence. Peter is not saying that we purify our souls, but that our souls get purified by God when we obey His truth. The "born again" concept is mentioned a few times in the New Testament. In this context, it seems to refer to the process whereby we were dead in our sins, and then our life is renewed in the Spirit when we become believers. A child who comes out of the womb, which is of the flesh, has a new type of life out of the water into breathing air when they come out. We have a new life with the Spirit when we breathe in the Spirit of God and the abundant life with God that the Spirit has for us (John 10:10; John 3:3-8; Ephesians

2:1). With the Spirit, our eyes open the Kingdom of God. Like the air, we cannot see the Spirit, but it is there. The flesh is temporary, but the one born of the Spirit is eternal because God is eternal, and those in the Spirit of God will live in eternity.

1 Peter 2:4 Coming to Him *as to* a living stone, rejected indeed by men, but chosen by God *and* precious, 5 you also, as living stones, are being built up a spiritual house, a holy priesthood, to offer up spiritual sacrifices acceptable to God through Jesus Christ. Note that Christ, the living stone is better than the stones used to build a temple or stones used to make idols. We are living stones that build up a spiritual house (the church). This is better than a stone temple. All of us living stones are like priests in the old testament in that we have the privilege and responsibility to worship God. We are a living sacrifice and should offer praise and thanks to His name (Romans 12:1, 2; Heb. 13:15, 16).

1 Peter 2:9 But you *are* a chosen generation, a royal priesthood, a holy nation, His own special people, that you may proclaim the praises of Him who called you out of darkness into His marvelous light; 10 who once *were* not a people but *are* now the people of God, who had not obtained mercy but now have obtained mercy. This scripture lets us know how special we are to God; chosen, royal, holy. And, we have a purpose which is to praise the one who called us into His marvelous light. We once were a very diverse group of individuals going every which way, but now are a cohesive group called "the people of God" who have a specific mission in life. We are set apart from the world to do God's work here on earth. We are adopted into His family and will receive His inheritance (Ephesians 1:11; Colossians 3:24; Hebrews 9:15). We previously deserved condemnation due to our unbelief, but now we have been pardoned from the just sentence of judgment. We are now just visitors here for a short while with a specific mission.

1 Peter 2:15 For this is the will of God, that by doing good you may

put to silence the ignorance of foolish men—16 as free, yet not using liberty as a cloak for vice, but as bondservants of God. 17 Honor all *people*. Love the brotherhood. Fear God. Honor the king. The verse immediately before this verse talks about submitting ourselves "**to *every* ordinance of man for the Lord's sake.**" Other scripture talks about potential exceptions when an ordinance of man contradicts the laws of God (Acts 5:29; Luke 20:25), but those exceptions appear to be very rare given that the statement here uses the word "every" in describing which ordinances of man that we should follow. So, should we pay our taxes? Even Christ made it clear in His time that we should "**Give to Caesar what is Caesar's and to God what is God's:** (Matthew 22:25). He also provided an example for us through paying taxes himself (Matthew 17:24-27). In Romans 13:1, Paul clarifies that we should submit ourselves to the governing authorities. He goes on to say that if we rebel against these authorities, we are rebelling against what God has instituted, "**and those who do so will bring judgment on themselves**." That is *not* something we should want to do.

1 Peter 2:18 Servants, *be* submissive to *your* masters with all fear, not only to the good and gentle, but also to the harsh. The scripture goes on to say that if we do good and suffer for it and take it patiently, "**this *is* commendable before God.**" The question is asked: why do bad things sometimes happen to good people? One answer is that only one was good (sinless) on earth. That was Christ, and He willingly suffered death on our behalf. We are told to be submissive to harsh masters, but how many of us are willing to do so? We are told to **follow His steps** in suffering for others. He did not return pain for the pain He suffered, but rather endured knowing that His father's will was more important than what He was going through. Thus, we should treat everyone with love and respect even if they are harsh with us. Such suffering has great reward (Matthew 5:10-12; Romans 8:17, 18; Philippians 1:19; 2 Timothy 1:12). Remember that these rewards do not come from deserved punishment but rather undeserved. So we may want to try enduring some undeserved punishment along the way of discipleship with a heavenly-minded attitude rather than the attitude that everything needs to be just for us while we are here on the earth.

1 Peter 3:3 Wives, likewise, *be* submissive to your own husbands, that even if some do not obey the word, they, without a word, may be won by the conduct of their wives, 2 when they observe your chaste conduct *accompanied* by fear. Here's a great verse to start a chapter. Note the ultimate reason for the submission - to win them over without a word. That is discipleship in its pure form. Discipleship through actions rather than words. If a wife is a believer, what higher calling could she have? What would be more important than winning the one you love and have committed to spend your life with, to be a disciple of Christ? The chapter encourages the wife to have additional adornment beyond the appearance. That adornment is the adornment of the heart. The beauty of the heart is the incorruptible beauty of a gentle and quiet spirit, **which is very precious in the sight of the Lord.** We should spend more time on this inner beauty than the outside appearance (1 Samuel 16:7). So this book starts with submission to government leaders, then to employers, and then to a spouse.

1 Peter 3:7 Husbands, likewise, dwell with *them* with understanding, giving honor to the wife, as to the weaker vessel, and as *being* heirs together of the grace of life, that your prayers may not be hindered. Now, how should husbands treat their wives? They should be understanding and honor them. If the husband does not do this, their prayers could be hindered. That's not a good thing to happen. Yes, that goes against our old nature of returning evil for evil and reviling for reviling, but that is what believers are to do in our marriages. If our wife does evil to us, we are to return a blessing. If she reviles us, we are to return a blessing. Note: **"the face of the Lord is against those who do evil"** (3:12). We do not need to try to do the Lord's job, nor does he want us to.

1 Peter 3:15 But sanctify the Lord God in your hearts, and always *be* ready to *give* a defense to everyone who asks you a reason for the hope that is in you, with meekness and fear;... We are to provide a reason for our hope, not with arrogance but with meekness and fear. Scripture says that **it is better, if it is the will of God, to suffer for doing good than for doing evil.** What a different concept. Again, this concept goes against our old nature. We might be willing to take the punishment in the world system if we knew we deserved it. But, to accept punishment or suffering for something we were not guilty of is totally against our old nature. The old concept is turned on its head. This scripture implies that we should be more willing to take punishment when wrongly condemned than justly condemned. Come to think of it that is what Christ did for us. Thus, suffering from something we did not do allows us to identify with what He did for us. That perspective provides a very different concept, which may be part of God's plan for a believer (see Matt. 5:10-12).

1 Peter 4:3 For we *have spent* enough of our past lifetime in doing the will of the Gentiles—when we walked in lewdness, lusts, drunkenness, revelries, drinking parties, and abominable idolatries. Before our salvation, we followed after what the unsaved did. We don't need to do that anymore. Unbelievers cannot understand why we are different and don't want to run with them and hang out with them when they are involved in drunkenness, revelries, and idolatries. They will ridicule those who don't want to join in with them in these activities. They will think that something is wrong with you if you don't want to run with them in the "good times." "Good times" is a euphemism for these frivolous and wicked activities. Not only that, but they speak evil of you and ridicule you for not joining in.

Remember that it is good to be ridiculed for not joining in with some potentially sinful activity. Don't let it influence you to join in. They think there are no repercussions for their sins if they don't believe in God and are not caught. However, their beliefs don't change the fact that there is a God, and one day, they will have to stand defenseless before Him and account for what they have done (Revelation 20:11-15). Also, even here on earth, there are multiple repercussions/consequences for sinful behavior. These consequences may not come immediately, but they will usually come.

1 Peter 4:8 And above all things have fervent love for one another, for "love will cover a multitude of sins." Here is a very important scripture regarding what our priorities should be. It says "above all things." That is a very high priority. And, what does it say for us to do? It says to love one another and have "fervent" love for one another. That would be love with great warmth, with an intensity of spirit, feeling, and enthusiasm for one another. That would mean our family members, friends, and other brothers and sisters in the faith. How many of us demonstrate this type of love? There is a reward even in the here and now for this type of love. It will cover a multitude of sins.

1 Peter 4:12 Beloved, do not think it strange concerning the fiery trial which is to try you, as though some strange thing happened to you; 13 but rejoice to the extent that you partake of Christ's sufferings, that when His glory is revealed, you may also be glad with exceeding joy. This scripture turns the response to trials on its head. We are to rejoice when we are tried to the extent that we partake of Christ's sufferings. His sufferings are generally hundreds of times more difficult than anything we experience. Remember that His glory will be revealed at some point and then we will fully comprehend and have an excellent reason for rejoicing. But along the way, our trials appear to give us a better understanding of what Christ went through for us.

Note that there is a reason for our suffering. Is it not that which proves our true character? Thus, we should expect and prepare for suffering because it will be a part of our experience until Christ returns (Rom.

8: 18-22). At that time, we will be **delivered from the bondage of suffering into the glorious liberty of the children of God**. When we are criticized for following Christ, we do not need to worry. This type of reproach brings a great reward in the next life (Matt. 5:10-12). Scripture says to be **exceedingly glad** about this type of situation. That is probably impossible unless we are what I call heavenly minded or eternally minded; that is: focusing on eternity with Christ rather than the short life here on earth. This life is here for a while, and then, it is gone just like a vapor. While we are here, we need to keep in mind that some of us will suffer **according to the will of God** (v. 19).

1 Peter 5:2 Shepherd the flock of God which is among you, serving as overseers, not by compulsion but willingly, not for dishonest gain but eagerly; 3 nor as being lords over those entrusted to you, but being examples to the flock; 4 and when the Chief Shepherd appears, you will receive the crown of glory that does not fade away. Here is something that is difficult for many "elders" to do. They are called to be examples of not lording it over people in their congregation. They need to remember that this is not their flock but God's. They are not to boss people around but set an example of humble servant leadership for all to see. They do need to hold people accountable, but not by compulsion. They need to be servants who encourage people to live according to God's word, being an example and teaching them how to do this. They should not be as masters who use punishment and harsh directions (John 13:15). A leader who will not humble themselves in the sight of the Lord will be resisted by God Himself (vs. 5:5). We are to be **"clothed with humility"** (vs. 5:5), and it appears that even our leaders should be submissive to one another.

1 Peter 5:6 Therefore humble yourselves under the mighty hand of God, that He may exalt you in due time, 7 casting all your care upon Him, for He cares for you. This is a hard thing to do for anyone. It is especially hard for an authority who views a challenge to their authority as improper. We sometimes fail to remember that the warning to **be vigilant** comes right after the scripture tells us to be humble. This scripture appears to indicate that the ruler of this world is looking for every opportunity to destroy your humility and make you a proud resistor.

What did Job do when the Lord allowed Satan to sift him like sand? He humbled himself and continued to trust in the Lord. He did not allow himself to rise with pride and turn on the Lord (Job 13:15). Satan wanted him to turn on the Lord with pride and try to fix things himself without God. We need to (a) be vigilant about not getting puffed up with pride or anger, (b) be self-controlled and disciplined enough not to let the attacks of the devil fuel our anger or pride, and (c) to remain steadfast and immovable in our faith and humility.

We do not want to try to take things into our own hands against what God is doing. God is in control. If you become proud, remember who will be resisting you. It is as clear as day in this part of scripture. God, Himself will be resisting you. Satan will do everything he can to make you proud because he knows how God feels about pride, and he wants you to be an enemy of God just like he is. He could even assist you in being disciplined about not committing other sins like lying, adultery, or coveting so that your pride is built up, which is one of the worst spiritual sins. The old saying is that "misery loves company." This saying does have truth to it when it comes to Satan wanting you to join him in pridefully turning away from faith in God.

1 Peter 5:9 Resist him, steadfast in the faith, knowing that the same sufferings are experienced by your brotherhood in the world. Note that we are not commanded to run but to resist. We are apparently to stand fast in our faith. Of course, there are times when we should avoid discussions that might lead to anger (Colossians 3:8-13; James 1:20; Psalm 37:8) and times when we should walk the other way to avoid trouble.

1 Peter 5:10 But may the God of all grace, who called us to His eternal glory by Christ Jesus, after you have suffered a while, perfect, establish, strengthen, and settle *you*. Here is a great reason to benefit from suffering. We can gain strength, stability, and maturity when we go through it.

61

2 Peter

[61] **2 PETER** - This book is partly about sanctification.

2 Peter 1:5 But also for this very reason, giving all diligence, add to your faith virtue, to virtue knowledge, 6 to knowledge self-control, to self-control perseverance, to perseverance godliness, 7 to godliness brotherly kindness, and to brotherly kindness love. We begin the Christian life through faith. Then begins the walk of obedience and good works. Believers were previously spiritually dead but now have eternal life. The reason for this list of additions was explained as "**corruption that is in the world through lust.**" So we are to add to our faith, virtue, knowledge, self-control, perseverance, godliness, brotherly kindness, and finally, love. That is a long list of essential building blocks to the ultimate of love.

2 Peter 1:20 ...knowing this first, that no prophecy of Scripture is of any private interpretation, 21 for prophecy never came by the will of man, but holy men of God spoke *as they were* moved

---

[61] NSB quotations are from the Nelsons Study Bible, copyright (c) 1997 by Thomas Nelson, Inc., Nashville, TN; used by permission; scripture taken from the New King James Version, Copyright (c) 1979, 1980, 1982 used by permission. All rights reserved.

by the Holy Spirit. So, prophecy does not come from the ability of a man to discern what the future holds. It comes from God through His Holy Spirit working through holy men of God. Therefore, God is to be glorified for all prophesies, not man.

2 Peter 2:9 ...*then* the Lord knows how to deliver the godly out of temptation and to reserve the unjust under punishment for the day of judgment, 10 and especially those who walk according to the flesh in the lust of uncleanness and despise authority. God delivers us out of trials, but we still have to go through them to develop perseverance (James 1:3). Unfortunately for the unjust, God reserves judgment and punishment for them. It may look like God is allowing the unjust to prosper, but that will no longer be the case in the end. God is just, and justice will be served when all is said and done.

2 Peter 2:12 But these, like natural brute beasts made to be caught and destroyed, speak evil of the things they do not understand, and will utterly perish in their own corruption, 13 *and* will receive the wages of unrighteousness, *as* those who count it pleasure to carouse in the daytime. Reveling in the daylight by the unrighteousness is something those who will perish in their corruption like to do. "These" appears to be referring to false teachers. They are compared to animals who do not plan for the future but simply react to the present. They denigrate God and do not even understand who God is and how they will perish in their corruption. After this, they will receive the wages of their corruption, which is their just deserts.

2 Peter 2:14 ...having eyes full of adultery and that cannot cease from sin, enticing unstable souls. They have a heart trained in covetous practices, *and are* accursed children. Not only does the one who has a hardened heart toward God corrupt themselves, but they also entice unstable people to join them in their trespasses. As a result, they are accursed, which means detestable. Being detestable to God is not a good thing to be.

2 Peter 3:2 ...that you may be mindful of the words which were spoken before by the holy prophets, and of the commandment of us, the apostles of the Lord and Savior, 3 knowing this first: that scoffers will come in the last days, walking according to their own lusts, 4 and saying, "Where is the promise of His coming? For since the fathers fell asleep, all things continue as *they were* from the beginning of creation." This paragraph gives us a preview of what to expect in the last days. We can expect scoffers who do whatever they want and mock those of us who await the second coming and say that everything remains the same. They will have ignored the creation, which points to God.

2 Peter 3:7 But the heavens and the earth *which* are now preserved by the same word, are reserved for fire until the day of judgment and perdition of ungodly men. Right now, God is maintaining the incredible balance required for life on earth through what Christ has done and is doing. There will be a day of judgment for the ungodly at a time unknown to us. For now, they get to enjoy God's creation just as believers do.

2 Peter 3:10 But the day of the Lord will come as a thief in the night, in which the heavens will pass away with a great noise, and the elements will melt with fervent heat; both the earth and the works that are in it will be burned up. Now we know what the Bible says the end of the earth will be. It will burn up. Scientists also predict the end of the earth as we know it when the sun runs out of fuel. That will be a long time away, but it will eventually come, and when it does, the earth will no longer sustain our type of life. The point is that our world is temporary from a secular or Biblical perspective.

I don't mean to cause alarm, but if the earth is going to burn up, it makes sense to be ready for the afterlife. Maybe that is the most critical point of this verse in the Bible. We should continue to watch and prepare (Hebrews 9:28: Matthew 25:13). It might also be worth keeping in mind that God made the world for His good pleasure. He sustains it, and He will allow it to melt with fervent heat in His timing. Then, He will make a new earth and a new heaven (2 Peter 3:13).

62

1 John

[62] **1 JOHN** - Jesus Christ is God and, at the same time, human. He is God incarnate. This book covers how to identify someone who believes this is the truth.

1 John 1:6 If we say that we have fellowship with Him, and walk in darkness, we lie and do not practice the truth. The simple message here can be summarized as follows: "actions speak louder than words." This is especially true in determining what someone believes. If we believe in God, we do our best to follow His commandments and not just provide lip service. We have sin in us and always will. Nevertheless, we should be doing our best to avoid sin.

1 John 2:2 And He Himself is the propitiation for our sins, and not for ours only but also for the whole world. What is propitiation? It is to appease or conciliate. Jesus Christ was our propitiation because He paid the price for our sins past, present, and future to gain us favor with God. He did that for each of us and everyone else on the earth.

---

[62] NSB quotations are from the Nelsons Study Bible, copyright (c) 1997 by Thomas Nelson, Inc., Nashville, TN; used by permission; scripture taken from the New King James Version, Copyright (c) 1979, 1980, 1982 used by permission. All rights reserved.

1 John 2:9 He who says he is in the light, and hates his brother, is in darkness until now. This verse lets us know that we can't just talk the talk; we need to walk the walk. In this example, we have to love our brothers to walk the walk.

1 John 2:15 Do not love the world or the things in the world. If anyone loves the world, the love of the Father is not in him. 16 For all that *is* in the world—the lust of the flesh, the lust of the eyes, and the pride of life—is not of the Father but is of the world. If we are believers in Jesus Christ, things in our desires should change. As more than one pastor has said: "If there's been no change, there's been no change." Then the verse talks about the kinds of things that we desire when we love the things of the world, like lust and pride. When we recognize who God is, our perspective on these issues is forever changed, and we are humbled.

1 John 2:18 Little children, it is the last hour; and as you have heard that the Antichrist is coming, even now many antichrists have come, by which we know that it is the last hour. This verse appears to warn that we are in the last hour when many Antichrists are active. First, who is an Antichrist? It is someone who (a) is not a believer (v. 19), (b) lies (v.21), (c) denies that Jesus is the Christ (v. 22; 1 John 4:2,), and (d) who denies that Jesus came in the flesh (2 John 1:7). In general, these people worship the creation, not the Creator.

What is the last hour? It seems to be the current Church age which can be called the dispensation of grace which is the sixth dispensation in God's work with humanity. It is the time between the day of Pentecost (Acts 2) and the second coming of Christ (1 Thessalonians 4:3: 2 John 1:5). It is called the dispensation of grace. Grace is God's forgiveness of the undeserving. There are a lot of Antichrists running around during this age. No one knows, except the Father, when this Church Age will end (Matthew 24:26).

1 John 2:22 Who is a liar but he who denies that Jesus is the Christ? He is antichrist who denies the Father and the Son. This verse points out one of the character traits of an Antichrist.

1 John 3:1 Behold what manner of love the Father has bestowed on us, that we should be called children of God! Therefore the world does not know us, because it did not know Him. God's love for us is beyond our imagination. We are adopted into His family. Why doesn't the world know believers? They do not know God, and without knowing God, they cannot understand what makes believers believe what they do. Therefore, they cannot know believers. Believers will always be a mystery to them.

1 John 3:4 Whoever commits sin also commits lawlessness, and sin is lawlessness. Lawless people are against the law and generally against God because sin and lawlessness are the same. It involves going against the rules or laws laid out by God or the government. It points out that those willing to violate God's laws will also violate man-made laws.

1 John 3:8 He who sins is of the devil, for the devil has sinned from the beginning. For this purpose the Son of God was manifested, that He might destroy the works of the devil. The devil is against God and influences those who sin regularly, encouraging them to sin more and not be concerned about what God thinks about it.

1 John 3:9 Whoever has been born of God does not sin, for His seed remains in him; and he cannot sin, because he has been born of God. The Holy Spirit within true believers does not sin. However, the flesh can and does. However, that sin should be diminishing as the edification process continues.

1 John 3:13 Do not marvel, my brethren, if the world hates you. 14 We know that we have passed from death to life, because we love

the brethren. He who does not love *his* brother abides in death. This is such a comforting scripture. That is because God knew that those who hated Him would also hate those of us who believe in Him. So, He provides us with foreknowledge of this fact so we will not be surprised when some people hate us and will be encouraged by this situation because it demonstrates that we are true believers who love our brothers and sisters in the faith. It is encouraging to know that we abide in life.

1 John 3:15 Whoever hates his brother is a murderer, and you know that no murderer has eternal life abiding in him. Just like with adultery, if we think about murdering someone in our hearts, it is a sin, just as if we had murdered the person. In God's economy, it is just as if we had committed the sin.

1 John 4:1 Beloved, do not believe every spirit, but test the spirits, whether they are of God; because many false prophets have gone out into the world. How do we test a spirit? One way is to ask: do they confess that Jesus Christ came in the flesh (1 John 4:2)? Note that there are false prophets and that we need to be aware of them and test to make sure that they are of God.

1 John 4:2 By this you know the Spirit of God: Every spirit that confesses that Jesus Christ has come in the flesh is of God, 3 and every spirit that does not confess that Jesus Christ has come in the flesh is not of God. And this is the *spirit* of the Antichrist, which you have heard was coming, and is now already in the world. Not only does this verse provide a way to determine how to discern what type of spirit a person has, but it also tells us who the other spirit is. So, how do we tell who is led by the Holy Spirit? One way is to check whether the person confesses that Jesus Christ came in the flesh. If they do *not*, they are the opposite of a Christian believer. They are anti-Christian. Another way is to observe whether they exhibit the fruits of the spirit like love, peace, kindness, goodness, faithfulness, gentleness, and self-control (Galatians 5:20). If their life exhibits the opposite of these fruits, they may have the spirit of the Antichrist instead of the Spirit of God. Note that Christians can go against their normal personality and exhibit the opposite traits at times. This might happen if they wind up under the influence of too much alcohol or drugs. That is why Christians should avoid too much mind-altering substances that can interfere with self-control, motor control, and rational thinking.

1 John 4:7 Beloved, let us love one another, for love is of God; and everyone who loves is born of God and knows God. 8 He who does not love does not know God, for God is love. Here is another test for whether a person is a true believer. Do they show love for their brothers and sisters in the faith? If not, since love comes from God those who do not display it do not know God. If a person says they know God but do not show love for other believers, they do not really know God.

1 John 4:13 By this we know that we abide in Him, and He in us, because He has given us of His Spirit. 14 And we have seen and testify that the Father has sent the Son *as* Savior of the world. There are many tests of faith in this book of the Bible. Here is another on a more personal level. When we know that God has sent Jesus Christ to the world to provide salvation to men, and we tell others about the good news, we know that this knowledge has been given to us by God.

1 John 4:21 And this commandment we have from Him: that he who loves God *must* love his brother also. This scripture somewhat goes along with the other scriptures about those who love their fellow brethren. It shows that they know God because God is love. If we love God, we will love our brothers in the faith. If we do not, we don't know God. To love other believers is not optional. It is mandatory.

1 John 5:1 Whoever believes that Jesus is the Christ is born of God,

and everyone who loves Him who begot also loves him who is begotten of Him. This verse speaks of the process of being born again. We are physically born from our mothers, and we can also be spiritually born. When we believe that Jesus is the Christ, we are spiritually born from God. Thus, we are born a second time, first physically and then spiritually.

1 John 5:3 For this is the love of God, that we keep His commandments. And His commandments are not burdensome. If we love God, we will want to keep His commandments. As noted elsewhere in this commentary, we are not the light, but we can reflect His light when we love God. When we reflect His light, the power comes from Him. We are like the moon reflecting the sun. All the light comes from the sun and is reflected off of the moon. We just reflect His light.

1 John 5:4 For whatever is born of God overcomes the world. And this is the victory that has overcome the world—our faith. As I have said before, the importance of faith cannot be overstated. Faith is a life-and-death issue. It is important. Faith overcomes the world. It is that important.

1 John 5:7 For there are three that bear witness in heaven: the Father, the Word, and the Holy Spirit; and these three are one. Of course, the Father is God. However, we can't completely understand how the Son (the Word) Jesus Christ is God, and the Holy Spirit is God. They are all one God. Like I said, with our limited capacity, we can find this concept complex, but we know it is true.

1 John 5:11 And this is the testimony: that God has given us eternal life, and this life is in His Son. God is the one who says he gives us eternal life that is in His Son, who is Jesus Christ. We cannot earn eternal life. It is something that is given to us by God as a gift. As repeated many times in the Bible, it is not something that we can work to earn.

1 John 5:16 If anyone sees his brother sinning a sin *which does* not *lead* to death, he will ask, and He will give him life for those who commit sin not *leading* to death. There is sin *leading* to death. I do not say that he should pray about that. What is the sin leading to death? Could it be the continual refusal to acknowledge Jesus Christ has come in the flesh? Other similar ideas may be part of the same attitude. Other scripture regarding the sin leading to death says that it is to blaspheme the Holy Spirit. This is called out in scripture as an unforgivable sin (Mark 3:28-29; Matthew 12:31-32; Luke 12:10). Blasphemy is continual irreverence, disrespect, contempt, slander, or abuse. More specifically, in some scriptures, blasphemy against the Holy Spirit appears to be attributing miracles that Christ performed to the power of Satan (Matthew 12:32; Mark 3:28).

63

2 John

[63] **2 JOHN** - The truth is that Jesus Christ came in the flesh.

2 John 6 This is love, that we walk according to His commandments. This is the commandment, that as you have heard from the beginning, you should walk in it. We might ask why God wants us to follow His commandments. It looks like part of the reason is that they protect us from harmful consequences. Another is that God says to follow them. As noted elsewhere, we do not gain salvation through following the ten commandments, but they do set us apart as we should be. Freedom is doing what we should. If you think following ten laws is difficult, consider that our various levels of government enacted approximately 40,000 new laws in 2010. Like traffic rules, these ten laws allow us to be more free and safe.

2 John 7 For many deceivers have gone out into the world who do not confess Jesus Christ *as* coming in the flesh. This is a deceiver and an antichrist. This verse makes it clear that there will be many

---

[63] NSB quotations are from the Nelsons Study Bible, copyright (c) 1997 by Thomas Nelson, Inc., Nashville, TN; used by permission; scripture taken from the New King James Version, Copyright (c) 1979, 1980, 1982 used by permission. All rights reserved.

deceivers. That can be easily observed today. The truth taught in the Bible is that Christ came to the earth and took on a physical body. Those who do not teach this fact are deceivers. Jesus Christ was God and man at the same time. Even historians mentioned Jesus Christ, but that is an issue for another commentary.

2 John 9 Whoever transgresses and does not abide in the doctrine of Christ does not have God. He who abides in the doctrine of Christ has both the Father and the Son. 10 If anyone comes to you and does not bring this doctrine, do not receive him into your house nor greet him;11 for he who greets him shares in his evil deeds. We are not to believe more than the truth as presented by the apostles nor less. If someone teaches something beyond the scriptures, they are probably adding to the Bible and would be considered transgressors even though they act more spiritual. They, in reality, are probably less spiritual. They do not have God, as this verse describes. Sometimes we have people come to our door, and we don't know what doctrine they share, so we let them in. Once we understand what their doctrine is, if it goes against the doctrine of Christ, we don't need to entertain their ideas again. If we help such a transgressor spread their doctrine, we share in their evil deeds and do not want to do that.

64

3 John

[64]**3 JOHN** - Struggles within a church can be destructive.

3 John 2 Beloved, I pray that you may prosper in all things and be in health, just as your soul prospers. This is a pleasant greeting. John is praying that they prosper both physically and spiritually. That is a good position.

3 John 11 Beloved, do not imitate what is evil, but what is good. He who does good is of God, but he who does evil has not seen God. If we were to see God perfectly, we probably would not sin anymore. However, we cannot see God in the same way we see a person. We can see Him through knowing what Christ did while He was physically present on the earth and what the Holy Spirit does in our hearts.

Other than what we see of the actions of Christ while He was on the earth, I'm not sure how we see God. What we do should directly reflect what we see of God. We can observe what is good and seek to follow that

---

[64] NSB quotations are from the Nelsons Study Bible, copyright (c) 1997 by Thomas Nelson, Inc., Nashville, TN; used by permission; scripture taken from the New King James Version, Copyright (c) 1979, 1980, 1982 used by permission. All rights reserved.

example. We do not want to follow those who are doing what is evil. If we do not know and follow God, we will probably do more evil.

65

Jude

[65]**JUDE** - More than most others, this book has a lot to say to the modern generations. Those who would like to distort the beliefs of Christianity may not enjoy the focus of this book. It contains accurate descriptions of false teachers so that they are easily recognized. It focuses on three things: faith, believers, and God. It appears that the main thing we are to do with false teachers is to avoid them. It is apparently not a Christian's job to confront false teachers or even discredit them other than to accept that they are marked for the condemnation of God.

Of the six people named Jude in the Bible, this book was probably written by Jude, the brother of James and half-brother of Jesus. Jude organizes his thoughts in threes. He points out errors and judgment and encourages righteous living.

Jude 1:2 Mercy, peace, and love be multiplied to you. In this second verse, Jude wishes us three things: mercy, peace, and love. Though we don't deserve mercy from God, He gives it to us. It is interesting to

---

[65] NSB quotations are from the Nelsons Study Bible, copyright (c) 1997 by Thomas Nelson, Inc., Nashville, TN; used by permission; scripture taken from the New King James Version, Copyright (c) 1979, 1980, 1982 used by permission. All rights reserved.

note that each of the four times a greeting in the New Testament wishes the reader mercy; it is a preamble to a warning about false teaching (1 Timothy 1:2; Timothy 1:2; Titus 1:4; 2 John 3). It appears that we need God's undeserved mercy in these situations of understanding false teachers.

Jude 1:4 For certain men have crept in unnoticed, who long ago were marked out for this condemnation, ungodly men, who turn the grace of our God into lewdness and deny the only Lord God and our Lord Jesus Christ. These subtle men were "long ago" marked out for condemnation. How could they long ago be marked for condemnation? Hard to say, except that God is the potter and can do what he wants with what He has made (Isaiah 64:8; Romans 9:21). God can, and has the authority to, make one person for honor and one for dishonor. He is God. These men are clever enough to infiltrate the Christian community. Watch out for false teachers who corrupt the teaching on grace and use it to do whatever lewd thing they feel like doing while denying God and our Lord Jesus Christ.

Jude 1:5 But I want to remind you, though you once knew this, that the Lord, having saved the people out of the land of Egypt, afterward destroyed those who did not believe. It is clear from this scripture that people, who should believe because they have been saved in some physical way, can then be destroyed due to their unbelief. In other words, false believers are not fooling God one bit, and they will suffer the consequences at the appropriate time. They will be judged by God. God even condemns angels who do not keep their proper domain to chains and darkness (Jude 1:6). There are three things that these unbelievers are said to do: **defile the flesh, reject authority, and speak evil of dignitaries** (Jude 1:8).

Jude 1:9 Yet Michael the archangel, in contending with the devil, when he disputed about the body of Moses, dared not bring against

him a reviling accusation, but said, "The Lord rebuke you!" Here, Michael, the archangel, is an example that it is not our job to rebuke even these false believers. Any rebuking is to be left to the Lord. These are those for whom He has reserved **the blackness of darkness forever.** That is plenty of rebuke and punishment. We don't need to add any more.

Jude 1:16 These are grumblers, complainers, walking according to their own lusts; and they mouth great swelling words, flattering people to gain advantage. This verse gives us some idea of how to identify false Christians. It is not that anyone who does any of this is a false Christian. However, if this is all you hear from someone, they may be a false Christian, Even if they are not, these people may not be the best people to be around since **"These are sensual persons, who cause divisions, not having the Spirit"** (v. 19).

66

Revelation

[66]**REVELATION** - Predictions for the Future

Revelation 1:3 Blessed *is* he who reads and those who hear the words of this prophecy, and keep those things which are written in it; for the time *is* near. The word "blessed" is said to mean spiritually happy. Thus, the verse indicates that those who read the words of the prophecy in Revelation will be happy. When the verse says **the time is near,** it would appear to mean that the time is close in God's economy because many of the prophecies are yet to be fulfilled. A day to the Lord is like a thousand years (2 Peter 3:8). He is patient and does not want anyone to perish (2 Peter 3:9). Note that God does not appear to be bound by time as we are. He created time, and therefore, it makes sense that He is not bound by it.

Revelation 1:7 Behold, He is coming with clouds, and every eye will see Him, even they who pierced Him. And all the tribes of the earth will mourn because of Him. Even so, Amen. This seems to be

---

[66] NSB quotations are from the Nelsons Study Bible, copyright (c) 1997 by Thomas Nelson, Inc., Nashville, TN; used by permission; scripture taken from the New King James Version, Copyright (c) 1979, 1980, 1982 used by permission. All rights reserved.

a prediction about the second coming of Christ. Everyone will see Him this time, coming with the clouds. Even the family of those who rejected and crucified Him will see Him this time. Note that the phrase "**those who pierced him**" appears to refer to the people in current times who continue to reject His deity. They will mourn because they rejected the Lord, and now there is no way that they can rationalize this rejection.

Revelation 1:10 I was in the Spirit on the Lord's Day, and I heard behind me a loud voice, as of a trumpet, 11 saying, "I am the Alpha and the Omega, the First and the Last," and, "What you see, write in a book and send *it* to the seven churches which are in Asia: to Ephesus, to Smyrna, to Pergamos, to Thyatira, to Sardis, to Philadelphia, and to Laodicea." What does John mean by the statement "**I was in the Spirit**"? In this case, it appears to suggest that John was hearing and seeing what the Spirit of God was communicating to him. He was "**in the Spirit,**" which means that he was in a state of spiritual readiness to receive these visions of the Apocalypse. The Apocalypse, according to dictionary.com is: "assumed to make revelations of the ultimate divine purpose." Or, it is: "a prophetic revelation, especially concerning a cataclysm in which the forces of good permanently triumph over the forces of evil." John was spiritually ready to receive what the Spirit said and write it down. Now the question is, are we prepared to read what John wrote down and understand it. In this case, God referred to Himself as "**the First and the Last**" and directed John not only to write down what he heard but to distribute it widely. What John wrote is still being distributed widely, and those who read these words are blessed.

Revelation 1:20 The mystery of the seven stars which you saw in My right hand, and the seven golden lampstands: The seven stars are the angels of the seven churches, and the seven lampstands which you saw are the seven churches. There is often confusion about what specific parts of the Bible mean. Part of the reason is that God found it fair to use many literary techniques to communicate His plans to humankind. He appears to use parody, humor, exaggeration, figures of speech, poetic language, allegory, and parables to share what He wants to communicate to who He wants to know it. This verse gives the meaning of the seven stars and golden lampstands. Interestingly, we learn that the seven churches each have angels watching over them.

Revelation 2:11 "He who has an ear, let him hear what the Spirit says to the churches. He who overcomes shall not be hurt by the second death." Who has an ear to hear? Those whose names are written in the Book of Life (believers, 20:15) have an ear to hear. Those who do not have an ear to hear, are unbelievers. The second death is when those whose names are not written in the Book of Life are judged and experience the spiritual death of being cast into the lake of fire. Note that the first death is the physical death that most of us will experience at the end of our time here on earth.

Revelation 2:23 I will kill her children with death, and all the churches shall know that I am He who searches the minds and hearts. And I will give to each one of you according to your works. This verse is speaking of Jezebel, who called herself a prophetess. She taught and seduced church members in Thyatira to commit sexual sins. She was given time to repent but did not do so. Thus, she and her followers would receive the consequences of their works. This verse substantiates that the continual transgression of God's commandments has consequences even here on earth. The reference to "her children" comes directly after a sentence about those who commit adultery with her. Hence "her children" appears to be referring to adults who follow her teachings rather than to her biological children.

Revelation 2:26 And he who overcomes, and keeps My works until the end, to him I will give power over the nations— This is encouragement for the faithful who overcome the temptations to stray from the truth. In the end, these people will be the ones given oversight responsibility. Presumably, this will be in the Millennium. It will be a peaceful time when even animals will cease to eat other animals (Isaiah 65:25).

Revelation 3:2 Be watchful, and strengthen the things which remain, that are ready to die, for I have not found your works perfect before God. No one's works are perfect, so it makes sense to seek the forgiveness that comes by the grace of God through faith in Christ. We need to watch out for what God is doing and repent when we find ourselves straying off course.

Revelation 3:5 He who overcomes shall be clothed in white garments, and I will not blot out his name from the Book of Life; but I will confess his name before My Father and before His angels. Here Christ is telling us a couple of essential facts. One, we need to endure over time in the faith. This appears to be what is meant by the word "overcomes." Those who do will be rewarded with eternal life in addition to other rewards. Two, Christ can blot out a name from the Book of Life. The last thing we should want would be for our name to be blotted out of the Book of Life.

Revelation 3:10 Because you have kept My command to persevere, I also will keep you from the hour of trial which shall come upon the whole world, to test those who dwell on the earth. These admonitions to persevere are given numerous times in the Bible. The repetition lets us know how important it is to endure in the faith. We are pilgrims here. Our real home is in heaven so, while we are here, it makes sense to keep our focus on the end goal. I call this being heavenly-minded. What happens here is just a brief introduction and a sort of testing ground for eternal life.

Revelation 3:15 "I know your works, that you are neither cold nor hot. I could wish you were cold or hot. This verse seems to tell us that the Lord knows what we do and apparently, prefers us to be really for Him or not. Riding on the fence is not preferred by the Lord. The message seems to be either make a commitment or don't, but don't ride on the fence.

Revelation 3:17 Because you say, 'I am rich, have become wealthy, and have need of nothing'—and do not know that you are wretched, miserable, poor, blind, and naked— When people have a lot of money, they can come to depend on the money instead of God for their happiness and wellbeing. Depending on money is a fool's game. I once was in a country called Yugoslavia that had a tremendous inflation rate. Around 1989, the exchange rate for American dollars was 29,000 dinars to one dollar. Thus, when I exchanged $100, I came out of the bank with 2,900,000 dinars. I was a millionaire in dinars. The only problem was that a room for the night could cost close to 1,000,000 dinars. A few years later, the inflation rate is reported to have reached 313 million percent between 1992 and 1994, which is said to be the second-highest rate in world history. Not long after that, Yugoslavia had a war and ceased to be a country. Venezuela's inflation rate in 2019 was more than 65,000 percent year over year. Thus, the citizens of those countries who put their trust in money saw it become practically worthless quickly. These are modern-day examples confirming the folly of putting too much faith in having money.

But how could the people mentioned in this verse be both rich and poor simultaneously? They were rich with money but spiritually poor. The next verse explains that though they thought they were okay because they had money, they were spiritually naked and wretched, miserable, poor, and blind. They needed to put on the spiritual garments of faith in God rather than faith in their money.

Revelation 3:19 As many as I love, I rebuke and chasten. Therefore be zealous and repent. Believers still carry our old sin nature that battles with our new spiritual nature. God plays a part in helping us with this battle by rebuking and chastening us when we start getting off track. He is with us throughout these trials.

Revelation 3:20 Behold, I stand at the door and knock. If anyone hears My voice and opens the door, I will come in to him and dine with him, and he with Me. This verse indicates that Christ stands at the church's door (vs. 3:14) and knocks. Those who listen for His knock, hear it, and open the door will be rewarded with His presence.

Revelation 4:2 Immediately I was in the Spirit; and behold, a throne set in heaven, and *One* sat on the throne. In this situation, it appears that John was experiencing something outside of the natural world. Typically, we cannot see what is in the spiritual realm, but when John was in the Spirit, he could see a throne in heaven with One sitting on the throne. Also, being in the Spirit could describe John's openness to receiving the visions God was allowing him to have.

Revelation 4:5 And from the throne proceeded lightnings, thunderings, and voices. Seven lamps of fire *were* burning before the throne, which are the seven Spirits of God. What are the seven Spirits of God? Here they are described as "**lamps of fire.**" Isaiah 11:2-3 (NKJV) may provide some further enlightenment as follows:
[2] The Spirit of the LORD shall rest upon Him,
The Spirit of wisdom and understanding,
The Spirit of counsel and might,
The Spirit of knowledge and of the fear of the LORD.
[3] His delight is in the fear of the LORD,
And He shall not judge by the sight of His eyes,
Nor decide by the hearing of His ears;... So, the lamps seem to represent several concepts. This verse perhaps implies six spirits of God, including a Spirit of (1) wisdom, (2) understanding, (3) counsel, (4) might, (5) knowledge, and (6) fear of the LORD. Perhaps the seventh could be

righteous judgment. In another verse, it appears that the seven Spirits can be in one person (3:1). Farther along (5:6), we see the Seven Spirits represented by seven horns and seven eyes sent out throughout the earth. I'm not sure precisely what is meant by the Revelation 4:5 verse, but I look forward to finding out the exact meaning in the spiritual realm of heaven.

Revelation 4:8 *The* **four living creatures, each having six wings, were full of eyes around and within. And they do not rest day or night, saying:**

"**Holy, holy, holy,**

Lord God Almighty,

Who was and is and is to come!" From this verse, it appears that rest is not required in heaven as it is on earth. It also seems to say that God was in the past, is in the present, and the future. God is eternal. That is a difficult concept for us to understand because we are in the dimension of time. We can only be in the present at any one time, and as soon as we say we are in the present, that present just became the past and the future at that time just became the present. Since God created the dimension of time passing, it makes sense that He may be outside the dimension of time. Outside the dimension of time, eternity may have a different meaning beyond our comprehension.

Revelation 4:11

"**You are worthy, O Lord,**

To receive glory and honor and power;

For You created all things,

And by Your will they exist and were created." In just four lines, this verse covers a lot of territories that are essential to understanding life on earth. First, it reminds us of the importance of GOD and what our appropriate response to GOD should be. Then it states unequivocally why we owe our allegiance to Him. He created the earth. He created us and all we can see and all that we cannot see. Finally, we are told something about His motivation. He made all things, and He maintains His creation. In other words, His will created and supports our physical existence. If not for His continual will to keep our world and universe stable, it would extinguish.

Our world and everything in it could vanish without a trace if God did not continue His desire to keep us going. The history in the Bible shows us that there are times when God has not been pleased with how people expressed disdain and indifference toward their creator. In the end, their attitude did not work out so well for these people. The Bible recounts how many of them died in a massive flood. Some people put themselves above God and attempt to judge Him based on their idea of righteousness. They might ask if it is righteous for God to destroy some of His creation? Of course, it is. He is God. He appropriately makes the rules and is far above humans in acting righteously. By definition, if He does it, it is righteous. That is not true of us. Though some have tried, no human being can legitimately make that claim.

Revelation 5:6 And I looked, and behold, in the midst of the throne and of the four living creatures, and in the midst of the elders, stood a Lamb as though it had been slain, having seven horns and seven eyes, which are the seven Spirits of God sent out into all the earth. So here, the seven Spirits of God are described as having seven horns and seven eyes sent out by God into all the world. That is interesting. In Revelation 1:4, the seven Spirits are described as being before His throne and having something to communicate to the seven churches in Asia. In Revelation 3:1, the one who has the seven Spirits knows someone's works. In this verse, the seven Spirits are described as "**seven lamps of fire burning before the throne.**" What are we to make of all this? God has seven Spirits, and they (a) know a lot, (b) see a lot, (c) say a lot, (d) go a lot of places, (e) are closely connected to God, and (f) are like a fire burning before God's throne. That is significant but other than what the Bible says; I don't have any interpretation.

Revelation 5:8 Now when He had taken the scroll, the four living creatures and the twenty-four elders fell down before the Lamb, each having a harp, and golden bowls full of incense, which are the prayers of the saints. Here, it appears that the golden bowls of incense are the prayers of the saints or at least represent such. The verse says they are the prayers. It makes me wonder how prayers can be collected in a bowel in the spiritual realm. We know little about the spiritual realm, so the question makes sense in this context because of what the scripture clearly states.

It does appear that there are musical instruments in the spiritual realm because the 24 elders each had a harp. There would be no need for them to have harps if they didn't play them. There are also several references to singing in heaven. Thus, there is instrumental and vocal music in heaven. Maybe that is why music can seem to give us somewhat of a spiritual sense even here on earth. It can be a spiritual activity when used in the worship of God.

The saints are those who have been redeemed. It appears a bowl in heaven can contain their prayers. It is also interesting that the prayers of the saints play a role in this important event in heaven. They are part of the event. It will be fascinating to see how things are in the spiritual realm of heaven!

Revelation 5:13 And every creature which is in heaven and on the earth and under the earth and such as are in the sea, and all that are in them, I heard saying:
  "**Blessing and honor and glory and power**
  ***Be* to Him who sits on the throne,**
  And to the Lamb, forever and ever!" Back in Philippians 2, we see a verse that mentions, "**10 that at the name of Jesus every knee should bow, of those in heaven, and of those on earth, and of those under the earth, 11 and *that* every tongue should confess that Jesus Christ**

***is* Lord, to the glory of God the Father."** This verse contains a similar idea to Revelation 5:13, along with specifying what everyone will be saying.

Revelation 6:1 Now I saw when the Lamb opened one of the seals; and I heard one of the four living creatures saying with a voice like thunder, "Come and see." "Come and see" is the statement from one of the living creatures. Who or what are these living creatures? This is one of the questions people have asked over thousands of years. Though we may not know who they are short of heaven, we can figure out their primary job.

From scripture, we know they praise God and continually declare His holiness. In Revelation 5:6-13 we learn that these four living creatures worshiped Jesus Christ and God as co-equal. So why do they say "Come and see"? It appears John was supposed to see what happened when the Lamb opened the seals and write it down for the book of Revelation. We might not understand all of the imagery presented, but we can discern that there will be tribulation, war, bloodshed, famine, pestilence, and death. Then comes Hades ("the place of the unseen" in Greek). Death and Hades appear to be inseparable. All of us will experience death and become unseen. The unsaved will move on to Hell. The saved will move on to heaven and receive their glorified bodies when the time is right (Philippians 3:21; 1 Corinthians 15:42-44).

Revelation 6:11 Then a white robe was given to each of them; and it was said to them that they should rest a little while longer, until both *the number of* their fellow servants and their brethren, who would be killed as they *were*, was completed. This verse lets us know what happens with the martyrs. They wait for the time when all the other martyrs are killed. Then, God will justify their martyrdom. "**Vengeance is mine**," says the Lord (Deuteronomy 32:35). What is a martyr? It is a person who is unjustly killed for their beliefs.

Revelation 6:13 And the stars of heaven fell to the earth, as a fig tree drops its late figs when it is shaken by a mighty wind. This seems to be a description of how it will seem after a great earthquake causing the sun to become black and the moon to look like red blood. Soon after this happens, the great day of the wrath of the Lord will come. At that time, unbelievers will not be able to stand.

Revelation 7:3 ...saying, "Do not harm the earth, the sea, or the trees till we have sealed the servants of our God on their foreheads." As noted in the following passages, these servants were 144,000; 12,000 from each of the tribes of the children of Israel. It appears that these folk, along with a great multitude from every "tribe, nation, peoples, and tongues" (verse 7:9), will worship God.

Revelation 7:10 ...and crying out with a loud voice, saying, "Salvation *belongs* to our God who sits on the throne, and to the Lamb!" This is what the great multitude in heaven will be saying.

Revelation 7:14 And I said to him, "Sir, you know."
   So he said to me, "These are the ones who come out of the great tribulation, and washed their robes and made them white in the blood of the Lamb... So, this verse seems to confirm that some who will go through the great tribulation (predicted in Daniel 12:1) will become believers during this time and wind up in heaven worshiping the Lord.

Revelation 7:16 ...They shall neither hunger anymore nor thirst anymore; the sun shall not strike them, nor any heat; 17 for the Lamb who is in the midst of the throne will shepherd them and lead them to living fountains of waters. And God will wipe away every tear from their eyes." The same people praising the Lord in a previous couple of verses will be taken care of by God.

Revelation 8:6 So the seven angels who had the seven trumpets

prepared themselves to sound. These "trumpet" judgments are worse than the "seal" judgments. These will include judgments on the plant life, the sea, the rivers and springs, the sun, moon, and stars, and then on the men who did not have the seal of God on their foreheads.

Revelation 8:8 Then the second angel sounded: And *something* like a great mountain burning with fire was thrown into the sea, and a third of the sea became blood. When this trumpet judgment happened, it led to a third of the ships in the ocean being destroyed and a third of the sea creatures dying. That sounds pretty ominous.

Revelation 9:1 Then the fifth angel sounded: And I saw a star fallen from heaven to the earth. To him was given the key to the bottomless pit. This verse does not explain who the star from heaven is, so I don't know if it might be Jesus or Satan. Whoever it is, they will have the key to the bottomless pit. From what I can tell, the bottomless pit is like an interim jail where selected demons will be held in check (Luke 8:31) and where Satan himself will be held during the 1,000-year reign of Christ on earth (20:2,3). Apparently, it is God's plan that after 1,000 years, Satan will be released for a little while before he winds up getting sent into the lake of fire forever (20:10).

Revelation 9:4 They were commanded not to harm the grass of the earth, or any green thing, or any tree, but only those men who do not have the seal of God on their foreheads. Thus, the people who do not have the seal of God on their foreheads will be tormented for five months by locust-like creatures that have power, like scorpions (vs. 9:3). So what power do scorpions have? When they sting, they inject a powerful bunch of toxins that do not kill but give a lot of pain.

Revelation 9:15 So the four angels, who had been prepared for the hour and day and month and year, were released to kill a third of mankind. Wow! A third of mankind today would be about 2.6 billion people killed. That will be way more than any war we've ever had. The scripture also tells us how they will be destroyed. An army of 200,000,000 horsemen will kill them. In the vision, the horses' heads looked like heads of lions, and fire, smoke, and brimstone came out of their mouths (vs. 17).

When this was written, the world population was estimated to have been somewhere between 250,000,000 and 400,000,000. Thus, an army of 200,000,000 would not have been possible. Now, it is possible. At least a few countries could have a military force of that many, with less than one-fifth of their populations serving.

Revelation 9:20 But the rest of mankind, who were not killed by these plagues, did not repent of the (works of their hands, that they should not worship demons, and idols of gold, silver, brass, stone, and wood, which can neither see nor hear nor walk. Even after seeing all the plagues and tremendous loss of life, the rest of humanity did not repent of their worship of false gods, murders, sorceries, sexual immorality, or thefts.

Revelation 10:4 Now when the seven thunders uttered their voices, I was about to write; but I heard a voice from heaven saying to me, "Seal up the things which the seven thunders uttered, and do not write them." This is interesting. We are not privy to what the seven thunders said and do not know. This is one of the few places in the Bible where writers are told not to reveal what they learned. Humanity gets to know a lot, but there is a lot more to which we are oblivious and know nothing. Of course, some people think they know a lot because they know more than the average person, but compared to the knowledge of God, they are imbeciles.

Revelation 10:7 ...but in the days of the sounding of the seventh angel, when he is about to sound, the mystery of God would be

finished, as He declared to His servants the prophets. Much that was previously unknown will only be revealed when the events take place during the Apocalypse. These events apparently will take place over seven years, and then our earth as we know it will be finished.

Revelation 11:3 And I will give *power* to my two witnesses, and they will prophesy one thousand two hundred and sixty days, clothed in sackcloth." These witnesses that come with power in the middle of the tribulation period will testify by the Spirit of God (Zechariah 4:6) for about three and a half years (1260 days).

Revelation 11:6 These have power to shut heaven, so that no rain falls in the days of their prophecy; and they have power over waters to turn them to blood, and to strike the earth with all plagues, as often as they desire. The people will fear them and eventually kill them and rejoice over their dead bodies for three and a half days, and then the witnesses will be resurrected by God, and the people will be terrified.

Revelation 11:8 And their dead bodies *will lie* in the street of the great city which spiritually is called Sodom and Egypt, where also our Lord was crucified. When the two witnesses finish their testimony, the beast (a world ruler empowered by Satan, according to some commentators) will kill them, but they will not be buried. The interesting thing about this verse is that the great city is spiritually called Sodom and Egypt. What could that mean? The great city they are talking about here is Jerusalem because that is where Jesus was crucified. It could be that Jerusalem becomes corrupt like Sodom and, therefore, is spiritually like Sodom. The reference to Egypt might have to do with the idolatry of Egypt in ancient times. Whatever the reason, from a spiritual perspective, Sodom and Egypt have a lot in common with Jerusalem when the tribulation time comes.

Revelation 11:9 Then *those* from the peoples, tribes, tongues, and

nations will see their dead bodies three-and-a-half days, and not allow their dead bodies to be put into graves. These people will be rejoicing that the witnesses are dead and can't torment them with their words and actions. These seem to be the people upon whom (6:10; 8:13) God's judgment falls.

Revelation 11:10 And those who dwell on the earth will rejoice over them, make merry, and send gifts to one another, because these two prophets tormented those who dwell on the earth. How did these witnesses torment people? They told the unrepentant world what would be happening to them for three and a half years. They were also actively devouring their enemies and those who wanted to harm them with fire and bringing plagues and droughts.

Revelation 11:11 Now after the three-and-a-half days the breath of life from God entered them, and they stood on their feet, and great fear fell on those who saw them. You can see why the people who were rejoicing at the witness's death would now be afraid. At that time, they will know that God was involved and would be judging them.

Revelation 11:19 Then the temple of God was opened in heaven, and the ark of His covenant was seen in His temple. And there were lightnings, noises, thunderings, an earthquake, and great hail. This seems to designate where the ark of the covenant is located. However, Moses's ark could have been a model of the one mentioned in this verse.

Revelation 12:3 And another sign appeared in heaven: behold, a great, fiery red dragon having seven heads and ten horns, and seven diadems on his heads. In verse 9 this fiery red dragon is interpreted as Satan. This verse may be where red came to be associated with the Devil. However, the imagery of this verse is very different from what we generally see. The next verse indicates that this dragon would attempt to devour the newborn child who became the person taken up into heaven by God who will eventually rule all nations (Christ). This makes me think that Herod's attempt to kill Jesus Christ when He was a baby was satanically inspired since that is what Satan wanted to happen.

Revelation 12:10 Then I heard a loud voice saying in heaven, "Now salvation, and strength, and the kingdom of our God, and the power of His Christ have come, for the accuser of our brethren, who accused them before our God day and night, has been cast down. First, the accuser was cast down from heaven to the earth, and the angels who followed were cast out with him. Later, he will be cast down again, this time to the bottomless pit for a thousand years (20:1-3).

Revelation 12:12 Therefore rejoice, O heavens, and you who dwell in them! Woe to the inhabitants of the earth and the sea! For the devil has come down to you, having great wrath, because he knows that he has a short time." When Satan was cast down to earth, he was angry and had many angels who became the demons who do his bidding here. His time is limited, and he knows it, so he is full of wrath that he takes out on the earth's inhabitants. Eventually, he will make war with all the believers who keep the commandments of God and have the testimony of Jesus Christ (12:17).

Revelation 12:17 And the dragon was enraged with the woman, and he went to make war with the rest of her offspring, who keep the commandments of God and have the testimony of Jesus Christ. Christians appear to be the offspring referred to here.

Revelation 13:2 Now the beast which I saw was like a leopard, his feet were like *the feet of* a bear, and his mouth like the mouth of a lion. The dragon gave him his power, his throne, and great authority. This verse appears to refer to the second beast, who is a leader also empowered by Satan. The second beast is some kind of false prophet who directs the people to worship the first beast, the world leader empowered by Satan. The false prophet and the other beast who is a world leader will be directed by the dragon (Satan) against God.

Satan was against God in heaven and is against God now that he has some time on earth. This may be the unstated underlying conflict in a lot of disputes in life. You can talk about God in abstract terms, and everyone can be happy. However, when the name of Jesus Christ is brought into the discussion, everything can change. If you think about it, that is appropriate because God came to the earth as Jesus Christ and paid the price for our sins so we could be reconciled to God. That changed everything on the earth for the past, present, and future. The earth and the universe in which it resides have a lot going on in the spiritual realm, and it is not just about human beings.

Revelation 13:4 So they worshiped the dragon who gave authority to the beast; and they worshiped the beast, saying, "Who is like the beast? Who is able to make war with him?" This will be a hectic time on earth. Those who do not believe in God will be enticed (12:9) to worship one of the beasts. This beast may be a world leader. [Thus, at some point, it sounds like the globalists will triumph, and there will be some world leader who has authority over all countries. Maybe it could be the head of a united nations type of entity, but all the other countries are made to submit. Some type of global issue could be used as a catalyst for setting up this world governing authority.] This leader will have control for forty-two months. Since we know that idolatry is ultimately demonic (1 Corinthians 10:20-23), this will be a highly regarded leader and thought to be invincible so that no one will make war against him. Still, he will make war with the saints (Christians) and overcome them during this time (12:7). People who do not believe in God will worship this leader (13:8).

Revelation 13:8 All who dwell on the earth will worship him, whose names have not been written in the Book of Life of the Lamb slain

from the foundation of the world. The Book of Life of the Lamb is the book that has all of the names of people who will have eternal life as opposed to the Lake of Fire (20:12, 15). There seem to be a few options regarding how God could write down the names of the Saints in this book before they even lived their lives. One is that God can see the past, present, and future because He is not in time since He created time.

Another might be that He just knows everything. I don't know how He can do this, but since He created our universe, I imagine that it is not too difficult for Him to know our future before we even live our life. It seems that God can see the past, present, and end at the same time. That is difficult for us to comprehend because we are stuck in only the present.

Revelation 13:14 And he deceives those who dwell on the earth by those signs which he was granted to do in the sight of the beast, telling those who dwell on the earth to make an image to the beast who was wounded by the sword and lived. Apparently, the first beast was wounded severely but recovered. The unbelievers are wowed by the recovery and wind up making an image of the first beast. The scripture does not say precisely why the first beast was wounded.

Revelation 13:15 He was granted *power* to give breath to the image of the beast, that the image of the beast should both speak and cause as many as would not worship the image of the beast to be killed. The second beast can do things that will influence people, and this beast is the one who convinces the people to make an image of the first beast. The image is given the ability to speak and anyone who does not worship the image is killed. Note that there were no microphones, recorders, amplifiers, or speakers when this was written. In modern times, these inventions, along with artificial intelligence, could easily be used to make it seem like an idol can speak even without a miraculous process.

Videos can also be made to show whatever the videographer wants them to show. This is where the faith of the Christians really could be tested. The believers at that time will become martyrs for their refusal to worship the image of the beast. To buy or sell, everyone will have to have the mark, the name of the beast, or the number of his name, which is 666.

Revelation 14:1 Then I looked, and behold, a Lamb standing on Mount Zion, and with Him one hundred *and* forty-four thousand, having His Father's name written on their foreheads. Mount Zion is generally taken to mean Jerusalem. This Mount Zion may be a reference to Mount Zion in heaven. The 144,000 are people from **all the tribes of the children of Israel** (Revelation 7:4).

Revelation 14:4 These are the ones who were not defiled with women, for they are virgins. These are the ones who follow the Lamb wherever He goes. These were redeemed from *among* men, *being* firstfruits to God and to the Lamb. The 144,000 with the Father's name written on their forehead were (a) the only ones who could learn the new song, (b) were redeemed from the earth, (c) were virgins (spiritually pure), (d) they followed the Lamb (Christ), (e) they were redeemed from among men, (f) they were among the first to believe in God and the Lamb, and (g) they were without deceit or fault before God (vs. 5). Of course, they had faults while on earth, but they were forgiven and therefore without deceit or fault in heaven.

Revelation 14:6 Then I saw another angel flying in the midst of heaven, having the everlasting gospel to preach to those who dwell on the earth—to every nation, tribe, tongue, and people— This process will be a fulfillment of Matthew 24:14 which says the Gospel will be preached to all the world. Note that this verse says that the angel is flying in heaven. Perhaps the imagery of angels with wings comes from this verse. I don't expect angels to need wings to fly in heaven. That would mean air would have to be present to provide lift. Air would seem to be an element of the physical world. I don't think there would be air in the spiritual realm. Also, I don't find any descriptions of angels with wings in the Bible.

Revelation 14:9 Then a third angel followed them, saying with a loud voice, "If anyone worships the beast and his image, and receives *his* mark on his forehead or on his hand, 10 they, too, will drink the wine of God's fury, which has been poured full strength into the cup of his wrath. They will be tormented with burning sulfur in the presence of the holy angels and of the Lamb. This is not a very pleasant prediction for those who oppose God. He will not permanently withhold His wrath.

Revelation 16:2 So the first went and poured out his bowl upon the earth, and a foul and loathsome sore came upon the men who had the mark of the beast and those who worshiped his image. This is just the first of the seven bowls of judgment for all those who have the mark of the beast and worship his image. After these things, the kings of all the world will gather at Armageddon. This will be the battle of the great day of God almighty (16:16). After the seventh bowl of judgment (16:17-20), which results in the plague of the hail, men will blaspheme God.

Revelation 16:13 And I saw three unclean spirits like frogs *coming out of the mouth of the dragon, out of the mouth of the beast, and out of the mouth of the false prophet.* As noted, the dragon appears to represent Satan (12:9). The great deception in the signs of the dragon will influence the kings of the world to come out to do battle with God. That, of course, will be a feeble effort on the part of the kings. The dragon, the beast, and the false prophet appear like an anti-trinity. They work together to draw the nations into the battle. The beast is known for his blasphemy (Daniel 7:8; 7:11; 7:20; 7:25; 11:36; Revelation 13:6+). These three will be very persuasive, along with the false prophet and the unclean spirits.

Revelation 17:9 "Here *is* the mind which has wisdom: The seven heads are seven mountains on which the woman sits. The mind that has wisdom would seem to be a mind that understands wisdom from God rather than from man. There are different interpretations about the seven mountains and the woman. I will leave it to the reader to come up with your thinking on this issue.

Revelation 18:11 "And the merchants of the earth will weep and mourn over her, for no one buys their merchandise any more: This verse is speaking about the city of Babylon. It will be judged and destroyed by fire. The merchandise sold in Babylon also includes the slave trade (18:13).

Revelation 18:22 The sound of harpists, musicians, flutists, and trumpeters shall not be heard in you anymore. No craftsman of any craft shall be found in you anymore, and the sound of a millstone shall not be heard in you anymore. With the destruction of Babylon, the music that was there will be silenced, and there will not be any more craftsmen working there.

Revelation 19:4 And the twenty-four elders and the four living creatures fell down and worshiped God who sat on the throne, saying, "Amen! Alleluia!" It appears that the twenty-four elders and four living creatures worship God all the time (4:2-11; 5:8-14; 11:16; 14:3).

Revelation 19:7 Let us be glad and rejoice and give Him glory, for the marriage of the Lamb has come, and His wife has made herself ready." Of course, the Lamb refers to Christ, and His wife refers to believers who were faithful to God.

Revelation 19:9 Then he said to me, "Write: 'Blessed *are* those who are called to the marriage supper of the Lamb!' " And he said to me,

"These are the true sayings of God." This will be great for those who are blessed in this way.

Revelation 19:11 Now I saw heaven opened, and behold, a white horse. And He who sat on him *was* called Faithful and True, and in righteousness He judges and makes war. The earlier verse questions about who could make war with the beast is answered here. It is the one who is Faithful and True. That is Jesus Christ.

Revelation 19:16 And He has on *His* robe and on His thigh a name written: KING OF KINGS AND LORD OF LORDS. This says a lot about Christ. He is the one who is over all the other rulers on the earth.

Revelation 19:19 And I saw the beast, the kings of the earth, and their armies, gathered together to make war against Him who sat on the horse and against His army. This is where the beast and the false prophet get captured and cast into the lake of fire (20). The rest of their army will be killed (19:21), and the birds will eat their flesh.

Revelation 20:2 He laid hold of the dragon, that serpent of old, who is *the* Devil and Satan, and bound him for a thousand years;... After a thousand years in the bottomless pit, Satan must be released for a little while. Why? I don't know other than apparently that is part of God's plan. We do not get to know everything while here on earth. That is the way it is for now.

Revelation 20:5 But the rest of the dead did not live again until the thousand years were finished. This *is* the first resurrection. There will be two resurrections; one of the believers before the Millennium and one after but before the great white throne judgment (vs. 11-15). At the great throne judgment, anyone whose name is not in the book of life will be cast into the lake of fire. That sounds harsh, but these people choose their path, so why would God not grant what they chose to them?

Revelation 20:6 Blessed and holy *is* he who has part in the first resurrection. Over such the second death has no power, but they shall be priests of God and of Christ, and shall reign with Him a thousand years. I interpret this verse to say that believers in Christ will wind up serving as priests in the Millennium. The second death is the one after which comes the great white throne judgment.

Revelation 20:13 The sea gave up the dead who were in it, and Death and Hades delivered up the dead who were in them. And they were judged, each one according to his works. Note that those judged by their works are not the people of faith. They are the ones who refused the offered gift of salvation by the grace of God through faith. The alternative is to be judged by your works, and no flesh can be justified by works of the law (Romans 3:20). A person cannot save themselves no matter what they do. The second death is spiritual and is final from what the Bible says.

Revelation 21:10 And he carried me away in the Spirit to a great and high mountain, and showed me the great city, the holy Jerusalem, descending out of heaven from God,... John received his vision of the Apocalypse while in a spiritual state. He reports that he was carried away and shown things in this state. What he saw was the new city of Jerusalem for believers.

Revelation 21:14 Now the wall of the city had twelve foundations, and on them were the names of the twelve apostles of the Lamb. From this verse, we see how the predictions in Ephesians 2:20 are fulfilled and Christ is the chief cornerstone of the New Jerusalem.

Revelation 21:23 The city had no need of the sun or of the moon to shine in it, for the glory of God illuminated it. The Lamb *is* its light. So, there will be no need for the sun or moon to provide light in this New Jerusalem because Christ (the Lamb of God) will be there and provide any light needed. Only those whose names are in the Lamb's Book of Life will be in this city.

Revelation 22:3 And there shall be no more curse, but the throne of God and of the Lamb shall be in it, and His servants shall serve Him. Many years ago, the curse came upon humankind (Genesis 3:14-19) when Adam disobeyed God. The good news is that this curse will be removed, and all the people will serve God.

Revelation 22:7 "Behold, I am coming quickly! Blessed *is* he who keeps the words of the prophecy of this book." This blessing is one of the beatitudes in Revelation. The visions in this book inform believers about what to expect. We don't know when this will happen, but we know there is a plan. We know who wins the war between good and evil, and we know we can have hope for eternity in heaven with no more pain, death, sorrow, or crying (Revelation 21:4). We need to keep the prophecy in Revelation in mind as we keep heavenly-minded even as we live our lives in the fallen state of the current dispensation in which we are living.

Revelation 22:12 "And behold, I am coming quickly, and My reward *is* with Me, to give to every one according to his work. This is a different consequence than the consequence for unbelievers. Unbelievers will receive the wages of their unbelief (20:13), which is death. This second death is after the bodies have been re-united with the souls. Then they are cast into the Lake of Fire.

Note that there seem to be four types of death mentioned in the Bible. One is spiritual death. A person can have a body and soul but be dead spiritually (Isaiah 59:2; Ephesians 2:1). Two is physical death when the physical body dies and turns back to dust (James 2:26; Genesis 35:18). After the body dies, the soul continues to live. Three is when the soul is cast into Hell without the body or spirit (Luke 16:19-21; Ezekiel 18:4). Four is what is referred to as the second death in the scriptures. It is the final death after the Millennium when the body and soul of the unsaved are cast into the Lake of Fire (Matthew 25:41; Revelation 20:14). I'm sorry for these poor people, but this is what the Bible says. On the other hand, believers will receive rewards for their good works (2 Corinthians 5:10).

Revelation 22:14 Blessed *are* those who do His commandments, that they may have the right to the tree of life, and may enter through the gates into the city. The tree of life mentioned in this verse could be taken literally or figuratively. The point seems to be that those who express their faith by obeying the commandments will have the right to life and enter New Jerusalem.

Revelation 22:16 "I, Jesus, have sent My angel to testify to you these things in the churches. I am the Root and the Offspring of David, the Bright and Morning Star." Jesus makes many claims about Himself. He leaves no intellectually viable option for those who want to deny that He is who He says He is. If He is not God, He has to be either a mentally ill person who doesn't know what he is saying or a liar because of the substantial claims He makes about Himself.

Claims that He was a great moral teacher or a wonderful ethical guru, or simply a prophet are intellectually untenable based on what He is quoted as saying about Himself. Apparently, that is the way He wanted it. For those who study the scriptures, we have a clear choice to make. Either we believe He is who He said He is, or we believe one of only a few other options. Who gives us the freedom to make that choice? He does.

Love is not coerced. It is a free-will choice and probably cannot be forced anyway. No other spiritual leader or guru makes these claims that I know of unless they have a mental health condition or are lying. In the case of Christ, not only does He provide a way of salvation, He pays the just price for all our sins and leaves us justified by His death on the cross in our place. He calls us and does the work for us. All we do is decide to accept the gift and get on the salvation plane to the destination where God created us to go.

Revelation 22:18 For I testify to everyone who hears the words of the prophecy of this book: If anyone adds to these things, God will add to him the plagues that are written in this book; 19, and if anyone takes away from the words of the book of this prophecy, God shall take away his part from the Book of Life, from the holy city, and *from* the things which are written in this book. This stern warning should not be taken lightly.

67

Conclusion

FINAL THOUGHTS: Why would God allow His Word to be subject to misinterpretation? Could it be that we are finite beings in our current state and as such, may be incapable of fully understanding that which is eternal or spiritual? Or, maybe God is divinely fair to the point that those who choose not to believe in the authority of the Bible are provided a rationale for justifying their position through using literal interpretations when other interpretations are more appropriate or vice versa.

Inspiration: Since early humanity's written history, the "Word of God" (the Bible) has been accused of *not* being inspired by God. The Christian Bible states that the question of who inspired it is spiritually discerned (1 Corinthians 2:14 - **But the natural man does not receive the things of the Spirit of God, for they are foolishness to him; nor can he know *them*, because they are spiritually discerned.**).

I started reading the Bible as a curious natural man who did "**not receive the things of the Spirit of God.**" I had three college degrees (A.A., B.A., M.A.) but my initial understanding was considerably limited. Most of my professors avoided any biblical references like the plague. Still, how could I consider myself educated if I had not read what appeared to be the world's most influential book? Thus, I read and read. As I did, I found the Bible to be absolutely unique. In my experience, there is nothing like it and no other theological book with its level of authoritative narrative. Eventually, I was inspired to write this commentary as a means of understanding as much as I could about it.

For most people who call themselves Christians, the supernatural creator is God. Simple observation of the physical universe seems to demand such a creator. I know there are those who maintain that the natural world just always existed and that time and chance resulted in all we see today of the universe. That does not make logical sense to me. How could that be possible when, based on what we know from logic and science, everything in the natural world always has a cause? It is possible to believe that nothing created everything, but a logical defense of that belief seems difficult?

My conclusion is that the supernatural (God) created the natural (our physical universe). Just because this reasoning makes logical and spiritual sense to me, doesn't mean it will to others. As reported above, scripture in the Bible supports the conclusion that reason alone will not convince someone of the Biblical worldview. The Bible says the issue of the inspiration of the Word of God is spiritually discerned. Thus, if one convinces themself that there is no supernatural, they may find themselves in a quest for an explanation of life that will never come.

I encourage anyone who has read this commentary to seriously consider what the rest of the Bible says, and not let your mind be blinded (2 Corinthians 4:4). My experience is that there is nothing else that can even compete with the grace offered in the Bible through the sacrifice of Jesus the Christ.

About the Author

After working as a musician to put himself through college and gaining a Master of Arts Degree in Psychology, the author obtained various other credentials and worked with people coming out of federal and state prisons and the mentally ill before becoming the Chief Executive Officer of a nonprofit social service agency. While heading the agency, it grew from about 60 to over 650 employees serving tens of thousands of people in need. The author has served on various nonprofit boards of directors in officer capacities, including Secretary of the Board for the Nonprofit Insurance Alliance of California, Regional Vice President for the International Community Corrections Association, President for Quality Comp, Incorporated, and as President of the California Council of Community Mental Health Agencies. Other activities include serving on church boards of directors and leading church music teams.

www.ingramcontent.com/pod-product-compliance
Lightning Source LLC
Chambersburg PA
CBHW071654170426
43195CB00039B/2191